D1073737

ADVANCE PRAISE FOR

Colleges at the Crossroads

"Higher education seems in flux and confused in the 21st century. Students are rising up, faculty life is changing rapidly, leaders are becoming more difficult to find, and funding is uncertain. In *Colleges at the Crossroads*, Joseph L. DeVitis and Pietro A. Sasso invite readers to grapple with current issues in higher education from multiple perspectives while also urging them to challenge the very notion of higher education as we know it."

> —*Marybeth Gasman, Judy and Howard Berkowitz Professor of Education,*
> *University of Pennsylvania, and Director of the Penn Center*
> *for Minority Serving Institutions*

"Joseph L. DeVitis and Pietro A. Sasso go beyond presenting provocative, controversial topics by addressing their pros and cons and providing questions that will generate robust dialogue among students, faculty, and higher education professionals. I look forward to using this book in a wide range of courses, for example, law, ethics, organizational administration, disability education, social justice issues, and internships. The possibilities are endless. This is a must read and a must use!"

> —*Karen A. Myers, Associate Professor and Program Director,*
> *Higher Education Administration, and*
> *Director of the Ability Institute, Saint Louis University*

Colleges at the Crossroads

Studies in Criticality

Shirley R. Steinberg
General Editor

Vol. 517

The Counterpoints series is part of the Peter Lang Education list.
Every volume is peer reviewed and meets
the highest quality standards for content and production.

PETER LANG
New York • Bern • Berlin
Brussels • Vienna • Oxford • Warsaw

Colleges at the Crossroads

Taking Sides on Contested Issues

Edited by
Joseph L. DeVitis
& Pietro A. Sasso

PETER LANG
New York • Bern • Berlin
Brussels • Vienna • Oxford • Warsaw

Library of Congress Cataloging-in-Publication Data
Names: DeVitis, Joseph L., editor. | Sasso, Pietro A., editor.
Title: Colleges at the crossroads: taking sides on contested issues /
edited by Joseph L. DeVitis and Pietro A. Sasso.
Description: New York: Peter Lang.
Series: Counterpoints: studies in criticality; v. 517 | ISSN 1058-1634
Includes bibliographical references.
Identifiers: LCCN 2017021599 | ISBN 978-1-4331-3421-0 (pbk.: alk. paper)
ISBN 978-1-4331-3422-7 (hardback: alk. paper)
ISBN 978-1-4331-4580-3 (ebook pdf)
ISBN 978-1-4331-4581-0 (epub) | ISBN 978-1-4331-4582-7 (mobi)
Subjects: LCSH: Education, Higher—Aims and objectives—United States.
Education, Higher—Effect of technological innovations on—United States.
Education, Higher—Economic aspects—United States.
Academic freedom—United States.
College teachers—Tenure—United States.
College teachers—Workload—United States.
College students—Social conditions—United States.
College sports—Moral and ethical aspects—United States.
Universities and colleges—United States—Administration.
Classification: LA227.4 .C6444 | DDC 378.73—dc23
LC record available at https://lccn.loc.gov/2017021599
DOI 10.3726/b11364

Bibliographic information published by **Die Deutsche Nationalbibliothek.**
Die Deutsche Nationalbibliothek lists this publication in the "Deutsche
Nationalbibliografie"; detailed bibliographic data are available
on the Internet at http://dnb.d-nb.de/.

The paper in this book meets the guidelines for permanence and durability
of the Committee on Production Guidelines for Book Longevity
of the Council of Library Resources.

© 2018 Peter Lang Publishing, Inc., New York
29 Broadway, 18th floor, New York, NY 10006
www.peterlang.com

All rights reserved.
Reprint or reproduction, even partially, in all forms such as microfilm,
xerography, microfiche, microcard, and offset strictly prohibited.

Printed in the United States of America

Dedication

To Maurice R. Berube and Kenneth Teitelbaum—
two menches, in and out of academe.
(JLD)

To my students and colleagues who have challenged
my romanticism about higher education and urged
me to be more curmudgeonly about it. To them, I
owe my maturation toward a more critical view of
postsecondary issues. As a progressive, I remain
cautiously optimistic about the future.
(PAS)

Table of Contents

List of Charts, Figures, Tables

Introduction

Joseph L. DeVitis and Pietro A. Sasso

Freedom is, first of all, the chance to formulate the available choices, to argue over them—and then, the opportunity to choose.
　　　　　　　　　　　　　　　　　　　　　　　　　　—C. Wright Mills

If students are not going to have controversial ideas on college campuses, they're not going to have them in America.
　　　　　　　　　　　　　　　　　　　　　　　　　　—Donna Shalala

At their best, human beings have practiced reasoned and passionate discourse on different points of view on an infinite variety of subjects. In colleges and universities, such debates have been fundamental to the search for truth(s). Indeed, yearning for truth(s) has been captured in myriad mottoes of American campuses and epitomized by Harvard's one-word mission: Truth. The journey toward truth(s) serves to sharpen crucial thinking skills and enables its participants to develop fuller forms of conceptual knowledge and even wisdom. Conceived from that perspective, dialogue is part and parcel of how we come to understand the world—in this case, the often contentious terrain of higher education. It also prepares students to better serve civic responsibilities: "Individuals who can weigh truth claims, evaluate sources of evidence, and understand how knowledge evolves...are essential to the effective functioning of democratic societies" (Hofer & Sinatra, 2010, p. 118). And, given the most recent presidential campaign, let us hope we are not inhabiting a post-truth(s) world.

Historically, there have been two competing arguments regarding institutions of higher learning. The first argument contends that they have largely intersected with external social forces and thus have never functioned in a vacuum. The second argument claims that the academy operates mainly within its own walls and iron gates. That is to say, it is an insular pocket of knowledge transfer. Both arguments posit a complex view of academic reality, especially as we consider the seemingly endless web of external and internal intersecting factors. The outcome is typically caught in a storm of conflict (in lively arenas of debate and criticism) that may, with a heavy dose of luck, result in a dialectic of convergence.

At the same time, readers should note that this collection is hardly value-neutral; it is strewn with ideological premises and arguments. This is inevitable since any form of education is deeply political. It is wise to take care in analyzing political discourse about any level of schooling and to be wary of sloganeering and posturing. The latter can come from the Left or the Right; words and phrases such as "excellence," "standards," "rigor," "world class," and the like are typically used to persuade when they more truly offer empty bromides. No matter what one's political preferences, education is too precious to be left to undiscerning policymaking based on public-relations platitudes. Furthermore, it does not help that strident headlines often portray the "ivory tower" in shadowy images:

> News media attention to what happens on college campuses make policymakers and the public aware of such less-than-flattering topics on campus crime, drug and alcohol abuse by students, poor graduation rates of athletes, work habits and productivity of faculty members, and million-dollar-a-year athletic coaches. (Heller, 2003, p. 3)

Granted, higher education is facing serious questions about its efficacy and integrity as never before. No longer does an appreciable portion of the public view it without blinders. It has legitimate concerns about college costs, worth, and relevance in their daily lives, especially when economic downturn affects so many people. Yet a majority of the public still views our colleges and universities as national treasures—indeed, major purveyors of a key element in achieving the American Dream. After all, over 20 million people attend postsecondary institutions in the United States (Johnson, 2013). But some social critics wonder if the Dream itself is on the wane (DeVitis & Rich, 1996; Newfield, 2008). That dichotomous set of circumstances paints a puzzling portrait of confusion and a yearning need for clarity on contemporary higher learning.

The chief aim of this text is to prod students, faculty, administrators, and other college student personnel—in fact, all those concerned with higher education—to wrestle with some of the most controversial issues now confronting the academy with a sense of open-minded inquiry. Philosopher Williams Hare (2002) says it well: "Do not pretend to know more than you do or assume that what you think you know is beyond challenge" (p. 23).

In that spirit, this compendium offers a rich opportunity to deliberate with other participants and to gain new slants of comprehension on important mutual concerns. Yet dialogue can be messy; it normally generates twists, turns, and detours in our thinking before we reach any sort of resolution. And genuine dialogue demands that we respect each other by listening, with care, to differing arguments and then appraising their merits and deficiencies as gleaned from those shared ideas.

In preparing this book, we initially explored *The Chronicle of Higher Education, Inside Higher Ed*, and similar publications in order to ascertain which issues were most often cited as "controversial" in the academic community. After this inquiry, we developed a set of themes based on divergent perspectives on these critical contemporary concerns: the purposes of higher education; liberal education; academic freedom; freedom of expression and political correctness; tenure issues; faculty governance; faculty workload; standardized admission tests; college student learning; the relevance of Greek life; the worth of a college education; the efficacy of social justice and equity on college campuses; the coexistence of academics and athletics; student entitlement; technology and distance education; and university spending on amenities.

The editors hope that the presentation of those topics will generate the kind of stimulating discussion that ideally underscores why universities can be so vital to individuals and society. Engagement in such dialogue is crucial to the collegiate experience; it fosters a sense of connectedness for student learners (Astin, 1996). Effective outcomes occur when students engage in active learning and feel that they are invested in the process (Chickering & Gamson, 1987). As David Thornton Moore (2013), a critical theorist and proponent of service learning in higher education, puts it, "Learning is not simply an intellectual matter located inside the head...it changes the way one relates to the actual world" (pp. 3–4). We heartily concur: that kind of cultivation should be pervasive throughout the campus, in *both* the formal academic curriculum and cocurricular activities. Additionally, to practice collegiate education in its fullest dimensions, it is imperative that we recognize the import of *social* learning and the continuing need to infuse campuses with an increasingly diverse array of students. In particular, intergroup dialogue can be useful in bringing together different social identity groups to address critical campus concerns (Zuniga, Nagda, Chesler, & Cytron-Walker, 2011).

The editors recommend that instructors using this text seek to insure engaged sessions with students by emphasizing provocative questioning in their pedagogy. We further suggest that these types of questions form the basis for starting and sustaining rich dialogue:

1. Does the author(s) present the necessary facts to sustain her argument?
2. What are the underlying assumptions of her argument, and are they sound?
3. Do you perceive any hidden motives or agendas behind the author(s)'s argument?
4. Does the author(s) appear to be biased in explaining her views?
5. Does the author(s) connect ideas in a reliable way and adequately support them?
6. Does the author(s) leave out factors that you consider to be important? Which factors?
7. What are the overall strengths and weaknesses of the author(s)'s argument?
8. In the final analysis, which side of the issue do you accept most fully? Why? And why do you tend to reject the other side? (Davis, 2009)

Finally, we will begin each section of the text with a brief introduction to the pertinent controversial question. We present a "pro" and "con" format of sorts; however, readers should be assured that every essay offers an informed, thought-provoking response that is typically more nuanced than might appear at first blush. Life doesn't promise easy decisions or simple solutions. Thus, our audience should be cautious about any hard and fast assumptions it might hold on a given topic. Perhaps Maxine Greene (1995), an eloquent educational philosopher, sums it up best: "Teaching and learning are matters of breaking through barriers—of expectations, of boredom, of predefinition" (p. 14).

Let us begin the dialogue in earnest.

References

Astin, A. W. (1996). Involvement in learning revisited: Lessons we have learned. *Journal of College Student Development, 37*(2), 123–134.

Chickering, A., & Gamson, Z. (1987). Seven principles of good practice in undergraduate education. *AAHE Bulletin, 39*, 3–7.

Davis, B. G. (2009). *Tools for teaching* (2nd ed.). San Francisco, CA: Jossey-Bass.

DeVitis, J. L., & Rich, J. M. (1996). *The success ethic, education, and the American dream.* New York, NY: State University of New York Press.

Greene, M. (1995). *Releasing the imagination: Essays on education, the arts, and social change.* San Francisco, CA: Jossey-Bass.

Hare, W. (2002). Teaching and the attitude of open-mindedness. *Journal of Educational Administration and Foundations, 16* (2), 103–124.

Heller, D. E. (2003). Introduction: The changing dynamics of affordability, access, and accountability in public higher education. In D. E. Heller (Ed.), *The States and public higher education: Affordability, access, and accountability.* Baltimore, MD: Johns Hopkins University Press.

Hofer, B. K., & Sinatra, G. M. (2010). Epistemology, metacognition, and self-regulation: Musings on an emerging field. *Metacognition Learning,* 5, 113–120.

Johnson, J. (2013, September 14). Today's typical college students often juggle work, children, and bills with coursework. *Washington Post,* p. C8.

Moore, D. T. (2013). *Engaged learning in the academy: Challenges and possibilities.* New York, NY: Palgrave Macmillan.

Newfield, C. (2008). *Unmaking the public university: The fifty-year assault on the middle class.* Cambridge, MA: Harvard University Press.

Zuniga, X., Nagda, B. A., Chesler, M., & Cytron-Walker, A. (2011). *Intergroup dialogue in higher education: Meaningful learning about social justice.* San Francisco, CA: Jossey-Bass.

Part One: What Should Be the Purposes of Higher Education?

In "What Is College for?" Johann N. Neem contends that the essential aim of collegiate education should be to develop the student's learning in an atmosphere as unfettered as possible by external pressures. The liberal arts and sciences are the core drivers of his abiding faith in immersing students in a kind of Aristotelian kind of education: providing them deep knowledge of the human and natural world, habituating them to asking questions about it, and building their curiosity about all things under the sun. While arguing that college is not for everyone, Neem characterizes liberal education as fundamental for those who choose to attend and have the ability to benefit from their intellectual desire for lifelong thinking about "thoughts worth thinking."

Patricia A. McGuire, in "Modernizing College Purposes to Save a Troubled World," offers a broad analysis of the imperative to redefine the purposes of higher education in ever-changing times. The author traces the historical nature of college purposes from traditional frameworks to what she describes as one that required "the new college student of the 21 century." She does not relinquish her firm commitment to liberal education, but views it from more contemporary perspectives. Focusing on the needs of an increasingly diverse student population, McGuire calls for more relevant curricula, pedagogy, and delivery systems as well as more serious attention to academic governance and accountability issues. Finally, she underscores the necessity for revival of civic education to equip students for future leadership roles.

1. What Is College for?

JOHANN N. NEEM

A college education is distinguished from other kinds of education because it embodies ideals distinct from the rest of students' lives. If we take college seriously, we need students to spend a good amount of time on campuses isolated from the world so that they can cultivate their intellect. Students should leave college different than when they entered. The best test of a good college education, therefore, is whether a student has been transformed—whether she has developed the fundamental intellectual virtue of curiosity about the world, and whether she has the knowledge and skills to produce deep insights about the human and natural worlds. In short, the purpose of college education is to take students out of the "real world" and place them on campuses devoted to learning as the highest ideal.

From this perspective, a university dedicated to training for business or jobs does not offer a college education. Neither do online institutions that promise to allow students to earn their degrees in their spare time as fast as they can complete their course work. Both fail the test of taking students out of their normal lives in order to reorient them around the specific goal of learning. Our daily lives are filled with all kinds of responsibilities (such as jobs and children) and distractions (such as mass entertainment). Colleges offer a retreat where these can be, at least temporarily, put aside. Ideally, one would reenter the world with new perspectives and new ideas. As the philosopher Michael Oakeshott has said, our world "is crowded." We confront "a ceaseless flow of seductive trivialities which invoke neither reflection nor choice but instant participation" (Oakeshott, 1975). He was writing in 1975, but with the Internet, his comments have become only more true. It is more important than ever, therefore, that colleges pull people away from the world, if even for just a little while.

Taking time out to learn is, of course, easier for traditional-aged students right out of high school than it is for returning students who have all the trappings of the real world. Adults with jobs, credit card debt, mortgage payments, and young children at home simply cannot abandon their lives for several years. These "nontraditional" older and/or working adults now make up the majority of American college students. For this reason, many reformers argue, we must transform colleges—make them more focused on job training; provide more education online; and make degrees faster and easier. Certainly, colleges need to work harder to reach working and older students. Yet even as colleges become more flexible to help older students earn degrees, they must remain true to their mission (Scobey, 2016). In short, if we really believe in expanding access to college education, and not just access to college degrees, we must find ways to offer older students access to the real thing.

There is no reason that adults cannot devote a good part of their week to colleges, just as so many Americans do to their churches. Churchgoers know that they cannot have the same kinds of transformative and sustaining experiences online as they can by attending churches where they interact with and learn from both ministers and each other. They know that relationships formed over years are vital to sustaining their faith. While they work during the day, churchgoing adults devote time on Sundays, and often on other evenings during the week, to meet together for study and worship. They hope that by taking time away from their daily routines, by forming communities, and meeting in specific buildings designed for worship, they will grow in their faith. They hope that their faith will inform what they do in their daily lives. Adult college students should be able to have similar experiences. Colleges should structure programs that allow working adults to participate, and working adults must be committed enough to devote their time to attending. While being a full-time student on campus is the best option, there is no reason that colleges cannot do more to approximate that experience for working people.

We must also address the primary reason that so many older students are returning to college. While many adults may appreciate the opportunity to cultivate their intellect, others are there because they believe that they have no other options. Americans have been told again and again that they need a college degree to make it in today's economy. This is in part because of larger changes in the economy, but it is also about politics. In the past decades, we have allowed the rich to get richer, while wages for the majority have stagnated. Competition from abroad, technological innovation, and the declining strength of labor unions have combined to drive down wages, but not every industrial country has permitted the gap between rich and poor to grow as large as it has become in the United States. Countries with similar levels of education, facing the same kinds of technological change, have chosen to promote more equal outcomes. America has not, and as a result, going to college now appears to be one of the only ways for Americans to get ahead (Dougherty, 1997).

Ironically, despite all the rhetoric, it's not clear that the American economy requires as many college degrees as we often assume. It is possible that we are producing more college-educated workers than the economy demands. There is no doubt that Americans with a college degree earn more on average than those without one. There is also no doubt that the economy requires highly skilled workers. The question is whether we should conflate highly skilled workers with college-educated workers. Surprisingly, many of the country's fastest growing positions require technical training but not a college education. The US Department of Labor's Bureau of Labor Statistics (2016), for example, estimates the fastest-growing occupations to be:

1. Wind turbine service technicians
2. Occupational therapy assistants
3. Physical therapist assistants
4. Physical therapist aides
5. Home health aides
6. Commercial divers
7. Nurse practitioners
8. Physical therapists
9. Statisticians
10. Ambulance drivers and attendants, except emergency medical technicians
11. Occupational therapy aides
12. Physician assistants
13. Operations research analysts
14. Personal financial advisors
15. Cartographers and photogrammetrists
16. Genetic counselors
17. Interpreters and translators
18. Audiologists
19. Hearing aid specialists
20. Optometrists

All these positions require specialized skills, but most do not require a college degree. There are, in other words, good reasons for the United States to offer better alternatives to college. Technical programs would allow students to incur less debt while leading to high-paying skilled jobs (Holzer, 2015; Steinberg, 2010). Certainly, all students who want and are able to pursue a college education should be encouraged to do so. We do not want college to be reserved for the elite. But for the many others who are in college but don't really want to be there, apprenticeships and technical programs could be a better alternative. Providing these alternatives would also free four-year colleges and universities to do what they do best: provide a liberal education.

The Liberal Arts and Sciences

The liberal arts and sciences are at the heart of a serious college education—subjects such as biology, chemistry, history, literature, mathematics, philosophy, and physics. But today, business is the largest major in America. Most American students do not go to college to receive a liberal education but to get a better-paying job. But undergraduate business programs actually deny students a college education. Why is that? First, the very purpose of a business degree is to prepare for work, not to cultivate the intellect. As philosopher Tal Brewer has written, the idea of going to school to study business is an "oxymoron." The words scholar and school derive from the Greek word for leisure. Schools are places where people step aside from the world of need—from the world of business—to engage in reflection. Colleges, "devoted to discussion and thought unfolding under its own internal demands," cannot with integrity offer "training for the sort of life that has no place for such thought." Business schooling is "a scholé of the negation of scholé" (Brewer, 2014).

In addition, business programs are less effective at developing the high-level thinking skills that employers value most, and that our democracy needs from us as citizens. In their book *Academically Adrift* (2011), sociologists Richard Arum and Josipa Roksa found that students taking courses in the arts and sciences produce significantly greater gains in critical thinking (as measured by the Collegiate Learning Assessment, or CLA) than business majors. They attribute the result to the fact that students in the natural and physical sciences study the most hours and students in the humanities read and write the most. In their follow-up book, *Aspiring Adults Adrift* (2014), Arum and Roksa acknowledge that the data is messy. First, students move between majors quite a bit. Second, a good part of the difference may have to do with differences between selective and less-selective institutions. Third, because of self-selection, less academically able students probably opt out of arts and science majors. Yet, they conclude, "students who majored in traditional liberal arts fields—social sciences, humanities, natural sciences, and math—demon-strated greater improvement on the CLA than did students who majored in business."

What do the liberal arts and sciences offer? Ultimately, they offer three things. First, studying the liberal arts and sciences offers insight into how the human and natural worlds work. Second, they develop in students a habit of asking questions about the world, fostering the curiosity to keep asking questions. Finally, they provide the knowledge and skills to help students develop better, more profound answers to their questions than they otherwise would have come up with. Thus, a good college education, by steeping students in the liberal arts and sciences, leads to more insightful graduates who can enrich their personal lives, and be thoughtful citizens and effective contributors to the economy.

To understand why this is the case, imagine going for a walk in the forest. You see a lot of green, but have no idea what the green things are. Slowly, you become aware, perhaps by what you learn from parents or in school, that those green things are trees. They come from seeds, need water, air, and sun. Over time, you learn there are different kinds of trees. If you keep at it, and keep learning, soon you realize that there are ecosystems, in which those different trees interact with the soil, with each other, with the climate, and with animals. You start to know the names of the trees, and specific things about them. Now, when you go for a walk, you can interpret what you see, and offer your insights to your walking companion, who sees nothing but green. That is what liberal education is about, gaining insight into the natural and human worlds to enable each person to make sense of it—as citizens, and as workers—and to enrich their own experience of the world as a result.

Some people argue that skills like critical thinking matter more than the subjects one studies. This is a false distinction. Knowledge gained from actual subjects like biology and history is an essential tool for thinking critically. One cannot walk into a forest, no matter how good one's critical thinking skills might be, without some knowledge of trees, how they work, and their differences. One cannot answer questions without using prior knowledge to build new knowledge. If colleges do not offer students access to serious subject matter, students will not graduate with the capacity to think critically about the world they inhabit. As one scholar of student learning explains, "knowledge is foundational: we won't have the structures in place to do deep thinking if we haven't spent time mastering a body of knowledge related to that thinking" (Lang, 2016, p. 15; see also Willing-ham, 2006). The ancient philosopher Plato once noted that one has to have an inkling of the answer to a question before one can even ask it. Even in the age of Google and Wikipedia, one needs knowledge to know what to search for and how to make sense of the answers that are found. That is because the ability to ask sophisticated questions and to evaluate potential answers is premised on what one already knows, not just on skills like critical thinking. To think well, therefore, requires knowledge. It therefore matters very much what subjects one studies and how deep one's exposure to subject matter is. A person cannot ask good questions, much less come up with good answers, about trees, much less forests, without some prior understanding of trees and forests. The same is true for history and politics, for economics and physics. It takes prior knowledge to gain new knowledge.

Thus, when reformers argue that it does not matter what one studies in college so long as one learns how to think, they are making an argument that is simply wrong. Take another analogy: what it means to play and to appreciate music. On the one hand, it is arbitrary which instrument one decides to learn. But this does not mean it does not matter. It makes a big difference if one chooses to study oboe or violin—so even if it is arbitrary, it is important. Being an oboe player is as different from being a violin player as being a chemistry major is from being an English major. But both oboists and violinists are musicians, just as both chemistry and English are part of liberal education. But imagine if someone came along and said that the real purpose of playing oboe and violin is not to become better musicians, but instead to develop the manual dexterity skills that employers want on the job. And, moreover, to develop these skills one need not play either oboe or violin, but can gain the same dexterity from yardwork or knitting. This may be true, but you are no longer learning to be a musician. The same is true of studying business, or simply learning skills—at some point, it is no longer a college education because one is no longer studying the liberal arts and sciences.

Time

A good college education takes time. There is a reason that students spend several years on a college campus taking classes. Class time is formative. It enables students to gain specific insights into the world under the mentorship of professors. Every course is a vista point that provides students new perspectives on the world. These perspectives are different for all students because they depend on the teacher, the texts or material studied, and the student herself or himself. But these perspectives lead to new insights which, in turn, form the lenses by which students view the world. They provide understanding, cultivate the imagination, and are the basis for asking new, better questions. This all takes time.

Time is formative. It takes time to foster students' dispositions, or their virtues and habits. It is not enough that students demonstrate the ability, for example, to write a research paper. Some reformers have called for a competency-based approach to education, in which students pass through predetermined competencies as fast and efficiently as they can. Not only does this approach reduce students' exposure to the kinds of vistas that foster insight, but it denies students the time required to change. College students must come to think of intellectual inquiry as an end in itself, something that they cannot, and would not, avoid. Students should not seek credits, grades, or competencies, but understanding (Neem, 2013).

Most of us do not naturally devote our time to thinking about history or politics or how cells replicate. We have to develop the habit of seeing the world historically or sociologically or economically. We have to learn to think as intellectuals. To do that we have to study history or sociology or economics. But to do more than pass tests, we must become people who think *as* historians, sociologists, or economists. And to do that, we must do, over and over, history, sociology, and economics, until it becomes a kind of second nature to see the world in new ways and ask thoughtful questions about it. And when we have developed this habit—or what is better called intellectual character—it will be sustained after college, leading us into the world with the desire to make sense of it by asking new kinds of questions of it.

Time is also required to develop skills in any meaningful way. Real skills come from repetition. For example, one can pass a driver's exam by cramming and taking written and skills-based tests. Yet that does not a driver make. A driver becomes a driver through repeated practice, until driving becomes something that one does skillfully. The same is true for intellectual skills (Lang, Chapter 5).

Finally, time on campus is vital to developing the deeper relationships that help students learn and increase student retention rates (Chambliss & Takacs, 2014). Thus, time is required to gain insights, to develop new dispositions or habits, to gain new skills, and to develop relationships. Ideally, college students do not just learn skills or knowledge; they become the kind of people who use their intellectual skills and knowledge to seek new knowledge. And to do that well, they need actual knowledge and actual vistas that provide interesting perspectives on the world. That is why efforts to make college degrees faster and quicker are bound to fail, at least if we take the idea of a college education seriously.

Money

Time is money. If a good college education takes time, what are we supposed to tell all the Americans who cannot afford it? The newspapers are filled with stories about rising tuition and student debt. Reformers argue that, given rising costs, college reform is a moral imperative if we are to increase access. The old system is simply an outdated luxury that we can no longer afford. Campuses and professors are too expensive. Degrees take too long and should be available online; earning them should be faster and more convenient. Yet, as I argued earlier, if degrees were fast and convenient, they would also be ineffective. Many Americans do not care. They want access to college degrees, but not to college education. Yet, many of the reforms proposed in the name of college access actually increase inequality by offering some students, especially working Americans, a subpar product rather than access to the real thing, while wealthier students get the benefits of going to college campuses, where they learn from professors, and spend time cultivating their hearts and minds. That betrays our country's commitment to equal access. We can do better. Indeed, we have done better.

To clear some space, we must first address the claim that college is too expensive. It is not. While the small number of the nation's most prestigious institutions has been raising tuition through the roof, they also offer significant financial aid to help poorer students attend. On the other hand, the cost per student for most public four-year institutions and community colleges has not increased as dramatically. (Cost refers to the amount a college spends per student; tuition is the amount of that cost paid for by students.) The reason tuition has grown so rapidly at most American schools is because tax support has declined dramatically. Legislators, responding to budgetary pressures and public opposition to new taxes, have cut higher education funding, leading colleges to raise tuition. This is not to say that college is not expensive. Colleges are labor-intensive institutions. Rising health care costs, the cost of new technology, the growing number of administrators and staff, and the cost of expensive facilities all contribute to college costs. Yet, surprisingly, even with these factors included, the primary reason for increasing tuition is public defunding. From this perspective, it is not that colleges cost too much, but that they no longer receive tax support. This is about politics, not costs (Desrochers, 2014; Matthews, 2013).

Moreover, the student debt crisis is overstated. Few students attend the nation's most expensive colleges. Harvard and Princeton, or even Berkeley and the University of Michigan, are not representative. Instead, most students attend regional four-year public universities or community colleges, where the cost per student is much less. As a result, the monthly education debt burden for Americans has stayed the same, or even declined a little, over the past two decades. The average student debt for the 2010–11 academic year was about $26,000, about the price of a new car. Only four percent of students had debt burdens over $100,000. College graduates' lifetime earnings, moreover, have grown significantly faster than their debt burden. In short, for most graduates, college debt is minimal and manageable (Akers & Chingos, 2014).

If the cost and debt problems are exaggerated, then we do not need to destroy college education in order to save it. We just need to pay for it. And this means giving students the freedom to study. By making college more expensive and privatizing the costs, however, we have limited students' freedom to engage in the liberal arts and sciences. If students are taking out large loans, they will think of their education solely in terms of how much money they can earn, especially if they are worried about paying off their student loans. If students are told again and again that the primary purpose of college is to get a better job, they will not come to school to study but instead to get a degree as quickly and painlessly as possible. Yet this is not what college is for. Students need the time and freedom to think. This requires leisure, or free time away from everyday concerns. We need to democratize access to that kind of leisure so that students can focus on the hard work of learning. We have done so in the past. After World War II, the GI Bill enabled thousands of Americans to attend college without incurring too much debt. For decades, taxes supported low tuition at public schools. We can therefore ease the burden on students if we choose to. It's a question of public will.

Conclusion

American colleges are exceptional in their desire to offer every student a liberal education. Today, many policy makers are asking whether the liberal arts are relevant for the 21st century. "The question is un-American," journalist Fareed Zakaria recently argued (2015). America, after all, led the world in increasing access to liberal education at the K–12 and higher education levels. Americans understood that a democracy requires educated citizens and leaders. They also recognized that the liberal arts and sciences endow people with flexible, creative skills and the insight necessary for economic success. Yet, increasingly, the United States treats liberal education as a luxury good. Expensive private liberal arts colleges even market their programs as "boutique" products for privileged students (Cohen, 2014). We have denied too many people access to a good college education in the name, ironically, of access. In reality, we have not committed ourselves to expanding access to college education. Instead, we have forced more students into college who do not wish to be there, offered them subjects that do not belong in college, and then pretended to be committed to equal access.

To put it simply, we do need a revolution in college education, but a revolution in the literal meaning of that term, a return to core purposes. Colleges have been adrift. They have been offering more vocational degrees, shifting programs online, hiring temporary faculty, and offering students quicker but less meaningful educations. We must find ways instead to offer all students, young and older, richer and poorer, access to a real college education, on campuses with professors, where they can spend a portion of their lives living in a community devoted to thinking. This costs money, but not that much if we reinvest in the public universities that provided previous generations access to a real college education. We can offer equal opportunity to all Americans who desire to go to college and are capable of it. For other students, we should offer alternative options to gain training and education after high school. Not everyone wants to or should go to college. But for those who do, colleges have an obligation to offer them a serious education in the liberal arts and sciences, not quick, easy, and cheap degrees. The measure of success is not whether college graduates earn more than noncollege graduates (and why should college graduates necessarily earn more than other highly skilled workers?) but whether college graduates are able to produce new insights because of their time on campus. In the end, the benefits of a good college education accrue not just to individuals who may lead more fulfilling lives, but to our democracy and economy. Because we all benefit, we, as taxpayers, all have a reason to subsidize it.

The purpose of college, then, is to teach people to think, to make them love thinking, and to provide them with the knowledge and intellectual skills that will enable them to have thoughts worth thinking. This takes time, and thus costs money, but it's worth it.

References

Akers, B., & Chingos, M. M. (2014). *Is a student loan crisis on the horizon?* Brown Center for Education Policy, Brookings Institution, Washington, DC.

Arum, R., & Roksa, J. (2011). *Academically adrift: Limited learning on college campuses.* Chicago, IL: University of Chicago Press.

Arum, R., & Roksa, J. (2014). *Aspiring adults adrift: Tentative transitions of college graduates.* Chicago, IL: University of Chicago Press.

Brewer, T. (2014). The coup that failed: How the near-sacking of a university president exposed the fault lines of American higher education. *The Hedgehog Review, 16,* 2. Retrieved from http://iasc-culture.org/THR/THR_article_2014_Summer_Brewer.php

Bureau of Labor Statistics. (2016, April 18). *Fastest growing occupations, 2014 and projected 2024* [accessed July 25, 2016]. Retrieved from http://www.bls.gov/emp/ep_table_103.htm

Chambliss, D., & Takacs, C. G. (2014). *How college works.* Cambridge, MA: Harvard University Press.

Cohen, S. (2014). The boutique liberal arts? *Liberal Education, 100,* 4. Retrieved from https://www.aacu.org/liberaleducation/2014/fall

Desrochers, D., & Kirshtein, R. (2014). *Labor intensive or labor expensive? Changing staffing and compensation patterns in higher education.* Delta Cost Project Issue Brief. Retrieved from www.deltacostproject.org/sites/default/files/products/Delta CostAIR_Staffing_Brief_2_3_14.pdf

Dougherty, K. (1997). Mass higher education: What is its impetus? What is its impact? *Teachers College Record, 99* (Fall), 66–72.

Holzer, H. (2015, May). *Creating new pathways into middle class jobs.* Progressive Policy Institute *Policy Brief.* Retrieved from http://www.progressivepolicy.org/issues/economy/creating-new-pathways-into-middle-class-jobs/

Lang, J. M. (2016). *Small teaching: Everyday lessons from the science of learning.* San Francisco, CA: Jossey-Bass & Pfeiffer.

Matthews, D. (2013, August 28). The tuition is too damn high, Part III: The three reasons tuition is rising. *Washington Post* [accessed July 26, 2016]. Retrieved from https://www.washingtonpost.com/news/wonk/wp/2013/08/28/the-tuition-is-too-damn-high-part-iii-the-three-reasons-tuition-is-rising/

Neem, J. N. (2013). Experience matters: Why competency-based education will not replace seat time. *Liberal Education, 99,* 4. Retrieved from https://www.aacu.org/liberaleducation/2013/fall/neem

Oakeshott, M. (1975). A place of learning. In M. Oakeshott (Ed.), *The voice of liberal learning* (pp. 1–34). Indianapolis, IN: Liberty Fund.

Scobey, D. (2016). Marginalized majority: Nontraditional students and the equity imperative. *Liberal Education, 19,* 1. Retrieved from https://www.aacu.org/diversitydemocracy/2016/winter/scobey

Steinberg, J. (2010, May 5). Plan B: Skip college. *The New York Times.* Retrieved from http://www.nytimes.com/2010/05/16/weekinreview/16steinberg.html?pagewanted=all&_r=0

Willingham, D. T. (2006, Spring). How knowledge helps. *Teachers College Record*. Retrieved from http://www.aft.org/periodical/american-educator/spring-2006/how-knowledge-helps

Zakaria, F. (2015, May 7). Book excerpt: In defense of a liberal education. *ABC News Online* [accessed July 26, 2016]. Retrieved from http://abcnews.go.com/Politics/book-excerpt-defense-liberal-education-fareed-zakaria/story?id=29901850

2. Modernizing College Purposes to Save a Troubled World

PATRICIA A. McGUIRE

Imagine an enterprise that includes scores of Nobel Prize winners across the spectrum of learned disciplines; major sports teams with millions of fans worldwide; obscure poets reciting their verses in mellow basement coffee-houses; renowned hospitals whose doctors innovate path-breaking treatments; community legal aid clinics, particle accelerators, art museums, investment companies, technology incubators, hotels, and restaurants; Olympic champions, labor unions, thousands of newspapers and magazines and media outlets; acapella groups, real estate ventures, law enforcement agencies, soaring gothic chapels, molecular laboratories developing bioterrorism defenses, and libraries whose voluminous holdings would circle the earth many times over.

Oh, and the enterprise also has millions of customers and staff, aka students and faculty, engaged in thousands of classrooms virtual and physical, teaching and learning and conducting research and producing papers on just about every intellectual topic imaginable. American higher education in the 21st century is a vast enterprise, a holding company with thousands of diverse businesses loosely affiliated under the banner of "postsecondary education"—government nomenclature mashing together colleges and universities that often can barely recognize their common educational purpose amid the remarkable diversity of their many endeavors.

While many scholars and leaders in the industry agree that American higher education is "...the greatest system of higher learning that the world has ever known..."[1] critics also insist that the flaws in the system are so serious that nothing short of wholesale reinvention must occur. The enormous scope of the enterprise can mask severe deficiencies in fulfillment of the core mission according to critics who assail the corporatization of the university. Whether real or perceived problems, they point to high tuition prices, oppressive debt burdens, inadequate access for low-income students, low graduation rates, and weak correlation between curricula and job markets as the reasons why change is essential for higher education to fulfill its purpose more effectively.

What, exactly, is the purpose that sparks so much intense debate about higher education today?

Purpose: From Classical College to Big Business

Originally established as early as the 17th and 18th centuries as colleges to educate future ministers and other aristocratic young male adults in the classical curriculum, the modern American university developed in the late 19th and 20th centuries as an enterprise with multiple lines of business involving not only teaching, but also research and myriad extracurricular activities. The idea that higher education is a "business" with many different "product lines" or "income streams" is, in itself, cause for agita among traditionalists who long for simpler times in the academy, arguing that the many activities of the university have come to obscure the essential purpose. But by the second decade of the 21st century, even the remaining small colleges have found it difficult to sustain themselves financially if they do only the one thing that most people think of as the whole "purpose" of higher education: teaching undergraduates in the liberal arts.

Diversification of the collegiate business model began in earnest with the 19th century as the emerging scientific demands of business and the nation gave birth to the modern research university first at Johns Hopkins and soon thereafter at Harvard, Yale, and other elite colleges. By the middle of the 20th century, the intense spirit of institutional competition made improving the bottom line a top priority in order to expand campus infrastructures and recruit better faculty talent, leading to diversification of institutional mission, goals, programs, and delivery systems. This expansion generated more diverse revenue streams that had the general effect of improving profitability and per-ceived prestige, and supporting reinvestment in ever-more glamorous facili-ties and renowned scholars.

Coincidentally, four external phenomena contributed to transforming the American collegiate model from a genteel educational enclave to a serious business enterprise, notably:

- *Scientific Investments for National Defense:* World War II triggered grave concerns about the future of U.S. scientific advancement, leading to the creation of the National Science Foundation and spawning massive public investment in university laboratories to stimulate research and development largely for defense purposes.

- *Federal Financial Aid:* The postwar era also fostered greater concern for advanced education for citizens for both economic and defense reasons. Broad public funding for college students, originating with the G.I. Bill of 1944 and expanding into the Higher Education Act of 1965, rapidly broadened the collegiate audience from the children of the aristocracy to a broad cross-section of the American population.
- *Civil Rights and Women's Rights:* After *Brown v. Board of Education* triggered the desegregation of public schools starting in the 1950s, the Civil Rights Movement in the 1960s forced the integration of major universities and opened pathways for rapid social and economic advancement for African-Americans in larger numbers than ever before. Meanwhile, the drive for equality for women led to the enactment of Title IX in 1972, and soon coeducation became the norm throughout American higher education.
- *Intercollegiate Sports:* Even as civil rights, women's rights, and defense investments were transforming college campuses, intercollegiate athletics became a major revenue-producing industry, at least for the institutions that organized the NCAA Division-I in the early 1970s.

These four forces—government investment in the sciences, federal funding for college students, equality for women and students of color, and the rise of big-time college sports—fundamentally reshaped higher education in the latter decades of the 20th century. Yet, despite so many remarkable changes in collegiate structures and activities across a relatively short period of time, critics of higher education decry the enterprise as slow to change, resistant to innovation, and protective of traditional ways of doing business.

Why is there such a disconnect between the reality of institutional change and the perception of stasis?

The New College Student of the 21st Century

When politicians and pundits talk about the "purpose" of college, they invariably mean full-time undergraduate liberal arts education for traditional-aged students in traditional campus settings. On many campuses, such students are no longer the majority population. However, federal and state education policy—and the basic premise of many critiques of the industry—still revolves around the halcyon ideal of the 18- to 22-year-old full-time undergraduate majoring in English, living in a dormitory with parents paying tuition and supporting a romantic collegiate lifestyle that includes rushing for Greek houses, winter break ski trips, alcohol-soaked weekends, semesters abroad, and plenty of indulgence on getting serious about postgraduate occupations.

The facts belie that stereotype. According to data from the U.S. Department of Education, nearly 75% of all undergraduates have one or more "nontraditional" characteristics[2] like paying for their own education, commuting to the campus, attending in part-time as well as full-time patterns, parenting and caring for family members, holding down a full-time job while in school, and other characteristics that are very different from the once-prevalent stereotype of the "college kid."

This new American college student is so prevalent on many campuses today that the adjective "nontraditional" no longer applies. Many universities today hail these "new traditional" students as the force driving significant change in campus practices and delivery systems, from more child care and flexible course scheduling to hybrid and online course options.

Gidget doesn't go to college any more, but public policy as well as institutional governance, programs, and curricula still often function as if that mythical coed is the only student on campus. The curricula and delivery systems of undergraduate education remain largely the same as they were in the 1950s, with enough marginal adjustments to accommodate social changes in the ensuing years, but still insistent on academic conventions such as 120-credit B.A. degrees, required courses that often seem irrelevant to modern work, major programs frozen in faculty memories of their own undergraduate days—all supported by a funding structure subsidized by states and the federal government that offers little incentive for change.

Indeed, despite political lip service to the imperative of change in the collegiate model, federal and state regulations often reinforce some of the most outmoded traditions of the collegiate model, e.g., basing financial aid on traditional semesters and seat time, declaring financial aid eligibility based on numbers of credits taken, reinforcing regional and state boundaries for approval to operate programs and accreditation, retrenchment from offering year-round Pell Grants, reduction in the number of semesters of eligibility for loans and Pell Grants despite evidence that many students (particularly adult students or low-income students of color who often work full-time while supporting families) proceed through college in radically different pathways than the more economically secure predominantly white middle-to-upper-middle class students of previous generations.

Amid all of its more glamorous business enterprises, American higher education needs to refocus its energy and resources on developing a more effective model for undergraduate education to reach new and remarkably different student populations across multiple generations, social classes, races, ethnicities, cultures, and world views. All of these students will be the citizen leaders of a dramatically transformed national and global society in the next half century.

To participate as the effective economic, social, and civic leaders they must become, these students need the more complex knowledge and skills, competencies, and global perspectives that a transformed collegiate curriculum can and should deliver. That curriculum needs to reach the new American college student in more creative, more flexible, and more effective and affordable ways. That curriculum is not necessarily one decoupled from liberal arts, but rather, one that achieves a new articulation of the broad foundation of liberal learning more urgently attuned to the critical demands of contemporary work and public life in each ensuing era of American and global social, economic, and political development.

Redefining Collegiate Purpose in the Mid-21st Century

While a great deal of change actually did occur in the organizational form, business activities, and audiences of many colleges and universities throughout the last half century, key elements of the core collegiate mission remained steadfastly rooted in deeply traditional ideas about undergraduate education. The collegiate innovators who did such a good job building massive sports and entertainment empires, research institutes, and incubation campuses need to turn their attention to the largely outmoded structures and delivery systems of undergraduate education.

To satisfy its public purpose in the education of diverse populations of students across generations for the challenges of middle-to-late 21st-century work and civic life, higher education must address the urgent need for change in four fundamental areas: students, curricula and delivery systems, governance, and accountability.

Welcoming New Populations of Students

While some colleges and universities experienced a major paradigm shift in the kinds of students enrolling in the last two decades, many other institutions avoided the rising tide of low-income students, black and Hispanic students, and students with nontraditional characteristics. Elite colleges and sports powerhouses, in particular, had the market appeal to continue to enroll traditional students through intense competition; and wealthier families had the means to pay increasingly burdensome tuition prices and the related total cost of attendance bills.

The institutions that changed earlier and more rapidly to welcome the new American student were largely less selective public institutions and special mission private colleges such as women's colleges in urban centers that lost their original population of traditional-aged young women in the migration to coeducation. These colleges and universities became the incubators for models of adult education (e.g., Weekend College, accelerated degrees, and competency-based credits) and, increasingly, outreach to historically marginalized populations of low-income students of color, including undocumented students. The successful change models studied the shifting demographic and enrollment landscapes of their regions as well as the nation and learned to create new academic programs and delivery systems largely out of necessity, and often with scant venture capital.

Collegiate enrollment boomed nationally in the 1980s and 1990s, but beginning around 2010, the pace of growth in higher education enrollment began to slow and change demographically. According to data from the National Center for Education Statistics (NCES), enrollment of traditional-aged students (18–24 years) grew 45% between 1998 and 2012, but was projected to grow just 15% between 2012 and 2023.[3] Meanwhile, enrollment of students over the age of 25, while also slowing, was projected to increase by more than 20% between 2012 and 2023.[4] Not surprisingly, more colleges and universities started enrolling more working adults, particularly women who had stepped out of college to support spouses and raise families. The growth in the population of "returning women" is one of the factors driving the increasingly large majority of women throughout higher education.

Additionally, spurred by a national policy agenda to increase both high school and college graduation rates and the proportion of Americans with college degrees while recognizing the dramatic demographic changes that will occur in the U.S. population by mid-century, the movement to enroll more low-income students of color became increasingly popular. NCES data forecasts that the collegiate enrollment of Hispanic students will rise 34% between 2012 and 2023, 25% for black students, 14% for multiracial students, 11% for Asian students, but just 7% for White students.[5]

As previously noted, federal data indicates that nearly 75% of all undergraduate students today have at least one "nontraditional" characteristic such as working full-time, attending part-time, caring for children, being self-supporting, and similar characteristics. Adult working women, low-income students—particularly low-income black and Hispanic students—are a significant part of the growth of students with nontraditional characteristics.

The new college student of the 21st century cannot simply step into the old patterns of attendance, rituals and traditions, course schedules, and extracurricular activities that characterized the idea of college for generations of traditional students. Colleges and universities must make major changes in programs and services, policies and practices, cost structures and financial aid support, staffing patterns and course schedules in order to make a college education truly accessible and successful for this new college student.

Simply admitting more low-income students, students of color, and students with nontraditional characteristics is insufficient. In the final years of the Obama administration, much public policy discussion about access in higher education focused on efforts to encourage, or force, elite institutions to accept more low-income students using Pell Grant eligibility as the marker for low income. However well-intentioned, this effort rests on an assumption that simply admitting (and, by implication, funding) more Pell Grantees will ensure the ultimate success of these students.

This argument assumes that because elite schools have high graduation rates, low-income students will graduate from them at similarly high levels. But graduation rates are not really a function of the institution itself, but rather a proxy for the economic and social advantages that the students bring with them to the school. Elite colleges have high graduation rates because they draw their students primarily from social elites whose wealth and status ensure excellent preparatory education for their children and enough financial support to remove all distractions such as having to work long hours in menial jobs to pay for housing and books rather than concentrating on studies (and social life!).

It is a grave disservice to students with different characteristics—economic status, race and ethnicity, age and life responsibilities—to assume that they will blend into an elite campus culture and become just like every other student. Rather than assuming that the new populations of students will change to adapt to the prevailing elite culture, the colleges and their campus communities need to transform their practices, services, programs, and cultural perspectives to ensure true success in a more broad-based educational mission.

Institutions that have welcomed and successfully managed majorities of new populations of college students have learned important lessons that others need to study and adopt. From practices as obvious as having service offices such as the Registrar, Advising, Bookstore, and Financial Aid open when students are in attendance (yes, even at 8 pm on a weeknight or Saturday morning), to educating faculty to be responsive to students with work and family obligations, to addressing once-hidden issues such as homelessness and hunger among students, to providing greater academic support and improved gateway programs for students who have been away from the classroom for a long time, or who did not have the advantages of prep schools in their run-up to college, the institutions that have enrolled the new college student in large numbers know that "business as usual" must change. With the right changes aligned to student needs, the students can and will be successful.

Curriculum, Pedagogy, and Delivery Systems

Higher education must transform curricula, pedagogy, and delivery systems to educate the new college student of the 21st century successfully across a range of disciplines and demands for greater alignment with workforce needs.

Curriculum. The undergraduate liberal arts curriculum, with its large menu of general education requirements and even broader array of majors, is remarkably constant despite decades of tinkering to allow more or less student choice with each passing curricular fashion. That curriculum is increasingly the object of scornful punditry and even political threats[6]—why force students to study Rembrandt or Skinner or Beowulf if those topics do not lead to an immediate job and demonstrable improvement in the student's purchasing power, that is, starting salary[7] after college? In an age that fetishizes data as proof of results, even though intellectual growth defies strict linear categorization, the notion that a broad liberal arts education is the best possible preparation for a lifetime of change and choices requiring critical thinking is dismissed as a hopelessly outmoded academic excuse for protecting the status quo.

On the other hand, some of the best defenders of liberal learning are corporate CEOs and professionals who know that the most important intellectual skills for the workforce are the ability to analyze, write coherently, solve problems, conduct research and discover new ideas, master new fields of knowledge, innovate, persuade, motivate, and take good risks—all among the desired learning outcomes of the liberal arts—along with a broad knowledge of human civilization, history, behaviors, languages, literature, ethics, and the scientific keys to understanding numbers, molecules, and chemical structures. Academics may debate forever whether the foundational collegiate-level knowledge and skills need 50 or 60 required credits and specific courses (deliberation on the foreign language requirement alone can take months), but, in the end, most agree on the desirability of a strong general education program.

The new college student needs writing, logic, numeracy, historical perspective, research skills, and scientific understanding as much, if not more so, than more traditional students of prior eras. Older professional students also often have deeper appreciation of literature, psychology, politics, and ethics, and bring real-world experience to their studies. Critics who dismiss the liberal arts foundation as frivolous or irrelevant to work clearly have not spent much time with adult students who thirst for the perspectives on human behavior that they find in great literature and philosophy, and who want to exert well-formed intellectual leadership on workplace and community debates about everything from climate change to racism in policing to school reform and pay equity—all topics that students should encounter for research and debate in college.

Critiques of the undergraduate curriculum often fail to distinguish among components of general education, liberal arts majors, and professional majors that may also have general education requirements. Nurses and accountants need ethics and behavioral insights and cultural sensitivity as much as, if not more than, aspiring artists and English professors. Nationally, in fact, the majority of undergraduates major in professional disciplines, with the largest concentrations in Business, Health Professions, Psychology, Education, and Biology/Biomedical Sciences; and this group of concentrations has stayed fairly consistent at about 46% of all baccalaureate degrees awarded from 1970 to 2014. By contrast, the population of English majors has declined from 63,000 in 1970 to 50,000 in 2014, or from 8% of all degrees awarded to about 3%.[8] The claim that most college students major in subjects that do not meet workforce needs is simply untrue. According to the Georgetown Center on Education and the Workforce, Business and STEM majors are among the highest earning majors, and this correlates with the most popular majors in the NCES data.[9]

Ultimately, the undergraduate curriculum must satisfy not one narrow purpose but multiple worthy goals for the student, the institution, and the society in which the student lives and works. Critics who create a false dichotomy between the study of the liberal arts and preparation for careers are just wrong. Undergraduate education, including not only baccalaureate programs but also many associate degree programs, certainly prepares students for professional work in specific fields. It also provides them with sufficient intellectual breadth and ballast to help leverage mere curiosity into purposeful lifelong learning. Few students or employers will benefit for very long from specific job training—skills acquired in job training are useful only until the next software upgrade when the student or worker must learn again. A college education is not job training at all, but rather a pathway through intellectual development that makes it possible for the graduate to respond effectively to continuously changing demands for new skill sets, new knowledge bases, and new ways of solving problems.

Pedagogy. Notorious political attacks on the utility of Anthropology and Art History aside, the problem is not so much the content of the curriculum as the manner in which faculty teach. Great pedagogy can make Falstaff as real as the colleague in the next cubicle, but in the wrong hands he's just one more flat fat figure in a parade of obscure and, to the bored student, seemingly irrelevant medieval characters. When the student is preoccupied with her preparation for tomorrow's staff meeting at work, her parent's increasingly unstable health, her children's babysitting arrangements, and that menacing note from the landlord, she may be distracted from giving her full time and attention to a long lecture. But she wants to learn, and actually finds the subject interesting, but would be more engaged if she could do just that—*engage* with the material rather than simply absorbing the lecture. Working professionals want to discuss how a particular lesson relates to their own experience; and from this kind of discussion they extract all of the important learning value of the liberal arts—whether analyzing Plato's cave in terms of an office retreat, or perfecting their writing skills using real business cases, or coming to understand economics through the lens of people who make serious financial decisions all the time at work and in their personal lives.

In the same way, colleges and universities that have served significant populations of low-income students and students of color have learned that engaging pedagogy is fundamental to student success. Students who have never been inside a major art museum might not respond to a thousand Renaissance slides projected in a dark auditorium; but when given the opportunity to explore and express art in their own lives, and to see and experience art in the field, they become animated and engaged in ways that eventually lead them back to a serious academic discussion of old masters. It may not be only a coincidence that the arguments in favor of diminishing liberal learning in favor of a more utilitarian workforce-focused curriculum have grown louder in a parallel track to the demand for more access for low-income students of color. Such students should not be denied the full glories of the study of history and art and literature and, yes, anthropology, that more traditional students enjoyed as a matter of privilege. Liberal learning should illuminate all souls, not just the wealthy leisure class; and a deep respect for the aesthetic and cultural dimensions of human life enriches the entire society.

Developing pedagogies across all disciplines that actually engage students in active learning is not a new concept, but too often remains a matter of faculty choice rather than institutional commitment. To ensure transformed pedagogy across the enterprise, colleges and universities must include pedagogical development in faculty education and assessment, including assessments leading to promotion and tenure.

Delivery Systems. Along with transformed pedagogy, the new college student needs the opportunity to learn in new formats and delivery systems. Fewer than 20% of today's college students can afford the luxury of attending full-time while living on campus to pursue a very traditional course schedule delivered in ivy-covered buildings joined by leafy quads. The new college student is just as likely to need and enjoy her American Fiction course or Macroeconomics seminar on a home computer at 3 am, or in a downtown corporate conference room, or in a hotel room while traveling for work, or on a ship in a remote military outpost. The question can no longer be how to get more students to have more time and funding to move onto campus, but rather, how colleges and universities must extend the classroom in new ways to students in a remarkable range of locations and time zones.

Online learning, MOOCs (massive open online courses), hybrid courses, downtown campuses, remote delivery—all have become essential features for delivery of contemporary higher education instruction. Yet, for too many institutions, these innovations remain as exotic or marginal as "night school" once was in the postwar era. While Blackboard and Moodle are increasingly standard tools for course management on many campuses—and some highly traditional institutions have created partnerships with companies like Coursera or EdX and others to experiment with MOOCs—the pervasive use of technology to deliver instruction in new ways remains more conceptual than real in too many colleges.

Regulation has stifled, rather than encouraged, innovation in delivery systems. Federal and state regulations have failed to keep pace with the rapid changes in instructional technology; and they impose outmoded ideas about who goes to college, how students learn, how faculty teach, and what is necessary to earn a degree. These outmoded regulatory environments, in turn, affect how accrediting agencies review institutions. So, for example, accreditors are increasingly consumed with the verification of the award of credit using federal rules that embrace truly outmoded ideas about time-in-place for learning. State authorization rules affecting online learning have chilled many institutional plans to create more flexible delivery systems since few institutions have the time or resources to seek out and pay hefty fees for state approval in every state where a student might be online. Institutions are wary of innovation that might put their federal financial aid funds at risk, or invite greater regulatory and accreditation review. The system works to maintain stasis in delivery rather than encouraging innovation.

The new college student often wants to complete her degree on a faster timetable—to attend year-round, to earn credit by demonstrating competency and experience, to accelerate semesters, and to attend in different patterns than those imposed by federal rules for financial aid. Sometimes the student needs to change directions and majors, only to find out that narrowing eligibility requirements mean that she has run out of financial aid.

Federal and state regulatory oversight of colleges and universities, and financial aid programs, should encourage innovation and new models for delivery that will help more students to earn more degrees on a faster timetable. In no way does a more innovative delivery system or faster timetable to degrees short-change excellence in teaching and learning; in fact, learning outcomes could be measurably better if students do not feel caught in regulatory webs and requirements that seem to elongate their time in school for no good purpose.

Governance

While politicians and editorial writers demand that college presidents take action to ensure that colleges produce more students who can start at higher salaries more quickly—that is, produce more engineers and computer scientists, the highest paying professions in 2016—presidents have little control over the curriculum. Academic governance is the province of the faculty, and decisions about reform of general education requirements or changes in major programs can take years to enact. In order for higher education to make more rapid and meaningful change in curricula and delivery systems, the governance system must change—but this very suggestion is likely to evoke years of heated debate in the faculty lounge as well as in board rooms. With presidential tenure averaging just a little over six years at doctoral institutions, according to the most recent *American College President*[10] study of the American Council on Education, the faculty with lifetime tenure often simply wait out the incumbent.

Boards, presidents, and faculty need to have an honest discussion about the ways in which the existing governance policies and practices of most universities inhibit innovation and transformation of curricula and programs, pedagogy and faculty reward systems, and then devise delivery systems more favorable to the lives and schedules of the new college students of the mid-21st century.

In the next ten years, a major generational change will sweep through faculties and executive offices on most college campuses, creating a great opportunity for revolution in governance policies and practices. Just as today's college students bore quickly when their older faculty start waxing eloquent about Woodstock and Vietnam, so, too, many younger college faculty roll their eyes at tales from the 1960s when every faculty right came with a bitter struggle against evil administrators. The new generation of faculty, like most millennials, want respect, security, good pay and great perks, time off and flextime, advancement sooner than later, an opportunity to have a say in what affects them, and clear guidance about what is expected of them to advance in the workplace. Guess what? The new generation of presidents will also be millennials and they want exactly the same things. Millennial presidents and faculty will have more in common than differences, and they should move as quickly as possible to form common cause in transforming the ways in which they make decisions for the benefit of their students and institutions.

Rather than tying them down to "the way we've always done it," boards of trustees should give the new generation of faculty and presidents broad mandates to remake the institutions for the rising new generations of college students. The absolute worst advice a board can give to a president is to declare war on the faculty in order to create necessary change—and yet, too many boards have done just that because of the fear they feel as bottom lines erode along with shrinking traditional student populations. However true the fundamental charge may be in some schools, the tendency of boards and presidents to blame faculties for the failure of institutions to change is ultimately a strategy for catastrophe—costly battles will ensue, reputations will shred, search firms will get rich, and stasis in what needs to change will prevail.

Reforming collegiate governance is an area where philanthropy that cares about educational reform and improvement could invest constructively. Incentivizing change in forms of governance to produce more effective results more quickly could take the form of grants for campus-based teams to create new models, consultation to facilitate discussion of change across all players, awards recognizing exemplary new models, and continuing education programs for boards, presidents, and faculty to participate together in learning about new modalities for decision-making.

Accountability

Higher education is, or should be, the backbone of a free society, the place where people can gather to acquire the knowledge and skills for lifelong productivity, and also where the clash of ideas, discovery of knowledge, and invention of new products and services flourish for the benefit of the society. Because the outcomes of this enterprise are so vital to the health and vitality of the nation, and given the large public financial investment in higher education, colleges and universities face demands for increasingly detailed accountability for results and full transparency in strategy and operations.

Higher education can and should be held accountable for playing a large part in the intellectual, social, and economic progress of the nation; for contributing important inventions and new ideas developed through the best research and development; for leading and shaping national and community conversations about the future of the society, its leaders, and organizations and values and culture.

Unfortunately, in the last several decades, higher education has lost the high ground in proclaiming such lofty outcomes. Instead, while presidents have been busy with developing diversified businesses and raising some stunning sums of money, the public has grown increasingly disenchanted with the spiraling cost of college and, according to some, perceived poor outcomes for too many students who have taken on large debt but have not reaped promised benefits. Enter the federal government whose investment—billions in Pell Grants, more than a trillion in student loan debt—is used as a wedge to justify forcing a form of "accountability" through published data points on each institution, aka the College Scorecard.[11]

The College Scorecard is an interesting but largely unripe collection of factoids drawn from federal databases—enrollment, net price, graduation rates, average salaries of borrowers ten years after starting at the school as derived from IRS data. Nothing in the College Scorecard reveals what the students learn, how well the college experience fulfills their aspirations, what kinds of career pathways the graduates pursue whether investment banking or teaching or missionary work. In that the College Scorecard offers not a whit of nuance about the relationship between what students actually learn, what aspirations they have in college, and how they choose to live their lives upon completion, the presentation of data such as the median earnings of borrowers sets up grossly unfair comparisons among institutions while not offering much by way of real accountability for results.[12]

College presidents, boards, and faculty must reclaim their rightful roles and responsibilities for accountability for real results in higher education. Data sets are not results, they are simply information that may or may not tell the story about student learning and satisfaction. Growth in the bottom line is also not the right result to tell the accountability story. Nor is achieving a high place in a magazine ranking. Higher education has wasted a decade or more while telling the wrong story about collegiate value and effectiveness. The voices that want to diminish the idea of the university into a series of job training exercises are growing louder; the smart wonks who want to reduce all of this complex enterprise to a few random data points on a scorecard are winning the short-term battle for credibility.

To return the role of higher education to a place of importance and value in a world that must have more purposeful moral and intellectual leadership more quickly, college leaders—presidents, trustees, faculty—must do a far better job reporting real results to the public and making the case for the critical role of higher education as essential for democracy to flourish.

Educating Competent and Compassionate Citizen Leaders

One of the more startling comments of the 2016 presidential campaign came when one of the candidates blurted out, "I love the poorly educated."

Polls for that candidate, Donald J. Trump, repeatedly indicated strong support for him among portions of the population with the least education, particularly white males without college degrees. Conversely, Hillary Clinton had her strongest polls among college graduates. While researchers and pundits plumb the many other strands of identity and demographics in the electorate, the clear education divide of the 2016 electorate signifies the widening economic and philosophical gaps in American life.

Mr. Trump's campaign exposed the fears and resentments of citizens who felt left out of the economic recovery after the Great Recession of 2008. A 2016 study by the Georgetown Center for the Workforce[13] reveals that workers with only a high school education were, indeed, largely left out of the recovery; that study found that of 11.6 million jobs created after the recession, 11.5 million went to people with college degrees. The recovery added large numbers of managerial and professional jobs while obliterating many blue collar jobs.

Adding to the stress and fear of the portion of the populace with less education is the malicious incitement against "the other"—whether Muslims or Mexicans or Syrian refugees or undocumented immigrants or people of color, 2016 reached a nadir in America's long struggle with respect for the diversity of our nation. While pure racial hatred certainly stoked some of the more virulent expressions of contempt for diverse populations during the presidential campaign, two major threads clearly brought together disparate groups of people who felt alienated and threatened—a nativist thread claiming that Mexicans and other immigrants are taking jobs away from more deserving white citizens, and a more fascist thread claiming that Muslims, in particular, are responsible for terrorism and waging religious war with America. Many of the same sources of right-wing fearmongering also made a habit of mocking serious reports on climate change, dismissing science as a cover to deflect public attention from the alleged threat of terrorists lurking in local mosques or bodegas.

Fear—the fear of being left on the margins of the economy, the fear of suffering real physical and psychological harm at the hands of unknown evil forces—is a deeply negative emotion that demagogues and terrorists alike exploit to reinforce their own power.

Knowledge is one of the greatest antidotes to fear, and a robust system of higher education must have as one of its overarching purposes the development of enlightened citizen leaders who have the capacity to confront fear while offering a more hopeful and productive vision for the communities they influence. The late John Gardner, founder of Common Cause, put it best when he wrote that, "...the first and last task of a leader is to keep hope alive."[14]

Remaking the purpose of higher education to achieve greater good in the nation and world approaching the middle of the 21st century must mean more than adapting to new technologies, welcoming more low-income students of color, recognizing the realities of adult and professional students, and changing the way institutions make decisions. While important, these actions must ultimately support enlargement and reinvigoration of higher education's most important purposes for the influence and leadership its graduates exercise beyond the campus quad.

Colleges and universities must never apologize for the intellectual luxuries of the liberal arts and sciences, even as higher education must act with a greater sense of urgency to make studies in these disciplines more clearly relevant to the great issues of this and future ages. Stewardship of the treasury of knowledge, a fundamental obligation of colleges and universities, requires constant replenishment of that treasury through creative cultivation of the climate for invention and discovery of new knowledge, not simply maintenance of all that is past.

The new American student must renew the commitment of the nation to the purpose and value of education for all citizens to the highest possible levels. This student must find honor and purpose in the profession of teaching at all levels, and find in the act of sharing knowledge the greatest possible satisfaction. This student will become the new inventor, the creator of technologies and medical cures and plays and books and laws and new ideas about work and culture and the social compact for the generations to come.

Among many current and future intellectual demands, the new American college student must know even more about the real science behind the grave planetary danger of climate change and the essential responsibility of citizens, corporate and community leaders to promote environmental sustainability for the sake of future generations.

The new American college student must know in some detail the history and sociology and psychology of religious and racial conflict in order to build more peaceful and just communities and corporations as the United States moves closer to the bright line at mid-century when the majority population will be people of color. This new student must also understand why some people feel so threatened by the approach of demographic change, and with that understanding develop strategies to reduce the fear and inchoate sense of loss, changing anger to acceptance and positive engagement with new communities over time.

This student must develop a deeper and more nuanced understanding of movements like Black Lives Matter, LGBTQ rights, rights for persons with disabilities, and other social phenomena that reflect the yearning of historically marginalized communities for greater justice, equality, and participation in mainstream society. And, after understanding, the student must know how to organize and lead communities away from conflict toward more peaceful and lasting solutions to complicated social problems. The moral goal of American society to be the exemplar to the world for justice, for freedom, for hope, and for peace needs the continuous care and frequent fierce advocacy of those with not only knowledge but the compassionate commitment to make sure that every person has the same opportunity to enjoy freedom and justice.

This is the modern purpose of American higher education—not to curate a museum to past achievements of the academy, but to spark a new American revolution for the sake of the people whom higher education must serve with ever greater effectiveness in a world where freedom and equality remain more hope than reality for too many citizens of the global village. This ongoing revolution demands well-educated citizen leaders to organize and motivate disparate interest groups to work in concert to defeat fear and its constant companions of poverty and despair; to deny power to the demagogue; to disrupt convention whenever necessary; to speak up for the voiceless; to advocate necessary change in laws and social structures to achieve the common good; to move the society ever more confidently along the moral arc of justice that ensures that the promise of inalienable rights and the blessings of liberty are a heritage that truly belong to all of the people.

Notes

1. Cole, J. R. (2012). *The Great American University.* New York, NY: Public Affairs.
2. U.S. Department of Education. National Center for Education Statistics. (2015, September). *Demographic and enrollment characteristics of non-traditional undergraduates: 2011–2012.* Retrieved from USDE website at http://nces.ed.gov/pubs2015/2015025.pdf
3. U.S. Department of Education. National Center for Education Statistics. (2016, April). *Projections of education statistics to 2023.* Retrieved from https://nces.ed.gov/pubsearch/pubsinfo.asp?pubid=2015073

4. *Ibid.*
5. *Ibid.*
6. Jaschik, S. (2014). Obama vs. art history. *InsideHigherEducation.com.* Retrieved from https://www.insidehighered.com/news/2014/01/31/obama-becomes-latest-poli tician-criticize-liberal-arts-discipline
7. Carnevale, A., Cheah, B., & Hanson, A. R. (2015). *The economic value of college majors.* Georgetown Center on Education and the Workforce. Retrieved from https://cew.georgetown.edu/cew-reports/valueofcollegemajors/
8. U.S. Department of Education. National Center for Education Statistics. *Digest of Education Statistics 2014.* Retrieved from http://nces.ed.gov/fastfacts/display. asp?id=37
9. Carnevale, *Ibid.*
10. American Council on Education. (2012). *The American College President.* Retrieved from http://www.acenet.edu/the-presidency/columns-and-features/Pages/The-Americ an-College-President-Study.aspx
11. U.S. Department of Education. *College scorecard.* Retrieved from https://col legescorecard.ed.gov/
12. McGuire, P. (2015). College scorecard sandbags equity in higher education. *Huff ington Post.* Retrieved from http://www.huffingtonpost.com/patricia-mcguire/coll ege-scorecard-sandbag_b_8129780.html
13. Georgetown Center on Education and the Workforce. (2016). *America's divided recovery: College haves and have nots 2016.* Retrieved from https://cew.georgetown. edu/cew-reports/americas-divided-recovery/
14. Gardner, J. (1968). *No easy victories.* New York, NY: Joanna Cotler Books.

Part Two: Should Liberal Education Be Modified?

In "The Urgent Need for Liberal Education in Today's Troubled World," Bruce W. Hauptli interprets how and why liberal education is under assault in the contemporary environment, both within and outside of the academy. He takes a classical view of liberal studies—one firm enough to encompass its perennial relevance for fostering rationality, ethics, and democratic education. Arguing against the notion that liberal arts is out of tune in the modern age, Hauptli sees those disciplines as inherently *vocational* in equipping students to sustain their personal and professional lives in ever-changing times. Thus, he believes that there is no better kind of learning for the individual in society.

In "Civic Engagement and Higher Learning," Richard Guarasci offers civic preparation in the form of service learning as a significant way to modify more traditional types of liberal education. He points to a renaissance in that kind of learning throughout American higher education and uses his own campus curriculum, the Wagner College "Plan for the Practical Liberal Arts" to illustrate its power in uniting work and the public and academic disciplines with service. For Guarasci, service and learning are inseparable; the neighborhood, families, and college community become as one.

3. The Urgent Need for Liberal Education in Today's Troubled World

BRUCE W. HAUPTLI

We live in a time of deep political divisions and intolerance. Moreover, both at home and abroad religious fanaticism confronts us (whatever "side" we are on).[1] While many say we live in a "scientific" age, there are many (again, both at home and abroad) who believe scientists and their "theories" are egregiously promoting hoaxes on a too-gullible public.[2] While we live in an "information age" where the best available information known to human beings is readily available to a far greater portion of humanity than ever before, it seems that fewer and fewer are able to separate the wheat from the chaff; and many confuse "popular sources" and "talking points" with authoritative information sources.[3]

Within our cultural tradition proponents of liberal education have held it to be the preferred strategy for addressing such challenges. Today, however, the very idea of a liberal education[4] is under attack from multiple sides (again, both at home and abroad).[5] Relativists claim it lacks tolerance for diversity and difference, while theologically minded individuals claim it promotes atheism and destroys fundamental enduring values. Differing individuals and groups claim it is useless; too expensive, that it is really indoctrination, or that it should be replaced by "education for the workplace." Some, of course, just don't understand what a liberal education is, and thus they cannot see it as even potentially valuable or important.[6]

The challenges to liberal education arise both from outside higher education and from within it. Clearly the cost–benefit criticisms engender internal calls for reallocation of resources, and the push for education for the workplace often finds a receptive audience in the professional schools. In his *Respecting Truth: Willful Ignorance in the Internet Age*, Lee McIntire discusses contemporary misunderstandings of the scientific methodology and misinterpretations of evolving understandings of our cognitive processes contending that:

> it is regrettable that we as individuals suffer from cognitive irrationalities that prevent us from finding or recognizing the truth. It is deplorable that so many ideologues choose to exploit this weakness by lying about the truth in their own self-interest. Yet it is almost criminal that so many in the media and academics... have done so little to counter those weaknesses and lies by standing up for truth. It is one thing to overlook the truth. It is worse to obfuscate it. But almost as bad is to remain complicit when those methods that lead to truth are being attacked. Science may not be perfect, but it is arguably the best method that we have for the discovery of truth.[7]

Indeed, both within the society at large and within the academy, the misunderstanding of scientific methodology has developed into a nascent relativism in society at large (engendering the confusion of talking points and social media posts with facts), and a full-blown relativism in parts of the academy that denies any connection of "theory" with facts and any "privileging" of one theory over any other.

Since I believe a liberally educated citizenry can best address the political divisions, help overcome the religious intolerance, assist in separating the signal from the noise, promote tolerance for differing conceptions of the good life, and prepare individuals for both an evolving information economy and for democratic citizenship, I believe it is important that we promote an understanding of what such an education is and of its importance today. To make this case, I first need to quickly clarify what such an education is like.[8]

A liberal education should transform the student.[9] As Brand Blanshard said, "to educate a human mind is not merely to add something to it. It is to transform it at a vital point, the point where its secret ends reside."[10] What is central to such an education is not that the student comes to acquire specific bits of information (certain basic units of cultural literacy, for example), but rather that *a habit of reasonableness* (often referred to as "critical thinking") becomes inculcated. According to Harvey Siegel, such an individual is "appropriately motivated by reasons: she has a propensity or disposition to *believe and act* in accordance with reasons; and she has the ability properly to assess the force of reasons in the many contexts in which reasons play a role."[11] Reasonable individuals must not simply *understand* how to critically assess a position, they must be *moved by reason*.

As the Lawrence University *Catalog* once stated: "open and free inquiry, a devotion to excellence, the development of character, the mastery of competencies, the ability to think critically, the excitement and rewards of learning—these are the aims and principles of a liberal arts education."[12] This sort of education cannot promise to produce happiness; indeed both Plato and J.S. Mill contend that even were it to produce dissatisfaction, the sort of life it engenders is preferable to the life of a "contented pig," which does not pursue these ends. As Blanshard says:

> ...Socrates' life was better because, whether more pleasant or not, it involved a completer fulfillment of powers. Grant the pig as generous a gastronomic capacity as one wishes, still one must admit that its intellectual, moral, and aesthetic horizons are limited, while those of Socrates are all but unlimited. What gave Socrates' life its value was the free play of a magnificent mind, the fulfillment in thought, feeling, and practice of a great intellect and a great heart.[13]

While many have been proponents of "the examined life," holding it to be the *sole* good life for *all* human beings, I believe that a truly democratic society will allow that there are *numerous distinct conceptions of the good life,* and *many intrinsic values,* while also believing there need not be a single hierarchy which orders them. That is, there is much to recommend John Dewey's criticism that while there may be much to recommend Plato's "ideal state," even if it did ultimately provide for the best possible society and individual:

> humanity cannot be content with a good which is procured from without, however high and otherwise complete that good. The aristocratic idea implies that the mass of men are to be inserted by wisdom, or if necessary, thrust by force, into their proper positions in the social organism...when an individual has found that place in society for which he is best fitted and is exercising the function proper to that place, he has obtained his completest development, but...the truth omitted by aristocracy, [and] emphasized by democracy...[is] that he must find this place and assume this work in the main for himself.[14]

Martha Nussbaum contends that the classical view of a liberally educated "world citizen" emphasizes three "capacities":

> ...the capacity for critical examination oneself and one's traditions....[15]
> ...an ability to see themselves not simply as citizens of some local region or group but also, and above all, as human beings bound to all other human beings by ties of recognition and concern.[16]

and

> ...narrative imagination...the ability to think what it might be like to be in the shoes of a person different from oneself, to be an intelligent reader of the person's story, and to understand the emotions and wishes and desires that someone so placed might have.[17]

I see these three capacities not as a three-legged stool, but as an elaboration of the core unified character Siegel characterizes as someone with "...a propensity or disposition to *believe and act* in accordance with reasons; and...the ability properly to assess the force of reasons in the many contexts in which reasons play a role."[18] The capacity to be motivated by reason is not a capacity of an isolated individual, but, rather, of someone who is concerned with the intersubjective activity of subjecting her beliefs, emotions, wishes, and desires to critical scrutiny. This activity requires that one see oneself as bound to others who also adopt this stance, but who may not share the same beliefs, desires, emotions, wishes, etc.

Nussbaum notes that to foster a democracy that is reflective and deliberative we must promote students whose "Socratic ignorance" of both their own and of other cultures ensures they will not take platitudes and claims about either at face-value. Instead they will approach both:

> ...with good intellectual equipment for the further pursuit of understanding. These traits, so important in a citizen of today's interdependent world, are very unlikely to be developed by personal experience alone. At present we are not doing well enough at the task of understanding, and these failures are damaging our nation— in business, in politics, in urgent deliberations about the environment and agriculture and human rights. We must, and we can, cultivate understanding through a liberal education; and an education will not be truly "liberal" (producing truly free and self-governing citizens) unless it undertakes this challenge.[19]

Of course, where questions regarding ends are addressed in a context where it is *not* presupposed that there are single answers applicable to all, the critical and reasonable capacities enhanced by a liberal education become *all the more important*. For it is only by critically and reasonably examining various differing conceptions that individuals will be able to assess properly their own, make informed choices, and develop a tolerance for others' choices of ends. Amy Gutmann discusses the importance of allowing for a diversity of ends for democracy maintaining that "democratic education" should:

> ...help students understand the merits (and limits) of tolerating competing conceptions of the good life, and thereby respecting the rights of all individuals to pursue their conception of the good life to the extent that these conceptions are consistent with respecting the equal rights of other individuals. Agreeing to disagree about conceptions of the good life is essential to securing the basic liberty of all individuals. Religious differences have long been among the most salient cultural differences in democratic societies. Deliberative democracy is committed to protecting religious freedom along with other basic liberties, such as freedom of speech. On matters of basic liberty, a democratic education teaches toleration of cultural differences on grounds of reciprocity: mutual respect for the personal integrity of all persons.[20]

Fostering such "reasonable individuals" is not a simple process. They *may* arise without attending a college or university—indeed both Socrates and J.S. Mill leap to mind as examples here. Moreover (and unfortunately) colleges and universities do not always foster either reasonableness or critical thinking. Indeed, all too frequently American colleges and universities praise the ideal of a liberal education but go about their business without any serious efforts to instantiate that ideal. It is the ideal of a research university which often dominates the American higher educational scene. Such institutions claim that they dedicate themselves to research, teaching, and service, but they truly devote themselves to transmitting, extending, and publishing specialized domains of human knowledge, values, and culture. In such educational institutions undergraduate education is seen as preparatory—its aim to produce individuals who are capable of pursuing graduate work in one of the specialized scientific, scholarly, creative, or professional fields. This is a noble goal, but it should not be the central goal of undergraduate education. Students can become skilled in the methodologies, doctrines, and values of a particular field or profession without becoming critical thinkers or reasonable individuals.

Of course extensive training in a particular science, scholarly, creative, or professional field, *can* generate individuals who are excellent critical thinkers—indeed John Dewey thought that critical thinking could be best fostered while pursuing particular scientific, professional, or practical problems. The hallmark of a liberal education, however, is not training for a particular field; instead a liberal education trains one for *life*. Individuals frequently find that they need or want to (or need to) change professions as their lives progress, and even where one is lucky enough to find a fulfilling life path and pursue it from the start, there is *more* to life than one's professional endeavors.

In the ideal case liberally educated individuals approach *all* their cognitive, axiological, professional, and practical undertakings as reasonable individuals. Thus, as Siegel notes, "when we take it upon ourselves to educate students so as to foster critical thinking, we are committing ourselves to nothing less than the development of a certain sort of person."[21] A liberal education is a challenge because the student must learn to make considered choices if she is to acquire the traits noted above. One cannot "learn how to learn" without acting and critically observing the consequences of these actions—one must learn by doing, and such learning is a function of choice and self-discipline. A liberally educated individual asks "Why" rather than "What," and proceeds to critically consider the various proposed responses. Such critical abilities are not easily developed and the challenge posed by a liberal education is that of choosing to become a critical thinker—of choosing to accept the responsibility, discipline, and effort that this involves.

While an individual may impose such a responsibility upon herself without ever attending a college or university, the enterprise of becoming such an individual is sufficiently difficult that most are aided by becoming part of a *community* which can foster and instantiate such a life. The college or university which would educate reasonable individuals who are critical thinkers must foster diversity, skepticism, and debate. This is not important because diversity, skepticism, and debate are themselves worthwhile—a diverse society of skeptical debaters might be a woefully uncritical community. These traits are important because a liberal education requires an intellectual community wherein individuals can cooperatively, collegially, and responsibly explore, debate, and consider the problems of this and other ages (and of this and other cultures)—here we see the connections between the three capacities Nussbaum mentions.

A college or university seeking to promote reasonableness must seek to develop critical thinkers who do not simply limit their critical activities to one specialized problem or area of human concern. A liberal education does this by promoting a community which values both specialized and general knowledge. The liberally educated individual thinks critically, writes clearly, and speaks effectively whether considering a mathematical problem, a scientific theory, a political argument, or a musical composition. By being exposed to a wide range of subject matters while also focusing her attention on a single area of knowledge, the liberally educated individual acquires the ability to respond to the unforeseen and unexpected—her education enables her to make considered judgments, and to treat ideas (whether her own or others') critically, reflectively, and reasonably.

If such an education is to be possible, the educational community itself must be committed to this ideal and it must provide models of critical thinking which the undergraduate student may observe and emulate. For this reason, teaching in such a community takes time and effort. Such teachers must adopt Israel Scheffler's model of teaching which holds that:

> to teach...is at some points at least to submit oneself to the understanding and independent judgment of the pupil, to his demand for reasons, to his sense of what constitutes an adequate explanation. To teach someone that such and such is the case is not merely to try to get him to believe it: deception, for example, is not a method or a mode of teaching. Teaching involves further that, if we try to get the student to believe that such and such is the case, we try also to get him to believe it for the reasons that, within the limits of his capacity to gasp, are *our* reasons.

Teaching, in this way, requires us to reveal our reasons to the student and, by so doing, to submit them to his evaluation and criticism. ...To teach is thus... to acknowledge the "reason" of the pupil, i.e., his demand for and judgment of reasons.[22]

Oftentimes people believe that a liberal education is not "useful"—it requires that one study fields, acquire information, and understand methodologies which one may never employ in one's professional life. This criticism is very wide of the mark however. Reasonable individuals will be most able to deal successfully with the complex problems and challenges which arise for today's workforce. Moreover, such an education is *essential* for sustaining a democracy. Where the citizens are not critical thinkers, it is all too easy for their thought, actions, and values to be manipulated by others. A true democracy requires that the citizens *themselves* critically assess both the means and the ends which society is to foster and pursue. Plato favors the rule of the state by philosopher kings because he believed that the ship of state must be directed by a skilled "navigator" who has a special kind of knowledge. As Dewey noted, Plato's ship of state metaphor flounders when it is recognized that navigators do not generally choose this ship's destination—the members of the crew of the ship of state are not simply hired hands. They *are* the state, and they are vitally interested in the choice of a destination as well as the course selected to attain the destination.[23] If they are not critical thinkers, however, their preferences may result from manipulation rather than rational contemplation, and their fate may not be greatly different from that of satisfied pigs.

To attempt to justify liberal education by appealing to our nature as rational animals, the "higher pleasures," the possibility of "moral self-sufficiency," or the prerequisites for "democracy" do not end the justificatory responsibility which arises here. Someone may well ask what justifies *these* ends—asking "What assures you that humans are rational," "What justifies the stated preference for democracy," or "Why should we seek to become moral, autonomous, or self-sufficient?" Such questions lead to lengthy philosophical debates, but I will not pursue these issues here.[24] I do not presume that everyone shares these ends—the fideist, skeptic, egoist, and fascist will certainly have reservations which I cannot meet here without going too far afield.

I will, however, appeal to Winston Churchill's justification of democracy since it offers a point worth noting in regard to such extended debates. Churchill notes that:

> many forms of Government have been tried, and will be tried in this world of sin and woe. No one pretends that democracy is perfect or all-wise. Indeed, it has been said that democracy is the worst form of Government except all those other forms that have been tried from time to time; but there is the broad feeling in our country that the people should rule, continuously rule, and that public opinion, expressed by constitutional means, should shape, guide, and control the actions of Ministers who are their servants and not their masters.[25]

I think that Churchill's justification of democracy may apply quite well to the justification of a liberal education in our current context. While such an education is not perfect, given the expectations we have, it is not clear that there are any truly viable alternatives. While there are other educational models, they do not facilitate the ends we actually need to achieve to sustain our democracy, provide for individual autonomy, and ensure the sorts of adaptive and reasonable personnel our society and economy need to flourish. Unfortunately, a liberal education is something one must actually work at—the challenge of accepting the responsibility to become a critical thinker and a reasonable individual is a difficult challenge to accept when one is a member of a passive consumer society.

A liberal education is a privilege because it is not the educational norm within our larger community—relatively few citizens actually receive such an education (although such an education is, truly speaking, something all citizens *should* receive). Those who receive such an education become not only personally empowered, but they also have a civic responsibility. The American "founding fathers" clearly believed, and acted, upon this—and Adams and Jefferson did much to mandate and facilitate the liberal education of the populous. As their example shows, liberally educated individuals have the ability to improve society and better the lot of all citizens.

Liberally educated individuals who do not direct at least some of their energies in an effort to improve their society act irresponsibly and betray the fact that they have acquired but the veneer of a liberal education. Socrates and J.S. Mill were social activists—neither pursued the higher pleasures simply to make himself exceedingly happy. Each believed that their happiness was intimately tied to the happiness of others, and each worked selflessly to help others improve their lot. While their examples may be hard acts to follow, liberally educated individuals find that the privilege of empowerment carries the *responsibility* of social commitment.

In the truest sense, a liberal education *is* vocational—it prepares individuals for lives as responsible and critical agents and citizens. It equips them with the skills requisite to master new vocations rather than limiting them to a single niche in a continuously evolving world, and it equips them with the tools necessary to help sustain our democratic institutions. While it has been valued and valuable throughout our cultural history, I hope I have made some headway toward showing that the challenges we confront make it *urgently necessary* for today's society.

Notes

1. *Cf.*, Craig Biddle, "Islamic Jihad and Western Faith," *The Objective Standard* v. 10 (Spring 2015).
2. An interesting source which questions our "scientific" presumptions while also addressing religious differences is: Gerardus Bouw, "Why Geocentricity?" http://www.geocentricity.com/geocentricity/whygeo.html, last modified May 7, 2001, and accessed on June 3, 2016.
3. *Cf.*, Lee McIntyre, *Respecting Truth: Willful Ignorance in The Internet Age* (New York, NY: Routledge, 2015).
4. It should be clear that "liberal" here refers not to the current political distinction between liberals and conservatives, but, rather, the "etymological roots of the word 'liberal,' used in regard to education, are found in the Latin *liberalis*, an adjective applied for centuries to various words regarding education: *disciplinae liberales, studia liberalia, doctrinae liberales, litterae liberales*, an, especially, *artes liberales*. These terms abound in writings from the Renaissance, from the late Middle Ages, and on back from Isidore in the seventh century, Cassiodorus in the sixth century, Augustine in the fourth century, Quintilian in the first century C.E., and Cicero in the first century B.C.E.", Roger Kimball, "Foundation of the *Artes Liberales*," in his *Orators and Philosophers: A History of the Idea of Liberal Education* (expanded edition) (New York, NY: College Entrance Examination Board, 1995), p. 13.
5. *Cf.*, Martha Nussbaum, *Not For Profit: Why Democracy Needs The Humanities* (Princeton, NJ: Princeton University Press, 2010); Fareed Zakaria, *In Defense of Liberal Education* (New York, NY: W.W. Norton, 2015; Michael Roth (New Haven, CT: Yale University Press, 2014); and Robert Orrill (ed.), *The Condition of American Liberal Education: Pragmatism and a Changing Tradition* (New York, NY: College Entrance Examination Board, 1995).
6. Of course such challenges are not new, and this model of education has been challenged throughout the cultural tradition. Kimball and Roth artfully trace this history in the works cited in note 4 above.
7. Lee McIntire, *Respecting Truth: Willful Ignorance in the Internet Age* (New York, NY: Routledge, 2015). Kindle version location 3010.
8. A fuller discussion of the *nature of such an education* can be found on my webpage.
9. A Wittgensteinian should be suspicious when she is tempted to define the essence of anything, and a naturalist should be wary of those times when she is tempted to speak about intrinsic values, but there are centrally important aspects of a liberal education which stand out if one pauses to reflect on such educational programs and experiences. What I have to say on this matter is by no means original, and I have borrowed particularly heavily from the *1989–1990 Course Catalog* of my *alma mater*, Lawrence

University (Appleton, WI: Lawrence University, 1989). That description of a liberal education is excellent.

10. Brand Blanshard, "The Uses of A Liberal Education," in his *The Uses of a Liberal Education* (La Salle, IL: Open Court, 1973), pp. 42–43.

11. Harvey Siegel, *Educating Reason* (New York, NY: Routledge, 1988), p. 23. Emphasis added to the passage.

12. Lawrence University's *Course Catalog, op. cit.,* p. 13.

13. Brand Blanshard, "What Is Education for?" in his *The Uses of a Liberal Education, op. cit.,* p. 98.

14. John Dewey, "The Ethics of Democracy" (1888), reprinted in *John Dewey: The Early Works: Early Essays and Leibniz' New Essays 1882-1889* v. 1, ed. Jo Ann Boydston (Carbondale, IL: SIU Press, 1969) p. 243; and in *John Dewey: The Political Writings* ed. Debra Morris and Ian Shapiro (Indianapolis, IN: Hackett, 1993), pp. 59–65, p. 61.

15. Martha Nussbaum, Cultivating *Humanity: A Classical Defense of Reform in Liberal Education* (Cambridge: Harvard University Press, 1997), p. 9

16. *Ibid.,* p. 10.

17. *Ibid.,* pp. 10–11.

18. Harvey Siegel, *Educating Reason op. cit.,* p. 23. Emphasis added to the passage.

19. Martha Nussbaum, Cultivating *Humanity: A Classical Defense of Reform in Liberal Education* (Cambridge: Harvard University Press, 1997), p. 147.

20. Amy Gutmann, *Democratic Education* (Princeton, NJ: Princeton University Press, 1987), p. 308.

21. *Ibid.,* p. 41.

22. Israel Scheffler, *The Language of Education* (Springfield, IL: Charles C. Thomas, 1960), p. 57.

23. *Cf.,* Renford Bambrough, "Plato's Political Analogies," in *Philosophy, Politics, and Society,* ed. P. Lasslet (Oxford: Blackwell, 1956), p. 105.

24. My *The Reasonableness of Reason: Explaining Rationality Naturalistically* (Chicago, IL: Open Court, 1995) develops an extended defense of the commitment to reason against skeptical and fideistic challenges which contend that such a commitment is arbitrary, unjustified, or only justifiable in a question-begging manner.

25. W.S. Churchill, *W.S. Churchill: His Complete Speeches 1887–1963,* R.R. James (ed.), v. 7 (New York, NY: Chelsa House, 1974), p. 7566.

4. Civic Engagement and Higher Learning

RICHARD GUARASCI

In the midst of the most substantive fiscal and demographic challenges to higher education since the Great Depression, universities and colleges face dramatic problems in reconfiguring the pricing and delivery of undergraduate education. Tuitions rise along with increasing student debt. According to the national narrative, students and families confront the rising cost of college with uncertainty, fearing that for too many, higher education may be priced beyond their means. Families worry that tuition debt burdens will overwhelm them, particularly if their students are unable to secure adequate post-graduation employment set at meaningful levels of compensation.

Universities respond by offering ever-rising levels of student financial aid, essentially discounting tuitions so that net tuition revenue has remained either flat or in decline. Their budgets are unsustainable, their faculty members anxious, academic programs threatened. Competition for enrollment is acute, particularly in public institutions in which state legislatures search for fiscal relief and find higher education a convenient target for reduced appropriations. The large majority of private colleges suffer from unsustainable levels of student financial aid that reduce net tuition prices by more than 50%, and result in severe pressure on their fiscal health and educational needs.

At the same time, university admission and marketing offices produce volumes of data demonstrating the economic value of a college degree. Legislatures and government policy makers insist on evaluating colleges on the employability and compensation levels of recent graduates, essentially reducing higher learning institutions to first-job training centers. In short, the new American narrative presents higher education in strictly material terms, forgetting the original missions of land-grant universities, religiously founded private colleges, and 20th-century urban and metropolitan universities. All were founded on mission statements promising broad learning for professional and career success as well as the preparation of a literate and engaged democratic citizenry. Clearly, this new American narrative contrasts with the respective visions of Benjamin Franklin and Thomas Jefferson, who both envisioned a nation founded on a vibrant democracy born of a highly educated and participatory electorate.

With such a materialistic public discourse surrounding higher education, there is a missing media notice of a rather profound rediscovery of the public purpose of higher education. Civic engagement has emerged as an essential part of the fabric of American higher education.[1] More than 1,100 colleges and universities are members of Campus Compact, the largest national higher education organization that promotes public service, civic engagement, community-based learning courses, and university-community partnerships. More than 500 individuals belong to the Anchor Institutions Task Force, a grouping of individuals and institutional representatives who promote neighborhood and place-based partnerships involving university students, faculty, and staff with local agencies and public leaders. The Anchor goal is to contribute and sustain large amounts of social capital into distressed communities. The list goes on to include a large number of other higher education organizations supporting campus work in civic engagement. An extraordinary number of students are actively involved in community work, both in courses and co-curricular campus efforts, often using the power of social media to partner with community organizations in addressing social issues such as reducing abysmal high school graduation rates. In addition, campus stakeholders are effectively engaging local economic development, environmental sustainability, racial stereotyping, anti-poverty work, immigration issues, and severe health disparities in economically distressed communities.

Although often idiosyncratic and scattered, civic engagement work has emerged as a central feature of college campuses. Why has this happened and why now? And why has it developed as a nearly universal element in American colleges and universities? Are civic learning and civic practice necessary elements of undergraduate education and, if so, why? What are the goals of civic engagement and are universities assessing this work thoroughly? What are the expected outcomes? Finally, is civic engagement an essential element in a more effective type of undergraduate education, one reconciling theory and practice, text and field-based learning, liberal arts, and professional studies?

The Renaissance of Civic Engagement

The past twenty-five years have been witness to the renewal of the civic mission of universities and colleges. No one expects to find vibrant civic engagement programs on American campuses. Regional accreditors account for such efforts in their respective protocols for student learning outcomes and campus life programs.[2] University leaders point to the importance of such programs in their speeches and we find student civic involvement prominently placed in college admissions and promotional literature. In its popular annual rankings issue, *U.S. News* features the top schools renowned for service learning. How did this relatively recent renewal occur and why at this point in American higher education history?

We can trace the origins of this renewal to the founding of Campus Compact, now the largest national higher education civic engagement association, which includes more than 1,100 universities and colleges. In 1985, the Compact began at a meeting led by some key university presidents from Brown, Georgetown, and Stanford universities and the Education Commission of States. Their intention was to combat a perceived growing materialism and narcissism of undergraduates by agreeing to a presidential compact promoting community service on college campuses. Soon after, a number of other presidents signed on and eventually 34 state compacts emerged in addition to the establishment of a national office. Although a number of other national higher education organizations emerged that specialized in student involvement in community service, Campus Compact provided the initial impetus. Today, the civic landscape includes a large number of critically significant programs. Often specialized in particular educational sectors, specific policy arenas, or academic programs, the national organizational growth is expansive.

Campus Compact grew steadily in the 1980s. Its work concentrated on student engagement in community service and direct service delivery in distressed communities and with local social agencies. By the 1990s, Compact was one of the leaders in linking community service to the curriculum, introducing service-learning courses. Initially controversial among faculty and administrators, Compact established baseline guidelines for the effective use of experiential learning and student responsibility in honoring community partners and their needs and expectations. Compact's guidelines suggested minimal standards for student and community outcomes. By the turn of the century, millennial students sought out service-learning courses in greater numbers and more faculty members found greater educational value in field-based learning when effectively coordinated with civic work. As the field matured, both curricular and co-curricular efforts produced a vast amount of direct service to local communities worth millions of dollars in voluntary labor.

During this decade, a number of fellow higher education organizations focused on discrete dimensions of civic work. A few examples include the Association of State Colleges and Universities (ASCU), which formed the American Democracy Project in conjunction with the *New York Times*, promoting democratic literacy and voter education among university students. ASCU's efforts involved 240 campuses and potentially 2.3 million students. The Association of American Colleges and Universities (AACU), which has a membership of more than 1,300 colleges and universities, developed numerous initiatives linking classroom pedagogy, civic and personal responsibility, and campus diversity in support of engaged citizenship and an inclusive democracy. AACU's work brought greater intellectual substance to the civic work, which elevated the diversity and justice agendas into the mainstream of democracy building. Instead of perceiving the need for greater diversity and increased university access as exclusively the claims of the underrepresented on campus, AACU promoted a greater vision. Their civic work elevated social inclusion to the larger agenda of building a vibrant and socially rich version of an American democracy appropriate for the 21st century. This rekindled Franklin's and Jefferson's original vision for an educated and active citizenry molded by universities, committed to educating for democracy as well as for personal growth.

Other examples of the reach of civic engagement in higher education include two fascinating organizations that speak to a specific aspect of undergraduate learning and personal growth. Bringing Theory to Practice (BToP) concentrates on the relationship of civic practice with the psycho-social development of undergraduates. Most specifically, BToP develops programs that integrate student learning, civic engagement, and personal reflection with the goal of increasing student flourishing.[3] Often this work is found to increase students' self-esteem as they become valuable to others through civic work. In a somewhat ironic way, BToP focuses on increasing social betterment by equally improving the lives of engaged students and the community residents with whom they are involved. Autobiography and biography are joined together as each becomes involved with the other. Both are recipients of the gifts of volunteerism and civic practice. BToP finds that undergraduates with barriers to learning (addictions, health issues, learning disabilities, social stereotyping, etc.) have a greater probability of surmounting them through the connection of community engagement. Community residents find hope, if not direct service, from a generation of young persons with whom they develop mutual respect, common empathy, and a sense of social reciprocity. The Engelhard Foundation and the Christian A. Johnson Endeavor have funded and supported BToP programs on more than 450 campuses.

Imagining America is another niche civic engagement organization that focuses on the unique and important role of the arts and humanities in engaging civic prosperity, addressing social inequality, enhancing diversity, and enabling community engagement. Through the promotion of public scholarship, Imagining America supports faculty, artists, performers, and students in their work with challenged communities. I will discuss this below in many ways using a local example of musical and theatrical performance. The arts and public history are remarkably effective in breaking stereotypes. This type of civic work creates an authentic community narrative that recognizes social differences and elevates the common shared lives of those often divided within a local community. This is a unique approach in the civic engagement work of higher education. It demonstrates the growth of this work and its adoption by specific domains within the campus. As with other stakeholder areas such as student and alumni affairs and discrete disciplines, the growth and maturation of civic engagement is yielding an expansive footprint throughout the academy and, one would hope, providing critical social capital and measurable impacts inside communities and institutions suffering severe social dislocations and a declining base of personal opportunity.

There are many other important national organizations in the higher education space. Each plays a significant role in building the agenda of democracy. The Coalition of Urban and Metropolitan Universities (CUMU) includes more than 90 universities and colleges as members. They focus on the special role that their urban locations demand. Many of these institutions were focused on the working-class, immigrant populations, and the social dislocations of urban and industrial life in the dawn and later the closing of the 20th century. Social work, allied health, and education programs served usually underrepresented populations excluded from bucolic residential campuses. Their constituencies required attention to service for their geographic neighbors. Students were mostly if not exclusively commuters for much of the past century.

Founded in 1989, CUMU has grown in size and substance. CUMU promotes active engagement of its member institutions through civic work in partnering with the cities and their neighborhoods, usually involving increasing economic development, bettering the local K–12 schools, providing essential services addressing health disparities and needs of new immigrants, and building civic prosperity. Above and beyond educating young and old to be credentialed professionals in these occupations, CUMU institutions are committed to being fully civically engaged inside and outside of the curriculum. They share many values with the other national organizations already mentioned but they bring a unique focus to the metropolitan and urban space.

The Democracy Commitment (TDC) is a national initiative of community colleges that promotes civic engagement for their students through course work, volunteer projects, and community partnerships. Like the other national organizations, TDC promotes the development of civic skills and civic learning through public work for community college students. TDC also serves as a national clearinghouse for these projects and interfaces with universities and the other national organizations.

I have just touched the surface of the long list of national higher education civic groups. There are some key players such as the Kettering Foundation and the Bonner Foundation, which provide research, dialogue, leadership training, and similar assets for the civic work of campuses and the work of the national organizations. There are smaller coalitions such as Project Pericles, a group founded by philanthropist Eugene Lang, which is made up of approximately 30 member institutions, mainly private liberal arts colleges committed to the civic agenda in higher learning. The Center for Information and Research on Civic Learning and Engagement (CIRCLE) is housed at Tufts University. It provides important data and analysis on civic development of high school and college students. The Democracy Imperative was founded in 2007 and is a national network of civic and campus leaders that supports deliberative dialogue on campuses and in communities. The roster of national civic organizations in the higher education sector is much larger than accounted for in this chapter. In addition to them, there are many vital campus centers that play a local and national role such as the Netter Center at the University of Pennsylvania, the New England Resource Center for Higher Education, and many others. One can see that in the past 30 years civic engagement has exploded within the higher learning sector.

The renewal of civic engagement is just that, not a new element of higher learning in the United States but rather the rediscovery of one of its founding virtues. This explosion of activity in the past three decades may be as much the rediscovery of a basic American instinct as the influence of new educational leadership. One is reminded of Alexis de Tocqueville's prescient observation in the 1830s about the unique American character built on personal liberty and democratic impulse but residing on the ugly truth of the dramatic denial of basic freedoms for women, slaves, and those without property. He argued that the fate of the new nation and its radical experiment in liberal democracy hung on the fact that personal volunteerism and community service developed "the habits of the heart" within these new citizens and that alone would soften the other impulse to personal selfishness. So, witnessing civic engagement within American higher education is not new, particularly because these values and practices were present in its history and part of the bedrock of spiritual, humanistic, and cultural values responsible for its creation. The evidence lies in the founding and present mission statements of virtually every college and university in the United States, although the materialistic narrative championed by some current elected officials would seek to deny or replace them.

The scope and currency of the civic is omnipresent in American higher education. It ebbs and flows in size and importance in different eras. During the Nixon era, the National Center for Service Learning was established to support efforts in community service. It virtually died in the Reagan administration only to be reborn under President George H. W. Bush's "thousand points of light" program for increasing citizen volunteerism. It reemerged under President Clinton as the Learn and Serve program, which spent well over $2 million annually to fund service-learning efforts. Again, these funds did not survive the budget rescissions of George W. Bush's administration. Little has been reclaimed under President Obama and the national legislative political stalemate in Washington.

The Promise and Limits of Service Learning

Although the footprint of civic engagement in higher education may be vast, I would contend that it is far from strategic and falls far short of its potential. Its growth is impressive. It has added much in the way of deep learning for undergraduate students. It has increased their civic awareness and their civic sensibilities. It has affected communities for the better, most likely on the level of service delivery. But the possibilities for civic learning and social impact are much greater than the amount of social capital dispensed by universities, their faculty, and students. The potential is vast but we tap so little of it. My standard for assessing the impact of civic engagement for any university or specific campus program is quite simple. The work must increase student learning, increase the civic competency and engagement of participating students as well as participating community partners, and finally the civic work must have a measurable impact on the community and its residents. The civic work must not only elevate student citizenship but also begin to reduce the coefficients of inequality that define so many of the communities and neighborhoods with whom colleges are partnered. To achieve these objectives, civic assessment protocols are an essential and obvious piece of any formula defining success.

We need a new and unified direction for this work that moves past good intentions and idiosyncratic efforts to achieve community prosperity.

The good news is that the civic engagement paradigm is evolving once again. While maintaining the best of service learning and community service, the leaders in civic engagement now are prioritizing comprehensive and strategic neighborhood and community partnerships. From its recent reappearance in 1985 as a campus-based volunteer service that was inspired by the founding of Campus Compact and later the introduction into college curriculums through service-learning courses, the universities focused on civic engagement as the preparation of college students as engaged democratic citizens. First, administrators encouraged their student affairs staffs to encourage students and their campus organizations. Community service moved away from a requirement for those students in recovery from disciplinary violations to active student participation on and off campus. Gradually, over a decade or more, the concept of service gained legitimacy as an essential component of student development. Campus Life offices promoted community service as an integral part of social development and character formation.

Once service learning began to find favor in isolated but important parts of the curriculum, the footprint of the civic work expanded. Newfound faculty allies began to see value when service was indeed integral to the classroom goals of specific subjects. The primary curricular home of service learning was usually found in the social science departments and to a degree in the helping professions. By the turn of the century, community involvement was lodged in two places, student affairs–organized co-curriculum and distinct curricula offerings. The natural sciences and, to a large extent, the humanities found community involvement outside of their responsibilities and outside of their disciplines. These barriers have been slowly broken down during the past 10 years. Service learning was evolving too. It began as an auxiliary field based on experience that provided students with the ability to observe course issues in community contexts, such as poverty, social welfare policy agencies, and immigration communities. The local community became an object of study from a somewhat "voyeuristic" perspective. As the faculty emphasized greater academic rigor in service learning, ethical as well as educational values became important. This is not to say that these were not valuable civic experiences for both students and community participants. In its best moments, service learning promoted basic democratic encounters for each. Students would engage individuals and neighborhoods outside of their personal experience and so too would community residents. When done responsibly, service learning allows students to connect formal learning, texts, and subjects directly with the biographies of communities and residents who are often left outside the media narratives available to young students. At its best, these two disparate groups find friendship, empathy, and social connections. All of this can lead to a greater understanding of their respective social worlds and it may foster authentic democratic moments for each. This is how democratic cultures develop from narcissism and materialism of the "me" to the connectedness and reciprocity of "we." After all, this is what the original signers of the Campus Compact had envisioned, the renewal of democratic sensibilities among college youths.

In my personal teaching as a political science professor and dean of the college in the mid-1990s, I introduced the first service-learning courses on the campus of Hobart and William Smith Colleges, a small, private liberal arts institution in upstate New York. The course was called "Politics, Community and Service," and students read widely on theories of democracy and race, gender, and class.[4] We included numerous perspectives, and students were assigned community placements in settings appropriate to the overall course themes and as fitting the needs of the local community. Geneva, New York, remains a racially diverse upstate city of approximately 30,000 residents. It was a site for the Underground Railway prior to and during the American Civil War. But it was a divided city racially. Separate cultures remained distant although individuals would maintain personal interracial friendships across the class divisions.

My class was fully engaged in the course materials. Although they were divided politically across the usual political orientations, they maintained an enthusiasm for the materials and carried out a respectful discourse. They kept journals on their fieldwork, which required them to divide their reports into three categories, simple weekly field notes on what happened in their field placements, reactions to the weekly assigned readings, and the integration of the field experiences and their observations with concepts they found useful from the assigned weekly readings. We invited community agency partners to class to give presentations on their field placements. Additionally, students wrote traditional college analytic papers on the course readings. They finished the course with a "citizenship autobiography" that asked them to more thoroughly compare, contrast, and integrate their fieldwork with any authors or readings they found most helpful or most repugnant. The citizenship autobiography was organized along the lines of an intellectual autobiography in the sense that I asked them to write about who they were becoming as engaged citizens as a result of this course. They were to integrate the readings with the personal impact of the community work.

The results of this course (and others I have taught since) were quite remarkable. The students engaged material thoroughly and differently from what was typical of undergraduate experience at the time. Community involvement consisted of placements in interracial settings of poverty, hunger, addictions and recovery, mental health agencies, and related social agencies. Often stereotypes fell hard from both liberal and conservative perspectives. Personal relationships developed between students and Geneva residents. They emerged across differences in age, race, ethnicity, gender, and sexuality. Agency leaders developed personal relationships with students and so did their clients, who were drawn from community residents. Differences became part of open conversations among all of the class stakeholders. The course readings gave students an intellectual compass to place individuals and neighborhoods into a larger context. My students were becoming liberally educated as both learners and citizens.

I realized that in previous years of effectively teaching many of the same concepts, students failed to rise to this new standard of engagement that transcended a Deweyan experiment of simply connecting course texts and fieldwork with the goal of deepening learning. This course experience linked the personal and the intellectual through civic engagement. The result was much deeper learning of the course material. This course met the standard of increasing student civic competence as judged by the remarkable and revealing citizen autobiographies. One student wrote about her community work in a residential center for drug- and alcohol-addicted mothers who were required to live there for at least three months and to bring their young toddlers. My female student, a brilliant and strong independent white feminist, expected to encounter women her mother's age but met mothers younger than she. She was taken aback. The civic work helped her cross a cultural divide composed of inner-city young black and brown teenagers, too young to be mothers and too bright to be addicted. She wrote in her citizenship autobiography, "Through the accident of history, twenty one years ago I was born into my comfortable life, and she was unfortunately born into a life of material poverty, almost insurmountable barriers and limited opportunities. I thought a lot about God that night."[5] In ways a text can rarely create, my student began to confront issues of race, gender, and inequality. The combination of an intellectually challenging course and real-life civic experience provided her with a much more profound educational moment. Some of her assumptions about these issues were now to be better informed and subject to further interrogation.

These types of learning experiences can be profound, as in this case. In some ways, they are analogous to the best of what study abroad may offer students, a deep immersion outside their own culture, experiences, and comfort. Assumptions are challenged and new cultural experiences require deeper personal introspection and cultural reflection. Of course, there are many service-learning courses in which the opposite can occur, when there is little responsibility and direct community involvement provided by the instructor and/or supporting civic engagement staff. Without supervision and cultural context, old stereotypes of race, class, and gender may harden. I found that my visits to the sites with my students helped us to reflect together on what and why things were as they found them in their field sites and neighborhoods. "Why is this a failing school?" I would ask. "What teachers work here? What resources do they have and who decides that? What is the constellation of political, social, and economic forces that surround this community?" My job was to get my students past the superficial and beyond regurgitation of the text materials.

After several courses like this one and with similar outcomes, I began to realize the power and limits of service learning. Indeed, the best results do create the possibility of the encounter with "the stranger" for both students and community residents. They open up democratic moments rich with personal stories that expose similar values, individual hopes, and personal dreams. The connectedness created by civic work opens a door for democratic sensibilities to emerge.

But does any of this amount to changing the social conditions that underlie persistent class, race, and gender inequalities? In other words, will service learning lead us to real social and personal agency that produces engaged citizens and nonpartisan community leadership to contest the foundation of despair? Does service learning lead to Franklin's and Jefferson's dreams of a vibrant democracy characterized by genuine equality of opportunity and the deliverance of substantive legal equality? In other words, does service learning create better moments that may dispense with social stereotypes and simultaneously open up democratic participation and call up Walt Whitman's hope for "democratic vistas"? I think service learning may attend to the former but we need the civic work to be more impactful, intentional, and strategically aligned to realize the latter.

From Service Learning to Neighborhood Partnerships

Neighborhood partnerships may be in the offing with higher education and civic engagement. The paradigm is deepening if not shifting. As the civic becomes more and more embedded into the fabric of campus life, it influences the institutional self-narrative. Those original founding mission statements find new champions among students, engaged faculty, and staff. Narratives of service-learning courses as well as those student stories lauded by student affairs, career development, university chaplains, impressed community partners, and local officials all find their way to the president's office and the senior managers. Sometimes it works in reverse and presidents champion the civic and spawn the civic practice and civic culture on their campuses. What emerges is a more comprehensive institutional vision, the "civically engaged" university. The new ambition promotes and supports civic engagement as a virtue and as an intentional institutional goal that transcends the entire campus—the classroom, the co-curriculum of learning outside the classroom, the extracurricular activities, neighborhood and community relations, alumni affairs and career development programs, and government relations. What began in the 1980s as the promotion of community volunteering is now emerging as part of the university brand.

Concurrently, a more ambitious vision of civic engagement is now prospering. Pioneered as an organizing concept by a small task force with its center of gravity at the Netter Center at the University of Pennsylvania, civically engaged universities are encouraged to view themselves as critical agents for creating local civic prosperity. As placed-based institutions, colleges and universities are critical and one of a number of "anchor institutions" within their local communities. Along with churches, schools, hospitals, local foundations, and many nonprofit organizations, colleges and universities are not likely to uproot. They stay in place.

The anchor institution identity is a powerful and potentially high-impact reconceptualization of the civic mission of universities. It is one that promises a comprehensive relationship with local communities. It transcends the elliptical calendar that limits the civic mission to become solely a prisoner of the academic calendar. It incorporates all of the other dimensions of college civic commitments, service, community-service programs, and individual one-off volunteer events. It includes all of these within a strategic alignment of sustainable university social capital with the appropriate community challenges and local partners in the pursuit of greater local civic, economic, educational, and social prosperity. The anchor institution concept meets my formula for increasing student learning and student and community civic competency, while impacting meaningfully.[6] It meets the original mission and goals of most if not all of the higher education sector. This is education for the advancement of a vibrant democracy and a successful economy.

Anchor universities and colleges are taking root across all sectors of nonprofit two- and four-year degree-granting institutions. Some examples of nationally recognized leaders include large universities such as the University of Pennsylvania, the University of Louisville, Syracuse University; regional institutions such as Portland State, Indiana University–Purdue University at

Indianapolis (IUPUI), Nebraska-Omaha; two- and four-year local institutions such as Miami-Dade College; branch campuses such as Rutgers-Newark; and, private liberal arts colleges such as Wagner College (New York City) and Widener University (Chester, Pennsylvania).[7] A host of community colleges are also leading the way.

What does an anchor institution do? How does it operate as an anchor? Syracuse and Louisville as well as Wagner offer helpful portraits. Under the leadership of Chancellor Nancy Cantor, Syracuse University created ongoing and deep relationships with the Syracuse public schools as well as a remarkable arts corridor in a depressed area of the city. Long suffering from a declining economy in upstate New York and existing as a racially divided city, Syracuse was championed by Chancellor Cantor. She took on the challenge of turning the city toward revitalization through direct intervention by the university. A number of service-learning courses and civically minded departments directly aligned student and faculty engagement in the spectrum of issues surrounding the K–12 city schools. An aggressive scholarship program was put in place to open opportunities at the university for students unable to afford Syracuse. The chancellor championed a comprehensive support system from pre-kindergarten through high school to stimulate readiness, persistence, and high school completion in schools that have very low graduation rates. Linking Syracuse service courses, internships, university financial aid programs, grant writing, and numerous other assets, Syracuse University became the facilitating anchor institution that invigorated the other anchors in corporate, nonprofit, and governmental offices. Alliances were formed across sectors that aligned social and monetary capital with the entire pipeline of the school trajectory that children experience from preschool through high school. Simultaneously, Syracuse University forged ahead with the redeployment of its own capital resources and physical plant facilities to create a vibrant arts corridor that involved local youths and college students. All of this activity stimulated economic confidence within the region.

The University of Louisville played a similar role but under somewhat different circumstances. The city of Louisville faced the very real threat that its major employer would exit the city in the near term because the failing school system was unable to provide employers with skilled and capable employees. The mayor and others turned to the university for assistance. The university realigned its civic work to foster educational excellence in the K–12 schools. The goal was to increase the number of two- and four-year degrees dramatically over the next 10 years. As with Syracuse, engaged senior leadership at the university, reinvigorated faculty, and engaged students became a staple within the civic work required to support city youngsters who would be prime candidates for school failure at those critical junctures throughout the school system. Unprepared for kindergarten, unable to read at the third-grade level, unprepared for high school in the seventh grade, and failing at the second and third year of high school set the predictable pattern for inner-city public school failure. Through curricular, co-curricular, and extracurricular engagement, Louisville students were involved in tutoring and supporting students. Applying their own acquired college learning to students and their families, successes were realized. Many other anchors joined in, from nonprofits in health and social welfare to company internships, mentorships, and numerous other youth programs. The anchor model is persistent. It is embedded in the mission. It aligns university resources with community challenges. And as with all civic engagement programs, it bears genuine results for the success of college students by increasing their persistence, academic achievement, and completion. Purposeful college student engagement demonstrates measurable academic success as well as increased civic competency and discernible positive impact within the local community.

This pattern is evident throughout the profiles of those universities and colleges attracted and committed to the anchor model. It provides a more efficient strategy for the civic institution. And this approach is gaining currency within the international higher education sector. For instance, Queens University in Belfast, Northern Ireland, employs the anchor vision for its comprehensive engagement with the Protestant and Catholic communities in and around Belfast. It is a key agent for fostering religious and class reconciliation after so many years of extreme violence. I visited recently and was pleased to find genuine civic engagement through courses, student organizations, the contribution of faculty expertise, community-based research, administrative leadership, and deep and wide partnerships throughout many challenged communities in Belfast. The schools are still divided by religion but Queens assists with teacher visitations, tutoring, and after-school programs in community centers across the school divides. Queens students expressed how their involvement in helping their own communities heal and prosper gave them a renewed sense of purpose in their college studies and for their career aspirations. In one community center visit, I spoke with former prisoners who are facilitating reconciliation of groups of Protestant and Catholic residents living in religiously segregated communities. Many of the participants are former enemies.

The Wagner Anchor Model: The Port Richmond Partnership

At Wagner College, the civic is becoming the defining element of the under-graduate identity. Located on Staten Island, the smallest of the five boroughs of New York City, Wagner, until recently, was not centrally involved in much local community work outside of the one-off food and blood drives. Staten Island maintains a population of 480,000 residents. It is larger in population than Cleveland, Detroit, Oakland, St. Louis, and a number of other cities. It is, however, dwarfed by the other 8 million New Yorkers residing in the other four boroughs. One community on Staten Island is Port Richmond, located approximately a mile from the famous Staten Island Ferry. Long ago a center of commerce prior to the building of the Verrazano Bridge that united it with Brooklyn in 1964, Port Richmond now is home to 12,000 residents, 60% of whom are Mexicans, mostly undocumented; 20% African Americans; and the remainder working-class whites. The neighborhood lies about two miles from the Wagner College campus, itself pitched on Grymes Hill overlooking New York Harbor and Manhattan. Wagner enrolls 2,100 students from 46 states and 29 nations. Eighty percent of its students reside on campus. It is a private liberal arts college with a healthy component of professional programs in business, education, and allied health disciplines.

Although the college was founded as a Lutheran institution, that pro-prietary relationship lapsed in 1970; however, the commitment to the social purpose of a broad and deep education was forged with renewed vigor with the advent and ensuing development of the Wagner Plan for the Practical Liberal Arts in 1998.[8] Linking learning and location as the core concept for the entire four-year undergraduate program, experiential learning was required of all majors and throughout the general education programs. As the Wagner Plan grew, it dramatically identified the college with its urban location.[9] The civic purpose inherent in its founding mission organically reemerged, and by 2007 civic engagement was deeply incorporated into major programs. The required first-year program for all undergraduates combined experiential and often civic learning with learning communities of approximately 25 students each. Students selected course combinations, formed into themed learning communities, and joined to create reflective tutorials (RFT) that emphasized interdisciplinary integration of the theme uniting the two respective disciplinary courses. The RFT also emphasizes analytic writing and research, but most important are field-based learning placement and experiences that link to the local community and New York City institutions.

Over the first half dozen years, civic engagement informed many of these field experiences in the first-year and in the senior-year program in all the majors. By 2007, Wagner decided to significantly realign and deepen the civic work by moving away from the idiosyncratic placements across many nonprofits and different communities in the spirit of the former service-learning model. The college joined with Port Richmond in a strategic anchor partnership across five policy areas and with a year-round commitment.[10] Approximately two-thirds of its civic work relocated to this one inner-city, challenged neighborhood. The five policy areas include education in partnership with the K–12 community, immigration justice, entrepreneurship and small business development, addressing health disparities particularly around diabetes and obesity, and the development of the arts and humanities in conjunction with the college's national partners in Imagining America. The partnerships include approximately 30 local partner organizations and are supported by the Wagner Center for Leadership and Community Engagement. Each policy area is led by a faculty fellow, by a Wagner student selected as a Port Richmond Engaged Scholar, and a community partner drawn from one of Wagner's partner institutions. The Wagner Center oversees the larger Partnership by stewarding partner relations, cultivating and supporting Wagner faculty participants, supporting a small army of co-curricular organizations formed by Wagner students for this purpose, and assisting the academic departments in the deployment of students and courses around the policy goals of the Port Richmond Partnership. The level of activity in the community on any given day throughout the calendar year is somewhat daunting for a very professional and hardworking staff of five and another army of interns.

This program is becoming an indelible mark of a Wagner education. Wagner students are heavily engaged in the Partnership and our other civic programs in other local communities as well as our international sites. Now the community is becoming significantly engaged. Port Richmond High School now is a major partner. Together, Wagner College and Richmond High School created a leadership academy for high school students not oriented to college but certainly capable of attending, given the right support and encouragement through a demanding academic and civic program. The large majority of Leadership Academy students have no or little knowledge of or experience with post-secondary education in their families. As in many cities and inner-city schools, graduation rates hover at around 50%. The academy is structured to intervene and see that these youngsters succeed in high school; graduate with pride, self-esteem, and full of confidence; and go on to attend and graduate from the college of their choice.

Academy students take courses at Wagner during the summer from sophomore through senior year. Two of these summers consist exclusively of college courses taught by full-time Wagner faculty members. In the high school sophomore summer, students take enriched high school math and English. Each summer, students live on the Wagner campus. They are mentored and chaperoned by Wagner students and staff from the Center.

There is one other critically distinctive component of the success of this work. In the summer and throughout the school year, these high school academy students enroll in a civic studies seminar in which they learn the theory and practice of civic engagement, democracy, and social change. They are involved in local civic engagement with Wagner students and staff in their home neighborhood of Port Richmond. They begin by building an asset map of their own community, identifying those institutions that are assets in building change, opportunity, and civic prosperity. These students will complete a full semester of college as they graduate from high school; Wagner will contribute full four-year scholarships for one-quarter of them (roughly a $4,000,000 commitment when operational costs are added to run this one program in Port Richmond). The academy promotes interdisciplinary courses and civic competency to high school as well as Wagner students in and around a neighborhood rife with racial stereotypes, youth and domestic violence, little opportunity, and too often unrelenting despair. By aligning college social capital with strategic fund-raising and by working with highly dedicated local partners, we expect these dynamics to lessen and for optimism and achievement to take root. To date, we see success in high school persistence. (There are equally powerful pieces in the other policy areas in this partnership. The college and the community are allies as well as anchors for each other.)

The larger lesson for higher education becomes the need to join forces with local communities in the enhancement of our local neighborhoods and in revitalizing our colleges and universities in pursuit of their original missions. The anchor concept is infusing other national higher education civic organizations with new national priorities in promoting comprehensive partnerships as the organizing strategy for their civic programs. Both Campus Compact and the Coalition of Urban and Metropolitan Universities have adopted community partnerships, particularly K–12/university partnerships as their national priority. Others are moving to this position. This new civic work aligns vast amounts of institutional higher education social capital with the ever-deepening crisis in inner-city high schools. In short, comprehensive K–12/university partnerships join the agendas of school effectiveness and educational excellence to inequality and civic work. This makes for a promising alliance of often-divided institutions in addressing the very real and highly consequential social challenge of building a vibrant democracy and a successful economy for this American century.

The Civic as the Core of the Practical Liberal Arts

The reemergence of the civic within higher education promises a more expansive view of undergraduate education. Although we can easily point to the founding missions of universities and colleges as a basis for understanding the civic as an essential element of higher learning, there is an even more fundamental argument lodged in the ancient philosophy of Aristotle in which the social nature of knowledge underscores "polis" as the arena for the usefulness and power of learning and inquiry. In this long-honored view, the practice of engaged citizenship within the public arena defines our essential humanity. It is the engagement among humans within a democratic society that propels the human project. Democratic character is required to support the public purpose, and democratic character is a function of open inquiry, formulated argument, and responsible action.

This approach is fundamental to the case for liberal education and it is well accepted within higher education. There is, however, another way to assess the fundamental importance of the way we conceive of liberal learning and the role of civic engagement. It begins with the reconciliation of professional studies and liberal education, long seen as separate and distinct forms of learning. Their integration holds great promise for expanding our understanding of the civic. Liberal education offers the student an opportunity to explore the breadth and width of the human experience. Here learners are exposed to the vast variety of cultures, historical epochs, distinct philosophies, and the underlying construction of personality, the formation of authority and social institutions, and, of course, the construction of the natural world and the place of humans within it. In short, liberal education provides the context in which to understand the experiences of individuals and societies. Professional studies focuses on applied learning. It has been stereotyped as vocational learning by some of liberal education traditionalists who prize learning in and of itself as true education. From this critique, vocational learning is regarded as devoid of intellectual activity. It presumes that applied learning is limited to the linear application of disciplinary knowledge. It neglects to account for the variability and discretion in applied learning in areas such as engineering, architecture, medicine, and so on. Professional disciplines require similar intellectual habits of mind as does liberal studies. Both include critical thinking, careful judgment, and reliable evidence. They both require social context to fully engage their subjects. In short, both liberal and professional studies contain the key elements of a refined and cosmopolitan intellect.

In seeking to bring these different but related forms of learning into common cause, the practical liberal arts emerge. Both modalities offer the intellectual tools for interpretation and meaning making. In this new synthesis, the clinical and field-based learning, of which the civic is a primary component, provide the public arena not only for the social usefulness of knowledge but also as the vessel for the creation of new knowledge.

The concept of civic professionalism is the organizing principle for the practical liberal arts.[11] Every undergraduate learner will ultimately choose a career path and each will be involved in a loose sense in a profession that serves related publics. Practicing that career involves a level of responsibility to those publics regardless of field. For instance, business students will ultimately be responsible to investors and consumers; theater majors may become performing artists responsible to texts and audiences. The helping professions are engaged with students, parents, patients, and families. Civic professionalism unites work and publics, learning with the civic, disciplines with service.

Wagner College's "Wagner Plan for the Practical Liberal Arts" provides a case study for an educational model predicated on educating its students for civic professionalism. Experiential and civic engagement is tied to the four-year undergraduate experience, which combines liberal and professional studies through the use of multidisciplinary learning communities. The anchor institution model for civic engagement in the Port Richmond neighborhood creates applied learning opportunities, civic commitments, and social agency. The Partnership becomes the public arena for democratic practice and intercultural community. Civic engagement is at the center of this form of learning by doing.

Higher education is at a new inflection point. It must adapt to the new realities of fiscal limits, dramatic technological opportunities, and a renewed civic purpose. This last dimension holds great promise to conceptualize the better use of the other two challenges so that the greater public rediscovers higher learning as an authentic public good as well as a means to personal advancement.

Notes

This chapter was previously published as "Civic Engagement and Higher Learning," pp. 61–80, in DeVitis & Sasso, *Higher Education and Society* (Peter Lang, 2015).

1. As reported in *Volunteering and Civic Life in America Report 2012* and cited by Center for Civic Engagement, Oregon State University, 3.1 million college students volunteered more than 312 million hours.

2. National Task Force on Civic Learning and Democratic Engagement. (2012). *A crucible moment: College learning & democratic engagement.* Washington, DC: Association of American Colleges and Universities.
3. Love, A. G. (2013, Spring). Wagner College: Establishing positive links between civic engagements and student well-being. *Bringing Theory to Practice* [Newsletter].
4. Guarasci, R. (2001, January–February). Developing the democratic arts. *About Campus.*
5. Guarasci, R., & Cornwell, G. (1997). *Democratic education in an age of difference.* San Francisco, CA: Jossey-Bass.
6. Anchors Institutions Task Force. (2010). *Task force statement.* Marga, Inc., 20.
7. Hodges, R., & Dubb, S. (2012). *The road half traveled: University engagement at a crossroads.* East Lansing, MI: Michigan State University Press.
8. Guarasci, R. (2006, Winter). On the challenge of becoming the good college. *Liberal Education, 92*(1). 14–21.
9. Guarasci, R., & Lieberman D. (2009, November–December). Sustaining transformation: Resiliency in hard times. *Change.*
10. Guarasci, R. (2014). Civic provocations: Higher learning, civic competency and neighborhood partnerships (pp. 59–62). In J. N. Reich (Ed.), *Civic engagement, civic development, and higher education.* Washington, DC: Bringing Theory to Practice.
11. Sullivan, W. (2004). *Work and integrity: The crisis and promise of professionalism in America* (2nd ed.). San Francisco, CA: Jossey-Bass.

Part Three: Is Academic Freedom Still Necessary?

In "'Flipping' the Tenure Debate and the Continuing Need to Protect Academic Freedom," Neal H. Hutchens and Frank Fernandez discuss the meaning and importance of academic freedom, its dilution in certain institutional structures, and why it should be safeguarded. They worry that the failure to support tenure and academic freedom sabotages intellectual and scientific development—one of the academy's chief functions. Hutchens and Fernandez also point to political and ideological assaults on higher education that weaken professional autonomy and the search for truth. Thus, they call for stronger protection for nontenured faculty and those in nonfaculty roles as well as for full-time faculty. In modern times, the authors fear that administrative authority has grown too powerful.

In "What Is Academic Freedom for?" Ashley Thorne isolates which forms of academic freedom she claims are legitimate and which should be considered objectionable. On the one hand, she points to the right of professors to teach their subject (so long as they remain within subject bounds) and students' rights to learn that subject. On the other hand, she argues that academic freedom should not protect indoctrination. Thorne is critical of classroom and published arguments that do not respect reasoned, civil debate; she is also sensitive to the need to listen to other points of view before either accepting or rejection them. Lastly, she searches for more ultimate truth against contemporary philosophies of subjectivism and postmodernism.

5. "Flipping" the Tenure Debate and the Continuing Need to Protect Academic Freedom

NEAL H. HUTCHENS AND FRANK FERNANDEZ

The negative social, political, and economic consequences incurred by nations that disallow or substantially curtail intellectual freedom for college faculty serve as a stark reminder of the fundamental importance of academic freedom to higher education. The case of Turkey provides a recent cautionary tale, as professors there have faced escalating intimidation and retaliation for espousing views disfavored by governmental leaders (see, e.g., Albayrak, 2016; Göçek, 2016). Pressure on Turkish academics only increased following a failed military coup in 2016, as the government's response included the dismissal of thousands of university department heads and a call by the nation's top higher education official for university leaders to provide a list of traitors (Grove, 2016). Regrettably, infringements on academic freedom in higher education abound in other countries as well (e.g., Jacobs, 2013; *New York Times*, 2013; Redden, 2013; Reuters, 2014; Sataline, 2015; Shahin, 2014).

While a long-accepted facet of American higher education, challenges to academic freedom also exist in the United States. These include increased reliance on part-time, adjunct faculty teaching with severely limited employment protections, adoption of management models and strategies more appropriate for business than for higher education, and concerns raised by international partnership efforts—such as the establishment of branch campuses—with nations that may not share a strong commitment to intellectual freedom in higher education. In this chapter, we discuss what is academic freedom, the weakening of traditional arrangements (namely tenure) meant to safeguard it, and the continuing need to protect academic freedom.[1]

Academic Freedom in American Higher Education

Faculty members afforded the protections of academic freedom have helped shape our understanding of human rights; produced knowledge, insights, and creative contributions of intrinsic value to the human experience; and supported scientific and economic development (e.g., Baker, 2014). Academic freedom represents one of the essential characteristics of American higher education, integral to the ways that colleges and universities contribute to individual well-being and development, the nation, and beyond. For much of American history, however, college faculty were not engaged in the creation of new knowledge or free to challenge established dogma. Instead, professors sought to inculcate students with accepted truths. This state of affairs began to change during the latter part of the 19th century, with American higher education influenced by conditions in Germany, which had adopted concepts of freedom in teaching and research for professors (Scott, 2006).

As a new generation of academics in the United States—initially earning their PhDs from German institutions and then later from burgeoning American research universities such as Johns Hopkins—sought to engage in research and knowledge production, they periodically encountered backlash. Faculty members who upset presidents, trustees, or other influential figures could and did lose their positions (Cain, 2012). One of the most well-known examples involved the dismissal in 1900 of economist Edward Ross from Stanford University. The reasons for Ross's dismissal stemmed from stances he took regarding the use of immigrant labor and railroad monopolies. His views upset the widow of Leland Stanford, the university's original benefactor and namesake who was a railroad magnate and well-known "robber baron" of the era (Cain, 2016).

In response to the dismissals of professors such as Ross, professional academic organizations began to call for safeguards to protect professors in their work (Cain, 2016). A key moment in the advancement of academic freedom protections for professors in the United States came with the establishment of the American Association of University Professors (AAUP). The association was founded by academics from leading higher education institutions. These inaugural members issued the 1915 Declaration of Principles on Academic Freedom and Academic Tenure, articulating the need to provide meaningful protection for intellectual freedom in our nation's higher education institutions.

Later, the AAUP and an association of institutions and academic leaders would jointly produce and endorse another pivotal statement on academic freedom—the 1940 Statement of Principles on Academic Freedom and

Tenure. This foundational document played a key role in the adoption of academic freedom as an integral professional value in higher education. The drafters of the 1940 Statement asserted that teachers should possess independence in research and its dissemination in the classroom (AAUP, 2014).

An important point to keep in mind (including for professors) in considerations of academic freedom involves a recognition that, rather than primarily for the individual benefit of faculty, academic freedom protections are intended for the benefit of the public. In this sense, college and university faculty are akin to other professional actors (e.g., doctors, lawyers) that require sufficient autonomy to carry out their work. Academic freedom is meant to provide professors with basic protections so that they can do their work without being subject to unreasonable oversight that inhibits them from exchanging ideas and pursuing new knowledge. Without academic freedom, professors are unable to carry out effectively their roles to their students, institutions, and societies.

Tenure and Academic Freedom

Tenure provided the dominant mechanism, one based in contract, to advance the intellectual rights articulated in the 1915 Declaration, 1940 Statement, and later documents and commentaries. Tenure represents a special type of contractual relationship. Absent incompetence or misconduct on the part of the professor or institutional financial emergency, an institution agrees to an ongoing employment contract with a faculty member. It is not, however, a lifetime appointment. Instead, a college or university can end a professor's tenured appointment for appropriate reasons, such as professional misconduct.

Critiques of tenure are abundant, but an important point in discussions about academic freedom involves recognition that tenure applies to an increasingly shrinking portion of the faculty. It now extends to no more than a third of higher education faculty (Kezar & Maxey, 2012). Most faculty teaching in colleges and universities are part-time adjuncts, with institutions exercising extensive control over their dismissal or nonrenewal. Another group of professors is employed on a full-time basis, but with varying types of appointment arrangements. While some are on year-to-year appointments that require annual renewal, others have multiyear contracts that operate on a rolling basis and provide employment safeguards more akin to those afforded through tenure (Baldwin & Chronister, 2001). For some groups of faculty, collective bargaining rights also constitute an important—and expanding—source of legal protections (Hutchens, 2011).

One might assume that First Amendment speech protections provide an ample alternative source of legal safeguards to protect academic freedom in the context of public higher education. In reality, substantial legal uncertainty and debate exists regarding the extent of First Amendment protections for professors' academic freedom, including in the context of teaching and research. Despite language in several Supreme Court opinions supportive of constitutional protection for professors' academic freedom (e.g., *Keyishian v. Board of Regents*, 1967), courts have failed to develop a set of definitive legal standards establishing a constitutional framework for faculty First Amendment academic freedom rights. A 2006 Supreme Court case, *Garcetti v. Ceballos*, raised further questions and debate over the extent to which faculty possess First Amendment rights related to speech arising in carrying out their professional duties or, alternatively, whether such speech is subject to institutional control, at least for First Amendment purposes.

As the AAUP recognized a century ago, realization of academic freedom in colleges and universities requires more than simply institutional aspiration and the goodwill of individual administrators. Professors require legally enforceable employment safeguards to exercise adequately their intellectual independence. Tenure now covers a decreasing percentage of the professoriate. For public higher education faculty, the First Amendment could provide some degree of legal protection for faculty academic freedom. But, the scope of constitutional protection for faculty speech arising in teaching, research, or carrying out other professional duties is unknown and subject to legal disagreement. Simply put, for academic freedom to flourish in colleges and universities, it must be backed by more than the largesse of institutional leaders. Currently, uncertainty encompasses the available mechanisms to protect professors' academic freedom, whether through employment arrangements such as tenure or the First Amendment.

Importance of Academic Freedom

Intellectual openness and the creation of new knowledge serve as the currency in higher education. Failing to protect academic freedom undermines the ability of colleges and universities to fulfill their basic functions to their direct constituents and to society more broadly. Academic freedom plays an important role in the creation of research agendas, advancing new ways of thinking and knowledge creation, and teaching students.

Rather than only abstract benefits, academic freedom has resulted in identifiable (and at times especially noteworthy) outcomes coming from the work of faculty. Simon Marginson (1992) described how three Nobel Prize winning economists, James Buchanan, Milton Friedman, and Friedrich von Hayek, used their time at the University of Chicago and their careers in academia to profoundly change the way that leaders across the political spectrum think about economics and public policy. Buchanan, Friedman, and von Hayek were staunch proponents of free markets and limited government, and their scholarly writings influenced politics and policy in England and the United States. While their theories on free markets and political libertarianism are not without controversy, they were able to advance ideas with significant impacts by working in universities to deliberately develop research and publication agendas that took many decades to work their way into mainstream political thought (Marginson, 1992).

Other notable examples include scholars such as Elinor Ostrom, who also won a Nobel Prize for her scholarly work on shared natural resources (often referred to as "the commons"), and Charles Tiebout, whose eponymous model is the foundation for the idea that people "vote with their feet" and will move to places with lower taxes, better public services, or fewer regulations. Kenneth Clark was a professor whose research was influential in the Supreme Court's decision to declare segregated schooling unconstitutional in *Brown v. Board of Education* (Beggs, 1995). To provide just two more notable examples, higher education faculty also played an important role in areas that include the consequences of marketing cigarettes to children (Fischer, 1996) and the health effects caused by the use of paint containing lead (Kaiser, 2005).

Each of these scholars benefited from working in a university environment where they had professional autonomy to write, teach, and research. Professors can devote themselves to advancing new ways of thinking when they have job security and need not fear censorship from their employers. In other words, academic freedom allows professors to develop research agendas over many decades and to contribute to public discourse throughout entire careers. In addition to their own work, professors are able to build departments and develop programs to train graduate students over many years who later educate other students or help to develop and implement policy and expand the knowledge base in particular areas.

Universities and faculty research are also increasingly important for economic competitiveness in the 21st-century knowledge economy (Goldin & Katz, 2009). University faculty members played an important role in supporting science, technology, engineering, and mathematics (STEM) scientific research during the 20th century. In fact, during the last century, the United States produced a plurality of the world's scientific research in STEM fields (Zhang, Powell, & Baker, 2015). Many scientists choose to work at universities because they have academic freedom to select their own research projects and develop research agendas. In this sense, academic freedom prevents research projects from being ended prematurely or never begun at all because they are not perceived as cost-effective. Industries and individuals later benefit and derive technological innovations from faculty research (Aghion, Dewatripont, & Stein, 2008).

The dean of the Computer Science department at Carnegie Mellon University offered his views on a well-publicized incident in which Uber, in its efforts to develop a self-driving car, hired four professors and 36 technical staff from the university (Moore, 2016). Rather than taking a negative view of the situation, the author described the significant role played by colleges and universities as places for leading scientific researchers to go—even if rotating periodically back into industry—to find the kinds of creative spaces needed to engage in research and discovery not generally available in for-profit contexts in industry. The fact that Uber sought to recruit individuals from the university helped show the important role of higher education institutions in nurturing top intellectual talent.

Failing to support academic freedom in higher education undercuts the kinds of intellectual and scientific advancements that have made American higher education a model looked to by the rest of the world. Institutions that fail to safeguard the academic freedom for faculty are placed at a competitive disadvantage, either to other universities (including those outside the United States) or to private industry. Policymakers, governing boards, and institutional leaders should consider carefully before diluting what has constituted one of the key ingredients in making the United States a world leader in higher education and in scientific development.

Challenges to Academic Freedom

In this section, we provide an overview of several prominent challenges to academic freedom in American colleges and universities. As discussed, most higher education faculty do not possess tenure-stream appoints. The lack of meaningful academic freedom protections for many nontenure-track faculty, most of whom are part-time adjuncts, raises troubling questions, especially in the context of teaching. As higher education has taken a more consumeristic turn, teaching evaluations can comprise an important part of decisions to retain adjunct professors. While student evaluations of instructors are a valuable part of assessing teaching, notable problems exist with overreliance on them in making reappointment decisions for nontenure-track faculty. The evaluations may not accurately capture teaching quality but, instead, reflect student pushback against quality, but rigorous, instruction or against instructors who challenge students to identify and reflect upon the soundness of their own preconceived notions. Research also indicates that women and faculty of color are subject to disparate treatment in student evaluations.

A tenure-stream professor—or at least one on a multiyear contract—is placed in a better position to overcome the limitations, unfairness, and vicissitudes that are all too often part of the student evaluation process. In contrast, many nontenure-track faculty are potentially faced with the need to placate rather than educate students to maintain an appointment based on favorable student evaluations. Currently, a lack of meaningful employment protections for too many faculty in higher education coupled with inappropriate use of student evaluations results in a significant challenge to academic freedom in the classroom for many faculty, most notably those in the "new faculty majority" employed off the tenure track.

Academics are also subject to outright attack in their work, including, at times, by elected officials or other powerful individuals or groups. For example, leading climate scientist Michael Mann has been subjected to long-term harassment by climate change skeptics. Based on his employment at the University of Virginia between 1999 and 2005, the then attorney general of Virginia, Kenneth Cuccinelli, who was also a candidate for governor, sought to gain access to a wide range of documents from Mann in efforts to discredit the scientist's work. Initially, the university was going to comply with the request and only launched a challenge after Mann, who was by then at Penn State University, sought to intervene in the litigation. Eventually, the Virginia Supreme Court in 2012 held that the university did not have to disclose the documents. Other professors have faced similar efforts to use open records requests as a means to harass or discredit their work (e.g., Murray, 2013; O'Neil, 1996).[2] Notably, such efforts have not come from only groups or individuals associated with either the political left or right, as requests have spanned the political and ideological spectrum.

Debate and uncertainty over First Amendment protection for faculty in public higher education also present a serious challenge to academic freedom. The majority of college and university faculty have appointments at public colleges and universities. Even for those professors at private institutions, the constitutional speech standards applicable to their public counterparts likely contribute to the speech norms at private colleges and universities. In litigation, a number of public colleges and universities have challenged that professors possess First Amendment speech rights that apply to their professionally based speech, including in the realm of teaching and research. That is, institutions have sought to advance legal positions that curtail faculty academic freedom rights via the constitution (e.g., *Adams v. Trustees of the University of North Carolina-Wilmington*, 2011; *Demers v. Austin*, 2014; *Sadid v. Idaho State University*, 2011).

The issues raised in this section reveal several ongoing challenges to academic freedom. The arrangements (i.e., tenure and the First Amendment) looked to as important sources to protect academic freedom face an unknown future. What is next for higher education in relation to meeting the challenges to protecting academic freedom? In the next section, we consider "flipping" the tenure debate as one way to advance discussion and reflection on this issue.

"Flipping" the Tenure Debate

In debates over academic freedom, much of the focus is on the privileges of tenured faculty and various anecdotes of individuals failing to live up to the responsibilities that come with tenure. Tales of recalcitrant faculty, however, fail to address the issue of the continuing need to safeguard intellectual independence in colleges and universities. Stories of particular examples of "failed" faculty members offer little in the way of advancing our thinking of how academic freedom advances the needs of students, institutions, and society when exercised by individuals acting in good faith in regard to the use of academic freedom.

One way to reorient discussion on tenure and academic freedom is to "flip" the tenure debate. Instead of asking why professors should have or not have tenure, perhaps it is, in fact, time to debate and consider expanding professional independence and autonomy to other professionals in higher education. That is, we could discuss "why not" expand professional autonomy safeguards, including speech protections, to nontenure-stream and to nonfaculty professionals in colleges and universities. Flipping the tenure debate in this way might help us to question the wisdom of current management trends in higher education of consolidating authority and control into a smaller and smaller cadre of campus decision-makers.

Rather than conceptions based on family, community, or citizenship, colleges and universities increasingly rely on the language of customer and employee to depict the higher education enterprise. Flipping the tenure debate could help us examine whether we have become too reliant on hierarchical administrative models in higher education and, by extension, senior managerial authority, as opposed to reliance on professional knowledge and expertise. Likewise, we could also examine sensible limits to the consumer model of higher education. With such an inquiry, we might find that, rather than the specter of tenure, a greater risk to the long-term vitality of higher education in the United States comes from the outsized role that managerial authority and business models have increasingly come to play at many colleges and universities. Beyond faculty roles, institutions could examine whether nonfaculty professionals, particularly those working in front-line positions with students in such areas as student affairs and academic advising, possess sufficient professional independence to voice their views and opinions in discussions and debates over institutional policies and practices. And this would include being able to offer views contrary to tenured faculty. If such basic professional autonomy protections and safeguards do not exist, then institutions could examine "why not" extend professional autonomy protections rather than continuing to curtail them in higher education.

A reconceptualization of the professional autonomy issue in higher education away from a singular focus on tenure could yield interesting realizations. Stakeholders serious about student and overall institutional success might conclude that, rather than less professional independence, more professional autonomy safeguards should exist at colleges and universities, including for nontenure-track faculty and nonfaculty professional staff. By reframing and expanding considerations of professional autonomy in higher education, tenure might be afforded the opportunity to be considered in a new light, one focused on the benefits derived from intellectual independence. If not debated in isolation, rather than presented as a problem to be eliminated, tenure might potentially be viewed alongside a refashioned continuum of levels of professional autonomy and independence needed for professionals in colleges and universities to do their jobs effectively and with sufficient professional independence, both in faculty and nonfaculty roles.

Amidst the seemingly continual stream of rhetoric against tenure, higher education institutions and policymakers should reflect carefully before jumping too quickly on the "let's get rid of tenure bandwagon." Empowering more professionals at institutions, including in nonfaculty roles and those in nontenure-stream faculty positions, could help to sustain and enhance the kind of knowledge production and creativity needed to address the multifaceted challenges facing our nation and world. At the least, "flipping" the tenure debate is a conversation worth having in debates over academic freedom.

Conclusion

Reasons to protect and to enhance academic freedom in American colleges and universities have not diminished in the years since the 1915 Declaration and 1940 Statement. Academic freedom is necessary because it not only protects faculty who may come under attack for publishing scholarship that is controversial in the short term (such as those who spoke out against lead paint or cigarette advertisements), but also enables faculty members to develop new knowledge and ways of thinking that inform and shape public discourse or scientific and technological advancements over the long term. Discussions of academic freedom and tenure need to take into account not only the "bad apple" examples but also need to consider carefully the advantages and benefits lost when faculty academic freedom is curtailed.

Notes

1. For much of the chapter, we largely focus on the need to protect faculty academic, but the authors recognize the importance of intellectual freedom for students and, indeed, other members of our campus communities (see, e.g., Sun, Hutchens, & Breslin, 2013). In fact, that is why later in the chapter we discuss the idea of "flipping" the tenure debate in relation to issues of academic freedom.
2. It is important to note that we are not against the use of all open records request pertaining to faculty, such as those that would reveal funding sources. Instead, we are referring to efforts to use expansive document or records requests in ways that impede the research process or present information to the public in a manner that unfairly distorts the actual quality or integrity of the research.

References

Adams v. Trustees of the University of North Carolina-Wilmington, 640 F.3d 550 (4th Cir. 2011).

Aghion, P., Dewatripont, M., & Stein, J. C. (2008). Academic freedom, private-sector focus, and the process of innovation. *The RAND Journal of Economics, 39*(3), 617–635.

Albayrak, A. (2016, January 15). Turkey Cracks Down on Critics of Campaign Against Kurdish Rebels. *Wall Street Journal.* Retrieved from http://www.wsj.com/articles/turkey-cracks-down-on-critics-of-campaign-against-kurdish-rebels-1452886393

American Association of University Professors. (2014). *Policy documents and reports* (11th ed.). Baltimore, MD: The Johns Hopkins University Press.

Baker, D. (2014). *The schooled society: The educational transformation of global culture.* Stanford, CA: Stanford University Press.

Baldwin, R. G., & Chronister, J. L. (2001). *Teaching without tenure: Policies and practices for a new era.* Baltimore, MD: Johns Hopkins University Press.

Beggs, G. J. (1995). Novel expert evidence in federal civil rights litigation. *American University Law Review, 45*(1), 1–75.

Cain, T. R. (2012). *Establishing academic freedom: Politics, principles, and the development of core values.* New York, NY: Springer.

Cain, T. R. (2016). A historiography of academic freedom for American faculty, 1865–1941. In M. B. Paulson (Ed.), *Higher education: Handbook of theory and research* (pp. 157–215). New York, NY: Springer International Publishing.

Demers v. Austin, 746 F.3d 402 (9th Cir. 2014).

Fischer, P. M. (1996). Science and subpoenas: When do the courts become instruments of manipulation? *Law and Contemporary Problems, 59*(3), 159–167.

Garcetti v. Ceballos, 547 U.S. 410 (2006).

Göçek, F. (2016, July 26). Why Turkey wants to silence its academics. *The Conversation*. Retrieved from https://theconversation.com/why-turkey-wants-to-silence-its-academics-62885

Goldin, C. D., & Katz, L. F. (2009). *The race between education and technology*. Cambridge, MA: Harvard University Press.

Grove, T. (2016, July 21). Turkish crackdown puts spotlight on education sector. *The Wall Street Journal*. Retrieved from http://www.wsj.com/articles/turkish-crackdown-puts-spotlight-on-education-sector-1469129606

Hutchens, N. H. (2011). Using a legal lens to better understand and frame issues shaping the employment environment of non-tenure track faculty members. *American Behavioral Scientist, 55*(11), 1443–1460.

Jacobs, A. (2013, December 10). Chinese professor who advocated free speech is fired. *The New York Times*. Retrieved from http://www.nytimes.com/2013/12/11/world/asia/chinese-professor-who-advocated-free-speech-is-fired.html?_r=2

Kaiser, J. (2005). Lead paint experts face a barrage of subpoenas. *Science, 309*(5733), 362–363.

Keyishian v. Board of Regents, 385 U.S. 589 (1967).

Kezar, A., & Maxey, D. (2012). Missing from the institutional data picture: Non-tenure-track faculty. *New Directions for Institutional Research, 2012*(155), 47–65.

Marginson, S. (1992). Education as a branch of economics: the universal claims of economic rationalism. *Melbourne Studies in Education, 33*(1), 1–14.

Moore, A. W. (2016, August 2). It's not 'corporate poaching'—it's a free market for brilliant people. *The Conversation*. Retrieved from https://theconversation.com/its-not-corporate-poaching-its-a-free-market-for-brilliant-people-61846

Murray, F. (2013). Boston College's defense of the Belfast Project: A renewed call for a researcher's privilege to protect academia. *Journal of College and University Law, 39*, 659–713.

O'Neil, R. M. (1996). A researcher's privilege: Does any hope remain? *Law and Contemporary Problems, 59*(3), 35–49.

Redden, E. (2013, October 21). Has China failed key test? *Inside Higher Ed*. Retrieved from https://www.insidehighered.com/news/2013/10/21/peking-u-professor-fired-whats-seen-test-case-academic-freedom

Reuters. (2014, March 24). *Russian professor sacked over criticism of actions in Ukraine*. Retrieved from http://www.reuters.com/article/us-ukraine-crisis-professor-idUSBREA2N1BM20140324

Sadid v. Idaho State University, 265 P.3d 1144 (Idaho 2011).

Sataline, S. (2015, August 14). Hong Kong's academic freedom under fire. *Boston Globe*. Retrieved from https://www.bostonglobe.com/ideas/2015/08/13/hong-kong-academic-freedom-under-fire/hJ6upYtbMalJgE9Ez0MmWI/story.html

Scott, J. C. (2006). The mission of the university: Medieval to postmodern transformations. *The Journal of Higher Education, 77*(1), 1–39.

Shahin, E. (2014, March 7). Opinions are dangerous as Egypt cracks down on dissent. *The Conversation*. Retrieved from https://theconversation.com/opinions-are-dangerous-as-egypt-cracks-down-on-dissent-24039

Sun, J. C., Hutchens, N. H., & Breslin, J. D. (2013). A (virtual) land of confusion with college students' online speech: Introducing the curricular nexus test. *University of Pennsylvania Journal of Constitutional Law, 16*, 49–96.

Zhang, L., Powell, J. W., & Baker, D. P. (2015). Exponential growth and the shifting global center of gravity of science production, 1900–2011. *Change: The Magazine of Higher Learning, 47*(4), 46–49.

6. What Is Academic Freedom for?

Ashley Thorne

Stranded on an uninhabited island, a senior FedEx manager—played by Tom Hanks in the movie *Castaway*—uses an ice skate blade to knock out his own abscessed tooth. The incident shows his resourcefulness during his exile from civilization. It's also an illustration of something being employed for a purpose other than its intended use.

You *can* use ice skates to knock out a sore tooth, but that's not what ice skates are for.

Academic freedom too has its rightful purposes.

Prepositions are important here. Most thinking about academic freedom is on academic freedom *to*. The concern is to know what a person with academic freedom is entitled to do. Is she free to teach and to research according to his or her professional judgment? Is she free to speak her political opinions in class? Free to criticize the university?

There's also the question of *to whom* academic freedom belongs. Does it belong only to tenured faculty members, or is it also rightly claimed by assistant professors or adjuncts? What about students, administrators, campus speakers, and the university as a whole?

All these questions matter, but the one I take up here is academic freedom *for*. For what purpose does academic freedom exist?

Robert P. George, McCormick Professor of Jurisprudence at Princeton University, put it well: "Academic freedom is freedom for something, something profoundly important—namely, the intellectual excellence that makes self-mastery possible."[1] He said that academic freedom is a means to higher ends: "We should honor academic freedom as a great and indispensable value because it serves the values of understanding, knowledge, and truth that are greater still."

Here I will focus on four purposes of academic freedom. It is freedom (1) for teaching a particular subject, (2) for respectful scholarship, (3) for debate, and (4) for the pursuit of truth.

Each of these purposes provides a border hemming academic freedom in, giving it conditions—in essence, limits. Freedom with limits may sound like an oxymoron. But all freedoms have their domains, and limits can be a helpful thing. A city without limits isn't a city. A square with no sides is just blank space.

These particular purposes are meant to apply mainly to faculty members, and most of the examples below are of teachers and professors. When faculty members use their academic freedom toward these goals, they are also protecting the academic freedom of students to learn (*Lernfreiheit* in German).

Academic Freedom Is for Teaching a Subject

The most basic reason students attend college is to learn particular academic subjects. Their role is to learn and the professor's role is to teach. The professor is responsible to impart his expertise and knowledge in such a way as to give students the opportunity to take on that knowledge as their own. He is to bequeath the legacy of civilization to the next generation.

A professor's charge is to teach his subject without deviating into unrelated political opinions. The 1915 founding Declaration of Principles of the American Association of University Professors (AAUP) directed:

> The teacher ought also to be especially on his guard against taking unfair advantage of the student's immaturity by indoctrinating him with the teacher's own opinions before the student has had an opportunity fairly to examine other opinions upon the matters in question, and before he has sufficient knowledge and ripeness of judgment to be entitled to form any definitive opinion of his own.[2]

The temptation to influence a captive audience, however, can be great; and some faculty members do attempt to indoctrinate.

Bradley E. Schaefer, Louisiana State University

In 2010, Louisiana State University professor of physics and astronomy Bradley E. Schaefer provided an example of an unnecessary intrusion of partisan politics into the classroom when he berated his students for their views on climate change.

A video from a class in his "Solar System" course showed Schaefer asking the class to sit on certain sides of the room according to actions they believed the government should take to address global warming, ranging from "U.S. should do nothing" to "Mandatory birth control" and "Eliminate all engines." He then mocked the students who sat on both the far right and the far left of the room.[3]

"Oh boy, that's really good for you, at least for the next decade or two," he said to the students on the "do nothing" side. "And then you will remember having sat on that corner, because you will not want to tell your children, if they live, why you're sitting on that corner, that you were part of the trouble, right? Do you realize that?"

Schaefer went on, "The more you're sitting over here, the more you're wanting to keep your hedonistic luxury at the cost of your children." To one student he said, "Too little, too late. Blood will be on your hands."

He continued the scare tactics in the exercise he gave to the class, in which the students on the "do nothing" side were to estimate the probability that they or their children "will die in ugly ways due to your current decision." The exercise informed them, "Your professed policies have a substantial likelihood of leading to the death of a billion people or more."

During the class Schaefer announced his opinion that "Global warming is real; it's caused by humanity." He repeatedly said, "It's only going to get worse."

Not only did Schaefer introduce a subject unrelated to his course, he also sought to indoctrinate his students into his own politically motivated views.

Louisiana State University, rather than suspending or even reprimanding Professor Schaefer, doubled down. The LSU officials adopted the narrative told in *The Chronicle of Higher Education* and *Inside Higher Ed* that Schaefer had nobly "challenged" the students, and that he had done so with students on both sides of the question. "This is not a case of irresponsible teaching," LSU provost John Maxwell Hamilton wrote.[4]

Irresponsible teaching seems the only accurate way to describe what happened in that class. Professor Schaefer haranguing students according to his personal political views—even on both sides of an issue—was an abuse of professional responsibility to teach and guide those under his academic care. That he insisted on his own view foreclosed the possibility of open debate. That he inserted politics unrelated to the course topic violated students' freedom to learn the subject for which they enrolled.

Kenneth Howell, University of Illinois

In some courses ideology and politics *are* relevant to the subject being taught, and it is appropriate to include controversial ideas in the course.

An example of a faculty member whose teaching was protected by academic freedom is Kenneth Howell. An adjunct professor of religion at the

University of Illinois, Urbana-Champaign, Howell was fired in 2010 after being accused of preaching to his students religious views on homosexuality. Howell taught an "Introduction to Catholicism" course under an arrangement with the campus-based St. John's Catholic Newman Center. One of the classes in the course was on "The Question of Homosexuality in Catholic Thought." He gave a lecture and followed up the next day in an email to his students with additional thoughts on morality and sexuality. His focus was on the Catholic teaching on natural law, contrasted with the standard of "consent." An excerpt from his email reads:

> This is where Natural Moral Law (NML) objects. NML says that Morality must be a response to REALITY. In other words, sexual acts are only appropriate for people who are complementary, not the same. How do we know this? By looking at REALITY. Men and women are complementary in their anatomy, physiology, and psychology. Men and women are not interchangeable. So, a moral sexual act has to be between persons that are fitted for that act. Consent is important but there is more than consent needed.[5]

Howell was subsequently informed that a student, not in his class, had submitted a complaint and called his email "hate speech." He was told that his email "violate[d] university standards of inclusivity" and that he would not be permitted to teach at the University.[6]

Cary Nelson, President of the AAUP at Illinois, defended Howell as a professor who had the right to preach to his students in his classroom. Yet he wasn't preaching—and if he was, he wouldn't be protected by academic freedom.

Rather, Howell was faithfully rendering the teachings of Catholicism, which were the subject of his course. His personal agreement with these teachings should not have disqualified him from presenting the arguments for them. As National Association of Scholars President Peter Wood wrote in an article on the story, "There is no evidence that Howell used his classroom or his email to students in this fashion [preaching]. Howell leaves no doubt that he himself believes in Catholic teachings, but a mere statement of belief is not the same as an effort to win converts."[7]

Within a few weeks, the University did the right thing. It reversed its decision and reinstated Howell to his teaching position.[8]

Neutrality as an Institution

Not only should individual professors keep their teaching to their academic subjects, but likewise, the institution itself must remain politically neutral in order to protect academic freedom. The University of Chicago Kalven Committee report of 1967 declared, "To perform its mission in the society, a university must sustain an extraordinary environment of freedom of inquiry and maintain an independence from political fashions, passions, and pressures."[9]

In 2012, Bowdoin College President Barry Mills published a letter in the student newspaper exhorting students to vote in favor of same-sex marriage in an upcoming Maine ballot initiative.[10] Mills' fervent appeal was a misuse of his position of authority in the College, and it placed Bowdoin as an institution firmly on one side of a political debate.

In a manner similar to a professor insisting on his partisan view as the correct one, a top administrator urging students to follow his lead in an election both silences those on the other side and misconstrues the academic mission as political more than educational. College and university leaders would do better to seek to adhere to the Kalven Committee's principle of institutional neutrality on political questions.

Freedom to Learn a Subject

If faculty members teach their subjects competently and fairly, then students will enjoy the freedom to learn that material in the context of open inquiry.

Academic Freedom Is for Respectful Scholarship

In debates some people want to win the argument rather than be content with a friendly exchange of views. It is natural to become defensive, attack opponents, interrupt, mock, or try to silence the other side.

The academic calling requires disciplining that instinct. To paraphrase a line from the Bible, "To whom much is given, much is required."[11] Scholars are given academic freedom so that they may model reasoned debate. They are to show respect for those with whom they disagree—to attack the idea, not the person.

The AAUP 1915 statement says:

> The liberty of the scholar within the university to set forth his conclusions, be they what they may, is conditioned by their being conclusions gained by a scholar's method and held in a scholar's spirit; that is to say, they must be the fruits of competent and patient and sincere inquiry, and they should be set forth with dignity, courtesy, and temperateness of language.[12]

Here the authors referred mainly to the presentation of research findings, but they provided a portrait of the "scholar's spirit" that ought to characterize everyone in the academic community.

The First Amendment, of course, protects freedom of all kinds of expression, not just that which is said in a patient or temperate way.

In an academic context, however, there is a higher standard than that governing the public square. Academic communities exist to cultivate knowledge, intellectual friendship, and wisdom. Those aims are best served when the members of these communities treat one another with respect.

There will always be faculty members who are by temperament cantankerous. These individuals are still covered by academic freedom. Rather than trying to change someone's personality, a president, provost, dean, or chair can set the expectation that faculty members will abide by reasonable standards of politeness. If anyone has difficulty understanding what those standards are, his job is not in jeopardy; but he will need to talk with the person setting the standards.

Colleges and universities cannot legislate courtesy, but they can enunciate ideals and conventions; and their faculty members and administrators can set the example. They can also make clear that nastiness is no basis for intellectual community.

That doesn't mean everyone on campus must avoid confrontation, or agree to disagree. But it does mean that debate is conducted with basic respect for one's ideological opponents.

Two faculty members who illustrated this in the negative are Steven Salaita and Melissa Click.

Steven Salaita, University of Illinois

In 2014, the University of Illinois at Urbana-Champaign revoked its offer of a faculty appointment to Steven Salaita after he posted on Twitter a series of angry, often vulgar, comments about Israel. In one he wrote, "Let's cut to the chase: If you're defending #Israel right now you're an awful human being." In another, he wrote, "You may be too refined to say it, but I'm not: I wish all the f——ing West Bank settlers would go missing" (he spelled out "f——ing").[13] This was after three Israeli teenagers were reported kidnapped—and were later found murdered, evidently at the hands of Palestinian terrorists in Hamas.[14]

About a month after the University's decision not to hire Salaita, Chancellor Phyllis Wise published a statement providing a rationale. She wrote: "I firmly believe that a tenured faculty position at the University of Illinois is a tremendous honor and a unique privilege. Tenure also brings with it a heavy responsibility to continue the traditions of scholarship and civility upon which our university is built."

Chancellor Wise emphasized the need for an academic community built on "civil, thoughtful, and mutually respectful" discourse. She wrote that the decision not to hire Salaita was based not on his views but on the way they were expressed.

After he lost the job offer, Salaita expressed no regret for taking the tone he had. Rather, he insisted that his language was warranted; and that he preferred "moral clarity" over "the meek platitudes of civility."[15]

Salaita sued the University, which in 2015 awarded him a settlement of $875,000.[16]

Melissa Click, University of Missouri

Another instance of serious incivility was when Melissa Click, communications professor at the University of Missouri, clashed with a student journalist, Mark Schierbecker. He was filming the November 2015 campus protests that led to the resignation of University President Tim Wolfe.

"You need to get out," Click told the student, grasping at his phone as he filmed. When the student stayed, Click called out to the protestors, "Hey, who wants to help me get this reporter out of here? I need some muscle over here. Help me get him out. Who's gonna help me?"[17] Click joined hands with the protestors and moved forward with them to edge Schierbecker away. She instructed: "You guys need to make room for this guy to come through. He shouldn't be in here. And don't let him back in."

The University Board of Curators terminated Click's employment following this incident. The Board specified that she had the right to express her views, but that in trying to intimidate students, she "did not meet expectations for a university faculty member."[18]

Nicholas Christakis, Yale University

A faculty member who did show restraint in the face of malice directed at him is Yale sociology professor Nicholas Christakis.

He and his wife Erika Christakis were "co-masters" in Silliman College, a Yale residential community. In October, 2015, Ms. Christakis sent an email to the students in Silliman regarding Halloween costumes. Responding to an email sent earlier by Yale's Intercultural Affairs Committee with guidelines for choosing culturally inoffensive costumes, she said that students should be treated like adults and should feel free to make their own decisions about what to wear.

Many students took her email as a sign of insensitivity toward minorities and an invitation to racism, and over 1,000 signed an open letter saying so.[19] Some took out their anger on her husband Nicholas. A video taken on the campus quad shows him surrounded by about 100 students,[20] with one shouting at him ("Be quiet!" "You're disgusting!") in crude language ("Who the f—— hired you?").[21]

The student's outburst is another example of the incivility that doesn't belong on a college campus. Mr. Christakis, however, didn't take the occasion to lash out at the student in return. He looked her in the eye, listened calmly, and nodded occasionally. At a pause in the student's rant, he said simply, "I don't agree with that."[22]

Civility

Even though he was not speaking within a campus context, Salaita's comments on Twitter, and his subsequent remorselessness, showed him publicly belittling those who disagreed with him. His actions ran directly in opposition to the spirit of the scholar.

So did Melissa Click's. She showed no interest in a two-way conversation and resorted instead to threats and coercion.

Christakis, by contrast, set an example of patient toleration in response to vituperation.

Again, although First Amendment freedoms allow for expressions of rage, vulgarity, and threats, it is right for academic communities to hold themselves and their members to higher standards in the interest of sustaining a culture of civility. That culture, in turn, makes it possible for people to debate ideas without malice toward one another.

Academic Freedom Is for Debate

Acting with respect for others finds an application in debate, which is one of the core purposes of academic freedom. A faculty member must be willing to listen to and teach competing ideas. He must also be open to criticisms of his own ideas.

Once again, the AAUP 1915 statement is helpful; it says that "The claim to freedom of teaching is made in the interest of the integrity and of the progress of scientific inquiry; it is, therefore, only those who carry on their work in the temper of the scientific inquirer who may justly assert this claim."[23]

The temper of the scientific inquirer entails approaching the world of knowledge with humility, acknowledging that one's hypotheses may be mistaken, being open to correction, and listening to others' perspectives. It doesn't mean that academics should not seek to prove their own views by means of sound arguments and evidence. But they ought to be generous in the way they hear people out.

Sandra Korn: "Academic Justice"

Academic freedom allows controversial topics to be discussed freely in the spirit of open inquiry. Contemporary campus culture tends to favor choosing a side, then preventing the other side from speaking. Harvard undergraduate student Sandra Korn, in 2014, provided a term for this mindset: "academic justice." She wrote in the *Crimson*, "If our university community opposes racism, sexism, and heterosexism, why should we put up with research that counters our goals simply in the name of 'academic freedom'?"[24]

One of Korn's examples of "research that counters our goals" was Harvard Professor Harvey Mansfield's assertion in his 2006 book *Manliness* that "to resist rape a woman needs...a certain ladylike modesty."[25] Korn wrote: "I would happily organize with other feminists on campus to stop him from publishing further sexist commentary under the authority of a Harvard faculty position. 'Academic freedom' might permit such an offensive view of rape to be published; academic justice would not."[26]

For her, "academic justice" means preventing offensive perspectives from being heard. Korn gave expression to something already widely believed, a concept that has motivated colleges across the country to cancel talks by invited campus speakers.

George Will and Scripps College

A few months after Korn's *Crimson* op-ed, Scripps College disinvited conservative *Washington Post* columnist George Will from speaking. The revocation of the invitation came after Will published a column in which he argued that college women, incentivized by colleges having made "victimhood a coveted status," were mislabeling their regrettable hook-ups as rapes.[27]

Scripps President Lori Bettison-Varga justified her decision to disinvite Will because he "authored a column questioning the validity of a specific sexual assault case that reflects similar experiences reported by Scripps students."

Sexual assault should indeed be taken seriously and dealt with as a crime, but there is room for reasonable people to discuss the differences between rape and regrettable sex. Scripps' disinvitation of George Will precluded that discussion from happening and prevented students from hearing a perspective they might not otherwise encounter. Will is just one of dozens of speakers who have been disinvited from campuses because of their views.[28]

Hearing the Other Side

John Stuart Mill wrote in *On Liberty* that "He who knows only his own side of the case, knows little of that."[29] He argued that a healthy competition of ideas keeps both sides more reasonable and more awake to the possibility of finding truth in unexpected places.

"Only through diversity of opinion is there, in the existing state of human intellect, a chance of fair-play to all sides of the truth," wrote Mill. He thus arrives at the fourth purpose of academic freedom, and the one to which the first three point.

Academic Freedom Is for Pursuing the Truth

Academic freedom exists to empower scholars to seek truth.

To some modern academics, truth is seen as an outdated idea, or at least an overrated one. Professor emeritus of psychology David Moshman wrote:

> The subjectivist conception of knowledge represents an important advance over simplistic objectivist assumptions that professors discover and teach the truth. Knowledge is always subjective in the sense that it reflects, in part, the viewpoint of the knower.[30]

As postmodern relativism has come to dominate higher education, the pursuit of *the* truth has been subordinated to the idea that every person has his own truth. Duke's Center for Sexual and Gender Diversity sponsors "My Truth Panels" in which gay and lesbian students can share their coming out stories.[31] Hit singer Nicki Minaj starred in a reality TV series called "My Truth."[32] In 2016, University of Maryland, Baltimore County, hosted an event during Black History Month called "Speak Your Truth."[33] More and more it is assumed that what is real and knowable is limited to individual feeling.

Setting the Goal

While each person does have his or her own perspective, opinions, and tastes, objective truth still exists, even if it is sometimes elusive. In some disciplines it is more elusive than in others. Mathematics is a field of objectively right answers, whereas philosophy is a field of theories and interpretations. Still, in every subject, students should be taught to evaluate, "Does this conform to reality?" "Is this true?" "Are the arguments against this idea stronger than the ones for it?"

The teacher does not need to answer all these questions but should lead students in seeking the truth, hearing dissents, and weighing competing ideas on their merits.

James Enstrom, University of California, Los Angeles (UCLA)

Epidemiologist James Enstrom provides an example of a scholar devoted to the truth, even when that devotion cost him his job. He was fired from UCLA after 34 years there, following his blowing the whistle on a fraudulent scientific paper.

Dr. Enstrom had questioned the reigning orthodoxy about the dangers of pollution from particulate matter (abbreviated PM2.5). Enstrom discovered that the published research on this subject, on which new California environmental regulations were based, was written by someone who had faked his doctoral degree by buying it from a diploma mill.[34]

Between 2005 and 2010, Enstrom worked to expose the scam as well as shine a light on the science itself—he brought up evidence that PM2.5 is much less dangerous than the research author had indicated.[35] Enstrom also gave testimony in California state hearings in 2008.[36]

After he was fired in 2011, he brought a lawsuit against UCLA and won a settlement four years later for $140,000 and the revocation of his termination.[37]

In 2016 Enstrom spoke to UCLA students and told them that good scientists "pursue the truth whether it is politically correct or incorrect."[38]

Nothing but the Truth

Making the search for truth the aim of a college education gives students and faculty members a plumb line by which to measure ideas. It frees colleges to prioritize some subjects over others. It motivates students to wrestle with difficult concepts and not just cram for the test.

Pursuing truth is a lifelong endeavor. Adults exercise this muscle when they follow the news, do their work, vote, make moral choices, and reach for meaning after losing loved ones. Trying to find out what is true and real never ends; so it serves students well to train them early.

Free for Good

It is understandable that a castaway alone on an island—with no ice—would find an alternate use for ice skates. Academic freedom too is put to desperate uses when left marooned in the desolate realm of academic justice. LSU tried to justify Bradley Schaefer's bullying of students. Steven Salaita attempted to defend his bid for violence against Israelis. The AAUP protested on both his behalf and Melissa Click's. In these cases academic freedom was misapplied to situations where it was irrelevant.

Colleges and universities need true academic freedom as much today as ever. They need this important ideal in order to teach students the subjects they need to know; to model civil debate; and to seek the truth.

A person alone in exile may seem free—he is bound by no moral standards, social norms, or laws. But cut off from civilization, life is cramped. Isolation on an island is its own sort of prison. Society is where friendships can flourish, new generations can innovate, and history can be made.

Likewise, academic freedom doesn't exist to be a license to indulge the whims of maverick faculty members acting on their impulses. Colleges and universities should give serious thought to the academic culture best suited to raising up men and women who think clearly, make prudent decisions, and put others ahead of themselves. They need to cultivate a living community of people who disagree with one another, sometimes strenuously, but always with forbearance, putting the pursuit of truth ahead of their personal agendas. That kind of community releases its members from the stifling effects of conformity and empowers them to explore uncharted territory.

That's what academic freedom is for.

Notes

1. Robert P. George. (2014, May). "Why Academic Freedom Matters (Now More Than Ever)." *Intercollegiate Review*, Digital. Retrieved from https://home.isi.org/node/68449

2. 1915 Declaration of Principles on Academic Freedom and Academic Tenure. American Association of University Professors. Retrieved from https://www.aaup.org/NR/rdonlyres/A6520A9D-0A9A-47B3-B550-C006B5B224E7/0/1915Declaration.pdf

3. "Full Video: LSU Astronomy Class" [Video]. (2011). Retrieved from https://vimeo.com/16649140

4. Ashley Thorne. (2010, December 1). "LSU Covers Up for Astronomer Who Bullied Class: NAS Replies." National Association of Scholars. Retrieved from https://www.nas.org/articles/LSU_Covers_Up_for_Astronomer_Who_Bullied_Class_NAS_Replies

5. Jodi Heckel. (2010, July 9). "E-mail that prompted complaint over UI religion class instructor." *News-Gazette*. Retrieved from http://www.news-gazette.com/news/local/2010-07-09/e-mail-prompted-complaint-over-ui-religion-class-instructor.html

6. "FIRE Letter to UIUC Chancellor Robert A. Easter." (2010, July 16). Foundation for Individual Rights in Education. Retrieved from https://www.thefire.org/fire-letter-to-uiuc-chancellor-robert-a-easter/

7. Peter Wood. (2010, July 16). "The Illinois Railroad: Making Quick Work of a Catholic Prof." National Association of Scholars. Retrieved from https://www. nas.org/articles/The_Illinois_Railroad_Making_Quick_Work_of_a_Catholic_ Prof

8. David French. (2010, July 30). "A Victory for Academic Freedom at the University of Illinois." *National Review.* Retrieved from http://www.nationalreview. com/phi-beta-cons/242141/victory-academic-freedom-university-illinois-da vid-french

9. *Kalven Committee: Report on the University's Role in Political and Social Action* (Vol. 1, Publication No. 1). (1967, November 11). Retrieved from http://www-news. uchicago.edu/releases/07/pdf/kalverpt.pdf

10. Barry Mills. (2012, October 25). "Now's the Time to Stand Up for Civil Rights and Freedoms in Maine: Vote 'Yes' on Question 1." Letter to the editor, *Bowdoin Orient.* Retrieved from http://bowdoinorient.com/article/7583

11. English Standard Version. Luke 12:48. (2011). In *Bible: English Standard Version.* Wheaton, IL: Crossway. A paraphrase of: "Everyone to whom much was given, of him much will be required."

12. 1915 Declaration. AAUP.

13. Subir Grewal. (2015, August 18). "The Salaita Tweets: A Twitter/Outrage Concordance," *Daily Kos.* Retrieved from http://www.dailykos.com/story/2015/8/18/1412900/- The-Salaita-Tweets-A-Twitter-Outrage-concordance

14. "Live Updates, July 1: Teens' Bodies Found." (2014, July 1). *Haaretz.* Retrieved from http://www.haaretz.com/israel-news/1.602189

15. "Steven Salaita Lashes Out against University of Illinois at Urbana-Champaign after Twitter Rant Leads to Firing" [Video]. (2014, October 7). *Chicago Tribune,* 2.49. Retrieved from http://www.chicagotribune.com/news/local/ breaking/-steven-salaita-lashes-out-against-university-of-illinois-at-urbana-champ aign-20141007-premiumvideo.html. Featured in: Jodi S. Cohen. (2014, October 7). "Professor Who Lost U. of I. Job Offer Lashes Out at Administrators." *Chicago Tribune.* Retrieved from http://www.chicagotribune.com/news/local/ breaking/ ct-salaita-speaking-tour-met-1007-20141007-story.html

16. Jodi S. Cohen. (2015, November 12). "University of Illinois OKs $875,000 Settlement to End Steven Salaita Dispute." *Chicago Tribune.* Retrieved from http:// www.chicagotribune.com/news/local/breaking/ct-steven-salaita-settlement-met- 20151112-story.html

17. Kayla Schierbecker. (2015, November 10). "Clash between Media and Concerned Student 1950 (Full)" [Video]. Youtube. Retrieved from https://www.youtube. com/watch?v=1S3yMzEee18

18. Pam Henrickson. (2016, February 25). "Statement from University of Missouri Leadership." *Inside UM System.* Retrieved from https://www.umsystem.edu/ums/ news/media_archives/022516_statement

19. Open Letter to Associate Master Christakis. (2015, October 31). *DOWN Magazine.* Retrieved from http://downatyale.com/post.php?id=430

20. Hilary Hanson. (2015, November 7). "Yale Admins' Comments on Offensive Halloween Costumes Spark Protest." *Huffington Post.* Retrieved from http://www.huff- ingtonpost.com/entry/yale-halloween-costumes-offensive-free-speech_us_563e3 f9ce4b0b24aee4a8fef

21. TheFIREorg. (2015, November 6). "Yale University Students Protest Halloween Costume Email (VIDEO 3)" [Video]. Youtube. Retrieved from https://www.youtube.com/watch?v=9IEFD_JVYd0
22. *Ibid.*
23. 1915 Declaration. AAUP.
24. Sandra Y.L. Korn. (2014, February 18). "The Doctrine of Academic Freedom: Let's Give Up on Academic Freedom in Favor of Justice." *Harvard Crimson.* Retrieved from http://www.thecrimson.com/column/the-red-line/article/2014/2/18/academic-freedom-justice/
25. H. Mansfield. (2007). *Manliness.* New Haven, CT: Yale University Press.
26. Korn. "The Doctrine of Academic Freedom."
27. Valerie Strauss. (2014, October 8). "Scripps College uninvites George Will because of column on sexual assault." *Washington Post.* Retrieved from https://www.washingtonpost.com/news/answer-sheet/wp/2014/10/08/scripps-college-uninvites-george-will-because-of-column-on-sexual-assault/
28. Foundation for Individual Rights in Education, Disinvitation Database. Retrieved from https://www.thefire.org/resources/disinvitation-database/#home/?view_2_page=1&view_2_sort=field_6|desc
29. John Stuart Mill. (1869). *On Liberty.* London: Longman, Roberts & Green.
30. David Moshman. (2016, July 26). "Truth, Knowledge, and Academic Freedom." *Huffington Post.* Retrieved from http://www.huffingtonpost.com/david-moshman/truth-knowledge-and-acade_b_11170492.html
31. "My Truth Panels." Duke University. Center for Sexual and Gender Diversity, Training and Resources. Retrieved from https://studentaffairs.duke.edu/csgd/training-resources/my-truth-panels
32. IMDb. (2012). "Nicki Minaj: My Truth," [TV Mini Series]. Retrieved from http://www.imdb.com/title/tt2498356/
33. "Speak Your Truth: UMBC Edition." My UMBC, Race, Equity, Inclusion, and Justice, Events. Retrieved from http://my.umbc.edu/groups/race-equity-inclusion-justice/events/38425
34. Peter Wood. (2011, April 1). "The Smog of Reprisal." *Chronicle of Higher Education.* Retrieved from http://chronicle.com/blogs/innovations/the-smog-of-reprisal/29054
35. Jacob Kohlhepp. (2016, February 4). "UCLA whistleblower encourages students: Fight for the truth against all odds." *The College Fix.* Retrieved from http://www.thecollegefix.com/post/26103/
36. Matt Lamb. (2015, March 12). "VINDICATED: Researcher Punished for Exposing Climate Fraud Beats UCLA." *The College Fix.* Retrieved from http://www.thecollegefix.com/post/21611/
37. Shreya Maskara. (2015, March 5). "Former UCLA Researcher James Enstrom Reaches Settlement with UC." *Daily Bruin.* Retrieved from http://dailybruin.com/2015/03/05/former-ucla-researcher-james-enstrom-reaches-settlement-with-uc/
38. *Ibid.*, Kohlhepp.

Part Four: Should Tenure Be Abolished?

In "The Contingency of Tenure," David Shiner affords a balanced, yet provocative, analysis of how the tenure system has historically prevailed in higher education and why more recent arguments against it are gaining some steam. He presents a detailed review of the literature on tenure as well as personal interviews with colleagues to marshal his case. Shiner also takes readers on an interesting tour of his own campus, Shimer College, to illustrate its alternatives to tenure, as well as highlighting examples from other universities. He concludes that individual institutions should be careful to respond to their own unique features in any deliberation about tenure policies and practices.

In "Why Tenure Needs Protection in These Troubled Times," Philo A. Hutcheson points to salient factors related to its erosion. He details the historical and social foundations for tenure in the professoriate, especially its stewardship by the American Association of University Professors (AAUP). In particular, Hutcheson emphasizes the McCarthy era of the 1950s and the rising tide of anti-intellectualism in American life. In contemporary times, he cites a growing trend toward non-tenure track positions, i.e., "at-will employees" with little or no protection. Finally, Hutcheson argues that tenure and academic freedom serve to oppose current threats to research in such vital scientific areas as global warming and anti-vaccination efforts, to name a few.

7. The Contingency of Tenure

David Shiner

In the introduction to his 1973 book *The Tenure Debate,* Carthage College professor Bardwell Smith penned the following words: "Some at present are predicting that the incidence of tenure will climb to 75 or 80 percent in the near future."[1] Smith did not identify the "some" who predicted that increase. That proved to be fortunate for them, as they could hardly have been further off base.

The incidence of tenure in higher education had already begun its decline at the time Smith was writing, and it has resolutely continued in that direction ever since. According to the United States Department of Education, well over half of all college and university faculty members nationwide were tenured or on the tenure track in the mid-1970s. By 2007, that number had fallen to 31%.[2] According to the American Association of University Professors (AAUP), the percentage of tenure-track faculty members has dipped even further in the past decade; and there is no evidence that a reversal is in the offing.

The persistence of this trend has led some observers to predict the eventual demise of tenure altogether. Among their number is Daniel J. Ennis, English professor at Coastal Carolina University in South Carolina. "[W]e are reaching the end of a long cycle," Professor Ennis writes in an aptly titled article, "The Last of the Tenure Track." "Today some institution somewhere has, unaware, hired its last tenured professor. To be sure, there will be tenure-track hires next year, and the year after, and perhaps for a decade or more, but today somebody accepted a tenure-track job, and that person will outlive tenure at his or her institution."[3] Ennis's article has a distinctly rhetorical tone, and in fact the decline in tenure-track appointments is a relative matter. College and university faculties have grown considerably over the years and, as the AAUP notes, the total number of tenured and tenure-track faculty members has increased by more than 25% since 1975. Part-time appointments, however, have exploded during that same period, mushrooming by some 300%. "[T]he big story across academia is more or less the same," notes Jordan Weissmann in a recent article in *The Chronicle of Higher Education*. "[I]f it were a movie, it'd be called 'Rise of the Adjuncts.'"[4]

These facts will not be news to anyone who has paid even a modicum of attention to recent hiring trends in colleges and universities. Various circumstances facing higher education, especially economic ones, have led to increasing utilization of part-time faculty members, the vast majority of whom are hired on short-term contracts. Ennis argues that "tenure will not be eliminated because the merits of the system have been carefully weighed and found lacking.... [It] will be killed not by irresponsible academics or the barbs of the commentariat, but instead by the tightening grip of the American economy. Those who have criticized tenure may find its incremental oblivion less emotionally satisfying than a formal abolition, but the results will be the same."[5]

Not everyone who shares Ennis's assessment of the current state of the tenure system concurs with his claim that its decline has resulted from "the tightening grip of the American economy." Ennis evidently endorses the interpretation of commentators who have attributed the growth of so-called "contingent faculty" primarily to financial pressures that took place during an economic downturn in the 1990s. The AAUP, on the contrary, argues that "the greatest growth in contingent appointments occurred during times of economic prosperity."[6] The reality appears to be more nuanced than either of those positions would suggest. As researchers Samantha Bernstein and Adrianna Kezar have shown, substantive growth in the hiring of part-time faculty began in the 1970s, when market fluctuations led to significant changes in hiring patterns. "Between 1945 and 1975, college enrollment increased in the United States by 500 percent," Bernstein and Kezar remark. "However, rising costs and a recession in the late 1970s forced administrators to seek out part-time faculty to work for lower wages in order to accommodate these students. The practice increased dramatically thereafter. In addition to enrollment changes, government funding for higher education decreased in the late 1980s and '90s. The demand for new courses and programs was uncertain, and so campuses needed more flexibility in faculty hiring."[7] This confluence of events created administrative quandaries for which an increase in nontenure-track faculty has—for better or worse—been the most frequent solution.

Other economic factors aside from uncertainty about the future have contributed to the sea change in faculty demographics. Salaries and benefits for tenured faculty members often comprise a substantial portion of an institution's annual budget. The expected long-term commitment of funds that is likely to result from positive tenure decisions multiplies that effect, which has been further exacerbated by the legal abolition of mandatory retirement. NYU sociology professor Dennis Wrong points out that, as a result of these factors, "an institution's commitment to tenure may now cover as much as fifty years rather than roughly thirty years as in the past; moreover, the added years are when salaries for senior faculty are at their highest."[8] Such considerations have led some observers of higher education to argue that tenure is at least partly responsible for its own decline, particularly when coupled with the priority of research over teaching that is often associated with tenured status.

In this vein, Naomi Schaefer Riley refers to "tenure's stranglehold on university budgets"[9] as a key factor in continued increases in the hiring of adjuncts and part-timers. Riley's view of tenure is understandably unpopular with tenured faculty, but many of those who are responsible for institutional budgets share at least some of her antipathy. As Jack Stripling notes, "Less than a quarter of college leaders who responded to a Pew Charitable Research Center survey, done in association with *The Chronicle*, said they would prefer full-time, tenured professors to make up most of the faculty at their institutions." Stripling comments further, "Instead, 69% said they would prefer that a majority of faculty work under long-term or annual contracts."[10]

Among those who are not surprised by the Pew survey's findings is Cathy Trower, Research Director at the Collaborative on Academic Careers in Higher Education at Harvard University's Graduate School of Education. As a matter of simple economics, she observes, it is reasonable for college presidents to want to reduce the number of well-compensated faculty members who "are with you until death, essentially."[3] Trower's many years of research on issues in higher education have led her to view the tenure system as problematic for reasons beyond those related to institutional finances. "Like the old work rules of newspaper guilds and auto workers," she writes, "the tenure system, hatched in another era by a generation of mostly white males, does not fit contemporary economic realities, nor does it accommodate today's faculty who work within the system under very different, and increasingly complex, expectations." She concludes by opining that the inertia of the tenure system has resulted in "a status quo where tenured and tenure-track members are an endangered species."[11]

Trower's view of the increasing obsolescence of the "status quo" is echoed in a recent report with decidedly greater tangible implications. That report, ominously entitled "The Trouble with Tenure," was researched and written by the Wisconsin Policy Research Institute (WPRI) in order to inform state policy on faculty hiring and retention. In his introduction to the report, WPRI President Mike Nichols states, "The University of Wisconsin Board of Regents is just weeks away from adopting a new policy on tenure, and it's no surprise that most of the professors who have it or are on track to get it want to preserve the status quo.... You won't find a defense of the status quo in these pages."[12] In calling the "status quo" into question, Nichols and his colleagues champion the perspective of the regents rather than that of tenured and tenure-track faculty. Predictably, this leads them to adopt conclusions that have more in common with the views of the college and university presidents who responded to the Pew survey than those of tenured faculty and the AAUP. Those conclusions, subsequently approved by the UW Board of Regents, further underscore the fact that governing boards and presidents often view the tenure system much differently than tenured and tenure-track faculty members do.

Unsurprisingly, this difference in perspective can play a role in hiring and retention decisions. College presidents might not be able to curtail the tenure system at their institutions, but they can and do involve themselves in the tenure process in other ways. Colleen Flaherty reports on a study of college presidents in which 58% of those surveyed claim to have blocked the hiring of scholars because of qualms about their competence, and 54% say they have blocked scholars from receiving tenure for the same reason. As intrusive as some would find that practice, most presidents would like to go even further. Flaherty notes that more than half of the presidents responding to the survey believe they should take a more active role in faculty hiring decisions, while two-thirds think they should take a more active role in deciding which faculty members qualify for tenure. Only a handful of presidents strongly disagree with those views.[13]

Opinions about the merits of those practices vary. Carol Christ, director of the Center for Studies in Higher Education at the University of California at Berkeley, considers them "an important safeguard for the quality of the institution." Christ regards presidents as providing a necessary "check" on faculty tenure recommendations, noting that a positive tenure decision is a "lifetime commitment that this person is going to be an extraordinary faculty member. It's a very solemn responsibility."[14] Others, particularly tenure-track faculty members and the AAUP, take exception to the practice. Among other concerns, they question the ability of those who do not teach or conduct research in a given faculty member's area of expertise to make definitive and binding judgments on that person's professional qualifications and ability.

Another aspect of tenure that some researchers view as problematic is its purported prioritization of research over teaching. Bernstein and Kezar regard the surge in nontenure-track appointments as having resulted from "the tenure model's failure to adapt with the significant and rapid changes that have occurred in colleges and universities over the last 50 years." The most significant of those changes, they believe, is "the rise of teaching-focused institutions, the largest growth being in the community college, technical college and urban institutions that have a primary mission to educate students with little or no research mission."[15] The view that the status of tenure is more oriented toward research than teaching while contemporary trends in higher education augur in the opposite direction is held by many, including a sizable number of nontenure-track faculty members. Brannon and Philip Coyle recently conducted a survey of faculty in the University of Wisconsin system who are off the tenure track but teach at least 75% of a full load and are therefore eligible for institutional benefits such as health insurance. They chose to seek responses from this group, who teach on fixed-term renewable contracts, "in order to get a picture of attitudes toward tenure among a group of individuals who have an excellent perspective on the performance of professors but who themselves have a limited vested interest in the benefit." Their results are telling. A clear majority of those faculty members believe that tenure is a good indication of the quality of research of tenured professors, but many fewer—less than a third—regard it as a reliable indicator of instructional quality.[16]

A number of empirical studies have confirmed, in varying degrees, the perspectives of the faculty who responded to the Wisconsin survey. Research conducted by Martin Trow, a predecessor at the Center for Studies in Higher Education at the University of California at Berkeley, showed that frequency of academic publication correlates tightly with tenure. Trow found that the correlation between tenure and recent publication is particularly pronounced in so-called "elite" institutions of higher education.[17]

Those institutions were the focus of a more comprehensive study conducted some years after Trow published his findings. In *Off-Track Profs: Non-tenured Teachers in Higher Education*, John G. Cross and Edie N. Goldenberg present and discuss their research on nontenure-track faculty appointments at elite universities such as MIT and Cornell. Tenure in those schools is earned largely through research and scholarship, and those who are granted tenure are expected to continue in that vein for the remainder of their professional careers. While the authors are understandably cautious about making broad generalizations vis-à-vis a group of schools that have significant differences among them, they conclude that the tenure system as currently practiced in those universities is generally not productive of an atmosphere in which teaching is regarded as primary.[18]

When tenured faculty members in institutions of the sort studied by Cross and Goldenberg do not teach to capacity, nontenure-track personnel are engaged to fill the gap. Paul Strieleman is one such professor. Strieleman, a senior lecturer in Biological Sciences at the University of Chicago, teaches introductory courses in biochemistry and common core courses in nutritional science. He also directs and develops the laboratories for the university's undergraduate biochemistry courses. "The university needs people like me because the faculty who have tenure, at least in the sciences, have major research responsibilities," Strieleman says. He adds that, when he began teaching at the university in the mid-1990s, any tenured faculty member in the sciences had the right to not be assigned classes simply on the basis of not wanting to teach them.[19]

The status of untenured teachers such as Strieleman underlines some of the conceptual problems with the currently fashionable term "contingent faculty." According to the AAUP's definition, this category includes full-time faculty who are off the tenure track. That characterization would have been of little significance a half-century ago, when such instructors held just over 3% of all faculty positions in higher education;[20] but they have become much more prevalent since then. Alternative definitions of "contingent faculty" do not include full-time faculty of any sort. Strieleman has heard his position characterized as "noncontingent," although he doesn't think that is a formal designation on the part of the University of Chicago. The categorization of the nontenure-track, almost-full-time University of Wisconsin faculty members surveyed by Brannon and Coyle is more ambiguous; and in fact the researchers do not use that term in their report.

Appropriate categorization of faculty members such as Strieleman and many of those studied by Cross and Goldenberg depends in part upon the circumstances in which they work. In the United States, tenure has traditionally been regarded as assuring that faculty will be treated in a manner befitting the dignity of their profession. The AAUP cites two primary purposes of tenure: "1) freedom of teaching and research and of extramural activities, and 2) a sufficient degree of economic security to make the profession attractive to men and women of ability."[21] Strieleman believes that both of those conditions are fulfilled for lecturers at the University of Chicago, even though they are not on the tenure track. He notes that he and his untenured colleagues are eligible to serve on committees and accrue benefits, and he believes that they have the same freedom as tenured professors to teach and publish within their discipline as they see fit. With respect to job security, senior lecturers receive renewable contracts for terms of increasing length and can only be released from service due to cuts in position, professional malfeasance, or poor performance. Those are essentially the conditions that the AAUP recognizes as legitimate for the purposes of ending a given faculty member's term of service, as will be discussed later in this chapter.

The University of Chicago's solution to the problems raised by the research orientation of the tenure system as it practices it is creative and functional, but it is unclear whether it is fully desirable or ultimately sustainable. The University formally classifies senior lecturers as "non-academic faculty," a category that also includes librarians and research associates. This is a somewhat labored way of reserving privileged "academic faculty" status for those who are on the tenure track. Furthermore, although Strieleman reports that his tenured colleagues willingly take part in undergraduate instruction, the fact that positions such as his are only possible because of the emphasis on research for those on the tenure track does little to mitigate the gap between tenured professors and undergraduate students. That gap is evidently greater at most of the schools examined by Cross and Goldenberg than at the University of Chicago (which was not part of their study), as they saw fit to recommend that tenured professors at elite universities teach introductory courses in their disciplines on a regular basis.

Conditions for most nontenure-track faculty in the United States are considerably less agreeable than those under which Strieleman works, and the educational effects of their labors are more problematic. Considerable use of part-time faculty with short-term contracts can be helpful with respect to short-term flexibility and budgeting, but the adverse educational consequences of that practice are well documented. Bernstein and Kezar note that recent research has identified "consistent and disturbing trends related to student outcomes.... These include poor performance and lower graduation rates for students who take more courses with contingent faculty, and lower transfer rates from two-year to four-year institutions."[22]

Paul D. Umbach has also undertaken such research. Professor of Higher Education and Educational Evaluation and Policy Analysis at North Carolina State University, he conducted a study revealing that part-time faculty members "challenged their students significantly less and spent significantly less time preparing for class then their more permanent peers" and that "contingent status, particularly part-time status, is negatively correlated with faculty job performance related to undergraduate education."[23] Umbach's findings have been reinforced by a subsequent analysis by educational researchers Audrey Jaeger and Kevin Eagan that correlated the incidence of such faculty members with student attrition. In a study that controlled for student background characteristics, prior achievement, financial aid measures, and enrollment traits, Jaeger and Eagan found that "high levels of exposure to part-time faculty instruction in the first year appear to have significantly negative relationships with student persistence into the second year."[24]

Studies such as these are of particular importance because of their direct relevance to issues of concern to college administrators and trustees. Jaeger and Eagan speak the language of those constituencies by emphasizing the bottom-line consequences of engagement of part-time faculty at the expense of full-timers. Noting that "many systems of higher education throughout the country...face financial constraints," they argue persuasively that, given those constraints, those systems "are not only demanded to reduce costs but also improve outcomes; one such outcome is retention."[25] Jaeger and Eagan further observe that "[t]he key issue for administrators and policy makers to consider is the extent to which increasing the number of part-time faculty members at an institution to save on instructional costs reduces the likelihood of a student persisting and thus adds a significant cost to the institution."[26]

Other "bottom line" factors also augur against excessive reliance on part-time faculty. One such factor is alumni relations. "Alums who visit their alma mater love to see that good old Professor Chips is still around," observes Roger Meiners, a professor of business at the University of Texas at Arlington. "If everyone comes and goes every few years, there will be lower institutional loyalty on the part of alums. That means lower revenue." Therefore, Meiners concludes, "[F]or long-term relationships, a core stable faculty is valuable."[27]

As examples such as the senior lecturer system at the University of Chicago suggest, a "core stable" faculty is not necessarily the same as a tenured faculty. That is a consideration for boards and administrators who understand the myriad problems that can result from employing a surfeit of part-time faculty and are attempting to strike a balance between that concern and others they face. Many faculty members also understand this difficulty; but the faculty's role in determining how to best achieve such a balance is diminishing, particularly in public institutions.

Several recent high-profile cases can be cited to that effect. In late 2015, the Board of Trustees of the State College of Florida voted overwhelming to abolish tenure for incoming faculty members, instead offering annual contracts that the colleges can decline to renew at their discretion. A few months later, the University of Wisconsin Board of Regents, following the recommendations in the aforementioned WPRI Report, loosened the provisions concerning tenure as a means of faculty protection—a move that had been presaged a year earlier when the Wisconsin state legislature voted to permit the Regents to make binding decisions on such matters. In both cases, those changes were heralded by their supporters as signaling the dawn of a new era in faculty employment and decried by their opponents as unnecessarily risking the educational integrity of the colleges and universities affected by those decisions.

Some schools have devised policies which, while considerably less controversial than those implemented in Florida and Wisconsin, have had the effect of calling the value of tenure into question, while attempting to maintain a stable cadre of capable full-time faculty members. Aside from the aforementioned cases of nontenure-track instructors at elite universities, some schools have decreased their percentage of tenured faculty by creating a non-tenure-track status which includes benefits that tenured faculty do not have. Professors at Webster University in Missouri, for example, may opt to eschew tenure in favor of "faculty-development leave" (FDL) status, which qualifies them for semester-long sabbaticals every five years instead of the customary seven. Professors in this category undergo comprehensive review every five years, which theoretically makes them more vulnerable to dismissal than their tenured colleagues; however, members of the Webster faculty say that there is little precedent for such dismissal.[27] Interestingly, the FDL alternative was implemented at the behest of the Webster faculty; the University administration and board of trustees approved it as a way to reduce permanent fixed costs and improve the quality of instruction. It seems to have worked well for all concerned: two-thirds of the university's current senior faculty members have opted for FDL status, rather than tenure.[28]

Webster is a private institution, and efforts to balance concerns about tenure with qualms about the prevalence of part-time faculty are generally easier to achieve at private than public schools. Nevertheless, private and public institutions are broadly similar in many respects, including employment of part-time faculty members. It might be thought that private schools employ adjuncts and part-timers at significantly lower rates than public ones, but a report recently published by the Council of Independent Colleges (CIC) proves otherwise. According to the CIC report, only slightly more than half the faculty members at private institutions nationwide are full-timers, a virtually identical percentage to that at public colleges and universities.[29] Given such similarities between types of institutions, it seems plausible that practices such as those at Webster and the University of Chicago might be considered by administrators and trustees at public universities who oppose tenure, especially when their opposition is not motivated primarily by short-term economic concerns. Decision-makers at both public and private institutions might also find it useful to better understand practices concerning faculty employment at schools that do without tenure entirely.

Concordia University in Wisconsin is one such institution. Concordia, a Lutheran liberal arts institution with a strong service orientation, operates on the basis of a contract system, with professors receiving three- and five-year "rollover" contracts instead of tenure. Professors who meet expected standards of academic performance have their contracts extended; those who do not may be terminated when their contracts expire. Concordia University President Patrick Ferry believes that this system assures educational quality while providing sufficient security for full-time faculty, adding that he can recall only one faculty member's contract not being extended during his quarter-century on campus.[30]

Another private school that eschews tenure is Hampshire College in Massachusetts. Hampshire is an avowedly secular college that bears little resemblance to Concordia in most respects. It was founded almost half a century ago with a strong belief that academic freedom was vital but not necessarily linked to tenure. That conviction has continued for the entirety of the College's existence. All members of the Hampshire faculty teach on the basis of contracts of various lengths, and academic freedom is explicitly granted in the by-laws of the College's Board of Trustees.[31]

The contract system at Hampshire is based on what Kristen Luschen, Dean of Multicultural Education and Inclusion and Professor of Education Studies, characterizes as "a continual process of review." Each faculty member is periodically required to prepare a professional statement and a file of their achievements and plans, as well as to receive input on their performance from students, colleagues, and external scholars. That process can be arduous and even anxiety-provoking, but it has been valued by the Hampshire faculty since the College's inception. "I could imagine someone saying, 'I wish I had tenure,' but that's not what I've heard from our faculty," Luschen asserts. "Instead, they express appreciation for the opportunity to receive feedback from colleagues and students, and to learn about the amazing things their colleagues are doing in their teaching and scholarship. Faculty members here are expected to innovate and experiment, and having to share our work with colleagues encourages us to take on those challenges."[32] Hampshire boasts a faculty consisting of 82% of full-timers, well in excess of the national average.[33] This is fairly typical of private colleges that operate without tenure, although by no means universally so, Concordia being one of a number of counterexamples.

While private schools such as Hampshire and Concordia claim a degree of institutional autonomy that public institutions by their nature cannot, their policies concerning faculty employment include features that larger and more complex institutions might wish to consider. Their success in retaining full-time faculty indicates that they appear to be able to meet the AAUP goals for those professors, namely academic freedom and job security, without utilizing tenure as the means to achieve them. One reason for this is undoubtedly the exceptional character of such institutions. Most schools that operate without tenure, Naomi Schafer Riley claims, "have strong and clear missions. Few professors would even apply to these schools if they did not believe fully in the schools' missions."[34] This appears to be the case for Concordia and Hampshire. It is certainly true of Shimer College, a small private college in Illinois which has served as this author's academic home for the past 40 years.

The Shimer College Mission reads as follows:

> Shimer College provides and preserves education centered on discussion of enduring questions and issues. Historically influential original sources are studied through Socratic questioning in small seminar classes, following the kind of Great Books curriculum advocated by Robert Maynard Hutchins. The core values informing education at Shimer are free inquiry, dialog, critical open-mindedness, and integration of disciplines. The College offers all members of its community the opportunity to participate meaningfully in deciding the future of the institution. A Shimer education demands much of both the intellect and the character of students, and prepares them for responsible citizenship and the examined life.[35]

While some aspects of Shimer's mission statement would be unexceptional for many liberal arts colleges ("free inquiry," "responsible citizenship," and so on), the statement as a whole betokens a purpose that is decisively different from most. Very few colleges and universities claim to utilize a "Great Books" curriculum; only a handful feature "Socratic questioning in small seminar classes" as a uniform pedagogic principle. As Riley notes, newly minted PhDs who are not interested in teaching in that type of environment are unlikely to apply to such a school, nor are they likely to be hired if they do choose to apply.

The Shimer faculty's shared commitment to the school's mission is closely related to its historic lack of concern about tenure. The key goals of tenure as espoused by the AAUP are not regarded as under threat at Shimer. Academic freedom is considered to be unproblematic for the following reasons, all of which are made clear to prospective faculty members when they apply:

1) Concerning *public statements*, the Shimer faculty is governed by the following assertion in the *Shimer College Faculty Handbook*: "In expressing opinions, the faculty member needs to be careful not to imply the voicing of what might be construed as a College position on any issue unless the College has formally endorsed such a position."[36] Aside from this caveat, faculty members are free to "go

public" without fear of institutional recrimination, and several have done so in recent years.

2) Concerning *statements in class*, the faculty is permitted, indeed encouraged, to speak as they see fit, as is implied in the Mission Statement. The so-called "unwritten rules" about how to do this mostly involve the duty of faculty members to recognize the implications of their position of authority in the classroom. Any problems in this regard are generally minor, and they are handled informally and collegially.

3) Concerning *choice of teaching materials*, this is not permitted in the required courses that comprise two-thirds of the Shimer curriculum, nor does the faculty expect that it will be. It is in the nature of a "core" curriculum such as Shimer's that decisions concerning course materials are decided upon by the faculty as a whole rather than by any individual. Faculty members are welcome to assign materials of their choosing in elective courses as long as those materials qualify as "original sources," since Shimer eschews the use of textbooks as instructional materials.

These factors are an important part of the explanation of why Shimer lacks tenure, but only a part. Other characteristics of the College are also important. In her article "Rethinking Tenure," Trower states that qualities valued by 21st-century faculty members include "collaboration, not competition; transparency, not secrecy; community, not autonomy; flexibility, not uniformity; diversity, not homogeneity; interdisciplinary structures, not disciplinary silos; and family-work life balance, not 'publish or perish' careers."[37] With few exceptions, those qualities are also valued by the teaching staff at Shimer. Indeed, that has been the case for much of the long history of the school, which was established in 1853.

Like the faculty, Shimer's Board of Trustees endorses the mission and concomitant conception of academic freedom described above. The Board is supportive, indeed protective, of faculty security and general well-being. Most Board members are Shimer alumni; their commitment to Shimer is a consequence of their satisfaction with, and appreciation for, the education they received there. They have shown no interest in terminating faculty members for any reason, not even during conditions of extreme financial hardship (of which Shimer has had more than its share). For its part, the faculty repays the Board's trust by assuring that instructional quality takes place at a very high level, which involves a good deal of conscientious "self-policing." The faculty also defers to the administration and Board on matters concerning use of financial resources, even when those decisions result in the elimination of planned pay increases for the teaching staff. This high level of mutual trust has not always been present at Shimer, but it has been for the vast majority of the time in recent decades.

Conditions of faculty hiring, evaluation, and promotion at Shimer are spelled out in considerable detail in the *Shimer College Faculty Handbook* (henceforth *Handbook*), as are the circumstances under which members of the faculty can be released from service to the College. Adjuncts are hired only occasionally, and then almost exclusively to teach courses for which the Shimer faculty is not qualified, for example, elective offerings in Eastern Studies. The percentage of full-time faculty members has rarely been less than 90% at any time in the College's history.

The conditions of release from service for faculty at Shimer may be of special interest, since that issue is directly addressed at most other schools by tenure stipulations. All incoming faculty members at Shimer undergo a regimen of formative and summative evaluation during their early years at the College. If and when they qualify for Senior Faculty status (normally after four years), they receive a renewable three-year contract. At that point, as the *Handbook* states, "it is assumed that they will continue to serve on the Shimer faculty as long as they are willing and able to do so. However, the College guarantees no member of the Senior Faculty employment in perpetuity."[38] Members of the Senior Faculty continue to receive three-year contracts for the remainder of their employment at Shimer if all goes well, but exceptions are possible under certain explicitly stated conditions.

The AAUP recognizes two types of circumstances in which faculty members may be relieved of service: "termination" and "dismissal." The former may result when the college is in a state of financial exigency; the latter, from "lack of fitness of faculty members in their professional capacities as teachers or researchers."[39] Broadly speaking, those definitions inform the conditions under which senior faculty members at Shimer may be subject to nonretention.

Regarding termination, the AAUP stipulates that the following conditions must be met: a demonstration of financial exigency must be "demonstrably bona fide," untenured faculty are the first to be terminated, and terminated faculty are given right of first refusal if their position is to be filled within three years.[40] Other than the "tenure" stipulation, those conditions are reflected in Shimer's policies on this subject. This is significant because, as Philo Hutcheson, the author of the companion chapter on tenure in this volume, has pointed out, "More often than not, it is the administration that makes the determination of exigency. Several cases suggest that, in actuality, the institution suffers from financial discomfort rather than exigency."[41] At Shimer, termination of faculty may take place only when the President and the Finance Committee of the Board of Trustees have publically declared and demonstrated a state of financial exigency. Since such declarations potentially have clearly negative consequences, for example, with respect to fund-raising and financial audits, institutions are unlikely to make them unless the condition of the institution is unmistakably dire rather than merely uncomfortable. Drake University defines financial exigency as "a critical financial condition of the university as a whole, such that a failure to dismiss tenured faculty members would threaten the welfare of the university."[42] While Shimer has no explicitly stated definition of financial exigency, its history strongly suggests that its tacit definition is at least as strict as that of Drake.

Even in the case of financial exigency, the contract status and academic performance of faculty members at Shimer play no role in termination decisions, which must be "based on an assessment of the College's teaching needs, financial considerations, and the desire to adversely and significantly affect as few individuals as possible." Also in line with AAUP guidelines, such terminations are explicitly intended to serve as involuntary leaves of absence rather than permanent departures from the college. The *Handbook* states that "any terminated faculty member has an open 'right of return' under whatever terms of employment the College's financial or enrollment exigencies permit and the faculty member is willing to accept"[43] for up to three years after the date of termination.

Formal procedures regarding faculty dismissals at Shimer are somewhat more complex. Because Shimer operates on a contract system rather than a tenure system, Shimer distinguishes two types of cases that fall under the heading of "dismissal" as rendered in AAUP guidelines. "Dismissal" *per se* may take place if the Academic Dean determines that a faculty member has committed "serious breaches of standards of expected conduct or if he or she is otherwise found to have engaged in personal or professional behavior that demonstrably impedes her or his ability to carry out academic and/or administrative duties effectively."[44] In other words, the category of "dismissal" at Shimer covers the sorts of egregious acts for which even tenured professors would be likely to lose their positions, those which are sometimes categorized as "gross professional misconduct."

The other sort of dismissal, for which Shimer utilizes the term "nonrenewal," is related directly to consistently subpar teaching performance. Like all matters concerning faculty hiring and evaluation at Shimer, it is decided upon by a college-wide committee, the Academic Planning Committee (APC). The APC, which is chaired by the Academic Dean, is comprised of faculty members, students, and a member of the administrative staff who is directly involved in the academic enterprise. That committee has sole authority for deciding whether to renew faculty contracts, and it may decline to do so in cases of inadequate teaching performance. This has not occurred in any case of a senior faculty member in my four decades at the College, although in rare cases diminished performance has led to a shorter-term contract with stipulations for what the faculty member must accomplish in order for further contracts to be offered in the future. Nonrenewal is far more frequent for junior faculty members, as the balance between quality assurance and faculty security depends upon comprehensive evaluation and assessment during a faculty member's early years at Shimer. Any faculty member who wishes to contest an APC decision is welcome to file an appeal. Appeals are to be heard by a faculty hearing panel, the composition and charge of which is rendered in the *Handbook*.[45] This is strictly an "on the books" policy; while it is carefully worded and quite extensive, it has never been used.

Shimer's model of faculty employment has functioned effectively, even admirably, in the eyes of the vast majority of Shimer's teaching staff, administrators, and Board of Trustees members. That is not to say that it would work as well elsewhere. Consideration of various models of faculty employment must be undertaken with a number of caveats, including those regarding the particular nature of the college or university in question.

After pointing out that the data resulting from his research on tenure reflects large-scale generalizations that may obfuscate equally significant differences between institutions, Martin Trow concludes, "Whatever forces of competition or emulation have given rise to such remarkably similar patterns of employment across such a heterogeneous range of institutions, academic tenure has quite different consequences in research universities than it has, for example, in small local colleges. And that raises the question whether there can be any national policy on academic tenure that does not do violence to the quite different roles tenure plays in the different institutions which together make up American higher education."[46] Trow's observation suggests that there can be no suitable "one-size-fits-all" approach to issues regarding employment policies for college and university faculty.

Faculty employment policies that do not involve tenure (such as those practiced at schools like Concordia, Hampshire, and Shimer) inevitably reflect the institutional qualities of the schools that implement them. The same is true of universities that practice hybrid systems, such as Webster and the University of Chicago. There are many similarities between institutions of higher education in the United States, as noted earlier; but their differences are equally striking, and each school is best served when both its unique features and the qualities it shares with other schools are reflected in its policies and practices.

It is advisable, indeed essential, for college presidents and boards to make every effort to understand the broad range of considerations regarding faculty employment at their institutions beyond the short-term bottom line. Awareness of successful practices at other schools, including those that are very different from their own, can help them in considering and devising policies that accurately reflect that understanding. It is also important for college and university faculty, especially those whose voices are likely to be heeded by administrations, state boards, and the general public, to imagine and encourage new or revised models of faculty employment that can respond productively to the various concerns facing higher education in the complex intellectual and economic environment of the early 21st century.

Notes

1. Bardwell L. Smith, "What Price Tenure?" in Bardwell L. Smith and Associates, *The Tenure Debate* (Washington, DC: Jossey-Bass Inc., 1973), p. 7.
2. Daniel J. Ennis, "The Last of the Tenure Track," *The Chronicle of Higher Education,* July 3, 2011.
3. *Ibid.*
4. Jordan Weissmann, "The Ever-Shrinking Role of Tenured College Professors (in 1 Chart)," *The Chronicle of Higher Education*, April 10, 2013.
5. Ennis, *op cit.*
6. "Background Facts on Contingent Faculty," AAUP website (www.aaup.org).
7. Samantha Bernstein and Adrianna Kezar, "Is It Time to Eliminate Tenure for Professors?," *The Conversation* (online journal), June 28, 2016.
8. Dennis Wrong, "The Challenge of Tenure," *Dissent*, Summer 1998.
9. Naomi Schaefer Riley, *The Faculty Lounges and Other Reasons You Won't Get the College Education You Paid For* (Chicago, IL: Ivan R. Dee, 2011), p. 93.
10. Jack Stripling, "Most Presidents Prefer No Tenure for Majority of Faculty," *The Chronicle of Higher Education,* May 15, 2011.
11. Cathy A. Trower, "Rethinking College Tenure," *New York Times*, August 12, 2010.
12. Mike Nichols, "President's Note," in *The Trouble with Tenure* (WPRI Report, Volume 29 Number 1, February 2016), p. 2.
13. Colleen Flaherty, "Wanting More Say," *Inside Higher Ed*, March 13, 2015.
14. *Ibid.*
15. Bernstein and Kezar, *op cit.*
16. Ike Brannon and Philip Coyle, "A Survey of System Instructional Staff Opinions Regarding Tenure," in *The Trouble with Tenure, op cit.*, p. 17.
17. Martin Trow, "The Distribution of Academic Tenure in American Higher Education," in Smith, *op cit.*, pp. 244–249.

18. John G. Cross and Edie N. Goldenberg, *Off-Track Profs: Nontenured Teachers in Higher Education* (Cambridge, MA: MIT Press, 2009).
19. References to comments by Paul Strieleman are based on his conversation with the author on June 1, 2016.
20. Martin J. Finkelstein and Jack H. Schuster, "Assessing the Silent Revolution: How Changing Demographics Are Reshaping the Academic Profession," *AAHE Bulletin,* October 2001, p. 5.
21. "Recommended Institutional Regulations on Academic Freedom and Tenure," AAUP website (www.aaup.org).
22. Bernstein and Kezar, *op cit.*
23. Paul D. Umbach, "How Effective Are They? Exploring the Impact of Contingent Faculty on Undergraduate Education," *Review of Higher Education*, Volume 30 Number 2, Winter 2007, pp. 91-123.
24. Audrey J. Jaeger and M. Kevin Eagan, "Examining Retention and Contingent Faculty Use in a State System," *Educational Policy*, June 13, 2010, p. 530.
25. *Ibid.*, p. 531.
26. *Ibid.*, p. 530.
27. Stripling, *op cit.*
28. Jennifer Epstein, "In Lieu of Tenure," *Inside Higher Ed*, March 10, 2010.
29. Christopher Morphew, Kelly Ward, and Lisa Wolf-Wendel, "Changes in Faculty Composition at Independent Colleges" (Council of Independent Colleges, June 2016), pp. 10–11.
30. Mike Nichols and Michael Flaherty with Charles Sorenson, "How the University of Wisconsin Board of Regents can Make Professors Accountable to Taxpayers and Students," in *The Trouble with Tenure, op cit.*, p. 13.
31. Hampshire College website (www.hampshire.edu).
32. References to comments by Kristen Luschen are based on her conversation with the author on August 10, 2016.
33. Hampshire College website (www.hampshire.edu).
34. Riley, *op cit.*, p. 139.
35. Shimer College website (www.shimer.edu).
36. *Constitution and Handbook of the Shimer College Faculty 2015–16,* p. 9.
37. Trower, *op cit.*
38. *Constitution and Handbook of the Shimer College Faculty 2015–16,* p. 19.
39. "Recommended Institutional Regulations on Academic Freedom and Tenure," AAUP website (www.aaup.org).
40. *Ibid.*
41. Philo A. Hutcheson, "The Corrosion of Tenure: A Bibliography," *The NEA Higher Education Journal*, p. 92.
42. Cited in Trower (editor), *Policies on Faculty Appointment* (Boston, MA: Anker Publishing Company, 2000), p. 252.
43. *Constitution and Handbook of the Shimer College Faculty 2015–16*, p. 21.
44. *Constitution and Handbook of the Shimer College Faculty 2015–16*, p. 20.
45. *Constitution and Handbook of the Shimer College Faculty 2015–16*, pp. 22–23.
46. Trow in Smith, *op cit.*, p. 250.

8. Why Tenure Needs Protection in These Troubled Times

Philo A. Hutcheson

Tenure is a popular target, and it has been a popular target for well over a century. Critiques range from the perspective that it is nothing better than job protection for lazy or incompetent (or lazy and incompetent) professors to its failure to protect nontenured professors from attacks on their academic freedom. It is important to acknowledge that both conditions exist. There are also concerns about tenured professors seemingly enforcing their social or political or economic norms in classrooms or the degree to which tenure-track professors exercise caution in their research and teaching in order to avoid challenging the work of tenured professors who will vote on their tenure. Yet two broader questions are the most important to consider: What do we achieve with a tenure system? And who could benefit?

The concepts of academic freedom and tenure are inextricably and necessarily linked; hence, I will begin with a discussion of academic freedom and then move to a discussion of tenure, concluding with some thoughts about recent events and possible threats to academic freedom that require the protection of tenure—more specifically, to the need to extend the protection of tenure in terms of those who do not currently have tenure as well as institutional commitment to tenure.

Professors engage in a variety of tasks in their daily work; in general, these tasks fall under the headings of research, teaching, and service. In both research and teaching, and at times in service, inquiry is a central part of what professors do. Professors must examine traditional and new ideas, using any number of methods, and draw conclusions; they share information and knowledge with students, raising questions and at times offering answers about issues. In service, professors bring their expertise to a problem, using inquiry to aid in the solution. These fundamental activities give rise to a complex and challenging notion, that is, academic freedom. Simply stated, to what extent does society at large as well as institutions of higher education accept inquiry? Are professors to engage in inquiry only to the point of reaffirming an established order, or are we willing, as citizens and academics, to allow professors to inquire even if troubling questions and answers arise about our individual and social behavior? My analysis will indicate that professors themselves often accept limitations on academic freedom, which means that tenure is all the more important since it is meant to protect an already limited notion of the freedom to inquire.

Another concern is that there are disparate views regarding academic freedom, and there is also a tendency toward individual interpretation. One of the most threatening periods in regard to attacks on professors was McCarthyism during the early 1950s, when Senator Joseph P. McCarthy (Republican, WI) led attacks on intellectuals and professors, accusing them of being former or current members of the Communist Party of the United States. A thorough treatment of wide-ranging interpretations of the meaning of academic freedom during McCarthyism and the attacks on professors is Schrecker's *No Ivory Tower* (1986). This work documents the varying perspectives on academic freedom within the professoriate as well as among college and university administrators and trustees and such public groups as state and federal government officials, business people, and journalists. Given those varying perspectives, it is important to offer a specific definition of academic freedom and, later in the chapter, of tenure.

In the early 1900s the American Association of University Professors (AAUP) initiated the consideration of academic freedom and tenure after two faculty dismissal cases came to its attention. A leader of the AAUP, Arthur O. Lovejoy, upon reading about one of the cases in *The New York Times,* proposed to the Association president, John Dewey, that the AAUP could gain favorable publicity by coming to the defense of the dismissed professors. Dewey concurred, and he noted in his presidential address that the topic of academic freedom was thrust upon the AAUP (Hutcheson, 2000; Metzger, 1961b). The earliest report of the AAUP on academic freedom, the 1915 "Declaration of Principles on Academic Freedom and Academic Tenure," represented a critical first step toward defining academic freedom and tenure—including the link between academic freedom and a necessary protection of that freedom, that is, tenure.

The AAUP coordinated with other organizations to extend the 1915 statement, clarifying faculty, administrative, and institutional roles, with the 1926 "Conference Statement on Academic Freedom and Tenure." Of particular importance in regard to this Statement is the fact that the AAUP collaborated with other national organizations to define academic freedom and tenure (Metzger, 1961a). Further negotiations resulted in the 1940 "Statement of Principles on Academic Freedom and Tenure" (often referred to as the 1940 Statement), and ever since then institutions of higher education and a wide range of organizations have endorsed the 1940 Statement. As of the fall of 2016, over "240 national scholarly and education associations were endorsers" (https://www.aaup.org/our-work/protecting-academic-freedom). The introduction to the Statement offers a clear reason for academic freedom and tenure, arguing, "Institutions of higher education are conducted for the common good and not to further the interest of either the individual teacher or the institution as a whole." It also specifically addresses research and teaching:

1. Teachers are entitled to full freedom in research and in the publication of the results, subject to the adequate performance of their other academic duties; but research for pecuniary return should be based upon an understanding with the authorities of the institution.

2. Teachers are entitled to freedom in the classroom in discussing their subject, but they should be careful not to introduce into their teaching controversial matter which has no relation to their subject. Limitations of academic freedom because of religious or other aims of the institution should be clearly stated in writing at the time of the appointment. (https://www.aaup.org/report/1940-statement-principles-academic-freedom-and-tenure)

The Statement also indicates that professors should exercise care in their public utterances in view of their special positions as experts.

Even institutions of higher education that do not specifically cite the 1940 Statement offer language in faculty handbooks that echo it. For example, Frank Phillips College (a community college in Texas) indicates in its employee handbook:

Institutions of higher education are conducted for the common good. The common good depends upon a free search for truth and its free expression. Hence, it is essential that the faculty member is free to pursue scholarly inquiry without undue restriction and to voice and publish conclusions concerning the significance of evidence considered relevant. The faculty member must be free from the fear that others inside or outside the college community, because their vision may differ, may threaten a professional career or the material benefits accruing from it.

Each faculty member is entitled to full freedom in the classroom in discussing the subject being taught. (http://www.fpctx.edu/InsideFPC/documents/FPC%20Employee%20Handbook%202016%20-%202017.pdf, retrieved November 2, 2016)

This language is instructive because the college has been on the AAUP list of censured institutions longer than any other college or university on the list (since 1969) (Censure List, 2016a). Even institutions that the AAUP has judged as remiss may have institutional policy language that clearly echoes AAUP language on academic freedom.

Despite some degree of widespread support for the principles of academic freedom, there is a fundamental problematic condition of academic freedom; indeed, academic freedom began with a set of philosophical limitations. In the United States a slow and piecemeal adoption of principles of academic freedom, institutional and professional limitations were developed. From there I will then move to McCarthyism as a period when a number of key illustrations about limits of academic freedom were obtained, and conclude with some thoughts about general criticisms of professors as well as the current climate for freedom of inquiry in research and teaching and the need for what protection tenure offers.

Academic Freedom and Its Philosophical Limits

U.S. professors have willingly and knowingly sacrificed principles of academic freedom for public service to the nation and the government, especially in times of crisis such as world wars or the Cold War (Gruber, 1975; Lazarsfeld & Thielens, 1958; Schrecker, 1986; Slaughter, 1980). Yet these examinations uniformly suggest that the social and political conditions of the academic profession and the environment, rather than the philosophical context of academic freedom, are primary influences on deviation from academic freedom in this country. Is this the case, or has the academy inherited and accepted an academic freedom that is inherently restrictive?

The literature on the history of academic freedom typically refers to its German origins, the requisite nod to *Lehrfreiheit*, roughly speaking, the freedom to teach and to conduct research. In general, scholars ascribe the origins of Western notions of academic freedom to Immanual Kant and ideas he initially developed in a 1784 essay, "An Answer to the Question: What is Enlightenment?" He wrote:

> But only a ruler who is himself enlightened and has no fear of phantoms, yet who likewise has at hand a well-disciplined and numerous army to guarantee public security, may say what no republic would dare to say: *Argue as much as you like and about whatever you like, but obey!* (Kant, 1784/1977)

Kant acknowledged this "paradoxical" condition of human affairs and suggested that "a lesser degree of civil freedom gives intellectual freedom enough room to expand to its fullest extent." Kant (1798/1992) extended the argument about academic freedom in three essays, *The Conflict of the Faculties*. These essays specifically provide an argument about academic freedom—one which German educators furthered in their development of the German university (Herbst, 1965; Ringer, 1969), and which later arose in the arguments of key leaders in the initial development of academic freedom interpretations in the United States.

The 1915 Statement on Academic Freedom and Tenure served as the basis for the two major ensuing statements, the 1925 Statement and the 1940 Statement on Academic Freedom (Metzger, 1961a). The 1940 Statement remains the central and dominant expression of academic freedom in the United States—no other statement on academic freedom and tenure has secured so many external endorsers; and the 1915 statement is a critical moment in the development of academic freedom interpretations in this country. Eight of the authors of the 1915 Statement had studied in Germany. The most influential author (Gruber, 1975, p. 166, note 5), Arthur O. Lovejoy, not only studied in Germany but also studied the works of Immanuel Kant (Lovejoy, 1959, 1961; Wilson, 1980); thus Lovejoy's work on the 1915 Statement is highly important. And, in fact, the 1915 Statement does defer to civil authority in its institutional form, noting that presidents and trustees may be right, and professors wrong.

It would not take long for the AAUP to have to address the role of the professor in times of crisis, highlighting the professor's role relative to external authority. Increasing U.S. involvement in World War I brought many professors to the forefront of duty to the state, to the tension between arguing and obeying. An AAUP committee chaired by Lovejoy wrote a report on academic freedom and war. The report was clearly a call for limiting the academic freedom of the professor in the name of the civil freedom restrictions in wartime America, arguing, for example, that professors who espoused "absolute nonresistance" to aggression should be suspended (Report of Committee on Academic Freedom in Wartime, 1918, p. 37). In response to a critical evaluation in *Nation* magazine, Lovejoy wrote that colleges could choose to be "accomplices" to those who could cause defeat or refuse to "countenance" those who would aid the enemy. He argued that times of crisis demanded the suspension of rules on such matters as academic freedom (Lovejoy, 1918, p. 255). This limitation, a manifestation of argue but obey, was not the only limit on academic freedom, and the period of McCarthyism in the 1950s is instructive as to additional limitations.

McCarthy and McCarthyism: The Limits of the Power of the Professor

Suspension of the rules was to occur again during World War II and during McCarthyism (Schrecker, 1986). A great deal has been written about Senator Joseph McCarthy, especially his undocumented attacks on people accused of being Communists and McCarthyism, as well as a fair amount on McCarthyism and professors. This literature highlights several important characteristics of academic freedom in the United States.

McCarthyism occurred in the 1950s, when the academic profession was often the subject of vituperative charges against its members' loyalty to the nation and the society. In a number of cases, the attacks destroyed professors' chances for successful careers (Schrecker, 1986). Despite these problems, higher education also continued its business at large. As Caplow and McGee (1958) point out in *The Academic Marketplace*, higher education appointed new professors much as it had in the recent past, emphasizing their disciplinary distinction and institutional prestige. How was higher education able to conduct much of its work as usual, and why did the enterprise choose to act in that way?

Senator Joseph McCarthy represents the epitome of the attacks on professors, although he focused on other groups, particularly government officials. Those who agreed, in one way or another, with McCarthy and his arguments and methods were more likely to attack professors and formed the era known as McCarthyism. Both McCarthy and McCarthyism strike at the heart of the search for truth—the professoriate's 20th-century mission—because the attackers generally did not provide direct evidence of subversive activity. The professoriate is dependent not only upon argument but also direct evidence; as was remarkably clear during McCarthyism, it is very difficult to develop responses to attacks that have no evidence.

The biographical literature on Joseph McCarthy is extensive. Among the works that are often in support of McCarthy, Roy Cohn's *McCarthy* (1969) provides a startling reminder of the claims offered during the presidential primary campaigns of 2016. Cohn worked with the Senator and was a fervent supporter. In reference to McCarthy's infamous 1950 speech in Wheeling, West Virginia—when the Senator announced that there were 205 Communists working in the State Department (a figure he later revised to 57, then later again to 81)—Cohn stated that although the figures varied,

> Let us never forget that the substance of his charges was true. There *were* persons working in the State Department whose activities and associations indicated that had pro-Communist leanings. Could any American rest easily, knowing

pro-Communists may have been helping to shape our foreign policy? (Cohn, 1969, p. 277)

This form of attack, when evidence is not especially relevant, had very real consequences even for those who were not attacked directly.

Lazarsfeld and Thielens (1958) produced an extensive analysis in response to their question, "How did the general tension affect social science teaching?" in their work, *The Academic Mind*. In terms of the emotional reaction to McCarthyism, just under half of the social science professors in their sample felt apprehensive, but not paralyzed. Overall, the work documents "patterns of caution" (p. 192) among professors in their teaching, research, and professional obligations.

Even biographers who were critical of McCarthy acknowledged his abilities. Rovere (1959) offered sharp criticism in contrast to Cohn, introducing his subject as a "most gifted demagogue" whose "access to the dark places of the American mind is unequaled" (p. 9). He continues by suggesting that McCarthy's followers were from "the world of the daft and the frenzied," but then acknowledges his substantial support from "regular Republicans" (p. 23). Rovere concedes that regardless of the accuracy of McCarthy's charges, the Senator held the attention of the U.S. public and media, the Congress and two presidents of the country, and even the world. In another biography, Reeves (1982) agreed with Cohn and Rovere that Senator McCarthy did not heed the facts, but was able to command great public and political attention.

Another important aspect of political support for McCarthyism is the role of liberals during this period. Their efforts, or in many cases the lack thereof, reveal the extraordinary depth and breadth of McCarthyism as well as its historical extent. According to Fried (1990), "The names of John F. Kennedy, Paul Douglas, and other famous liberals do not often appear in the chronicle of opposition to McCarthy" (p. 261). The political context of McCarthyism is neatly summarized by Wolfe (1981), "Communism *was* outside the postwar consensus, the ideas of the radical right *were not*" (p.12); and Griffith (1987) argued that, in investigating McCarthy and McCarthyism, he found "a thoroughly conventional politics rooted in political parties and interest groups" (p. xi).

McCarthyism, then, in part represents a conservative political position with liberal acquiescence or even acceptance, with appeals to the working class, although its actual support derives from probusiness antilabor groups. It occurred at a time when international political developments threatened the status of the United States.

Nevertheless, McCarthy and McCarthyism meant more than political anti-Communist fears and attacks. Wiebe (1977) argued that McCarthy used both national and local standards to sustain his attacks, establishing a mass movement. Attacks on Communism meant attacks on "atheism, sexual freedoms, strange accents, civil rights, or whatever most threatened a particular group's sense of security" (p. 1122). In its broadest manifestation, beyond the political framework, McCarthyism represented attacks on those who were different—whether their differences were religious, ethnic, sexual, or other.

Examinations of McCarthyism and the professoriate tend to fall into two categories. The first category is composed of examinations that typically conclude that the professoriate, or higher education, could have, but failed, to defend professors. The second group is composed of examinations that suggest the capacity of McCarthyism to influence, if not control, higher education.

MacIver wrote *Academic Freedom in Our Time* (1955) when McCarthyism was still a powerful movement; activities such as censorship of books and loyalty oaths indicated the depth and breadth of the "new wave of intolerance" (p. 34). He also pointed to the considerable lack of evidence in investigations by governmental and private agencies and the extraordinary number of such groups engaged in investigations. Yet he too revealed the ambiguity of this period, suggesting, "The problem of how to deal with the minute proportion of scholars who are communists is only a minute part of the master problem of how to deal with communism in the world, communism as a world power" (p. 52). He also documented the range of attacks on Keynesians, atheists, nonconformists, and the sexually immoral as well as on supposed communist affiliations. His solution was reasoned defense rather than emotional outbursts. MacIver reminded his readers that it was essential for faculties as collectivities of professors to maintain a corporate identity, especially when times require the defense of colleagues.

Slaughter (1980) offered a critical view of the AAUP defense of academic freedom and tenure principles during McCarthyism, stating that the Association "sacrificed individuals and substantive principles in order to gain compliance for procedural safeguards from university officials for the profession as a whole" (p. 46). While more critical than MacIver's analysis, Slaughter argued that the AAUP could have done more to defend professors. Schrecker's work, *No Ivory Tower* (1986), is the most comprehensive of the examinations of McCarthyism and the professoriate. She argued that academe "came to adapt itself to the suppression of dissent" (p. 11). She concluded her examination with a chapter on the academic profession's response to McCarthyism, especially the AAUP. Criticizing the General Secretary of the Association, Schrecker suggested that if professors had chosen to act, they could have stopped some of the dismissals. The nation's professors were complicit, evidencing liberal ambiguity and hence leaving colleagues to the mercy of the attacks.

In contrast, Lazarsfeld and Thielens (1958) concluded, "The clear, if unconscious, implication is that the initiative would have to come from someone else" (pp. 233–234). They found little in the academic mind to suggest it had the capacity or the means to resist McCarthyism. Furthermore, institutional histories of McCarthyism on campus tend to indicate the precarious status of professors and the limits of reasoned defense. Two early and notable academic freedom cases arose at the University of Washington and the University of California; they are instructive for their portrayal of the complex and often supportive responses to McCarthyism. Sanders' work, *Cold War on the Campus* (1979), captures both the administrative and professorial support for anticommunism at the University of Washington in the late 1940s and early 1950s. It was not only the administration that was concerned about professors and Communism; a majority of those belonging to the local AAUP chapter supported a statement opposing the right of professors to belong to the Communist Party (Sanders, 1979). At the University of California, in 1949, the regents required professors to swear that they were not members of the Communist Party. Stewart suggests in *The Year of the Oath* (1950) that a collective approach served the faculty members well, as they were able to forestall the implementation of the oath. He concludes, however, that the result of the opposition was a Pyrrhic victory at best given that the Regents, at the time of the book's publication, had begun to dismiss professors. Other institutional histories, such as Lipset (1975), Holmes (1989), Lewis (1993), and McCormick, also tend to highlight the limits of reasoned defense and the fragile nature of academic freedom. McCormick's (1989) examination of the dismissal of an art professor, Luella Mundel, at Fairmont State College in West Virginia, captured the broad social conditions of McCarthyism. McCormick noted that a socially conservative local elite used Red-baiting to arouse public animosity, that the university president was an anticommunist liberal, and that there was never any direct evidence that the dismissed professor was in any way connected with Communism. The attacks appear to have centered on issues of "female nudity, nontraditional female behavior, and homosexuality," which were somewhat characteristic of recent doctoral recipients "affecting varied styles of intellectual searching—bohemianism or political dissent or avant garde cynicism" (p. 33) and, ultimately, on the issue of atheism. Both local and national forces pressured the university administration and faculty into the eventual dismissal of Professor Mundel.

The University of Wisconsin provides a substantial example of the problematic nature of reasoned defense. O'Brien (1980) argued that the president of the University of Wisconsin, Edwin B. Fred, withstood several attacks on the University. President Fred succeeded in his defense in great part because administrators "had carefully cultivated relations with government officials," many of whom were alumni and alumnae (p. 197). O'Brien concluded, "Most important were the traditions, coordinated power, and constant vigilance of political forces in Wisconsin, ranging from Socialists to moderate Republicans" (p. 202). Political alliances rather than reasoned defense protected the University of Wisconsin.

Advocates of McCarthyism used lack of evidence as a means to attack and as a way to effect sanctions against professors. McCarthyism included the widespread denial of appointment and promotion (or even the retention of one's position) as well as apprehension among professors and administrators in regard to both possible attacks and sanctions. McCarthyism also included attacks on marginal groups. McCarthyism highlights the professoriate's vulnerability in the face of both subtle and heavy-handed political maneuvering. Faculty solidarity and reasoned defense might slow the maneuvering, but there is little more than faith to suggest that a collectivity could halt the political power.

Higher education was able to continue business as usual because McCarthyism represented in great part struggles as old as higher education in this country—whether those struggles were the result of the accommodation of external political interference or internal disagreement. In great part, then, McCarthyism and the professoriate represent the standard, rather than the exception, in the history of academic freedom.

While most scholars writing on the issue of McCarthyism and the professoriate acknowledge the tenuous nature of academic freedom, it is far less common in the literature to find expressions of concern about the vulnerability of the professoriate. Even the members of the Association of American Universities—elite research universities with presumably strong foundations for academic freedom and identified as tending toward defenses of attacked professors—offered unanimous support for a 1953 document clearly violating policies and processes of the 1940 Statement (*The Present Danger: A Report from the University Presidents*). What is important is professors' political condition: When those who can wield power choose to do so against professors, professors have little power to respond. It is not that McCarthyism or other popular movements critical of academe are ominous, but rather that the condition of the professor is ominous. The professoriate is politically vulnerable and organizationally dependent. As McCarthyism shows, when the public and the polity decide that professors are not sufficiently American, professors suffer. In addition, professors themselves often limit their inquiry, either out of apprehension or, more problematic, because they refer to what they see as deeper basic values, centered on patriotism and allegiance to the state. Argue but obey.

Some Thoughts Concerning Tenure

The efforts to codify tenure in the 1940 Statement signaled the AAUP's remarkable achievement in the area of academic freedom and tenure. Such processes as tenure review by the seventh year of a tenure-track professor's appointment are so ensconced in academe that they are taken for granted at a vast number of colleges and universities in the United States.

The Statement indicates that "After the expiration of a probationary period, teachers or investigators should have permanent or continuous tenure, and their service should be terminated only for adequate cause, except in the case of retirement for age, or under extraordinary circumstances because of financial exigencies" and that moral turpitude may be cause for dismissal. The Statement also indicates that professors should exercise restraint in their public utterances in view of their special positions as experts (2016b) (https://www.aaup.org/report/1940-statement-principles-academic-freedom-and-tenure). Tenure is the device that protects, to some degree, professors' academic freedom; in fact, by and large AAUP Committee A (the organization's committee for review of academic freedom and tenure complaints) cases are actually about the institution's failure to provide the very sort of due process that tenure is meant to provide.

As is clear in the discussion of McCarthyism, professors all too easily face sanctions or dismissal in times of crisis, in troubling times; and tenure stands as a first line of defense, although it is a tenuous line. While it is rare for an institution to dismiss a tenured faculty member (other than for reasons of financial exigency—and even in those cases institutions may not follow due process for tenured professors), it happens. When Ward Churchill (2016) outraged conservatives on- and off-campus upon belated review of his comments about the 9/11 attacks on the World Trade Center, many of them sought to withhold state or private monies. The University of Colorado instituted a supposedly unrelated investigation of possible research misconduct; and despite the fact that the investigating committee did not reach a uniform conclusion about sanctions, the University dismissed him (www.wardchurchill.net). Whether it is recent events or decades past, the evidence is clear: If institutional and faculty defenses are not stalwart, then a core characteristic of higher education, inquiry based on rational means, becomes subject to political, social, and economic threats. Furthermore, there is a strong under-lying assumption in that inquiry that expects professors to argue but obey, and those working to defend tenure and tenured professors must stay aware of that problematic condition.

What is more troubling, and a most serious indication of the need for improvement, is the large proportion of faculty members who, in the words of the lawyers, are "at-will employees" (i.e., employees who can be dismissed without cause). A process of detenuring the academy began in the 1970s (Hutcheson, 1996) and continues unabated. In 2003, 31% of all faculty members were tenured; by 2013, 21% were tenured according to a study by TIAA-CREF (2016) (https://www.tiaainstitute.org/public/pdf/taking_the_measure_of_faculty_diversity.pdf). This march toward the university and college as a home for at-will employees carries with it serious repercussions in regard to the face of the academy because increasing numbers of white women and people of color are entering the professoriate, but they are fun-neled into nontenure-track positions. Hence those who may want to raise questions about social justice and equity based on their experiences are placed in the more vulnerable employment positions. It is not that we need tenure, it is that we need to extend the protections of tenure, even as tenuous as they can be, to faculty members who honor the centuries-old tradition of critiqu-ing society in the effort to create a more perfect society.

And, finally, what does an endorsement mean? Herein lies one area admit-ting of improvement, because endorsing a set of principles is not the same as acting upon them. Colleges and universities that espouse academic freedom but do not act vigorously to defend it, as McCarthyism showed, leave profes-sors vulnerable to attacks that can ruin their careers. Fear of the different and challenging, whether it is political affiliation, sexual identity, or any number of characteristics, too easily leads to attacks on the professor. In an age when even scientific proof of such matters as climate change or the overwhelming benefits of vaccination for both one's own children and those who come into contact with one's children are subject to question and even denial, arguing but obeying may all too easily lead to far greater problems.

References

American Association of University Professors. (2016a). Censure List. Retrieved from https://www.aaup.org/our-programs/academic-freedom/censure-list

American Association of University Professors. (2016b). *The 1940 statement of princi-ples on academic freedom and tenure*. Retrieved from https://www.aaup.org/report/1940-statement-principles-academic-freedom-and-tenure

American Association of University Professors. (2016c). *Protecting academic freedom.* Retrieved from https://www.aaup.org/our-work/protecting-academic-freedom

Caplow, T., & McGee, R. J. (1958). *The academic marketplace.* Garden City, NY: Basic Books.

Cohn, R. (1969). *McCarthy.* New York, NY. New American Library.

Fried, R. M. (1990). *Nightmare in red: The McCarthy era in perspective.* New York, NY: Oxford University Press.

Griffith, R. (1987). *The politics of fear: Joseph r. mccarthy and the senate* (2nd ed). Amherest, MA: University of Massachusetts Press

Gruber, C. (1975). *Mars and Minerva: World War I and the uses of the higher learning in America.* Baton Rouge, LA: Louisiana State University Press.

Herbst, J. (1965). *The German historical school in American scholarship: A study in the transfer of culture.* Ithaca, NY: Cornell University Press.

Holmes, D. R. (1989). *Stalking the academic communist: Intellectual freedom and the firing of Alex Novikoff.* Hanover, NH: University Press of New England.

Hutcheson, P. A. (1996). Faculty tenure: Myth and reality 1974 to 1992. *Thought and Action, 12*(1), 7–22.

Hutcheson, P. A. (2000). *A professional professoriate: Unionization, bureaucratization, and the AAUP.* Nashville, TN: Vanderbilt University Press.

Kant, I. (1798/1992). *The conflict of the faculties* (M. J. Gregor, Trans.). Lincoln, NE: University of Nebraska Press.

Kant, I. (1977). An answer to the question: What is enlightenment? (pp. 54–60). In H. Reiss (Ed.) and H. B. Nisbet (Trans.), *Kant's political writings.* New York, NY: Cambridge University Press.

Lazarsfeld, P. F., & Thielens, W., Jr. (1958). *The academic mind: Social scientists in a time of crisis.* Glencoe, IL: The Free Press.

Lewis, L. S. (1993). *The Cold War and academic governance: The Lattimore case at Johns Hopkins.* Albany, NY: State University Press of New York.

Lipset, S. M. (1975). Political controversies at Harvard, 1636 to 1974. (pp. 1–278). In S. M. Lipset & D. Riesman (Eds.), *Education and politics at Harvard.* New York, NY: McGraw-Hill Book Company.

Lovejoy, A. O. (1918, March 7). Letter to the editor, *Nation,* 255.

Lovejoy, A. O. (1959). Kant and evolution. In B. Glass, O. Temkin, & W. L. Straus Jr. (Eds.), *Forerunners of Darwin: 1745–1859* (pp. 173–206). Baltimore, MD: The Johns Hopkins University Press.

Lovejoy, A. O. (1961). *The reason, the understanding and time.* Baltimore, MD: The Johns Hopkins University Press.

MacIver, R. M. (1955). *The pursuit of happiness: A philosophy for modern living.* New York, NY: Simon and Schuster.

McCormick, C. H. (1989). *This nest of vipers: McCarthyism and higher education in the Mundel affair, 1951–52.* Urbana, IL: University of Illinois Press.

Metzger, W. P. (1961a). *Academic freedom in the age of the university*. New York, NY: Columbia University Press.

Metzger, W. P. (1961b, Autumn). The first investigation. *AAUP Bulletin, 44*(3), 206–210.

O'Brien, M. (1980). *McCarthy and McCarthyism in Wisconsin*. Columbia, MO: University of Missouri Press.

Reeves, T. C. (1982). *The life and times of Joe McCarthy: A biography*. New York, NY: Stein and Day.

Report of Committee on Academic Freedom in Wartime. (1918). *Bulletin of the AAUP, 4*(1), 35–37.

Ringer, F. K. (1969). *The decline of the German Mandarins: The German academic community, 1890–1933*. Cambridge: Harvard University Press.

Rovere, R. H. (1959). *Senator Joe McCarthy*. London: Methuen & Co.

Sanders, J. (1979). *Cold War on the campus: Academic freedom at the University of Washington, 1946–1964*. Seattle, WA: University of Washington Press.

Schrecker, E. (1986). *No ivory tower: McCarthyism and the universities*. New York, NY: Oxford University Press.

Slaughter, S. (1980, March). The danger zone: Academic freedom and civil liberties. *Annals of the American Academy of Political and Social Science, 448*, 47–48.

Stewart, G. R. (1950). *The year of the oath: The fight for academic freedom at the University of California*. Garden City, NY: Doubleday & Company.

The Present Danger: A Report from the University Presidents. (1953, June). *Atlantic Monthly*, pp. 44–46.

TIAA Institute. (2016). *Taking the measure of faculty diversity*. Retrieved from https://www.tiaainstitute.org/public/pdf/taking_the_measure_of_faculty_diversity.pdf

Ward Churchill Solidarity Network. (2016). Retrieved from www.wardchurchill.net

Wiebe, R. H. (1977). Modernizing the Republic (p. 32–67). In B. Bailyn (Ed.), *The great Republic: A history of the American people*. Lexington, MA: Heath Press.

Wilson, D. J. (1980). *Arthur O. Lovejoy and the quest for intelligibility*. Chapel Hill, NC: The University of North Carolina Press.

Wolf, A. (1981). Sociology, liberalism, and the radical right. *New Left Review, 128*, 3–27.

Part Five: Is Higher Education Stifling Free Expression in an Era of Political Correctness?

In "Free Expression at Public Colleges and Universities: Why Students Should Care About It and Why Campus Officials Should Make Sure It Is Protected," Dennis E. Gregory contends that public higher education should maintain a "free marketplace of ideas"—as much as is legally permissible and regardless of trends toward political correctness and campus speech codes. While sympathetic to the good intentions of the latter movement, he presents an array of court decisions to sustain his argument. In his view, First Amendment rights are more fundamental than efforts to establish "safe spaces." Gregory calls for students to become more aware of judicial history on these important matters and for academic leaders to be more diligent in performing their Constitutional duties to defend free expression.

In "Free Expression and Political Correctness: Contextualizing the Controversies and Finding a Way Forward," R. Scott Mattingly, J. Bennett Durham, and Matthew R. Shupp claim that free speech requires that our society and college campuses become more adept at insuring dialogue among persons of different cultural and ideological groups. Instead of reducing venues for free expression, they argue that creating a larger stage for communication of multiple perspectives would strengthen both civic and academic discourse. The authors stress the need to "humanize politics" in the often hyperactive world of technology, social media, and morally offensive hate groups. For the writers, the resolution lies in habits of the heart: emotional sensitivity, mutual respect, cultural competence, dialogical thinking, embrace of ideological diversity, and improvement of self-awareness and individual coping skills.

9. Free Expression at Public Colleges and Universities: Why Students Should Care About It and Why Campus Officials Should Make Sure It Is Protected

DENNIS E. GREGORY

Introduction

American higher education, while arguably the best higher education system in the world, faces many challenges today. Decreases in state and federal funding; low retention and graduation rate; concerns about crime and violence on campus (with gun violence and sexual violence at the top of the list); unfunded federal mandates that cause the addition of new administrators to focus on compliance; growing student activism; and burgeoning numbers of adjunct faculty and the resulting decrease in tenure track positions (the list goes on and on). All claim the attention of administrators and faculty alike. Another issue today, which is at the heart of the spirit of American higher education—and which is not getting the attention it deserves—is the retreat from support for free expression on our public college campuses. Those familiar with landscape of American higher education praise its diversity of institutions and understand that the private sector of higher education (both not-for-profit and for-profit) faces many of the same problems as do their public counterparts, but issues of free expression are not necessarily the same on independent campuses. As a result, this chapter focuses upon the issue of free expression on public college and university campuses.

The April 8, 2016, edition of the "Chronicle Review" section of *Chronicle of Higher Education* contains an article entitled, "What Students think about Free Speech," by Erwin Chemerinsky who is the Dean and professor of the University of California-Irvine School of Law and Howard Gillman, Chancellor and professor at UC-Irvine. In their article Chemerinsky and Gillman (2016) describe a class they taught to a group of freshmen students and that after doing so, they came to the conclusion that:

> ...strong free speech advocates...cannot assume that the social benefits of broad free-speech protections will be automatically appreciated by a generation that has not lived through decades-long struggles against censureship and punishment of protesters, dissenters and iconoclasts. (B6)

Chemerinsky and Gillman (2016) go on to indicate that:

> The necessity of creating supportive and nondiscriminatory learning environments must be acknowledged, and advocates will need to be explicit about how broad protections for speech—including offensive and hatefull speech—can be reconciled with this commitment. (B6)

A Gallup survey of college students and adults about issues of free expression on campus (Free expression, 2016) provided interesting results. According to the report of the poll results,

> This study leaves little doubt that college students believe First Amendment rights remain strong in this country—but raises questions about how they interpret those rights. College students are more likely than the U.S. adult population overall to believe First Amendment rights are secure, and they tend to view their student cohort as more respectful of free speech than the broader population. They also believe First Amendment rights are stronger now than in the past, and believe a free press is more important to democracy today than it was 20 years ago, even as newer information sources challenge the press' once-dominant position as Americans' primary news source.
>
> At the same time, students are willing to accept some limitations on free expression, particularly that which is done to intentionally hurt or stereotype members of certain groups. Most college students believe that the steps their school has taken to discourage certain kinds of speech are appropriate, even though more agree than disagree that such steps may create an environment that inhibits free expression. And, while students also mostly agree in the abstract that the press has a right to cover campus protests even over the objections of protesters, they are almost evenly divided on the legitimacy of specific reasons that protesters might want to block reporters.

This chapter will describe some of the problems that the observations above create and the ongoing situation on our public campuses in which institutional administrators take the above-mentioned need to create "supportive and non-discriminatory learning environments" too far and trample on the constitutionally protected rights of those who value free expression over comfort and political correctness. I do not disagree with the contention that discrimination and hateful expression are abhorrent and that institutions need to do their best to make their campuses safe places to live and learn. However, I would contend that creating policies violates free expression in order to make campuses free from a robust and open learning environment. The true university allows discomfort and challenge—one in which the "marketplace of ideas" can be open and active at the heart of the academy. Just like the axiom that one cannot be a "lite bit pregnant," a little bit of First Amendment limitation, outside that already laid out by the Supreme Court, is not appropriate even when the supposed ends of that limitation may be perceived to further positive goals (Free Expression, 2016).

Benjamin Franklin is famously quoted as saying "They who can give up essential liberty to obtain a little temporary safety deserve neither liberty nor safety" (1755). Unfortunately, campus leaders seem much too quick to abandon this liberty for safety and to appease students, as those described earlier. What these students do not understand—and which is demonstrated by how the newfound student activists are being forced to deal with speech codes and codes that limit activism on campuses—is that when liberty is taken away from one group or person in the name of protecting the feelings of others, those same rules can be used against those seeking these limitations when the time comes. It may be that today's students and administrators have no sense of history. Chemerinsky and Gillman (2016) imply as much in their article. One needs only to look back to the 1960s to get a brief, but vivid, history lesson that should be instructive to today's administrators and students (Sorey & Gregory, 2010).

According to the *American freshman: National norms fall 2015* (Eagan et al., 2015), the incoming freshman class is more likely to be involved in protests on campus than any in the last fifty years. While the numbers are still small (8.5% in 2015 as opposed to 5.6% in 2014), this change comes after years of lack of apparent interest in activism in previous studies. Kueppers (2016), in her *Chronicle* article about this study, also reports other items that may be of interest about this class of new students which support their activism and concern about the direction of American society.

There are indeed controversies about what should be included in free speech policies, or whether they should exist at all. Martinez (2016) reports that a debate is occurring within the City University of New York system about just this issue. She notes that some students want absolutely no limits on free speech to protect their ability to demonstrate for social causes such as the Black Lives Matter. She quotes Hamad Sindhi, a student leader in the protest movement as saying: "We are advocating for a policy that guarantees free speech and does not have any restrictions on time, place, and manner," .... "We denounce any efforts by the police to suppress protests." This, of course, shows either an ignorance of First Amendment jurisprudence or a disregard for the consequences of such actions. When no limits are put on expression, that is, those basic ones imposed by the Court, then those in opposition to the protests are equally free to do and say what they wish.

In *The Coddling of the American Mind* (2015) Lukianoff and Haidt argue that colleges and universities are "protecting" students from ideas and speech and that, in doing so, the institutions are not only acting problematically on First Amendment grounds, but may actually be damaging to students. They suggest that more speech and informing students about how to debate and argue their positions peacefully are better focuses than limiting speech, even that speech that some may see as harmful.

While many campuses, according to the Foundation for Individual Rights in Education (FIRE)—vide their website (n.d.)—still have speech codes that violate the First Amendment, some institutions have recently explicitly rejected calls for limiting speech on their campuses. A March 4, 2016, "Trends Report" from the Chronicle of Higher Education provides several brief articles about issues. One of these articles, (Schmidt, 2016) lists several institutions that have rejected speech codes. This group is led by the University of Chicago, whose policy on free expression has been seen as one of the best. Johns Hopkins University has also adopted a similar free expression statement, as have Chapman University, Princeton University, Purdue University, Winston-Salem State University, and the University of Virginia College at Wise.

The Legal Backdrop of Free Expression on Campus

Fora for Speech and Expression

There are three types of fora for speech and expression on public college and university campuses. These include: (1) Traditional Public Forum, in which the institution may impose only time, place, and manner restrictions and in which other restrictions must pass strict scrutiny and must demonstrate a compelling state interest (Alexander & Alexander, 2011; *Perry Education Association v. Perry local Educator's Association*, 1983; *Sword v. Fox*, 1970, 1971); (2) Limited or Designated Public Forum, which the institution designates as such a public forum and which, when used as such, maintains the same limits on abridging speech, but which does not need to remain public all of the time, and; (3) Closed forum, which the institution designates as closed and only available to specific persons and for specific reasons (Alexander & Alexander, 2011). In none of these fora may the institution limit speech based on content once certain types of speech are allowed. For instance, a university may not allow a demonstration supporting Black Lives Matter in a public forum and then disallow a counterdemonstration based upon its approval or disapproval of the nature of the speech. Of course, *reasonable* time, place, and manner restrictions can be made for both groups.

Types of Restricted Speech

The Court has indicated that some types of speech are not protected. These include:

1. **Fighting Words:** These are words that are directly spoken to another individual and "which by their very utterance inflict injury or tend to incite an immediate breach of the peace" (*Chaplinsky v. New Hampshire*, 1942, 572). Racist or sexist chants, or other language addressed to a group or other expression that is hateful or disrespectful, do not fall into this category (Alexander & Alexander, 2011; Bader, 2014; *Chaplinsky v. New Hampshire*, 1942; *Iota XI Chapter v. George Mason University*, 1993).

2. **Defamation:** This is a tort that involves making untrue statements about another person which damages the reputation of that individual. Oral defamation is known as slander, and written or broadcast falsehoods are known as libel. In order for a public figure to win a defamation action, she must show that the falsehood was done with malicious intent (Legal Information Institute, n.d.).

3. **Obscenity:** According to *Roth v. United States* (1957), obscenity is language or expression without "any redeeming social importance" (484) and which "to the average person, applying contemporary community standards, the dominant theme of the material, taken as a whole, appeals to prurient interest" (489). According to Justice Brennan, writing for the Court,

> The fundamental freedoms of speech and press have contributed greatly to the development and wellbeing of our free society and are indispensable to its continued growth. Ceaseless vigilance is the watchword to prevent their erosion by Congress or by the States. The door barring federal and state intrusion into this area cannot be left ajar; it must be kept tightly closed, and opened only the slightest crack necessary to prevent encroachment upon more important interests. (internal footnotes removed) (488)

The Court has had difficulty in deciding obscenity cases because of the definition stated above. (Please see, *Alberts v. California*, 1957; Alexander & Alexander, 2011, p. 251; *Miller v. California*, 1973.) In *Jacobellis v. Ohio* (1964),
Justice Potter Stewart, commenting in a concurrence on whether hard core
pornography was obscene material in this case, famously stated,

> I shall not today attempt further to define the kinds of material I understand to
> be embraced within that shorthand description, and perhaps I could never suc-
> ceed in intelligibly doing so. But I know it when I see it.... (199)

**4. Incitement of Disruption or Illegal Activity Intended to Breach
the Peace:** Speech or any other expression that creates a clear and present
danger of disruption to the lawful operation of the institution need not be
allowed if it can be demonstrated that failure to do so will result in imminent danger or damage and that creates "true threats" (Alexander & Alexander, 2011). In a concurring opinion in *Whitney v. California* (1927), Justice
Brandeis indicated that:

> ...no danger flowing from speech can be deemed clear and present unless the
> incidence of the evil apprehended is so imminent that it may befall before there is
> opportunity for full discussion. If there be time to expose through discussion the
> falsehood and fallacies, to avert the evil by the processes of education, the remedy
> to be applied is more speech, not enforced silence. (377)

Outside of these limitations, institutions proceed at their own peril if they
choose to impose speech or other codes that limit students' and employees'
speech and expression, even if done with the most benevolent of motives.
As Justice Brandeis noted earlier, the response to horrible racist, sexist, and
other negative speech should not be repression of speech, but more speech
to blunt the negative aspects of the bad speech. For instance, if a group of
fraternity members hang sexist banners outside of the windows of a fraternity
house on campus or from a nearby apartment rented by fraternity members
during freshman move-in, the students should not be punished and the signs
should not be forcibly removed by campus police. Speech may not be limited
based upon the content of the speech. Instead, the president of the university
should make formal forceful statements decrying such sexism to the entire
community. Student affairs staff should work with student organizations to
create fora in which sexism can be discussed, and faculty members may raise
the issue in their classes. Colleges and universities should do what they do
best: educate!

While there are some situations, such as those described earlier in which
speech is restricted and in which the speaker may face criminal or civil penalties

from local courts, and from which policies of the university may also result in sanctions, these are very limited. In a general sense, the Supreme Court has made it very clear that speech and expression are among the most cherished of Constitutional rights and that the state does not have the authority to treat speech lightly or limit it unnecessarily.

Case Law Related to Colleges and Universities

Fundamental Cases in Support of Free Expression
While not specifically about speech (although speech was a subsidiary to each) two cases form the bedrock from which future cases have followed. These cases included the following:

In *Sweezy v. New Hampshire* (1957), the Court was faced with evaluating whether "subversive persons" (read: Communists) were in the state and whether more legislation was needed to control these persons. Sweezy refused to testify about certain matters, including a lecture that he had provided at the University of New Hampshire. Upon his refusal to testify, he was held in contempt. The Court found that New Hampshire's action was a violation of the Fourteenth Amendment Due Process Clause, and in the opinion supported the concept of academic freedom and the right NOT to speak in some situations. In his concurrence, Justice Franfurter indicated:

> When weighed against the grave harm resulting from governmental intrusion into the intellectual life of a university, such justification for compelling a witness to discuss the contents of his lecture appears grossly inadequate. Particularly is this so where the witness has sworn that neither in the lecture nor at any other time did he ever advocate overthrowing the Government by force and violence. (261)

Another case which laid the groundwork for freedom of expression and academic freedom on college and university campuses was *Keyishian v. Board of Regents of the State University of New York* (1967), in which employees of the State University contested the Constitutionality of loyalty oaths, and which were declared vague and overbroad. Here the Court indicated that

> Our Nation is deeply committed to safeguarding academic freedom, which is of transcendent value to all of us and not merely to the teachers concerned. That freedom is therefore a special concern of the First Amendment, which does not tolerate laws that cast a pall of orthodoxy over the classroom. (603)

Academic freedom exists for the university, for faculty, and for students. The balance of these freedoms, given the First Amendment, has largely been contextualized around freedom of expression and freedom of association and can only be limited within those constraints described earlier, and then only with strict scrutiny of the regulations created by the state (in this case, the university).

In a case that more directly focuses upon the limits of freedom of expression, the Fourth Circuit Court found in favor of a fraternity at George Mason University (*Iota Xi Chapter of Sigma Chi Fraternity v. George Mason University*, 1993), which engaged in an "ugly woman contest" at which racial and gender-based stereotypes were displayed through costumes and language. This event was deeply offensive to members of the community, particularly to minority students, women, and international students. The question before the Court was "whether Sigma Chi's 'ugly woman contest' is sufficiently expressive to entitle it to First Amendment protection" (390). The Circuit Court affirmed the District Court, which had ruled that the speech and expression of the fraternity, no matter how offensive, is protected expression.

A number of other cases could also be added to this list, including *Tinker v. Des Moines Independent School District* (1969), which dealt with freedom of expression and peaceful protest in public schools and which indicated the need for content-neutral speech policies; and *Healy v. James* (1972), which dealt with a number of First Amendment issues including freedom of association and expression. In addition, *Widmar v. Vincent* (1981) dealt with the use of university space by a religious group and the limitations on freedom of expression and content neutrality implied by that policy; and *Rosenberger v. Rector and Visitors of the University of Virginia* (1995) looked at content neutrality in funding expression based upon religion. Three cases that examined employee speech include *Pickering v. Board of Education* (1968), *Garcetti v. Ceballos* (2006), and *Demers v. Austin* (2013). The latter case examined whether speech by faculty was different than that of other public employees.

While the cases above are not directly related to the issue of limiting speech on college and university campuses as focused upon in this chapter, they do address the issue in other ways. There is a plethora of other cases that could be reported upon which clearly show the concern by the courts for protecting speech and expression on campus, emphasizing that any regulations, when and if they exist, must be content-neutral and clearly lay out the limits of speech.

Speech Codes

In 1973, the Supreme Court heard the case of *Papish v. University of Missouri Curators*. This case revolved around a student who had been expelled from the University of Missouri for distributing a newspaper which allegedly violated the Code of Student Conduct because it contained "indecent speech." In a PER CURIUM opinion, the Court reversed the Circuit Court ruling in favor of the University and ordered Papish reinstated. The Court, citing the recently decided case of *Healy v. James* (1972), decided, "We think Healy makes it clear that the mere dissemination of ideas—no matter how offensive to good taste—on a state university campus may not be shut off in the name alone of 'conventions of decency'" (670).

In *Doe v. University of Michigan* (1989) the eastern District Court of Michigan ruled that a speech code created by the University that prohibited "any behavior, verbal or physical, that stigmatizes or victimizes an individual on the basis of race, ethnicity, religion, sex, sexual orientation, creed, national origin, ancestry, age, marital status, handicap or Vietnam-era veteran status" (p. 855) violated the First Amendment. The Court noted that "While the Court is sympathetic to the University's obligation to ensure equal educational opportunities for all of its students, such efforts must not be at the expense of free speech. Unfortunately, this was precisely what the University did" (p. 868). The Court ruled that the code was overbroad and vague and thus created inappropriate limitations on protected speech.

Two years later, in *UWM Post v. Board of Regents of the University of Wisconsin System* (1991), the eastern District Court of Wisconsin similarly ruled that a "hate speech code which limited and punished, ...racist or discriminatory comments, epithets or other expressive behavior directed at an individual or on separate occasions at different individuals, or for physical conduct, if such comments, epithets or other expressive behavior..." if they were demeaning or created a hostile environment related to, "...race, sex, religion, color, creed, disability, sexual orientation, national origin, ancestry or age of the individual or individuals." Here, too, the Court indicated that the code was too vague and overbroad and thus in violation of the First Amendment.

Similarly, in *Dambrodt v. Central Michigan University* (1995), the Sixth Circuit upheld the decision from the District court granting summary judgment for the plaintiffs in that the discriminatory harassment policy of the University was unconstitutional. While the Court supported the firing of a coach that used harassing words to allegedly motivate his players, it stated that the policy itself was overbroad and vague.

Descriptions of these and various other cases that involve courts overturning speech codes may be found on the FIRE website. Rather than repeat all of the reviews of these cases, a referral to this website is in order. FIRE has shown itself to be the foremost advocacy organization available in support of First Amendment rights on college and university campuses. The leaders of this organization have produced plentiful literature on this topic and the organization has worked with campuses across the United States to eliminate speech codes. Where persuasion has not worked, lawsuits have followed: and, at this writing, I am not familiar with any occasions in which FIRE's lawsuits have resulted in losses. Its success should be taken as a cautionary tale to those well-intentioned institutions that seek to protect marginalized populations from harassment and abuse through a comfortable learning environment. There are other ways to do this besides violating the speech and expression rights of students, employees, and visitors.

Conclusion

Today student activism is increasing. We recently viewed the controversy at the University of Missouri, where student demonstrators (including a faculty member) allegedly sought to ban student journalists from the demonstration. We note that confrontations between campus police and demonstrators are occurring more regularly. Calls for unlimited speech protection for protesters have been issued, and protection of speech is an issue at the forefront of the minds of many—both on and outside of campus. These circumstances are countered by a large number of institutions of higher education that are seeking to protect students and create safe learning environments by instituting and maintaining speech codes of various types. Meanwhile, many students themselves are not aware of the history of speech on campus and are willing to limit speech that is hurtful or discriminatory despite its Constitutional protection in countless cases over the past sixty years. Hence advocacy groups have often had to force public colleges and universities to abide by their Constitutional responsibilities. Instead, it would be preferable for institutional leaders do stand up and do the right thing without external pressure.

While I abhor those who would demagogue and use hateful language and expression to injure and bully others by threatening their education—and even their ability to exercise basic Constitutional and civil rights—I do not condone the violation of the rights of everyone to stop those who would pervert our freedoms. More speech is better than limiting speech. When we see injustice, such as verbal attacks and demagoguery, we should confront it and expose it to the light of a free society, not respond in kind and seek to ban it by violating everyone's rights. No one, especially not the leaders of our postsecondary institutions, should impose restrictions on expression and punish those who utter speech with which we disagree. While we should condemn racist and sexist speech, we must respond to it rather than try to ban it. Colleges and universities that maintain speech codes that seek to limit protected speech should be ashamed of themselves for institutionalizing political correctness.

It seems appropriate to end this chapter with another quote from Benjamin Franklin who, among the Founding Fathers, seems to have best captured the importance of freedom of speech and expression. Perhaps this is true since he was a newspaper writer and publisher during the late Colonial period. What he said in 1739 rings just as true now as it did then. Public colleges and universities are part of the public trust, and as such, must always be mindful of Franklin's admonition: "Freedom of Speech is a principal pillar of a free government; when this support is taken away, the constitution of a free society is dissolved, and tyranny is erected in its ruins" (1739).

References

Alberts v. California. (1957). 354 U.S. 476.

Alexander, K.W., & Alexander, K. (2011). *Higher education law: Policies and perspectives.* New York, NY: Routledge.

Bader, H. (2014, February 7). *Right to free speech includes offensive speech.* Competitive Enterprise Institute. Retrieved from https://cei.org/blog/right-free-speech-includes-offensive-speech

Chaplinsky v. New Hampshire. (1942). 315 U.S. 568.

Chemerinsky, E., & Gillman, H. (2016, April 8). What students think about free speech. *Chronicle of Higher Education,* Chronicle Review. B-4 & B-6. Retrieved from http://chronicle.com/article/What-Students-Think-About-Free/235897

Dambrodt v. Central Michigan University. (1995). 61 F.3d 487 (6th Cir. Mich. 1995).

Demers v. Austin. (2013). No. 11-35558 D.C. No. 2:09-cv-00334-RHW (9th Cir. 2013).

Doe v. University of Michigan. (1989). 721 F. Supp. 852 (E.D. Mich 1989).

Eagan, K., Stolzenberg, E. B., Bates, A. K., Aragon, M. C., Suchard, M. R., & Rios-Aguilar, C. (2015). *The American freshman: National norms fall 2015.* Los Angeles, CA: Higher Education Research Institute, UCLA. Retrieved from http://www.heri.ucla.edu/monographs/TheAmericanFreshman2015.pdf

Foundation for Individual Rights in Education (FIRE). Retrieved from https://www.thefire.org/

Franklin, B. (1739). On freedom of speech and the press. *Pennsylvania Gazette.* November 17, 1739.

Franklin, B. (1755). *Reply to the Governor* (Letter for the Pennsylvania Assembly). November 11, 1755.

Free Expression on Campus: A Survey of U.S. College Students and U.S. Adults. (2016). Gallup poll sponsored by the Knight Foundation and the Newseum Institute. Retrieved from http://www.knightfoundation.org/media/uploads/publication_pdfs/FreeSpeech_campus.pdf

Garcetti v. Ceballos. (2006). 547 U. S. 410.

Healy v. James. (1972). 408 U.S. 169.

Iota Xi Chapter of Sigma Chi Fraternity v. George Mason University. (1993). 993 F.2d 386 (4th Cir., 1993).

Jacobellis v. Ohio. (1964). 378 U. S. 184.

Keyishian v. Board of Regents of the State University of New York. (1967). 385 U.S. 589.

Kueppers, C. (2016, February 11). Today's freshman class is the most likely to protest in half a century. *Chronicle of Higher Education.* Retrieved from http://chronicle.com/article/Today-s-Freshman-Class-Is/235273

Legal Information Institute. (n.d.). *Definition of defamation.* Retrieved from https://www.law.cornell.edu/wex/defamation

Lukianoff, G., & Haidt, J. (2015, September). The coddling of the American mind. *The Atlantic.* Retrieved from http://www.theatlantic.com/magazine/archive/2015/09/the-coddling-of-the-american-mind/399356/

Martinez, A. (2016, July 12). In a time of tension, universities craft new free-speech policies. *Chronicle of Higher Education.* Retrieved from http://chronicle.com/article/In-a-Time-of-Tension/237086/?key=Wqv3wuwMM8pX1wWtL_lczQXpTHCez6je3M-2e2Cwvs1CR0ZSckpQYndwLU81Wi14RkFaQlNaS-21wWEpVNi1UY2NRUWt6djF5YXE4

Miller v. California. (1973). 413 U.S. 15.

Papish v. University of Missouri Curators. (1973). 410 U.S. 667.

Pickering v. Board of Education. (1968). 391 U.S. 563.

Rosenberger v. Rector and Visitors of the University of Virginia. (1995). 515 U.S. 819.

Roth v. United States. (1957). 354 U.S. 476.

Schmidt, P. (2016, March 4). Colleges draw hard lines against calls to restrict speech. *Chronicle of Higher Education,* Section B, B8.

Sorey, K. C., & Gregory, D. E. (2010). Protest in the sixties. *College Student Affairs Journal, 28*(2), 184–206.

Sweezy v. New Hampshire. (1957). 354 U.S. 234.

Sword v. Fox. (1970). 317 F.Supp. 1055, W.D. VA.

Sword v. Fox. (1971). 446 F.2d 1091, U.S. App. (4th Cir.).

Tinker v. Des Moines Independent School District. (1969). 393 U.S. 503.

UWM Post v. Board of Regents of the University of Wisconsin. (1991). 774 F. Supp. 1163 (E.D. Wis. 1991).

Whitney v. California. (1927). 274 U.S. 357.

Widmar v. Vincent. (1981). 454 U.S. 263.

10. Free Expression and Political Correctness: Contextualizing the Controversies and Finding a Way Forward

R. Scott Mattingly, J. Bennett Durham,
and Matthew R. Shupp

Introduction

Is higher education stifling freedom of expression in an era of political correctness? Yes, as a broad trend across many institutions, it is. It seems hard to argue otherwise, considering the implications of the many recent controversies at colleges and universities over campus protests, disinvited speakers, microaggressions, trigger warnings, and more. This was evidenced at a recent Intelligence Squared debate featuring public intellectuals with relevant expertise, as two-thirds of the audience left in agreement that free speech is threatened on campuses today (Intelligence Squared U.S., 2016).

However, it is our contention that the national conversation about political correctness and threats to freedom of expression in higher education is generally missing the root cause of the problem. While the public and pundits alike tend to fixate on symptoms, the true crisis is the growing inability of our culture to promote dialogue between individuals from diverse cultural and ideological groups. We believe that education is the way forward and that colleges and universities have an obligation to lead by example in creating campus cultures that embrace our common humanity while equitably addressing the needs of diverse constituencies. Below, we provide context for the concepts of free expression and political correctness, analyze their relationship to the current environment of higher education, and make suggestions for continued improvement.

Choose Your Words Carefully: Free Expression in an Era of Political Correctness

As an ideal, free expression has been woven into the fabric of our nation since its inception. For centuries, Americans have agreed that the right to freedom of expression is an essential liberty in a free society that embraces diverse cultures, identities, and ideologies. However, most have also agreed that citizens should be protected from harm by reasonable limits to absolute free speech (e.g., defamation, obscenity, true threats, etc.). Such exceptions open the door to disagreement about where to draw lines of limitation around protected speech. In contemporary American culture, there is a growing divide about the merits of efforts to silence specific language, actions, and ideologies that are deemed offensive (and indefensible) by one group or another. This clash over rights to freedom of expression is often framed around "political correctness," the definition of which is generally dependent on the ideology of the person who invokes it. In order to better understand the intersection of free expression and political correctness (and the implications for institutions of higher education), we must first consider the context and objectives of the modern movement of political correctness.

In contrast to free expression, the concept of political correctness is a relatively recent development in our nation's history. Hall (1994) notes that both liberals and conservatives began using the term more heavily in the late 1980s and early 1990s to challenge speech deemed to be offensive. Those on the right have employed it in an effort to defend the constitution and the moral fabric of the nation. Those on the left have used it in an attempt to defend marginalized or oppressed groups. Lukianoff and Haidt (2015) argue that, originally, the "movement sought to restrict speech (specifically hate speech aimed at marginalized groups)" (para. 5). In this manner, both parties have emphasized the use of appropriate or "correct" language, though their primary objectives differ. As polarization has increasingly characterized our politics, views on political correctness have broadened to the extent that no universal definition exists. Chait (2015a) explains that now "people use the phrase to describe politeness (perhaps to excess), or evasion of hard truths, or (as a term of abuse by conservatives) liberalism in general" (para. 16). Many conservative politicians use the term as a scapegoat for "the presumed illegitimacy of ideas or movements they oppose" (Ferriss, 2016, para. 8), which contributes to a wider embrace of the movement among liberals, in defiance of perceived attacks.

Taub (2015) responds directly to Chait's criticisms of the movement, expressing concern that such critiques represent "a way to dismiss issues as frivolous in order to justify ignoring them" and, worse, that they are "often used by those in a position of privilege to silence debates raised by marginalized people—to say that their concerns don't deserve to be voiced, much less addressed" (para. 3). She takes issue with Chait's apparent failure, when discussing examples of perceived oversensitivity, to "[consider] their merits, or why they matter to the people who put them forward" (Taub, 2015, "Politically correct," para. 5). Ferriss (2016) cautions that defense of political correctness can become excessive and harm efforts at change by disengaging otherwise well-meaning offenders. Chait (2015b) himself counters Taub, arguing that a critique of the excesses of political correctness need not equate to an endorsement of privileged thinking: "We can oppose both racism and inappropriate responses to racism" (para. 13).

On many college campuses, recent arguments about politically correct speech have shifted in focus from a moral debate over the language people *should* use to a policy debate over the language people should be *allowed* to use. Political correctness, then, represents an argument about where the lines should be drawn around the right to free expression. In practice, this has led to an increase in campus speech codes that attempt to foster respectful communities through the regulation of speech. However well-intentioned these efforts may be, they are often problematic because they unreasonably limit free speech at the loosely defined discretion of campus administrators. As of this writing, the Foundation for Individual Rights in Education (FIRE) rates nearly two hundred colleges and universities in the United States as "red light" institutions with "at least one policy that both clearly and substantially restricts freedom of speech," a staggering number when one considers that the organization only claims to rate over 400 institutions (Foundation for Individual Rights in Education, n.d., Red Light, para. 1).

Lukianoff and Haidt (2015) condemned this state of affairs:

> The ultimate aim, it seems, is to turn campuses into "safe spaces" where young adults are shielded from words and ideas that make some uncomfortable. And more than the last [movement of political correctness], this movement seeks to punish anyone who interferes with that aim, even accidentally. You might call this impulse *vindictive protectiveness*. It is creating a culture in which everyone must think twice before speaking up, lest they face charges of insensitivity, aggression, or worse. (para. 5)

Certainly, some speech is problematic and not all speakers are well-intentioned. However, a culture of vindictive protectiveness has created environments in which a person can face severe consequences for a single statement that would historically be considered protected speech in this country. At best, this chills speech as well-meaning individuals become afraid to communicate freely out of fear that they will misstep. Chait (2015a) argues that this fear, across the political spectrum, is counterproductive. Reason, he suggests, is a healthier alternative, as "politics in a democracy is still based on getting people to agree with you, not making them afraid to disagree" (para. 41).

Despite their objections to the use of offensive or hurtful language, college students widely believe in the importance of free expression. A recent survey conducted by Gallup found that:

> When asked to choose, 78% of college students believe colleges should strive to create an open learning environment that exposes students to all types of speech and viewpoints, even some that are biased or offensive toward certain groups of people. Just 22% believe colleges should create a positive learning environment for all students that would be achieved in part by prohibiting certain speech or the expression of views that are offensive or biased against certain groups of people. (Gallup, Inc., 2016, p. 12)

However:

> Despite college students' clear preference for an open environment, they are willing to restrict some speech—particularly speech that intentionally seeks to hurt or offend. Roughly two-thirds of college students say colleges should be allowed to establish policies that restrict slurs and other language that is intentionally offensive to certain groups (69%), as well as the wearing of costumes that stereotype certain racial or ethnic groups (63%). (p. 12)

Though the combination of these views may at first appear contradictory, they are best understood as an argument not about whether free expression should be protected, but rather how it should be defined. Gallup concluded, "This study leaves little doubt that college students believe First Amendment rights remain strong in this country—but raises questions about how they interpret those rights" (p. 31).

While we, the authors, support the desire for respect and equity that often drives student concerns about offensive language and actions, we believe that attempts to achieve these goals by narrowing the protections of free expression are misguided. The right to free expression is an essential prerequisite to civil discourse and is at the very foundation of academic inquiry. Accordingly, in order to protect the integrity of our campuses, we must end speech codes and other policies that restrict or chill speech. However, the protection of free expression alone will not resolve the issues that drive much of the controversy under the banners of political correctness and free expression. Instead, we must focus on improving our ability to engage in meaningful dialogue with diverse groups.

Humanizing Politics: Why Free Expression Isn't Enough

In an ideal society with multiple voices safely able to express varying opinions and worldviews, the level of discourse should be elevated such that it enables each citizen to consider a variety of perspectives on a topic until arriving at a defensible conclusion. In other words, free expression should facilitate productive discourse. However, free expression without the willingness to acknowledge the differing viewpoints of others is not constructive and will not lead to progress. In the current higher education climate, a simple policy approach to protecting the right of individuals to speak their minds will only widen the chasms that divide certain ideological groups. Instead, we must look beyond the surface to understand the ideas and emotions that shape the language of our debates. In particular, we must consider the intersection of two factors: the impact of technology and social media on our ability to communicate effectively and the practice of fortifying our moral identities in social groups that often reject the worth of individuals outside those groups.

In the past decade, the accelerating developments in digital technology have altered the way we process and communicate information. The 24-hour news cycle and social media have given rise to networks through which every citizen can offer his or her own commentary on any topic of interest, including local, national, and global issues. In this hyperactive state of news and opinion, an overabundance of information exists about all issues. Internet searches and social media posts rule much of our lives; the Nielsen Report's (2016) Total Audience Report indicates that in the first quarter of 2016, the average adult in the United States spent 10 hours and 39 minutes per day consuming media. This constant flow of information dictates how much we "know" about any given topic. With so much information available, the path of least resistance or effort is often sought, and the first search result accepted as sufficient. This tendency is not only an isolated decision in favor of efficiency over effectiveness (Carr, 2011). The cumulative consequence of repeated speed searches is altering our brains such that we are losing the ability to evaluate information critically. This problem may be most associated with digital natives, but it is affecting all of us.

When our increasingly short attention spans are combined with our lack of information literacy skills, we easily become overwhelmed by complex issues. Instead of investing time and effort in thoughtful consideration, we take up positions quickly and hold fast to them, with little regard for the accuracy or relevance of information. This often results in an inability to engage in meaningful dialogue with those who hold different values and viewpoints. Collectively, groups divide along sharp lines of "us vs. them." We speak different moral languages and, yet, we refuse to acknowledge any possibility of mistranslation—"we" are completely right and "they" are completely wrong.

Our natural tendency to cling to existing opinions, blinded by confirmation bias, is exacerbated by political polarization. Lukianoff and Haidt (2015) point out:

> Part of what we do when we make moral judgments is express allegiance to a team. But that can interfere with our ability to think critically. Acknowledging that the other side's viewpoint has any merit is risky—your teammates may see you as a traitor. (How Did We Get Here? para. 4)

It is no surprise, then, that Nyhan and Reifler (2010) found that attempts to correct misinformation tend to fail, particularly when individuals have made strong ideological commitments. In fact, they noted a "backfire effect," in which misperceptions are actually strengthened after others' attempts at correction. McIntyre (2016) noted that this *motivated reasoning*—forming arguments to support your predrawn conclusions—can gradually shift to willful ignorance, denialism, and even demonization. Zaretsky (2016) identified recognition of differing values and the ability to negotiate those values as essential skills for moderation in thinking. Yet, our societal tendency to view most things in dualistic terms, denying that any ambiguity can exist, is having a negative impact on our ability to engage in discourse.

Instead of responding to legitimate concerns or debating ideas, we shout past each other with our own versions of the truth as we reinforce allegiance to our tribes by vilifying the others. Many defenders of political correctness shut down conversation by attacking perceived offensives in an abrupt and aggressive manner that intimidates the recipient. Rarely does the aggression result in the change of heart or the justice that is desired. Many opponents of political correctness shut down the conversation by using accusations of political correctness as an excuse to delegitimize others and refuse dialogue completely. Some even react to attacks by embracing political incorrectness, wearing the rejection of orthodoxy like a badge of honor. Neither side seems to be truly interested in promoting a change of heart, each believing that its own principles are sufficiently self-evident. It is as if the recipients of their accusations are deemed either unworthy of effort or incapable of change. Through this, we begin to lose our humanity. Instead of debating the merits of ideas, we judge the worth of the individuals who don't seem to share our views. In the current politics of morality, it is convenient, yet damaging, to find far more bad *people* than bad *ideas*.

Kohn (2013) suggests another way to think about our divide over political correctness. The way to bring about change, she argues, is not political correctness but emotional correctness: "the tone, the feeling, how we say what we say, the respect and compassion we show one another" (2:07). In other words, we should find greater compassion by focusing on *how* we say what we say. By first demonstrating empathy and a desire for mutual understanding, we can more effectively persuade with ideas, facts, and data. This allows us to make progress through our shared humanity. Some may contend that it is not another's responsibility to protect the feelings of either of those with privilege or those who are marginalized. Others may argue that disruption is the only way to achieve the social justice they seek. Perhaps this is true; but our default should not be an environment in which we speak over one another, attempting to be the loudest or even the most outrageous voice. In that world, needs go unmet, valid points go unheard, and opportunities to learn are missed.

The Way Forward: Bringing People Together

As we stated earlier, higher education policies should protect free speech much more broadly than is the current trend in many institutions. However, an approach based strictly on policy that regulates speech will not adequately solve the cultural problems represented by competing views on political correctness and freedom of expression. Upon a foundation of free expression, institutions must build a framework for cultural competence and mutual respect. In order to do so, campus leaders must create environments that are safe, but not sheltered. Efforts should be focused on bringing people of difference together and fostering opportunities for growth through the exchange of ideas. In particular, this can be accomplished through efforts to embrace cultural and ideological diversity, develop self-awareness and coping skills, and balance education with accountability.

Embrace Cultural and Ideological Diversity

As a first step, we must make individuals from diverse backgrounds feel welcomed as full members of our campus communities. All members of the community must strive to become more culturally competent by seeking to learn about others' worldviews and lived experiences (Pope, Reynolds, & Mueller,

2014). In these efforts, there is a recognition of our shared humanity; but it is coupled with a recognition that our beliefs, values, attitudes, and experiences are not necessarily shared. Some critics might contend that a world of policies, structures, and ideas does not require either an emotional connection or recognition of another's background. However, if the purpose of an organization is to serve people, as most are, then the successful development of that organization requires an understanding of the emotions and cultures represented by the people it serves. This approach could lead to better results in many campus conflicts involving protests over issues such as systemic bias and racism.

It is also critical that diverse ideologies are welcomed. In an interview, Williams argues that students, as well as faculty members, should be given opportunities to challenge knowledge (Flaherty, 2016). On the other hand, she balances this point:

> This doesn't mean I think all ideas are equally valid or equally deserving of a place on the curriculum. But I do think it is incumbent upon academics to put before students knowledge and perspectives they will find challenging or [that] may even make them feel uncomfortable. This is how learning takes place! (para. 10)

While faculty members can express their own views, ultimately students should "make up their own mind on a particular issue" (para. 12). Furthermore, Williams believes that institutions need ideologically diverse faculty members, a feeling shared by Lukianoff and Haidt (2015). Shanahan (2016) makes a similar point:

> Lectures by professors and campus protests rightly focus attention on important topics, but both are inherently one-sided. College students also need thoughtful opportunities to participate in structured debates outside their filter bubbles, so they can practice listening to and arguing dissenting points of view. (para. 18)

In short, learning experiences require the expenditure of time and energy in synergistic, real-time exchanges with individuals who possess different backgrounds or hold different viewpoints. An approach that incorporates such opportunities could lead to better results in conflicts over issues such as the invitation of speakers with controversial viewpoints.

We must help students embrace critical thinking in dialogue rather than fearing potentially divisive consequences. If we validate our ideas through discourse, then we can move forward even more confidently and perhaps gain new allies. If, however, we discover that our ideas require clarification or change, then no harm has been done; on the contrary, it is an opportunity to grow. Even if some disagreement remains after dialogue between two or more parties, the mutual understanding and respect garnered through emotionally correct (Kohn, 2013) discourse may open the door to compromise. The existence of a deep mutual understanding should remove political correctness from the equation entirely, liberating our speech by enabling us to challenge one another's ideas vigorously without fear of offending. By assisting one another with the process of reflecting upon and committing to beliefs and values, we can grow closer in community even as our individual positions may diverge. In time, members of a strong community will find more common ground than members of a fragmented community, leading to collaborative solutions.

The achievement of a culturally competent postsecondary community in which dialogue is valued requires an understanding of the roles of power and privilege, particularly the ways in which institutional systems can impede discourse and equity. A system governed predominantly by majority voices can silence individuals from groups that have historically been marginalized. In this way, a position of powerlessness stifles free expression inside and outside the classroom. This can provoke a fight-or-flight response, often manifested as activism, such as protests, or as withdrawal. As faculty members and administrators seeking to achieve more just educational environments, we must acknowledge our roles in perpetuating existing social structures and accept the existence of unconscious bias. Rather than being concerned with our own emotions or rushing to judge the merits of protesters' demands, our initial response as educators should be to listen actively to understand the emotions that underlie complainants' viewpoints and to validate their concerns. With an investment of time, effort, and desire, we can accomplish mutual understanding and pave the way for practical solutions.

Such an approach is described by an Emory University vice president as a response to campus conflicts involving race:

> The context that I got from that conversation [with students] was that our students are seeking change. They mean for the demands to be provocative and jarring, and if we look at the demands just at face value, we're missing something. We're missing an opportunity to open up a conversation and educate not only our students, but for us to be educated on the lived experiences of our students. And so for me, it was a critical moment in making sense of the demands and unpacking the demands as a community. (Brown, 2016, Transcript, para. 8)

Rather than dictating a resolution, Emory administrators sought input from the students about the development of a process. Their conversations went beyond a point-by-point reaction to the students' demands and examined underlying desires and systemic issues, aiming for recommendations that could "transform the community" (Brown, 2016, Transcript, para. 13).

Later, they published the recommendations online and sought feedback from all members of the community, including alumni and parents (Brown, 2016; Ruff, 2016). Finally, they held a racial-justice retreat with 100 attendees to promote deeper dialogue about the recommendations. Participants acknowledged that the work was challenging, but fruitful (Ruff, 2016).

Not only does exposure to cultural and ideological diversity lead to improved critical thinking for individuals in their personal and civic lives, it prepares students for work in a globalized society and produces better results for diverse organizations, including institutions of higher education (Kristof, 2016; Page, 2007; Reisberg, 2016). If a state of passivity and disengagement is the alternative, then, for the good of our students in the present and the future, we ought to encourage them to protest passionately, albeit in a manner that facilitates dialogue and, hence, progress. For administrators, simply providing a forum is not enough. We should lead by example, which involves honoring students' courage; listening as a means to understand emotions, concerns, and core issues; and a willingness to learn and grow.

Develop Self-Awareness and Coping Skills

In order to improve our capacity to build community, we must become more self-aware. The ability to engage in discourse requires comfort with one's own identity. If our identities are so fragile that the questioning or criticism of a single one of our positions by another person is enough to cause an identity crisis, then it will be difficult for us to address effectively either our differences of opinion with others or broader systemic problems. Specifically, institutions must engineer environments with opportunities for students to consider existential questions and achieve greater confidence and clarity. With this foundation, it becomes easier for students to engage in difficult conversations.

Related to self-awareness, coping strategies can help everyone on campus to better consider ideas for their merits, rather than for the emotional response they may elicit. This, in turn, will help us to advocate more effectively for our own needs and learn to compromise with others. This point is argued convincingly by Lukianoff and Haidt (2015):

> Universities should rethink the skills and values they most want to impart to their incoming students. At present, many freshman-orientation programs try to raise student sensitivity to a nearly impossible level. Teaching students to avoid giving unintentional offense is a worthy goal, especially when the students come from many different cultural backgrounds. But students should also be taught how to live in a world full of potential offenses. (What Can We Do Now?, para. 6)

Specifically, they encourage the use of cognitive behavioral therapy, claiming that:

> the outcome could pay dividends in many ways. For example, a shared vocabulary about reasoning, common distortions, and the appropriate use of evidence to draw conclusions would facilitate critical thinking and real debate. It would also tone down the perpetual state of outrage that seems to engulf some colleges these days, allowing students' minds to open more widely to new ideas and new people. (What Can We Do Now?, para. 6)

These student outcomes could lead to healthier relationships with peers and loved ones as well as to more constructive political and civic engagement. Rampell (2016) asserts that "colleges are supposed to be places where young adults develop the critical thinking and social skills to peacefully, productively engage with people with whom they disagree, whose ideas they may even find detestable" (para. 17). Lehfeldt (2016) adds that they are "sometimes naïve, sometimes overly ambitious.... But that's OK. They're college students. College should be the place where they try on controversial ideas, push the envelope, make demands. And get things wrong sometimes" (para. 7). Unfortunately, many postsecondary institutions are not doing an adequate job of helping students learn how to resolve conflicts, too frequently intervening to protect students from perceived discomfort and, therefore, preventing teachable moments (Rampell, 2016). When the lines around protected expression are drawn so narrowly, they often result in confusion, frustration, and missed opportunities for learning.

Instead, institutions should create respectful environments, but distinguish them from *safe spaces*, which overemphasize protection from discomfort. These spaces often go far beyond ensuring safety and instead shelter students from exposure to anything that might run counter to their worldviews. Zaretsky (2016) goes so far as to claim that safe spaces serve as opportunities for students "to fixate on their pain" (para. 22). One example of a practice that at times overemphasizes sheltering is the recent phenomenon of trigger warnings, which involve advance notification about any upcoming content with the potential to cause discomfort (Lukianoff & Haidt, 2015). Because of the variety of backgrounds and perspectives present in any given classroom, the topics that might cause discomfort are countless. This can have a chilling effect, with some instructors avoiding even seemingly vapid topics in an attempt to prevent problems.

Arao and Clemens (2013) suggest *brave spaces* as an alternative to *safe spaces*, with the major difference being that participants in brave spaces recognize they will be challenged and may even welcome such exchanges. Exposure to a variety of ideas and even conflicts, particularly when discussions are facilitated by effective educators, should serve as a stimulus for moving from absolute thinking, to relativistic thinking, to reflective commitment, in keeping with Perry's (1970) Stages of Intellectual Development. Upon reaching the stage of reflective commitment, students should demonstrate the ability to consider multiple perspectives fairly, make rational choices in favor of some perspectives, and commit to those perspectives. Original viewpoints may change or remain the same; but either way, the issues are understood more completely and individuals demonstrate greater maturity in addressing them. If we do not have the skills or the opportunities to challenge our viewpoints through consideration of alternatives, then our positions end up hollow; and we are unable to articulate them with substantive evidence or to withstand any assault on our thinking, no matter how defensible our positions or how weak the alternatives.

Balance Education with Accountability

In response to offensive language or behavior, the intent should be to educate rather than first seeking to punish. With the exception of violent or repeat offenses, institutions should generally be more cautious than the zero-tolerance approach that seems to be trending on many campuses. Rather than building a culture of vindictive protectiveness (Lukianoff & Haidt, 2015), we would be served better by employing the principles of restorative justice. There is a significant moral difference between seeking to argue with (or educate) someone who holds a different opinion and seeking to punish that person for holding that opinion, even if her views are ignorant or incorrect. As an illustration, Derald Wing Sue, whose research with several colleagues informed the contemporary understanding of microaggressions, claims that the original intent of the term was to serve as a tool for education, not to punish or shame as some have begun to use it (Zamudio-Suaréz, 2016). While we advocate for fairness and justice, we also must uphold the value of social education in our campus cultures.

This is particularly important for students who are in a critical phase of development. Even when many of us believe that a student(s) is misguided or immature, strong public reproach is unlikely to help that student or group. On the contrary, it might push a person or group to become defensive and hold fast to misguided views or stifle his or her development. If given guidance and space to consider the implications of a mistake, students are more likely to learn a better approach or attitude and attempt either to make amends to those whom they have slighted or to seek opportunities that stretch them and promote growth.

A particular challenge for digital natives is the impact of social media on the quality of discourse. On the one hand, social media provides students with direct outlets to express themselves in powerful ways. However, deep, meaningful dialogue is not possible in a Twitterverse limited to 140 characters. Most often, it seems that online posts are designed to elicit simple, emotional reactions such as likes, retweets, or emojis. "Dialogue" often presents as a series of fragmented opinions with no real effort to introduce accurate data or to understand underlying emotions. Gallup has found that college students are aware of the conflicting realities of communication in social media environments:

> Students are positive about the role of social media as a way to express oneself, but are divided about the chilling effects of certain social media behaviors and phenomena. At least eight in 10 college students agree that people use social media to effectively express their views (88%) and that social media allows people to have control over their story (86%). At the same time, less than half (41%) agree that the dialogue that occurs on social media is usually civil, and 74% agree it is too easy to say things anonymously in this space. (Gallup, Inc., 2016, p. 28)

This bifurcated viewpoint about social media reflects broader challenges in attempting to determine the differences between protected and unprotected forms of expression.

The problems students experience with dialogue on social media are also manifestations of a greater breakdown in cultural communication. Herbst (2016) argues:

> The real challenge to free speech on campuses is that students seem unable or unwilling in critical instances to talk to each other, especially on the digital platforms that are closely associated with their identities. That has led them down the dangerous path of being too willing to endorse and even demand restrictions on the very speech they are trying to exercise in the service of their own ideas and causes. It is this system of informal censorship that is the most significant challenge to the idea that campuses might still be marketplaces of ideas. (para. 12)

To help ensure that students' desire to protect their peers from threats and dehumanizing slurs does not countermand their desire to protect free speech, Herbst advocates for disarming anonymous voices:

> Our message should be incessantly to everyone, starting with young people, that the superior solution on a campus (and in society) is not to try to censor anonymous speech but rather to ignore it. Students should not pay attention unless the author is willing to put a name on it. Our society still has enough social capital that a great amount of obnoxious speech will probably disappear if the author has to be listed to have an audience.

Of course, anonymous violent threats have to be investigated, but the generation that has been raised on the Internet should be taught that credibility and audience can only be gained with a name. (para. 14–15)

In order to promote and defend their ideas, students must be encouraged to own them publicly in forums that protect their ability to do so. There is perhaps no better forum than a diverse college community comprised of introspective, resilient individuals who seek to make progress through the substantive debate of ideas.

Conclusion

We believe the evidence is clear that freedom of expression is being stifled on many college campuses today. However, the real threat to that freedom is not political correctness, but a basic lack of respect and appreciation for cultural and ideological diversity as a component of shared humanity, which is manifested in our inability to dialogue civilly with one another. True and lasting change can only occur through mature discourse, including reflection on the fundamental meaning and purpose of free expression from multiple perspectives and in multiple contexts. Regardless of the substance of any given debate that we might encounter in our higher education community or beyond, the goal should be to see ourselves in others, holding respect for our common humanity as a core value and striving to rise together toward our highest standards. This cannot happen without ample humility to acknowledge that we all have something to learn. If this is the attitude that we want our students to display and if we desire receptivity to the standards that we espouse, then we must model it ourselves. As Joel (2016) summarizes:

> It is time that all of our colleges and universities think and act seriously about cultivating and promoting civility on our campuses. It will not tamp down the crucial exchange of ideas. It will make this exchange more dignified, more meaningful and even more productive. (para. 10)

To this end, "all colleges and universities must make clear that free, meaningful expression can only survive in an environment where there are appropriate rules of engagement" (para. 11), not to restrict the content or mask the meaning of language, but to serve as guidelines regarding how to frame dialogue with appropriate civility. This is among the most critical objectives for higher education in our dynamic contemporary society.

Although the contexts may vary from one institution to the next—with different histories, missions, structures, and demographics—we believe that all colleges and universities can create environments that support healthy discourse without limiting speech. It is true that, as state actors, public universities are held to a stricter legal standard with regard to the First Amendment than are private universities. However, because we believe the root of the problem is social, not legal, it is our contention that the principles outlined in this chapter must be applied in all types of institutions. Each campus will need to exercise discretion in determining how to apply these principles appropriately within its unique context. Still, in any context, it is possible to facilitate opportunities for dialogue about a wide range of issues, fostering students' ability to engage in conversations inside and outside the institution with individuals who have different perspectives.

All institutions have a responsibility to prepare students for the future. While this might include specific job skills, even more important are the foundational skills that enable graduates to thrive in changing or uncertain environments as well as to contribute to the strengthening of their communities. As Roth (2014) concludes:

> In our age of seismic technological change and instantaneous information dissemination, it is crucial that we not abandon the humanistic foundations of education in favor of narrow, technical forms of teaching intended to give quick, utilitarian results. Those results are no substitute for the practices, sometimes painstaking, of inquiry and critique that enhance students' ability to appreciate and understand the world around them—and to respond innovatively to it. A reflexive, pragmatic liberal education is our best hope of preparing students to shape change and not just be victims of it. (para. 16)

As citizens, we share responsibility for the future of our society. As educators, we must lead by creating balanced educational environments that foster the debate of challenging ideas while treating all people with dignity and respect.

References

Arao, B., & Clemens, K. (2013). From safe spaces to brave spaces: A new way to frame dialogue around diversity and social justice. In L. Landreman (Ed.), *The art of effective facilitation: Reflections from social justice educators* (pp. 135–150). Sterling, VA: Stylus.

Brown, S. (2016, March 25). Video: How one university took its student protesters seriously. *The Chronicle of Higher Education*. Retrieved from http://chronicle.com/article/Video-How-One-University-Took/235834

Carr, N. (2011). *The shallows: What the internet is doing to our brains.* New York, NY: W.W. Norton & Company.

Chait, J. (2015a, January 27). Not a very P.C. thing to say: How the language police are perverting liberalism. *New York Magazine*. Retrieved from http://nymag.com/ daily/intelligencer/2015/01/not-a-very-pc-thing-to-say.html

Chait, J. (2015b, January 30). Secret confessions of the anti-anti-P.C. movement. *New York Magazine*. Retrieved from http://nymag.com/daily/intelligencer/2015/01/ secret-confessions-of-the-anti-anti-pc-crowd.html

Ferriss, L. (2016, January 14). The new 'politically correct' boondoggle. *The Chronicle of Higher Education*. Retrieved from http://chronicle.com/blogs/lingua franca/2016/01/14/the-new-politically-correct-boondoggle/

Flaherty, C. (2016, April 8). May the best idea win. *Inside Higher Ed*. Retrieved from https://www.insidehighered.com/news/2016/04/08/new-book-critiques-campus-censorship-movement-and-pushes-marketplace-ideas

Foundation for Individual Rights in Education. (n.d.). *Using the database*. Retrieved from https://www.thefire.org/spotlight/using-the-spotlight-database/

Gallup, Inc. (2016). *Free expression on campus: A survey of U.S. college students and U.S. adults*. Retrieved from http://www.knightfoundation.org/media/uploads/publica tion_pdfs/FreeSpeech_campus.pdf

Hall, S. (1994). Some 'politically incorrect' pathways through PC. In S. Dunant (Ed.), *The war of the words: The political correctness debate* (pp. 164–184). London: Virago.

Herbst, J. (2016, May 31). The real threat to free expression. *Inside Higher Ed*. Retrieved from https://www.insidehighered.com/views/2016/05/31/students-value-free-expression-only-if-its-not-derogatory-or-hurtful-essay

Intelligence Squared U.S. (2016, March 1). *Free speech is threatened on campus*. Retrieved from http://intelligencesquaredus.org/debates/past-debates/item/1500-free-speech-is-threatened-on-campus

Joel, R. M. (2016). Disagreeing agreeably. *Inside Higher Ed*. Retrieved from https:// www.insidehighered.com/views/2016/04/01/bds-movement-highlights-need-res tore-civil-discourse-campuses-essay

Kohn, S. (2013, October). *Sally Kohn: Let's try emotional correctness* [Video file]. Retrieved from https://www.ted.com/talks/sally_kohn_let_s_try_emotional_cor rectness

Kristof, N. (2016, May 28). The liberal blind spot. *The New York Times*. Retrieved from http://www.nytimes.com/2016/05/29/opinion/sunday/the-liberal-blind-spot. html

Lehfeldt, E. A. (2016, January 12). The moment we've waited for? *Inside Higher Ed*. Retrieved from https://www.insidehighered.com/views/2016/01/12/student-act ivism-provides-institutions-opportunities-essay

Lukianoff, G., & Haidt, J. (2015, September). The coddling of the American mind. *The Atlantic*. Retrieved from http://www.theatlantic.com/magazine/archive/2015/09/ the-coddling-of-the-american-mind/399356/

McIntyre, L. (2016, January 10). Willful ignorance on campus. *The Chronicle of Higher Education.* Retrieved from http://chronicle.com/article/Willful-Ignorance-on-Camp us/234820

The Nielsen Company. (2016). *The total audience report: Q1 2016.* Retrieved from http://www.nielsen.com/us/en/insights/reports/2016/the-total-audience-rep ort-q1-2016.html

Nyhan, B., & Reifler, J. (2010). When corrections fail: The persistence of political misper- ceptions. *Political Behavior, 32,* 303–330. doi:10.1007/s11109-010-9112-2

Page, S. E. (2007). *The difference: How the power of diversity creates better groups, firms, schools, and societies.* Princeton, NJ: Princeton University Press.

Perry, W. G., Jr. (1970). *Forms of intellectual and ethical development in the college years: A scheme.* New York, NY: Holt, Rinehart, and Winston.

Pope, R. L., Reynolds, A. L., & Mueller, J. A. (2014). *Creating multicultural change on campus.* San Francisco, CA: Jossey-Bass.

Rampell, C. (2016, May 19). College students run crying to daddy administrator. *The Washington Post.* Retrieved from https://www.washingtonpost.com/opinions/coll ege-students-run-crying-to-daddy-administrator/2016/05/19/61b53f54-1deb- 11e6-9c81-4be1c14fb8c8_story.html

Reisberg, L. (2016, April 19). Internationalization begins at home. *Inside Higher Ed.* Retrieved from https://www.insidehighered.com/blogs/world-view/internationali zation-begins-home

Roth, M. S. (2014, May 19). The false promise of 'practical' education. *The Chronicle of Higher Education.* Retrieved from http://chronicle.com/article/The-False-Pro mise-of/146549

Ruff, C. (2016, April 21). One university's response to students' demands on race: Radical transparency. *The Chronicle of Higher Education.* Retrieved from http://chronicle. com/article/One-University-s-Response-to/236187

Shanahan, M. K. (2016, January 31). Yes. Campuses should be safe spaces—for debate. *The Chronicle of Higher Education.* Retrieved from http://chronicle.com/article/ Yes-Campuses-Should-Be-Safe/235114

Taub, A. (2015, January 28). *The truth about "political correctness" is that it actually doesn't exist.* Retrieved from http://www.vox.com/2015/1/28/7930845/polit ical-correctness-doesnt-exist

Zamudio-Suaréz, F. (2016, June 26). What happens when your research is featured on 'Fox & Friends.' *The Chronicle of Higher Education.* Retrieved from http://chroni cle.com/article/What-Happens-When-Your/236949

Zaretsky, R. (2016, February 7). In defense of moderation. *The Chronicle of Higher Education.* Retrieved from http://chronicle.com/article/In-Defense-of-Moderat ion/235160

Part Six: What Has Higher Education Done About Inclusion and Social Justice?

In "Tokenizing Social Justice in Higher Education," Cristobal Salinas Jr. and Valerie A. Guerrero trace the evolution of the term "social justice" and contend that it is now used as a mere buzzword—without any real meaning amid countless pages of discourse and policy on diversity and inclusion. Salinas and Guerrero further argue that negative neoliberal undertones and stereotypical mocking of "social justice warriors" have stifled opportunities for genuine dialogue and sustainable change. To truly engage students, the authors suggest the need for a fuller understanding of oppression, privilege, and the internalization of beliefs. They proffer a new concept of "multicontextual thinking" for today's colleges and universities.

In "Creating Inclusive Classrooms as an Imperative for Historically Underrepresented Groups in Higher Education," Michael Sean Funk first reflects on his own initial learnings about social justice and inclusion. He tracks historical trends in student activism, ending with the current examples of #BlackLivesMatter and other student rights movements. Funk recommends some strategies for establishing inclusive dialogue in the college classroom. He contends that higher education acts as a mirror reflective of our larger world and that we must not live in a vacuum, but instead confront the serious issues of the day in our wider society as well as postsecondary education.

11. Tokenizing Social Justice in Higher Education

CRISTOBAL SALINAS JR. AND VALERIE A. GUERRERO

Though the term "social justice" has been in use in numerous contexts for hundreds of years, within higher education, the term has evolved to represent a myriad of connotations. The use of the word itself has become controversial in some circles, while meaningless in others. In section one of this chapter, we will explore some of the most common ways higher education currently engages with the concept of social justice. First, a brief review of terms conflated with social justice, then a deconstruction of social justice as a nonperformative, and finally an overview of how social justice is used as a barrier to engagement. Section two offers recommendations for effective engagement in social justice at individual, institutional, and cultural levels. Within each level, we provide examples and conceptual models to guide further study. Through this chapter brave spaces and multicontext thinking are presented as new practices to cultivate more effective engagement of social justice.

Section 1: What Is Social Justice?

While the notion of a common good attributed to St. Thomas Aquinas embodies components of social justice, the term itself was not in wide use until the 1840s when the phrase was introduced by a scholar generalizing the work of Aquinas (Gilson, 2013). Debate still exists about Aquinas' meaning of justice, which has influenced a complicated relationship between Christian values and social justice. Presently, some argue that social justice has a liberal agenda that is in conflict with Christianity, while others specifically interpret the New Testament as support for the goals of social justice (Deuteronomy 10:18; Galatians 3:28; Matthew 25:40; Mattson, 2015). Coupled with its storied history, the politically charged connotation of the term "social justice" in modern United States has become difficult to weave from its numerous definitions. Nonetheless, over time, ideals of promoting a just society have woven their way into many facets of modern life. Though language embodying equality and justice has an established history within education and later higher education, the specific term "social justice" has only become integrated into higher education discourse in recent decades.

At present, numerous groups ranging from social conservatives to freedom of speech advocates dismiss and oppose the concept of social justice as a radical agenda to overthrow the existing societal structure in favor of the least advantaged. While such rhetoric is used to delegitimize the goals of social justice, it also serves to diminish engagement in the *process* of social justice. As defined by Adams, Bell, and Griffin (2007), social justice is both a goal and a process. When understood as a goal, social justice allows us to envision a society mutually shaped to meet individual and group needs and in which all individuals have equal participation, distribution of resources is equitable, and all members are safe and secure both psychologically and physically (Adams et al., 2007). Those who are not committed to these goals might claim that such a society already exists, thus there is no need to participate in the process of social justice. However, the lifelong process of achieving social justice is both democratic and participatory (Adams et al., 2007; Landreman & MacDonald-Dennis, 2013). It must be inclusive while fostering and affirming the agency of humans to work together to effect socially just change. Unfortunately, the term "social justice" has become integrated into higher education without dedication to and engagement in its processes and goals.

How Did We Arrive at Social Justice as a Buzzword?

Social justice is a "concept and a practice that is often widely misunderstood" (Landreman & MacDonald-Dennis, 2013, p. 3). Many individuals use it interchangeably with terms like diversity, multiculturalism, and inclusion in an effort to demonstrate a commitment to these words (Goodman, 2011). Unfortunately, demonstrating "commitment" does not require actual engagement with these concepts and, instead, merely requires that an individual or institution invoke the implications of a word (Ahmed, 2012). Through this process, these concepts become mere trending buzzwords that act as nonperformatives or inactions. To better understand the ways that higher education is currently "engaging" with social justice, we will review recent related buzzwords in the field and the nonperformative inactions posing as engagement, then finish the section with a discussion around the ways in which social justice is utilized as a barrier to dialogue.

Evolution of Words

After the Civil Rights Act of 1964 changed the demographics of students participating in higher education, learning to "value diversity" was embraced by businesses and educational systems alike well into the 1990s, but primarily focused on adding difference to an existing environment (Ahmed, 2012; Smith, 2015). Generally, the term "diversity" is understood to mean difference or variety (Smith, 2015). When reframed through the context of assessment, we can also utilize the term "diversity outcomes," which refers to learning that occurs through exposure to diversity. Encouraging access has increased diversity (the representation of different groups, e.g., women and people of color) within arenas from which these groups were previously excluded, but has not fostered the systematic change that social justice seeks (Landreman & MacDonald-Dennis, 2013). Within higher education, valuing diversity typically involves the administration of an institution claiming as much as possible is being done in order to increase the presence of nonwhite individuals (Smith, 2015).

Another term turned buzzword is "cultural pluralism" that aims to promote the acceptance and appreciation of cultures beyond one's own as a means toward improving individual and interpersonal dynamics. However, similar to valuing diversity, striving for cultural pluralism does little in regard to fostering the equitable distribution of resources (Goodman, 2011). Moving away from a celebratory melting pot of cultural pluralism, the multicultural education movement sought to act as a radical approach to education with the goal of effecting social change (Banks, 1993; Gorski, 2010). Multicultural education is actually challenging to define because it is multifaceted and has numerous approaches with varying amounts of success (Gorski, 2010). Multicultural education views schools as sites for transformation and "is grounded in ideals of social justice, education equity, critical pedagogy, and a dedication to providing educational experiences in which all students reach their full potentials as learners and as socially aware and active beings, locally, nationally, and globally" (Gorski, 2010, para. 5). Unfortunately, while this transformative movement was prevalent within education studies and had some success becoming incorporated into K–12 settings, within higher education, multiculturalism generally invokes the sentiment of a buzzword and an additive method similar to that of diversity and cultural pluralism.

While multicultural education assumes an intentional curriculum, multiculturalism in higher education is an oft used slogan aimed to recruit and retain students from minoritized social groups (Quaye, 2008). Voicing an institution's commitment to multiculturalism has become the primary mode of "facilitating" cross-cultural learning rather than promoting intentional and structured opportunities to engage (Ahmed, 2012; Quaye, 2008). Literature within higher education frequently purports that exposure to multiculturalism in college ultimately achieves educational learning outcomes that lead to benefits to society (Hurtado, Milem, Clayton-Pedersen, & Allen, 1999). Some of these outcomes include: more democratic engagement (e.g., more likely to vote, greater concern for the public good); cognitive skills (e.g., critical thinking skills, sociohistorical thinking); cultural awareness, cultural acceptance, and reduction of prejudice (Astin, 1993; Milem, 1994). These outcomes occur as the result of a variety of experiences and circumstances in the campus environment and ultimately provide ongoing developmental opportunities for students. However, in higher education this version of multiculturalism has failed to effectively challenge oppression and inequity (Landreman & MacDonald-Dennis, 2013).

While higher education has invoked the meaning of diversity, cultural pluralism, and multiculturalism for a considerable length of time, little progress has been made toward transformative and structural change. As defined previously, social justice refers to both a process and a goal (Adams, Bell, & Griffin, 1997). Though the goals of multiculturalism included a vision of an organization that values the perspectives and achievements of all and promotes communication knowledge, some have called for more intentional strategies to actualize a more equitable environment (Manning & Coleman-Boatwright, 1991). The use of the term "social justice" has been employed to guide efforts toward structural transformation; however, its meaning has become diminished, mocked, and culturally linked to radical leftist politics in the United States. While it was previously difficult to untangle the term from its relationship with religion, it is currently nearly impossible to separate the word social justice from culturally charged political beliefs and movements. Many campuses are experiencing a debate on their campus between those who support social justice and those who do not, making meaningful engagement challenging. It is easy to become engulfed by evolving terms and divisive rhetoric; however, leaders and administrators in higher education have discovered how to make these terms work in their favor regardless of a lack of intentional action.

Social Justice as a Nonperformative

Embedded within the process of becoming a buzzword, is the implication that the meaning of a concept has become so eroded that it no longer has value. Unfortunately, within higher education, we frequently continue to champion terms that have lost their meaning after years of misuse. After becoming a buzzword, a term no longer has a meaningful, shared cultural definition to guide intentional engagement. Instead, we use the buzzword to invoke the suggestion of action, turning it into a nonperformative (Ahmed, 2012). Ahmed explains that asserting a commitment to diversity, multiculturalism, or social justice, for example, *becomes* the action rather than actually taking action; this is what the nonperformative intends to do. The nonperformative takes the place of actual action, while still portraying the message that something is happening.

Within higher education, nonperformatives are frequently summoned in the form of "commitment to diversity statements" conveyed via campus leadership. Such statements typically indicate that an institution does not condone discrimination or bias based upon a myriad of social identities. Through this commitment, when incidences of bias occur or systematic oppression is pointed out to an administration, it is possible for campus leadership to refer to the commitment statement as proof that the institution has already self-declared that they are not aligned with those ideas. In this sense, the speech act declaring commitment becomes the only action. There is not a change in practice or policy to actually effect change, rather we *name* our so-called commitment as a way to *not* effect change (Ahmed, 2012). Statements of commitment are often examples of self-declaration, or "a declaration of principles that the institution already has" (Ahmed, 2012, p. 115). Ahmed (2012) elaborates, "The org can be committed to a new policy without anything happening. Indeed, a new commitment defined as a policy can even be a way of keeping old commitments in place" (p. 126). These "commitments" involve little effort on the institution's part and merely add the declaration to what already exists rather than revisioning any part of the institution (Ahmed, 2012; Nkomo, 1992). In this way commitment is merely a tick box. If an organization can just tick a box, it gives the illusion of being committed even though the institution is not taking any action to engage with the process of social justice. This current method of engagement is actually a direct barrier to effective engagement in social justice within higher education.

Social Justice as a Barrier to Actual Engagement

In addition to the plethora of buzzwords that dilute engagement in social justice and the use of commitment statements as a replacement for action, debates around the level of "political correctness" on a college campus also serve as a distraction and barrier. One of the defining components of social justice is to facilitate dialogue where multiple perspectives are considered and explored, and all can participate. The term politically correct refers to an agreement with the belief that one should not engage in behavior that might offend a particular group of people (Merriam-Webster, 2015). Over time, this term has gained an offensive connotation, and through the lens of social justice implies that someone might alter their behavior against their will to satisfy social expectations rather than due to a genuine belief that the behavior is morally correct. On its own, this term can shut down productive discussion; however, some argue that there are levels of political correctness that are acceptable and do not act as barriers, and other more extreme levels that are in conflict with the goals of higher education (Zimmerman, 2016).

An Inside Higher Ed article published in the summer of 2016 described two types of "political correctness" the author asserts have become commonplace in education (Zimmerman, 2016). What was named PC-1 refers to changing one's language in an effort to describe human differences without demeaning others (Zimmerman, 2016). An example provided was a professor who refers to his women students as "girls." The author argues that by using "girls," the professor is questioning their place as adults in society and in order to comply with an "appropriate" level of political correctness should use the word "women" instead. Zimmerman describes PC-2 as "political correctness which inhibits dialogue by imposing liberal political orthodoxies" (Zimmerman, 2016). This definition is also an example of keywords that have become culturally linked to social justice movements and cultivate a negative connotation for some. PC-2 implies that an expected set of liberal beliefs should be adhered to, for example, individuals should use the restroom that corresponds with their gender. When aligned with the definition of social justice provided by Adams et al. (1997) who view this as both a process and a goal, these two topics could be ripe with possibilities for discussion and engagement. The process component requires engaging individuals in dialogue and critical thinking about the issue. The goal is a "vision of society in which the distribution of resources is equitable and all members are physically and psychologically safe and secure" (Adams et al., 1997, p. 3). To make progress toward the goal, engagement in dialogue from numerous perspectives is crucial to promote growth and complex thinking. However, by declaring something acceptably PC-1 versus aggressively PC-2, discussion is brought to a halt as participants prepare their best arguments for debate. When positioned on the offensive, it is difficult to foster space for vulnerability.

As stated, the term "social justice" can carry a negative stigma that implies a monolithic liberal agenda that seeks to restrain the beliefs of others (Zimmerman, 2016). This perception of the "social justice warrior" stifles the potential for dialogue before the opportunity even arises. Conservative students in recent years have consistently voiced feeling silenced, ridiculed, and targeted for their beliefs, discouraging them from participating in such dialogue (Vaccaro, 2010; Zimmerman, 2016). Without an opportunity to truly engage with one another, individuals with differing beliefs are not able to jointly participate in the process of social justice as described by Adams et al. (1997). For the authors, within our own personal development and as educators working with students, critical self-reflection, dialogue with numerous perspectives, investigating historical context, and developing brave spaces (Arao & Clemens, 2013) have been instrumental in engaging with the process of social justice. This process is not possible when we are consumed by categorizing what is an "appropriate level of political correctness."

Section 2: Engaging in Social Justice

How Can We Effectively Engage in Social Justice within Higher Education?

In order to effectively engage in social justice, we must first seek to understand two key concepts that are entwined with social justice: oppression and privilege. Scholars have proposed multiple frameworks to guide one's understanding of oppression (Adams et al., 1997; Goodman, 2011; Harro, 2000; Vaccaro, 2013; Young, 1990), each illuminating aspects of the complexities of oppression within modern society. To begin facilitating what we will call "multicontext thinking," we favor utilizing Vaccaro's Three-Level Model of Oppression (2013) and applying it to our understandings of both oppression and privilege. Through this multilevel analysis, we are actively practicing applying multiple contexts to one idea or situation which we argue results in a more thorough and inclusive engagement with the process and goals of social justice. We will also provide examples and recommendations for more effective engagement with the process of social justice at individual, institutional, and cultural levels.

As we previously asserted, the first steps to engaging in social justice require an understanding of oppression and privilege. The term "oppression" encompasses more than bigotry, prejudice, and bias; instead, it fuses these with systematic and institutional discrimination "to emphasize the pervasive nature of social inequality woven throughout social institutions as well as embedded within individual consciousness" (Adams et al., 1997, p. 4). Adams et al. (1997), scholars of seminal works in social justice education, describe oppression as consisting of five defining features. First, it is *pervasive* and embedded in all aspects of our individual, institutional, and cultural lives (Adams et al., 1997; Vaccaro, 2013). Next, it is *restricting*, meaning that it constrains one's sense of possibility and options in their life. Oppression is also *hierarchical*, it facilitates a social system where some groups are granted privileges where others are not. Additionally, since individuals hold multiple simultaneous identities that cut across social groups (e.g., young Japanese woman with college degree), oppression exists within "*complex, multiple, cross-cutting relationships*" in our lives (Adams et al., 1997, p. 5). It is here that we begin to understand oppression as intersectional (Collins, 1990) and in applying an intersectional framework, we can "consider the interconnections among systems of oppression, not only as they influence individual identity and experience, but also as the systems themselves are entangled, co-constructed, and mutually dependent" (Shlasko, 2015, p. 351). The last defining feature of oppression is the ways in which it is *internalized*. This feature draws attention to the prevalence of oppressive ideas within the human psyche, in addition to external social institutions, for example, believing individuals with black skin are more dangerous than individuals with white skin. Internalizing this belief not only has repercussions individually, it has a systematic impact that, for example, might look like a pattern of excessive force is used by policing agencies against nonviolent black individuals. These five features of oppression illuminate some of the challenges of social justice work and strive toward the goal of social justice. Given the vast role oppression plays in our everyday lives, it is critical to strategically inform and align individuals and institutions with the goals of social justice.

A second concept one must explore in order to effectively begin engaging in social justice is *privilege*. Privilege is generally defined as "unearned access to resources (social power) only readily available to some people as a result of their social group membership" (Adams et al., 1997, p. 73). The nature of privilege lends to the creation of a false dichotomy based on one's membership in social groups who either benefit from privilege (agent groups) or who gain less power and benefits compared to their agent counterparts (target groups) (Adams et al., 1997; Merrill, 2013). This division of social groups might look like heterosexual individuals as agents and LGBTQ+ individuals as targets, or white individuals as agents and people of color as targets.

Such a dualistic framework can result in disengagement with the process of social justice as some individuals might feel attacked, vulnerable, or defensive (Merrill, 2013). While this exploration is challenging, one must both consider the previously discussed *complex, multiple, and cross-cutting relationships* within oppression, while also investigating and implicating one's own role in oppression through the unconscious or conscious acquisition of privileges in our society. Without an understanding of one's own role in the reproduction of oppression through a set of privileges, one's engagement in understanding social justice remains shallow. Given the psychological challenge of admitting that we all have a role in continuing oppression, we suggest two strategies explained in the next section in order to effectively and ongoingly engage in social justice: multicontext thinking and applying Vaccaro's three-level model of oppression.

Multicontext Thinking

In their work, Bolman and Deal (2008, p. 18) introduce the practice of "multiframe thinking" or intentional *reframing* as a way to allow one's thinking to move beyond narrow and unconscious approaches to understanding organizations. Bolman and Deal (2008) offer four frames to aid in reframing one's initial assessment of a situation: structural, human resource, political, and symbolic. The goal of this process is to deepen one's own understanding and appreciation of an organization through consistent use of multiframe thinking. Multiframe thinking provides multiple "sets of ideas and assumptions—that you carry in your head to help you understand and negotiate a particular territory" (Bolman & Deal, 2008, p. 10). While we are not prescribing the use of Bolman and Deal's specific four-frame model, we do believe that this practice facilitates critical thinking skills required for effective engagement in social justice. To that end, we offer a similar but new term, *multicontext thinking*. Using multicontext thinking allows individuals to consider different perspectives and frameworks to understand the world around them.

Multicontext thinking aims to cultivate more effective engagement of social justice by individuals, institutions, and communities. Through a multicontext thinking process, one can seek to understand the simultaneous and multiple realities that exist in the world around them. Given that this can feel like an intimidating process, we suggest employing Vaccaro's model of individual, institutional, and cultural oppression as a starting point to utilizing multicontext thinking. Beginning with these three contexts provides a structure as we train our minds to use multicontext thinking, and avoid using a one-size-fits-all approach, which can lead to inaction, a lack of imagination, and the reproduction of oppression. In alignment with Bolman and Deal, we assert that engaging in multicontext thinking facilitates liberation as one "realize[s] there is always more than one way to respond to any problem or dilemma" (2008, p. 19).

Adapted from Hardiman, Jackson, and Griffin (2007), Vaccaro (2013) asserts that oppression can be understood from the individual, institutional, and cultural contexts in order to meaningfully understand the various forms oppression takes. We would like to extend this model to better understand privilege. In our experience, when asked to identify or explore how one might be implicated in systems of oppression and privilege, individuals have a tendency to disengage. To maintain and even increase engagement, we suggest conceptualizing oppression and privilege as phenomena that happen in individual, institutional, and cultural contexts. By diffusing some of the pressure upon the individual to two additional contexts, potential participants can begin to unveil the pervasive nature of oppression and privilege rather than internalizing responsibility and shutting down. This addition to the three-level model of oppression allows us to cultivate meaningful engagement in the concept of privilege instead of avoiding or glossing over a potentially challenging discussion.

Individual

Individual oppression refers to the conscious or unconscious attitudes, beliefs, and behaviors of an individual person that maintains oppression (Adams et al., 1997). Often, this type of oppression manifests through interpersonal actions, beliefs, and behaviors (Vaccaro, 2013). While most individuals do not explicitly intend to convey, for example, racist attitudes, frequently one does not recognize their own beliefs and/or behaviors as oppressive. An example that could be conscious or unconscious includes a white woman who automatically crosses the street as a black man approaches along her path. These types of actions serve to further oppression at the individual level.

Applying Vaccaro's model to privilege, we define individual privilege as benefiting from or gaining social capital that provides opportunities or advantages to someone as a result of their social group membership in a dominant or agent group. It is important to note that privilege is frequently utilized without the user noticing. This is possible because privilege is based upon a preference for whiteness that saturates society in the United States (and beyond but we are limiting our analysis to this nation). This preference can influence a given situation without notice from the individuals involved. For example, a parent who selects a white realtor when choosing between equally qualified black and white realtors, and reasons that it is because they can relate better to the white candidate. Since any two individuals can relate along numerous categories or experiences, selecting race as one's preferred shared dominant group membership bestows additional social capital to that identity and that individual. Given the unconscious nature of both oppression and privilege, we recommend intentional personal exploration guided by four main strategies: (1) critical reflection; (2) dialogue with numerous perspectives; (3) investigating historical context; and (4) developing brave spaces (Arao & Clemens, 2013).

We make these recommendations knowing that they also offer the opportunity to be applied to the institutional and cultural contexts. This overlap highlights the fluidity and interconnected relationship between the three levels. For example, an individual influences and affects institutions through their experiences living (working, teaching, voting, purchasing) in the dominant (white) culture (Adams et al., 1997). Further, by incorporating these strategies, individuals practice multicontext thinking; all of these components foster intentional engagement with the process and goals of social justice. In addition, these practices are aligned with the professional competencies for student affairs educators developed by ACPA (College Student Educators International) and NASPA (Student Affairs Administrators in Higher Education) to establish a common and standard set of skills/competencies (2015). One of ten skillsets, the social justice and inclusion competency is shaped by the student affairs educator's "sense of their own agency and social responsibility that includes others, their community, and the larger global context" (p. 30). This type of intentional development requires that a person critically reflect, dialogue with others from numerous perspectives, investigate historical context, and foster brave spaces (Arao & Clemens, 2013).

To begin, explorations into critical self-reflection should be grounded in better understanding and contextualizing one's own life experiences and social identities. Such reflection requires examining the ways in which you hold, participate in, and reproduce multiple levels of privilege and oppression. Often this looks like identifying your own social group memberships, doing research and learning about their histories, and negotiating the reality and impact of your role in upholding oppression. Next, as someone gains a deeper understanding of their own existence they must begin to dialogue with others from a wide range of perspectives. By this I do not mean find a minoritized person and ask them about their life. Instead, this requires participating in opportunities to discuss challenging topics with others, for example, seeking out events on campus that provide an opportunity to listen and learn from a perspective different than your own. Frequently, student organizations representing social group identities sponsor public events that share an aspect of their unique perspective. While these types of programs have varying levels of success (Razack, 2007), they do provide the ability to practice multicontext thinking and imagine realities different than one's own.

Similar to investigating one's own history via the internet, local library, or living family member, one can investigate historical contexts and time periods. This can be done at the individual, institutional, and cultural levels and we will provide examples in our suggestion lists. This might include asking your eldest family member to describe their schooling experiences or social interactions with other youth growing up. Such engagement will strengthen one's multicontext thinking abilities. Lastly, one must engage participation in brave spaces (Arao & Clemens, 2013). The brave space concept evolved from the idea of safe spaces. Safe spaces generally imply an environment where people feel comfortable to fully participate, safe from harm, and are willing and able to participate in discussion about challenging issues (Arao & Clemens, 2013). A brave space acknowledges that these discussions involve discomfort, vulnerability, resistance, denial, guilt, risk, and courage. These spaces can occur in the classroom, in the car, at the dinner table, attending a campus event, while watching a movie, and numerous other situations where more than one person is willing to engage in vulnerable discussion with agreed upon expectations for managing the dialogue. Arao and Clemens (2013) specifically provide five guidelines that we argue could be agreed upon formally or informally depending upon the existing relationships within the dialogue: (1) Controversy with civility; (2) Own your intentions and your impact; (3) Challenge by choice, but challenge your resistance; (4) Discuss the group's understanding of respect; and (5) Challenge an idea, do not attack the person. Environments with these conditions can easily be facilitated to practice participation in brave spaces throughout one's life.

As educators, we have incorporated these four strategies into our own intentional engagement with social justice. Though we did not approach our lives in this way from the start, our own process of engagement has developed over time and continues to evolve. In order to engage in individual engagement within social justice, we suggest the following:

- Students, faculty, staff, and administrators should develop an understanding of social justice. This includes identifying existing social justice programming and curriculum, as well as allies, social justice educators, and other sources of support on campus for individual-level engagement and exploration.

- Foster relationships among individuals who seek to engage in the processes and goals of social justice across all departments and units. This type of support network can provide a way to critically reflect and process.
- Design meaningful follow-ups postengagement for participants and facilitators to practice critical reflection and multicontext thinking.

Institutional Level

Institutional oppression is defined as "the systematic mistreatment of people within a social identity group, supported and enforced by the society and its institutions, solely based on the person's membership in the social identity group" (Cheney, LaFrance, & Quinteros, 2006, p. 1). These social institutions include "education, politics, health care, economy, media, religion, family, and the military, etc." (Vaccaro, 2013, p. 31) and they are both shapers of and shaped by the individual and cultural levels (Adams et al., 1997, p. 19). Adams et al. further explicate that "the application of institutional policies and procedures in an oppressive society run by individuals or groups who advocate or collude with social oppression produces oppressive consequences" (1997, p. 19). This oppression may manifest in housing or employment discrimination, or a tradition of leadership that all whole dominant social group identities (e.g., white, educated, male). Actively working against this might mean incorporating counterstories in an educational program to counteract the usual history shared in schooling. This might also look like intentional and culturally relevant outreach to communities that typically lack access to the institution. Rather than a one-time service project, try opportunities for longer-term engagement.

We must remember that social justice is *both* a goal and a process (Adams et al., 2007). As asserted in our exploration of the individual level, engagement requires us to "speak out against injustice but also to situate ourselves as benefactors of inequality" (Zyltra, 2011, p. 379). This process requires that higher education and educators create self-awareness of their own privilege and oppression before working to foster educational spaces for others. When educators at higher education institutions start enacting the importance and value of social justice, they "must begin to see their work in terms of advocacy rather than awareness" (Zyltra, 2011, p. 382). In order to facilitate institutional-level engagement with social justice and weaken the influence of oppression and privilege, we suggest the following:

- Individuals can facilitate an environmental scan to understand how the students, faculty, staff, and administrators describe the campus environment and culture; recognize the institution's traditions and expectations within the environment; and develop an understanding of the realities/challenges faced by the stakeholders of the institutions. Through this process, individuals are preparing for and designing institutional change.

- The mission or vision statement(s) regarding the diversity, inclusion, and/or social justice commitment of an institution, and its units or departments should be supported by an explicit action plan detailing how what is espoused in their mission or vision statement will be accomplished.
- Design leadership opportunities for individuals who seek to advocate and support social justice education and practices within their units.
- Develop a plan to facilitate engagement in social justice education and practices (e.g., training or workshops) and make these accessible to all employees (e.g., paid time to attend). This also requires identifying and training individuals that can facilitate social justice programming or establishing a campus unit to design and lead social justice education on campus.

Across the country higher education institutions have created social justice education and programs to advance and facilitate institutional change on their campuses with regard to access and inclusivity. Yet, many of the programming created is often developed out of urgency and in reaction to a problem that institutions are facing, and programs have been facilitated by individuals that do not understand or engage in social justice work. Most institutions of higher education are inherently rooted in dominant culture, some institutions create social justice programs as a way to attempt to fix the injustice and disparities populations of individuals face at these campuses. We must understand that social justice is a lifelong journey that requires individuals, institutions, and cultural organization to be engaged in creating brace space for all to reflect, advocate for equity, and create change.

Cultural Context

Cultural level of oppression can be demonstrated through "social norms, values, icons, ideologies, aesthetics, lore, jokes, music, popular culture, shared belief" (Vaccaro, 2013, p. 31). Cultural oppression manifests through the cultural and society stories that portray and divide individuals based on their privilege and oppression attached to their identities. One group might receive mistreatment, discriminations, and exploitation, while the other group holds hierarchy, power, and privilege. White supremacy is an example of cultural oppression. White supremacy is the belief that white individuals are superior, less violent, and better citizens than any other race, while individuals of other race might be portrayed as criminals, rapist, and drug dealers. These stereotypes toward marginalized populations have forced them to create brave spaces through activism to challenge the negative assumptions and to change the culture.

We live in a society where racism is present every day, and in a society that has been exposed to dialogue through educational settings and various media communication forms that recreate privilege and oppression (Katz, 1978, 2003). Some communities of people often feel threatened and sensitive to conversations in relationship to racism and other social justice topics. While these conversations occur in various forums, it appears that "race and racism seems nonexist...is mired in misinformation and miscommunication...[and] Instead of talking about racism, we deflect our conversation with vague references to 'culture,' 'diversity,' 'cross-cultural effectiveness'" (Katz, 2003, p. 3), and social justice. For example, we examine how the Black Live Matters movement was created by oppressed populations of people, and how it is associated with feelings of fear and misunderstood by privileged populations of people. The Black Lives Matter movement has been challenged by switching the significance of the statements to All Lives Matter and Blue Lives Matter. "#BlackLives-Matter is a call to action and a response to the virulent anti-Black racism that permeates our society. Black Lives Matter is a unique contribution that goes beyond extrajudicial killings of Black people by police and vigilantes" (BlackLivesMatter, 2013, para. 1). This is an example of cultural level oppression, how most privileged people have negatives associations when speaking of Black Lives Matter and communities of color, and how they continue to reestablish "White privilege, white power, and white ownership" (Katz, 2003, p. vii).

We used Black Lives Matter movement as an example of how oppressed populations have started to advocate for culture change in response to cultural oppression. Marginalized populations have created online and offline brave space to challenge and question the status quo that often assigns them to low positions in society. The Black Lives Matter movement is an example of how oppressed people have created a brave space online by using the #BlackLivesMatter and by creating rallies in communities to advocate for and validate the black lives.

Current movements and events such as Black Lives Matter, cultural oppression, privilege, and oppression can be analyzed from the multicontext thinking as it occurs in different forms when groups of individuals experience mistreatment, discriminations, and exploitation. In order to engage in cultural multicontext thinking, we suggest the following:

- Cultivate brave spaces for participants to critically reflect on their experiences participating in social justice activities and educational programs.
- Utilize community-based evaluation of social justice activities and programs to inform decision-making.
- Through the promotion of social justice education, actualize a culture where exploring and engaging in understanding social justice is common.
- Facilitate intentional opportunities to understand the different forms of power, privilege, social identities, and intersectionality in U.S. culture.
- Create cultural sensitivity and cultural multicontext thinking and intelligence to facilitate relationships, action work, and dialogue on social justice.
- Establish continuous social justice action goals and dialogues among others and hold others accountable.
- Create coalitions with communities of people to create cultural change through social activism.

Conclusion

In an attempt to understand the ways that higher education promotes, engages, and delivers social justice, we provide an overview of the evolution, history, and perspectives that communities of people have created about social justice. Counterpart to Adams et al.'s (2007) social justice definition, we believe that social justice is a goal that allow us to envision a society mutually shaped to meet individual and group needs and in which all individuals have equal participation, distribution of resources is equitable, and all members are safe and secure both psychologically and physically. And it is also a lifelong process that creates inclusivity while fostering and affirming the agency of humans to work together to effect socially just change. In this chapter, we encourage the use of multicontext thinking to allow individuals to consider different perspectives to understand the world around them. We promote critical self-reflection and dialogue to practice multicontext thinking with various perspectives to create and develop brave spaces in order to understand the various forms of individual, institutional, and cultural oppression and privilege. And, we provide recommendation for higher education and its stakeholders to effectively engage in social justice and equity, with the goal of developing multicontext thinking to cultivate more effective engagement of social justice by individuals, institutions, and communities. In order to become agents of change through social justice, we encourage you to examine your beliefs, values, attitudes, and behaviors.

Questions

1. How do you describe social justice, and how does your higher education institution and department define social justice?
2. At the individual, institutional, and cultural level, what forms of oppression and privilege do you have? Your institution? Your community?
3. Describe how you could apply multicontext thinking in programming, curriculum, and dialogue.

References

ACPA—College Student Educators International & NASPA—Student Affairs Administrators in Higher Education. (2015). *Professional Competency Areas for Student Affairs Educations.* Retrieved from: http://www.naspa.org/images/uploads/main/ACPA_NASPA_Professional_Competencies_FINAL.pdf

Adams, M., Bell, L. A., & Griffin, P. (Eds.). (1997). *Teaching for diversity and social justice: A sourcebook.* New York: Routledge.

Adams, M., Bell, L. A., & Griffin, P. (Eds.). (2007). *Teaching for diversity and social justice: A sourcebook (2nd ed).* New York: Routledge.

Ahmed, S. (2012). *On being included: Racism and diversity in institutional life.* Duke University Press.

Arao, B., & Clemens, K. L. (2013). From safe spaces to brave spaces: A new way to frame dialogue around diversity and social justice. In L. Landreman (Ed.), *The art of effective facilitation: Stories and reflections from social justice educators* (pp. 135–150). Sterling, VA: Stylus.

Astin, A. W. (1993). Diversity and multiculturalism on the campus: How are students affected? *Change: The Magazine of Higher Learning, 25*(2), 44–49.

Banks, J. A. (1993). Multicultural education: Historical development, dimensions, and practice. *Review of research in education, 19,* 3–49.

BlackLivesMatter. (2013). *About the Black Lives Matter network.* Retrieved from: http://blacklivesmatter.com/about/

Bolman, L.G., & Deal, T.E. (2008). *Reframing Organizations: Artistry, Choice, and Leadership.* (4th Ed). San Francisco, CA: Jossey-Bass.

Cheney, C., LaFrance, J., & Quinteros, T. (2006). *Institutionalized Oppression Definition*. Retrieved from: https://www.pcc.edu/resources/illumination/documents/institu tionalized-oppression-definitions.pdf

Collins, P.H. (1990). Black feminist thought: Knowledge, consciousness, and the politics of empowerment. Boston, MA: Unwin Hyman.

Gilson, E. (2013). *The Christian Philosophy of St. Thomas Aquinas*. New York, NY: Random House.

Goodman, D. J. (2011). *Promoting diversity and social justice: Educating people from priv- ileged groups*. Routledge.

Gorski, P. (2010). The challenge of defining "Multicultural Education." *EdChange*. Retrieved from: http://www.edchange.org/multicultural/initial.html

Hardiman, R., Jackson, B., & Griffin, P. (2007). Conceptual foundations for social justice education. In M. Adams, L. A. Bell, & P. Griffin (Eds.), Teaching for diversity and social justice (2nd ed., pp. 35–66). New York, NY: Routledge.

Harro, B. (2000). The Cycle of Socialization. In M. Adams, W. Blumenfeld, R. Castaneda, H. Hackmane, M. Peters, & X. Zuniga (Eds.), Readings for diversity and social jus- tice, pp. 16–21. New York: Routledge.

Hurtado, S., Milem, J., Clayton-Pedersen, A., & Allen, W. (1999). *Enacting Diverse Learning Environments: Improving the Climate for Racial/Ethnic Diversity in Higher Education. ASHE-ERIC Higher Education Report, Vol. 26, No. 8*. ERIC Clearing- house on Higher Education. Washington D.C.

Katz, J. H. (1978). White awareness: Handbook for anti-racism training. Norman, OK: University of Oklahoma Press.

Katz, J. H. (2003). White awareness: Handbook for anti-racism training (Second Edi- tions). Norman, OK: University of Oklahoma Press.

Mattson, S. (2015). *Social justice is a Christian tradition—Not a liberal agenda*. Retrieved from: https://sojo.net/articles/social-justice-christian-tradition-not-liberal-agenda

Goodman, D. J. (2011). *Promoting diversity and social justice: Educating people from priv- ileged groups*. Routledge.

Landreman, L. M. & MacDonald-Dennis, C. (2013). The evolution of social justice edu- cation and facilitation. In L. Landreman (Ed.), *The art of effective facilitation: Stories and reflections from social justice educators* (pp. 3–22). Sterling, VA: Stylus.

Manning, K., & Coleman-Boatwright, P. (1991). Student affairs initiatives toward a mul- ticultural university. *Journal of College Student Development, 32*(4), 367.

Merriam-Webster. (2015). *Politically correct*. Merriam Webster Dictionary. Retrieved from: http://www.merriam-webster.com/dictionary/politically%20correct

Merrill, K.C. (2013). The Evolution of a Social Justice Educator's Professional Identity: Impacts of professional maturation and multiple discourse perspectives on a personal practice. In L. Landreman (Ed.), *The art of effective facilitation: Stories and reflections from social justice educators* (pp. 45–63). Sterling, VA: Stylus.

Milem, J. F. (1994). College, Students, and Racial Understanding. Thought & Action (9), 2, 51–92

Nkomo, S. M. (1992). The Emperor Has No Clothes: Rewriting "Race in Organizations". *The Academy of Management Review*, *17*(3), 487–513.

Quaye, S. J., Lin, D. K., Buie, C. R., Abad, M., Labonte, A., Greenberg, J., & Hall, J. W. (2008). Student voices and sensemaking of multiculturalism on campus. *Creating Inclusive Campus Environments for Crosscultural Learning and Student Engagement*, 19–44.

Razack, S. H. (2007). Stealing the pain of others: Reflections on Canadian humanitarian responses. *The Review of Education, Pedagogy, and Cultural Studies*, *29*(4), 375–394.

Shlasko, D. (2015). Using the Five Faces of Oppression to Teach About Interlocking Systems of Oppression, Equity & Excellence in Education, *48*(3), 349–360.

Smith, D. G. (2015). *Diversity's promise for higher education: Making it work*. Baltimore, Maryland: JHU Press.

Vaccaro, A. (2010). What lies beneath seemingly positive campus climate results: Institutional sexism, racism, and male hostility toward equity initiatives and liberal bias. *Equity & Excellence in Education*, *43*(2), 202–215.

Vaccaro, A. (2013). Building a framework for social justice education: One educator's journey. In L. Landreman (Ed.), *The art of effective facilitation: Stories and reflections from social justice educators* (pp. 135–150). Sterling, VA: Stylus.

Young, I. M. (1990). Five faces of oppression. In I. M. Young (Ed.), *Justice and the politics of difference* (pp. 39–65). Princeton, NJ: Princeton University Press

Zimmerman, J. (2016, June 16). The Two Kinds of PC. *Inside Higher Ed*. Retrieved from https://www.insidehighered.com/views/2016/06/16/examination-two-kinds-political-correctness-essay

Zyltra, J. D. (2011). Why is the gap so wide between espousing a social justice agenda to promote learning and enacting it? What could student affairs educators do to genuinely enact a social justice ideology? Moving beyond good intentions. In P. M. Magolda & M. B. Baxter Magolda (Eds.), *Contested issues in student affairs; Diverse perspectives and respectful dialogue* (pp. 375–386). Sterling, VA: Stylus.

12. Creating Inclusive Classrooms as an Imperative for Historically Underrepresented Groups in Higher Education

MICHAEL SEAN FUNK

It is approaching twenty years since I flipped through the syllabus of my Diversity in Higher Education course while working on my Masters degree in Student Personnel Administration at New York University. I still possess a copy of the required book, *Campus Wars: Multiculturalism and the Politics of Difference*; it is now a keepsake that serves as a reminder of how music might change, but in the end, it is the same instruments that produce the sound. In other words, the language to describe the tensions on college campuses might be different; however, the essence of the issues persists.

The hot ticket topics that emerged from *Campus Wars* included: Race and Affirmative Action on campus, Free Speech/Code Speech, Sexual Assault and Date Rape, Multiculturalism (currently referred to as Diversity and Inclusion), Pluralism, and Identity Politics. With little effort, one can take a cursory glance at the first page of the *Chronicles in Higher Education*, *The New York Times*, *Huffington Post*, or *Inside Higher Education* to revisit similar issues within the Higher Education landscape. Without deeper investigation, a straightforward conclusion would prove that the polarity of perspectives on these issues remains unapologetically intransigent.

To be sure, a renewed display of activism is traversing throughout the country. Students are queering gender-binaries by challenging long-standing heteronormative practices. There is a regenerated decry to uphold the integrity of Title IX with the hope of quelling the culture of violence against women in society. In terms of race-based justice, the Midwest can take credit for its genesis as an unexpected fervor caught fire in Mizzou then billowed to the northeast corridor with an uprising at Yale's ivory tower, and has since persisted to reach a critical mass of colleges and universities spanning the United States. The current wave of organizing is producing an unsurpassed level of critical civic engagement that extends beyond a generation of college students. In turn, the student apathy I witnessed over the previous decade has been replaced by consciousness-raising campaigns orchestrated primarily from the ground up and most notably led by historically marginalized groups in higher education. The ground swell of student solidarity that aims to transform (not eradicate) the academy embodies a collective action for the purpose of creating change; however in some cases, not only has this been met with rebuke, it is also precariously framed by narratives condemning students for being overly sensitive, close-minded, anti-intellectual, and coddled (Lukianoff & Haidt, 2015).

Naturally, this is one perspective. And while I see this as the most exciting time in higher education since the moment I dedicated my life to it, others convey feelings of discontent and expressions of disappointment with recent unrest and what is articulated as a departure from the core values in academia. Meanwhile, as the discourse narrows its focus on the heavier of hands between essentially what is offered as only two points of view, I am finding in my own experience, facilitating dialogues on diversity and inclusion with my faculty peers, that even my own assumptions about the proclivity of faculty members to retreat from these "land mind topics" has been greatly contested. In other words, over the past year, I have witnessed a majority of faculty, while often clumsily, commit to reflecting on their practices and pedagogy in an effort to better meet the needs of the students they serve. Because of this, I find it important to be reminded of the willingness demonstrated by a vast number of faculty to reevaluate how and why experiences occur in the classroom. The shifting climate suggests educators are striving to customize pedagogy and curriculum to better serve today's student. With that said, there are still a considerable number of faculty that persist in resisting the call for change.

My position stands with creating an inclusive environment for our students, one that cultivates dialogue and exhibits a supportive learning community for all to learn. My charge here is to illuminate how the current discourse of "coddling" students not only invalidates the named experiences of a number of students within underrepresented and historically marginalized groups; it also misdirects the onus of responsibility. Placing blame on students relinquishes faculty accountability and evades an obligation to architect and maintain classroom settings that foster, not impede student learning.

For the purpose of this essay, I will: (A) provide a brief, historical overview of activism on college campuses with the goal of revealing how recent demands by students is a historical norm not an exception; (B) provide a summation of a condensed list of demands generated by student organizers across the United States; I contend that their demands are being mischaracterized as *vindictive protectiveness* and instead serve as a guideline that benchmarks inclusive educational practices (Lukianoff & Haidt, 2015); (C) disentangle the notion of academic freedom and examine how it is related, but distinguishable from freedom of speech; (D) provide comprehensive strategies that can assist in operationalizing an inclusive classroom that promotes a ripe environment for student learning.

Higher Education and Its History of Activism

While today's millennial student can be credited for a recent rise of student activism, to refer to today's action as remarkable is misleading. For instance, early manifestations dating back to the colonial period find students resisting the indoctrination of *in loco parentis* as well as religious dogma (Broadhurst, 2014). This also rang true during the centuries that followed where student mobilization was ignited by injustice both on campus and outside its parameters. Student rebellions and rallies were commonplace and they were anchored by attempts to address a range of issues including: the social reform of working-class conditions; antisocialism/communism; peace during times of war; Jim Crow laws; the invasion of the United States in Cambodia, which subsequently led to the death of four students at Kent University; Civil Rights; a call to divest from South African Apartheid; women's rights; LGBTQ rights; the Dream Act; Affordable Education; in addition to a host of other public concerns (Broadhurst, 2014; Rogers, 2012).

What may in part be different now is the emergence of social media. It is difficult to refute the impact of social media and its utility as a platform to propagate awareness surrounding daily activities on campus and beyond. While the concept of going viral is indeed a new one, social media has ushered in an unimagined level of transparency within a myriad of institutions and its ability to reach communities nationally and globally is unparalleled. More now than ever, students and parents alike have access to campus operations, which provides further insight into campus policies and practice. Perhaps more importantly, social media functions as an organizer that enables students to communicate more effectively for the purpose of mobilization.

Sparked by the tragic death of Michael Brown, a reawakening of racial consciousness is evolving among millennial students throughout the United

States. Subsequently, the #BlackLivesMatter campaign was formed as an attempt to validate the importance of Black lives. As the movement gains traction, a range of strategies are being exercised to protest the excessive force being practiced by law enforcement. An emphasis is being place on how these ostensible acts of violence are disproportionally exercised against communities of color. Die-ins, walkouts, hunger strikes, town halls, infiltration of political campaigners, and successful efforts to shut down the daily flow of traffic are being employed. Simultaneously, student leaders are crafting manifestos and extensive lists of demands as a call for action. The successes of these endeavors vary; however, it is undeniable how they have assisted with defining the present focus on issues of diversity and inclusion across the country.

Demands or Reasonable Requests

I have been sharing with my colleagues that from a developmental perspective, I do not think the word "demands" best describes what student protesters are seeking from university administration. In other words, students are pursuing reasonable requests, not unattainable demands. In the hope of gaining a better understanding of students' points of view it is useful to break down a momentous list of student demands at various colleges and universities throughout the United States comprised at http://www.thedemands.org/. The list typifies institutional diversity as it spans community colleges to Flagship schools, Research-I universities, small Liberal Arts colleges, Ivy League colleges, private and public four-year colleges, Historically Black Colleges and Universities, Hispanic Serving Institutes, women's colleges, and Asian American and Native American Pacific Islander Serving Institutions. The website Fivethirtyeight (http://fivethirtyeight.com/features/here-are-the-demands-from-students-protesting-racism-at-51-colleges/) aggregated the compiled list of demand of the first 51 of what is now up to 80 colleges and universities.

If you were to peruse the sight, you might find it striking that the most notable demand requested by students was the need to *diversify faculty members* (38 schools). This should come as no surprise as faculty members are significantly less represented than underrepresented student populations on college campus. This remains true even while underrepresented students of color on campus are rising. This is particularly true at four-year degree granting institutions. An aggregate of full-time degree granting institutions' faculty in 2013 offered by the National Center for Educational Statistics indicates that of all combined full-time faculty there were 79% White faculty; 10% Asian faculty; 6%, Black; 5%, Latino/a/x faculty with Native American/Indigenous making up less than 1% of this population (National Center for Educational Statistics, 2016).

The demand for more faculty of color is followed by a *mandate for diversity training* (35 schools). It is important to highlight *diversity courses for students* (21 schools) are distinguished further down in the chart. This denotes an urgent need for faculty training surrounding issues of diversity and inclusion. Attend any town hall where students are verbalizing their experiences on campus and you will learn that microaggressions perpetuated by faculty members are commonplace. While students are seeking their peers to become more educated, the most harmful behaviors are happening at the front of the classroom. Given the empirically documented consequences of stereotype threat (Steele, 1997) and the deleterious impact of unchecked implicit bias, it is critical for faculty members to lean in to the possibility of being more reflective about curriculum development and pedagogy.

Another significant request surrounds the creation or support of safe havens that support the developmental and psychosocial needs of historically marginalized students by *funding cultural centers* (25 schools). Given the historical context of marginalized populations of students on college campuses, the need for spaces on campus that nurture students' need for a "home away from home" reveals that such requests are warranted. For example, much of my early research focused on Black males in higher education. As I reviewed the literature, I thoroughly investigated the key theoretical and conceptual themes involving Black males in higher education from the Civil Rights Movement until the turn of the century. Below is a list of concepts and theories embedded in the literature about Black men primarily on college campuses.

Oppositional Identity (Ogbu, 1978), Camouflaging (Fordham & Ogbu, 1986), Racial Battle Fatigue (Smith, Yosso, & Solórzano, 2007), Chilly climate (New, 2015), Hostile environment (Rankin & Reason, 2005), Acting White (Fordham & Ogbu, 1986), Acting Black (Willie, 2003), Black box (FriesBritt & Griffin, 2007), Hyper-Surveillance (Smith, Yosso, et al., 2007), Racial profiling, Microaggressions (Sue et al., 2007), Institutional Racism (Adams, Bell, Goodman, & Joshi, 2014), Onlyness (Harper, 2012), Cool Pose (Majors & Billson, 1992), Buffering (Cross, 1991), Stereotype Threat (Steele, 1997), Implicit Bias (Statts, 2013), Deficit Models (Harper, 2012), Internalized Racism (Williams, 2011), Post-Traumatic Slave Syndrome (DeGruy, 2005), Victimization (McWhorter, 2001), Marginalization (Young, 2013), and Endangered Species (Washington, 2013).

Efforts to minimize this well-documented research is to ignore the long-term effects it poses to students' learning and development. Educating faculty about the harmful impact of this messaging does not intrude on academic freedom as much as it aids as an intellectual intervention.

Do any of these themes align with the quintessential college experience? In this case, the aesthetics of manicured lawns, spring flowers, unblemished neo-Gothic architecture, and a safe, gated community is replaced with an atmosphere that closely resembles a dystopian war-ground. This alarming contrast provides context as to why culturally pluralistic spaces serve as a beacon for underrepresented groups as well as necessitates the possibility of a more equitable campus. This is also why the recommendation to *track race-related racial hate incidents* (16 schools), akin to the spirit of the 1990 Cleary Act to document crimes on campus, is understandably less about censorship and more about implementing measures to yield accountability for actions that harm others in the classroom and on campus at large.

It is essential to emphasize that the bottom tier of the list includes: *apologies, speech/codes, and removal of selected officials* (7 schools or less). I find it fascinating that even though such pleas were the least prioritized by student activist, they serve as the bookends to the bulk of discourse that critiques student's unrest. Also notably absent is a requisite for *trigger warnings*, another topic dominating the discourse by those in opposition to student resistance. Notwithstanding the intense classroom dynamics students profess to experience in the classroom, the primary call to action resides with educational, not punitive solutions. Additionally, it becomes clearer that many faculty member do not possess the ability to appropriately facilitate topics surrounding diversity or other controversial topics. Moreover, they often lack the set of skills that will enable them to mitigate harmful behavior, which ultimately infringes upon the academic freedom and right of students as learners.

Academic Freedom or Freedom of Speech

If we as educators are committed to the notion articulated by bell hooks that education is the practice of freedom, it is incumbent on us to maintain the integrity of our students' right to learn (hooks, 1994). Too often academic freedom is conflated as freedom of speech. As a result of this misapplication, conversations about diversity and inclusion tend to lean toward preserving faculty speech and offer little recognition to the voices of our students.

Freedom of speech, housed within the First Amendment, stands as a pillar of democracy protecting self-determination with regard to the practice of religion and autonomy for self-expression. Its legacy reaches past three centuries. Academic freedom aspires to achieve similar goals, but instead champions principles predicated on the search for truth. This process enables teachers, researches, and students to engage in a process of inquiry and innovation in an effort to acquire and generate knowledge without fear of consequence.

In 1940 a Statement of Principles on Academic Freedom and Tenure was formed by a long-standing collaboration between the American Association of University Professors and the Association of American Colleges (later added "and Universities") https://www.aaup.org/. This document was revisited a generation later in 1969 by a joint committee involving both parties to reimagine and reinterpret the document given the demographic and institutional shifts in academia since its inception. In retrospect, the guideline not only serves to address the pertinent issues within the context of its time, but uniquely provides certain ground rules for today's hot topics. In particular, guidelines #2 and # 3 with regard to Academic Freedom read:

> Teachers are entitled to freedom in the classroom in discussing their subject, but **they should be careful not to introduce into their teaching controversial matter, which has no relation to their subject.** Limitations of academic freedom because of religious or other aims of the institution should be clearly stated in writing at the time of the appointment.

> College and university teachers are citizens, members of a learned profession, and officers of an educational institution. When they speak or write as citizens, they should be free from institutional censorship or discipline, but **their special position in the community imposes special obligations.** As scholars and educational officers, they should remember that the public may judge their profession and their institution by their utterances. **Hence they should at all times be accurate, should exercise appropriate restraint, should show respect for the opinions of others,** and should make every effort to indicate that they are not speaking for the institution.[6]

Key elements within the instructions strongly allude to the notion of controversial matters with warning to steer away from said topic(s), if the topic(s) transcends a faculty expertise or does not relate to the course. While it can be debated what constitutes controversial matter, the guiding principles explicitly urge faculty to teach within the scope of one's scholarship. This is critical as it frowns upon: "caviler controversial remarks", uninformed social commentary, the purporting of unexamined stereotypes, and the expression of unfavorable opinions about particular groups or cultural practices. Moreover the guidelines link a faculty's right to academic freedom with their ability to be accurate (competent) given their position of authority within the institution. In other words, a faculty member is not necessarily protected if they chose to engage in controversial issues outside the purview of their competency or expertise.

Copping Out About Trigger Warnings

Of the reoccurring headlines that surface when debating about issues of diversity and social justice, *trigger warnings* has earned top-5 recognition. I find this peculiar since I have not had one student take issue with its omission from my syllabi even while my subject material is explicitly provocative. I have watched countless videos and attended my full share of town halls and listening symposiums and not one anecdote regarding trigger warnings was raised. With that said, I think it is important that I clarify that I do recognize the reality of trauma and how it can debilitate one's process of learning if students are in fact triggered by classroom material primed to activate them. My point here is to emphasize that it does not seem to be a prevailing narrative among students. It is the inability or lack of interest to facilitate controversial subject manner in an inclusive manner that students object to. Students are not petitioning for political correctness; it is a call for academic correctness and critical pedagogy (Davis & Harrison, 2013).

Even if trigger warnings are, in fact, a big-ticket contention for students, it is for good reason. For instance, a moviegoer, who can expect to pay $20 for a ticket might take stock of the content of the film provided by the Motion Picture Association of America prior to buying one. The consumer is provided with a film rating and detailed explanations of the content contained in the film (e.g., profanity, graphic violence, strong sexual content, etc.). Similarly, you have students paying up to $5,000 for a 3-credit course. I find it appropriate for students to receive fair warning of what to anticipate in a course that potentially contains trauma-evoking subject matter. It simply boils down to responsible pedagogical practices that do not contradict with academic freedom.

Inclusive Teaching as a Practice

Know Yourself, Know Your Students

Knowing yourself and your students is a mantra I embrace and share with aspiring student affairs practitioners as they navigate the field of higher education. To be effective is to be more reflective. It is critical for educators to be aware of their positionality (the ways one might be privileged or historically disadvantaged), how that situates oneself as a professor in front of the classroom, and how one's own subjectivity factors in to classroom dynamics. Engaging in this process one might ask, *How do my social identities implicitly make room for or shut down students, consciously or unconsciously? How can I be intentional about taking into consideration various social groups and the dynamics that might manifest as a result into the classroom? What are my strategies for noticing and naming these dynamics when they occur* (Adams & Love, 2005; Bell, Goodman, & Varghese, 2016)? One strategy I implement for each of my courses is a *Learning Needs Assessment* form that enables students to provide me with a self-inventory of the student's needs as learners. For instance, students are offered an opportunity to provide preferred pronouns and name. If there is anything happening in their lives outside of the classroom that they are negotiating outside of course responsibilities there is space to share confidentially. Additionally there is a prompt to disclose which type of learning most meets their needs, albeit active experimentation; concrete experience; abstract conceptualization; or reflective observation (Kolb, 1984). I also invite students to share personal or professional goals for the course. Taking stock of students' inventory, I exhibit intentionality when tailoring my pedagogy to meet their stated preferences.

Power With Versus Power Over Pedagogy

While applying this to each classroom context varies, I believe it is important to resituate the hierarchy between student and instructor. Naturally, there is an inherent power dynamic that must be factored given there are evaluative outcomes based on students' ability to demonstrate new learning. However, the relationship does not have to be a superficial exchange, it can be a mutually beneficial process. As a professor, I have committed to create a setting where I can both teach and learn. Too often, professors believe they must have all of the right answers all of the time. In some instances, transparency about "not knowing" can create an educational opportunity for both faculty and students. I find it important to role model how to ascertain new knowledge much like we require our students to do. For example, this past year I inadvertently misgendered one of my student's pronouns. The student identified by the pronoun "they," but I sloppily failed to address their request during the first class meeting. With time, I gradually became more capable of utilizing "They's" pronoun even while the language at the time was unfamiliar to me. Based on students' evaluative feedback, I learned that the students appreciated witnessing me grapple with a new learning while committing to meeting the needs of my entire class. Although it seems counterintuitive, simply stating that you do not know enough about racism, classism, sexism, etc., but are committed to and working toward learning more builds more trust with students than improvising to impress or responding defensively. The classroom is an incubator for student growth and development and we must acknowledge that every conversation and transaction during our time spent with students' counts.

Check Your Assumptions

Chimamanda Ngozi Adichie (2009) warns of the danger of a single story. No matter the intent, it can lead to dehumanization. Operating from auto-pilot obstructs the possibility for new learning to take place. There is no social group or culture that acts as a monolith. The most successful class-rooms provide a canvass for self-authorship. As educators, we are charged with the difficult task of having an understanding of how our students' social identities might be situated within a rich and complex historical con-text. By doing so, we honor how that might affect their current experience in the classroom. Simultaneously, we must see our students as unique indi-viduals that transcend any particular social group narrative as we work to meet them where they are.

Recently, there has been an explosion of research on implicit-bias that affirms we are all accomplices (Amodio, 2014; Banaji & Greenwald, 2013; Statts, 2014). Given this, we must be relentless in our efforts to interrogate our own socialized assumptions about others and make significant strides to reenvision rote, autopilot, stereotypical narratives that can contaminate how we interact with the students.

Allows Space for Multiple Voices and Perspectives Rather Than One Voice

I recently attended a session where students expressed their concerns about microaggressions in the classroom. The student explained she is enrolled in a class that focuses on leadership, but her professor only used White males in his myriad examples of leadership. After observing this for a few class sessions, the student privately met with the instructor to inform him of what she had noticed. She probed about his sole use of male pronouns to describe lead-ership and she pressed about the professor's omission of people of color as representatives of leadership. Unfortunately, the professor responded defen-sively and did not take into account the gift (or feedback) offered by the student. After sharing her story, the student continued to articulate the need for diversity training for faculty, who she referred to as the primary culprits of insensitivity on campus. While I do not think this assessment is necessarily fair, I do believe it reveals a rising undercurrent of mistrust among students toward faculty.

In an effort to exemplify inclusive excellence in the classroom, faculty should be prepared to offer a variety of narratives and diverse perspectives anchored in their expertise. In some cases, this does mean more work. I find it useful to do a syllabus evaluation, have your colleagues provide feedback for you about what is missing, what works. Be thoughtful about including the voices and contributions of People of Color, Women, People with Disabilities, LBTQI communities, and other marginalized identities into your curriculum.

Creates Space to Receive and Provide Feedback

Conventional wisdom suggests professors wait until the end of the semester to anonymously receive feedback from students. We are then encouraged to modify curriculum and pedagogy based on the feedback we received. While all forms of feedback are valuable, the timing does little to serve the specific needs of the students we are currently in the classroom with. I suggest distributing quarterly index cards throughout the semester to request anonymous feedback about what is working, what is not working, and what students would like to see more of. This creates space for students to coconstruct curriculum and pedagogy and also enables them to be responsible for their own learning.

Why Us, Why Now

We must remind ourselves Higher Education is a microcosm for the world we live in, which demands that scholar practitioners be at the vanguard of inclusively centered leadership. As mutually invested educators it is imperative we exhibit *reflective-practice*. This intentional form of practice requires transparency, active listening, an effort to learn, and a willingness to be vulnerable. It involves an eagerness to develop curriculum and pedagogies that foster critical engagement, encourage civic responsibility, contribute to current research, and collaborate with community within and beyond campus parameters.

Once this is acknowledged then it is important to celebrate our triumphs as we also recognize our shortcomings. This is the reality of what the work is comprised of. The future of higher education is contingent on our ability to trust and depend on one another as we collectively work toward building sustainable and inclusive learning communities.

References

Adams, M., Bell, L., Goodman, D., & Joshi, K. (2014). *Teachings for diversity and social justice* (3rd ed.). New York, NY: Routledge.

Adams, M., & Love, B. (2005). Teaching with a social justice perspective: A model for faculty seminars across academic disciplines. In M. L. Ouellett (Ed.), *Teaching inclusively: resources for course, department & institutional change in higher education* (pp. 586–619). Stillwater, OK: New Forums Press.

Adichie, C. N. (2009, July). *The danger of a single story.* Retrieved from https://www.ted. com/talks/chimamanda_adichie_the_danger_of_a_single_story

American Association of University of Professors 1940 Statement of Principles on Academic Freedom and Tenure. (n.d.). Retrieved September 2016 from https://www. aaup.org/report/1940-statement-principles-academic-freedom-and-tenure

Amodio, D. M. (2014). The neuroscience of prejudice and stereotyping. *Nature Reviews Neuroscience, 15,* 670–682.

Banaji, M., & Greenwald, A. (2013). *Blind spot: The hidden biases of good people.* New York, NY: Random House Publishing.

Bell, L., Goodman, D., & Varghese, R., (2016). Critical self-knowledge for social justice educators. In M. Adams, L. Bell, D. Goodman, & K. Joshi (Eds.), *Teachings for diversity and social justice* (3rd ed.). New York, NY: Routledge.

Broadhurst, C. J. (2014). Campus activism in the 21st century: A historical framing. *New Directions For Higher Education, 2014*(167), 3–15.

Cross, W. E. (1991). *Shades of Black: Diversity in African American identity.* Philadelphia, PA: Temple University.

Davis, T., & Harrison, L. M. (2013). *Advancing social justice: Tools, pedagogies, and strategies to transform your campus.* San Francisco, CA: Jossey-Bass.

DeGruy, J. (2005). *Post traumatic slave syndrome: America's legacy of enduring injury and healing.* Portland, OR: Joy DeGruy Publications.

Fordham, S., & Ogbu, J. (1986). Black students school success: Coping with the burden of "acting White." *Urban Review, 18*(3), 176–207.

FriesBritt, S., & Griffin, K. A. (2007). The black box: How highachieving Blacks resist stereotypes about Black Americans. *Journal of College Student Development, 48*(5), 509–524.

Harper, S. R. (2012). *Black male student success in higher education: A report from the national Black male college achievement study.* Philadelphia, PA: University of Pennsylvania, Center for the Study of Race and Equity in Education.

Hooks, B. (1994). *Teaching to transgress: Education as the practice of freedom.* New York, NY: Routledge.

Kolb, D. A. (1984). *Experience as the source of learning and development.* Englewood Cliffs, NJ: Prentice-Hall.

Libresco, L. (2015, December 3). *Here are the demands from students protesting racism at 51 colleges.* Retrieved April 15, 2015, from http://fivethirtyeight.com/features/ here-are-the-demands-from-students-protesting-racism-at-51-colleges/

Lukianoff, G., & Haidt, J. (2015, September 15). The coddling of the American mind. *The Atlantic.* Retrieved from http://www.theatlantic.com/magazine/ archive/2015/09/the-coddling-of-the-american-mind/399356/

Major, R., & Billson, J. M. (1992). *Cool pose: The dilemmas of Black manhood in America.* New York, NY: Touchstone.

McWhorter. J. (2001). *Losing the race: Self-sabotage in Black America*. New York, NY: HarperCollins.

New, J. (2015). A 'chilly climate' on campus. *Inside Higher Education*, January.

Ogbu, J. U. (1978). *Minority education and caste: The American system in crosscultural perspective*. New York, NY: Academic Press.

Rankin, S. R., & Reason, R. D. (2005). Different perceptions: How students of color and White students perceive campus climate for underrepresented groups. *Journal of College Student Development, 46*, 43–61.

Rogers, I. H. (2012). *The black campus movement: Black students and the racial reconstruction of higher education, 1065–1972*. New York, NY, Palgrave Macmillan.

Smith, W. A., Allen, W. R., & Danley, L. L. (2007). "Assume the position...you fit the description": Psychosocial experiences and racial battle fatigue among African American male college students. *American Behavioral Scientist, 51*(4), 551–578.

Staats, C. (2013). *State of the science: Implicit bias review, 2013*. Columbus, OH: Kirwan Institute.

Staats, C. (2014). *State of the Science: Implicit Bias Review 2014*. Columbus, OH: Kirwan Institute.

Steele, C. M. (1997). A threat in the air: How stereotypes shape intellectual indentity and performance. *American Psychologist, 52*, 613–629.

Sue, D. W., Capodilupo, C. M., Torino, G. C., Bucceri, J. M., Holder, A. M., Nadal, K. L., & Esquilin, M. (2007). Racial microaggressions in everyday life. *American Psychologist, 62*(4), 271–286.

U.S. Department of Education, National Center for Education Statistics. (2016). *The condition of Education 2016 (NCES 2016–144), Characteristics of Postsecondary Faculty.* Retrieved September 9, 2016 from https://nces.ed.gov/fastfacts/display.asp?id=61

Washington, M. (2013). Is the black male college graduate becoming an endangered species? A multi-case analysis of the attrition of black males in higher education. *LUX: A Journal of Transdisciplinary Writing and Research from Claremont Graduate University, 3*(1), Article 20.

Williams, T. O. (2011). *A process of becoming: U.S. born African American and Black women in the process of liberation from internalized racism* (Unpublished dissertation). University of Massachusetts, Amherst, MA.

Willie, S. S. (2003). *Acting Black: College, identity, and the performance of race*. New York, NY: Routledge.

Young, I. M. (2013). Five faces of oppression. In M. Adams, W. J. Blumenfeld, R. Castaneda, H. W. Hackman, M. L. Peters, & X. Zuniga (Eds.), *Readings for diversity and social justice: An anthology on racism, anti-semitism, sexism, heterosexism, ableism and classism* (3rd ed.). New York, NY: Routledge.

Part Seven: What Should Be the Roles of Faculty?

In "It Is a Balancing Act: Faculty Workload," Isis N. Walton and Nicolle Parsons-Pollard offer an analysis of faculty functions, the variability of them by institutional type, and how faculty distribute their time and priorities. They challenge the stereotype of the professor having generous personal time and swaths of intervals to focus on research. At the same time, the authors suggest that the tensions among teaching, research, and service require appropriate balance for faculty to be more productive. They urge the professoriate to better educate the public and critics about the realities of faculty workload and productivity.

In "Faculty Work Life: Beyond the Tipping Point," Sean Robinson claims that neoliberal approaches to efficiency and productivity have created a "new managerialism" that has led to increasing administrative burdens on faculty. He further argues that changes in student demographics and public attitudes have generated a significant role shift for faculty: a decrease in research productivity and an acceleration of teaching and administrative responsibilities. According to Robinson, the traditional portrait of the "university professor" has unfortunately faded from the higher education landscape.

13. It Is a Balancing Act: Faculty Workload

Isis N. Walton and Nicolle Parsons-Pollard

When the authors accepted the assignment of contributing to this book the premise of the chapter was, "Are faculty working too little, especially as teachers?" We thought this is a great topic because each of us have been faculty for more than a decade and held administrative positions. So our hope was that as we weigh the question at hand we could see how to tease out the issues of the increasing cost of higher education, the feeling of being completely overwhelmed as a faculty member, and attempt to figure out what the appropriate workload should look like. However, these are very complex issues that cannot be addressed in one chapter and the more we review the literature on this issue the more exasperated we became about how our profession is seen by those inside higher education and those outside of it, in particular, the comparison of what we do as academicians to those in the business world. We will address not only what faculty do or at least are expected to do but also how it impacts workload to address the secondary question of "What should be the proper faculty workload?"

Public Scrutiny

The first sign of the public's growing scrutiny of higher education occurred with the passage of the 1992 Higher Education Reauthorization Act. The Act authorized the establishment of State Postsecondary Review Entities. In other words, it provided States to have some level of oversight and accountability for colleges and universities. Originally, the focus was on the disturbingly high rate in which students were defaulting on federal student loans; however, it did not take long before attention also turned to faculty workload and productivity. For example, South Carolina released performance measures that included mission focus, quality of faculty, instructional quality, and achievements of graduates (Middaugh, 2001). While these all sound reasonable, the measures received some criticism. All of the metrics led to one outcome, which was student achievement. Instructional quality was measured by things like the number of credit hours taught by faculty, class size, and faculty–student ratio. As stated by Middaugh, "they are important indicators that help to suggest whether there is an environment conducive to learning, but they do not measure whether learning is taking place" (2001, p. 29).

Likewise, the cost of higher education has created shock waves through America. The average student debt upon leaving college is at a historical rate of $28,950 for the class of 2014, which is a 2 percent increase from 2013 (Thomason, 2015). The concerns for students and their families are multiple—students leaving with debt, students not actually earning a degree and leaving with debt, students graduating with debt and no job, the impact debt has on the student's overall financial future, and the cost of higher education making it completely out of reach for most. The disparity between the haves and have nots is evident and continues to widen as "half of people from high-income families will get a college degree by age 25, just one in 10 people from low-income families do" (Flannery, 2015).

The Function of Faculty in the University

This chapter is written from the perspective of a full-time tenure eligible or tenured faculty member at a four-year institution. The reason for this perspective is not just because the authors come from these circumstances but also, more importantly, because this chapter would read very differently if we were to address the issues and concerns related to part-time faculty—as there are many from salary and the lack of benefits to the overall sense of value in the academic enterprise.

At the core faculty teach, conduct research/scholarship, and perform service. If you are a faculty member you probably told your parents or friends about your new tenure track job and they only understood that you teach and have summers off. And while they thought they understood your teaching responsibilities the fact of the matter is that most people equate teaching in higher education with that of K–12. So when a faculty member states that he or she teaches 12 hours a week (equivalent to four 3-credit courses) the reaction that ensues is generally disbelief and concern about how much students have to pay for college yet we do not appear to be working very hard.

The hierarchical relationship that exists among faculty in higher education creates various levels of engagement in teaching assignments, research productivity, and service commitments including multiple strains depending upon where you are in your career matriculation. The following will delineate teaching responsibilities among three distinctions of faculty ranks: assistant professors, associate professors, and full professors. An assistant professor is a recent Ph.D. recipient and who is primarily considered junior faculty with usually less than 5 years in the academy. The teaching load will typically be higher depending on the university with usually less advising responsibilities and service responsibilities. An associate faculty member is more seasoned, who earned their doctorate 5–7 years prior to receiving tenure and typically has some publications and an established service record within the university and the community at large. Finally, the rank of professor is the highest and most coveted ranking within the tenured faculty positions. A full professor has served the university with a significant number of years ranging from on average 10 years or more, has an established research agenda and publication record, as well as served on various departmental, school, and university committees and typically in an administrative capacity.

Research/scholarship is the faculty member's contribution to their field. It can include creative works, exhibitions, experimental research, grantsmanship, writing or reviewing articles and books, as well as presenting and attending professional meetings to remain current in one's field. For many the gold standard for disseminating this work is by publishing in peer-reviewed journals. And as indicated earlier, the mission of the university impacts the type of scholarship that is generally valued the most. For example, grantsmanship has become more significant at many institutions. As the cost of higher education has increased so has the desire to bring in more external funding to support faculty salaries and provide indirect costs recovery, which is the funding to support the operations necessary to fulfill the grant but are not identified as a part of the grant activity—such as lights and heating.

Lastly, there is service. Service involves the faculty member's involvement on the campus as well as away from campus. The primary obligation for faculty service is to sit on a plethora of committees as it is the faculty's responsibility to have domain over the program curricula. This vision of shared governance begins in the academic department and extends to the university level. Faculty are also actively engaged in the recruitment, retention, and promotion of their colleagues via the search committee and promotion as well as the tenure processes that exist at most institutions. In addition, faculty play a tremendous role in student life on campus. They generally serve not only as academic advisors but also as advisors for other groups like service or Greek life organizations as well as serving on disciplinary committees.

Distinctions of Faculty Expectations by University Typology

Although some standardization may be necessary to create a baseline, the type of university often dictates the actual roles of faculty. Thus, a "one-size-fits-all" is not a good analogy or best practice. This is no truer than in academe. All universities are not the same; they are commonly categorized as teaching or research institutions. This language has changed over the years and there are a number of categories that help to distinguish universities from one another. The Carnegie Classifications were first established in 1973 and developed to aid researchers that wanted to compare institutions (Carnegie Classifications, 2015a). The latest version of the classification system has eight categories: Doctoral Universities, Master's Colleges and Universities, Baccalaureate Colleges, Baccalaureate/Associates, Associate's Colleges, Special Focus: Two-Year, Special Focus: Four Year, and Tribal Colleges (Carnegie Classification, 2015b).

So when people refer to an institution as an R1 they are referring to a category within the Doctoral Universities classification. This classification ranks institutions based on their level of research—R1, R2, and R3, with R1s being the highest level. While doctoral universities only make up 7 percent of the more than 4,600 institutions in the United States, because of their size they enroll 32 percent of all students (Carnegie Classification, 2015b). This is important because an institution's classification largely reflects their mission. The expectations for faculty at R1s are very different than those at baccalaureate colleges. As aforementioned, faculty primarily are expected to teach, do research, and engage service. How this manifests itself varies depending on institutional mission. For example, the research productivity of faculty at a doctoral institution is "an index of departmental and institutional prestige and is strongly associated with an individual faculty member's reputation, visibility, and advancement in the academic reward structure" (Sax, Hagedorn, Arredondo, & Dicrisi, 2002). A "teaching" university is one where more emphasis is placed on faculty responsibilities to engage students in the classroom and other related duties, such as advising.

The Traditional Faculty Workweek

A typical day of the life of a teaching faculty member can best be explained by the following example provided. Arriving on campus and heading to your office to answer emails, meet students who have scheduled appointments, and/or attend a required meeting and encountering a student in the department who is looking for another faculty member. Being collegial you ask, "have you checked his/her office hours posted on the door, or did you knock on the door?" When asked these questions, student says, "No, I just got out of class early and decided to come over to discuss the class assignment." You are trying to get to your own office hours to complete your assigned tasks; however, you are compelled in some way to ensure that the student understands that we have posted office hours for a reason, typically because these are the times that we will sit with students in between teaching class, standing meetings, class preparation, and grading assignments. The student grimaces and states, "well this is the only time I can come because I have classes during her office hours and then I have work." You decide to assist the student and a 5-minute conversation turns into 20 minutes. Now the ripple effect of addressing this student's issues has now derailed the professor from other assigned tasks. And finally, the professor has to go to class. Next day, repeat.

We provide this example not as a complaint, but as an example to demonstrate that even outside of teaching, research, and service responsibilities, faculty are responsible for retention and graduation rates. So, if a student needs you—you help. By every measure imaginable, faculty work longer hours than most would believe based on the limited understanding of faculty work and the understanding that the average teaching load is 12 credit hours. So while faculty work is demanding, what most see as the ease of the job is really the flexibility of the job. Flexibility is one of the factors that helps to mitigate the impact the job has on family life (Jacobs and Winslow, 2004). Overwhelmingly, research supports that faculty generally work more than 40 hours per week. By all indications, faculty work between 50 and 60 plus hours per week (Flaherty, 2014; Jacobs, 2007). This long workweek includes weekends where some studies indicate 84.1 hours per week for male faculty and 89.3 for females (Jacobs, 2007). For example, Boise State faculty worked on average 54.4 hours per week, with about 58 percent of the time spent on teaching, 22 percent on research, and 20 percent on administrative and other tasks (Flaherty, 2014). According to the Digest of Education Statistics (2014), on average full-time faculty and instructional staff spent 58 percent of their time teaching in 2003, 20 percent on research and scholarship, and 22 percent on other activities. When researchers delve into discipline-specific work hours, they found that the number of hours remains relatively steady. For example, nursing faculty worked 53–56 hours per week (Ellis, 2013). Earlier in this article we mentioned that academicians are facing comparisons with those in the business world; nevertheless, when it comes to work hours, faculty are working more hours than many professionals (Jacobs, 2007; *Time spent working by full- and part-time status, gender, and location in 2014: The economics daily: U.S. Bureau of labor statistics,* 2015).

Typical Workload Formula

Allen (1997) defines workload as a "composite of all professional tasks per-formed by faculty: teaching or instructional activities, class preparation, research, administration, and public service" (p. 27). The American Associa-tion of University Professors (AAUP) reported that the general workload is distributed with 40 percent of time teaching, 40 percent on research, and 20 percent on service. This represents a change from the AAUP's 1994 study in which 40 to 65 percent of faculty time was focused on teaching (site 2000 and 1994). Likewise, the AAUP recommends that the maximum workload for undergraduate faculty should be 12 credit hours per semester and 9 credit hours for graduate level instruction.

So there is some recommended uniformity but is that recommendation appropriate for all institutions or all academic programs? The authors believe that it is, in part, this one-size-fits-all philosophy that contributes to the feel-ing of being overworked. There is little evidence to support that the AAUP recommendations are the most effective formula to accomplish the mission and goals of individual institutions or programs (Ellis, 2013). For example, Boise State implemented a policy that professors should teach 60 percent of the time (Flaherty, 2014). Whereas another study found that music educa-tion faculty should actually encompass less teaching and more service and research (Chandler, 2012). Consequently, when the workload is developed with the discipline and the mission of the institution in mind, faculty actually view their workload as "equitable and manageable" (Voignier, Hermann, & Brouse, 1998).

Subsequently, one of the best ways to combat the feeling of being over-worked is to really spend some time exploring workload allocations based on discipline and mission. The transparency that can come from the pro-cess may indeed be key to how faculty feel about their work. Now this is not to say that faculty do not work an inordinate number of hours as previously mentioned but it may indicate as to why we do it. The why is important because some of it is self-imposed. As faculty, we decide what is on our syllabus, have complete autonomy over the curriculum, decide what encompasses our research agenda, and choose to work at the type of institution that supports the level of scholarly activity. Lastly, while service is expected, the variety of service on a campus varies from highly engaged committee work to serving as a University Marshal at commencement (once or twice an academic year). This goes to the flexibility discussed earlier. The flexibility is not just about time or hours worked but is about working in a profession that really does allow you to decide a great many things. Some will read this portion of the chapter and totally disagree with the authors; however, think about the last time you tried to explain tenure or academic freedom to someone outside of the academy only to have them say, "Wow! A job for life unless you screw it up and you can say what you want for the most part!" The authors do not say this to demonize faculty, we say it to remember what a great profession it really is.

The Problem of Balance

The problem is a lack of balance that is appropriate for each institution and degree program. So are faculty overworked—yes some are but like any other industry there are others that are not working very hard at all. In this case, the public scrutiny is correct. The authors are not asserting that those teaching a workload less than 12 credit hours (or 9 at the graduate level) are not working at an appropriate rate that meets or even exceeds their university mission and goals, what we are saying is that just as there is no evidence to say that those teaching at AAUP recommended levels aren't being efficient with their time there is also no evidence that teaching more than 12 or 9 credit hours is not efficient either.

The prevailing wisdom would say that the competition is between teaching and research. In a recent meeting with faculty about not teaching overloads because it diminishes their research if they are provided a course reduction for such, one of the authors was told, "well nobody ever tells me that's too much service or advising." After thinking about his statement, it was clear he was wrong. There have been occasions in which that was exactly the message, especially with an ABD faculty and newly hired tenure track faculty. But he was probably right in that no one had ever told *him* he was doing too much—why? Maybe because he was not doing more than his peers but simply felt like it, or it is simply accepted that service and advising students comes with the territory at that particular type of institution or maybe he was doing the kind of low engagement service discussed earlier—important but not very taxing on one's schedule.

The expectations for research and scholarship have increased over time and not just at R1 universities. According to Leslie (2002), this began in the middle of the nineteenth century when institutions began to "expect faculty to achieve specialized training in a discipline." Institutions that never worried about publications or grants in the past have full scholarship definitions for tenure and promotion and while many emphasize teaching and service as indicators of the likelihood of getting tenure without the minimal levels of scholarship they are far less likely than someone who is not at great at teaching or did minimal levels of service.

The data shows that faculty like teaching; however, they would like more time for research and after tenure that level of teaching generally lessens; however, service tends to increase (Chandler & Russell, 2012; Emmert & Rollman, 1997; Leslie, 2002; Porter & Umbach, 2001). Some even believe that the greater emphasis on research has impacted the quality of teaching especially at the undergraduate level (Wolverton, 1998). This has been referred to as the "academic ratchet," which explains how the shift toward academic specialty and embracing a more "entrepreneurial spirit" has negatively impacted the academic curriculum (Zemsky & Massy, 1990). This ratchet has overly emphasized reward for research and scholarship and reduced the amount of time devoted to teaching.

The Balancing Act

The authors believe balance is needed. The conversations about the number of hours in which faculty work or the percentage of time spent is not nearly as important as the impact faculty are having. So while we do not dismiss the use of helpful tools like the Delaware Study of Instructional Costs and Productivity and increased efforts in managing teaching loads as well as resources, the balance between teaching, research, and service cannot be denied. It is critical that faculty teach students as that is the very core of every university's mission. The question is how do we do that? We do it by being really good at what we teach and we do that by being immersed in our disciplines and understanding what our students need to know for life after graduation and giving them opportunities to engage in the application of that knowledge.

The 1998 article by Krahenbuhl, *Faculty Work Integrating Responsibilities and Institutional Needs*, lays out the perspective of the authors. And while he references research universities, the authors believe that this can also apply to liberal arts institutions that have embraced undergraduate research. The public view of teaching, research, and service depicts the three as separate entities (see Chart 13.1).

Chart 13.1. The Public View of Faculty Work.
Source: Gary Krahenbuhl, Faculty Work, Change © 1998 UK: Taylor & Francis, Ltd.
Reprinted by Permission of the Author.

However, research and service do not take away from teaching; on the contrary, they improve it. Chart 13.2 illustrates how students are enriched by the natural overlap of the three major areas of faculty work. The sections labeled "A" and "B" represent learning opportunities. Higher education institutions must embrace a culture where knowledge generation produces chances for "shared discovery and student learning." And, the activities that result in section "C" demonstrate integrated knowledge transmission and application. As indicated in the chart, Krahenbuhl utilizes service learning; however, it could just as well be internships, clinical, or fieldwork.

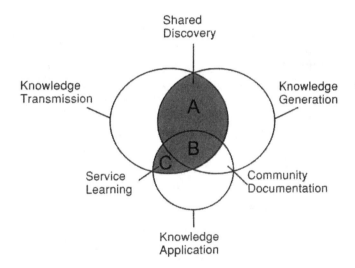

Chart 13.2. The Integration of Knowledge Transmission with Knowledge Generation and/or Application.
Source: Gary Krahenbuhl, Faculty Work, Change © 1998 UK: Taylor & Francis, Ltd.
Reprinted by Permission of the Author.

Faculty members know that students learn inside as well as outside of the classroom so engagement in research enhances learning; hands-on application and the like help students apply what they have learned. Faculty also know that when students participate in these types of activities, it creates a memorable experience for them. It is what Benjamin Franklin meant when he said, "Tell me and I forget. Teach me and I remember. Involve me and I learn." This level of student learning outcomes can be undervalued when too much emphasis is placed solely on classroom teaching.

There has to be a balanced approach with emphasis on the full complement of faculty work and appropriate evaluation of that work so that it is rewarded in a manner that aligns with the university mission (Colbeck, 2002). Unfortunately, the more time we spend on *just* teaching—the visible more well-known activity of faculty, the less likely students will get what they really need to be successful after graduation.

Krahenbuhl (1998) notes that other occupations understand the integration of work activities. As an example of this, he asserts that most surgeons spend a relatively small amount of their day in surgery, but they spend a great deal of time "seeing patients, continuing medical education, and service to the hospital board or AMA is important to his or her professional development and practice." Not only do those in the field of medicine understand this hypothesis but those outside of medicine understand it as well. It proves to be a great illustration of how faculty work is not and cannot just be about teaching in the classroom and how many hours that activity is performed. The research shows that faculty already do this—integrate their work roles—the failure is that others do not generally see it because they do not understand the nature of faculty work. With that said, we must do a better job of educating them as well.

References

1992 Higher Education Reauthorization Act.

Allen, H. L. (1997). *Faculty workload and productivity: Ethnic and gender disparities* (pp. 25–42). NEA 1997 Almanac of Higher Education. Washington, DC: National Education Association.

American Association of University Professors. (1994). The work of faculty: Expectations, priorities, and rewards. *Academe, 80*(1), 35–48.

American Association of University Professors. (2000). Interpretive comments on the statement on faculty workload (Committee on Colleges and University Teaching, Research, and Publications). *Academe, 8*(5), 69–72.

Carnegie Classifications. (2015a). Retrieved November 20, 2016 from http://carnegie classifications.iu.edu/

Carnegie Classification. (2015b, October 15, 2016). *Updated facts and figures.* Retrieved from http://carnegieclassifications.iu.edu/downloads/CCIHE2015-FactsFigures.pdf

Chandler, K. W. (2012). A comparison of contracted and ideal music education faculty workload. *Bulletin of the Council for Research in Music Education, 193,* 77. doi:10.5406/bulcouresmusedu.193.0077

Colbeck, C. L. (2002). Integration: Evaluating faculty work as a whole. *New Directions for Institutional Research, 2002*(114), 43–52. doi:10.1002/ir.45

Ellis, P. A. (2013). A comparison of policies on nurse faculty workload in the United States. *Nursing Education Perspectives, 34*(5), 303–309. doi:10.5480/1536-5026-34.5.303

Emmert, P., & Rollman, S. A. (1997). A national survey of tenure and promotion standards in communication departments. *Journal of the Association for Communication Administration, 26,* 10-23.

Flaherty, C. (2014). *Research shows professors work long hours and spend much of day in meetings.* Accessed October 8, 2016. Retrieved from https://www.insidehighered.com/news/2014/04/09/research-shows-professors-work-long-hours-and-spend-much-day-meetings

Flannery, M. E. (2015). *Who can afford a college degree today?* Accessed November 10, 2016. Retrieved from http://neatoday.org/2015/08/17/who-can-afford-a-coll ege-degree-today/

Jacobs, J. A. (2007). Faculty workloads in higher education. In B. Bank (Ed.), *Gender and education: An encyclopedia.* Santa Barbara, CA: ABC-CLIO. Retrieved from http:// bluehawk.monmouth.edu:2048/login?,   url=http://search.credoreference.com/ content/entry/abcge/faculty_workloads_in_higher_education/0

Jacobs, J. A., & Winslow, S. E. (2004). Overworked faculty: Job stresses and family demands. *The Annals of the American Academy of Political and Social Science, 596,* 104–129.

Krahenbuhl, G. S. (1998). Faculty work: Integrating responsibilities and institutional needs. *Change: The Magazine of Higher Learning, 30*(6), 18–25. doi:10.1080/00091389809602651

Leslie, D. W. (2002). Resolving the dispute: Teaching is academe's core value. *The Journal of Higher Education, 73*(1), 49–73. doi:10.1353/jhe.2002.0008

Middaugh, M. F. (2001). *Understanding faculty productivity: Standards and benchmarks for colleges and universities.* San Francisco, CA: Jossey-Bass.

Porter, S. R., & Umbach, P. D. (2001). Analyzing faculty workload data using multilevel modeling. *Research in Higher Education, 42*(2), 171–196. Sax, L. J., Hagedorn, L. S., Arredondo, M., & Dicrisi III, F. A. (2002). *Research in Higher Education, 43*(4), 423–446. doi:10.1023/a:1015575616285

Snyder, T., & Dillow, S. (2016). *Digest of education statistics 2014* (50th ed.). Accessed November 1, 2016. Retrieved from http://nces.ed.gov/pubs2016/2016006.pdf

Thomason, A. (2015). *Average student debt climbed higher in 2014, study finds.* Accessed November 20, 2016. Retrieved from http://www.chronicle.com/blogs/ticker/average-student-debt-climbed-higher-in-2014-study-finds/106084

Time spent working by full- and part-time status, gender, and location in 2014: The economics daily: U.S. Bureau of labor statistics. (2015). Accessed November 13, 2016. Retrieved from http://www.bls.gov/opub/ted/2015/time-spent-working-by-full-and-part-time-status-gender-and-location-in-2014.htm

Voignier, R., Hermann, C., & Brouse, S. (1998). Development of a faculty workload formula: The teaching component. *Nurse Educator, 23*(4), 35–39.

Wolverton, M. (1998). Treading the tenure-track tightrope: Finding balance between research excellence and quality teaching. *Innovative Higher Education, 23*(1), 61–79.

Zemsky, R., & Massy, W. (1990). Cost containment: Committing to a new economic reality. *Change, 22*(6), 16–22.

14. Faculty Work Life: Beyond the Tipping Point

SEAN ROBINSON

Within the past several decades, American colleges and universities have found themselves within a rapidly shifting context. These shifts have been not only philosophical, but also economic; driven by neoliberalism ideology and the ideas of marketization and managerialism, the idea of higher education as a public good has been replaced by the idea that higher education is a private good and is an investment on the part of individuals (Larabee, 1997). These shifts have introduced the notion of market forces into the higher education arena, which includes a newfound focus on competitiveness, efficiency, the relationship between resources to job performance, the restructuring of employment relationships and organizations themselves, and increased accountability measures. The impact within the academy is what Cummings and Finkelstein (2012) refer to as a diversified academic workforce, as seen by increasingly specialized job functions, differentiated career patterns and paths, and vastly different disciplinary backgrounds and work experiences. Given the changing context of higher education the purpose of this chapter is to discuss the impact such a neoliberal, market-driven environment has upon faculty, what I consider to be the true tipping of life in the academy. It is my position that the stronghold of managerialism and new measures of accountability within institutions greatly impact the character and quality of academic work along with the very nature of academic careers (in less than positive ways).

Faculty Workload Challenges

A number of scholars have documented the ways that faculty work has shifted over time, including increased financial constraints, additional accountability measures, an increase in managerial and administrative staff, the commodification of higher education, and changes in both student and faculty profiles (Cummings & Finkelstein, 2012; Gappa, Austin, & Trice, 2007; Schuster & Finkelstein, 2006). In response to these pressures, faculty have been expected to adapt their teaching, research, and service responsibilities and to rethink their roles within institutions. As Evans (2009) contends, faculty have become increasingly concerned about their ability to achieve balance, and to meet the ever-increasing challenges that confront them on a daily basis.

Drawing from the research exploring trends over the past three decades (Cummings & Finkelstein, 2012; Schuster & Finkelstein, 2006), it is clear that faculty are engaged in teaching more, while research productivity has decreased, in part due to diminishing resources, but also as a factor of an increase in demands on faculty time. As one example, James Lang (2005) describes the difficulty he had in his early years in a tenure-track job, teaching a four/three load, helping to raise two small children, and maintaining a disciplined writing schedule, to which he constantly had trouble adhering. Rice, Sorcinelli, and Austin (2000) contend that early career faculty cite as one of their primary stressors finding enough time to do all of their work; Gappa et al. (2007) found that this is not just for early career faculty, but that faculty at all ranks are faced with increased expectations for higher levels of productivity. One of the reasons for this *tipping point* stems directly from the neoliberal policies and practices that have found their way into all forms of higher education, most often represented by an increased focus on managerialism. This shift in perspective of the university as a business has resulted in structures, policies, and practices that require institutions to provide "services" to "clients." As Gumport (1997) postulated, the end result here under a "new" managerialism is that faculty work has morphed to serve the institution's managerial and corporate ends, and is no longer designed to serve historic vocational purposes; nor is such an enterprise seen any more as a public good. Furthermore, while many faculty are finding ways to work smarter out of necessity, they also appear to be working harder and longer.

The New Managerialism

As colleges and universities work to increase their reputation and ranking within a global environment, one way to gain a competitive edge is through the establishment of corporate structures and practices as a way to increase efficiency and effectiveness. This notion of corporate managerialism, driven by external market forces, represents a new normal in terms of university governance and administration. According to Geurts and Maassen (2005), institutional governance includes "the rules, structures and enforcement mechanisms...to do with the preparation of the decisions, the actual decision-making process and the implementation of the decisions taken" (p. 35). In exploring faculty perceptions and views of their environment, Geurts and Maassen found that academics had control over their basic teaching and research activities, but had little control over their actual working environment. In addition, the academics in their study had little involvement in governance and decision-making activities. Given the dissonance experienced, it is fair to assume that institutions are more likely to be operating from a top-down approach, maintain cumbersome bureaucratic and administrative processes and practices, and hold forth a strong performance-oriented culture. Since these very traits are often associated with managerialism (Deem & Brehony, 2005), it is no wonder that corporate culture and managerialism are seen as being incongruous with collegiality among faculty.

Managerialism has been defined as involving an "incorporation of approaches, systems, and techniques commonly found in the private sector, to the management and conduct of the public sector" (Anderson, 2006, p. 578). Anderson (2008) further contends that managerialism involves a "more muscular management style, an emphasis on particular forms of accountability, the development of a market orientation, a focus on securing non-government funding, and an increased concern with issues of efficiency and economy" maintained through "performance management schemes, quality assurance mechanisms, the restructuring of academic departments, and the implementation of budgetary devolution" (pp. 251–252). These set of practices that correspond to the nature of managerialism appear to be related directly to the ideas of neoliberalism, within which individuals advocate for the inherent efficiency of market-based services, including the provision of education. But as Levi-Faur and Jordana (2005) maintain, "The era of neoliberalism is also the golden age of regulation," with new regulatory systems in place that create and enforce marketization and corporatization of public services (p. 6).

The set of neoliberal managerialism practices help provide the context for the new focus on restructuring, new regulations, state and federal funding cuts, increases in academic workloads, job stress, job dissatisfaction, and the turn to corporate discourses and behaviors. With an ever-increasing reliance on student tuition as the financial driver, institutions across the country are in an arms race to maximize their status and reputation, while keeping tuition and overall costs low, which in turn necessitates greater accountability by administrators, and by faculty "doing more with less" (Schuster & Finkelstein, 2006). The work of faculty thus occurs not just in the context of corporate, managerialistic practices, but also one in which students are positioned as customers and clients, who are now concerned with maximizing their individual employment skill set and job prospects, rather than being educated as well-rounded, global citizens or scholars (Brule, 2004).

Changes to the Student Demographic

What does such a managerialistic and consumeristic shift on the part of institutions and students alike mean for faculty? Certainly one of the biggest changes comes in the form of student demographics as well as in sheer numbers. Student enrollments at all levels continue to grow, which means that faculty are confronted with a student body more diverse in backgrounds, experiences, expectations, and college readiness than ever before. According to the U.S. Department of Education National Center for Education Statistics (2016a), between 2003 and 2013, enrollment increased 20%, from 16.9 million to 20.4 million. Much of the growth between 2003 and 2013 was in full-time enrollment; the number of full-time students rose 22%, while the number of part-time students rose 18%. In this same time period, undergraduate enrollment rose 21% overall, from 14.5 million to 17.5 million and post-baccalaureate enrollment rose 19% from 2.4 million to 2.9 million (NCES, 2016b). In terms of changing student populations, from 2005 to 2015, there was an 84% increase in the number of international students enrolling in US institutions, from 564,766 to 1,043,839, with roughly 43% of these students coming from countries in Asia and the Pacific Rim (Institute for International Education, 2015).

Beyond the continued growth of the student body, there are additional changes that impact faculty. Students are expecting their individual programs and courses to be more relevant and more convenient than ever before. This means that faculty members are required to have at their ready a new set of skills, knowledge, and technology to support the breadth of student expectations and needs. Faculty members themselves are challenged to stay abreast of exponentially growing knowledge and new research in their individual domains, thus ensuring students' learning is indeed relevant and up-to-date. Faculty members are increasingly called upon to cross-disciplinary boundaries, thus necessitating an understanding of several disciplinary contexts. New technologies for research, collaboration, communication, and teaching require constant monitoring and training to stay abreast of the fast-paced developments in the IT arena. Finally, faculty must also become ever more knowledgeable about the cultures from which their students are coming to campus, and be prepared to spend more time teaching basic skills of critical reading and critical writing, especially for those international students with limited English proficiency enrolling in US institutions. The shift in student demographics could help to account for part of the growth in hours spent on teaching with the corresponding decline in hours spent on research, as reported by Cummings and Finkelstein (2012).

The Administrative Bloat of Faculty

Clearly, students are becoming more diverse, which requires more effort by faculty to meet the needs of students, while also fulfilling their basic research and service requirements, along with their increasing administrative responsibilities. As Altbach (2007) has said, "The traditional job of the professor is expanding to include entirely new kinds of responsibilities" (p. 153), beyond teaching, research, and service. The various tasks by faculty are becoming more diversified, and the growing demands are coming from different directions, including students, administrators, boards, legislators, funding agencies, and even employers alike. Indeed, the diversified activities and new demands foisted upon faculty by managerially, corporate oriented administrators have changed the balance between responsibilities, and seem to contribute to increases in stress and job dissatisfaction (Musselin, 2007).

Almost two decades ago, Currie and Vidovich (1998) documented the beginnings of increased managerialism. In their study comparing US institutions with Australian ones, they reported academics' perceptions of changes in university governments from more collegial models toward more corporate-managerial ones, which included smaller and frequently less representative decision-making bodies. Faculty discussed earlier participatory management styles versus current bureaucratic top-down managerial styles which had become the norm. Their study illustrates a complex relationship between collegiality and top-down managerial decision-making, with the general trend over time toward the latter, which suggests a higher degree of accountability and a potential silencing of academic faculty within universities.

Ranson (2003) defines accountability within managerialism as "a social practice pursuing particular purposes, defined by distinctive relationships and evaluative procedures" (p. 462). Accountability for academics can be seen in annual performance reviews, prescribed performance indicators, quality audits, graduate surveys, student evaluations, grants received, research publications, and teaching assessments. Within the neoliberal environments there has been an acceleration of these trends and metrics. According to Welch (2005),

The professor is also being pressured to account for their activities including ways in which they expend their resources and more detailed ways. This has given rise to something of an international cottage industry of developing and implementing so-called quality assurance mechanisms of higher education, although in practice many academics see little if any positive relationship between such exercises and games and quality. (p. 206)

Clearly, as Welch portends, there is a growing presence of external market forces and internal governance pressures that are impacting the work life of faculty, including workload issues and level of satisfaction as additional research suggests (e.g., Gappa et al., 2007; Jacobs & Winslow, 2004).

One of the primary ways that neoliberalism and marketization is showing up is in the various funding mechanisms within institutions. According to a report by the Pew Foundation (2015), a major shift has occurred in the relative levels of funding provided by states and the federal government in recent years. By 2010, federal revenue per full-time equivalent (FTE) student surpassed that of states for the first time in at least two decades, after adjusting for enrollment and inflation. From 2000 to 2012, revenue per FTE student from federal sources going to public, nonprofit, and for-profit institutions grew by 32% in real terms, while state revenue fell by 37%. The number of FTE students at the nation's colleges and universities grew by 45% during the same period. According to most recent data, at public colleges and universities in 2013, revenue from federal sources made up only 16%, while state sources made up 21% of total revenue; 21% comes from tuition and fees, 21% from self-supporting operations, 8% from private gifts endowments, and investments, 8% from other sources, and only 4% from local revenue (Pew Charitable Trusts, 2015). What these numbers suggest is that state support is on the decline, with most federal revenue coming in the form of research grants, Pell grants, subsidized student loans, and veterans' educational benefits. Given the decline in public funding, institutions must focus on revenue generation and resource allocation—increases in student tuition, commercialization of research, and the increase use of contract faculty over full-time tenure-track/tenured faculty. Likewise, institutions must also strive for maximum efficiency in such a competitive marketplace, which often translates into greater workloads for those full-time tenure-track/tenured faculty.

Changing Workforce, Changing Workload

In discussing the impact of managerialism on higher education, it is important to consider how faculty work has actually shifted in the past several decades. According to the *1992 Carnegie International Survey of the*

Academic Professions (Altbach, 1996), faculty reported working an average of 40–42 hours a week in the late 1970s to early 1980s. This rose sharply during the 1980s to almost 50 hours per week, with approximately 25% indicating that they worked more than 55 hours per week. Most of this rise could be attributed to the increase in research and scholarship activities; of note, however, is that this also coincided with a small decrease in the number of hours devoted to teaching. This is also the period when *U.S. News and World Report* began issuing rankings, drawing attention to such factors as faculty credentials, research productivity, and external grants received, which served to focus national attention on individual campuses that were able to attract the best and brightest students. The 1990s saw a slight correction to the research–teaching split, as legislators began to focus on undergraduate education once more, which resulted in both greater teaching loads for faculty and a slight decline in research productivity.

In their analysis of the changing academic profession from 1992 to 2007, Cummings and Finkelstein (2012) found a slight decline in actual working hours, to an average of 48 hours per week. But what is striking in their research is that time devoted to teaching increased by 12%, but that time spent on research activities declined by more than 27%. This decline in time spent on research and scholarship is evident in a 33% decline in actual research output (i.e., publications). Thus, two trends are clear regarding the primary nature of faculty work: while the teaching emphasis continues to grow, conceivably in part because of increasing student enrollments, resources and time spent on research have decreased. These trends are corroborated by other researchers as well (e.g., Schuster & Finkelstein, 2006).

Some of this shift in time spent on particular activities may be due in part to the rise of full-time nontenure-track, contract faculty who occupy specialized roles. According to Kezar (2013), part-time adjuncts represent 50% of all faculty in higher education, and are engaged almost exclusively in teaching activities; in addition, full-time nontenure-track faculty represent almost 20% of the workforce and a vast majority of these faculty (70%) are also focused primarily on teaching. Thus, roughly 30% of all higher education faculty are tenure-track/tenured, and are responsible for carrying out all of the duties typically associated with faculty life—teaching, research, and service, coupled with an increasing array of administrative activities once evenly distributed among more faculty. In fact, Schuster and Finkelstein (2006) trace the restructuring of academic work and careers that has occurred over the past several decades and document the decline in support staff including clerical, technical, and para-professional employees and the increase in professional, executive, and managerial staff, which has accompanied the shift in responsibilities among faculty. Among these responsibilities are escalating involvement in departmental affairs and administration and within campus-wide committees, task forces, and governance bodies; roughly 90% of faculty report being involved at the departmental level, up from 60%, whereas only 40% report being involved at the campus level (Schuster & Finkelstein). Given that less than one-third of faculty are considered "regular" faculty, it is no wonder that the burden has shifted so that fewer faculty are bearing greater responsibility for governance and administrative tasks; it's also no wonder that more faculty unions are now crafting stipulations around workload issues.

In considering the impact of neoliberalism and managerialism upon faculty work life, it is necessary to also consider faculty satisfaction. There is a social and historical construction to the concept of work satisfaction, but that satisfaction with work had indeed declined in the 1990s and 2000s. Past studies on work life satisfaction and well-being of faculty have found that while faculty are relatively happy with the intrinsic nature of their work, such as autonomy and flexibility, many faculty are unhappy with the extrinsic aspects of their jobs, namely rewards, promotion, and recognition (Houston, Meyer, & Paewai, 2006). Nonetheless, there is still a stronghold belief that neoliberal trends and ideologies have not delivered such freedom and flexibility, but has instead enacted greater bureaucratic policies and practices, supporting arguments that the greatest drivers of decreasing work satisfaction are an increased workload and perceived loss of control (Gappa et al., 2007). It may very well be that many well-intentioned efforts by university administrators could actually be undermined by the general effects of neoliberalism and managerialism.

Conclusion

As I have suggested in this chapter, neoliberal ideologies and managerialistic practices have caused the work life of faculty as a whole to reach a "tipping point" wherein the balance among teaching, research, and service obligations has shifted, and faculty responsibilities now include a preponderance of administrative duties and accountability measures. This in turn has created what some see as a diversified workforce along functions, career patterns, and background/experience (e.g., Cummings & Finkelstein, 2012). For those 30% of the faculty fortunate to be among the tenure-track/tenured, they will certainly be shouldering more of the burden and responsibility for program administration, decision-making, and institutional governance, thereby raising the overall workload for this sizable minority of faculty.

The challenges faculty face stem in part from changing funding structures coupled with pressures for privatization and marketization, new corporate structures and practices, increased accountability, and decreased autonomy (Welch, 2005). Most, if not all, of these have been spurred on by neoliberalist shifts toward greater efficiency and effectiveness. Today's increasingly diversified faculty body, who believe that there are imperatives for faculty to do more (Schuster & Finkelstein, 2006), continue to take on more roles and responsibilities, and seem to experience greater faculty stress and less job satisfaction than in prior generations of faculty. The golden age of the "university professor" has now passed, and academic faculty now face a shifting frontier, one not driven by their own passion for teaching, quest for basic research answers, or love of esoteric subject matter, but one driven by institutional goals, managerial directives, and external measures of productivity and efficiency. A sense of loss, or even nostalgia is sure to permeate the ranks of senior faculty, as institutions of higher education continue to embrace even more managerial and corporate approaches to the business of education. It is clear that a transformation is under way within higher education, and with this is a significant impact on academic faculty. Time will tell if the changes to our institutions do indeed create sustainable, efficient practices that serve not only the institutions themselves, but society as a whole.

References

Altbach, P. (1996). *The international academic profession: Portraits of fourteen countries.* Princeton, NJ: Carnegie Foundation for the Advancement of Teaching.

Altbach, P. (2007). *Tradition and transition: The international imperative in higher education.* Chestnut Hill, MA: CIHE/Boston College.

Anderson, G. (2006). Carving out time and space in the managerial university. *Journal of Organizational Change, 19*(5), 578–592.

Anderson, G. (2008). Mapping academic resistance in the managerial university. *Organization, 15*(2), 251–270.

Brule, E. (2004). Going to market: Neoliberalism and the social construction of the university student as an autonomous consumer. In M. Reimer (Ed.), *Inside the corporate U: Women in the academy speak out* (pp. 255–281). Toronto: Sumach Press.

Cummings, W., & Finkelstein, M. (2012). *Scholars in the changing American academy.* New York, NY: Springer.

Currie, J. and Vidovich, L. (1998). Microeconomical reform through managerialism in American and Australian universities. In J. Currie and J. Newson (Eds.), *Universities and Globalization. Critical Perspectives (pp. 153–172).* Thousand Oaks/London/New Delhi: Sage Publications.

Deem, R., & Brehony, K. (2005). Management as ideology: The case of 'new managerialism' in higher education. *Oxford Review of Education, 31*(2), 217–235.

Evans, D. (2009, September 14). Redefining faculty roles. *The Chronicle of Higher Education*. Retrieved from http://www.chronicle.com/blogs/onhiring/redefining-faculty-roles/8016

Gappa, J., Austin, A., & Trice, A. (2007). *Rethinking faculty work: Higher education's strategic imperative*. San Francisco, CA: John Wiley & Sons.

Geurts, P., & Maassen, P. (2005). Academics and institutional governance. In A. Welch (Ed.), *The professoriate* (pp. 35–58). Dordrecht: Springer.

Gumport, P. (1997). Academic restructuring: Organizational change and institutional imperatives. *Higher Education, 39*, 67–91.

Houston, D., Meyer, L., & Paewai, S. (2006). Academic staff workloads and job satisfaction: Expectations and values in academe. *Journal of Higher Education Policy and Management, 28*(1), 17–30.

Institute of International Education. (2015). *Project Atlas: International Students in the United States*. Retrieved from http://www.iie.org/Services/Project-Atlas/United-States/International-Students-In-US#.WGE041MrKpo

Jacobs, J. A., & Winslow, S. E. (2004). Overworked faculty: Job stresses and family demands. *The Annals of the American Academy of Political and Social Science, 596*, 104–129.

Kezar, A. (2013). *Changing faculty workforce models*. New York, NY: TIAA Institute. Retrieved from https://www.tiaainstitute.org/public/pdf/changing-faculty-workforce-models.pdf

Lang, J. M. (2005). *Life on the tenure track: Lessons from the first year*. Baltimore, MD: The Johns Hopkins University Press.

Larabee, D. (1997). Public goods, private goods: The American struggle over educational goals. *American Educational Research Journal, 34*, 39–81.

Levi-Faur, F. J., & Jordana, J. (2005). Preface: The makings of a new regulatory order. *The Annals of the American Academy of Political and Social Science, 598*, 6–9.

Musselin, C. (2007). Transformation of academic work: facts and analysis. In M. Kogan & U. Teichler (Eds.), *Key challenges to the academic profession* (pp. 175–190). Paris: International Centre of Higher Education Research, University of Kassel.

Pew Charitable Trusts. (2015). *ISSUE BRIEF: Federal and State Funding of Higher Education*. Philadelphia, PA: Pew Foundation. Retrieved from http://www.pewtrusts.org/en/research-and-analysis/issue-briefs/2015/06/federal-and-state-funding-of-higher-education

Ranson, S. (2003). Public accountability in the age of neoliberal governance. *Journal of Educational Policy, 18*(5), 459–480.

Rice, R., Sorcinelli, M., & Austin, A. (2000). *Heeding new voices: Academic careers for a new generation*. New Pathways Working Paper Series, No. 7. Washington, DC: American Association for Higher Education.

Schuster, J. H., & Finkelstein, M. J. (2006). *The American faculty: The restructuring of academic work and careers*. Baltimore, MD: The Johns Hopkins University Press.

U.S. Department of Education, National Center for Education Statistics. (2016a). *Digest of Education Statistics, 2014* (NCES 2016-006), Chapter 3. Retrieved from http://nces.ed.gov/programs/digest/d14/ch_3.asp

U.S. Department of Education, National Center for Education Statistics (2016b). *Digest of Education Statistics.* Total postbaccalaureate fall enrollment in degree-granting postsecondary institutions, by attendance status, sex of student, and control of institution: 1967 through 2025. Retrieved from http://nces.ed.gov/programs/digest/d15/tables/dt15_303.80.asp?current=yes

Welch, A. (2005). Conclusion: New millennium, new milieu? In A. Welch (Ed.), *The professoriate* (pp. 205–215). Dordrecht, the Netherlands: Springer.

Part Eight: What Should Be the Role of Faculty in Shared Governance?

In "Faculty Governance as a Thorny Problem," Michael T. Miller and Everett A. Smith tackle the complex question of how to include today's faculty in shared governance and policy-making. They trace the half-century of decline in faculty involvement and, as a possible solution, look toward more collaborative approaches between campus administrators and teachers. Important concerns about student rights, legal restraints, and accountability restrict how far faculty can be involved, as have public stereotypes about the so-called "aberrant" professor. Ultimately, Miller and Smith seek a new model for faculty governance that is broad and stable enough to serve both institutional and individual goals and interests.

In "The Erosion of Faculty Governance," Dilys Schoorman profiles the continuing decline of faculty participation in shared governance. In a kind of schizotypal paradox, faculty seem to call for a democratic, collegial governing process, but also want a highly structured arrangement for institutional management. Increasing bureaucratization and corporatization constitute their weightiest challenges. Suggesting that faculty participation is the exception rather than the rule, Schoorman calls for radical action: faculty need to create a fuller identity and become more like public intellectuals on accountability and oversight of curricular matters. Dialogue across difference and genuine representation should be central to faculty voice: the waging of a common, collective struggle that requires faculty to assume more institutional stewardship.

15. Faculty Governance as a Thorny Problem

MICHAEL T. MILLER AND EVERETT A. SMITH

Higher education, as a set of institutions and as an industry, continues to evolve and change to meet different demands. Campuses have physically changed to reflect consumer preferences, business operations have increased efficiencies, and the entire operation of curriculum management has become technology-based (Miller & Nadler, 2016). State and federal governments and other governing bodies have advocated for student rights, with even the Obama administration advocating for a clear disclosure of college-related costs and debt information. At the state level, legislators and coordinating bodies have advocated for improved access to institutions and success rates for students, forcing states to develop articulation agreements between community and four-year colleges and requiring institutions to offer courses on a regular basis so that students can graduate in four years. State policy makers engage in these activities because they perceive that faculty members and institutional leaders regularly and consistently inhibit student progress. Generations of literature on the professoriate seem to support allegations of inefficiency and bureaucratic bloat (Cahn, 2011; Campbell, 2000; Professor X, 1973).

The idea of inefficient higher education can be traced to multiple issues, including inappropriate stakeholder demands, the distractions of college sports (Sperber, 2001), marketing that responds to personal comforts rather than intellectual pursuits (Greene, Kisida, & Mills, 2010), and, ultimately, leader aspirations that may or may not reflect a public good-driven agenda (Sibley, 1998). And as administrators, college leaders, and policy makers fumble through the discussions of higher education's purpose, the college faculty member has been left to use self-determination as a guiding ideology. This notion of self-determination means that faculty members have largely driven curricular requirements, scheduling, and admission standards and processes. This self-determination has become problematic on multiple fronts, specifically including the evolution of the academy to embrace technology and efficiency measures that are common in most other industries (Halsted, 2015).

Higher education institutions have become complex, multibillion dollar industries that rely on technologically sophisticated programs to manage millions of students. With over 15 million students enrolled throughout higher education in the United States alone (Hammond, 2015), data management systems have become critical to institutional operations. These management systems regulate classroom assignments based on instructional needs and class size; they regulate enrollment timelines (giving preferences to students who need certain enrollments the most); they control temperatures in buildings based on when they are scheduled to be used; they monitor and compute the impact of published research; and among many other tasks, they monitor and report student progress. In the contemporary higher education institution, the student experience has changed from being faculty-driven to being faculty-assisted (Miller & Nadler, 2016).

Today's college faculty member is engaged in a variety of tasks and activities; and increasingly, these activities are of a divergent nature. Offering instruction, for example, now includes expertise in multiple technological platforms in addition to interpersonal communication skills that engage a unique generation of college students, "The Millennials" (Howe & Strauss, 2007). Compounding new challenges for instruction, faculty must also be proficient in advising software, face a more competitive grant writing environment, and rely on their own self-directedness to keep track of massive advances in knowledge production. In short, faculty members are challenged more now than at any time in their history; and questions about their ability for self-government reflect these challenges.

The purpose of this discussion is to illustrate the difficulties of engaging contemporary faculty in shared governance activities, particularly highlighting the challenges of faculty behavior in institutional decision making.

Faculty Governance: Gone for Good?

The history of academic faculty members provides a story of teachers who initially undertook all of the responsibilities of creating and offering their lessons, in addition to operating the institution—including arranging for student housing, collecting and administering barters and tuition, finding students jobs upon their degree completion, and determining who would be admitted and when (Schuster & Finkelstein, 2006; Veysey, 1965). This holistic approach provided for a foundation of faculty-based decision making; the faculty *were* the institution and they had primary responsibility for all of their actions, content, and clientele. As society evolved to a more popula-tion-dense, complex environment of rapid knowledge production, the scope and role of the faculty member has, out of necessity, changed. Faculty members have become the providers of instruction and the leaders of research, and many faculty members have embraced this change to pursue their intellectual directions rather than worrying about institutional liabilities.

Faculty involvement in governance has generally seen nearly 50 years of decreased interest and activism, beginning with the end of the activist move-ment in the mid-1970s (Miller, 2003; Rosser, 2003). Although there have been ebbs in faculty governance activity, these bodies have generally taken on minor actions that have significance for a campus, but rarely have a major impact on institutional or state policy. For example, the faculty senate at Ala-bama's Jefferson State Community College (Armstrong, 1999) fought to have the Confederate flag removed from campus, an important action, but one distinctly outside of the academic enterprise for which the faculty mem-bers were hired. And recently the faculty at the University of Iowa protested and contested the hiring of the campus's president over his lack of academic experience, to no avail (Miller, 2016).

The primary question to be considered is defining the purpose for shared governance in the contemporary academy and what can be realistically expected from shared governance participants (Langland, 2011). In an ideal situation, faculty would contemplate significant issues and poll their constit-uents to have informed discussions about what is best for the collective, an approach to decision making rooted in the foundations of democracy (Birn-baum, 2004). The practice, however, has become one of serving self-inter-ests, territorialism on campus, and highly inefficient approaches to decision making, both in terms of timeliness and comprehensive constituent consider-ation (Gerber, 2014).

The overriding issue for shared governance, and faculty governance in particular, is only partially in the quality of implementation, but also resides in the organizational management of contemporary businesses and industries (Langland, 2011). And although there may be some dispute about the extent that a college or university is considered a "business," these organizations largely resemble the complex organizations that require software purchases, data security, police forces, capital facility construction, etc. This is to reflect that the $500 billion higher education enterprise is no longer the "mom and pop" shop where students can negotiate tuition prices individually with a professor and move into the president's basement!

Even the most cursory reflection on the state of higher education shows how compartmentalized the role of faculty members has become. Faculty members are expected to teach, conduct research, and provide service; and although these responsibilities are to be apportioned differently at different types of institutions, faculty are primarily employed to interact with students. With a hugely complex industry to operate, the ability of a faculty member to negotiate a data security contract or adequately review construction bond ratings seems both unimaginable and inappropriate. And as these elements of institutional life become central to how a college or university operates, the role of the faculty member seems best fitted to those of working with students (Rixom, 2011; Waugh, 2003).

The perceived tradition of shared governance does not allow for a relinquishing of shared governance opportunities; rather, the history of shared governance calls for a collaborative approach to making decisions and setting priorities among faculty and administrators (Jones, 2012). This means that the role of faculty in institutional decision making must be negotiated in a manner that allows faculty members to have a trusted and respected role in institutional life, and recognizes that these individuals can be unequipped for some of the managerial-related decisions that must be made for higher education.

The typical domain of shared governance falls within the framework of the academic life of an institution. Faculty members have historically developed admission standards for programs, curricular requirements, grading scales, etc. One major difficulty in the 21st century is that these decisions are integrated within larger contexts than what a faculty member has traditionally had to consider. For example, many institutions are part of larger, state-supported systems; and students transfer within those systems bring different types of transfer courses and skill levels upon completion of a course. Should, for example, a faculty member at one system-related institution be able to accept or deny a transfer course from another institution; and if so, which campus should have the right to determine some minimal level of course completion competence? Similarly, if institutions are to serve a state's interest, should faculty members be immune from these interests in determining a curriculum or making decisions about accepting out-of-state students ahead of in-state students?

A similar level of complexity surrounds even the most basic activity within the university, for example, enrollment periods for students. The rather simple task of logging into an enrollment management system and then selecting courses for which to register requires multiple complex judgments. For instance, should certain students holding a particular class level be given priority registration, suggesting that seniors who need a first opportunity to enroll in required classes to graduate be entitled to enroll first? And what about students with disabilities, student-athletes, students in honor societies, and students with lower graduate point averages who need additional academic help? These matters seem to have left the faculty ranks as a priority discussion and, instead, have become the domain of enrollment management and the campus registrar who consumes data to predict which model of enrollment period results in the highest level of retention and matriculation.

The complexity of institutional management does not necessarily preclude faculty members from being involved in institutional decision making, but it does challenge the fundamental assumption that faculty have the right, expertise, and authority to govern an institution (Miles, 1997). Further, such shared governance becomes problematic in a variety of dimensions, including the legal parameters that faculty can be involved in, ranging to the scope of state authority over which institutions are to operate. Indeed, it has been convincingly noted that the ideal shared governance to which so many faculty have alluded has in fact never existed (Baldridge, 1982). A selection of these dimensions is discussed in the next section of this chapter to illustrate how difficult a model of true shared governance might be in contemporary higher education.

Challenges of Faculty Governance

Legal Limitations

Perhaps one of the most significant issues restricting faculty involvement in governance are the legal parameters placed on rights to decision making. At least three significant legal decisions have influenced the ability of faculty to be involved in institutional decision making, including *Ballard v. Blunt, Connick v. Myers,* and *Harleston v. Jeffries.*

In *Ballard v. Blunt* (1983), a public employee's comments were taken into consideration during the employee's evaluation. The comments were outside of the realm of the individual's job expectations, but were critical of the organization. The court ruled that individual comments outside of specific job duties can be used in evaluations. Similarly, in *Connick v. Myers* (1983), the court determined that public employees do not have the right to make comments about areas of their employer that are not directly aligned with job responsibilities. These decisions were refined in *Harleston v. Jeffries* (1994) that, when applied, indicate that faculty members can make comments and judgments about their specific academic disciplines, but that these comments do not include judgments or public statements about the employer. In short, these decisions reflect a public thinking that faculty members can indeed comment on their disciplines, that is, about what they teach, but that this legal right does not extend to how the campus is operated (Miles, 1997).

The founding of the American Association of University Professors (AAUP) is consistent with the legal limitations of recent court decisions, specifically, that the AAUP was created to protect academic freedom and not necessarily to allow faculty to have leverage in institutional operations. Even the AAUP has a specific committee, Committee A, designed to help protect academic freedom, tenure, and due process; but the committee does not advocate for broad institutional control. An important element in this discussion is that tenure and academic freedom are vital to the creative scholarly role, but there is a serious question as to whether or not this extends to areas in which faculty have no formal knowledge, training, or even constituent-based rationale for decision making. Anthony (2004) reported consistent, mixed results as to whether shared governance made a difference in institutional performance.

Individual Behaviors

A faculty role is one that requires tremendous effort and dedication, one that is based on a demonstration of content mastery and skill in some specific area of effort, such as teaching or research. These types of skills, however, are not necessarily consistent with those necessary for management. This is not to suggest that faculty members are incapable of managing large complex operations, but at least one significant trend in higher education suggests that other types of experiences and skills are more apt in leading a large organization: the trend is toward hiring nonacademic higher education leaders (Braswell, 2006). And although some faculty groups will see this trend as a threat to their existence on campus, the other perspective is that there are a wide variety of needs for a contemporary university, and the person who provides the leadership and management of this enterprise must be well versed and understand not only the academic underpinnings of the institution, but also all of the other managerial aspects of institutional life.

There are also concerns, however, for some of the behaviors of faculty members that have been characterized by self-interest promotion rather than promoting the welfare of others (Cahn, 2011). The self-interest focus is not unique to the college faculty member and can readily be seen in the behaviors of elected officials in various statehouses, but the lack of altruism is particularly troubling when the realm of decision making and representation is limited to a few hundred acres and a single campus. Decision making can become what is in the best interests of a few or what is personal rather than representing the welfare of the whole. Such thinking is particularly destructive to the idea of shared governance.

Faculty behaviors in other areas of campus life have also proven to be somewhat difficult to justify, with reports of academic or sexual misconduct; and the popular depiction of the college faculty member is one of an esoteric individual incapable of employment outside of higher education. Although these are hugely stereotyped perceptions of the professoriate, there is some grounding in these broad projections, often fueled by the popular reporting of individual actions.

Specialization

The evolution of American higher education emphasized creating specializations and silos to cluster faculty expertise, a rough interpretation of the German university model (Gerber, 2014). This specialization requires not academic citizens for faculty members, but what has been called membership in an academic "tribe" (Becher & Trowler, 2001). In this conceptualization of the modern university, a faculty member is most concerned about the welfare and significance of personal academic disciplineship rather than the broad welfare of the contemporary campus. This is more than political protectionism, and is seen as a way of life, of finding professional identity, and the lens through which faculty members see their worlds. This inward thinking, a process that allows so many academic faculty members to excel in their work, also means that faculty are ill-prepared to lead or take an active role in faculty governance, which is increasingly professional in nature (Johnston, 2003).

Specialization has traditionally been part of a larger issue of faculty motivation for involvement in campus activities and governance, but the movement to quantify individual work has made specialization of efforts even more rigid. Faculty members are expected to measure the impact factor of their academic writings as well as pursue grants that have a high rate of indirect cost, meaning that collaboration even with one other professor can become problematic. This notion of service to self and to an individual's own academic discipline results in less well-rounded faculty members and subcommunities of practice rather than a singular "university." Miller (2003) noted this tendency to collate around individual interests and drew a parallel with the Native American tribes that only banded together when faced with self-protection.

Accountability

To state legislatures, university administrators, and members of the press and public, many faculty have an undemanding lifestyle and work requirements, resulting in CareerCast citing the professoriate as the least stressful job in America (Jaschik, 2013). These perceptions are likely influenced by the nature of faculty work schedules and responsibilities. However, research has suggested the opposite (Wilson, 2012). The results of multiple studies on faculty involvement in governance show that faculty work well over 40 hours a week and experience burnout in their roles on campus (Brown & Miller, 1998). The pressure to perform well in their teaching, research, and service to the university impacts decisions for participating in the governance process, and the level of accountability of faculty can often depreciate over time. The protection of academic freedom, promotion of equity, and support for professional growth are critical components for accountability (Mamiseishvili, Miller, & Lee, 2016). When institutions lack these elements, as situational and interpretational literature have demonstrated, faculty become deterred from playing increasingly more responsible roles in decision making for institutional affairs. For new faculty, especially those who are on a tenure-track appointment, being involved in the shared governance process is beneficial. However, new faculty witness the plateaus of bureaucracy and its effects: tension, weariness, and overall frustration from senior faculty—all of which can be disheartening.

An additional consideration for faculty members is the extent to which they are held accountable for their actions within governance units. Faculty members who faithfully serve on faculty or academic senates may indeed find, for example, that their attendance at meetings goes largely unnoticed or that the lack of debate and consideration of different perspectives on issues yields little difference in senate voting outcomes (Miller, Williams, & Garavalia, 2003). And further, faculty members typically do not view their roles on faculty senates as elected, constituent-driven appointments, and as a result, senators respond to immediate questions as they perceive they respond to their own individual self-interests. This scenario thus challenges the notion that shared governance bodies are democratic organizations working for the collective welfare of the campus (Miller, 2003).

Diverse Reward Systems

Due to a wide variety of factors, including consistent funding sources, faculty members have been hired to do different kinds of tasks and take on different roles on the contemporary campus (Boyer, 1990). Increasingly, nontenurable faculty are hired to provide instruction, while other faculty are hired exclusively to conduct research. The result is that the professoriate, generally, is responding to different workplace demands and drawing rewards from different activities. Some faculty, for instance, are rewarded for writing large grants and conducting solitary research, while others teach multiple sections of large classes. Such variations in reward systems confound the shared governance process, as involvement in campus activities becomes a less prominent variable deeming a high reward (Knefelkamp, 1990).

Differences in reward systems can also vary based on career stage of a faculty member, as newer faculty members can be fully engaged in all aspects of teaching, research, and service; and senior faculty might find less enjoyment or reward from such engagement. Such was the foundation of Knefelkamp's (1990) observations on how rewards change for faculty members throughout their lives, and that rarely is any single activity powerful enough to engage a professor at the same level through an entire career. One result of this might be that those with the least experience on campus or with the least knowledge of other programs and constituent needs might become the faculty with the highest level of engagement, while those with the most to share and give back to the campus might be the least engaged.

Nature of Higher Education Agendas

Colleges and universities are driven by multiple stakeholders with often highly divergent interests (Manning, 2013). These stakeholders are as varied as employers, sports fans, politicians, local school districts, and even local business owners who rely on students as customers want and expect different things from higher education. Some of these constituents demand rigor and selectivity, while others look to factors such as winning teams, a high volume of student consumers, and in-service professional development activities. These demands all receive significant attention from different campus leaders, but ultimately, they result in differentiated work for different individuals with often similar titles. "Professors" recruit students, advise other students, teach new approaches or criteria to employees, while simultaneously teaching classes, conducting research, and providing service to their professions. The work of a higher education institution is dissipating rather than coalescing around central ideas, resulting in a campus agenda that is difficult, at best, to align among faculty members in a singular governance body (Sibley, 1998).

Conclusion: Time for a New Model of Shared Governance

The concept of sharing authority via governance models has a strong foundation in human resource development theory, meaning that people feel better and perhaps do their jobs better because they have some say in how the organization is operated and what it has for goals (Evans, 1999). With incredible advances in knowledge and a rapid pace of change in instructional methods, higher education leaders must construct some contemporary way to share authority in specific areas and maintain the enthusiasm, efforts, and productivity of faculty members. This, of course, assumes that faculty traditions give way to the contemporary realities of providing a state service through education.

The question of the philosophy of higher education as a private endeavor or as a publicly sponsored social support must be carefully navigated as role and mission statements are framed to allow for shared governance. One perspective that keeps the academy an isolated protector and creator of knowledge could be the power of faculty over decision making. When higher education institutions are used, however, to produce a workforce, assess and create programs for the public welfare, and serve as a component in a larger public-good-driven policy for quality of life and civic engagement, then faculty might play a very different role in decision making. Ultimately, the purpose of the academy must determine its shared governance philosophy.

Shared governance, including the involvement of students, clearly fits within the framework of academic affairs management, meaning that faculty can and should have a great deal of authority to make decisions related to academic matters. With increasingly complex accreditation guidelines and automated curriculum management, in their role with student engagement faculty would appear to best serve as a consultative body. With the power and ability to consult institutional leaders, faculty could better focus their attention at the jobs to which they are assigned. This would require, however, that institutions consider and keep the student development experience as a primary activity of the institution. Generally, there are misconceptions about what higher education has been and what it has done, but broadly, selected institutional leaders must consider more than the financial realities of their institutions and take student needs, concerns, and ultimately what is best for student development at the core of their decision making. If faculty have proven unable to do this, trustees in concert with the leaders they select must bear this torch.

Institutions must engage in a realistic and purposeful discussion about which constituent body has authority and responsibility for different matters of institutional life, and from this, build a plan that shares authority and responsibility respectively. This mutual development of expectations, responsibilities, and authority must be done within the legal context of public agencies and must include elements of accountability. Such accountability measures will be helpful in making assessments as to whether or not different constituents are upholding their responsibilities and exercising their authority judiciously. In a sense, what the higher education community needs is a "reset" of shared authority to clearly define roles.

Faculty leaders must not wait for administrative leaders to begin the conversation of the role, scope, and purpose of shared authority and must engage in such discussions among themselves—and in a responsible, timely fashion that best represents the potential of faculty engagement. Administrative leaders are pulled in different stakeholder directions, and faculty leaders must take the primary responsibility for assuming control over selected institutional aspects if for no other reason than it is they who desire such.

Shared governance can work and can effectively bring different points of view into the decision-making process, but the current system of attempted engagement is problematic at best. There must be a restructuring of who is involved, how they are selected for involvement, and how they are held accountable for this involvement. Further, there must be a clear delineation of who is responsible for which decisions, and how these decision outcomes are to be addressed. Higher education, as an industry and indeed as a multibillion dollar business, does not have room for amateur approaches to decision making, nor does it have room for a lack of public responsiveness. The academy of the future has a specific role to play in society—one that is complex and rooted in personal development as well as academic preservation, and to achieve such a goal, broad and responsible decision-making structures must be in place.

References

Anthony, M. K. (2004). Shared governance models: The theory, practice, and evidence. *Online Journal of Issues in Nursing, 9*(1), Retrieved from www.nursingworld.org/MainMenuCategories/ANAMarketplace/ANAPeriodicals/OJIN/TableofContents/Volume92004?No1Jan04?SharedGovernanceModesl.aspx

Armstrong, W. P. (1999). *Trends and issues of a community college faculty senate: The Jefferson State case study* (Unpublished doctoral dissertation). University of Alabama, Tuscaloosa.

Baldridge, J. V. (1982). Shared governance: A fable about the lost magic kingdom. *Academe, 68*(1), 12–15.

Becher, T., & Trowler, P. R. (2001). *Academic tribes and territories* (2nd ed.). Suffolk: Society for Research into Higher Education and the Open University Press.

Birnbaum, R. (2004). *The end of shared governance: Looking ahead and looking back.* In W. Tierney & V. Lechuga (Eds.), *Restructuring shared governance in higher education.* New Directions for Higher Education No. 127 (pp. 5–22). San Francisco, CA: Jossey-Bass.

Boyer, E. L. (1990). *Scholarship reconsidered: Priorities of the professoriate.* Princeton, NJ: Carnegie Foundation for the Advancement of Teaching.

Braswell, K. (2006). *A grounded theory describing the process of executive succession at Middle State University* (Unpublished doctoral dissertation). University of Arkansas, Fayetteville.

Brown, C., & Miller, M. T. (1998). Diversity in decision-making: Minority representation in student affairs administration. *College Student Affairs Journal, 18*(1), 25–32.

Cahn, S. M. (2011). *Saints and scamps, ethics in academia, 25th anniversary edition.* Lanham, MD: Rowan & Littlefield.

Campbell, J. R. (2000). *Dry rot in the ivory tower.* Lanham, MD: University Press of America.

Evans, J. (1999). Benefits and barriers to shared authority. In M. T. Miller (Ed.), *Responsive academic decision making* (pp. 29–54). Stillwater, OK: New Forums Press.

Gerber, L. A. (2014). *The rise and decline of faculty governance: Professionalization and the modern American university.* Baltimore, MD: Johns Hopkins University.

Greene, J., Kisida, B., & Mills, J. (2010). *Administrative bloat at American universities: The real reason for high costs in higher education.* Policy Report No. 239. Phoenix, AZ: Goldwater Institute.

Halsted, D. G. (2015, March 24). The read divide in higher education today is between faculty members and the education technology industry. *Inside Higher Ed.* Retrieved from www.insidehighered.com

Hammond, R. (Ed.). (2015). *Chronicle of higher education almanac, 2015-2016.* Washington, DC: Chronicle of Higher Education.

Howe, N., & Strauss, W. (2007). *Millennials go to college* (2nd ed.). Great Falls, VA: Lifecourse Associates.

Jaschik, S. (2013, January 7). Least stressful job? Really? *Inside Higher Ed.* Retrieved from https://www.insidehighered.com/news/2013/01/07/claim-college-professor-least-stressful-job-infuriates-faculty

Johnston, S. W. (2003). Faculty governance and effective academic administrative leadership. In S. L. Hoppe & B. W. Speck (Eds.), *Identifying and preparing academic leaders.* New Directions for Higher Education, No. 124 (pp. 57–63). New York, NY: Wiley.

Jones, W. A. (2012). Faculty involvement in institutional governance: A literature review. *Journal of the Professoriate, 6*(1), 117–135.

Knefelkamp, L. L. (1990). Seasons of academic life. *Liberal Education, 76*(3), 4–12.

Langland, E. (2011). Shared governance in an age of change. *Pedagogy, 11*(3), 554–562.

Mamiseishvili, K., Miller, M. T., & Lee, D. (2016). Beyond teaching and research: Faculty perceptions of service roles at research universities. *Innovative Higher Education, 41,* 273-285

Manning, K. (2013). *Organizational theory in higher education.* New York, NY: Routledge.

Miles, A. S. (1997). *College law* (2nd ed.). Tuscaloosa, AL: Sevgo.

Miller, M. T. (2003). *Improving faculty governance.* Stillwater, OK: New Forums.

Miller, M. T., & Nadler, D. P. (2016). Creating a value added college environment: The role of the hidden curriculum. In. W. Nuninger (Ed.), *Handbook of research on quality assurance and value management* (pp. 89–104). Hershey, PA: IGI Global.

Miller, M. T., Williams, C., & Garavalia, B. (2003). Path analysis and power rating of communication channels in a faculty senate setting. In M. T. Miller & J. Caplow (Eds.), *Policy and university faculty governance* (pp. 59–74). Greenwich, CT: Information Age.

Miller, V. (2016, February 23). Outbursts, interruptions dominate first Bruce Harreld forum. *The Gazette.* Retrieved March 1, 2016 from www.thegazette.com/subject/news/education/higher-education/outbursts-interruptsions-dominate-first-bruce-harreld-forum-20160223

Professor X. (1973). *This beats working for a living, the dark secrets of a college professor.* New Rochelle, NY: Arlington House.

Rixom, A. (2011). *Professionalism and decision making in higher education management: New collegiality and academic change* (Unpublished doctoral dissertation). University of Bath, UK.

Rosser, V. J. (2003). Historical overview of faculty governance in higher education. In M. Miller & J. Caplow (Eds.), *Policy and university faculty governance* (pp. 3–18). Greenwich, CT: Information Age Publishing.

Schuster, J. H., & Finkelstein, M. J. (2006). *The restructuring of academic work and careers: The American faculty.* Baltimore, MD: The Johns Hopkins University Press.

Sibley, W. A. (1998). *University management 2010.* Stillwater, OK: New Forums.

Sperber, M. (2001). *Beer and circus: How big time college sports is crippling undergraduate education.* New York, NY: Holt.

Veysey, L. R. (1965). *The emergence of the American university.* Chicago, IL: University of Chicago.

Waugh, W. L. (2003). Issues in university governance: More "professional" and less academic. *Annals of the American Academy of Political and Social Science, 585,* 84–96.

Wilson, R. (2012, June 3). Why are associate professors so unhappy? *Chronicle of Higher Education, 58.* Retrieved from http://chronicle.com/article/Why-Are-Associate-Professors/132071/

16. The Erosion of Faculty Governance

DILYS SCHOORMAN

Faculty governance has been central to the historical identity of higher education. The academy has been long regarded as a bastion of democratic practice,
through the free exchange of ideas intended to broaden the mind and elevate
the civic consciousness of all involved. This core mission of higher education is
increasing losing ground in the face of the "unfettered corporate-based market
model" that "continues to predominate [our] thinking about every aspect of
society" (Gerber, 2014, p. 165). Thus, faculty governance itself has become an
embattled undertaking. Given the drastic shift in the external pressures faced
particularly by state-funded institutions, there has been considerable discussion
about the desired institutional responses to these pressures and the role and relevance of faculty governance in this context (Kezar & Eckel, 2004; Schrecker,
2010; Slaughter & Rhoades, 2009). Supporters of faculty governance argue
that it is even more important under contemporary pressures, though many call
for significant changes in how faculty governance operates. This chapter will
explore the political, economic, and ideological contexts that threaten faculty
governance and will recommend ways in which faculty can reclaim or resist the
erosion of their collective power. Such a process will require faculty conscientization[1] about the power dynamics within which universities operate, the shifting ideologies that govern decision making in public education, and the actual
and potential role of collective faculty voice in such contexts.

Public Education Under Siege

Scholarship on faculty governance has consistently documented both the
strengths and limitations of faculty senates and other governance structures
(Birnbaum, 1989; Minor, 2004; Tierney & Minor, 2003). Although faculty

governance emerged as a central facet of higher education in the United States in the 20th century, the perennial criticism of such governance has revolved around its perceived impracticality in a fast-paced world and the tensions between the academic vs. business models in the nature and function of its decision making. Proponents of a corporate model slash budgets and call into question matters of faculty governance, tenure, and the traditional hallmarks and services of higher education in an effort to reconceptualize public education in terms of its economic profitability (Kelderman, 2016). The most recent manifestations of corporatization have been state-imposed performance metrics, part of the wave of accountability that has swept through public education. While active senates might prove to be responsive to such pressures, it is crucial for faculty and administrators to not merely accede to these pressures without question, but to problematize the legitimacy of corporatization as a catalyst for desired change and its impact on the mission and identity of higher education institutions.

Critical scholars have foreboded corporatization's problematic impact on education policy and practice (Apple, 2004; Aronowitz & Giroux, 2000). Echoing their concerns about globalization (contrasted with internationalization), scholars argue against corporatization's liberal market logics, which have resulted in standardization and homogenizing practices (Burbules & Torres, 2000; Stromquist, 2007). This often results in the recruitment of international students, less for their cultural or academic contributions but more for the out-of-state fees that they pay. With little impact on the curriculum, the global recruitment of students results more successfully in the "Americanization" of the world, rather than the internationalization of learning.

This market logic has led to the efforts in accountability that first hit public schools and that now impact public higher education institutions in the United States. Given the highly varied and individualized nature of learners, and the organic and creative process of effective and engaging instruction, the standardization and homogenization of education that frame desired education practice primarily in terms of efficiency typically result in ineffective educational outcomes. This has been the realization of educators around the nation as they reckon with the colossal failure of No Child Left Behind and the standardization and accountability regimes that such legislation spawned (Meier & Wood, 2004; Watkins, 2012). Externally imposed mandates deprofessionalized educators and ended up squandering the public education of a generation of students, while their more affluent counterparts, including children of many who imposed such an educational mandate, remained academically unscathed in the safety of private schools (Ma, 2013). No one has been held accountable for this academic genocide. As the accountability movement enters the higher education arena, the parallels with these reforms in public schools should not be lost in our understanding of current efforts to regulate the activities of publicly funded higher education institutions.

How faculty governance systems respond to this reality in higher education will vary across institutions and according to the consciousness of the governance leaders. For externally dependent institutions faculty governance activities are often framed by the politics of funding. What is crucial, however, is whether governance leaders and faculty understand their responses in political and strategic terms, or as required ideological shifts as well. It is one thing to have to recognize that we might have to "feed the beast" or "render unto Caesar" data, evidence, or program structures that attend to the necessities of the purse strings; but it is quite a different matter to allow those efforts to transform our professional or institutional identity, especially when they fail to make good educational or moral sense. We have seen the script before: While all K–12 schools recognized that they had to do better on test scores, those that focused solely on the test ultimately robbed their students of the joy of learning.

The business model has wrought a strange irony. Rather than making for a better educational experience for the students, it has led to further inequities as increasingly standardized practices marginalize those who need differentiation. Instrumental notions of education combined with an efficiency orientation have yielded performance metrics that demand "timely graduation" (i.e., within six years for undergraduate), job placement, and starting salaries (each dependent on marketplace vagaries over the quality of education) and fewer course credits as hallmarks of the desired college education. High academic quality is now reduced to "productivity" measured by headcount and full-time enrollment, graduation rates, and speed of completion. The language of the marketplace has recast students as clients, professors as workers, university presidents as CEOs whose attention must be paid to the "bottom line" rather than to the quality of the educational experience offered in the institution (Ginsberg, 2011; Giroux, 2011; Slaughter & Rhoades, 2009). Under these circumstances failing students for underperforming becomes a performance problem for educators as the cost of a degree (something that can be lowered by paying instructors less, or raising class sizes regardless of pedagogical soundness) and time to graduation become a measure of a successful higher education institution.

This stands in stark contrast to the experiences of students in elite private institutions who are encouraged to venture outside their comfort zones in innovative and unusual courses that may or may not relate to their major or profession, to pursue a double major or minor, study abroad, or even take a year off. This disparity raises both educational and moral questions. How might faculty governance and collegial decision making enhance our ability to be more adept at responding to the funding policies that frame our work without compromising the quality of what we do? It is within these broader political, economic, and ideological contexts in which our more micro, localized decision making in the name of faculty governance should occur.

The Faculty Governance We Desire

As scholars have pointed out, the corporatization of higher education has been in direct conflict with the traditional role of higher education institutions as spheres of democratic deliberation and collegial governance, exhibiting "a deep disdain, if not outright contempt, for both democracy and publically engaged teaching and scholarship" (Giroux, 2010, p. 187). This is further exacerbated by the fact that the corporate—rather than academic—view of higher education holds that the purpose of education is job preparation. The role of education in developing social consciousness, democratic leaders, and/or critical citizens is irrelevant within this perspective. Given this tension, active and effective faculty governance is both necessary and urgent.

The governance we desire must be understood both historically and contemporaneously. As Tierney and Lechuga (2004) observe, shared governance has been a hallmark of higher education in the United States since the early 20th century. They also note that while in 1915 Dewey, who helped to start the American Association of University Professors (AAUP), underscored the role of faculty in decision making, as early as 1918 Veblen also "lamented the control that business interests had over academics" (p. 1). Thus the academic vs. market tensions in the framing of the identity of higher education institutions are not new. Although the central role of the expertise of faculty in decisions about composition of the faculty (hiring, promotion, and tenure), the curriculum, and the student body (admissions requirements, grading) as laid out by the AAUP in 1966 has been hitherto accepted, contemporary challenges to this tradition emerge in the form of skepticism among state politicians about tenure, the lack of faculty control over the budget related to faculty hiring, and the decisions about admissions, delivery models, and even the mission of the university based on budget priorities. Faculty governance advocates must be able to address these challenges directly and unambiguously and continue to demonstrate through governance practices how shared decision making is of advantage to the institution. Such a response may well entail a shift in how governance is currently practiced in our own institutions.

Birnbaum (2004) points out that faculty governance is not only more than a decision-making structure but also a symbol and ideology of academic life and that a diminution of the faculty role in governance is likely to decrease institutional effectiveness. However, Birnbaum's observations must also be tempered with the reality that many faculty (a) have not been socialized into the value of faculty governance; (b) do not think critically about the shifting ideologies underlying the potential movement from democratic and collegial governance to corporate models, and (c) have limited interest in engaging in governance because of the increasing performance pressures particularly in teaching and research for promotion and tenure. Thus, the form of faculty governance that we would desire will have more to do with an institutional culture that values faculty expertise and input in decision making and engages in collegial decision making as integral to its standard operating procedures. This shifts the question from "should the faculty be involved?" to "how do we effectively involve the faculty?" Desired faculty governance would entail multifaceted opportunities in diverse arenas of decision making that demonstrate a comprehensive approach and explicit commitment to seeking multiple perspectives on key institutional decision making. This means that faculty and administrators should readily recognize the opportunities and obligations for collegial decision making both within and beyond the formal structures such as university and college senates and university governing boards, including multiple levels of the system and in a range of contexts such as department meetings, committee deliberations, and leadership and strategic visioning teams at the university and state level. On the other hand, if neither faculty nor administrators have been socialized on the value and/or the processes for engaging in effective collegial governance, more groundwork for trust building through formal governance structures may be a logical starting point.

There is ample evidence about what we should not want as faculty governance. The criticisms of faculty senates include concerns about structures being too slow, inefficient and unresponsive, sand box politics that focus on individual interests rather than more collective concerns, a preoccupation with microconcerns such as faculty parking, or serving as a forum dominated by a small proportion of disgruntled faculty who often see all administrators as the collective and undifferentiated enemy of shared governance (Birnbaum, 1989; Hollinger, 2001; Kezar & Eckel, 2004). Concomitantly, many have cited faculty governance processes as being to maladroit to effectively handle the complex issues of diversity, financial stress, or corporatization, although Birnbaum (2004) argues that these criticisms are rarely substantiated. Effective faculty governance of the future will require a collegial partnership between administrators and faculty, one that upholds the values of democracy while responding effectively to the business model of/for education advanced by the advocates of corporatization.

Problematizing the business model is of particular relevance. The corporate model of management is antithetical to the collegial model of governance, hence the emerging concern about the erosion of faculty governance. Nevertheless, the realities highlighted by the corporate model must also be heeded. While supporters have underscored the crucial role of faculty governance in interrupting or minimizing corporatization, governance leaders cannot ignore the fact that colleges and universities are currently beset by intense competition, diminishing funding sources, and political antipathy (Verburg, 2015). The failure to adequately attend to these pressures could have multiple outcomes. Where democratic deliberations are perceived as inefficient and time consuming, the corporate model could subvert collegial governance practices. On the other hand, the naïve acceptance of and/or the failure of governance leaders to interrogate the business model could lead to governance practices that consciously or unconsciously perpetuate corporatization. Under these circumstances, "effective" and active governance structures could actually subvert democratic governance processes.

Corporatization and subsequent diminished public funding have effected specific changes that raise legitimate concerns about the future of faculty governance. Chief among them is the decline in the number and work conditions of the faculty (Gerber, 2014; Ginsberg, 2011). The deprofessionalization of the faculty in the form of the "adjunctification" (Delbanco, 2012) of the teaching force (where more part-time instructors are being hired to fulfill the teaching mission of the university) is one clear and alarming indicator of corporatization. While more adjunct instructors might reduce the cost of education this places a greater burden on the diminishing number of tenure-track faculty to continue the governance activities and diminish the potential power and voice of the faculty. Ginsberg (2011) also draws attention to the growth of administration, to the detriment of faculty autonomy and voice, laying the ground for attacks on tenure and academic freedom (Moshman, 2004; Reichman, 2015). Faculty must respond, less viscerally and more strategically. Demonstrating the nature and scope of what we do in quantifiable terms will become a necessity. Helping the public to understand our work as contributing to the public good will be key.

New challenges such as the role of e-Learning, and its implications for curriculum, student learning, equity, access, and intellectual property concerns will need to be debated in well-informed faculty governance processes. The ramifications of equating research with the amount of money brought into the university, the need for researchers to fund themselves through grants and the impact of private funding on research in public universities, the temptation to admit students based on their ability to pay fees, or equating massification and class size with effectiveness must be explored. Efficiency and standardization (in the form of schedules, programs of study, predictability) must be balanced with equity, differentiation, and effectiveness, as the needs of students will vary considerably. Ultimately, we need to build faculty governance structures and processes unique to each of our institutions that will weather the storm of corporatization (see Tierney, 2004) and its attendant threats to democratic processes, faculty governance, and what some see as the slow death of the university itself (Eagleton, 2015; Giroux, 2011).

Restoring Faculty Governance as a Public Good

The reframing of faculty governance in embattled times of competition, scarce resources, and political antipathy will require an understanding of the role of shared governance as a public good. Giroux (2011) argues that academics should be in the forefront of the defense of the university as a public good and democratic public sphere. We must begin to recognize (and help all participants involved in the system recognize) that effective faculty governance and faculty input in decision making can and will strengthen the institution, but will require purposeful and urgent action. To this end, I offer several recommendations that draw on both the extant literature and on my experiences as a faculty governance leader. Each recommendation is also grounded in my philosophical perspectives as a critical multicultural educator for whom the principles of critical pedagogy (see Freire, 2000) are central to my professional practice. They are offered as a starting point for debate and reflection on how each might be adapted to suit different institutional realities.

Facilitating Conscientization About the Necessary Role of Faculty Governance

Although Tierney and Minor (2003) found that 80% in their study of 3,500 educators and 70 academic leaders agreed that shared governance was an important part of their institution, faculty involvement in governance continues to be the exception rather than the rule. Therefore, it is important to raise the critical awareness of faculty about governance matters on multiple levels. Faculty need to be conscious of the opportunities for shared governance and input that exist (or are absent) in the institution. This includes being aware of formal governance structures such as senates and governing boards and recognizing the manner in which faculty can (and should!) participate in decision making through these structures, while also engaging in shared decision making at department meetings and on committees that review curriculum, promotion and tenure, awards and petitions. Faculty members need to recognize that they can have an impact in institutional decision making, rather than taking a fatalistic perspective that their actions will not make a difference, or making the assumption that such activities are optional compared to their teaching and research obligations. Thus, faculty consciousness must be raised on the possibilities *and* the responsibility for greater engagement.

Conscientization among faculty members will be necessary at the levels of individual and collective consciousness. They need to become critically conscious of the ideological, political, and economic dynamics that frame decisions being made within the university and the impact on their professional work. Faculty members should guard against acquiescing to the trend toward corporatization, and failing to recognize this as a symptom of a broader ideological shift. Forging a collective consciousness about our roles in faculty governance will require of some a cultural shift from entrenched professional habits of working in isolation with individual goals and responsibilities. A form of double consciousness, vis-à-vis how shared governance is viewed within broader political circles, might be prudent in responding to the critics of shared governance.

Involvement in faculty governance also reinforces the crucial role of faculty in protecting the university as a champion of the public good. In a recent debate within our own institution about corporate sponsorship and our moral obligation as an educational institution, we recognized that many faculty members had not considered the role of the institution in terms of its moral responsibility to the public it served (Schoorman, 2013). An administrator in the "hard sciences" quipped that these moral questions were the domain of social sciences. The recognition that all faculty can and should have a voice in whether we ought to accept corporate funding from donors with a record of unethical practice was a catalyst in reconceptualizing the role of faculty involvement in governance.

Dialogue Across Difference

Within a critical multicultural perspective, dialogue—as opposed to conversation or debate—entails a deliberate effort to forge a satisfactory response to a collective problem; dialogue emerges from a genuine process of listening and entails no winners and losers (see Freire, 2000). For those socialized toward actions and task achievement, long discussions and deliberations are often seen as a waste of time. For others used to being experts in their fields, debating to win or argumentation for its own sake is typical. Many view disagreement as a basis of unpleasant conflict rather than as a valued opportunity to forge dialogue across divergent perspectives. Dialogue is crucial to building trust within the organization, demonstrating that faculty views are valued in institutional decision making.

Successful leaders in governance are necessarily skilled communicators who are able to engage in dialogue across difference and build trust. These are capacities forged over time in the cauldron of daily practice and intentional, purposeful learning. This can occur at a microlevel in a myriad ways in the typical life of a professor. How we interact with students and their divergent views, interests, and personalities; how we participate as colleagues in committees where we deliberate across our difference to reach an agreement; how we respond collectively as a department to new challenges or opportunities in our programs all represent the multiple opportunities to learn to listen and to learn to lead. The socialization of faculty in these micro contexts to (a) appreciate and, over time, to expect the ability to value difference as constructive in decision making, (b) actively solicit broad-based and (even) underrepresented perspectives, and (c) recognize the difference between argument for its own sake and productive dialogue to address collective problems will lay the foundation for an institutional culture that supports genuine inclusivity.

Representation

In most traditional governance structures such as senates, participants serve as elected representatives of their units. Yet criticisms of governance have frequently alluded to those who have used governance processes to advance individual agendas or to represent their own views as those of their colleagues. Governance structures themselves should include ways to prevent and/or interrupt such practices. For instance, in our leadership of a college faculty assembly, in a memo sent out in writing, we instructed departments to elect representatives who would be comfortable carrying forward the diverse perspectives of the unit and who could be trusted to do so with fidelity and without animosity (Schoorman & Acker-Hocevar, 2013). Furthermore when deliberating, nothing prevents the question, "Do all your colleagues feel this way?" "What is the range of diversity on this topic?" When, as faculty governance leaders, we presented the results of a faculty survey and highlighted the bases of faculty disagreements on certain points, we were puzzled by how relieved our colleagues and administrators were that we represented divergent positions without causing tension. It revealed that difference of perspective is often avoided rather than addressed head on. In the case of our discussion, the acknowledgement of divergence allowed us to identify common ground more readily, instead of being caught up in a debate of disagreement.

Department policies and practices also play a key role in supporting representation. At the department level, we call for the (re-)election of our governance representative to the college each year and provide an opportunity on the department agenda for governance concerns to be brought back to the faculty. This also elevates the role and responsibilities of the person serving. This intentionality contrasts sharply with practices where administrators seek a faculty member's perspective, but with little opportunity for the person to consult with those whom s/he is supposed to represent. Although representative governance might be blamed for delaying decision making within the institution, as we have found in the context of institutional crisis, well-established systems for procuring feedback from those one represents can facilitate broad-based input on key decisions quite expeditiously (Schoorman, 2013). For this to be successful, lines of communication, networks, and trust must be well established.

Make Being an Academic Central to the Faculty Governance Project

Faculty governance is predicated on the unique expertise of faculty in institutional decision making. While this expertise has traditionally been linked to matters of curriculum, it is crucial for us to recognize the tremendous potential of the faculty to take on, at least discursively, the underlying ideologies and logics of the external pressures we face as an institution. Higher education institutions and public educators in general have traditionally enjoyed a moral standing in society that require us, as a profession, to be moral upstanders rather than bystanders in the face of inequity. As Schrecker (2010) points out, our role is particularly relevant to protecting the American mind in a world of sound bites and bullet points. "Professors are the nation's public intellectuals; they raise the questions with which an informed citizenry must deal. They are, therefore, essential to the preservation of the reasoned debate and unfettered expression that our democratic system requires" (p. 4). We have watched as a generation of children has been robbed of the joy of learning under the misguided accountability regimes of NCLB. That same logic is now being visited upon higher education institutions.

Taking my own state—Florida—as an example, there is much to be addressed, not merely in an oppositional stance, but as a matter on engaged public intellectualism. How might the educationally privileged of a state (as we might reasonably cast the professors in a university) respond to the very disturbing logic of performance metrics that allows the state to penalize the bottom three "performers" regardless of how well they meet performance criteria? As academics and intellectuals we know this is flawed and that it adversely impacts our state's students and betrays our taxpayers. Yet we have been unable to mount the intellectual, political, and discursive counterpoint that responds with data on the misguided system of accountability that is being visited upon the state's public higher education system. Not only does placing the norm-referenced system of ranking over criterion-referenced evaluation set institutions in competition against one another instead of much-needed collaboration, it makes as little sense as telling a family of ten that only the first seven to wake up will be allowed breakfast. The assumption that competition will spur quality has limited applicability in the context of education and by and large is a dereliction of public responsibility.

My point here is that academics are expected to provide intellectual leadership in a society. While we are called upon to engage collectively in a response to a system that is flawed, our collective support of our institution should not preclude pointing out the problems of the system. We should not merely acquiesce to data gathering related to the salaries of our graduates, or the low price of our education, without simultaneously pointing out the alarming lack of validity and the ideological quicksands on which these accountability schemes are based. All faculty members are affected in one way or the other by the vagaries of corporatization. How difficult would it be for each of us as researchers, teachers, or concerned members of our communities of practice to provide an academic counterpoint to corporatization? That professors of business, science, social sciences, education, nursing, the arts, mathematics, etc., might individually and collectively be resources in our understanding of the challenges we face should be the strength within which we ground our collective and shared decision making. We might not all agree on each of our points, but if we can learn to listen, dialogue, and lean on each other's strengths, we will have formed a formidable coalition from which to respond to external pressures.

Collegial Governance as Organizational Culture

Faculty governance emerges in a variety of forms, with each institution yielding different structures and processes for effective governance (Tierney, 2004). Recognizing this, Tierney (2004) called for a conceptualization of faculty governance as a matter of organizational culture that integrates a variety of opportunities for shared governance in which all members of the academy might participate. This includes formal structures for participation (e.g., senates, departments, committees) as well as symbolic, consultative, and communicative practices in which norms and values about broad-based input, faculty voice, and leadership listening are facilitated, serving to socialize faculty into collegial governance practices. Such norms may include how agendas get set (solicitation of items or developed with no input or distributed prior to meetings or at meetings) or whether deliberations get mired in arguments about Roberts Rules, or if parliamentary procedures facilitate thoughtful and better decisions.

As Tierney (2004) points out, central to the successful facilitation of faculty governance as a central facet of the organizational culture is the demonstration of trust, a shared language, the ability to walk the talk, and the development of a core institutional identity. Trust and the development of a shared language are built up over time. They are embedded in statements and actions that are both codified and not, in the standard operating procedures as well as the informal communications of the system. In my own experiences of governance, establishing clear mechanisms for gathering faculty input, not proceeding with decisions when there has been limited input, identifying ways in which to gather broad-based input expeditiously have forged a culture where faculty voice has been demonstrably valued. On those occasions where faculty have felt that decisions were made outside of governance structures, governance structures themselves have been used to counter and, in some cases, interrupt administrative decision making.

A culture that values governance is also comfortable with divergent perspectives and participants are free to disagree without interpersonal or personal repercussions. However, most significantly, faculty experience a collective identity, belongingness, and responsibility to be engaged. None of this can be forged through a standardized set of recommendations. For governance leaders, administrators, and faculty alike such engagement is achieved through contextual, nuanced, deliberative, and inclusive practices.

Conclusion

This essay issues a wake-up call to all who care about governance and about the current precarious predicament that institutions of higher education find themselves. The wake-up call is not merely to heed the erosion of faculty governance, but to understand the ideological, political, and economic challenges on the traditional role of academics in shared governance. The debates on the desired way forward do not entail the question about whether faculty governance is relevant in contemporary contexts, but rather how faculty governance might retain its central role as the sine qua non of academic life, while being responsive to the changing dynamics of within which the institution is contextualized. A key component of these changing dynamics is the deleterious impact of corporatization and the business model on the higher educational institution. While it is imperative that the institution must respond in order to remain viable and weather the current political, ideological, and economic storms, it is also crucial that we do not lose our institutional identity in our response. Navigating these tensions will require a sophisticated and critical awareness on the part of a hitherto largely disengaged faculty for whom their professional identity was predominantly individual and isolated. This essay calls for a greater conscientization of all faculty, but particularly governance leaders, to recognize the need for a collective consciousness in the face of external pressures that could significantly impact the institution, to understand the political and ideological dynamics at play in current performance-based funding models, to reclaim their unique role as academics with specific expertise to serve as engaged public intellectuals and upstanders for the interests of the diverse communities that our institutions serve. Academic institutions are uniquely poised to analyze policy, provide data, and serve as the public's educators on what is best for our students and our states. There can be little doubt that identifying a way forward toward equitable and fiscally responsible education lies well within the infinite talent of our institutions. If governance processes can harness this talent in ways that serve the public good we will not only have revitalized faculty governance, but we might also save public education from further erosion.

Note

1. I draw on the work of Freire (2000) throughout this essay. Conscientization is a process of becoming critically aware of the power dynamics that underlie the contexts in which we work, and the recognition of our own potential, as those marginalized by these relationships, to transform these realities. Such transformation will require dialogue and collective struggle.

References

Apple, M. (2004). Creating difference: Neo-liberalism, neo-conservatism and the politics of educational reform. *Educational Policy, 18*(1), 12–44.

Aronowitz, S., & Giroux, H. (2000). The corporate university and the politics of education. *The Educational Forum, 64*(4), 332–339.

Birnbaum, R. (1989). The latent organizational functions of the academic senate: Why senates do not work but will not go away. *The Journal of Higher Education, 60*(4), 423–443.

Birnbaum, R. (2004). The end of shared governance: Looking ahead or looking back. *New Directions for Higher Education, 127*(Fall), 5–12.

Burbules, N., & Torres, C. A. (Eds.). (2000). *Globalization and education: A critical perspective.* New York, NY: Routledge.

Delbanco, A. (2012). *College: What it was, is, and should be.* Princeton, NJ: Princeton University Press.

Eagleton, T. (2015, April 6). The slow death of the university. *The Chronicle Review.* Retrieved from http://www.chronicle.com/article/The-Slow-Death-of-the/228991/?cid=wb

Freire, P. (2000). *Pedagogy of the oppressed* (30th anniversary ed.). New York, NY: Continuum.

Gerber, L. (2014). *The rise and decline of faculty governance: Professionalization and the Modern American University.* Baltimore, MD: John Hopkins Press.

Ginsberg, B. (2011). *The fall of the faculty and the rise of the all-administrative university and why it matters.* New York, NY: Oxford University Press.

Giroux, H. (2010). Bare pedagogy and the scourge of neoliberalism: Rethinking higher education as a democratic public sphere. *Educational Forum, 74*(3), 184–196.

Giroux, H. (2011). Once more with conviction: Defending higher education as a public good. *Qui Parle: Critical Humanities and Social Sciences, 20*(1), 117–135.

Hollinger, D. A. (2001). Faculty governance, the University of California and the future of academe. *Academe, 2001*(May/June), 30–33.

Kelderman, E. (2016). Unshared governance: New pressure on the faculty's role in leadership. *The Chronicle of Higher Education,* February 29, 2016.

Kezar, A., & Eckel, P. (2004). Meeting today's governance challenges: A synthesis of the literature and examination of a future agenda for scholarship. *Journal of Higher Education, 75*(4), 371–399.

Ma, K. (2013). *Standardization as a tool of oppression: How the education system controls thought and serves as a gatekeeper to the ruling elite.* Retrieved from http://www.hamptoninstitution.org/gatekeeper.html#.V9coEYWM0TJ

Meier, D., & Wood, G. (Eds.). (2004). *Many children left behind: How the no child left behind act is damaging our children and schools.* Boston: MA: Beacon Press.

Minor, J. T. (2004). Understanding faculty senates: Moving from mystery to models. *The Review of Higher Education, 27*(3), 343–363.

Moshman, D. (2004, April 10). Tenure under sneak attack at UNL. *Lincoln Journal Star,* p. 5.

Reichman, H. (2015). Does academic freedom have a future? *Academe* (November–December). Retrieved from https://www.aaup.org/article/does-academic-freedom-have-future#.V9gjEI4kZMA

Schoorman, D. (2013). Resisting the unholy alliance between a university and a prison company: Implications for faculty governance in a neoliberal context. *Cultural Studies <=> Critical Methodologies, 13*(6), 510–519.

Schoorman, D., & Acker-Hocevar, M. (2013). Faculty governance in neoliberal educational contexts: Challenges for democratic decision making. *Interchange, 43*(3), 265–285.

Schrecker, E. (2010). *The lost soul of higher education: Corporatization, the assault on academic freedom, and the end of the American university.* New York, NY: New Press.

Slaughter, S., & Rhoades, G. (2009). *Academic capitalism and the new economy: Markets, state and higher education.* Baltimore, MD: John Hopkins University Press.

Stromquist, N. (2007). Internationalization as a response to globalization: Radical shifts in university environments. *Higher Education, 53*(1), 81–105.

Tierney, W. (2004). Improving faculty governance: Utilizing a cultural framework to improve organizational performance. In W. Tierney (Ed.), *Competing conceptions of academic governance* (pp. 202–214). Baltimore, MD: Johns Hopkins University Press.

Tierney, W., & Minor, J. (2003). *Challenges for governance: A national report.* Center for Higher Education Policy Analysis, Los Angeles, CA.

Tierney, W. G., & Lechuga, V. M. (2004). Editor's notes. *New Directions for Higher Education, 127*(Fall), 1–4.

Verburg, S. (2015, June 10). UW-Madison faculty challenge lawmakers on tenure changes. *Wisconsin State Journal.* Retrieved from http://host.madison.com/wsj/news/local/govt-and-politics/uw-madison-faculty-challenge-lawmakers-on-tenure-changes/article_d235ded5-57ef-5ba6-a320-fff2c5adc25c.html

Watkins, W. (2012). *The assault on public education: Confronting the politics of corporate school reform.* New York, NY: Teachers College Press.

Part Nine: How Much Are College Students Learning?

In "Limited by Design? A Critical Sociohistorical Analysis of Postsecondary Learning Outcomes," Ezekiel Kimball, Juan Manuel Ruiz-Hau, and Fermin Valle employ the concept of "interest convergence" to show how the most powerful groups in society acquire benefits while appearing to act for the public good. The authors claim that practice pervades higher education and has produced differential collegiate experiences and learning outcomes depending upon students' political, social, and economic status. This class division is relevant to controversial issues of knowledge acquisition in our educational institutions. More hopefully, Kimball, Ruiz-Hau, and Valle close by reminding us that many marginalized students are pressing the academy to create more authentic and emancipatory learning.

In "Are College Students Learning More or Less Than in the Past," Sergio Ossorio and Kimberly A. Kline first consider the meaning of student learning and how college personnel can most effectively provide for and assess the ends and means of that complicated notion. They posit that structural changes are needed in both curricula and pedagogical methods. The authors are especially sensitive to *affective* factors that are often missing in traditional forms of classroom practice that emphasize cognitive acquisition. Accordingly, Ossorio and Kline recommend that universities enlarge upon such alternative pathways as collaborative learning and authentic assessment.

17. Limited by Design? A Critical Sociohistorical Analysis of Postsecondary Learning Outcomes

EZEKIEL KIMBALL, JUAN MANUEL RUIZ-HAU, AND FERMIN VALLE

Limited by Design?

Policymakers, employers, and students alike expect that participation in post-secondary education will result in concrete learning outcomes that lead to both individual and collective good. Furthermore, higher education researchers have devoted a great deal of attention to this issue. As Renn and Reason (2013) have noted, research on learning outcomes has proliferated since the formalization of the field: in the roughly forty years prior to Feldman and Newcomb's (1969) *The Impact of College on Students*, some 1,500 pieces on student learning in college were published. As noted in the first volume of *How College Affects Students*, the twenty-two-year period from 1967 to 1989 saw the production of roughly 2,600 studies of learning outcomes (Pascarella & Terenzini, 1991). The second volume, which covered a comparatively scant thirteen-year period, reviewed roughly the same number of studies (Pascarella & Terenzini, 2005). However, despite the widespread belief that postsecondary education results in learning outcomes and a wealth of empirical studies from which to draw, the evidence concerning student learning is decidedly mixed.

Students have been shown to realize domain-specific learning outcomes in their major field of study but have not appeared to gain significant content knowledge in other areas (Renn & Reason, 2013). Likewise, most studies have shown that students leave college with improved critical thinking and postformal reasoning (Pascarella & Terenzini, 2005). However, much of this literature is limited in scope (Renn & Reason, 2013), and large-scale studies using more robust instrumentation and research designs have yielded less positive outcomes (e.g., Arum & Roksa, 2011; Bowen, Chingos, & McPherson, 2009). Evidence has also shown that students leave college as more complex and fully realized versions of themselves—experiencing positive outcomes related to civic engagement, identity development, multicultural-ism, and moral development (Renn & Reason, 2013). Nonetheless, much of this literature is not longitudinal in design and has rarely been replicated, which makes it difficult to draw causal conclusions related to the role postsec-ondary institutions play in learning outcomes (Renn & Reason, 2013).

Even if we were able to demonstrate convincingly that learning occurs in college, this conclusion would neglect two important realities: first, public faith in the efficacy of postsecondary educations is waning. This shift is prompted by both empirical and conceptual arguments that capture the public consciousness by challenging the return on investment realized by many postsecondary institutions. For example, a recent high-profile study of critical thinking demonstrated limited within-college gains (Arum & Roksa, 2011) while another showed how a party culture and social striving sub-vert real learning (Armstrong & Hamilton, 2013). These empirical pieces are joined by prognostications and recriminations that decry the state of higher education. For example, recent high-profile works have argued against higher education's narrow credentialism (Delbanco, 2012), rewarding of conformity (Deresiewicz, 2015), technological backwardness (Selingo, 2013), and cre-ation of a late adolescent Disneyland (Seaman, 2005). In addition to waning public faith in higher education's efficacy, treatments of postsecondary learning outcomes often ignore variations in experiences across the student population. That is to say, it may well be the case that some people in post-secondary institutions learn more than others. As Bowen et al. (2009) have demonstrated, outcomes such as attendance, persistence, and graduation are mediated by race and class as the higher education system shuffles some stu-dents into better institutions than others. Racial and class stratification could create variations in learning outcomes as poorer students of color are more likely to attend less selective institutions (Astin & Oseguera, 2004; Posselt, Jaquette, Bielby, & Bastedo, 2012) and selectivity serves to structure educa-tional quality (Hoxby, 2009).

Notably, most critiques of higher education tend to treat these two ideas—limited learning and stratification—as unfortunate, perhaps even unintentional elements of the educational system. In this chapter, however, we contend that the educational system functions precisely as it has been designed to function: by maintaining a status quo ostensibly based on merit but wherein definitions of merit incorporate dominant forms of habitus that serve to promote different outcomes for different students (Baker, 2014; Kett, 2013). This argument is far from new and is often employed in other areas of educational research (e.g., Foley, 1994; Nasaw, 1981; Spring, 2016). Within higher education, it has also been incorporated into studies that explore the maintenance of a social elite via admissions practices (Stevens, 2009), patterns of degree award (Mullen, 2010), and postgraduation social networks (Rivera, 2015).

To advance our argument throughout this chapter, we employ a broadly critical lens to understand the epistemological and ontological foundations for higher education learning environments (Giroux, 2003). In our analysis, we draw heavily on prior conceptualizations of interest convergence (e.g., Bell, 1980; Gasman & Hilton, 2012) and intersectionality (e.g., Crenshaw, 1989; Núñez, 2014). The theory of interest convergence holds that people in positions of power and privilege support actions intended to promote social justice only when those actions also benefit them—and typically to a greater degree than those from historically marginalized or minoritized populations (Bell, 1980). We posit that alterations in higher education learning environments have tended to be (re)framed in ways that (re)inforce the intersecting social and economic logics of capitalism and multiple systems of identity-based oppression. Intersectionality expands on this insight by demonstrating that identity-based oppression arises from overlapping systems of power and privilege that serve to produce widely variant experiences based on the differing combinations of social identities (Crenshaw, 1989). In this chapter, we follow bell hooks (1981, 2003) in arguing that privilege is inextricably linked to a system of "imperialist white-supremacist capitalist patriarchy" utilized to perpetuate the long-running social, economic, and corporeal domination of persons holding historically marginalized and minoritized identities. While we focus principally on the use of postsecondary education to create, challenge, and resist oppression based on race and class in this chapter, we believe that our arguments can be extended to other social identities—for example, gender, sexuality, (dis)ability, nationality, ethnicity, and religious faith. Indeed, understanding identity as intersectional in nature helps to explain the wide divergences in perceptions of climate (Hurtado, Alvarez, Guillermo-Wann, Cuellar, & Arellano, 2012) and postsecondary outcomes (Astin & Oseguera, 2004; Posselt et al., 2012) among students from historically marginalized or minoritized populations. Based on the intersection of students' various social identities and varied campus environments, radically different postsecondary experiences for different groups of students result.

Our argument thus holds that evidence both of the presence and absence of learning outcomes can be explained if higher education institutions are not really in the business of producing learning outcomes as conceptualized by many scholars but rather making students fit into and become complicit with broader systems of capitalism (Bowles & Gintis, 1976/2011; Giroux, 2001; Welch, 2015). However, as critical theorists consistently argue, the fact that an educational system does not intrinsically serve the interests of some or all participants does not mean that those participants cannot sometimes use that system for their own ends (Apple, 2011; Brookfield, 2004; Freire, 1970/2000). Thus, it is entirely possible that the same system can result in no learning by design and also be repurposed for learning. To demonstrate how that can be the case, we contextualize other social science findings and theories in the Diverse Learning Environments (DLE; Hurtado et al., 2012). We adopt the DLE because it utilizes an inherently critical approach to understand the community, policy, and sociohistorical contexts for student experience alongside institutional contexts such as the campus climate, curriculum, and cocurriculum. It also suggests that the social identities of students intersect with the campus environment in ways that produce differential learning outcomes, which helps to explain why the same college environment can both result in and not result in learning.

Societal, Policy, and Community Contexts for Learning

In keeping with critical theory, we do not believe that higher education systems can be socially reproduced in a politically neutral way; instead, systems of power, oppression, and privilege that operate across the whole of human life shape colleges and universities in profoundly important ways. Dominant political, social, and economic classes largely define the way that learning is structured both within institutions and across the broader political economy. Language used to describe the purposes of higher education to meet "societal," "economic," or "national" interests often obfuscates the underlying imperialist white-supremacist capitalist patriarchy—as well as other systems of oppression—that dictates what learning is and for whom it is accessible. To demonstrate how these largely hidden processes operate in the creation of higher education systems, we utilize two historical examples: (1) the way in which slavery shaped the early history of American higher education and its continued legacy in impacting colleges and universities in the present day; and (2) the way in which the college access logic undergirding financial aid policy shifted over time.

Both the founding charters and the demographic censuses make it clear that the early American colleges were the exclusive domain of affluent white men (Geiger, 2015; Trow, 1999). Indeed, while some early American colleges did permit indigenous persons to enroll, they did so in an overt attempt to strip them of their cultural heritage (Wright, 1988). Beyond these restrictions in enrollment, the growth of American higher education both benefited from and reinforced the social reproduction of racist ideology utilized to legitimize slavery (Wilder, 2013). As Wilder (2013) has shown, American colleges actively cultivated donations from wealthy Southern planters and Northern merchants who profited directly from the exploitation of slave labor. Yet, even as college presidents sought these donations and professors propagated racist pseudo-science, the college campus also saw itself repurposed by students seeking to learn more about, and introduce others to, the burgeoning abolitionist movement. Even today, the legacy of slavery on many college campuses remains in the form of statues, buildings, and restricted funds—leading some students to challenge these artifacts as reflective of a negative climate for their learning (Wilder, 2013).

In a more recent context, the passage of legislation like the G.I. Bill and the Higher Education Act of 1965 provided more, even if not equal, access to higher education for historically marginalized and minoritized populations (Gilbert & Heller, 2013). With funding available to subvent the cost of attendance for students without the ability to pay tuition costs out-of-pocket, greater equity in access briefly seemed realizable (Kimball, 2011). However, the economic crisis of the 1970s precipitated a political and economic turn toward neoliberalism with an emphasis on privatization (Harvey, 2005). A decades-long trend would begin wherein policymakers increasingly framed educational policy around parity rather than equity, state appropriations declined, tuition rose dramatically, and students assumed ever higher debt loans in ways that benefited some but not necessarily all students (Giroux, 2014; Harvey, 2005; Lapon, 2015; Welch, 2015). While presented as part of a broader policy shift designed to ensure equal opportunity, divestment in financial aid saw the relative value of Pell Grants fail to keep up with rising tuition costs amidst tepid legislative support (Lapon, 2015; Mettler, 2014). Compounded by declining state appropriations, the access promised to low-income students through federal legislation failed to produce a proportional number of graduates from low-income populations, and, instead, legislation enabled student loans to become a trillion-dollar corporate industry (Lapon, 2015; Mettler, 2014). However, here once again a systemic mechanism for the perpetuation of the status quo also serves as the catalyst for students to repurpose that same system for learning: an active student movement has sprung up to protest the limited available financial aid, advocate for affordable postsecondary education opportunities, and seek the abolition of student debt (Giroux, 2014; Nathanson, 2016).

While we provide just two examples, we believe that they adequately demonstrate the extent to which the societal, policy, and community contexts within which colleges and universities reside replicate the status quo. However, these same examples also demonstrate the very real possibility that students can transcend the imperative toward social reproduction and repurpose postsecondary institutions for real learning that will in turn result in social change.

Institutional Contexts for Learning

Kerr (1963) has called American colleges and universities a "prime instrument[s] of national purpose" (Kerr, 1963). However, as Kerr (1963) also pointed out colleges that once served a single, well-defined purpose—the replication of a social, economic, and political elite—have grown into diffuse organizational structures that serve many different ends. Best captured by the idea of the "multiversity," the contemporary postsecondary institution is a pluralistic community with myriad purposes and multiple centers of power that responds to a number of interests and concerns (Kerr, 1963).

Such institutional reprioritization introduced unprecedented levels of complexity in the way postsecondary institutions operate. For example, federal and state policymakers, employers, donors, and others have emerged as key stakeholders in institutional decision-making and accountability. Faculty tenure review processes that value the principles of teaching, research, and service have similarly shifted to include professional growth, quality of patient care (in the healthcare fields), and patents or commercialization of research in response to the knowledge-intensive economic priorities of the 21st century. Postsecondary institutions have become increasingly complex enterprises open to a wide range of understandings and interpretations (Birnbaum, 1988), and as a result are "familiar yet hard to describe, unpredictable though sometimes rational, rooted in history yet forward-looking, traditional yet teaching others to anticipate change" (Manning, 2013, p. 11). They have become prototypic organized anarchies, characterized by "problematic preferences, unclear technologies, and fluid participation" (Cohen & March, 1972, p. 1). Despite shifting priorities, competing interests, and circles of influence, modern postsecondary institutions nevertheless maintain systems of privilege and inequality that privilege those with access to dominant forms of habitus and oppress those without it. Indeed, as Foucault (1978/2000) has noted, power is totalizing.

Nonetheless, the totalizing effect of higher education as an instrument of expanding political, social, and economic power also creates the need for ever more college-educated specialists to replicate the system (Clark, 1960). While those with access to dominant forms of habitus benefit most from this replication and students from historically marginalized and minoritized populations remain underrepresented throughout postsecondary education systems, the need for more college-educated specialists has also resulted in the expansion of educational opportunity. Well-resourced private liberal arts colleges, for example, reproduce the values of the elite through stringent admissions requirements and high tuition. Through education, affluent children become increasingly well-suited for social and economic positions that demand wealth and power, a process recently described as a hereditary meritocracy (Economist, 2015). However, elite liberal arts colleges also increasingly value access for students from historically marginalized and minoritized populations—if only for purposes of public perception—and, in so doing, provide a mechanism to interrupt the strict system of social reproduction that might otherwise pervade.

Likewise, many public colleges and universities, meanwhile, admit students en masse through rolling admissions policies and lower admissions standards; offer large courses that can comprise pedagogical effectiveness; and are subject to tougher legislative oversight and budgetary constraints. However, the same institutions enroll roughly the same numbers of National Merit Scholars and other high-achieving students as elite liberal arts colleges (Geiger, 2015); employ a highly trained faculty drawn by the prospect of graduate teaching (Hoxby, 2009); and generate opportunities for social mobility (Baker, 2014). While these opportunities for social mobility are unequally stratified (Bowen et al., 2009), they do nonetheless exist. This trend can also be seen at community colleges, which despite having been plagued by low retention and graduation rates throughout their history (Brint & Karabel, 1989) do allow some students access to professions and further education that would otherwise not be attainable (Clark, 1960). However, a more cynical reading of that same structuring of opportunity would suggest that community colleges exist in order to mitigate differences between students' educational aspirations and the material, social, and economic realities that interfere with them. This "cooling out" process gradually recenters students' educational aspirations toward more achievable goals and maintains structural inequalities (Clark, 1960). The net effect of the institutional structuring of opportunity is that some students do realize profound learning gains and others do not.

Campus Climate for Learning

The DLE developed by Hurtado et al. (2012) holds that campus climate is a multidimensional construct that directly influences learning outcomes. Consisting of historical, organizational, compositional, behavioral, and psychological dimensions, climate has a direct effect on the way that students experience the postsecondary learning environment. Empirical research on campus climates has shown that climate is experienced negatively by those from historically marginalized and minoritized populations (Hurtado, Griffin, Arellano, & Cuellar, 2008). Negative climate-related experiences, in turn, constrain students' social and academic experiences in ways that limit learning for all students (Hurtado et al., 2012).

Beginning with the historical dimension of a campus climate, many institutions have overlooked their own past and present roles in the maintenance of slavery, exploitative economic practices, white supremacy, and other oppressive systems (e.g., Biondi, 2012; Brint & Karabel, 1989; Wilder, 2013). In response, students have organized to demand that the troubling historical legacies on many college and university campuses be addressed (Black-Liberation Collective.org, 2015; Kelley, 2016). This activism has reshaped higher education institutions and curricula in profound ways (e.g., Biondi, 2012; Rojas, 2010), which reflects the way in which multiple systems of social oppression also intrude into the organizational dimension of a campus climate. Student activism has often also targeted the need for more diverse staff, faculty, and administrators (Boren, 2001)—a clear attempt to alter the compositional dimension of the campus climate. Finally, recent attention drawn to microaggressions and calls for more diversity training for university staff are just two examples of the psychological and behavioral dimensions of student attempts to reshape campus climates (BlackLiberationCollective.org, 2015; Kelley, 2016). Even though students are not typically addressing campus climate explicitly in their demands, the demands themselves target the dimensions of campus climate, which in turn impacts the learning of all students (Bowman, 2010).

Student Identity and Learning

The unresolved and continued legacies of slavery, white supremacy, capitalism, racism, and other systems of power and oppression mean that most higher education institutions are still premised on an institutional habitus that privileges affluent, cisgendered, heterosexual, able-bodied, white men. The privileged dividend comes into conflict with today's increasingly diverse student population across race, ethnicity, class, gender, gender identity and expression, sexual orientation, age, immigration status, and ability (Renn & Reason, 2013). Despite the tendency to view diversity through the lens of a single historically marginalized or minoritized population at a time, the reality is that the vast majority of students are navigating multiple identities that are connected to larger systems of oppression (Wijeyesinghe & Jones, 2014). The connection between learning, student identity, intersectionality, and larger structures of power, oppression, and privilege is reinforced by the decades of campus climate research concentrated in the DLE (Hurtado et al., 2012). As a whole, intersectionality provides us with a lens to push beyond singular and static notions of identity to view students much more holistically as a necessary condition for understanding each student's unique learning process. Without embracing a more holistic, complex, and intersecting notion of student identity higher education could very well inhibit student learning.

The Curriculum, Cocurriculum, and Learning

Curriculum, "the formal academic experience" expected of students as part of the completion of degree program (Ratcliff, 1997), varies considerably from institution-to-institution and program-to-program (e.g., Barnhardt, 2015; Brint, Cantwell, & Hanneman, 2008; Knight, Lattuca, Kimball, & Reason, 2013). In fact, as Lattuca and Stark (2009) have indicated, the curriculum results from a series of decisions made by a variety of actors that result in a "plan" for a student's education. That plan comprises disparate elements such as: the goals for expected outcomes held by individuals, institutions, governments, and other social actors; the content included and excluded; the sequencing of coursework; instructional techniques; facilities and techno-logical resources; and the alignment (or lack thereof) between students and other curricular elements (Lattuca & Stark, 2009; Toombs & Tierney, 1991, 1993).

However, as Lattuca and Stark (2009) have noted, many of the deci-sions that comprise institutional curricula are either made in a way that is less than deliberate and planful. The shared governance environment dictates that many actors have a vested interest in the construction of curricula—including individual faculty members, department chairs, academic administrators, and academic senates (e.g., Birnbaum, 1989; Del Favero, 2003; Knight & Holen, 1985; Minor, 2004). This overlapping system of responsibility has led some to label higher education an organized anarchy (Cohen & March, 1986) and others to compare institutional decision making to herding cats (Hammond, 2005). Curricula, which are comprised of many intersecting and overlapping decisions, lay bare the full complexity of colleges and universities, and notably, a focus on the cocurriculum only serves to clarify the ambiguity. In the cocurriculum, institutions are limited in their ability to ensure student participation even when intentional in the creation of cocurricular experiences (Harper, 2011). Indeed, by its very definition the cocurriculum is intended to support the curriculum by "serv[ing] as an applied curriculum that often presents students with the opportunity to put into action what they have learned in the classroom, whether that learning is content based...or interpersonally based" (Benjamin & Hamrick, 2011).

By design, the curriculum and cocurriculum contribute to learning. However, given the complexity of organizational decision making in colleges and universities, we suggest that their default tendencies are toward the replication of the dominant societal habitus; examining reports on the design of both curricula and cocurricula reveals as much. For example, the Liberal Education & America's Promise initiative (2011), one of the Association of American Colleges and Universities' signature programs, described three outcomes for their proposed liberal education that are of broad societal interest. These included preparation to participate in both "a globally engaged democracy" and "a dynamic, innovation-fueled economy" (AAC&U, 2011, p. 6). Both goals were focused on making a student fit a broader social structure. Only the third outcome—"the development of individual capability"— actually afforded students agency and suggested the potential for largely self-directed learning (AAC&U, 2011, p. 6). Likewise, the Lumina Foundation's Degree Qualification Profile [DQP] juxtaposed societal interest and individual student outcomes: "The DQP recognizes that U.S. higher education is in the midst of significant change, challenged to deliver a 21st century higher education system that effectively balances the learning needs of students with the rapidly changing economic needs of the U.S.—and indeed the global— community" (Lumina Foundation, 2014).

The cocurriculum is also constructed with a view toward broader societal interests. For example, in a synthesis of the major outcomes of the postsecondary experience intended for novice student affairs professionals, Hamrick, Evans, and Schuh (2002) listed five types of outcomes. These included the production of: (1) educated persons, (2) skilled workers, (3) democratic citizens, (4) self-aware and interpersonally sensitive individuals, and (5) life skills managers. Societal interests rather than individual outcomes undergird many of these goals; however, perhaps reflecting the value that the student affairs profession places on holistic, person-centered development, several goals also reflect individual learning processes. Individual learning processes do occur in colleges and universities: they may just be a secondary or unintended outcome.

Indeed, the history of higher education suggests that students have frequently found formal curricula and cocurricula to be lacking and have used the student-led creation of learning spaces like libraries, development of literary societies, debate clubs, academic organizations, Greek Life, student activities, and athletics programs as mechanisms to recraft higher education to suit their learning needs (Geiger, 2015; Thelin, 2011). At times, these interventions have even directly modified the formal curricula and cocurricula offered by colleges and universities; for example, student movements in the 1960s and 1970s led directly to the creation of academic programs that addressed issues of race, ethnicity, sexuality, gender, geography, and economy that the institutionally developed curriculum did not (Boren, 2001; Ferguson, 2012). In many cases, the students who precipitated the expansion of these curricula also indicated their desire for ongoing independence from standard institutional proscriptions of curricula and robustly supported the curricula that they developed using cocurricular learning opportunities such as student organizations and periodicals (Biondi, 2012; Rojas, 2010). In almost every case, however, both these curricular and cocurricular developments were quickly subordinated to formal mechanisms of institutional control (Ferguson, 2012).

Learning and Postsecondary Outcomes

Despite the proliferation of research on learning outcomes such as critical thinking, postformal reasoning, civic engagement, identity development, multiculturalism, and moral development (Pascarella & Terenzini, 2005; Renn & Reason, 2013), there are few agreements as to what is actually meant by learning in higher education research (Bloland, Stamatakos, & Rogers, 1994; Reason & Renn, 2008). Arguments regarding learning and the related process of development further complicate attempts to find a resolution (e.g., King & Baxter Magolda, 1996; Schroeder & Hurst, 1996). While ambiguity exists as to what is and is not meant by learning in higher education literature, we contend that some of the ways in which learning has been described are more meaningful than others. The domain-specific learning gains described in the introduction of this chapter (Renn & Reason, 2013) may not fully prepare students for the complexities of life after college, as the challenges individuals face across their lifespan become increasingly complex (Kegan, 1982). As long as the call for knowledge remains bounded within a domain of specialization, this kind of learning is useful. However, when separated from their domain of origin, the knowledge that has been mastered becomes obsolete.

Expanding on Freire's (1970/2000) banking model of education analogy, mastery of domain-specific knowledge is akin to depositing funds in a single savings account. Meanwhile, the realities of life across the lifespan may demand more than one account, more than one bank, and more than one way of accessing these funds. A broader understanding of the banking system as a whole yields additional information as to the nature of money, capital, and potential inequities that exist within such a system as well as one's own location within it. This awareness, a kind of critical consciousness, represented true learning for Freire (1970/2000) because it emancipates the learning from perpetual indebtedness to oppressive systems linked to educational institutions. We believe this to be a more meaningful form of learning in the struggle to combat knowledge obsolescence. Furthermore, in the development of critical consciousness, personal and social transformation cannot be separated from the other (Freire, 1970/2000); thus, as the individual learns and grows, so too do the communities in which they live.

Transformative learning similarly explains how our expectations, framed within cultural assumptions and presuppositions, directly influence the meaning we derive from our experiences (Mezirow, 1996). Understood as "the process of using a prior interpretation to construe a new or revised interpretation of the meaning of one's experience in order to guide future action" (Mezirow, 1996, p. 162), transformative learning theory explains changes in meaning structures in two areas: instrumental learning and communicative learning. *Instrumental learning* is achieved through task-oriented problem solving, and through the internalization of cause and effect relationships. *Communicative learning* involves problematic ideas, values, beliefs, and feelings, and "critically examining the assumptions upon which they are based, testing their justification through rational discourse and making decisions predicated upon the resulting consensus" (Mezirow, 1996, p. 58). In transformative learning theory, changes in instrumental and communicative learning perspective catalyze transformation in three dimensions of self: (1) psychological (changes in the understanding of self); (2) convictional (revisions of belief systems), and (3) behavioral (modifications in the way we live). These three work in concert with one another to produce a deeper understanding of the self as contextualized within a set of environmental conditions for the purposes of personal and communal growth.

In our discussion on learning in higher education, we contend that Freire's critical consciousness and Mezirow's transformative learning are significantly more meaningful forms of learning, yet nearly impossible to measure. While we argue that many of the examples described earlier of students repurposing or attempting to modify colleges and universities to facilitate their own learning are both transformative and emancipatory, we cannot demonstrate the frequency with which they occur on campuses. Indeed, when we measure learning, we seldom explore these dimensions at all. As a result, it may well appear that learning is not happening on college campuses when in fact some students learn a great deal simply by confronting an institutional habitus, climate, and environment hostile to them.

(In) Conclusion

Throughout this chapter, we have advanced the argument that structures of colleges and universities do not inherently lend themselves to learning but rather toward social reproduction and the maintenance of the status quo. Empirical evidence has shown gains in domain-specific learning, critical thinking, postformal reasoning, and holistic development (Pascarella & Terenzini, 2005; Renn & Reason, 2013). However, we question the extent to which this learning is accessible to all as well as the extent to which the very notion of learning is constrained by societal interests. Students whose social, political, and economic statuses afford them greater privilege enroll in and graduate from postsecondary institutions at a much higher rate than do students from historically marginalized and minoritized populations (Bowen et al., 2009). Government policy, prevailing social logics, and institutional structures all contribute to this disparity. Meanwhile, institutional climates, curricula, and cocurricula replicate the dominant societal habitus such that exploitative economic practices, white supremacy, and other oppressive systems shape the experiences of all students. Nonetheless, students have historically challenged these ideas and continue to do so to this day (Boren, 2001).

We argue that these challenges to the status quo open the door for authentic learning, which we describe in emancipatory, transformative terms (Freire, 1970/2000; Mezirow, 1996). That is to say, authentic learning is self-directed and unfettered by societal interests. Both the existing evidence for and against student learning in higher education can be explained in this way. We find evidence of learning when we define learning in a manner consistent with social reproduction and seek evidence for it among students whose social, political, and economic statuses mean that we will benefit most from this learning. We find more limited evidence of learning when it is operationalized holistically or across all student populations. However, we contend that it is precisely among historically marginalized and minoritized student groups that authentic learning is most likely to occur. In their struggle to repurpose higher education institutions not made for them and perhaps even hostile to their existence, they are engaged in a form of emancipatory, transformative practice that leads to learning. We simply seek out and measure that type of learning far too rarely.

References

Apple, M. (2011). *Education and power* (3rd ed.). New York, NY: Routledge.

Armstrong, E. A., & Hamilton, L. T. (2013). *Paying for the party: How college maintains inequality.* Cambridge, MA: Harvard University Press.

Arum, R., & Roksa, J. (2011). *Academically adrift: Limited learning on college campuses.* Chicago, IL: University of Chicago Press.

Association of American Colleges and Universities. (2011). *The LEAP vision for learning: Outcomes, practices, impact, and employers' views.* Washington, DC: Association of American Colleges and Universities.

Astin, A. W., & Oseguera, L. (2004). The declining "equity" of American higher education. *The Review of Higher Education, 27*(3), 321–341.

Baker, D. (2014). *The schooled society: The educational transformation of global culture.* Stanford, CA: Stanford University Press.

Barnhardt, C. L. (2015). Campus educational contexts and civic participation: Organizational links to collective action. *The Journal of Higher Education, 86*(1), 38–70.

Bell, D. A. (1980). Brown v. Board of Education and the interest-convergence dilemma. *Harvard Law Review, 93*(3), 518–533.

Benjamin, M., & Hamrick, F. A. (2011). How does the perception that learning takes place exclusively in classrooms persist? In M. B. Baxter Magolda & P. M. Magolda (Eds.), *Contested issues in student affairs: Diverse perspectives and respectful dialogue* (pp. 23-24). Sterling, VA: Stylus.

Biondi, M. (2012). *The black revolution on campus.* Berkeley, CA: University of California Press.

Birnbaum, R. (1988). *How colleges work: The cybernetics of academic organization and leadership.* San Francisco, CA: Jossey-Bass.

Birnbaum, R. (1989). The latent organizational functions of the academic senate: Why senates do not work but will not go away. *The Journal of Higher Education, 60*(4), 423–443.

Black Liberation Collective. (2015, December 10). *Black liberation collective.* Retrieved August 1, 2016 from http://www.blackliberationcollective.org/our-demands/

Bloland, P. A., Stamatakos, L. C., & Rogers, R. R. (1994). *Reform in student affairs: A critique of student development.* Greensboro, NC: ERIC Counseling and Student Services Clearinghouse.

Boren, M. E. (2001). *Student resistance: A history of the unruly subject.* New York, NY: Routledge.

Bowen, W. G., Chingos, M. M., & McPherson, M. S. (2009). *Crossing the finish line: Completing college at America's public universities.* Princeton, NJ: Princeton University Press.

Bowles, S., & Gintis, H. (2011). *Schooling in capitalist America: Educational reform and the contradictions of economic life.* Chicago, IL: Haymarket Books (Reprint of original work published in 1976).

Bowman, N. A. (2010). College diversity experiences and cognitive development: A meta-analysis. *Review of Educational Research, 80*(1), 4–33.

Brint, S., Cantwell, A. M., & Hanneman, R. A. (2008). The two cultures of undergraduate academic engagement. *Research in Higher Education, 49*(5), 383–402.

Brint, S., & Karabel, J. (1989). *The diverted dream: Community colleges and the promise of educational opportunity in America, 1900-1985.* New York, NY: Oxford University Press.

Brookfield, S. D. (2004). *The power of critical theory: Liberating adult learning and teaching.* San Francisco, CA: Jossey-Bass.

Clark, B. (1960). The "cooling-out" function in higher education. *American Journal of Sociology, 64,* 569–576.

Cohen, M. D., & March, J. G. (1972). *The American College President.* New York, NY: McGraw-Hill, Carnegie Commission on the Future of Higher Education.

Cohen, M. D., & March, J. G. (1986). *Leadership and Ambiguity: The American College President* (2nd ed.). Cambridge: Harvard Business School Press.

Crenshaw, K. (1989). Demarginalizing the intersection of race and sex: A black feminist critique of antidiscrimination doctrine, feminist theory and antiracist politics. *University of Chicago Legal Forum, 1989*(1). 139–167.

Delbanco, A. (2012). *College: What it was, is, and should be.* Princeton, NJ: Princeton University Press.

Del Favero, M. (2003). Faculty-administrator relationships as integral to high-performing governance systems: New frameworks for study. *American Behavioral Scientist, 46*(7), 902–922.

Deresiewicz, W. (2015). *Excellent sheep: The miseducation of the American elite and the way to a meaningful life.* New York, NY: Simon and Schuster.

Economist, The. (2015). America's elite: An hereditary meritocracy. *Economist, 414*(8922): 17–20.

Feldman, K. A., & Newcomb, T. M. (1969). *The impact of college on students.* New Brunswick, NJ: Transaction Publishers.

Ferguson, R. A. (2012). *The reorder of things: The university and its pedagogies of minority difference.* Minneapolis, MN: University of Minnesota Press.

Foley, D. E. (1994). *Learning capitalist culture: Deep in the heart of Tejas.* Philadelphia, PA: University of Pennsylvania Press.

Foucault, M. (2000). *Power.* (R. Hurley, Trans., J. D. Faubion, Ed.). New York; NY: New Press (Based on lectures originally given in 1978).

Freire, P. (2000). *Pedagogy of the oppressed* (M. B. Ramos, Trans.). New York, NY: Continuum (Reprint of original work published in 1970).

Gasman, M., & Hilton, A. (2012). Mixed motivations, mixed results: A history of law, legislation, historically Black colleges and universities, and interest convergence. *Teachers College Record, 114*(7), 1–20.

Geiger, R. L. (2015). *The history of American higher education: Learning and culture from the founding to World War II.* Princeton, NJ: Princeton University Press.

Gilbert, C. K., & Heller, D. E. (2013). Access, equity, and community colleges: The Truman Commission and federal higher education policy from 1947 to 2011. *The Journal of Higher Education, 84*(3), 417–443.

Giroux, H. A. (2001). Mis/education and zero tolerance: Disposable youth and the politics of domestic militarization. *Boundary 2, 28*(3), 61–94.

Giroux, H. A. (2003). Public pedagogy and the politics of resistance: Notes on a critical theory of educational struggle. *Educational Philosophy and Theory, 35*(1), 5–16.

Giroux, H. A. (2014). *Neoliberalism's war on higher education.* Chicago, IL: Haymarket Books.

Hammond, T. H. (2005). Herding cats in university hierarchies: Formal structure and policy choice in American research universities. In R. G. Ehrenberg (Ed.), *Governing academia* (pp. 91–138). Ithaca, NY: Cornell University Press.

Hamrick, F. A., Evans, N. J., & Schuh, J. H. (2002). *Foundations of student affairs practice: How philosophy, theory, and research strengthen educational outcomes.* San Francisco, CA: Jossey-Bass.

Harper, S. R. (2011). Strategy and intentionality in practice. In J. H. Schuh, S. R. Jones, & S. R. Harper (Eds.), *Student services: A handbook for the profession* (5th ed., pp. 287–302). San Francisco, CA: Jossey-Bass.

Harvey, D. (2005). *A brief history of neoliberalism.* Oxford: Oxford University Press.

hooks, B. (1981). *Ain't I a woman. Black women and feminism.* London: Pluto Press.

hooks, B. (2003). *Teaching community: A pedagogy of hope.* New York, NY: Routledge.

Hoxby, C. M. (2009). The changing selectivity of American colleges. *The Journal of Economic Perspectives, 23*(4), 95–118.

Hurtado, S., Alvarez, C. L., Guillermo-Wann, C., Cuellar, M., & Arellano, L. (2012). A model for diverse learning environments. In J. C. Smart & M. B. Paulsen (Eds.), *Higher education: Handbook of theory and research* (pp. 41–122). New York, NY: Springer.

Hurtado, S., Griffin, K. A., Arellano, L., & Cuellar, M. (2008). Assessing the value of climate assessments: Progress and future directions. *Journal of Diversity in Higher Education, 1*(4), 204–221.

Kegan, R. (1982). *The evolving self: Problem and process in human development.* Cambridge, MA: Harvard University Press.

Kelley, R. (2016, March 7). Black study, Black struggle. *Boston Review.* Retrieved from http://bostonreview.net/forum/robin-d-g-kelley-black-study-black-struggle

Kerr, C. (1963): The idea of a multiversity. In C. Kerr (Ed.), *The uses of the university* (pp. 1–45). Cambridge, MA/London: Harvard University Press.

Kett, J. F. (2013). *Merit: The history of a founding ideal from the American Revolution to the twenty-first century.* Ithaca, NY: Cornell University Press.

Kimball, E. (2011). College admission in a contested marketplace: The 20th century and a new logic for access. *Journal of College Admission, 207,* 20–30.

King, P. M., & Baxter Magolda, M. B. (1996). A developmental perspective on learning. *Journal of College Student Development, 37*(2), 115–117.

Knight, D. B., Lattuca, L. R., Kimball, E. W., & Reason, R. D. (2013). Understanding interdisciplinarity: Curricular and organizational features of undergraduate interdisciplinary programs. *Innovative Higher Education, 38*(2), 143–158.

Knight, W. H., & Holen, M. C. (1985). Leadership and the perceived effectiveness of department chairpersons. *The Journal of Higher Education, 56*(6), 677–690.

Lapon, G. (2015). The political economy of student loans. *International Socialist Review, 98,* 82–108.

Lattuca, L. R., & Stark, J. S. (2009). *Shaping the college curriculum: Academic plans in context.* San Francisco, CA: Jossey-Bass.

Lumina Foundation. (2014). *The degree qualifications profile: A learning-centered framework for what college graduates should know and be able to do to earn the associate, Bachelor's or Master's degree.* Indianapolis, IN: Lumina Foundation.

Manning, K. (2013). *Organizational theory in higher education.* New York, NY: Routledge.

Mettler, S. (2014). *Degrees of inequality: How the politics of higher education sabotaged the American dream.* New York, NY: Basic Books.

Mezirow, J. (1996). Contemporary paradigms of learning. *Adult Education Quarterly, 46*(3), 158–173. Retrieved September 2, 2008 from the SAGE Social Science Collections.

Minor, J. T. (2004). Understanding faculty senates: Moving from mystery to models. *The Review of Higher Education, 27*(3), 343–363.

Mullen, A. L. (2010). *Degrees of inequality: Culture, class, and gender in American higher education.* Baltimore, MD: Johns Hopkins University Press.

Nasaw, D. (1981). *Schooled to order: A social history of public schooling in the United States.* New York, NY: Oxford University Press.

Nathanson, R. (2016). The right to free college. *In These Times, 40*(1), 12–13.

Núñez, A. M. (2014). Advancing an intersectionality framework in higher education: Power and Latino postsecondary opportunity. In *Higher education: Handbook of theory and research* (pp. 33–92). New York, NY: Springer.

Pascarella, E. T., & Terenzini, P. T. (1991). *How college affects students: Findings and insights from twenty years of research.* San Francisco, CA: Jossey-Bass.

Pascarella, E. T., & Terenzini, P. T. (2005). *How college affects students: A third decade of research.* San Francisco, CA: Jossey-Bass.

Posselt, J. R., Jaquette, O., Bielby, R., & Bastedo, M. N. (2012). Access without equity longitudinal analyses of institutional stratification by race and ethnicity, 1972–2004. *American Educational Research Journal, 49*(6), 1074–1111.

Ratcliff, J. L. (1997). What is a curriculum and what should it be. In J. G. Gaff & J. L. Ratcliff (Eds.), *Handbook of the undergraduate curriculum: A comprehensive guide to purposes, structures, practices, and change* (pp. 5–29). San Francisco, CA: Jossey-Bass.

Reason, R. D., & Renn, K. A. (2008, November). *Why quibble over learning and development?* Paper presented at the Annual Meeting of the Association for the Study of Higher Education, Jacksonville, FL.

Renn, K. A., & Reason, R. D. (2013). *College student in the United States: Characteristics, experiences, and outcomes.* San Francisco, CA: Jossey-Bass.

Rivera, L. A. (2015). *Pedigree: How elite students get elite jobs.* Princeton, NJ: Princeton University Press.

Rojas, F. (2010). *From black power to black studies: How a radical social movement became an academic discipline.* Baltimore, MD: Johns Hopkins University Press.

Schroeder, C. C., & Hurst, J. C. (1996). Designing learning environments that integrate curricular and cocurricular experiences. *Journal of College Student Development, 37,* 174–181.

Seaman, B. (2005). *Binge: What your college student won't tell you.* Hoboken, NJ: Wiley.

Selingo, J. J. (2013). *College (un) bound: The future of higher education and what it means for students.* New York, NY: Houghton Mifflin Harcourt.

Spring, J. (2016). *Deculturalization and the struggle for equality: A brief history of the education of dominated cultures in the United States.* New York, NY: Routledge.

Stevens, M. L. (2009). *Creating a class: College admissions and the education of elites.* Cambridge, MA: Harvard University Press.

Thelin, J. R. (2011). *A history of American higher education.* Baltimore, MD: Johns Hopkins University Press.

Toombs, W., & Tierney, W. G. (1991). *Meeting the mandates: Renewing the college and departmental curriculum.* Association for the Study of Higher Education-ERIC Higher Education Report. Washington, DC: Association for the Study of Higher Education.

Toombs, W. E., & Tierney, W. G. (1993). Curriculum definitions and reference points. *Journal of Curriculum and Supervision, 8*(3), 175–195.

Trow, M. (1999). American higher education: Past, present and future. In J. L. Bess & D. S. Webster (Eds.), *Foundations of American higher education* (2nd ed., pp. 7–22). New York, NY: Pearson Custom Publishing.

Welch, N. (2015). Educating for austerity: Social reproduction in the corporate university. *International Socialist Review, 98,* 58–81.

Wijeyesinghe, C. L., & Jones, S. R. (2014). Intersectionality, identity, and systems of power and inequality. In D. Mitchell Jr., C. Y. Simmons, & L. A. Greyerbiehl (Eds.), *Intersectionality & higher education: Theory, research, & Praxis* (pp. 9–19). New York, NY: Peter Lang Publishing.

Wilder, C. S. (2013). *Ebony & ivy: Race, slavery, and the troubled history of America's universities.* London: Bloomsbury Press.

Wright, B. (1988). "For the children of the infidels?" American Indian education in the colonial colleges. *American Indian Culture and Research Journal, 12*(3), 1–14.

18. Are College Students Learning More or Less Than in the Past?

Sergio Ossorio and Kimberly A. Kline

From the historic colleges established during the colonial era to the cornucopia of contemporary institutions of higher education, which take shape in various forms (public and private colleges, for-profit colleges, four-year and two-year colleges, community colleges, and universities), student learning has been at the forefront of the central focus of these corporations. But what is student learning, and what do educators need to know to effectively measure it?

These questions have permeated systems of education throughout history. Faculty have deemed them the driving force of their curriculum. Student affairs professionals have adored the ideas, theories, and learning outcomes that sprout from posing them. Institutions have used them to assess the effectiveness of their faculty's teaching and the level of educational prowess gained by their students throughout their collegiate careers.

As these questions are considered, a hotly contested new topic of debate has risen: are college students learning more or less than in the past? It may be argued that the past and the present, in both higher education and student learning, are differentiated by cultural shifts and the introduction of technology; and these shifts have reconstructed the learning environments of today relative to yesterday. But these nuances of change do not alter the core function and purpose of higher education—student learning. Hence, to determine whether collegians are learning "more" than before, student success must be evaluated in all aspects of the term. Perhaps this question cannot be answered. Sure, we can attempt to assess student success today in comparison to the past. But it would be most beneficial to our students, faculty, staff—our living organism of education, and our world—to bestow light upon the mishaps of our current systems used to evaluate the learning processes taking place in our institutions of higher education. Our students are learning in the classroom, but we do not know what they are learning due to the inadequacy of our measurement tools.

Before we can measure student learning, we must understand what this word means. Student learning is a process that is demonstrated when a student does something as a means to learn, and this process can be understood in terms of the student's focus of attention (Laurillard, 1979). Essentially, student learning is a complex phenomenon; the context of this term includes social, political, psychological, and organizational forces that either indirectly or directly affect college student learning (Braxton, 2002). The effectiveness of the learning outcomes college students experience is highly, but not solely, determined by the instruction and curriculum prescribed to them in the classroom. Evans, Forney, Guido-DiBrito, and Patton (2010) describe the correlation between curriculum and student learning:

> A relevant curriculum is needed that is sensitive to individual difference, offers diverse perspectives, and helps students make sense of what they are learning. The assumptions about student learning that underlie the curriculum and the process by which learning takes place have as much impact on outcomes as the specific curricular content. (p. 70)

The curriculum encapsulates the framework for the learning experience. Therefore, the connection between each student and the curriculum needs to be harmonious to provide a high standard of quality education for the student. When rapport between the student and the curriculum is established, there is a link created that removes any hindering and unwanted distance between the two that can foster disinterest and dissent within the learning experience. If such a disruptive relationship is built, the student's learning experience will become fractured; the student will either fail or refuse to make sense of what it is she is learning. The curriculum needs to be founded in a jurisdiction of synchronization for the student, the faculty's instruction, and the curricular content; otherwise the impactful experience that is desired will not be reached.

When affective teaching strategies—such as "active learning, student-faculty interaction, timely feedback, high expectations, and respect for individual learning differences" (Evans et al., 2010, p. 70)—are paired with satisfactory curricular content and an appropriate bond shared between the student and the curriculum, the student will potentially be exposed to interpersonal sensitivity, cooperation, and interdependence (Evans et al., 2010). Such healthy attributes nurture self-development. The curriculum should provide a structure that yields information about the learning experience. It should also have a component in it that serves as a measurement tool for student learning. Reports, examinations, and projects serve as this component, but they are inadequate when they stand alone.

A pivotal piece is missing in this set of evaluation processes. That piece is the affective domain, which encompasses the abstract and intangible results of a student's learning experience. The affective domain is a principle found in a classification of learning objectives known as Bloom's Taxonomy of Learning (Weigel & Bonica, 2014). Bloom's Taxonomy is comprised of three domains: cognitive, affective, psychomotor (Weigel & Bonica, 2014). These domains were developed as principles to classify educational outcomes. The affective domain can be perceived as the "feeling/heart," or undertakings that influence emotions (Weigel & Bonica, 2014). A detailed discussion of the other domains is beyond the scope of this chapter. In the affective domain, the primary goal is to tailor student learning toward the student's emotions in an attempt to stimulate the student's feelings and create an in-depth learning experience that cannot be replicated or achieved with any other teaching method(s) where an emotional tie is absent. This approach toward education engages student learners and allows them to intimately and holistically immerse themselves in the atmosphere of interconnectedness that a classroom or educational experience is meant to deliver.

Juxtaposed with the affective domain model, it is not uncommon to witness the practice of the banking concept of education, a conception Paulo Freire (2000) denotes as a negative and oppressive form of education. Freire (2000) explains the banking concept of education as a process in which knowledge is considered a gift imparted by an individual who considers herself knowledgeable upon others who are considered to be ignorant. Freire (2000) provides a perceptible example to clarify this notion: "the teacher presents himself to his students as their necessary opposite; by considering their ignorance absolute, he justifies his own existence" (p. 72). Oppressive forces exercised in the classroom are intolerable and prohibited, and yet such painful affairs are still prevalent in the classroom. While the plight of our country's education system displays scattered concerns, the plea for educational aims and methods designed to manage mechanisms that support educational objectives in the affective domain remains highly justifiable. The emotional well-being of our students is a crucial element in student learning; this idea need not be a political conviction in a written exposition, but a work of art and action in the classroom.

Educational objectives in the affective domain entail objectives that relate to both feelings and commitment (West, 1969). A student's learning experience should be based on emotion just as strongly as it is currently based on cognition. The affective domain sets educational objectives that target the emotions of the student, so the learning experience becomes enriching when it is composed of this additional feeling-centered outcome. As sentient beings, humanity is fond and inseparable of emotion; it affords our existence purpose and meaning. To provide our educational experiences with the same substance is to enhance student learning—the practice of education—with purpose and meaning. Dewey and Dewey (1990) elaborate on this notion when they express the idea that behind the visible results—the outward product and the outward doing—is a fresh mental attitude, a wider and more compassionate vision, and the desire to intertwine capacity and insight with the interests of the world and humankind. The tangible and intangible fragments of our lives are equally important. Thus, college student learning would find benefit in investing equally in the affective domain as well as the cognitive domain.

From a dialogical perspective, postsecondary institutions do not sufficiently measure student learning. Instead, we are accustomed to measuring portions of student learning—portions pertaining to specific and limited learning outcomes that largely assess criteria of knowledge based on memorization of curriculum content. In essence, such assessment tools deprive educators of the understanding needed to effectively evaluate an educational experience. One prospective aid to this dilemma is coconstructed learning, or collaborative learning. Collaboration in this context can be defined as a joint effort toward the exploration of a cooperative "problem space" in hopes of solving a problem (Baker, 2015). Often, as previously noted, in the banking concept of education, students are seldom considered equals vis-à-vis prior knowledge and other social characteristics (Baker, 2015). The term "student" is a condition that excludes the consideration of collaboration within the interactions between teacher and student (Baker, 2015). Collaborative learning is a process in which a problem is solved with both others and alone to strengthen the grasp students have over their conceptualization of the problem (Baker, 2015). Consequently, collaborative learning, in postsecondary education, requires the student and the teacher, the student and the student(s), and the student and the professional staff to work in unison to achieve adequate student learning outcomes. It is the responsibility of each of these parties to pursue solidarity in the educative process. In this pursuit, collaborative learning performs as a set of partnerships created to foster creativity in the way we measure student learning. This approach offers each party with access to a calculation method that determines what the student has learned.

The ideas presented thus far may emerge as constructs of radical education, but these abstract philosophies are all grounded in concrete designs. For instance, Kolb's Theory of Experiential Learning (Evans et al., 2010) is similar to the domains of Bloom's Taxonomy of Learning. Kolb's theory consists of a four-stage cycle: concrete experience, reflective observation, abstract conceptualization, and active experimentation (Evans et al., 2010). Concrete experience is understood as a feeling dimension, abstract conceptualization is considered the thinking dimension, and active experimentation is perceived as a doing dimension (Evans et al., 2010). The cognitive, affective, and psychomotor domains of Bloom's Taxonomy are formulated much like three of the four stages in Kolb's cycle. Ultimately, both theoretical models argue that a wholesome educational experience should include these aforementioned principles. Evans et al. (2010) express the notion that, to work effectively, learners need each of the abilities characterized in the four parts of the learning cycle. Thus, again we see it argued that an all-inclusive educational experience derives from more than only a cognitive focus. Learning outcomes must be diverse in their nature, less strict, and more comprehensive in the various unique qualities and learning styles that make up the human experience. If we desire the best method(s) for college student learning, we must measure what is being learned and target the numerous constituents of human ontological being through creative means, while ensuring that our instruction refrains from oppressive teaching styles.

To continue our dialogue on the matter of creativity and its association with college student learning, let us consider the thought that creative expression is a necessity in the formula that constitutes a holistic student learning experience: "imagination and creativity are integral parts of our classrooms and their inclusion is as natural to most of us as breathing" (Young, 2009). Young (2009) introduces the idea of authentic assessment as a promising link in national and state education reform. Authentic assessment is alluded to as assessment practices that target the evaluation of critical thinking skills and creative problem-solving capabilities (Young, 2009). Young (2009) argues that creativity and imagination coincide with higher levels of thought processing, and they are pivotal factors in authentic assessment. Creativity and imagination are missing elements in college student learning assessment. These components of the student learning experience require measurement, not negligence. Like the affective domain principle, creativity and imagination may be perceived as intangible entities often found difficult to understand; thus, how will we attempt to measure such abstract human creations to ensure that they are adequately represented in our student learning experiences? Young (2009) suggests we avoid assessing creativity as a quantifiable product, and more as a process of student growth to which we cannot attach a number. With this assessment method, we can offer students the opportunity to focus on the presence of creativity in their work versus the level of creativity they produce in their work. This individualistic expression of freedom in the classroom develops the bond between the student and the overall learning experience. With this shift in mind, there is less pressure to accompany student work, which allows for a strengthened existential experience for the student, given that she is not compelled to tailor her work to the strictures of numeric criterion.

Authentic assessment invites humanity rather than expels it. When creativity is extracted from the student in exchange for a static, hollow, and alienated learning experience, the student falls subject to a form of instruction Freire (2000) refers to as narrative education. Narrative education annuls the creative power of the student and leads her to mechanically memorize the narrated content provided by the teacher (Freire, 2000). Lonka, Olkinuora, and Mäkinen (2004) describe this process of memorization as surface level learning, whereas deep level learning is a more intricate process where the student pays attention to the meaning and significance offered in the materials to be learned. As students take on the role of depository and the teacher serves as the depositor, students become containers whose purpose is to continue to be filled with deposits (Freire, 2000). There is no room for transformation or transcendence in this erroneous and oppressive system.

As student affairs professionals, it is our charge to ensure that the institutions we serve, and the services our institutions provide our students, is as free of oppressive taint as possible. We are called to the majestic responsibility of guiding our students toward enlightenment and liberation. Therefore, our educational objectives and tools used to measure those objectives must coexist with freedom.

References

Baker, M. J. (2015). Collaboration in collaborative learning. *Interaction Studies, 16*(3), 451–473. doi:10.1075/is.16.3.05bak

Braxton, J. M. (2002). Introduction: Influences on college student learning. *Peabody Journal of Education, 77*(3), 1–5. doi:10.1207/s15327930pje7703_1

Dewey, J., & Dewey, J. (1990). *The school and society; and, the child and the curriculum.* Chicago, IL: University of Chicago Press.

Evans, N. J., Forney, D. S., Guido-DiBrito, F., & Patton, L. D. (2010). *Student development in college: Theory, research, and practice* (2nd ed.). San Francisco, CA: Jossey-Bass.

Freire, P. (2000). *Pedagogy of the oppressed.* New York, NY: Continuum.

Laurillard, D. (1979). The processes of student learning. *Higher Education, 8*(4), 395–409. doi:10.1007/bf01680527

Lonka, K., Olkinuora, E., & Mäkinen, J. (2004). Aspects and prospects of measuring studying and learning in higher education. *Educational Psychology Review, 16*(4), 301–323. Retrieved from http://www.jstor.org/stable/23363874

Weigel, F. K., & Bonica, M. (2014, January–March). An active learning approach to Bloom's Taxonomy: 2 games, 2 classrooms, 2 methods. *U.S. Army Medical Department Journal*, 21+. Retrieved from http://proxy.buffalostate.edu:2101/ps/i.do?id=GALE%7CA361848302&v=2.1&u=buffalostate&it=r&p=AONE&sw=w&asid=1d5a27962b5b5be7bbf3de0a75bd861c

West, E. H. (1969). Editorial comment: The affective domain. *The Journal of Negro Education, 38*(2), 91–93. Retrieved from http://www.jstor.org/stable/2294266

Young, L. (2009). Imagine creating rubrics that develop creativity. *The English Journal, 99*(2), 74–79. Retrieved from http://www.jstor.org/stable/40503364

Part Ten: Can Technology and Distance Instruction Save Higher Education?

In "Instructional Technology as Revolutionary Savior of Higher Education Classrooms: An Analysis of Scope, Ethics, and Values," David S. Knowlton defines "instructional technology" as the "integration of media into a systematic teaching and learning process." Though granting that it alone will not save higher education, he suggests that online education, through instructional technology, can reinforce student identity and reduce the power differential between instructor and student through knowledge-based authority. He also bemoans the questionable assumption of some administrators that distance education cannot increase profit margins and faculty productivity. Knowlton concludes that instructional technology, as part of sound pedagogy and appropriate use of media, can indeed "revolutionize" postsecondary education.

In "Will Technology and Distance Instruction Save Higher Education?" Paul Gordon Brown contends that colleges and universities can be marginally enriched by the use of technology. He discusses various pedagogical methods, how distance education provides greater access for adult learners, and how technology can facilitate competency-based instruction. At the same time, he claims that for-profit institutions have eroded public trust in online learning. While arguing that technology offers no panaceas, he agrees that it should be considered as part of any number of teaching strategies. Finally, Brown affirms that technology has afforded a more flexible approach to a system that has been relatively impervious to competition, market demands, and consumer behavior.

19. Instructional Technology as Revolutionary Savior of Higher Education Classrooms: An Analysis of Scope, Ethics, and Virtues

DAVID S. KNOWLTON

When I was first asked to write a chapter arguing that technology could be the savior of the higher education classroom, I immediately felt unsettled, overwhelmed, and intimidated. I was surprised by my own negative reaction. After all, I am a professor of instructional technology, and I have done much faculty development promoting the use of technology in the higher education classroom. When I teach face-to-face courses, I regularly tell my students to boot their laptops, get out their cell phones, and fire up their tablets, as I have found that these tools can help elevate the quality of classroom discourse and provide pathways toward student engagement. Furthermore, these days, I mostly teach online courses, and I have been known to argue that online courses can be more pivotal and transformative than their face-to-face, traditional counterparts. Thus, enthusiastic advocacy of instructional technology as applied in both traditional and online classrooms would seem to be right up my natural alley.

Still, I was so overwhelmed by the task of arguing for a full embrace of instructional technology that I almost declined the invitation to write this chapter. Upon accepting the invitation, I began my own walk through a process of uncovering my apprehension. A first reason for apprehension related to clarity over definitions of terms.

(1) Do administrators share my assumptions about the very nature of instruction?
(2) Is there a common understanding of the definition of technology?
(3) When I use the term "online courses," will that mean the same thing to me, as a faculty member, that it means to an administrator?

To address this concern, this chapter will explicitly define instructional technology and its relationship to online courses. As a second point of apprehension, I had concern over the word "savior" to describe instructional technology's role in higher education. The many god terms that could be used in an advocacy chapter dripped with hyperbole to the point where I worried that my arguments could not be taken seriously: Instructional technology and online courses as *savior, virtuous, ideal, transformative, revolutionary, game changer*. On the one hand, who could be against such things? On the other hand, such terms merely add a cheerleading component to advocacy. But are readers of this chapter and I cheering for the same team or merely the same mascot? Thus, this chapter brings negative value judgments to various arguments about a few seeming virtues of instructional technology. The use of god terms must be put in appropriate context.

The two points of ill-ease that I have just described led me to a third apprehension: Many of my experiences suggest that administrators often are not open to hearing the ethereal and theoretical viewpoints of faculty members. After all, such viewpoints privilege complexity and ambiguity while marginalizing straightforward and metric-driven policies that are easy to implement. As I pondered this point of apprehension, I quickly realized that any simplistic argument about instructional technology and its virtues would inherently lead only to administrator support for the preservation of the status quo. If there is anything that I bemoan as a professor of instructional technology, it is the propping up of the status quo and a that's-the-way-it's-always-been mentality. Instructional technology must provide motivation for administrators to innovate higher education institutions. No, straightforward and cut-to-the-chase policy positions will not do within a chapter that advocates for instructional technology.

Defining the Parameters of Instructional Technology

Commonly, technology invokes images of things—a computer, tablet, cellphone, or other device. If such a view prevails, then asking if technology can save higher education is akin to asking if toothbrushes can save our teeth. Can any inanimate object garner the momentum to serve as savior? There is no suspense here; the answer is a resounding "no." After all, inanimate objects are...well, ..."inanimate," not to put too fine of a point on it. On one level, it may seem to be a statement of the obvious that computers and other devices are inanimate and have no power to save higher education classrooms. But, I regularly hear stakeholders express assumptions that, say, PowerPoint will create better learning than a chalkboard or that a computer adds learning power in ways that pen and paper do not. This line of thinking approaches the idea of technology in too narrow of a way.

If, however, we appropriately broaden our understanding of technology, then we suddenly might have a robust basis upon which to build the argument that technology has the potential to save the higher education classroom. I borrow Galbraith's (1967, p. 12) classic definition of technology is "the systematic application of...organized knowledge to practical tasks" (cited in Commission on Instructional Technology, 1970, p. 21). Building upon Galbraith's definition, Reiser (2001) has interpreted "technology" in plain language by noting that its root word is "technique." Technology, properly understood, then, is not an inanimate object; technology is an application or process. The inanimate objects that we use within the process best are described as hardware, software, media, or devices. In sum, instructional technology is the integration of media into a systematic teaching and learning process. Any arguments that aim toward instructional technology as savior of the higher education classroom must keep this definition within their sites.

Why does this distinction matter? Is it nothing more than academic word play and intellectual obfuscation meant to distract administrators from efficiency and progress? Absolutely not! Evidence is clear that media and devices do not, in themselves, lead to learning; rather, these are instructional strategies. This means that the cogent design and implementation of instruction and learning environments lead to learning (Clark, 1983, 1994a, 1994b, 2001). Certainly, there are those who disagree by offering conjecture that media does have power to create learning (see Kozma, 2001). Empiricism shows, however, that when instructional strategies are held constant, changes in media do not result in stronger learning outcomes or achievement (Morrison, 1994).

Superficially, the definition of technology and assertions about the impotence of media that have just been offered should call into question the quality of any argument about the merits or problems of instructional technology that merely defines technology as tool. More cogently, though, a broader understanding of technology leads to a fairly tight logical progression: *If* online courses depend upon technology and *if* technology, properly understood, is the thoughtful application of media, *then* distance education depends upon a process of soundly applying media as an abiding piece of a teaching and learning process. Such logic creates a context for the advocacy of instructional technology. Advocacy is not excitement over tools; rather, it is excitement over pedagogical process that might, but might not, work hand-in-hand with various tools. Instructional technology advocacy must depend on techniques both of designing and implementing the learning environment (Knowlton, 2000).

Unethical Notions of Instructional Technology as Savior of Higher Education Classrooms

Even with technology defined, the sense in which instructional technology can *save* the higher education classroom is not clear. One person's savior is another's arch fiend. Some purposes of harnessing instructional technology might initially seem virtuous, but they are not. This section addresses two purposes that should be rejected because the value added is an immature value, given the true potential of Instructional Technology. Each purpose focuses on online courses.

Online Courses as Fiscal Savior

I have heard administrators claim that online courses can save higher education. More online courses with larger enrollments are an algorithm for profits, so this line of reasoning goes; and profits can save a college or university. Such reasoning is faulty in multiple ways: To begin, within the structure of such reasoning, hidden costs remain hidden. Designing and developing online courses are quite expensive when compared to face-to-face courses. Faculty members need release time for design and development (Bailey & Card, 2009; Orr, Williams, & Pennington, 2009), but release time adds costs. Also, to maintain online courses, ongoing fiscal investment in technical support and equipment must be a priority (Fish & Wickersham, 2009; Orr et al., 2009).

The costs listed so far are necessary, but they are not sufficient. After all, the costs that I have just discussed suggest that faculty members have both the know-how to design online courses and the skill to use media productively. On average, though, faculty members are not experts in media use, online course design, and online pedagogy. Along with the investments of time and equipment, then, administration must support faculty members as they get trained *both* technically (Fish & Wickersham, 2009; Orr et al., 2009) *and* pedagogically (Knowlton, 2000; Palloff & Pratt, 2000).

Yet another hidden cost is associated with government oversight and regulation, as illustrated by the recent case of ITT Technical Institute, Inc. In bringing up this case, I am not taking a stand for or against private educational institutions involving themselves in online learning. I also am not taking a stand in the proper role of government in providing oversight of educational institutions, whether private or public. I merely am suggesting that, for better or worse, government oversight is a reality; and with the proliferation of various types of online courses, the financial burden placed upon institutions to comply with government regulations likely will continue to become heavier. As the press release announcing the closure of ITT Tech shows, these administrative burdens, while sometimes seeming unreasonable, are a reality that can have a huge impact on online course offerings (see ITT Tech, Inc. to Cease Operations, 2016). These increased costs need to be considered within administrators' claims that online courses will be of value in saving higher education.

Beyond the overlooking of hidden costs of online courses, administrative calls for the large-scale proliferation of online courses in the name of profits ignore a more egregious problem as learning becomes subservient to profit. Consider, for instance, the costs that have already been discussed in this chapter. How can such costs be mitigated? Profit only comes with a large scaling of online offerings.

As goes scaling, so goes class size; as goes class size, inversely goes faculty-to-student interaction (Sorensen, 2015). Decreasing these interactions through larger class sizes makes it less likely that students will receive personalized help and quality feedback from faculty members, yet such interaction may well be essential to ensure student learning in online classrooms (Knowlton, 2000).

I agree with Speck (2000) in arguing that any technology that is integrated into university classrooms must promote learning; any agenda prioritized above learning creates an ethical breach of an implied social contract between higher education institutions and society at large. Certainly, when such a breach occurs, faculty members rightly should stand up and become the academy's conscience, blowing the whistle of ethical breach loudly. Will administration stand in solidarity with whistle-blowing faculty to ensure that learning reigns supreme? I do not demean a profit motive. I do argue that any higher education stakeholders who undermine student learning in the name of profits are not on solid ground. Speck (2000) offers a solution to ensure that there is no ethical breach:

> Return to faculty the right and responsibility to determine pedagogical issues related to the use of technology in classrooms. The faculty should have the

authority to determine...good academic practice. ...I am concerned that the integrity of the academic enterprise not be compromised under the guise of educational progress that is driven primarily—perhaps solely—by economic gain. (pp. 80–81)

Online Courses to Free Up Faculty Time

The scarlet letter of guilt is worn not only by administrators who might be inclined to put profit over learning but also by faculty members who sometimes declare inappropriate uses of online courses to be a savior to higher education classrooms. Thus, the notion of faculty members reigning supreme as the arbiters of good academic practice is the proverbial double-edged sword, and it may well be online students who are gorged. For instance, I worry that some faculty members see online courses not through a lens of good academic practice but through one of convenience, as prefabricated course packages produced by publishing companies serve as teacher and metrics and analytics that track student behavior—when and for how long each student logged on and which links she/he clicked—serve as proxy for student achievement, intellectual growth, and learning. The professor, then, saves time and is more efficient in the work of teaching because there is less to be done. Any professor who thinks that he/she can be replaced by a computer probably should be!

Nevertheless, a course that is guided by media as opposed to being one guided by a pedagogical process is no savior; it is a sham. Virtuous pedagogical processes and techniques require a range of human efforts, including advising and facilitating of students' thinking. Strong pedagogy, human investment, and leadership are lost when a media-driven approach—as opposed to a technology-driven approach—reigns supreme.

This unvirtuous media-driven approach to saving higher education with online courses normalizes and exacerbates what Sperber (2000) calls "the non-aggression pact" (p. 112). Hagopian (2013) summarizes Sperber's concept by noting that the nonaggression pact is "a state of détente in which the needs, aspirations, and pathologies of individual learners are ignored so that professors may use the energies conserved to conduct and publish research" (p. 8). When online courses set aside and undermine student selfhood in the name of faculty ease and efficiency, the higher education classroom's central purpose of learning is compromised.

A virtuous technology-driven approach does not lessen the work of faculty members. In fact, some evidence suggests that technology increases the demands that students place upon faculty, as many students expect faculty to use the tools indicative of the online classroom to communicate frequently and quickly (see, for instance, Fullerton, 2013). Said differently, faculty members who enter the online teaching arena might notice that some time is "freed up" because they are not in the classroom, but they equally should recognize that "other time commitments will take its place, such as facilitating online interactions, supporting the development of social presence and building community" (Watwood, Nugent, & Deihl, 2009). In some cases, it takes over twice as much time to teach the same course online compared to in-class. This was true even while there were less than half the number of students in the online compared to the in-class section (Cavanaugh, 2005). The time commitment of teaching online relative to face-to-face is a constant issue within the literature of online teaching; consistently, it has been found that online teaching, when done well, takes *more* time on the part of the faculty member (Mandernach, Hudson, & Wise, 2013).

Typically, when I put forth this argument about the lack of virtue inherent to online courses serving as a time-saving device for faculty members, the response from many faculty members goes something like this: "Pedagogy is not part of my field as much as is content." In other words, these faculty members are declaring that bad pedagogy "didn't kill me as a student, and it won't kill these students either" (Cox, Harrison, & Hoadley, 2009, p. 151). This response is inappropriate, as it privileges an unthoughtful pedagogy that defies learning. As this chapter has made clear, though, the very word "technology" points to process; unthoughtful process is the antithesis, then, of sound instructional technology.

To summarize, putting profits and faculty member efficiency ahead of student learning is shameful. These uses of online courses are not a pathway toward saving higher education; rather, they provide potential ruin and pervert virtuous priorities. Using instructional technology to motivate profit and shift faculty priorities should be given no credence within higher education as an argument.

Three Virtues of Technology That Can Save Higher Education Classrooms

The arguments put forth in this chapter, thus far, create an implied theoretical framework for understanding instructional technology as a potential savior of higher education classrooms. This framework includes several key points: Technology is not a synonym for tool; it is a *synonym* for process. Thus, instructional technology is a process of instruction that sometimes happens to require media. Pedagogy is more important than are tools. Also, this framework has suggested the lack of ethics of putting institutional profits or efficiency in teaching above student learning. In fact, robust instructional technology will *increase* the amount of time that faculty members spend teaching. Only with this framework in mind can any arguments about the virtues of instructional technology be ethical.

In what ethical sense can instructional technology be a savior to the higher education classroom? Following the lead of Hagopian (2013), I argue that traditional and online classrooms must become "enchanted spaces" where students question their own assumptions about both the very nature of learning and themselves as learners (p. 13). Such a classroom defies the metrics that can be included within bureaucratic reports and grades that can be documented within transcripts. Enchanted spaces disrupt, rather than stabilize; and thus they defy administrative ease and embrace learning rebellion. College and university administrators need to broaden their perspective of classroom media and the technology that supports it in order to see a teaching and learning process that will save higher education from merely replicating obsolete rituals of classrooms from the past. Only through a revolution in the process of teaching and learning can instructional technology save higher education; administration must understand and embrace the revolution in order to best support it.

In what follows, I put forth three arguments about the virtues of instructional technology. Each argument is congruent with this chapter's implied theoretical framework; and each argument aims for disruption of traditional classroom moors and milieus. My purpose here is not pedagogical guidance for faculty members; rather, my purpose is to provide insight that might inspire administrators' visions of how instructional technology virtuously can save higher education classrooms.

Expansion of Time and Psychological Space

In traditional face-to-face classrooms, time often seems linear, episodic, and clearly demarcated. There is in-class time and out-of-class time. Curriculum often is based in a linear conception of time as students read a textbook from the first chapter to the last. A syllabus is crafted from week one forward and organized around isolated topics. Classroom activities often have time limits or absolute due dates according to a set time. Such traditional views of time rarely are questioned by administrators, faculty members, or students. After all, what else is there? With appropriate applications of today's media, though, more cyclical and fluid uses of time can be capitalized upon to shape virtuously the teaching and learning process.

Fluid approaches to time are virtuous because fluidity in time promotes well-considered doing and thinking. Thoughtful writing, for instance, is a nonlinear process that can be enhanced through a cyclical approach that integrates microbursts of drafting, revising, reconsidering, and redrafting such that each aspect of writing blurs in time with other aspects (Elbow, 1973; Lindemann, 1995). In terms of thinking, consider the role of time within creative thought. Essential to a creative process of thinking is incubation time where ideas can either percolate below the subconscious (see Csikszentmihalyi, 1996) or emerge through deliberate cognitive activity (see Knowlton & Sharp, 2015). In other words, sometimes thoughts come into focus through deliberate activity; other times, thoughts seem to appear out of nowhere in moments of respite. Similarly, essential to critical thinking is the time necessary for thoughts to shift from cognition to distributed cognition (see Jonassen & Carr, 2000) and toward metacognition (see Sitko, 1998). The use of time within these processes of doing and thinking are not stable and do not conform to linearity. Different students might need different qualities and quantities of time in order to have the necessary psychological space that creates achievement. If online courses can create a fluid sense of time such that students have their own psychological space for work, then it seems reasonable to conclude that students might better be able to harness time and reap dividends.

Can instructional technology help students harness time to create more meaningful psychological space? The answer is a resounding "yes," if professors will only apply media to allow it. In what follows, I focus on online classrooms to illustrate possibilities for fluid time and broader psychological space. Simonson (2000) gently alludes to this notion of fluid time when he argues that online learning should not provide standardized approaches to learning; rather, the strong application of media (i.e., the technology) should provide diverse opportunity for equivalent learning. Sugrue (2000) agrees: "[A]pplications [should] attempt to balance learner freedom and system control, perhaps providing feedback to students as data for self-reflection, but not dictating what they should do next" (p. 134). If online courses are designed well, then time becomes fluid and malleable; and students have different dimensions of psychological space in which to work, allowing them to weave and carve time as opposed to passively existing within it. A newly carved conception of time and psychological space can bring with it an intellectual and emotional vitality that might lie dormant in more linear courses. The following describes the result on time of a solid instructional technology.

With online courses that are based upon synchronous media and technologies, separation between in-class and out-of-class time disappears—any time is class time. Thanks to the ubiquitous nature of mobile media, students can engage in their coursework during students' lunch hours at their jobs, while sitting in a doctor's office, or in a local park. This melding of time allows students to shape the time of their learning efforts around their preferences, conveniences, and perceived proclivities. Both night owls and early birds can "attend class" on more of an equal footing. While one side of the coin allows students to shape time, the other side of the coin is the intrusion of coursework upon a student's nonschool time. Thus, students' day-to-day lives beyond their asynchronous time become more connected to what they are learning. Because any time is class time, then, an online course takes up psychological space in a student's life, even when that student wishes to turn off the class. For instance, in reflecting on a course assignment that required the submission of ideas through social media, one graduate student noted, "This assignment took up more space in my day-to-day life and forced me to think about school outside of my standard-scheduled homework time" (Nygard, Day, Fricke, & Knowlton, 2014, p. 7).

Beyond the blurring of the time for class, the online classroom can expand the dimensions of time while coursework is underway. Consider that during a face-to-face, traditional class session, only one person can talk at a time. This limits the number of voices heard within the given time span of a class session, and it diminishes qualities of thought, as developing quality and thought requires considerable time. Through the use of discussion boards, chat features, and other asynchronous media, giving ideas a voice and receiving those ideas becomes multidimensional. Multiple students can voice their ideas at any given moment in time, and those ideas can be received at other times. The interaction of discussion no longer is a horizontal construct; it is vertical, as well, since at any given moment in time multiple students can overtly share their insights, questions, and so forth, while multiple other students take in that which has been shared. That is, within online courses, media can provide time that is either "pointillist" (episodic moments of time that can later serve as building blocks for learning) or "cyclical" (the ebb and flow and tension and release inherent to online discussion) (Ihanainen & Moravec, 2011, p. 27). Because online communication is archived and more permanent than ineffable speech discussions are, the pointillist and cyclical types of learning are more easily achieved. And, both pointillist and cyclical time can overlap into moments of "serendipity" and "evolution of dialogue" (Ihanainen & Moravec, 2011, p. 31).

Reconstruction of Student Identity

Many students are out of touch with why they even are in college (Hassel & Lourey, 2005). Their identity on campus often is not aligned with their academic work but is, instead, aligned with a nonacademic "selfhood" that exists "in the dorms, bars, Greek houses, stadia, and other social spaces of the university" (Hagopian, 2013, p. 8). Traditional classrooms can unwittingly reinforce nonacademic student identities. After all, in a traditional classroom, students' physical presence becomes their identity, as there is the notion that students who occupy a chair or desk are "identified" by virtue of their embodied presence in the room. But, that physical presence might well create identity through personal demeanor, the Greek letters on students' chests, body posture, levels of extroversion, fashion sensibilities, or cultural conformity. Students who are poised with energy and anticipation in the front of the room have a very different identity than the ones who seemingly are slouching in the back to hide behind other more-prepared students.

The online classroom provides opportunity to facilitate a more substantive identity based upon students' ideas and thoughts. In fact, once superficial elements of physical presence are diminished through online media, students' identity depends on their expressed ideas, beliefs, and values. Student expression within a learning process is important, and "[u]ntil a classroom milieu fosters students' willingness to share their beliefs, pretense will take precedent over learning" (Knowlton, 2010, p. 75). If a student is not contributing ideas in an online course, then will anyone know that student even exists? (see Knowlton, 2000, or Palloff & Pratt, 1999). To rephrase the classical philosophical principle: In the online classroom, students are because they think. And because identity of a student is based upon that student's thoughts, identity becomes more productively complex and serves as a focal point upon which students can consider their own development, as well as the development of classmates. Several elaborations and extensions of this point reinforce the view that well-applied media can create a more substantive student identity in both online and traditional classrooms.

First, the argument that has been put forth here leads to an understanding that instructional technology can help students use computers as problem-solving tools to construct their identity. Mainstream news outlets claim alarming levels of unhealthy addiction to media among college students (Kardaras, 2016), and this addiction, so the line of argument goes, interferes with students' ability to express themselves cogently because students' sense of intellectual presence is squelched. Students' identity becomes one of inappropriate immersion in their social media presence. Instructional technology helps change this use of media as media becomes a more serious communication tool to enhance their intellectual identity, not a mindless distraction. For instance, in a large lecture hall, students often become detrimentally anonymous. But, within these halls, social media can provide backchannels for communication that create deeper intellectual engagement (Junco, Heiberger, & Loken, 2010), a broader presence (Elavsky, 2013; Elavsky, Mislan, & Elavsky, 2011), and, thus, a clearer identity. While a student might become physically lost as one student in a sea of faces, that students' ideas—and thus, his/her intellectual identity—can be transported to the screen for all to see.

Second, social interaction creates stronger identity than does mere contribution (Knowlton, 2005). Interaction takes the ideas that students express and enlarges them through dissemination. Dissemination creates opportunity for broader negotiation and debate, which adds additional dimensions to intellectual identity. Constructed, then, is an identity of ideas that become more productively complex through the mutual consideration of course content (see, for instance, Baxter & Haycock, 2014). *If* students' ideas about content become synonymous with that students' identity and *if* ideas become the basis of media-enhanced interaction, *then* in a myriad of ways, instructional technology is focused on the creation of complex identity through a consideration of course content.

Third, the absence of physical cues provides more of an opportunity for students to develop a better understanding of themselves through a metacognitive identity. Arguments come far and wide that mediated communication takes away needed cues and norms that accentuate and enhance communication, such as body language, facial expression, and nuance of voice. It is true, of course, but the result can be that students must find ways to insert these missing communication elements through emojis, parentheticals, and other devices to help the readers of their ideas—whether professors or other students—better understand the personality, nuance, and intended meaning of expressed ideas (Knowlton & Nygard, 2016; Weiss, 2000). By consciously inserting these cues, students are creating a type of metacognitive feedback loop for understanding themselves and their own intentions within mediated communication. The process of inserting one's self in extraverbal ways creates more self-awareness in one's own identity. And, such awareness adds substance within online classrooms (Knowlton, 2005).

I recognize, of course, that there are exceptions to my argument that instructional technology creates more substantive issues of student identity. For instance, students regularly use unthoughtful Snapchat photos as their course avatars. And, students sometimes contribute to, say, online course discussions with the same care and thoughtfulness that they upload an Instagram photo of their breakfast. Still, because sound uses of communication media depend on student constructions as a sign of student existence, there is more of an opportunity that students will become what they think and thus they think what they become.

The Leveling of Formal Authority

This final point about the potential of instructional technology to revolutionize higher education is related to classroom authority: Who holds authority? Who should hold authority? What perspective on authority is most useful to ensure meaningful learning for students? Professors traditionally hold formal authority by virtue of both their academic credentialing and their contract with a university or college. Formal authority often seems to be above reproach in the opinions of both faculty members and administrators. It is this formal authority that many professors and administrators seem to point to as the reason that students should respect and defer to faculty members (Knowlton, 2013; Speck, 2013). Reliance on formal authority, however, is inappropriate and does damage to meaningful learning opportunities (Hagopian, 2013; Knowlton, 2010, 2013; Speck, 2000, 2013). Formal authority can squelch classroom dialogue and questioning (Hagopian, 2013), and it can build counterproductive barriers between faculty members and students (Knowlton, 2013).

Instructional technology can undermine formal authority and level classrooms for a more appropriate balance of power. Some of the balance of power comes as a result of students having better access to information through the medium of the web. As early as 1998, predictions of the web's power as a source of information were clear: "Despite the seeming anarchy of the web—its transitory nature, its built-in information overload and search tools that cannot, as of yet, provide absolutely reliable and exhaustive results—we will find more and more useful materials moving into this ever expanding cyberspace" (Dobler & Bloomberg, 1998, p. 69). Those predictions have come true, and students no longer must rely solely on a professor's expertise for information and ideas. More of the leveling of authority is seen through a culmination of previous points in this chapter. As instructional technology promotes manipulation of time for more fluid student harnessing and provides opportunity for a stronger sense of student identity, the playground of the classroom becomes more leveled with regard to authority. The use of instructional technology allows students' voice to confidently emerge.

When formal authority is undermined, then what is left? One answer to that question is the professor's pedagogical authority (Speck, 2013). Another answer to that question is legitimate student authority (Hagopian, 2013; Knowlton, 2010). The leveling of authority that instructional technology can enable is far from unfortunate. As professors have to let go of formal authority and move toward pedagogical authority, it seems reasonable to conclude that opportunities for student learning will be elevated, not diminished. Pedagogical authority, after all, relies on a faculty member's ability to elicit information and ideas from students, not merely to input that information in a mechanical way. The result of less reliance on a faculty member's formal authority and more reliance on both pedagogical and student authority likely will be clear: Revolution of the learning environment and disruption of the status quo (Knowlton, 2010).

Conclusion

No doubt, instructional technology will change the landscape of higher education, in general, and higher education classrooms, more specifically. The real key is whether this change will catch university administrators and faculty flatfooted and reactively or agile and proactively. This chapter has put forth multiple ideas to help administrators inform their vision of what proactive leadership might entail with regard to instructional technology. Academic freedom of faculty members is not enough to move instructional technology forward. Administration must come to the forefront to help the use of instructional technology truly innovate and shape the university classroom. Administrative support is a necessary ingredient to help instructional technology serve as the savior of higher education classrooms.

References

Bailey, C., & Card, K. (2009). Effective pedagogical practices for online teaching: perception of experienced instructors. *Internet and Higher Education, 12*, 152–155.

Baxter, J. A., & Haycock, J. (2014). Roles and student identities in online large course forums: Implications for practice. *International Review of Research in Open and Distance Learning, 15*(1), 20–40.

Cavanaugh, J. (2005). Teaching online—A time comparison. *Online Journal of Distance Learning Administration, 8*(1). Retrieved from http://www.westga.edu/~distance/ojdla/spring81/cavanaugh81.htm

Clark, R. E. (1983). Reconsidering research on learning from media. *Review of Educational Research, 53*(4), 445–459.

Clark, R. E. (1994a). Media will never influence learning. *Educational Technology Research and Development, 42*(2), 21–29.

Clark, R. E. (1994b). Media and method. *Educational Technology Research and Development, 42*(3), 7–10.

Clark, R. E. (2001). The media versus methods issue. In R. E. Clark (Ed.), *Learning from media: Arguments, analysis, and evidence* (pp. 205–217). Greenwich, CN: Information Age Publishing.

Commission on Instructional Technology. (1970). *To improve learning: a report to the president and congress of the United States.* Washington, DC: US Government Printing Office.

Cox, C. D., Harrison, S., & Hoadley, C. (2009). Applying the "studio model" to learning technology design. In C. DiGano, S. Goldman, & M. Chorost (Eds.), *Educating learning technology designers* (pp. 145–164). New York, NY: Routledge.

Csikszentmihalyi, M. (1996). *Creativity: Flow and the psychology of discovery and invention.* New York, NY: Harper Perennial.

Dobler, B., & Bloomberg, H. (1998). How much web would a web course weave if a web course would weave webs? In J. R. Galin & J. Latchaw (Eds.), *The dialogic classroom: Teachers integrating computer technology, pedagogy, and research* (pp. 67–91). Urbana, IL: National Council of Teachers of English.

Elavsky, C. M. (2013). Activating ego-engagement through social media integration in the large lecture hall. In D. S. Knowlton & K. J. Hagopian (Eds.), *From entitlement to engagement: Affirming millennial students' egos in the higher education classroom* (pp. 61–67). San Francisco, CA: Jossey Bass.

Elavsky, C. M., Mislan, C., & Elavsky, S. (2011). When talking less is more: Exploring outcomes of Twitter usage in the large-lecture hall. *Learning, Media and Technology, 36*(3), 215–233.

Elbow, P. (1973). *Writing without teachers.* New York, NY: Oxford University Press.

Fish, W., & Wickersham, L. (2009). Best practices for online instructors. *The Quarterly Review of Distance Education, 10*(3), 279–284.

Fullerton, D. S. (2013). What students say about their own sense of entitlement. In D. S. Knowlton & K. J. Hagopian (Eds.), *From entitlement to engagement: Affirming millennial students' egos in the higher education classroom* (pp. 31–36). San Francisco, CA: Jossey-Bass.

Galbraith, J. K. (1967). *The new industrial state.* Boston, MA: Houghton Mifflin.

Hagopian, K. J. (2013). Rethinking the structural architecture of the college classroom. In D. S. Knowlton & K. J. Hagopian (Eds.), *From entitlement to engagement: Affirming millennial students' egos in the higher education classroom* (pp. 7–18). San Francisco, CA: Jossey-Bass.

Hassel, H., & Lourey, J. (2005). The dea(r)th of student responsibility. *College Teaching, 53*(1), 2–13.

Ihanainen, P., & Moravec, J. W. (2011). Pointillist, cyclical, and overlapping: Multidimensional facets of time in online learning. *International Review of Research in Open and Distance Learning, 12*(7), 27–39. Retrieved from http://www.irrodl.org/index.php/irrodl/article/view/1023/2040

ITT Educational Services, Inc. to Cease Operations. (2016, September 6). Press release. ITT Educational Services, Inc. to Cease Operations at all ITT Technical Institutes Following Federal Actions. Retrieved from http://www.ittesi.com/2016-09-06-ITT-Educational-Services-Inc-to-Cease-Operations-at-all-ITT-Technical-Institutes-Following-Federal-Actions

Jonassen, D. H., & Carr, C. S. (2000). Mindtools: Affording multiple knowledge representation for learning. In S. P. Lajoie (Ed.), *Computers as cognitive tools: No more walls* (pp. 165–196). Mahwah, NJ: Lawrence Erlbaum Associates.

Junco, R., Heiberger, G., & Loken, E. (2010). The effect of Twitter on college student engagement and grades. *Journal of Computer Assisted Learning.* doi:10.1111/j.1365-2729.2010.00387.x

Kardaras, N. (2016, August 27). It's "Digital Heroine": How screens turn kids into psychotic junkies. *New York Post Online.* Retrieved from http://nypost.com/2016/08/27/its-digital-heroin-how-screens-turn-kids-into-psychotic-junkies/

Knowlton, D. S. (2000). A theoretical framework for the online classroom: A defense and delineation of a student-centered pedagogy. In R. E. Weiss, D. S. Knowlton, & B. W. Speck (Eds.), *Principles of effective teaching in the online classroom* (pp. 5–14). San Francisco, CA: Jossey-Bass.

Knowlton, D. S. (2005). A taxonomy of learning through asynchronous discussion. *Journal of Interactive Learning Research, 16*(2), 155–177.

Knowlton, D. S. (2010). Take out the tests, and hide the grades; add the spiritual with all voices raised! Professor explications and students' opinions of an unconventional classroom milieu. *Critical Questions in Education, 1*(2), 70–93. Retrieved from https://academyedstudies.files.wordpress.com/2015/02/knowltonvol1no21.pdf

Knowlton, D. S., & Nygard, S. (2016). Twitter in the higher education classroom: Known fragmentations and needed frameworks. *Journal on Excellence in College Teaching, 27*(1), 117–151.

Knowlton, D. S., & Sharp, D. C. (2015). Students' opinions of instructional strategies in a graduate-level creativity course. *International Journal for the Scholarship of Teaching and Learning, 9*(2), article 6. Retrieved August 7, 2015 from http://digitalcommons.georgiasouthern.edu/ij-sotl/vol9/iss2/6

Knowlton, H. M. (2013). Affirming ego through out-of-class interactions: A practitioner's view. In D. S. Knowlton & K. J. Hagopian (Eds.), *From entitlement to engagement: Affirming millennial students' egos in the higher education classroom* (pp. 69–74). San Francisco, CA: Jossey-Bass.

Kozma, R. B. (2001). Kozma reframes and extends his counter argument. In R. E. Clark (Ed.), *Learning from media: Arguments, analysis, and evidence* (pp. 179–198). Greenwich, CN: Information Age Publishing.

Lindemann, E. (1995). *A rhetoric for writing teachers* (3rd ed.). New York, NY: Oxford University Press.

Mandernach, B. J., Hudson, S., & Wise, S. (2013). Where has the time gone? Faculty activities and time commitments in the online classroom. *Journal of Educators Online,*

10(2), 15 pp. Retrieved from http://www.thejeo.com/Archives/Volume10Num ber2/MandernachHudsonWise.pdf

Morrison, G. R. (1994). The media effects questions: "Unresolvable" or asking the right question. *Educational Technology Research and Development, 42*(2), 41–44.

Nygard, S., Day, M., Fricke, G., & Knowlton, D. S. (2014). Four students' perceptions of a twitter-based assignment in a graduate-level graphic design course. *Quarterly Review of Distance Education, 15*(3), 1–14.

Orr, R., Williams, M., & Pennington, K. (2009). Institutional efforts to support faculty in online teaching. *Innovative Higher Education, 34*, 257–268.

Palloff, R., & Pratt, K. (1999). *Building a community of learners in cyberspace.* New York, NY: Wiley & Sons.

Palloff, R., & Pratt, K. (2000). Making the transition: Helping teachers to teach online. *EDUCAUSE 2000* in Nashville, October 10–13, 2000. Retrieved from http://net. educause.edu/ir/library/pdf/edu0006.pdf

Reiser, R. A. (2001). A history of instructional design and technology: Part 1: A history of instructional media. *Educational Technology Research and Development, 49*(1), 53–64.

Simonson, M. (2000). Making decisions: The use of electronic technology in online class-rooms. In R. E. Weiss, D. S. Knowlton, & B. W. Speck (Eds.), *Principles of effective teaching in the online classroom* (pp. 29–34). San Francisco, CA: Jossey-Bass.

Sitko, B. M. (1998). Knowing how to write: Metacognition and writing instruction. In D. J. Hacker, J. Dunlosky, & A. C. Graesser (Eds.), *Metacognition in educational theory and practice* (pp. 97–115). Mahwah, NJ: Lawrence Erlbaum Associates.

Sorensen, C. (2015). An examination of the relationship between online class size and instructor performance. *Journal of Educators Online, 12*(1), 140–159.

Speck, B. W. (2000). The academy, online classes, and the breach in ethics. In R. E. Weiss, D. S. Knowlton, & B. W. Speck (Eds.), *Principles of effective teaching in the online classroom* (pp. 73–82). San Francisco, CA: Jossey-Bass.

Speck, B. W. (2013). The bruised ego syndrome: Its etiology and cure. In R. E. Weiss, D. S. Knowlton, & B. W. Speck (Eds.), *Principles of effective teaching in the online classroom* (pp. 81–88). San Francisco, CA: Jossey-Bass.

Sperber, M. (2000). *Beer and circus: How big time college sports is crippling undergraduate education.* New York, NY: Henry Holt.

Sugrue, B. (2000). Cognitive approaches to web-based instruction. In S. P. Lajoie (Ed.), *Computers as cognitive tools* (pp. 133–162). Mahwah, NJ: Lawrence Erlbaum Associates.

Watwood, B., Nugent, J., & Deihl, W. (2009). *Building from content to community: [Re] Thinking the transition to online teaching and learning.* Virginia Commonwealth University: Center for Teaching Excellence, pp. 1–22. Retrieved from http://www.vcu. edu/cte/pdfs/OnlineTeachingWhitePaper.pdf

Weiss, R. E. (2000). Humanizing the online classroom. In R. E. Weiss, D. S. Knowlton, & B. W. Speck (Eds.), *Principles of effective teaching in the online classroom* (pp. 47–52). San Francisco, CA: Jossey-Bass.

20. Will Technology and Distance Instruction Save Higher Education?

PAUL GORDON BROWN

The question of whether or not technology will "save" higher education presupposes that higher education is in need of saving. But what does it need to be saved from? The challenges to colleges and universities in the United States are well documented: soaring costs (United States Department of Education, 2016), increased demands for accountability (Leveille, 2006), and a societal and governmental shift toward a view of higher education as a private as opposed to a public good (Kezar, Chambers, & Berkhardt, 2005). Although a number of these challenges relate to issues of policy and administration, recent advancements in web-enabled instruction and technology hold the promise of ameliorating some of these challenges. Although the data is mixed, courses and educational materials delivered digitally hold the potential to reduce instructional costs (Aldridge, Clinefelter, & Magda, 2013). Online education can also provide more flexible educational opportunities to fit with the differing life circumstances of students.

Although distance education has been discussed for decades (Allen & Seaman, 2016), it wasn't until the arrival of the world wide web in the early 1990s, and with recent advancements in web technology, that the necessary tools to deliver an effective online education began to fall in place. In particular, the web has democratized access to information. Individuals are now able to access knowledge and experts in ways not previously possible when the academy and the library were physical gatekeepers to access. As a result, some individuals are experimenting with alternatives to the traditional college education.

In her 2010 book, *DIY U: Edupunks, Edupeneurs, and the Coming Transformation of Higher Education*, Anya Kamenetz chronicles some of these students and higher education entrepreneurs who are "hacking" higher education. There are "artisans"—who hope to leverage technology to reduce costs, increase educational access, and improve student learning. There are "monks"—who are engaging Web content by creating it, consuming it, and remixing it. And there are also the "merchants"—educational start-ups and for-profit groups trying to monetize higher education by providing services that traditional institutions cannot quickly match. The examples provided by these groups highlight the ways in which technology is challenging traditional higher education paradigms. Although the nature of the academy and the way it operates may be changing, colleges and universities remain vitally important centers for scholarly production and education.

This chapter explores some of the ways technology is helping to address higher education's challenges. The chapter is organized around three potential ways in which technology and related educational delivery innovations can help transform higher education. First, addressing issues of cost and access to higher education, this chapter discusses the opportunity for open educational resources to democratize course content access and potentially lower instructional costs. Second, amid calls for greater flexibility in learning environments and accountability to diverse learning styles, there is a discussion of the potential of asynchronous and self-directed learning, of social and digital media tools, and of flipped and hybridized classroom models. Lastly, in response for a need to provide continuous learning and accommodations for adult learners, the chapter discusses competency-based modular educational systems, and certifications through more portable and open standards such as badges.

Lowering Costs and Increasing Access

Higher education was once something reserved only for the elites in society. From Cambridge and Oxford in England to the colonial colleges of the United States, it was a privilege most reserved for the select, often rich, few (Thelin, 2011). In 1948, however, the United Nations recognized that access to higher education according to ability is a basic human right (Universal Declaration of Human Rights, Art. 26, Sec. 1). As colleges and universities have evolved since, access to higher education has expanded greatly. Martin Trow (1989) famously referred to this as a progression from elite, to mass, and finally to universal higher education.

Scaling traditional higher education systems to accommodate a higher volume of students, however, has number of challenges. Chief among these is cost. Within the United States, since 2000, tuition at public four-year institutions has more than doubled, and at private institutions, tuition has raised by nearly a third (The College Board, 2016). As tuition has increased, government and educational assistance programs have failed to keep pace with this rise (Mumper, Gladieux, King, & Corrigan, 2011; National Center for Education Statistics, 2010). As a result, there are increased demands for lower-cost higher education alternatives. Technology can be seen as playing an important role in this process through movements toward more open access to educational resources, content, and knowledge, and through experimentation with one-to-many methods of educational delivery, such as with Massively Open Online Courses (MOOCs).

The movement toward open access to educational content began in earnest around the turn of the century. Open access literature (including educational materials such as textbooks, journal articles, and other scholarly publications) is literature that is "digital, online, free of charge, and free of most copyright and licensing restrictions" (Suber, 2012, p. 4). The provision of these materials, which were formerly available only in physical, more copyright-restricted formats, allows individuals to better engage in self-directed learning and allows educators to engage with and enhance their educational offerings.

In 2000, the Massachusetts Institute of Technology (MIT) took open access one step further through their OpenCourseWare (OCW) initiative (Abelson, 2008). OCW, also known as Open Educational Resources (OER), is "the open provision of educational resources, enabled by information and communication technologies, for consultation, use and adaptation by a community of users for non-commercial purpose" (UNESCO, 2002, p. 24). OER takes the traditional proprietary content of the university and provides it in a free, readily accessible format online. These open resources often include the posting of a "course description, syllabus, calendar, and at least one of the following: [1] lecture notes, [2] demonstrations, simulations, illustrations, learning objects, [3] reading materials, [4] assessments, [and, 5] projects" (UNESCO, 2002, p. 5). Since its inception, OCW has grown exponentially (MIT OpenCourseWare, 2011) and expanded to other colleges and universities across the globe (Arendt & Shelton, 2009; MIT OpenCourseware Consortium, n.d.; Vladoiu, 2011).

Open education initiatives are not just focused on content, but also the way in which higher education is delivered. One of the best examples of this is the MOOC. MOOCs are courses that are "made available over the Internet without charge to a very large number of people" ("MOOC," n.d.). What sets MOOCs apart from other online courses is that they are "open access" and designed for "unlimited participation" (Allen & Seaman, 2016, p. 8). They are also typically for free and often provided to unregistered students, although with no formal credit given (Allen & Seaman, 2016). As of 2015, approximately 14% of higher education institutions in the United States reported offering or planning to offer MOOCs (Allen & Seaman, 2016). Educational delivery in this way democratizes access and provides individuals with college-level coursework at little to no cost. It also provides adult learners with avenues for reeducation and self-education in ways not previously possible.

Although open movements, on their surface, may seem to pose a threat to colleges and universities, open access still requires institutions to produce and curate content. In this way, colleges and universities remain vitally important sites for scholarly production. Furthermore, as will be discussed later, institutions of higher education remain important for their ability to credential and certify learning. By providing open access to educational materials, higher education institutions are able to provide more flexible learning opportunities to more individuals, thus increasing participation and the overall addressable audience.

Accommodating Diverse Learning Styles and Enhancing Instruction

The opportunities provided by open educational content and opportunities for self-directed learning also have the ability to democratize access to education in a way that can accommodate the needs of diverse learners. One of the promises technologically enabled learning holds is its ability to encourage the exploration of topics in an interdisciplinary way and through the use of distributed networks of people and information (Bull et al., 2008; Greenhow & Robelia, 2004; National Science Foundation, 2006, Section I, Introduction). Davidson and Goldberg (2010) refer to this as "digital learning" or "participatory" learning.

The sheer size and global nature of the Web allow one to engage in "many-to-many" and "many-to-multitudes" communication (Davidson & Goldberg, 2010). This communication allows one to decouple learning from the institution. Learning under this regime is "unschooled." Unschooling is described as "a learner-centered democratic approach to education...[where] the learner chooses what, where, how, and when they want to learn something... [and] is empowered and has a substantive say in the running of the spaces and places that they inhabit" (Ricci, Laricchia, & Desmarais, 2011, p. 141).

With digital and participatory learning, students are able to create their own, and more sophisticated, Personal Learning Networks (PLN). PLNs are the network of people and content that contributes to and supplements our knowledge and learning (Rajagopal, Joosten-ten Brinke, Van Bruggen, & Sloep, 2012; Warlick, 2009). Although evolving in practice, the concept of a PLN is not new. Modern PLNs leverage technology to expand networks beyond older geographical and technical barriers that limited access. Kamenetz (2010) refers to these PLNs as the "ultimate educational resource" (p. 158). They include "the universe of people, texts, books, Web sites, blogs, any and all knowledge resources and relationships that help situate you in a community of practitioners" (Kamenetz, 2010, p. 158). Open educational resources, and the colleges and universities that provide them, maintain an important role in these networks and can leverage them to enhance instruction.

These changes can also be seen in the growth of multimedia and technological tools in the classroom. Numerous faculty members have begun experimenting with social and new media tools in their courses ranging from learning management systems to social networking sites (Joosten, 2012, McHaney, 2011). There is growing evidence that these technologies can provide for better educational outcomes. For example, research into the use of the social media service, Twitter, has found that it increases student engagement and has the potential to raise grades (Ebner, Lienhardt, Rohs, & Meyer, 2010; Junco, Elavsky, & Heiberger, 2013; Junco, Heiberger, & Loken, 2011; Lin, Hoffman, & Borengasser, 2013). By engaging with tools that reach beyond the university, students are exposed to a broader network for personal learning. This has the potential to create lifelong learners that are better equipped for knowledge consumption, production, and exchange. Skills are increasingly of critical importance in the 21st century work context.

Other higher education institutions are experimenting with alternative classroom environments that leverage technology. These include blended and flipped courses. Blended courses include both "online and face-to-face delivery" and a "substantial proportion of the content is delivered online," reducing the amount of time in physical classroom (Allen & Seaman, 2016, p. 7). Flipped classrooms move lectures to out-of-class time, typically through video and other preclass media, and instead use classroom time to involve students in discussion and hands-on problem solving (Edelson, Gordin, & Pea, 1999). A benefit to blended and flipped courses is that they provide learners with the opportunity for more flexible learning time while also freeing up instructors to use classroom time for outcomes better suited to the environment, including discussion, application, and inquiry-based learning (Edelson et al., 1999).

Flipped classrooms and blended courses are not without their critics who question their pedagogical merits (Ash, 2012; Thompson, 2011), but online education has its adherents. Private corporations are also looking to use these models as opportunities to provide employees with access to lower cost degrees with the flexibility required for working adults. Starbucks is a notable pioneer in this area, partnering with Arizona State University to provide online degree programs for its workers (Bluenstyk, 2014). JetBlue Airways has taken this program one step further leveraging open educational resources and testing-for-credit options to expand pathways for its employees (Ruff, 2016). Although there are rightful concerns about educational quality, choice, and corporate motivations in providing these options, they nevertheless highlight how online coursework's flexibility and cost structure may be an important piece of the equation when developing working adult education and reeducation programs.

Promoting Lifelong and Adult Learning

Adapting teaching and learning to meet the needs and expectations of today's marketplace and student populations extends beyond content and delivery into issues of portability, credentialing, and certification. Traditional methods of measuring and certifying student learning are not able to the keep pace with the demands for modern education. For example, the college "credit hour," also known as the "Carnegie unit," was originally conceived of as a way to measure student seat time, as opposed to student learning, and each institution applies it differently (Laitinen, 2012, p. 4; Wellman & Ehrlich, 2003, p. 1). The monolithic college degree, itself a collection of these credit hours, also does not provide the flexibility for lifelong learning and changing demands for future skills training.

Whereas OER is making previously proprietary content free, the "Badges for Lifelong Learning Project" (Badges Project) represents an "alternative path to accreditation and credentialing" (Digital Media and Learning Competition, para. 6). Initiated in 2011 through a grant from the MacArthur Foundation, the Badges Project is a collaboration between Duke University's Humanities, Arts, Science and Technology Advanced Collaboratory, the Mozilla Foundation, and numerous other corporations and nonprofit organizations. It entails an open competition to develop a system to certify digital and lifelong learning.

The Badges Project recognizes that learning takes place in a variety of contexts including in "afterschool programs and online tutorials, through mentoring, playing games, interacting with peers in person and in social networks, with smart phone apps, in volunteer workshops, at sports camps, during military training, and in countless other ways and other places" (Digital Media and Learning Competition, n.d., para. 1). A badge, or a digital icon or credential, is "a validated indicator of accomplishment, skill, quality or interest that can be earned in any of these learning environments" (Digital Media and Learning Competition, n.d., para. 2). Additionally, badges "support learning, validate education, help build reputation, and confirm the acquisition of knowledge" (Digital Media and Learning Competition, n.d., para. 2).

What is interesting about the Badges Project is that it is seeking to certify previously unquantified learning. Additionally, the badge is unbundling learning by attempting to create more discrete forms of certified education. In the college and university context, this is akin to a picking apart of the monolithic four-year degree. Much like OER began to liberate the individual course, the Badges Project is liberating other forms of learning and certifying them in much the same way a degree operates. The Badge Project further seeks to provide a system whereby this learning can be quantified and displayed in a uniform and centralized way. If successful, it will "support, identify, recognize, measure, and account for new skills, competencies, knowledge, and achievements for 21st century learners regardless of where and when learning takes place" (Digital Media and Learning Competition, n.d., para. 5).

Beyond badges, organizations such as the Lumina Foundation and the Bill and Melinda Gates Foundation, with help from the federal Department of Education, have begun efforts to create competency-based degree programs (Fain, 2012, 2014). In 2011, the Lumina Foundation first published its Degree Qualifications Profile, and in 2014 updated it to "help build a learning-based, student-centered system" for higher education (p. 2). The Degree Profile is referred to as a "qualifications framework" that "describes what degree recipients should know and be able to do" (The Lumina Foundation, 2014, p. 6).

The Degree Qualification Profile represents a map for developing competency and student learning-based certification for degrees. The University of Southern New Hampshire is already using the Profile as a basis for awarding associate degrees in general studies, and Western Governors University, a pioneer in the space, continues to innovate (Fain, 2012). With the structures beginning to take shape by which to quantify student learning, the next step in the evolution is to create certifications for these competencies and outcomes that can serve as complements to or perhaps even replace the credit hour.

Technology has the potential to promote lifelong and adult learning in ways not previously possible when courses and credit were restricted to physical colleges and universities offering monolithic degrees. The next step in the revolution will be maintaining educational quality and integrity while modularizing educational units. The future of higher education is likely to be much more nomadic, mirroring changes in the work environment. This is especially to the benefit of adult learners, who, because of life circumstances, may not be able to afford the luxury of going back to school to obtain another degree. Badges and competency-based education hold the promise of allowing workers to continue updating their skills through microlearning certifications.

New Challenges

Although the integration of technology and related reforms holds much promise to help transform higher education in a way that makes it more accessible, more responsive, and more flexible, it is not without caveats. Technology alone cannot be the answer to address all of the challenges that face colleges and universities. Online courses, and self-directed and asynchronous learning may not be the best for everyone. Individuals possess a number of different learning styles and life circumstances when they enter higher education. Technology is but one answer to addressing these diverse needs and providing choices to students. Traditional residential college education remains an important option to many, however. Technology should be employed in a way that does not replace this system, but enhances it and provides individuals with other opportunities for achieving educational goals. The ideal for higher education lies somewhere in-between the purely digital and purely traditional modes of educational delivery.

Technological solutions to current educational problems also have the potential to create new problems of their own. One may question what happens to the academic tradition of research and scholarship if courses and degrees become consolidated and commoditized. One may also question if cheaper online alternatives to more expensive residential education models may have the effect of creating an elite stratified system of education. Furthermore, if education is reduced to career-focused microcourses, the traditional strengths of the American system's liberal arts and civic education may be eroded. This segregation runs the risk of "cultural fragmentation," or the erosion of a common set of values (Organization for Economic Co-operation and Development, 2007, p. 12).

Further complicating this situation is the rise of for-profit online universities and the influence of private technology companies whose motives may be brought into question. Proprietary for-profit universities, in particular, often have open enrollments and may be perverting the traditional economics and values of the university by hiring one-time instructors to teach specific courses and lacking the traditions of academic freedom and shared governance (Altbach, 2001). Although beneficial on the level of increasing access, they provide little benefit to the overall public good. Additionally, the "degrees" they offer are often so specialized and technical, and their academics of such poor unaccredited quality, that they can barely be said to be universities at all (Altbach, 2001). In this sense, technology may be solving some problems, while creating entirely new ones.

Conclusion

This chapter reviewed ways in which technology is transforming higher education. Beginning with attempts to lower costs and increase access, it discussed open educational resources providing freely available content to all, as well as MOOCs, which represent ways of distributing this type of content with open education. It then moved on to discuss digital and participatory learning, the cultivation of personal learning networks, and experiments with blended and flipped classroom environments. These innovations have the opportunity to accommodate diverse learners and enhance instruction. Finally, badges and experiments with competency-based education were examined. These new systems allow for more flexible adult and lifelong learning and are challenging the notion of the monolithic degree.

As discussed throughout this chapter, although technology holds much promise, there are also perils associated with it. Some are technology's own creation and some are a result of the way society may choose to enact it. Individuals learn in different ways and technologically enabled instruction may not be best for everyone. Furthermore, the development of stratified class-based systems of education has the potential to create systems where education is viewed as merely transactional for many and as a means of social capital accrual and elite education for others. The influence of private for-profit companies and technology providers may also erode the public trust and the integrity of higher education. Although these issues may arise, they are not inherently problems of the technology itself. Rather, technology should be seen as one solution to a number of problems while still requiring careful execution and development so as not to create or exacerbate others.

So technology will save higher education, but only if institutions of higher learning are willing to embrace it. Higher education, long an industry that was largely impervious to competition, is only beginning to feel the heat. Embracing technology, rather than running from it in fear, is the only way to ensure that colleges and universities will remain relevant. The beauty of technology is that it is forcing necessary change. It is helping push a more responsive, open, and flexible system of higher education. With the correct stewardship, technology holds promise to better serve the needs of 21st-century learners. When it comes to higher education's problems, technology alone is not the solution, but it is a necessary part of the equation.

References

Abelson, H. (2008, April). The creation of OpenCourseWare at MIT. *Journal of Science Education and Technology, 17*(2), 164–174. doi:10.1007/s10956-007-9060-8

Aldridge, S. C., Clinefelter, D. L., & Magda, A. J. (2013). *Online learning at public universities: Building a new path to a college degree.* Louisville, KY: The Learning House, Inc.

Allen, I. E., & Seaman, J. (2016). *Online report card: Tracking online education in the United States.* Babson survey research group and Quahog Research Group. Retrieved from http://onlinelearningsurvey.com/reports/onlinereportcard.pdf

Altbach, P. G. (2001). The rise of pseudouniversities. *International Higher Education, 25,* 2–3.

Arendt, A. M., & Shelton, B. E. (2009). Incentives and disincentives for the use of OpenCourseWare. *International Review of Research in Open and Distance Learning, 10*(5), 1–25.

Ash, K. (2012, August 27). Educators evaluate 'flipped' classrooms. *Education Week.* Retrieved from http://mublog.marymount.edu/MUBlog/teachingonline/files/2013/07/Best-Practices-Flipped-Classroom.pdf

Bluenstyk, G. (2014, June 15). Starbucks will send thousands of employees to Arizona State for degrees. *Chronicle of Higher Education.* Retrieved from http://chronicle.com/article/Starbucks-Will-Send-Thousands/147151

Bull, G., Thompson, A., Searson, M., Garofalo, J., Park, J., Young, C., & Lee, J. (2008). Connecting informal and formal learning: Experiences in the age of participatory media. *Contemporary Issues in Technology and Teacher Education, 8*(2), 100–107.

The College Board. (2016). *Tuition and fees and room and board over time, 1975-76 to 2015-16, selected years.* Retrieved from https://trends.collegeboard.org/college-pricing/figures-tables/tuition-and-fees-and-room-and-board-over-time-1975-76-2015-16-selected-years

Davidson, C. N., & Goldberg, D. T. (2010). *The future of thinking: Learning Institutions for the digital age.* Cambridge, MA: MIT Press.

Digital Media and Learning Competition. (n.d.) *Badges for lifelong learning.* Retrieved from http://dmlcompetition.net/Competition/4/badges-about.php

Ebner, M., Lienhardt, C., Rohs, M., & Meyer, I. (2010). Microblogs in higher education—A chance to facilitate informal and process oriented learning? *Computers & Education, 55,* 92–100.

Edelson, D. C., Gordin, D. N., & Pea, R. D. (1999). Addressing the challenges of inquiry-based learning through technology and curriculum design. *Journal of the Learning Sciences, 8*(3–4), 391–450.

Fain, P. (2012, October 1). A disruption grows up? *Inside Higher Ed.* Retrieved from http://www.insidehighered.com/news/2012/10/01/competency-based-education-may-get-boost

Fain, P. (2014, January 23). General Education's Remake. *Inside Higher Ed.* Retrieved from https://www.insidehighered.com/news/2014/01/23/association-wants-create-portable-competency-based-general-education-framework

Greenhow, C., & Robelia, B. (2004, June). Informal learning and identity formation in online social networks. *Learning Media and Technology, 34*(2), 119–140. doi:10.1080/17439880902923580

Joosten, T. (2012). *Social media for educators: Strategies and best practices.* San Francisco, CA: Jossey-Bass.

Junco, R., Elavsky, C. M., & Heiberger, G. (2013). Putting twitter to the test: Assessing outcomes for student collaboration, engagement and success. *British Journal of Educational Technology, 44*(2), 273–287. doi:10.1111/j.1467-8535.2012.01284.x

Junco, R., Heiberger, G., & Loken, E. (2011). The effect of Twitter on college student engagement and grades. *Journal of Computer Assisted Learning, 27*(2), 119–132. doi:10.1016/j.chb.2010.03.024

Kamenetz, A. (2010). *DIY U: Edupunks, edupeneurs, and the coming transformation of higher education.* White River Junction, VT: Chelsea Green Publishing.

Kezar, A. J., Chambers, T. C., & Berkhardt, J. C. (2005). *Higher education for the public good: Emerging voices from a national movement.* San Francisco, CA: Jossey Bass.

Laitinen, A. (2012, September). *Cracking the credit hour.* New America Foundation and Education Sector. Retrieved from http://higheredwatch.newamerica.net/sites/newamerica.net/files/policydocs/Cracking_the_Credit_Hour_Sept5_0.pdf

Leveille, D. E. (2006). *Accountability in higher education: A public agenda for trust and cultural change.* Berkeley, CA: Center for Studies in Higher Education.

Lin, M. G., Hoffman, E. S., & Borengasser, C. (2013, March/April). Is social media too social for class? A case study of twitter use. *TechTrends, 57*(2), 39–45.

The Lumina Foundation. (2014). *The degree qualifications profile.* Retrieved from https://www.luminafoundation.org/files/resources/dqp.pdf

McHaney, R. (2011). *The New digital shoreline: How Web 2.0 and millennials are revolutionizing higher education.* Sterling VA: Stylus Publishing.

MIT OpenCourseware. (2011). *2011 program evaluation findings summary.* Retrieved from http://ocw.mit.edu/about/site-statistics/11_Eval_Summary_112311_MITOCW.pdf

MIT OpenCourseware Consortium. (n.d.). *Our history.* Retrieved from http://ocw.mit.edu/about/our-history/

MOOC. (n.d.). *Oxford English Dictionary.* Oxford: Oxford University Press. Retrieved from http://www.oxforddictionaries.com/us/definition/american_english/mooc

Mumper, M., Gladieux, L. E., King, J. E., & Corrigan, M. E. (2011). The Federal government in higher education. In P. G. Altbach, P. J. Gumport, & R. O. Berdahl (Eds.), *American higher education in the twenty-first century* (3rd ed., pp. 38–69). Baltimore, MD: Johns Hopkins University Press.

National Center for Education Statistics. (2010). *Digest of education statistics.* Retrieved from http://nces.ed.gov/programs/digest/d10/

National Science Foundation. (2006). *Informal science education program solicitation (NSF 06-520).* Retrieved from www.nsf.gov/pubs/2006/nsf06520/nsf06520.htm

Organization for Economic Co-operation and Development. (2007). *Participative Web and user-created content: Web 2.0, wikis, and social networking.* Paris: Author.

Rajagopal, K., Joosten-ten Brinke, D., Van Bruggen, J., & Sloep, P. B. (2012). Understanding personal learning environments: Their structure, content and the networking skills needed to optimally use them. *First Monday, 17*(1), 1–8.

Ricci, C., Laricchia, P., & Desmarais, I. (2011, Winter). What unschooling is and what it means to us. *Our Schools/Our Selves, 20*(2), 141–151.

Ruff, C. (2016, April 18). JetBlue will pay employees college tuition upfront. *Chronicle of Higher Education.* Retrieved from http://chronicle.com/article/Jet Blue-Will-Pay-Employees-/236144

Suber, P. (2012). *Open access.* Cambridge, MA: MIT Press.

Thelin, J. R. (2011). *A history of American higher education* (2nd ed.). Baltimore, MD: Johns Hopkins University Press.

Thompson, C. (2011, July 15). How Khan academy is changing the rules of education. *WIRED Magazine.* Retrieved from http://resources.rosettastone.com/CDN/us/pdfs/K-12/Wired_KhanAcademy.pdf

Trow, M. (1989). American higher education: Past, present and future. *Studies in Higher Education, 14*(1), 5–22.

UNESCO. (2002, July). *Forum on the impact of Open Courseware for higher education in developing countries.* Paris: Author. Retrieved from http://unesdoc.unesco.org/images/0012/001285/128515e.pdf

United Nations. (1948). *Universal declaration of human rights.* Retrieved from http://www.un.org/en/universal-declaration-human-rights/

United States Department of Education, National Center for Educational Statistics. (2016). *Tuition cost of colleges and universities.* Retrieved from http://nces.ed.gov/fastfacts/display.asp?id=76

Vladoiu, M. (2011). State-of-the-art in Open Courseware initiatives worldwide. *Informatics in Education, 10*(2), 271–294.

Warlick, D. (2009, March/April). Growing your personal learning network. *Leading & Learning with Technology, 36*(6) 12–16.

Wellman, J. V., & Ehrlich, T. (Eds.). (2003, Summer). *How the student credit hour shapes higher education: The tie that binds.* New Directions for Higher Education, No. 122. San Francisco, CA: Jossey-Bass.

Part Eleven: *Should Standardized Tests Be Given More or Less Weight in College Admissions?*

In "The Importance of Standardized Tests in College Admissions," Martin C. Yu and Nathan R. Kuncel make the case for the utility of such tests. When controlling for high school course selection variability, standardized tests such as the SAT are seen as predictors of potential college grade point average. The authors seek to dispel myths about test bias, socioeconomic status, and coaching that assist with test–retest results. They note that the tests do not take into account noncognitive factors (e.g., study habits and attitude) and that they measure only academic potential, not all human dimensions. Given this severe limitation, Yu and Kuncel contend that tests should be given lesser consideration for admissions, but that they should still be continued because of their value.

In "Why Standardized Testing Is Not Necessary in College Admissions," Aaron W. Hughey points to what he considers "inherent flaws" in the SAT, ACT, GRE, and other specialty tests typically mandated for admission to higher education institutions (though a growing number are no long requiring tests for undergraduate admission). Hughey surveys the testing industry and its potent influence, maintaining that it tends to divide students along social class, race, and gender lines in both K–12 and postsecondary education. The author also treats the issue of dishonesty and cheating in test implementation. Hughey sums up the testing system as fundamentally discriminatory and unworthy of use in terms of either equity or effectiveness.

21. The Importance of Standardized Tests in College Admissions

MARTIN C. YU AND NATHAN R. KUNCEL

College Admissions

In the admissions process at many colleges and universities, standardized tests are commonly used in conjunction with other student information by admissions committees to help inform decisions about undergraduate and graduate school applicants. However, there are those who question whether these tests are effective predictors of college performance and raise concerns that they are unfair to certain groups of students (e.g., Hughey, 2009; Rooney & Schaeffer, 1998; Sacks, 1997). Some advocate that in college admissions, standardized tests should be given less weight, made optional, or eliminated altogether. In this chapter, we aim to demonstrate that standardized tests are highly valid predictors of college performance and that they play an important role in the admissions process. Additionally, it is also our goal to correct the record on several commonly misconceived issues concerning the use of standardized tests in admissions, and to discuss what is known about additional predictors that are used in conjunction with test scores and grades.

Predictive Validity of Standardized Tests

It is valuable to demystify the nature of tests as they ask people to do tasks that are directly relevant to academic and work success. Read a passage and understand it. Examine a graph and interpret it. Apply foundational mathematical skills to a problem. Even simple verbal analogy problems require a person to see the connections been words and are associated with academic success, job performance, and even creativity (Kuncel, Hezlett, & Ones, 2004).

There is now evidence based on studies of thousands and even hundreds of thousands of students that standardized tests are strongly predictive of grades earned at all levels (see Hunt, 2010, for a review). Just one example is Berry and Sackett (2009), who found that after accounting for differences in college course choice between students (167,816 of them), SAT scores had an estimated population validity between .54 and .67 for predicting college GPA. This was similar to high school GPA predicting college GPA, which ranged from .59 to .71. High school GPA, based on 4 years of behavior, is a somewhat more powerful measure, but note that standardized tests provide incremental predictive power (Berry & Sackett, 2009) and are a check on grade inflation and differences in high school quality.

Homeschooled students are a good example of this issue. We recently examined the college performance of 732 college students who were home-schooled, and compared them to a matched sample of 732 traditionally educated college students (Yu, Kuncel, & Sackett, 2016). Given that homeschooling regulations vary on a state-by-state basis (Ruger & Sorens, 2013), combined with the considerable variability in how children are homeschooled, we would expect that interpreting their high school grades would be especially difficult. This is exactly what we found. High school GPA was a poor predictor of college performance for homeschooled students compared to traditional students. On the other hand, standardized test scores predicted college performance equally well for both groups and provided the best information.

It is worth pausing and noting that although correlations are often discussed, other metrics are able to better convey the predictive power of these measures. Starting with an estimate of $r = .54$ for the SAT, this means that about 81% of the students in the top quintile will end up with an above average GPA but only 19% of those in the bottom quintile will earn such a GPA. Given these statistics, it is clear that test scores are useful predictors of academic performance and are a nice complement to prior grades for the purposes of admissions decisions. How much weight they should receive should be dependent on the priorities of the school and the context. In graduate admissions for example, test scores often are stronger predictors than college GPA for predicting many different outcomes (Kuncel & Hezlett, 2007). For college admissions, high school grades are currently somewhat better predictors and should receive more weight assuming predicting subsequent GPA is a priority.

However, grades are not always the primary concern. Depending on the outcome(s) of interest, more or less weight should be given to other measures in the decision process, with a combination of sources of information generally yielding the best predictions. Tests predict a large range of outcomes beyond grades earned in school. Some outcomes like the research productivity of Ph.D. students, job performance, leadership effectiveness, and creative accomplishments including earning patents and publishing literary works are nicely predicted by test scores (Kuncel & Hezlett, 2007; Lubinski, 2009) while available evidence suggests that college grades are inferior predictors (Roth, Bevier, Switzer, & Schippmann, 1996). Other outcomes, like obtaining the degree, are also positively related to test scores in both college and graduate school (Kuncel & Hezlett, 2007), but the relationship is weaker. For this outcome, other characteristics are equal or better predictors of this outcome, especially since degree attainment is largely determined by motivation and opportunity (including financial support). Finally, it is important to realize that some commonly used measures such as personal statements, letters of recommendation, and admissions interviews are generally very poor predictors of subsequent success. More on this later.

Testing Concerns

Although they predict a variety of important outcomes, it is important to evaluate common concerns raised about the use of tests. There are a number of arguments levied against the use of standardized tests for college admissions, with common claims including that test scores are just a proxy for socioeconomic status (SES) and put low-income students at a disadvantage, that these tests are biased against particular groups (e.g., ethnicity or gender), and that test coaching is unfair to students who do not have access to it. In this section, we aim to dispel these arguments and to alleviate these concerns toward standardized testing.

Socioeconomic Status: Some have argued that standardized test scores merely reflect SES and discriminate against less affluent students (e.g., Hughey, 2009; Sacks, 1997), and claims were made based on an analysis of University of California data that SAT I scores had virtually no relationship with college grades after controlling for SES (Crosby, Iyer, Clayton, & Downing, 2003). These claims have not stood up to more careful analysis.

Large multi-institutional datasets and new meta-analyses were examined by Sackett, Kuncel, and colleagues (Sackett, Kuncel, Arneson, Cooper, & Waters, 2009; Sackett et al., 2012) to test the relationships among SES, standardized test scores, and college performance. Overall, they found that SES was indeed related to test scores but the predictive power of tests was largely unrelated to family income and parental education. Controlling for SES had a trivial effect on the predictive validity of test scores for college performance. This remained the case even when high school GPA was controlled for.

Circling back around to the original claims that sparked media attention, the original analysis made by Geiser and Studley (2002) at the University of California included *both* SAT scores (Math and Verbal) and SAT II scores (Math, Verbal, plus a third test of the student's choice). What was actually observed was the unsurprising finding that two tests don't add anything beyond three tests. That is, the effect of a near-zero weight for the SAT was not due to SES (see Kuncel & Hezlett, 2010 for a more in-depth explanation), but it was rather due to the presence of the SAT IIs in the analysis. Therefore, although there is a relationship between test scores and SES, this in no way invalidates the use of standardized tests for college admissions, and the focus of our concern should instead be to address the causes of differential academic preparation of children depending on SES.

Finally, it is worth noting that the distribution of SES for students enrolled in college was similar to that of the applicant pool. This suggests that colleges do not systematically exclude students based on SES or indirectly screen out less affluent students based on test scores (Sackett et al., 2012). Tests are a piece of information to aid decision making; what truly matters is the admissions policy of the school. Ironically, an analysis of test-optional and test-requiring colleges found that test-optional colleges actually enrolled fewer low-income students with Pell grants than test-requiring colleges, and although there was an increase in the proportion of these students over time at test-optional colleges, this increase was no larger than that observed for test-requiring colleges (Belasco, Rosinger, & Hearn, 2014).

Ultimately, standardized admissions tests do not substantially contribute to the underrepresentation of low-income students in college, and access to these tests should not be considered a significant barrier in the college application process given the availability of fee-waivers for low-income students. Instead of narrowly focusing on criticizing standardized tests and blaming them for the underrepresentation of low-income students in college, it would be more productive for consideration of this issue to instead be more broadly focused on the fact that low-income students are underrepresented in the college admissions process as a whole (e.g., Walpole, 2003).

Group Differences and Test Bias: Another common allegation is that standardized tests show systematic differences between majority and minority groups, and that these differences indicate that the tests are biased against the minority group (e.g., Helms, 2006; Hughey, 2009). However, this is a half-truth. It is true that some minority groups, on average, have lower scores on standardized college admissions tests (Roth, Bevier, Bobko, Switzer, & Tyler,

2001), although the full range of scores is represented within each group. In other words, all groups have individuals who do brilliantly on tests and individuals who do poorly on tests.

What is not true is that tests are biased. Often, people interpret the scores as direct measures of innate talent. They are not. Tests measure skills developed over years and because of this, we should expect that individuals who have developed better skills will earn higher scores. Given that there are group level differences in opportunity to develop skills, support, and encouragement for skill development, or environmental factors that interfere with skill development, we would expect a legitimate measure of that skill to reflect these factors. For example, if a person only has access to poor baseball facilities, ineffective baseball coaches, and parents/peers/communities that discourage playing baseball, they probably won't become as good at baseball as someone who had access to good baseball resources. Under these circumstances, rather than criticizing a baseball skills test for being biased against this person, it would be more reasonable to explain the differences in test scores as being due to differences in actual skill and to then criticize the environment for not developing those skills. Similarly with standardized college admissions tests, research suggests that they may be capturing actual differences in verbal and quantitative skills that are the consequence of early developmental influences such as familial income, maternal education, maternal ability/knowledge, availability of learning materials in the home, parenting attitudes and practices, and child birth weight (Cottrell, Newman, & Roisman, 2015). Therefore, while group differences exist and we should try to find ways to reduce them, targeting standardized college admissions tests is by no means an effective way of doing so. We don't throw out thermometers just because they indicate a fever.

Moreover, these group differences are found in college outcomes as well, providing further evidence that these tests are capturing actual group differences rather than being biased against a particular group (see review in Sackett, Borneman, & Connelly, 2008). Test bias can be examined in more detail using the Cleary (1968) model, where the regression lines for predictor–criterion relationships in different groups are compared. In this model, bias would exist if the same predictor score is associated with a different criterion score for each group. A made-up illustration can be useful. Let's imagine that a score of 1800 on the SAT is associated with a 3.0 college GPA for White students, and a 3.2 GPA for Black students. In this case, we would say that the SAT is biased against Black students as they generally achieve a higher college GPA than their SAT score indicates. It is biased against them and underestimates their performance. In reality, however, the literature on test bias demonstrates that any bias that exists actually either favors the minority group or is not meaningful once other factors are accounted for (Young, 2001).

Coaching: With any form of high-stakes evaluation, a legitimate concern is with the extent to which it would be possible to coach test-takers to achieve a higher score as doing so may create significant and unfair disparities in scores between those who have access to coaching resources and those who do not. Obviously, those with higher SES could be expected to have more access to coaching, tutoring, or other forms of instruction that may better prepare them for taking a standardized admissions test. The belief that coaching confers significant benefits for increasing scores on standardized admissions tests is such that several well-known test preparation companies (e.g., Kaplan, 2016; Princeton Review, 2016) advertise a money-back guarantee for increases in test scores for students who fall within a range of initial test scores and who have completed the entire test preparation program.

However, the literature on coaching effects on standardized test scores tells a different story. In a review of previous research, Briggs (2009) reported that typical differences in test scores between formally coached and non-coached test-takers are quite small. This ranges from about 5–10 points on the critical reading section of the SAT, 10–20 points on the math section of the SAT, and about .4 points on the math section of the ACT. Using a stronger analytical method to isolate coaching effects from other factors that may influence test scores, Hansen (2004) matched formally coached and noncoached test-takers on other characteristics such as prior test scores, experience with the test, demographics, college preferences, high school grades, course load, and course choice. Here, the average scores of coached and non-coached test-takers were only separated by about .01 to .02 standard deviations. If we desire to further reduce these miniscule differences in test scores due to coaching, providing free coaching is one way of doing so. Luckily, there is a proliferation of free test preparation resources on the internet, such as from the test developer's own website (The College Board, 2016).

At first glance it may appear that there is a substantial discrepancy between advertised score improvements and actual coaching effects, but consider the fact that the former is a within-person comparison while the latter is a between-person comparison. While the extant research tells us that formal test coaching does not confer much additional advantage over test preparation that does not involve coaching, it has no bearing on the degree to which an individual test-taker's scores can be increased. Even without coaching, some test-takers are able to improve their SAT scores by 100 points or more (Powers & Rock, 1999). Taking all of this into consideration, it may be preparation in general rather than formal coaching in particular that helps test-takers to improve their scores on subsequent administrations of a test. Therefore, it is completely reasonable for test preparation companies to advertise gains in 100 points or more, even if the gain is mainly due to it being a case of test preparation in general rather than being specifically an effect of formal coaching.

Combining Information to Make Admissions Decisions

Success is clearly multidimensional and what a person brings to their journey through school is also multidimensional. It should be of no surprise that combining complementary sources of information is necessary to make the best possible admissions decision. Standardized tests were never intended to measure all possible determinants of college performance, and it's worth noting that they are also not used this way. Many studies have found that multiple pieces of information are considered and often tests are not the most important (e.g., Kuncel & Klieger, 2007; Schmitt et al., 2009).

Tests are intended as an integral, but also complementary, part of the admissions process. Other student characteristics such as personality (Poropat, 2009), and study habits, skills, and attitudes (Credé & Kuncel, 2007) have been shown to have moderate correlations with college performance. Since these other noncognitive characteristics typically exhibit low or no correlations with cognitive ability, they can be expected to produce useful amounts of incremental validity over standardized admissions tests which are largely measures of cognitive ability. Furthermore, these characteristics may be more strongly associated with other criteria of interest such as prosocial or counterproductive behavior than is cognitive ability. Additionally, given that test scores are highly valid but also show group differences, another benefit of combining test scores with other less cognitively loaded predictors (which may be less valid but show smaller group differences) is that group differences in the overall admissions system can be reduced (Sackett & Ellingson, 1997). In sum, it would be useful to incorporate measures of these noncognitive student characteristics into the admissions process if college admissions committees also value other criteria besides academic performance that are better accounted for by these characteristics.

Unfortunately, the research cited above employs carefully designed assessments often in a research context. They don't reflect what measures are typically used let alone HOW they are typically used. Many admissions settings emphasize letters of recommendation and personal statements. Letters of recommendation are useful supplementary predictors for degree completion but not much else based on evidence from a meta-analysis of the literature

(Kuncel, Kochevar, & Ones, 2014). A meta-analysis of the surprisingly sparse literature on personal statements and essays indicates that they are nearly useless for predicting subsequent grades and faculty ratings of student performance (Murphy, Klieger, Borneman, & Kuncel, 2009). Finally, interviews which are regularly used for admissions to medical school as well as private K–12 schools are often unstructured with very poor predictive power (Goho & Blackman, 2006). It appears that admissions are often based on a mixture of useful and moderately robust predictors (test scores and grades) combined with pretty lousy predictors (personal statements, unstructured interviews, and letters of recommendation) that we continue to use due to some combination of tradition, habit, and possibly laziness.

Another concern with the consideration of these noncognitive characteristics is that they typically rely on measures such as self-reports or other reports that have a large subjective component. Especially in a high-stakes situation such as college admissions, these measures would be susceptible to the problem of test-takers deliberately answering questions dishonestly in an attempt to represent themselves in a more favorable manner (i.e., response distortion or impression management), which could reduce the accuracy and predictive validity of these measures. Viable alternatives to more effectively capturing this information include standardized reports from others (Connelly & Ones, 2010) or self-reports based on modern forced choice methods (Salgado & Tauriz, 2014).

All of this together provides us with both bad news and good news. The bad news is that neither cognitive ability tests nor noncognitive measures are perfect. The good news is that they are both predictive of college performance and have incremental validity over each other, and that there is nothing preventing us from using only one over the other. Thus, by combining multiple predictors, we can maximize the information that we can obtain from each predictor, while minimizing the negative implications due to flaws or deficiencies in each predictor.

Conclusion

In this chapter, we have shown that standardized tests are highly predictive of college performance and should be considered an important component of the college admissions process. They show incremental validity over other predictors such as high school GPA and personality, and they have the advantage of being more objective predictors of college performance. Ultimately, best practices for the use of standardized tests in college admissions would include the provision of test preparation resources for students who plan to take these tests, and the consideration of these tests in conjunction with other predictors to maximize the ability of the admissions system to effectively judge a student's academic potential and predict his or her eventual academic performance in college.

Additionally, we have provided evidence to refute a number of common criticisms and concerns levied against the use of standardized tests for college admissions. This evidence demonstrated that (1) standardized tests are not merely proxies for SES and that they are not responsible for the underrepresentation of low-income students in college, (2) although there are group differences in mean scores on these tests, these differences are consistent with actual differences in performance, and these tests do not exhibit bias against minority gender or ethnic groups, and (3) formal test coaching does not significantly improve test scores. Given that standardized tests are strong indicators of academic potential and that hypothetically damning criticisms in fact do not hold, we would be remiss to assign lesser importance to the use of these tests, to make them optional, or to outright eliminate their consideration in college admissions decisions.

References

Belasco, A. S., Rosinger, K. O., & Hearn, J. C. (2014). The test-optional movement at America's selective liberal arts colleges: A boon for equity or something else? *Educational Evaluation and Policy Analysis, 37*(2), 206–223.

Berry, C. M., & Sackett, P. R. (2009). Individual differences in course choice result in underestimation of the validity of college admissions systems. *Psychological Science, 20*(7), 822–830.

Briggs, D. C. (2009). *Preparation for college admission exams.* NACAC Discussion Paper. Arlington, VA: National Association for College Admission Counseling.

Cleary, T.A. (1968). Test bias: Prediction of grades of Negro and white students in integrated colleges. *Journal of Educational Measurement, 5,* 115–124.

The College Board. (2016, June 15). *SAT practice.* Retrieved from https://collegereadiness.collegeboard.org/sat/practice

Connelly, B. S., & Ones, D. S. (2010). An other perspective on personality: Meta-analytic integration of observers' accuracy and predictive validity. *Psychological Bulletin, 136,* 1092–1122.

Cottrell, J. M., Newman, D. A., & Roisman, G. I. (2015). Explaining the white-black gap in cognitive ability test scores: Toward a theory of adverse impact. *Journal of Applied Psychology, 100,* 1713–1736.

Credé, M., & Kuncel, N. R. (2007). Study habits, skills, and attitudes: The third pillar supporting collegiate academic performance. *Perspectives on Psychological Science, 3,* 425–453.

Crosby, F. J., Iyer, A., Clayton, S., & Downing, R. A. (2003). Affirmative action: Psychological data and the policy debates. *American Psychologist, 58*, 93–115.

Geiser, S., & Studley, R. (2002). UC and the SAT: Predictive validity and differential impact of the SAT I and SAT II at the University of California. *Educational Assessment, 8*, 1–26.

Goho, J., & Blackman, A. (2006). The effectiveness of academic admission interviews: An exploratory meta-analysis. *Medical Teacher, 28*, 335–340.

Hansen, B. B. (2004). Full matching in an observational study of coaching for the SAT. *Journal of the American Statistical Association, 99*, 609–618.

Helms, J. E. (2006). Fairness is not validity or cultural bias in racial-group assessment: A quantitative perspective. *American Psychologist, 61*, 845–859.

Hughey, A. W. (2009). College admissions tests and socioeconomic/racial discrimination. *ACPA Developments, Fall 2009*. Retrieved from http://digitalcommons.wku.edu/csa_fac_pub/29

Hunt, E. B. (2010). *Human intelligence*. New York, NY: Cambridge University Press.

Kaplan. (2016, June 15). Retrieved from https://www.kaptest.com/sat

Kuncel, N. R., & Hezlett, S. A. (2007). Standardized tests predict graduate students' success. *Science, 315*, 1080–1081.

Kuncel, N. R., & Hezlett, S. A. (2010). Fact and fiction in cognitive ability testing for admissions and hiring decisions. *Current Directions in Psychological Science, 19*, 339–345.

Kuncel, N. R., Hezlett, S. A., & Ones, D. S. (2004). Academic performance, career potential, creativity, and job performance: Can one construct predict them all? *Journal of Personality and Social Psychology, 86*, 148–161.

Kuncel, N. R., & Klieger, D. M. (2007). Application patterns when applicants know the odds: Implications for selection research and practice. *Journal of Applied Psychology, 92*, 586–593.

Kuncel, N. R., Kochevar, R. J., & Ones, D. S. (2014). A meta-analysis of letters of recommendation in college and graduate admissions: Reasons for hope. *International Journal of Selection and Assessment, 22*, 101–107.

Lubinski, D. (2009). Exceptional cognitive ability: The phenotype. *Behavioral Genetics, 39*, 350–358.

Murphy, S. C., Klieger, D. M., Borneman, M. J., & Kuncel, N. R. (2009). The predictive power of personal statements in admissions: A meta-analysis and cautionary tale. *College and University, 84*, 83–86.

Poropat, A. E. (2009). A meta-analysis of the five-factor model of personality and academic performance. *Psychological Bulletin, 135*, 322–338.

Powers, D. E., & Rock, D. A. (1999). Effects of coaching on SAT I: Reasoning test scores. *Journal of Educational Measurement, 36*, 93–118.

The Princeton Review. (2016, June 15). *SAT test prep*. Retrieved from http://www.princetonreview.com/college/sat-test-prep

Rooney, C., & Schaeffer, B. (1998). *Test scores do not equal merit: Enhancing equity and excellence in college admissions by deemphasizing SAT and ACT results.* Cambridge, MA: FairTest.

Roth, P. L., Bevier, C. A., Bobko, P., Switzer III, F. S., & Tyler, P. (2001). Ethnic group differences in cognitive ability in employment and educational settings: A meta-analysis. *Personnel Psychology, 54,* 297–330.

Roth, P. L., Bevier, C. A., Switzer III, F. S., & Schippmann, J. S. (1996). Meta-analyzing the relationship between grades and job performance. *Journal of Applied Psychology, 81,* 548–556.

Ruger, W., and J. Sorens. 2011. Freedom in the 50 States 2013: An Index of Personal and Economic Freedom. Arlington, VA: Mercatus Center at George Mason University.

Sackett, P. R., Borneman, M. J., & Connelly, B. S. (2008). High-stakes testing in higher education and employment: Appraising the evidence for validity and fairness. *American Psychologist, 63,* 215–227.

Sackett, P. R., & Ellingson, J. E. (1997). The effects of forming multi-predictor composites on group differences and adverse impact. *Personnel Psychology, 50,* 707–721.

Sackett, P. R., Kuncel, N. R., Arneson, J., Cooper, S. R., & Waters, S. (2009). Socio-economic status and the relationship between admissions tests and post-secondary academic performance. *Psychological Bulletin, 135,* 1–22.

Sackett, P. R., Kuncel, N. R., Beatty, A. S., Rigdon, J. L., Shen, W., & Kiger, T. B. (2012). The role of socioeconomic status in SAT-grade relationships and in college admissions decisions. *Psychological Science, 23,* 1000–1007.

Sacks, P. (1997). Standardized testing: Meritocracy's crooked yardstick. *Change, 29,* 24–31.

Salgado, J. F., & Tauriz, G. (2014). The Five-Factor Model, forced-choice personality inventories and performance: A comprehensive meta-analysis of academic and occupational validity studies. *European Journal of Work and Organizational Psychology, 23,* 3–30.

Schmitt, N., Keeney, J., Oswald, F. L., Pleskac, T. J., Billington, A. Q., Sinha, R., & Zorzie, M. (2009). Prediction of 4-year college student performance using cognitive and noncognitive predictors and the impact on demographic status of admitted students. *Journal of Applied Psychology, 94,* 1479–1497.

Walpole, M. (2003). Socioeconomic status and college: How SES affects college experiences and outcomes. *The Review of Higher Education, 27,* 45–73.

Yu, M. C., Sackett, P. R. & Kuncel, N. R. (2016). *Educational Measurement: Issues and Practice, 35*(4), 31–39.

Young, J. (2001) *Differential validity, differential prediction and college admission testing: A comprehensive review and analysis.* New York, NY: College Entrance Examination Board.

22. Why Standardized Testing Is Not Essential in College Admissions

Aaron W. Hughey

As Strauss (2016a) has observed, "Test scores have consequences, some more than others. College admissions test scores are more far-reaching than many students might know." While this might not be the understatement of the century, it certainly qualifies as a finalist for that honor. Standardized testing has been endemic to academic culture for the last century; and although it is still woefully entangled in virtually every level of our educational institutions, telltale signs are beginning to coalesce, suggesting that perhaps the practice has reached the limit of its utility as an assessment tool. Nowhere is the growing tide of discontent with standardized testing more evident than within the realm of college admissions. Once seen as a way to ensure access to higher education for those capable of being successful in the academy, the inherent flaws of the SAT, ACT, GRE and a whole variety of specialty instruments are becoming more manifest as their true limitations are increasingly exposed.

As noted above, there is currently a movement away from using standardized tests in the college admissions process; among the schools that no longer require the SAT or the ACT are Brandeis University, Wesleyan University, Virginia Commonwealth, American University, and Catholic University (Anderson, 2016a). At George Washington University, applications saw a 28 percent increase after it dropped the requirement that prospective students submit SAT or ACT scores (Anderson, 2016b). One of driving forces behind the decision to move away from using standardized test scores in the admission process was a concerted effort to enhance the diversity of the student body, especially students who have been historically disadvantaged. Whereas standardized tests were once championed as a way to insure that those who had the ability to succeed were given the opportunity to demonstrate their potential, it has become obvious as we have developed a greater awareness of the limitations of these instruments that they do, in fact, measure a lot more than scholastic potential.

Although the writing is plainly on the wall with respect to the future of standardized testing as a college admissions criterion, it is important to acknowledge that these well-established vehicles for ostensibly separating those capable of successfully completing a degree program from those deemed more suited for other career choices are still in wide use at a majority of colleges and universities (Strauss, 2016a). Most institutions, especially those that are deemed more selective, continue to require that prospective students continue to submit their SAT or ACT scores as part of their application package. But why is this the case as the intrinsic limitations of these instruments have slowly become more recognized and understood by the psychometric community? In order to answer this question honestly, it is important to look at the testing business from an economic perspective. The bottom line is that there is a lot of money at stake, and there are powerful and influential forces advocating for colleges and universities to continue to rely on standardized tests as a key component of the collegiate admissions process (Zernike, 2016b).

It is also important to understand the extent to which financial considerations affect the decision-making process when it comes to standardized testing. The collegiate admissions process is only one aspect of a testing culture that has evolved to dominate the educational landscape over the past few decades. This can be seen clearly in the recent movement by the major testing companies to move into the public school market. Federally mandated testing in public schools, which is seen as a way to hold both students and teachers more accountable for the learning process, costs around $700 million a year (Zernike, 2016b). The idea here is fairly straightforward; well-established instruments such as the SAT and the ACT, although developed for the express purpose of predicting how well students can be expected to perform in college, can also be used to assess how well the public schools are meeting the challenge put forth by the last two Administrations to significantly improve the quality of the services they provide (Gewertz, 2016). Recent changes in federal law permit companies such as the College Board and The ACT to compete with examinations sanctioned by the executive branch for determining relative school performance (Zernike, 2016b). This shift in the laws governing public education has allowed the SAT and ACT to be used at the secondary level, creating a potentially lucrative market for these instruments. Students who have no intention of attending college may now be required to take standardized tests originally developed to screen potential college applicants. It is unclear how these instruments can serve this purpose, however, since they were not created to specifically meet the educational standards many school systems now have in place.

Swail (2016) succinctly captures the essence of traditional differences between the SAT and the ACT:

> Two days ago, more than a quarter million students around the country sat down for the inaugural debut of the newly revised SAT. The College Board had promised a new SAT to be more representative of their prior learning in school. Traditionally, the ACT is a test that is very reflective of school-based learning, whereas the SAT was broader and more abstract. For instance, while the ACT would ask very specific questions about academic school content, the SAT relied heavily on strategies such as analogies, which would ask the test-taker if they understood the relationship between a set of words. It is argued that students who had taken Latin in school had a unique advantage for this section because of their knowledge of root words. (para. 1)

Before proceeding with a more definitive critique outlining why standardized testing is inappropriate for making decisions about who should be admitted to college, it is first necessary to look at standardized testing in a more generic sense. Long before students get to the point of deciding whether or not they want to matriculate to an institution of higher learning, they have had extensive exposure to standardized testing. Indeed, the last few generations are so used to filling in the bubbles on Scantron forms that it has become something they can probably do in their sleep. And although that particular delivery method is now fading away and being replaced (like everything else, by the digital revolution), the current generation of public school students is perhaps the most scrutinized in history, especially if gauged by their exposure to, and involvement with, standardized tests. But what has been the legacy of this relatively new emphasis on educational efficacy, as succinctly captured by the passage of the infamous No Child Left Behind Act and its reliance on standardized testing as the cornerstone of assessment and accountability?

The results have been underwhelming. As Walker (2014) observed:

> Today, more than a decade later, the law is uniformly blamed for stripping curriculum opportunities, including art, music, physical education and more, and imposing a brutal testing regime that has forced educators to focus their time and energy on preparing for tests in a narrow range of subjects: namely, English/language arts and math. For students in low-income communities, the impact has been devastating. (para. 3)

Over a decade has passed since this monumental and well-intentioned legislation was enacted and the unintended and mostly detrimental consequences of "teaching to the test" could not be more disturbing (Quinlan, 2016). In too many schools across the nation, valuable instructional time and scarce resources are devoted to preparing students to take standardized tests intended to show mastery of material that is inherently impeded by the pedagogical process itself (Walker, 2014). Moreover, those most adversely affected by this unprecedented emphasis on the power of standardized testing to solve our educational, social, cultural, and economic problems have been those from less affluent families (Hirsch, 2006). While students from more well-off families engage in various enrichment activities designed to augment and reinforce their educational experience, those without similar access are more dependent on their teachers to provide them with the kind of insights that their more comfortable counterparts are able to achieve through other means. But when teachers' priorities are skewed toward preparing their students to take a high-stakes examination, they have very little time to coordinate these experiences for their less affluent students (Hirsch, 2006). It is not surprising, then, that students from less affluent families do not tend to do as well as their more well-to-do peers on standardized tests designed to assess how prepared an individual is to perform college-level work. It should come as no surprise that the introduction of Common Core in many school districts has only served to make the situation worse for many students (Brown, 2016).

Moreover, it has even been suggested that an emphasis on standardized testing is representative of a more wide-ranging agenda, supported by testing companies in conjunction with those opposed to unions, aimed at closing public schools and replacing them with charter schools (Taylor, 2016). In this scenario, the purpose of education is not so much to provide all members of the next generation with the knowledge and skills they will need to be productive members of society, but to keep those on the lower rungs of the social ladder "in their place." Among the educational community, there is a persistent myth that one of the purposes behind standardized testing is to help identify future criminals as well as those who may be predisposed to act in antisocial lifestyles (Taylor, 2016). One particularly outrageous claim, which seems to be totally without merit, is that there are states that use reading scores on standardized tests administered to elementary school students to predict future prison needs (Sanders, 2013).

Another dimension critical to evaluating the overall utility of standardized testing involves the technology increasingly used to administer the instruments. In recent years, there has been a seismic shift away from paper-based assessments and toward online formats. Whereas some forms of standardized testing can be readily adapted to a digital environment, difficulties arise when using computerized approaches to measure higher-order abilities such as critical thinking and creative problem solving (Brown, 2016). There is a huge difference between measuring acquired knowledge and skills with a multiple-choice or a true–false test and trying to accurately estimate acquisition of those same competencies using more sophisticated techniques such as open-ended short-answer and essay formats. Computers can accurately grade an objective test where student responses are compared to a predetermined scoring key; in fact, machines have been doing this for decades. Developing programs that can correctly deduce reasoning ability, taking into account such manifestations as humor, sarcasm, and other forms of out-of-the-box thinking is much more challenging (Brown, 2016).

The shift to digital standardized testing has also been plagued, almost from the start, by technical problems that often seem to take on a life of their own. It is not unusual to run across stories in the media of some of the difficulties routinely encountered by those attempting to implement standardized testing in a computerized format at virtually all levels: limited bandwidth, outdated computers and support equipment, inadequate technical support, and even electrical problems in some rural areas (Brown, 2016). Advocates for the technology consistently assert that these problems are all solvable, although those familiar with the history of technological innovation can attest to the fact that the process can be never-ending—once one set of difficulties has been overcome, it is often the case that a new set emerges that requires even more manipulation (Barber, 2014). Remember, this is not a trivial concern or a minor detail that can be easily dismissed. The trajectory of the lives of those who take standardized tests is often profoundly affected by the scores they receive on these instruments. It is sometimes easy to be dismissive when technical problems related to the testing process are brought to the forefront of the discussion.

Another area that everyone tends to agree is essential for success in a wide variety of life applications involves the role that noncognitive variables often play in the educational process. In fact, the federal government recently mandated that states must include a minimum of at least one nonacademic measure when attempting to determine school performance (Zernike, 2016a). On the surface, this seems like a legitimate request; after all, it is difficult to deny that factors such as motivation, emotional maturity, propensity for social integration, and perseverance exert a tremendous influence on the performance of any task (Garcia, 2014). As Zernike (2016a) cautions, however, this can be exceedingly difficult to do with a standardized test:

> The biggest concern about testing for social-emotional skills is that it typically relies on surveys asking students to evaluate recent behaviors or mind-sets, like how many days they remembered their homework, or if they consider themselves hard workers. This makes the testing highly susceptible to fakery and subjectivity.

> In their paper published in May, Dr. Duckworth and David Yeager argued that even if students do not fake their answers, the tests provide incentive for "superficial parroting" rather than real changes in mind-set. (para. 12)

It should also be noted that some researchers have suggested that standardized tests, in and of themselves, can be detrimental to students' self-esteem. As Swail (2016) has noted, standardized tests do an exceptional job of stressing out 16- to 17-year-olds. Furthermore, some students, particularly those from the lower socioeconomic classes, tend to interpret lower scores as an indication that they are somehow inferior to their more affluent peers and therefore more inclined to fail (Taylor, 2016). This is an important consideration that must be taken into account when using standardized tests to help students make educational and life decisions.

The idea that standardized tests give an objective, impartial, and accurate assessment of a student's potential for success in college is inherently suspect (Sternberg, 2012). Regardless of the capabilities claimed by those who have a financial stake in making sure institutions continue to use them, in actuality the SAT and the ACT tend to measure two things: socioeconomic status and how much an individual has spent preparing to take the exam (Kohn, 2016). As such, adopting either test for use in college admissions decisions or as a vehicle for determining if a school system has adequately met educational standards, Common Core or otherwise, is unsupported by empirical evidence. What is not in question, however, is the long-standing contention that standardized tests such as the SAT and the ACT, as currently employed by many colleges and universities, tend to favor white students from more affluent families (Zernike, 2016b). For this reason alone they should be excluded from the college admissions process.

Perhaps Hartocollis (2016b) sums it up best:

> The standardized testing industry has long grappled with questions of racial, socioeconomic and gender fairness. On average historically, whites and Asians do better than blacks and Hispanics on the SAT; wealthier children do better than poorer ones; and boys do better than girls—slightly better in verbal skills and considerably better in math. It is unclear why these gaps persist, test designers and social scientists say, but the differences are the subject of much study, including the research on negative stereotypes. (para. 11)

At the heart of the debate regarding the efficacy of using standardized tests to help facilitate the college admissions process is the role that background, race, and gender play in the scores they yield. Some proponents assert that the SAT and the ACT are simply the "messengers"—they alert us to the gaps that exist in our educational system and therefore serve as an indicator of what needs to be improved and with what population (Wartik, 2016). If, for example, test scores reveal that students from less affluent families do not read as well as those from more prosperous families, then we know where the system is flawed and therefore can formulate a viable plan to correct the deficiency. However, instruments that were originally designed for one function cannot be arbitrarily repurposed for an alternate use without significant modifications (FairTest, 2007). Using the results of these instruments as indicators of areas where we as a society can improve is also only useful if we use them expressly for that purpose and then actually implement a plan to correct the located discrepancies. Otherwise, the instruments are merely serving to further the societal injustices which they are purportedly being used to detect.

With respect to bias in the testing situation, the companies that develop the instruments on which colleges and universities rely to make admissions decisions claim that most of the results from studies on "stereotype threat" cannot be generalized to real-world situations (Hartocollis, 2016b). This seems to be a rather convenient declaration, although it does not appear to have a basis in fact (Steele, 1999). The conditions under which a student takes a standardized test do tend to exert a powerful influence on that student's performance on the test, much like a student's social and cultural heritage exert an influence on the performance of everything they undertake in life (Hirsch, 2006). Unfortunately, these considerations are seldom taken into account when using the results of standardized tests to make decisions that affect the test-taker's future.

As many readers may be aware, the College Board recently redesigned the SAT; the first cohort took the revised version in the spring of 2016 (Strauss, 2016b). What may be less familiar is the fact that the new test was developed to align much more closely with the Common Core State Standards and, as such, has evolved into something more akin to the ACT, which is a knowledge-based instrument, than previous incarnations of the SAT, which were specifically intended to measure the reasoning capabilities of the individual taking the examination (Anderson, 2016c). Those who have been following the progression should begin to realize that there is an overarching agenda slowly taking shape, with the Common Core driving the changes now being implemented. This raises a legitimate concern for institutions using the standardized test to augment college admissions decisions.

Specifically, the new SAT features a greater emphasis on reading, including more narrative description in math problems; as such, students from families and/or school systems where reading was not considered a priority—and especially where English was not the predominant language spoken—will not perform as well on the new version (Hartocollis, 2016a). It is interesting to note that the latest modifications to the SAT represented an attempt to satisfy college admissions and high school guidance counselors who have been advocating for an instrument that more closely aligns with what is being taught in school (Hartocollis, 2016a). Keep in mind this logic reflects several assumptions, including that the Common Core will be adopted by all states and therefore be used as the guiding criteria for all public school systems and that colleges and universities consider those standards to be evocative of what students should have mastered before matriculating to higher education. At this time, neither of these assumptions may turn out to be accurate.

The revised SAT has also triggered some conflict between the College Board and The ACT regarding how scores on the revised instrument should be interpreted, as noted by Anderson (2016c):

> First, the College Board released a set of charts Monday that showed how new SAT scores compare with the old SAT scores and ACT scores. It turns out that the new SAT scores are somewhat higher on the 1600-point scale than comparable results from the old version of the test. A new SAT 1300, for instance, corresponds to a 1230 on the sections of math and critical reading in the old version of the test.

> That meant families familiar with the old SAT scale would have to adjust their reflexive interpretations of what a score is worth. College admissions testing, after all, is an exercise in sorting. It is crucial not to overestimate or underestimate the relative strength of a given score, especially with an entirely new version of a test. (para. 2–3)

When relying on a standardized test that is purposefully designed to serve whatever perceived purpose, the user needs to make critical decisions about who is best prepared for college. Consequently, who should be admitted is problematic, especially given the previously described intrinsic limitations of these instruments. Once again, the motivation seems to be more economic than educational. Greed can be a powerful incentive; and it often trumps other, more pragmatic considerations when it comes to the efficacy of standardized tests.

For example, medical students in the United States are experiencing first-hand how economics often adversely affects the assessment process. In order to become a licensed physician in this country, medical students are required to pass three standardized tests, one of which is called the "Step 2 Clinical Skills" exam (Douglas-Gabriel, 2016). The test is designed to assess how well future physicians are able to relate to their patients and the extent to which they have mastered real-world problem-solving techniques. So far so good, but the fee to take the test is $1,275 and it is only offered in five cities—and the only results students receive are of the "pass/fail" variety. No substantive or developmental feedback is provided to those taking the standardized test. Providing more information, according to the company that administers the test, would "encourage cheating" (Douglas-Gabriel, 2016).

Testing companies, especially those that administer instruments like the SAT and the ACT, tend to be preoccupied with making sure that it is virtually impossible to cheat on their assessments—and for good reason. In a survey of 40,000 high school students, over 50 percent indicated they had cheated on a standardized test during the previous year; and 34 percent reported they had done it more than once (Strauss, 2016d). Many students see standardized tests as a game in much the same way they see video games and other aspects of their day-to-day lives; that is, they have been indirectly taught that in many respects the end always justifies the means and, as such, expediency is the critical criterion (Lancaster, 2015). And contrary to what some might surmise, the problem is not limited to the lower profile schools; cheating seems to be as prevalent in more affluent schools as it is in the poorer districts (Strauss, 2016d).

Cheating is a nontrivial problem when employing these instruments to make college admissions decisions, and it seems to be particularly acute when dealing with international students, as Strauss (2016d) explains:

> There's cheating, for example, on the SAT, administration after administration, in countries around the world, leading the College Board to withhold scores to investigate. There's cheating on the Test of English as a Foreign Language and the Graduate Record Examination, which allows foreign nationals to enter U.S. colleges and universities without actually knowing English and with falsified records. (Last year the U.S. Justice Department indicted 15 Chinese nationals in an elaborate cheating scheme to enter U.S. colleges.) (para. 3)

While cheating is a legitimate concern (Baer, 2015), when the desire to completely alleviate any possible instance of dishonesty (which can never be fully achieved) is taken to the extreme, it can adversely affect the validity and reliability of the instrument employed. The other problem with instituting measures designed to counteract cheating is knowing exactly how to define it and precisely where to draw the line. For instance, an entire industry has emerged to help prepare aspiring college students maximize their performance on the SAT and the ACT. If a student completes a test preparation course and it can be demonstrated conclusively that the course helped the student achieve a score that is significantly above what he or she would have attained without taking the course, then what is the instrument actually measuring? As Swail (2016) observes, most standardized tests do a great job of determining who is good at taking tests and only a minimal job of assessing whether or not a student has the ability to succeed in college.

In addition, what are the ethical implications about those involved in the test preparation industry who take the SAT or the ACT in order to learn how it can be "beaten?" This is a much more common practice that is generally acknowledged or appreciated; anytime there is an administration of either instrument, there are always a few scattered among the high school juniors and seniors who are taking the test so that they can be better at helping students who are willing and able to pay for their services (Hartocollis, 2016b). The College Board recognized this threat to the integrity of the SAT when it recently denied several well-known test prep providers the opportunity to take the revised version of their flagship instrument (Strauss, 2016b). In defending its decision, the testing company indicated that the new practice is a heightened security measure designed to restrict anyone from taking the SAT who is not planning to use the score for applying to college admission.

Although the practice of taking a standardized test in order to better prepare others to take the same examination can be seen as unethical, it sometimes yields positive results that can help to keep the companies from making these instruments more accountable and responsible to the customers they serve. Remember, most of the companies that develop and administer standardized tests used for college admissions purposes do not allow test-takers to directly challenge their scores. Witness the following anecdotal account from Hartocollis (2016b) regarding what some of these entrepreneurs uncovered earlier this year:

> Sprinkled among them in May, when the SAT was given for the second time since a much-ballyhooed revamping, were a number of people long past college—members of the test-prep industry who took the exam to see how those changes played out in practice so that they could improve their tutoring services. Armed with perhaps sharper pencils and a more jaundiced eye than the typical 17-year-old, they noticed two questions that some thought could throw off the performance of girls.
>
> Their concerns are fueling a debate in the industry–on Facebook and in private emails–over whether the test items were sufficiently vetted for gender bias, and whether the exam was unfair to female students. (para. 2–3)

The real concern here is socioeconomic discrimination. Those who can afford to pay for test prep services, which can cost several hundred dollars per hour (Staffaroni, 2015), obviously have an advantage over those who cannot afford those kinds of intensive, score-enhancing services. That being the case, what the SAT and the ACT measure, to a significant extent, is not a student's innate ability and potential but her access to resources capable of increasing her test scores. So unless those kinds of services are outlawed, or made available to everyone, it is pretty clear that what is being assessed by these instruments is not merit but privileged circumstances (Wade, 2012). In essence, standardized tests designed to level the playing field are perpetuating the social order by making it much more difficult for those from low-income families to effectively compete with their wealthier counterparts.

Given the indisputable evidence and acknowledged deficiencies with standardized tests such as the SAT and the ACT, it is incredulous that they are still widely used as part of the admissions process at a majority of colleges and universities. These instruments clearly do not serve the purpose for which they were originally intended. Instead, the primary reasons they continue to be used have more to do with economics (Rainesford, 2016) and less with their value as tools designed to differentiate between those who are adequately prepared for college and should be admitted and those who should probably choose an alternate life trajectory.

Finally, the notion that the SAT and the ACT continue to be used (even though their imperfections have been well-documented) because there are "no suitable alternatives" is not a valid argument for keeping them as criteria in the college admissions process. It is important to understand that standardized tests such as the SAT and the ACT do not need to be "replaced" by other mechanisms for augmenting decisions about whom should be allowed to attend a particular institution. The bottom line is that the SAT and the ACT serve no useful purpose, they do more harm than good, and they should be immediately discarded (Sheffer, 2014). It is not necessary to identify what should be used to provide the information and insights supposedly gleaned from these instruments in that whatever information and insights were obtained are essentially meaningless.

The core problem in our education system is grades, not standardized tests. If the integrity of the grading system could be restored; that is, if it could be reestablished that a student's grade-point average was truly indicative of her mastery of the material represented by that average, then the need for standardized tests to demonstrate either ability or potential would essentially evaporate (Jaschik, 2016; Katsikas, 2015). The only way to effectively deal with these circumstances is to take standardized tests out of the equation, thus forcing education institutions at all levels to deal with the root cause (Sanchez, 2015). The road ahead will be tricky to navigate, but the current move to eliminate the SAT and the ACT from the collegiate admissions decisions is a good start.

References

Anderson, N. (2016a, February 4). No test scores? No problem: Applications surge after GW goes test-optional. *The Washington Post*. Retrieved from https://www.washing tonpost.com/news/grade-point/wp/2016/02/04/no-test-scores-no-problem-app lications-surge-after-gw-goes-test-optional/

Anderson, N. (2016b, February 5). They took the tests. But they got into a selective college without sending scores. *The Washington Post*. Retrieved from https://www. washingtonpost.com/news/grade-point/wp/2016/02/05/they-took-the-tests-but-they-got-into-a-selective-college-without-sending-scores/

Anderson, N. (2016c, May 12). What's a college test score worth? An ACT-vs.-SAT dispute. *The Washington Post*. Retrieved from https://www.washingtonpost.com/news/grade-point/wp/2016/05/12/whats-a-college-test-score-worth-an-sat-vs-act-dispute/

Baer, J. (2015, October 16). Goldman firing about 20 junior staffers for cheating on tests. *The Wall Street Journal*. Retrieved from http://www.wsj.com/articles/goldman-firi ng-about-20-junior-staffers-for-cheating-on-tests-1445010241

Barber, R. (2014, April 23). Testing madness: A story of unintended consequences. *Douglas County School District*. Retrieved from https://www.dcsdk12.org/assess-ment-and-system-performance/testing-madness-a-story-of-unintended-consequences

Brown, E. (2016, April 14). Technical glitches plague computer-based standardized tests nationwide. *The Washington Post*. Retrieved from https://www.washingtonpost. com/local/education/technical-glitches-plague-computer-based-standardized-tests-nationwide/2016/04/13/21178c7e-019c-11e6-9203-7b8670959b88_story.html

Douglas-Gabriel, D. (2016, June 9). $1,300 to take one test? Med students are fed up. *The Washington Post*. Retrieved from https://www.washingtonpost.com/local/education/thousands-of-medical-students-fight-against-pricey-required-skills-exam/2016/06/08/a5b64a56-2357-11e6-aa84-42391ba52c91_story.html

FairTest. (2007, August 28). How standardized testing damages education (updated July 2012). *The National Center for Fair and Open Testing*. Retrieved from http://fairt est.org/how-standardized-testing-damages-education-pdf

Garcia, E. (2014, December 2). The need to address noncognitive skills in the educa-tion policy agenda (Briefing Paper #386). *Economic Policy Institute*. Retrieved from http://www.epi.org/publication/the-need-to-address-noncognitive-skills-in-the-education-policy-agenda/

Gewertz, C. (2016, January 4). Will States Swap Standards-Based Tests for SAT, ACT? *Education Week, 35*(15), 16–17. Retrieved from http://www.edweek. org/ew/articles/2016/01/06/will-states-swap-standards-based-tests-for-sat. html?r=1078705878

Hartocollis, A. (2016a, February 8). New, reading-heavy SAT has students worried. *The New York Times*. Retrieved from http://www.nytimes.com/2016/02/09/us/sat-test-changes.html

Hartocollis, A. (2016b, June 26). Tutors see stereotypes and gender bias in SAT. Testers see none of the above. *The New York Times*. Retrieved from http://www.nytimes.com/2016/06/27/us/tutors-see-stereotypes-and-gender-bias-in-sat-testers-see-none-of-the-above.html

Hirsch, E. (2006). *The knowledge deficit: Closing the shocking education gap for American children*. New York, NY: Houghton Mifflin.

Jaschik, S. (2016, March 29). Grade inflation, higher and higher. *Inside Higher Education*. Retrieved from https://www.insidehighered.com/news/2016/03/29/survey-finds-grade-inflation-continues-rise-four-year-colleges-not-community-college

Katsikas, A. (2015, January 13). Same performance, better grades. *The Atlantic*. Retrieved from http://www.theatlantic.com/education/archive/2015/01/same-performance-better-grades/384447/

Kohn, A. (2016, April 7). Standardized tests. *The New York Times*. Retrieved from http://www.nytimes.com/2016/04/08/opinion/standardized-tests.html

Lancaster, C. (2015, December 10). Are millennials ethical people? *Workplace Ethics Advice*. Retrieved from http://www.workplaceethicsadvice.com/2015/12/are-millennials-ethical-people.html

Quinlan, C. (2016, February 2). Why we need to improve standardized testing. *ThinkProgress.org*. Retrieved from http://thinkprogress.org/education/2016/02/02/3745204/standardized-testing-state-improvements/

Rainesford, A. (2016, April 27). The business of standardized testing. *The Huffington Post*. Retrieved from http://www.huffingtonpost.com/rainesford-alexandra/the-business-of-standardi_b_9785988.html

Sanchez, C. (2015, July 28). Is this the beginning of the end for the STA and ACT? *National Public Radio*. Retrieved from http://www.npr.org/sections/ed/2015/07/28/427110042/is-this-the-beginning-of-the-end-for-the-sat-and-act

Sanders, K. (2013). Kathleen Ford says private prisons use third-grade data to plan for prison beds. *Politifact Florida*. Retrieved from http://www.politifact.com/florida/statements/2013/jul/16/kathleen-ford/kathleen-ford-says-private-prisons-use-third-grade/

Sheffer, S. (2014, February 18). Do ACT and SAT scores really matter? New study says they shouldn't. *PBS Newshour*. Retrieved from http://www.pbs.org/newshour/rundown/nail-biting-standardized-testing-may-miss-mark-college-students/

Staffaroni, L. (2015, April 30). How much should you pay for SAT/ACT tutoring? *PrepScholar*. Retrieved from http://blog.prepscholar.com/how-much-should-you-pay-for-sat-act-tutoring

Steele, C. (1999, August). Thin ice: Stereotype threat and black college students. *The Atlantic*. Retrieved from http://www.theatlantic.com/magazine/archive/1999/08/thin-ice-stereotype-threat-and-black-college-students/304663/

Sternberg, R. (2012, September–October). College admissions: Beyond conventional testing. *Change*. Retrieved from http://www.changemag.org/Archives/Back%20Issues/2012/September-October%202012/admissions_full.html

Strauss, V. (2016a, January 31). The hairy hand of the SAT reaches far into your future. *The Washington Post*. Retrieved from https://www.washingtonpost.com/news/answer-sheet/wp/2016/01/31/the-hairy-hand-of-the-sat-reaches-far-into-your-future/

Strauss, V. (2016b, February 27). Something you should know about the new SAT. *The Washington Post*. Retrieved from https://www.washingtonpost.com/news/answer-sheet/wp/2016/02/27/something-you-should-know-about-the-new-sat/

Strauss, V. (2016d, March 2). Indian army makes recruits take test in underwear—to avoid cheating. *The Washington Post*. Retrieved from https://www.washingtonpost.com/news/answer-sheet/wp/2016/03/02/indian-army-makes-recruits-take-test-in-underwear-to-avoid-cheating/

Swail, W. (2016, March 7). Now that the SAT has been revised...let's revise how we use the SAT. *The Swail Letter on Education*. Retrieved from https://etwus.wordpress.com/2016/03/07/now-that-the-sat-has-been-revised-lets-revise-how-we-use-the-sat/

Taylor, K. (2016, April 23). Race and the standardized testing wars. *The New York Times*. Retrieved from http://www.nytimes.com/2016/04/24/opinion/sunday/race-and-the-standardized-testing-wars.html

Wade, L. (2012, August 29). The correlation between income and SAT scores. *The Society Pages*. Retrieved from https://thesocietypages.org/socimages/2012/08/29/the-correlation-between-income-and-sat-scores/

Walker, T. (2014, September 2). The Testing obsession and the disappearing curriculum. *NEAToday* (National Education Association). Retrieved from http://neatoday.org/2014/09/02/the-testing-obsession-and-the-disappearing-curriculum-2/

Wartik, N. (2016, February 11). Readers respond to redesigned, and wordier, SAT. *The New York Times*. Retrieved from http://www.nytimes.com/2016/02/12/us/readers-respond-to-redesigned-and-wordier-sat.html

Zernike, K. (2016a, February 29). Testing for joy and grit? Schools nationwide push to measure student's emotional skills. *The New York Times*. Retrieved from http://www.nytimes.com/2016/03/01/us/testing-for-joy-and-grit-schools-nationwide-push-to-measure-students-emotional-skills.html

Zernike, K. (2016b, April 5). Rejected by colleges, SAT and ACT gain high school acceptance. *The New York Times*. Retrieved from http://www.nytimes.com/2016/04/06/us/act-and-sat-find-a-profitable-market-as-common-core-tests.html

Part Twelve: Is College Worth the Cost?

In "Is Higher Education Worth the Cost?," Monica Galloway Burke, Colin Cannonier, and Aaron W. Hughey address the value of a bachelor's degree and conclude that it is worth its cost. They justify this finding with aggregate data that suggest college graduates enjoy more salary gains and a higher quality of life. These advantages are compared with those of individuals who did not attend college and thus face a widening wage gap throughout their lives. Despite the high price of many colleges, the authors maintain that foregoing college risks losing a lifetime of enriched experience based on undergraduate learning, in and outside the classroom.

In "Is Higher Education Worth the Cost? It Depends," Lindsey M. Burke critically analyzes both the demand for higher education and what she contends is the largely declining value of the bachelor's degree. She questions whether federal subsidies for colleges and universities are commensurate with the economic outcomes they presumably produce. Her further argument is that these subsidies lead to higher tuition and other costs. Finally, Burke worries about the huge amount of debt incurred by many undergraduates, especially minority students. Given this set of circumstances, she is not surprised that more Americans are growing less inclined to view higher education as a good investment.

23. Is Higher Education Worth the Cost?

Monica Galloway Burke, Colin Cannonier,
and Aaron W. Hughey

For many years, the path to economic upward mobility has been attached to higher education with the idea that earning a college degree is associated with social and economic opportunities and serves as a gateway to a better life, better job, and better pay. The value of a bachelor's degree became more widespread over the course of the twentieth century as more Americans became educated, prompting the emergence of a key axis of difference of life chances and lifestyles in society between the less educated and more educated (Fisher & Hout, 2006). As the benefits of higher education became more evident, college attendance and completion rates increased as well; in 1940, just under one in 20 Americans 25 years and older had completed at least four years of college (4.6% of the population). By 2000, almost one in four had earned a bachelor's degree or higher (24.4%), with more than half (52%) of the population completing at least some college education (Bauman & Graf, 2003; Suchan et al., 2007). For the most part, the percentage of individuals in the United States enrolled in college has risen significantly, with undergraduate enrollment increasing 47% between 1970 and 1983, 18% from 1985 to 1992 before stabilizing between 1992 and 1998, and 21% between 2003 and 2013 (U.S. Department of Education, National Center for Education Statistics, 2016b).

As the demand for, and enrollment in, higher education grew and the social and economic returns of a college degree became more evident, the cost of a higher education increased significantly. The costs associated with "investing in a college education include the direct costs of attendance (e.g., tuition, fees, room, board, books, and supplies) less financial aid, the opportunity costs of foregone earnings and leisure time, and the costs of traveling between home and the institution" (Perna, 2003, p. 451). According to the U.S. Department of Education (2016a), the average cost of a college education including total tuition, fees, room and board rates charged for full-time undergraduate students in all types of degree-granting institutions in the 1993–1994 academic year was estimated to be $9,151 (constant dollars) at public institutions and $24,901 (constant dollars) at private nonprofit and for-profit institutions. For the 2013–2014 academic year, the prices for undergraduate tuition, fees, room, and board were $15,640 at public institutions and $35,987 at private nonprofit and for-profit institutions. These changes represent a 71% and 44.5% increase at public and private institutions of higher education, respectively.

Over the 10-year period between the 2003–2004 and 2013–2014 academic years, prices for undergraduate tuition, fees, room, and board at public institutions increased by 34% and prices at private nonprofit institutions rose 25% after adjustment for inflation (U.S. Department of Education, National Center for Education Statistics, 2015). The most recent decade witnessed a lower increase in the average price of education at both types of institutions. This is remarkable since over this period, it should be noted that higher education faced a number of financial challenges emanating from the Great Recession, continued state budget cuts, and the increase in costs associated with meeting the needs of a more diverse student body. As suggested by Archibald and Feldman (2011), "changes in the economic environment combined with reasonable reactions by colleges and universities result in rapidly rising costs that have passed on in rapidly rising tuition and fees" (p. 83).

Beyond the Costs

When it comes to the increasing cost of higher education, some question whether a college degree continues to be worth the expense. The price tag for a college education has received increasing attention in some policy circles and intense, often contentious, debates have ensued throughout the media. The common queries in the debate revolve around the worth of a college degree, reasons for its high costs, the impact of student debt, the relationship between earnings and a college degree, the necessity for the high salaries of key leaders and coaches, and the effect of college costs on the lower and middle class. The question becomes: If there is an increase in costs, does that diminish the worth of a product or service? The considerations relevant to answering this question are both philosophical and pragmatic.

To illustrate the complexity of the problem, consider the cell phone. The costs of cell phones have increased over time, but so too have the productivity and the numerous new features available for its user. Cell phones have allowed users to undertake banking and transactions from the comfort of anywhere; families are able to connect with each other around the globe; people finding their way during travel has become easier due to GPS; and individuals are able to track their health and social media accounts through numerous apps, to name a few. The increase in costs has been accompanied by an increase in services and features. Importantly, the quality of the product that makes it easier, faster, and more efficient is often not fully taken into account. The importance of cell phones in meeting the needs of its user in most cases far exceeds the costs of the product and such benefits extend over a long time period. Looking at higher education from this viewpoint, over the years, the range of operations and services to meet the needs of diverse students (e.g., enhanced technology, enhanced counseling services, and modernized residential living), modes of educational delivery (i.e., online and hybrid courses and study abroad), and the quality of education (e.g., more qualified and varied faculty, discipline-specific accreditations, and service learning initiatives) have also increased in addition to its cost.

A college education operates in the same way as most investments. Acquiring a college degree or other certification requires large initial and oftentimes unrecoverable (sunk) cost obligations spread over multiple years. However, once acquired, a college education is often desirable to employers and, more importantly, provides the tools necessary for an individual to earn a future income that is on average significantly higher than the income of those with only a high school diploma. As will be discussed in more detail later, there are numerous nonmonetary benefits of earning a college degree, which along with income, are expected to yield substantial benefits well into the future, oftentimes outlasting the length of loan payments associated with financing these costs.

The basic question that must be answered is whether these future benefits are larger than the cost obligations. If the answer is in the affirmative, then pursuing a higher education is justified and a college education is a worthwhile investment. Unlike most investments, it is indestructible, long lasting, and remains with its investor for as long as he or she lives. In essence, the acquisition of a college degree is a permanent investment; it is something that cannot be taken away from an individual once earned. More specifically, individuals may not be separated from the knowledge and skills as a result of investment in higher education (Becker, 1993). Therefore, within the discussions related to the worth of a college education, an analysis of the benefits of a college degree such as the private and social returns, the development of human capital, and lifetime earnings is pertinent to the dialogue.

The Private and Social Returns of Higher Education

Historically, the individual and collective benefits of higher education have been emphasized in the United States. As World War II was drawing to a close in 1944, governmental leaders were concerned about a return to Depression-era unemployment rates and decided to implement a large-scale investment policy—The Serviceman's Readjustment Act (commonly known as the G.I. Bill)—to promote greater access to higher education to reduce unemployment rates, help restructure the US labor market by producing a more skilled labor force, and to fund another round of infrastructure development and expansion of public services by investing in higher education through grants for college (Douglass, 2010). This investment in human capital, which affects an individual and the economy at various levels, impacted the United States socially and economically by educating, training, and providing opportunities to many.

From a human capital perspective, when discussing the worth of a college degree, it must be noted that the benefits of higher education extend to the workplace, home, and community. There is a private benefit on various aspects in a person's life (i.e., wage, happiness, and health) from the accumulation of human capital (Card, 1999; Oreopoulos & Salvanes, 2009) associated with earning a college degree. For example, as explained by McMahon (2009), human capital can be used in the workplace to generate earnings. According to the human capital theory, it is presumed that the skills and knowledge gained from education raises the productivity of those who take part, thus increasing wages and the person's value in the labor market. This explains why higher wages are given to those with more education based on differences in productivity that arise from making the labor of educated workers more valuable than less educated workers (Becker, 1993; Hojo, 2003; Jorgenson & Fraumeni, 1993).

Higher education is viewed as contributing to the accumulation of human capital, which plays an important role in increasing not only personal income but in improving the economy as a whole (see Schultz, 1961). As Becker (1964) pointed out, higher education is viewed as an investment in which individuals forego current labor market earnings and take on direct costs in return for higher future earnings. Beyond the knowledge and experiences gained through higher education, being educated has been shown to promote positive outcomes for individuals, their communities, and the nation as a whole (Hout, 2012). The impact of higher education is directly related to the level of human capital both at the individual and the societal level. The presence of more educated workers also produces spillover effects that impact the productivity of the less educated (Burke & Cannonier, 2015). Of course, a college degree does not necessarily guarantee a good life, financial stability, or charity to the community; however, there is an array of public and private benefits often associated with higher education.

Labor Market Returns

It is well documented that higher education is associated with more private economic benefits (Leslie & Brinkman, 1988; Vedder, 2004). One public benefit related to higher education is its impact on the labor market. Higher education facilitates the attainment of new knowledge and skills that increase productivity, reflected in earnings and other work outputs in the labor market. By and large, labor market productivity influences both private and public economic returns (Becker, 1993; Bowen, 1964; Denison, 1984; Schultz, 1961, 1971) and although the gains are not evenly distributed across all disciplines, the return on investment is significant to both the individual and to society in general.

Individuals with Higher Levels of Education Earn More: One of the most touted reasons for why an individual should earn a college degree is that higher education enables them to earn more lifetime earnings. On average, completion of higher education leads to increased earnings. In reality, individuals who choose to obtain a higher education expect to obtain an income that exceeds the costs of earning a degree and the cost of losing wages while pursuing that degree (Sweetland, 1996). Research has shown that college graduates earn significantly more than high school graduates (Card, 1999; Pascarella & Terenzini, 1991, 2005) and are more likely to have a position with greater nonwage compensation (e.g., paid vacation, employer-provided health insurance (Department of Treasury, 2012)). It has been estimated that each year of educational attainment results in earnings gains averaging 10 to 15% per year (Card, 2001; Goldin & Katz, 2008). The difference between the earnings of college graduates and high school graduates has risen almost as much as tuition over the past 25 years, so the return is now almost as large as it was when tuition was lower (Hout, 2012).

Figure 23.1 provides graphical support of the large differences in earnings between college graduates and lower educated individuals. Specifically, the figure shows the evolution of average median real earnings by highest level of educational attainment for full-time workers who are 25 years and older over the period 1990 to 2014. The figure reveals that real income increased slightly only for college graduates whereas those with lower levels of education experience some decline, which was more pronounced for those with the lowest level education—those with less than a high school diploma and high school graduates. These results are striking because it points to two salient facts. First, based on these average median earnings, a college graduate today is better off in terms of real income compared to an equally educated individual 15 years ago. On the other hand, an individual with either a high school diploma or less is worse off than a person with the same level of education in 1990. The same is true for an individual who has pursued some level of college of education without completing the degree. In both cases, individuals who have not earned a college degree are on average likely to earn less than the average working individual. The upshot is that through increased earnings, an individual's capacity to obtain goods and services improves with the attainment of a college education. Individuals with a college education earn more than twice as much on average than those with the lowest level of education on average.

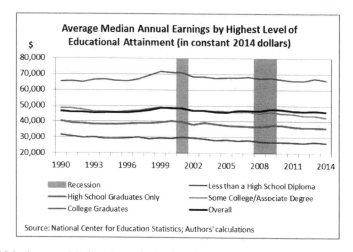

Figure 23.1. Average Median Annual Earnings by Highest Level of Educational Attainment, from the National Center for Education Statistics with Author's Calculations. *Source:* Author.

The pecuniary benefits associated with earning a college degree are large enough to repay the cost of obtaining it several times over. Carnevale, Smith, and Strohl (2010) estimated the lifetime earnings of individuals with a four-year college degree to be $1.6 million higher than those with a high school diploma, amounting to more than a 191% difference in lifetime earnings. Therefore, for individuals with higher education attainment, there are positive effects on earnings over the course of their lifetime (Tamborini, Kim, & Sakamoto, 2015). An increase in college graduates in the workforce also produces spillover effects by increasing the wages of high school dropouts and high school graduates each by 1.6% (Moretti, 2004).

Individuals with Higher Levels of Education Remain Employed, Get Promoted, and Receive Income Increases: Higher educational attainment is associated with positive career outcomes, including salary increases, number of promotions, development opportunities, and job mobility (Cappelli, 2000; Howard, 1986; Ng, Eby, Sorensen, & Feldman, 2005). Having a college degree also increases the probability that an individual will remain in the labor force and enjoy higher employment rates (Oreopoulos & Petronijevic, 2013). Figure 23.2 presents data from the Federal Reserve Economic Data showing the pattern of mostly seasonally adjusted monthly unemployment rates over the period January 1992 to June 2016 for individuals 25 years and older by educational attainment. It is evident that the lowest unemployment rates are associated with individuals having a college degree (not seasonally adjusted) while the highest unemployment rates are associated with individuals who have never earned even a high school diploma. Average unemployment rates for these educational categories of individuals were as follows: college graduates (2.8%), some college or associate's degree (4.8%), high school graduates only (5.8%), and less than high school diploma (9.3%), with the average unemployment rate being 6.1%.

Compared to those with a college degree or higher, the unemployment rate for those with less than a high school diploma is more than three times as large, twice as large for high school graduates, and more than one and a half times as large for those with some college education or an associate's degree. The unemployment rates for individuals with a high school diploma are about the same as the national average. Employment outcomes improve as educational levels improve and those with some exposure to college education or those with an associate degree experience far lower unemployment rates than the national average. The employment outcomes as shown suggest that some college education is better than none.

Individuals with a college education are better able to withstand economic crises like the Great Recession, which hit those with less education disproportionately hard, as those with a college degree or higher were largely protected against job losses and even some high education fields experienced job gains (Carnevale, Jayasundera, & Cheah, 2012). In the postrecession job recovery phase, more than half of the employment increases went to individuals with a bachelor's degree or higher, with the rest of the gains to those with some college education or an associate's degree (Carnevale et al., 2012).

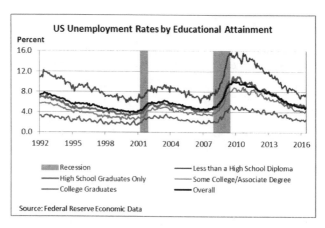

Figure 23.2. US Unemployment Rates by Educational Attainment.
Source: Author.

An individual with higher education attainment also has increased possibilities to be promoted to a higher level (Sicherman, 1991; Sicherman & Galor, 1990). Similarly, higher education can have a positive effect on productivity in the workplace, which leads to the possibility of enhanced individual as well as organizational income (Becker, 1993; Denison, 1962; Schultz, 1961, 1971). As results from Perna's (2003) research showed, the earnings premium increases with the level of educational attainment as both observed and adjusted earnings are higher for individuals who earn an associate, bachelor, or advanced degree than for individuals who attain only a high school diploma.

Individuals with Higher Levels of Education Are Viewed to Possess More Desirable Traits in the Workplace: Individuals with higher education attainment tend to be more productive in the workplace (Griliches & Regev, 1995; Rosen, 1999) and they seem to possess cognitive and noncognitive skills valued by an increasing number of employers (Fernandez, 2001; Heckman, Stixrud, & Urzua, 2006). Highly educated employees tend to display greater creativity, demonstrate more citizenship behaviors, and appear to engage in fewer counterproductive work behaviors like workplace aggression, workplace substance use, and absenteeism (Ng & Feldman, 2009).

Private Returns

Higher education has other nonfinancial beneficial effects other than its impact related to the labor market and income. The private benefits associated with higher education consist mostly of consumption and quality of life advantages (Williams & Swail, 2005). Some of the private benefits identified with attaining a higher education include improved health knowledge, better health and healthy lifestyles, longevity, better health and education for children, higher level of general happiness, better household management, a capacity to enjoy leisure, efficiency in making a variety of personal choices, and better understanding of political issues and civic engagement (Altindag, Cannonier & Mocan, 2011; Baum, Ma, & Payea, 2013; Haveman & Wolfe, 1984; McMahon, 2009; Mirowski & Ross, 2003). These benefits do not only reside with the individual, but can extend to others as well. Not only do more educated individuals tend to be better consumers of health for themselves (Grossman, 1972, 1975; Lleras-Muney, 2005; Mirowski & Ross, 2003), they are better consumers of health for their children (Currie & Moretti, 2003).

From a human capital perspective, a parent's educational attainment is an input into their children's human capital. Accordingly, they tend to be able to secure more human capital opportunities for their children (e.g., dance and music lessons, extracurricular activities, and educational resources such as better schools, private tutoring, as well as prep courses) (Becker, 1964; Haveman & Wolfe, 1994). Individuals with higher levels of education also tend to experience more socioeconomic mobility that enhances "intergenerational mobility, the ability of children to move up and down the economic ladder independent of their parents' economic status" (Department of Treasury, 2012, p. 15).

Social Returns

Societal gains are noted when more people are educated; these benefits include greater social equity, more cohesive communities, stronger sense of nationhood, and crime reduction (Mingat & Tan, 1996). Furthermore, "educated people read more about the issues, watch more news programs to stay informed, and take a more active interest in public affairs" (Joint Economic Committee, 2000, p. 9). Individuals with higher levels of education also have a reduced reliance on welfare and public assistance program (U.S. Department of Education, 1996). The impact of education on crime has been well-documented; an increase in education helps to lower crime through a decrease in incarceration rates, especially among Blacks (Lochner & Moretti, 2004). Since institutions of higher education are perceived as a primary means to develop and strengthen civic participation and engagement along several dimensions, including service learning, politics, community work, and volunteerism, the more educated have higher levels of awareness regarding sociopolitical issues and are usually more civically engaged citizens. Individuals with a college degree participate more fully in civil society and politics (Nie, Junn, & Stehlik-Barry, 1996; Putnam, 2000; Verba, Schlozman, & Brady, 1995) and have increased social consciousness of residents within a community (Beach, 2009).

Civic participation confers societal rewards by way of a vital democracy and well-functioning neighborhoods and is linked to individual rewards by way of job networks, occupational advancement, and physical and mental well-being (Putnam, 2000; Wilson, 2000). Higher education impacts voting behavior and partisanship; people with more education are efficient in processing information that allows them to make political choices on economic issues (Burke & Cannonier, 2015). As pointed out by Milligan, Moretti, and Oreopoulos (2004), higher education leads to more informed voters as reflected in their choice of candidates. Similarly, individuals who have attained higher levels of education are more likely to exhibit reduced prejudice and intolerance while increasing support for civil liberties and they are generally more trusting and are more tolerant toward migrants than the poorly educated (Borgonovi, 2012).

Conclusions

The evidence on the efficacy of obtaining a college education is abundantly clear: a college education is a worthwhile investment. The earnings premium associated with a college education is significant relative to other education categories, and this advantage, although not perfectly distributed, appears to be consistent across the entire spectrum of college majors (Abel & Deitz, 2014). A college-educated individual earns an average median annual income of approximately $35,000 more than a person who has never been exposed to any level of college education. College graduates experience an improvement in standard of living in real terms compared to a similar person a decade ago. Regrettably, the opposite is true for those without a college education as such a person today is worse off in terms of the amount of goods and services that can be acquired compared to a similarly educated individual 15 years ago. Despite the large financial benefits attributable to having a college education, there are nonmonetary benefits to both private individuals and society that are even larger, leaving little doubt about the comparative benefits of a higher education.

The past two decades witnessed a rise in the costs of attending college in the form of tuition, fees, room and board, even in spite of the fact that the rate of increase in these costs has declined in the more recent past. Coupled with the stagnant and to some extent the post-Great Recession decline in the real wages, an important question is whether, with these increasing costs, the pursuit of higher education is tenable. Indeed, it is! Despite the rising monetary costs of a college education, the net monetary benefits from a college degree continue to be robustly high. This is partly influenced by the steady decline in real wages of those earning a high school diploma or less. High unemployment rates associated with those with no college education seem to result in a lower opportunity costs to attending college and, thus, ensuring a decline in the total (direct plus opportunity) costs. Taken together, the claims that the value of a college education has declined and is not worth pursuing run counter to the overwhelming evidence that contradicts such notions. Those without a college education are falling further behind their college-educated peers and appear to be worse off today than similarly noncollege educated persons two decades ago. The argument that student borrowing to finance college education has become insurmountable appears to be exaggerated. Proponents who point to a rising student college debt payment to income ratio fail to provide any reliable evidence (Avery & Turner, 2012).

The larger question faced by today's younger prospective and current college students is one which relates to the decision-making process of choosing to attend college and more importantly, the due diligence undertaken during this process. There are other considerations for students' costs and debt in their higher education pursuit; that is, they should choose a course of study that provides a future earnings stream that is at least as great as the costs (both direct and opportunity) incurred in pursuing a college education. The choice of a course of study will be dependent on the prevailing as well as prospective labor market conditions relevant to that field. Students should seek out all available opportunities for obtaining scholarships and other forms of funding. It is imperative they research and choose an institution (including international where applicable) known for providing a high quality of education and where the probability of graduation is relatively high. This will help these individuals avoid the accumulation of significant amounts of college debt relative to future earnings.

Investing in a college education is likely to be the first major investment for most students. Despite the perceived high costs of acquiring a college education, there is ample evidence of significant overestimation of tuition cost by both students and their parents (Oreopoulos & Petronijevic, 2013).

As such, there is a responsibility and duty of care on the part of all those involved in this decision. This requires the use of all available information on costs to be incurred in undertaking this investment and the conditions of payment, expected future earnings stream, the quality of education, and probability of graduation. Although the relevant information is oftentimes freely available to the public, it is likely to require a considerable allocation of resources such as time in collecting, compiling, processing, and analyzing the information. Individuals tend to seek the expertise of financial advisors when deciding on the various types of financial instruments in which to place their savings. They do so in large measure because they lack the requisite knowledge on where and how to collect and process this type of information and they care about getting the highest return on their savings. When it comes to an investment in higher education, the stakes are just as high or perhaps higher. The role of high school guidance counselors, teachers, parents, and even higher education institutions is critical.

Ultimately, when determining whether higher education is worth the cost, it is important to assess the net benefit of obtaining a college education. If the benefits derived are higher than the costs, then pursuing higher education is a worthwhile endeavor. Higher education is one of our most robust investments, as it can withstand a variety of economic conditions, it can be transferred to a variety of uses, and it is long-lasting. In the final analysis, "The returns to higher education are large enough to offset even the full costs students now face" (Hout, 2012, p. 388). The value of a college education is worth the cost.

References

Abel, J. R., & Deitz, R. (2014). Do the benefits of college still outweigh the costs? *Federal Reserve Bank of New York Current Issues in Economics and Finance, 20*(3), 1–11.

Altindag, D., Cannonier, C., & Mocan, N. (2011). The impact of education on health knowledge. *Economics of Education Review, 30*(5), 792–812.

Archibald, R. B., & Feldman, D. H. (2011). *Why does college cost so much?* New York, NY: Oxford University Press.

Avery, C., & Turner, S. (2012). Student loans: Do college students borrow too much—or not enough? *Journal of Economic Perspectives, 26*(1), 165–192.

Baum, S., Ma, J., & Payea, K. (2013). *Education pays 2013*. The College Board. Retrieved from https://trends.collegeboard.org/sites/default/files/education-pays-2013-full-report.pdf

Bauman, K. J., & Graf, N. L. (2003). *Educational attainment 2000.* Washington, DC: U.S. Department of Commerce Economics and Statistics Administration, U.S. Census Bureau. Retrieved from https://www.census.gov/prod/2003pubs/c2kbr-24.pdf

Beach, M. J. (2009). A critique of human capital formation in the U.S. and the economic returns to sub-baccalaureate credentials. *Educational Studies: A Journal of the American Educational Studies, 45*(1), 24–38.

Becker, G. S. (1964). *Human capital: A theoretical and empirical analysis with special reference to education.* Chicago, IL: University of Chicago Press.

Becker, G. S. (1993). *Human capital: A theoretical and empirical analysis with special reference to education* (3rd ed.). Chicago, IL: University of Chicago Press.

Borgonovi, F. (2012). The relationship between education and levels of trust and tolerance in Europe. *The British Journal of Sociology, 6,* 146–167.

Bowen, W. G. (1964). *Economic aspects of education: Three essays.* Princeton, NJ: Princeton University.

Burke, M. G., & Cannonier, C. D. (2015). The social and economic landscape of Historically Black Colleges and Universities. In T. Ingram, D. Greenfield, J. Carter, & A. Hilton (Eds.), *Exploring issues of diversity within Historically Black Colleges and Universities* (pp. 73–107). Charlotte, NC: IAP Publishing.

Cappelli P. (2000). A market-driven approach to retaining talent. *Harvard Business Review, 78,* 103–111.

Card, D. (1999). The causal effect of education on earnings. In O. Ashenfelter & D. Card (Eds.), *Handbook of labor economics* (Vol. 3A, pp. 1801–1863). Amsterdam, Netherlands: Elsevier-North Holland.

Card, D. (2001). Estimating the return to schooling: Progress on some persistent econometric problems. *Econometrica, 69,* 1127–1160.

Carnevale, A. P., Jayasundera, T., & Cheah, B. (2012). *The college advantage: Weathering the economic storm.* Washington, DC: Center on Education and the Workforce, Georgetown Public Policy Institute, Georgetown University.

Carnevale, A. P., Smith, N., & Strohl, J. (2010). *Help wanted: Projections of job and education requirements through 2018.*Washington, DC: Center on Education and the Workforce.

Currie, J., & Moretti, E. (2003) Mother's education and the intergenerational transmission of human capital: Evidence from college openings. *The Quarterly Journal of Economics, 118*(4), 1495–1532.

Denison, E. F. (1962). *The sources of economic growth in the United States and the alternatives before of us.* New York, NY: Committee for Economic Development.

Denison, E. F. (1984). Accounting for slower economic growth: An update. In J. W. Kendrick (Ed.), *International comparisons of productivity and causes of the slowdown* (pp. 1–45). Cambridge, MA: Ballinger.

Department of Treasury. (2012). *The economics of higher education.* Retrieved from https://www.treasury.gov/connect/blog/Documents/20121212_Economics%20of%20Higher%20Ed_vFINAL.pdf

Douglass, J. A. (2010, February). *Higher education budgets and the global the global recession: Tracking varied national responses and their consequences* (Research and Occasional Paper Series: CSHE.4.10). Retrieved from Center for Studies in Higher Education website: http://cshe.berkeley.edu/publications/docs/ROPS.5Douglass. HEGlobalRecession.3.13.10.pdf

Fernandez, R. (2001). Skill-biased technological change and wage inequality: Evidence from a plant retooling. *American Journal of Sociology, 107,* 273–320.

Fisher, C. S., & Hout, M. (2006). *Century of difference: How America changed in the last one hundred years.* New York, NY: Russell Sage Foundation.

Goldin, C., & Katz, L. (2008). *The race between education and technology.* Cambridge, MA: Harvard University Press.

Griliches, Z., & Regev, H. (1995). Firm productivity in Israeli industry 1979-1988. *Journal of Econometrics, 65,* 175–203.

Grossman, M. (1972). On the concept of health capital and the demand for health. *Journal of Political Economy, 80*(2), 223–255.

Grossman, M. (1975). The correlation between health and schooling. In N. Terlecky (Ed.), *Household production and consumption* (pp. 147–211). New York, NY: Columbia University Press.

Haveman, R., & Wolfe, B. (1984). Schooling and economic well-being: The role of nonmarket effects. *Journal of Human Resources, 19*(3), 377–407.

Haveman, R. H., & Wolfe, B. L. (1994). *Succeeding generations: On the effects of investments in children.* New York, NY: Russell Sage.

Heckman, J. J., Stixrud, J., & Urzua, S. (2006). The effects of cognitive and noncognitive abilities on labor market outcomes and social behavior. *Journal of Labor Economics, 24,* 411–482.

Hojo, M. (2003). An indirect effect of education on growth. *Economics Letters, 80*(1), 31–34.

Hout, M. (2012). Social and economic returns to college education in the United States. *Annual Review of Sociology, 38,* 379–400.

Howard, A. (1986). College experiences and managerial performance. *Journal of Applied Psychology, 71,* 530–552.

Joint Economic Committee, United States Congress. (2000). *Investment in education: Private and public returns.* Retrieved from http://www.fsb.muohio.edu/evenwe/courses/eco361/f04/readings/investment%20in%20education.pdf

Jorgenson, D. W., & Fraumeni, B. M. (1993). Education and productivity growth in a market economy. *Atlantic Economic Journal, 21*(2), 1–25.

Leslie, L. L., & Brinkman, P. T. (1988). *The economic value of higher education.* Phoenix, AZ: American Council on Education/Oryx Press.

Lleras-Muney, A. (2005). The relationship between education and adult mortality in the United States. *Review of Economic Studies, 72*(1), 189–221.

Lochner, L. (2004). Education, work, and crime: A human capital approach. *International Economic Review, 45*, 811–843.

McMahon, W. W. (2009). *Higher learning, greater good: The private and social benefits of higher education.* Baltimore, MD: Johns Hopkins University Press.

Milligan, K., Moretti, E., & Oreopoulos, P. (2004). Does education improve citizenship? Evidence from the United States and United Kingdom. *Journal of Public Economics, 88*, 1667–1795.

Mingat, A., & Tan, J. P. (1996). *The full social returns to education: Estimates based on countries' economic growth performance.* Human Capital Development and Operations Policy Working Papers (No. HCD 73). Washington, DC: World Bank.

Mirowski, J., & Ross, C. E. (2003). *Education, social status, and health.* Hawthorne, NY: Aldine de Gruyter.

Moretti, E. (2004). Estimating the social return to higher education: Evidence from longitudinal and repeated cross-sectional data. *Journal of Econometrics, 121*, 175–212.

Ng, T. W. H., Eby, L. T., Sorensen, K. L., & Feldman, D. C. (2005). Predictors of objective and subjective career success: A meta-analysis. *Personnel Psychology, 58*, 367–408.

Ng, T. W. H., & Feldman, D. C. (2009). How broadly does education contribute to job performance? *Personnel Psychology, 62*, 89–134.

Nie, N. H., Junn, J., & Stehlik-Barry, K. (1996). *Education and democratic citizenship.* Chicago, IL: The University of Chicago Press.

Oreopoulos, P., & Petronijevic, U. (2013). Making college worth it: A review of research on the returns to higher education. *Future of Children, 23*(1), 41–65.

Oreopoulos, P., & Salvanes, K. G. (2009). *How large are returns to schooling? Hint: Money isn't everything* (NBER Working Papers No. 15339). Retrieved from National Bureau of Economic Research, website: http://www.nber.org/papers/w15339

Pascarella, E. T., & Terenzini, P. T. (1991). *How college affects students: Findings and insights from twenty years of research.* San Francisco, CA: Jossey-Bass.

Pascarella, E. T., & Terenzini, P. T. (2005). *How college affects students: A third decade of research* (Vol. 2). San Francisco, CA: Jossey-Bass.

Perna, L. W. (2003). The private benefits of higher education: An examination of the earnings premium. *Research in Higher Education, 44*(4), 451–472.

Putnam, R. D. (2000). *Bowling alone: The collapse and revival of American community.* New York, NY: Simon & Schuster.

Rosen, H. S. (1999). *Public finance.* New York, NY: McGraw-Hill.

Schultz, T. W. (1961). Investment in human capital. *American Economic Review, 51*, 1–17.

Schultz, T. W. (1971). *Investment in human capital.* New York, NY: The Free Press.

Sicherman, N. (1991). Overeducation in the labor market. *Journal of Labor Economics, 9*(2), 101–122.

Sicherman, N., & Galor, O. (1990). A theory of career mobility. *Journal of Political Economy, 98*(1), 169–192.

Suchan, T. A., Perry, M. J., Fitzsimmons, J. D., Juhn, A. E., Tait, A. M., & Brewer, C. A. (2007). *Census atlas of the United States* (Series CENSR-29). Washington, DC: U.S. Census Bureau. Retrieved from https://www.census.gov/population/www/cen2000/censusatlas/

Sweetland, S. R. (1996). Human capital theory: Foundations of a field of inquiry. *Review of Education Research, 66*(3), 341–359.

Tamborini, C. R., Kim, C., & Sakamoto, A. (2015). Education and lifetime earnings in the United States. *Demography, 52*(4), 1383–1407.

U.S. Department of Education, National Center for Education Statistics. (1996). *The condition of education 1996* (NCES96-304). Washington, DC: U.S. Government Printing Office. Retrieved from http://nces.ed.gov/pubs96/96304.pdf

U.S. Department of Education, National Center for Education Statistics. (2015). *Fast facts: Tuition costs of colleges and universities.* Retrieved from http://nces.ed.gov/fastfacts/display.asp?id=76

U.S. Department of Education, National Center for Education Statistics. (2016a). *Fast facts: Tuition costs of colleges and universities.* Digest of Education Statistics (NCES 2016-006). Retrieved from http://nces.ed.gov/fastfacts/display.asp?id=76

U.S. Department of Education, National Center for Education Statistics. (2016b). *Fast facts: Enrollment.* Digest of Education Statistics (NCES 2016-006). Retrieved from http://nces.ed.gov/fastfacts/display.asp?id=98

Vedder, R. (2004). Private vs. social returns to higher education: Some new cross-sectional evidence. *Journal of Labor Research, 25*(4), 677–686.

Verba, S., Schlozman, K. L., & Brady, H. E. (1995). *Voice and equality: Civic voluntarism in American politics.* Cambridge, MA: Harvard University Press.

Williams, A., & Swail, W. S. (2005). *Is more better? The impact of postsecondary education on the economic and social well-being of American society.* Washington, DC: Educational Policy Institute, Inc. Retrieved from http://www.educationalpolicy.org/pdf/gates.pdf

Wilson, J. (2000). Volunteering. *Annual Review of Sociology, 26,* 215–240.

24. Is Higher Education Worth the Cost? It Depends

LINDSEY M. BURKE

Higher education has become a rite of passage for those beginning the climb of upward mobility. In 2015, some 88 percent of adults in the United States had either a high school diploma or a general equivalency diploma, and one-third had earned at least a bachelor's degree—a figure that exceeded 30 percent for the first time in 2011[1] and had reached 33 percent by 2015.[2] The U.S. Census Bureau, which has consistently tracked educational attainment since 1940 on an annual basis, reports that just five percent of U.S. adults held a bachelor's degree or higher in 1940—a figure that had increased five-fold by 2015 to 33 percent.[3] Without question, higher educational attainment has been on the rise for the past 75 years, with more Americans now having earned a bachelor's degree than at any other point in history.

Increasing "Demand" for Higher Education

What has led to the increase in demand for higher education? Ohio University economist Richard Vedder cites the increase in the population of those 18 to 24, improvements in Americans' standard of living, and in part, a "revolution of rising expectations."[4] To a large extent, however, the demand curve has been shifted to the right by unrivaled access to federal subsidies, with third-party financing in the form of student loans and grants correlating with increases in college tuition.[5] During the 2011–12 academic year, for example, over 20 million undergraduate students (including full-time and part-time students) attended college in the United States. More than 70 percent of those students received some financial aid, with 6 out of 10 receiving a federal student loan.[6] When full-time, full-year undergraduates are isolated, the proportion receiving financial aid increases. Some 8.8 million students attended college full-time, for the full academic year, during the 2011–12 year. Among those students, over 84 percent received some form of aid, with more than 72 percent receiving federal aid in the form of loans and grants. The percentage of students receiving federal aid rose significantly over the course of a decade, increasing from 56.7 percent during the 1999–2000 academic year to 72.8 percent by the 2011–12 academic year.[7] Full-time, full-year undergraduates received on average $11,170 in federal aid during the 2011–12 academic year.[8]

Declining Value of a Bachelor's Degree

The unrivaled level of federal subsidies helps in part to explain increased demand for postsecondary education. Yet, although bachelor's degree attainment is at an all-time high, some scholars worry it has become an expensive signaling device, devoid of meaning, and a poor reflection of knowledge and skill acquisition.

The Sheepskin Effect

Although there may be advantages, in terms of time and financial commitment, to pursuing vocational education or not attending college altogether, many individuals continue to pursue bachelor's and other degrees even if uncertain about the necessity of having a degree for a given job. These individuals may be aware of the so-called sheepskin effect, wherein employers with imperfect information rely on college degrees to signal certain attributes—such as persistence—on the part of the applicant. Employers do not have perfect information on potential employees, therefore limiting their ability to choose rationally among an array of candidates. The bachelor's degree, attainable only after having earned one's way into college by demonstrating adequate scores on entrance exams such as the SAT and ACT, and by persisting through four years of coursework, signals to employers that job candidates have certain skills or attributes, such as grit. Yet as Tom Wood of the National Association of Scholars suggests,

> What is really happening is that employees signal their respective skills to employers by acquiring education. This is costly to all employees, but more costly to some than to others...According to this model of the labor market, it is not necessary for education to have any intrinsic value. All that is necessary in order for a credential to have value is that it convey valuable information about the employee to the employer that the employer would not otherwise have.[9]

The sheepskin effect is present in the literature from the 1970s forward. Notably, economists David A. Jaeger and Marianne E. Page found that, controlling for individual backgrounds, "sheepskin effects explain approximately a quarter of the total return to completing 16 years of education and more than half of the return to completing 16 years relative to 12 years."[10] As Wood explains, "The earnings of individuals holding a BA credential were 33% higher than matched individuals who had the same years of schooling but no BA credential."[11] To the extent that the sheepskin effect exists, it does not completely dismiss the cognitive gains attributable to college attendance, as it is possible— and indeed plausible—that "the B.A. has signaling value because credential holders are more productive in ways that are not visible to the researcher but are visible to the employer."[12] The sheepskin effect likely accounts for some of the earnings increase of bachelor's degree holders, but not all of the increase, with college graduates obtaining marketable skills as a result of their coursework and other experiences in college. Wood ultimately rejects the notion that there is no intrinsic value to higher education, concluding, "The evidence is clear that for a very large segment of our society, a high school education is not enough."[13] Setting aside the degree to which a sheepskin effect is present, is a bachelor's degree the best or most efficient way to signal knowledge and skill acquisition and grit to perspective employers? Additionally, is the potentially modest intrinsic value—which almost certainly varies based on institution attended, degree earned, and commitment of the student—enough to justify annual *federal* subsidies now exceeding $230 billion dollars?

Pushing Out Quality Alternatives

Although businesses and industry may look to the bachelor's degree as a proxy for employability, is a bachelor's degree a necessary prerequisite for everyone to climb the ladder of upward mobility? While some 65 percent of U.S. jobs will require some postsecondary education by 2020,[14] just one-third will require a bachelor's degree—a proportion roughly equivalent to the number of Americans currently holding a bachelor's degree. Yet policymakers' calls for increased access to higher education have grown louder, to include proposals for free community college[15] and free tuition at four-year institutions[16] completely subsidized by American taxpayers, with the goal of substantially increasing the number of bachelor's degree holders.

Yet according to the Bureau of Labor Statistics, only seven of the 30 fastest-growing jobs require a bachelor's degree. Within the next decade, among the top 10 fastest growing jobs, only two—accountants and college professors—require college degrees, the growth of which "is expected to be dwarfed by the need for registered nurses, home health aides, customer service representatives and store clerks,"[17] none of which require a bachelor's degree. Vedder notes that some of the individuals who hold bachelor's degrees in jobs that do not require them, such as the 15 percent of mail carriers who fall into that category, "could have bought a house for what they spent on their education."[18] This is not to say a student should not go to college or that earning a bachelor's degree is not worthwhile for many. Discussions about the value of the bachelor's degree should, however, include consideration of the opportunity costs and the financial burden placed on students, and the consequences of policymakers conferring preferential status through subsidies to one form of higher education over another. Often, for example, the decision to go to a traditional four-year college comes at the expense of alternatives that might better prepare individuals to enter the workforce, such as vocational and technical education. The *New York Times* reports that among German students who passed the national exam entitling them to taxpayer-funded college, some 40 percent opted to enroll in an apprenticeship program. Professor Robert I. Lerman of the American University explained that "some of the people coming out of those apprenticeships are in more demand than college graduates because they've actually managed things in the workplace."[19]

Moreover, as Wood notes, one prediction of human capital theory is that "education increases human capital, with each year of schooling adding to that capital until the diminishing marginal utility of education is cancelled out by the opportunity costs involved in getting the education." This could be seen as one argument for why K–12 education is publicly funded, whereas higher education is largely paid for by the individual pursuing the degree, rather directly or through loans that must eventually be repaid. There may be a diminishing point of returns when publicly subsidizing more than 12 years of K–12 education in terms of the opportunity and other costs involved. Literature from Canada, for example, suggests that the increase in acquired skills continues, but at a reduced rate, with every additional year of schooling. That is, cognitive skills increase by 3.2 percent for an additional year of schooling beyond the 12th year, but increase by only 2.1 percent for an additional year beyond the 16th year of schooling.[20] Yet some policymakers argue for not only increasing subsidies, but call for making college completely free at the point of delivery.

Unequal Returns on Investment

Is the bachelor's degree actually helping to climb the ladder of upward mobility? Scholars at the Brookings Institution found that the percentage increase in earnings for bachelor's degree holders was less for individuals from low-income backgrounds, with the proportional increase in earnings accrued from moving from a high school diploma to a bachelor's degree being much less for students from poor families than for individuals who did not grow up poor.[21] Students from low-income families (earning less than 185 percent of the federal poverty line) who earn a bachelor's degree earn 91 percent more than high school graduates over the course of their lifetimes. By contrast, nonpoor individuals earned 162 percent more on average over the course of their careers than those holding a high school diploma. It is a gap that widens over time. As Brookings report notes, "bachelor's degree holders from low-income backgrounds start their careers earning about two-thirds as much as those from higher-income backgrounds, but this ratio declines to one-half by mid-career."[22] Although a number of factors could be at play in the gap between initially poor and nonpoor bachelor's degree earners, such as the type of colleges attended by low-income students, these findings muddle the idea that a bachelor's degree is necessarily the key to economic mobility.

Further complicating matters is the amount of debt with which poor students often leave college. Although low-income students qualify for Pell Grants, which do not have to be repaid, poor students who qualify for the grants graduated from public universities with an average of $27,000 in debt during the 2012–13 academic year, and exited private universities with an average student debt load of $34,000. Students not receiving Pell Grants left with an average of $22,000 in debt from public universities, and graduated with an average of $30,000 in student loan debt accumulated at private institutions.[23]

Subsidies Lead to Higher Tuition and Fees

Growth in borrowing and debt may be driven by ever-increasing federal subsidies in the form of subsidized student loans and grants. The idea the subsidies encourage universities to raise tuition gained national attention in 1987 when the then U.S. Secretary of Education William Bennett wrote in the *New York Times* that "increases in financial aid in recent years have enabled colleges and universities blithely to raise their tuitions, confident that Federal loan subsidies would help cushion the increase."[24] His assertion, which would become known as the "Bennett Hypothesis," appears to have held true in the decades since it was first put forward. A recent evaluation by economists at the Federal Reserve Bank of New York found that for every additional dollar of Pell Grant funding, tuition increased by 40 cents. For every dollar increase in federally subsidized student loans, tuition increased 63 cents. As economists David O. Lucca, Taylor Nadauld, and Karen Shen note, those effects are highly significant "and are consistent with the Bennett Hypothesis." Moreover, although the benefits of Pell Grants and subsidized student loans are concentrated to those who qualify and receive the subsidy, the increased tuition costs are passed on to all students at a university.

This phenomenon is exacerbated by the reality that third-party payments have desensitized students to increases in tuition and fees. As Vedder explains, "Since most loans to students are subsidized—given at below-market interest rates with generous payback provisions—and others are even forgiven, students do not see loans as a burden equal to the dollar amount of the principal."[25] There is some truth to the notion that "in higher education, costs determine revenues, while in for-profit businesses, revenues determine costs."[26] Vedder identifies four primary drivers of increases in college costs: third-party payers, a lack of market discipline, lack of competition, and government regulation. The third-party payers critique is linked to a lack of market discipline. Universities are well aware of the fact that students have access to virtually unlimited federal subsidies—primarily through the Pell Grant program and Direct Loans—and, as such, are not subjected to the type of market discipline that comes with individuals directly paying for a good or service.

Pell Grants

The federal Pell Grant program provides financial aid to low-income students. The grants, which do not have to be repaid by recipients, are intended to ease the cost of college for eligible students. In 2014, the $33 billion Pell Grant program provided grants to nine million college students, making it the largest share of the federal education budget. Congress grew the Pell Grant program in 2007 by expanding eligibility and increasing funding, resulting in a doubling of the number of Pell recipients since 2008.

Direct Loans

The largest federal loan program authorized under the Higher Education Act (HEA) is in Title IV, part D—the federal Direct Loan program. The Direct Loan program includes subsidized and unsubsidized Stafford loans for undergraduate and graduate students, Parent PLUS and Grad PLUS loans, and consolidation loans. PLUS loans are loans to graduate students and the parents of undergraduate students. A graduate student or the parents of an undergraduate student may borrow up to the cost of attendance at a given school, less any other aid received.

Continuing to increase federal higher education subsidies has not eased the college cost burden for students, instead exacerbating the problem of escalating tuition. Since 1980, for example, tuition and fees at public and private universities have grown at least twice as fast as the rate of inflation. The result has been that 60 percent of bachelor's degree holders leave school with more than $26,000 in student loan debt, with cumulative student loan debt now exceeding $1.3 trillion. The growth in federal higher education subsidies has been authorized largely through the federal HEA, which governs federal higher education policy including student loans and grants.

History of the Higher Education Act

President Dwight D. Eisenhower laid the foundation for the HEA in 1958 when he signed into law the National Defense Education Act (NDEA). Title II of the NDEA established a federal student aid program, which, Eisenhower hoped, would "reduce the waste of talent" and aid national security.[27] President Lyndon B. Johnson then established a task force to study the role of the federal government in providing student aid. The 1964 task force argued that whether a student could afford to attend college should not be the determining factor in whether he did so.[28] One of the driving factors behind the task force's work was a study finding that one in six high school students who took the National Merit Scholarship test did not attend college, many times due to financial constraints. It was a finding that "in Johnson's eyes…reflected a loss of human capital."[29] It was that sentiment that drove the introduction and subsequent enactment of The HEA, which Johnson first signed into law in 1965 and constituted one of the many programs comprising his Great Society initiative. The law's primary purpose was to allocate federal student loans and grants to ease the cost of college—part of Johnson's goal to keep "the doors to higher education open for all academically qualified students regardless of their financial circumstances."[30] At only 52 pages, the HEA provided low-interest loans to students, offered grants to eligible students, and also provided authorization for programs for teacher training. The HEA's other titles were supplemental to the law's primary purpose—financial aid distributed through Title IV in the form of loans, grants, institutional aid, and work-study programs. Title IV "represented the first generally available aid program for postsecondary students."[31] Today, the 432-page HEA impacts nearly every aspect of federal higher education policy. The HEA was most recently reauthorized in 2008 as the Higher Education Opportunity Act, and is now divided into 11 titles. Notably, federal student aid authorized under Title IV of the act topped $169 billion in the 2013–14 academic year—an increase of 105 percent over the past decade.[32]

College Accreditation and the HEA

In addition to authorizing federal student aid programs through Title IV of the law, the HEA also authorizes the National Advisory Committee on Institutional Quality and Integrity (NACIQI) to "assess the process of accreditation and the institutional eligibility and certification of institutions of higher education." The NACIQI wields significant power over college accreditation by overseeing an exhaustive review process for approving prospective accreditors in conjunction with the US Department of Education. Applications to become an accrediting agency, for example, are reviewed by NACIQI and are placed on NACIQI's twice-yearly meeting agenda, and the NACIQI then recommends to the Department of Education whether to approve, limit, or deny a request to become an accreditor.[33] Federally sanctioned regional and national accrediting agencies are the sole purveyors of institutional accreditation. Institutions, for their part, do not have access to federal student loan and grant programs authorized under Title IV of the HEA unless they are accredited. The result has been a system that has created barriers to entry for innovative start-ups by insulating traditional brick-and-mortar schools from market forces that could reduce costs. Moreover, entire institutions are accredited instead of individual courses, rendering accreditation a poor measure of course quality and a poor indicator of the skills acquired by students.

Current Reform Efforts

Some policymakers have supported proposals to break the link between accreditation and Title IV funding, with proposals to decouple federal financing from accreditation having been introduced in the U.S. House and Senate. Sen. Mike Lee (R-UT), who introduced the Higher Education Reform and Opportunity Act, explained what he hopes to achieve through such a proposal:

> Qualified unions, businesses, and trade groups could start to accredit courses and programs tailored to their evolving needs. Churches and charities could enlist qualified volunteers to offer accredited classes and training for next to nothing. States could use innovative systems to attract new opportunities and businesses, investing in their own future by investing in the human capital of their citizens. Imagine having access to credit and student aid and for: a program in computer science accredited by Apple or in music accredited by the New York Philharmonic; college-level history classes on-site at Mount Vernon or Gettysburg;

medical-technician training developed by the Mayo Clinic; taking massive, open, online courses offered by the best teachers in the world, from your living room or the public library. Brick-and-ivy institutions will always be the backbone of our higher-education system, but they shouldn't be the only option.[34]

Reforms to accreditation have typically been bypassed in favor of policies designed to subsidize increases in tuition, which have historically failed to solve the college cost problem. Moreover, more recent regulatory changes have made federal subsidies and student loan forgiveness programs more generous, likely exacerbating college cost problems. Federal higher education subsidies have increased substantially over the past decade, and now represent 71 percent of all student aid. The federal government now originates and manages 93 percent of all student loans. By extension, taxpayers now bear primary responsibility for paying for student loan defaults, when they occur. As of April 2016, Americans owed more than $200 billion in defaulted or deferred student loan payments, with some 40 percent of federal borrowers not making payments on their loans. Of the 22 million Americans who had left college and entered the workforce with federal student loans in 2016, a full 43 percent were not making payments on their debt.[35]

During the Obama administration, loan forgiveness options were expanded to enable borrowers to have remaining debt forgiven after a fewer number of years, and were made more generous for individuals working in the public sector. The federal income-based repayment program was expanded in 2015, with new regulations capping the amount of money Direct Loan borrowers can be required to repay in a given month to 10 percent of their discretionary income. The same directive mandated that any borrower that still had student loan debt after 20 years of repayment would have that debt forgiven. Student loans are also now eligible for forgiveness after 10 years if the borrower works in the public sector, which is extended to some parents who borrow through the Parent PLUS program. With the near-disappearance of private lending, changes to loan forgiveness options mean taxpayers will bear more and more of the burden of paying for any remaining loan balances of federal borrowers. Not only do such options leave taxpayers on the hook for financing college (when most taxpayers themselves do not hold bachelor's degrees), these programs put no downward pressure on prices at universities, who can be even more confident that increases in tuition and fees will be met with little resistance from students, who rely on third-party payers and increasingly qualify for total loan forgiveness. These policies have an additional consequence: loan repayment caps and loan forgiveness leave taxpayers to finance a nontrivial number of leisure hours enjoyed by students.

College Students' Typical Days and the Academic "Arms Race"

As taxpayers increasingly bear the burden of financing higher education, through loan subsidies, repayment caps, and loan forgiveness, they also pay for the nonwork hours of college students, and an unrelenting race for higher-end campus facilities. Data from the Bureau of Labor Statistics' American Time-Use Survey indicate that the typical full-time college student spends just 2.76 hours per day on all education-related activities, including both studying and attending class, equating to 19.3 hours per week. Among those full-time college students who do not work, slightly more hours per day—3.56, or 24.9 hours per week—are spent engaged in education-related activities.[36] Limited education ours may be the reason fewer than half of the class of 2006 graduated college within six years. On average, individuals "will not work as little as they did at age 19 until they reach age 59, when significant numbers cut back on their work hours or enter retirement. With outstanding student loan debt currently at more than $1.2 trillion, these findings raise an important question: Why are taxpayers heavily subsidizing a period in some people's lives when combined education and work efforts are at their lowest?"

Table 24.1. Bureau of Labor Statistics: Many Full-Time College Students Put in Modest Hours. Full-time college students who are not employed spend an average of 25.8 hours a week on education and work-related activities.

		AVERAGE HOURS SPENT PER WEEK		
FT—full time, PT—part time	Population (in millions)	Work and work-related activities	Education	Total, work and education
FT college student/FT worker	2.7	39.1	8.4	47.5
PT college student/FT worker	3.4	39.6	7.0	46.6
Non-student/FT worker	110.0	41.2	0.2	41.4
FT college student/PT worker	4.5	18.7	19.9	38.6
High school student	13.3	4.6	29.5	34.1
PT college student/PT worker	1.1	23.4	10.4	33.8
FT college student/non-worker	4.7	0.9	24.9	25.8
Non-student/PT worker	25.1	22.5	0.3	22.8
PT college student/non-worker	1.1	2.0	15.9	17.9
Non-student/non-worker	72.9	1.0	0.3	1.3

SOURCE: Bureau of Labor Statistics, "American Time Use Survey—Multi-Year Microdata Files," http://www.bls.gov/tus/datafiles_0314.htm (accessed June 24, 2016).

IB 4589 ☎ heritage.org

Source: Author.

In addition to subsidizing many nonacademic hours, federal aid has also incentivized what has been deemed an academic "arms race." As Vedder explained during testimony before the Senate Budget Committee,

> A very good case can be made that federal student loans have fueled an academic arms race financed in large part by rising tuition fees, an arms race that has led to a proliferation in higher education bureaucracies, expensive recreational facilities, lower teaching loads that have funded largely unread esoteric research, bigger subsidies of intercollegiate athletics, and other spending unrelated to promoting the core university mission of disseminating and expanding our stock of knowledge and cultural capital.[37]

Indeed, administrative bloat within universities has become a growing problem in recent decades. The number of full-time university administrators per 100 students increased by 39 percent, compared with an 18 percent increase in employees working in research, teaching, and service, between 1993 and 2007. Inflation-adjusted spending on these individuals followed suit, growing 61 percent and 39 percent, respectively.[38] Jay P. Greene, Brian Kisida, and Jonathan Mills note that "One might think that as enrollments increase, universities would need relatively fewer administrators per student since they could spread those fixed costs over a larger base. Instead, the opposite is occurring. As universities increase their enrollment and receive more money, they expand the ranks of administrators even more rapidly." They continue:

> Rather than achieving economies of scale in administration so that more resources can be redirected to core functions, America's leading universities increased administration significantly faster than enrollment and almost twice as fast as teaching, research and service.

Federal subsidies appear to have fueled a lending and spending cycle in which federal aid is made easily available, typically with no credit check or regard for future ability to repay. In turn, universities appear to have responded to this easy money by raising tuition and fees, confident that students can return to the federal trough to access loans that, because they do not have to be repaid immediately (and sometimes not at all) desensitize them to increases in college costs.

So Is Higher Education Worth the Cost?

Undoubtedly, for many individuals, obtaining a bachelor's degree is a prerequisite to climbing the ladder of upward mobility. Yet for many people, they may be better served by vocational options or other paths that lead more directly into the workforce, avoiding what has been a lengthy, costly detour through the ivory tower. Americans appear to be quite skeptical that higher education always lives up to its promises, with just four in 10 respondents in a 2011 Pew Research Center poll reporting that college is a sound investment.[39]

Higher education in the United States has a long and celebrated history, predating federal spending and the numerous programs and requirements under the HEA. In order to increase access and affordability of higher education, policymakers should limit federal intervention, programs, and spending. In order to truly drive down college costs and improve access for students, policymakers should undertake major reforms to accreditation. College costs are at an all-time high even as access to knowledge is cheaper than at any other point in human history. The question, then, is not so much whether higher education is worth it. It is a question of whether the existing $230 billion per year system of federal subsidies creates perverse incentives, opportunity costs, preferential treatment of certain sectors, and burdens on taxpayers. The other side of the issue is, what can be done to ensure those who want and need to pursue postsecondary education can do so. Subsidizing increases in costs will not solve the problem or increase access. Those goals can, however, potentially be realized by decoupling federal financing from accreditation, restoring a private lending market by reducing federal subsidies, and by recognizing that there are manner ladders enabling the climb of economic opportunity.

Notes

1. Bernstein, R. (2012). Bachelor's degree attainment tops 30 percent for the first time, census bureau reports. *United States Census Bureau.* Retrieved from https://www.census.gov/newsroom/releases/archives/education/cb12-33.html
2. Ryan, C. L., & Bauman, K. (2016). Educational attainment in the United States: 2015. *United States Census Bureau.* Retrieved from: http://www.census.gov/content/dam/Census/library/publications/2016/demo/p20-578.pdf
3. *Ibid.*
4. Vedder, R. (2004). *Going broke by degree: Why college costs too much* (p. 18). Washington, DC: AEI Press.
5. Vedder, R. (2004). *Going broke by degree: Why college costs too much.* Washington, DC: AEI Press.
6. Table 331.10. Percentage of undergraduates receiving financial aid, by type and source of aid and selected student characteristics: 2011–12. (2014). Digest of Education Statistics. Retrieved from https://nces.ed.gov/programs/digest/d14/tables/dt14_331.10.asp

7. Table 331.35 (2014) Percentage of full-time, full-year undergraduates receiving financial aid, and average annual amount received, by source of aid and selected student characteristics: Selected years, 1999–2000 through 2011–12. Digest of Education Statistics. Retrieved from https://nces.ed.gov/programs/digest/d14/tables/dt14_331.10.asp
8. *Ibid.*
9. Wood, T. (2009). The sheepskin effect. *National Association of Scholars.* Retrieved from https://www.nas.org/articles/The_Sheepskin_Effect
10. Jaeger, D. A., & Page, M. E. (1996). Degrees matter: New evidence on sheepskin effects in the returns to education. *Review of Economics and Statistics, 78*(4), 733–740. In Wood, T. (2009). The sheepskin effect. *National Association of Scholars.* Retrieved from https://www.nas.org/articles/The_Sheepskin_Effect
11. Wood, T. (2009). The sheepskin effect. *National Association of Scholars.* Retrieved from https://www.nas.org/articles/The_Sheepskin_Effect
12. *Ibid.*
13. *Ibid.*
14. Carnevale, A. P., Smith, N., & Strohl, J. (2014). Recovery: Job growth and education requirements through 2020. *Georgetown Public Policy Institute*, Georgetown University. Retrieved from https://cew.georgetown.edu/wp-content/uploads/2014/11/Recovery2020.ES_.Web_.pdf
15. Reim, M. C. (2016). "Free" community college is a bad deal for taxpayers and students. *The Heritage Foundation.* Retrieved from http://www.heritage.org/research/reports/2016/07/free-community-college-is-a-bad-deal-for-taxpayers-and-students
16. Hillary Clinton, New College Compact. Retrieved from https://www.hillaryclinton.com/briefing/factsheets/2016/07/06/hillary-clintons-commitment-a-debt-free-future-for-americas-graduates/
17. Steinberg, J. (2010). Plan B: Skip college. *The New York Times.* Retrieved from http://www.nytimes.com/2010/05/16/weekinreview/16steinberg.html
18. *Ibid.*
19. *Ibid.*
20. *Ibid.*
21. Hershbein, B. (2016). A college degree is worth less if you are raised poor. *The Brookings Institution.* Retrieved from http://www.brookings.edu/blogs/social-mobility-memos/posts/2016/02/19-college-degree-worth-less-raised-poor-hershbein
22. *Ibid.*
23. Douglas-Gabriel, D. (2015). Minorities and poor college students are shouldering the most student debt. *The Washington Post.* Retrieved from https://www.washingtonpost.com/news/wonk/wp/2015/05/19/minorities-and-poor-college-students-are-shouldering-the-most-student-debt/
24. Bennett, W. J. (1987). Our greedy colleges. *The New York Times.* Retrieved from http://www.nytimes.com/1987/02/18/opinion/our-greedy-colleges.html
25. Vedder, R. (2004). *Going broke by degree: Why college costs too much* (p. 20). Washington, DC: AEI Press.
26. Vedder, R. (2004). *Going broke by degree: Why college costs too much* (p. 25). Washington, DC: AEI Press.

27. Angelica Cervantes et al., "Opening the Doors to Higher Education: Perspectives on the Higher Education Act 40 Years Later," TG Research and Analytical Services, November 2005. Retrieved from http://www.tgslc.org/pdf/hea_history.pdf
28. *Ibid.*
29. *Ibid.*
30. *Ibid.*
31. *Ibid.*
32. College Board, "Trends in Student Aid 2013," College Board Trends in Higher Education Series, 2013. Retrieved from http://trends.collegeboard.org/sites/default/files/student-aid-2013-full-report.pdf
33. Burke, L. M., & Butler, S. M. (2012). "Accreditation: Removing the Barrier to Higher Education Reform," Heritage Foundation Backgrounder No. 2728, September 21, 2012. Retrieved from http://www.heritage.org/research/reports/2012/09/accreditation-removing-the-barrier-to-higher-education-reform
34. Lee, M. (2013). What's next for conservatives? *The Heritage Foundation.* Remarks delivered on October 29, 2013. Retrieved from http://www.nationalreview.com/article/362515/whats-next-conservatives-sen-mike-lee
35. Mitchell, J. (2016). More than 40% of student borrowers are making payments. *The Wall Street Journal.* Retrieved from http://www.wsj.com/articles/more-than-40-of-student-borrowers-arent-making-payments-1459971348
36. Burke, L. M., Hall, J. B., & Reim, M. C. (2016). Big debt, little study: What taxpayers should know about college students' time-use. *The Heritage Foundation.* Retrieved from http://www.heritage.org/research/reports/2016/07/big-debt-little-study-what-taxpayers-should-know-about-college-students-time-use
37. Vedder, R. (2014). *Can college be made more affordable? It's about more than student loans.* Testimony of R. K. Vedder, Committee on the Budget. United States Senate. Retrieved from http://www.budget.senate.gov/imo/media/doc/Vedder%20Testimony.pdf
38. Greene, J. P., Kisida, B., & Mills, J. (2010). Colleges' bloated bureaucracy. *The Baltimore Sun.* Retrieved from http://articles.baltimoresun.com/2010-08-17/news/bs-ed-college-administrators-20100817_1_private-universities-public-universities-research-and-service
39. Is higher education worth it? *Pew Research Center.* (2011). Retrieved from http://www.pewsocialtrends.org/2011/05/15/chapter-3-public-views-and-experiences/

Part Thirteen: *Are Colleges Spending Too Much on Amenities?*

In "The College Arms Race: How It Is Destroying Higher Education in the United States," Matthew Varga and Scott L. Lingrell describe how private and public colleges use increases in tuition and student fees to support "unsustainable spending levels" in the face of economic downturn and recession. They charge that higher internal spending is part of efforts to remain competitive within changing student demographics and market shifts. Varga and Lingrell predict that any institutions unable to maintain sustainable enrollments through admissions and retention will shutter. They also paint a dim picture for private–public partnerships within state colleges and worry about the problematic consequences of further privatizing campus amenities.

In "The Need for College Amenities and Their Benefit to the Student and Institution's Success," Steven Tolman and Christopher Trautman define "amenities" as campus entities beyond the academic support system of academic advising and career services. They justify mainly those amenities connected to student development. Tolman and Trautman criticize the use of excessive amenities such as opulent resident and dining halls, palatial recreational centers, and the like. Yet they cite data indicating that some such amenities may be necessary to promote the now expected "student experience" in American higher education. In the end, the authors propose a responsible spending model related to student outcomes while acknowledging that the "college arms race" has benefits to students as consumers.

25. The College Arms Race: How It Is Destroying Higher Education in the United States

MATTHEW VARGA AND SCOTT L. LINGRELL

For a little over 400 years, the primary purpose of colleges and universities (colleges hereafter) has been to educate society by experts sharing their knowledge with novices (Brubacher & Rudy, 1958). Many colleges flourished and were established to educate specific populations; whether it was to educate clergy, the enslaved, Native Americans, or women, to name a few. However, now, postsecondary education has become more than a tool to transfer knowledge from an expert to a novice. It has become a competition between institutions to see who can outdo the other, by providing the better college experience, and building the fanciest residence halls, the grandest university unions, or the most expensive recreation centers. These construction projects occur despite the cost in the name of prestige, school pride, rankings, selectivity, and profits. This scenario is leading higher education in the United States down a very dangerous and destructive path in terms of affordability as well as market stability. In this chapter, we will explore the change in cost and affordability in higher education as it relates to the increased demand of amenities. The cost of higher education has increased, in large part, due to the college arms race, which is a competition between institutions to provide the best facilities, regardless of the cost.

World history tells us that competition between competing forces does not bode well in the end. We have seen two nations compete for the best military arsenal and for the most advanced space program; this competition unfolded over the years as the Cold War between the United States and the Union of Soviet Socialist Republics. Yes, we are comparing the figurative arms race in education, currently, to the literal arms and space race during the second half of the 20th century. As outlandish as this may seem initially, the similarities are eerie and demonstrate the severity of the situation facing higher education.

Two powerful nations with similar purposes and agendas in the world, which was to be the best country in the world with the best technology, military, and economy, all in the name of nationalism (concepts not that different from school pride, rankings, enrollment, and prestige). Both countries strived to provide the most for their citizens in ways they thought best, regardless of the cost to its coffers. A prime example is the space race and the financial commitment made by the United States to achieve its goal of supremacy. After the USSR successfully launched Sputnik into space, the race and rivalry begun (Brzezinski, 2007), and the United States vowed to be the first to orbit a man around the earth (Brzezinski, 2007). However, outdone by the USSR again, the order came from President John F. Kennedy to put a man on the moon because he recognized the declining reputation of the United States from both American citizens and the international community (Brzezinski, 2007). In John F. Kennedy's message to congress, in 1962 he requested an initial $531 million dollars ($4.2 billion dollars in 2015) and an additional $7 to $9 billion ($55 billion to $71 billion in 2015) over the next five years (John F. Kennedy Presidential Library and Museum, 2016). The United States spared no cost to become the top space agency program and nation in the world. Eventually, the space race collapsed from the inside after great feats were accomplished. The public was no longer impressed with either space program, as they wanted more; financially, it was no longer sustainable, as the cost had become too great for either country to bear—mirroring the question of affordability for colleges. Fast forward 50 years and the United States has all but dissolved the space program.

The comparison between the space race and the arms race of colleges is subtle, but very real. The United States spent an astronomical amount of money to achieve a goal designed to do nothing more than increase the prestige of the United States at home and abroad. Colleges are doing the exact same thing: they are spending hundreds of millions of dollars on amenities for students in order to increase their applications, enrollment, prestige, and national rankings (Ehrenberg, 2000; Gardner, 2005). Much like the USSR's dissolution, the result for some colleges and universities is a similar fate as they cannot sustain this model of "no matter the cost" any further as they have had to increase tuition to beyond what the market will bear. The outcome—some colleges and universities are closing their doors or losing their accreditation because they cannot compete with larger institutions that have increased their spending. This trend of increased spending over the last 20 years has not subsided despite an economic recession in 2008 and decreased state funding (Abramson, 2013; Desrochers & Hurlburt, 2014).

To properly evaluate and understand the college arms race, it is important to highlight the trends in college finance and the changes in the economic market. These two factors are directly related to an institution's need and desire to build college amenities as institutions of higher learning need to remain attractive to a declining student population despite the increase in tuition and fees (Jacob, McCall, & Stange, 2013). Once college finance and market demand is reviewed, the college arms race can be understood in terms of college amenities that are being offered, which is followed by legislative's response to these buildings that influence college affordability.

Trends in College Finance

In 2008, the United States experienced a severe recession, which would suggest a decrease in college spending as state-appropriated funds also decreased (Jacob et al., 2013; Samuels, 2013); however, from 2001 to 2011, colleges have consistently increased their overall spending, and spending by colleges and universities was higher than it had been in the previous five and 10 years (Desrochers & Hurlburt, 2014). According to the Delta Cost Project (2014), public research and master's colleges, as well as private research institutions, consistently increased spending over the 10-year period. Most notably are public research institutions that had an increase in spending for instructional activities (4.4%), research support (15.8%), student services (16.4%), and institutional support (10.9%). The increases in spending by public research institutions comes as states continually decreased financial support (Baum, 2015), so it is not surprising to see dramatic increases in tuition to support this spending. Private research institutions saw an even more dramatic increase in spending over the same 10-year period: instructional activities (18.7%), research support (31.3%), student services (29.8%), academic support (22.7%), and institutional support (23.4%). However, it is important to note the significant increases in spending from private institutions are less concerning because of the financial structure of private institutions, as they tend to have large endowments that support such spending.

The increase of college spending has been the result of two primary sources of revenue for colleges: student fees and tuition (Kelchen, 2016). Baum (2015) reports that the increase of student fees and tuition has steadily climbed since 1985. In fact, adjusting for inflation, public four-year institutions' tuition and fees are 3.22 times higher in 2015–2016 than they were in 1985–1984. Two-year public institutions saw a slightly lower increase at 2.42 times higher in 2015–2016 than in 1985–1984, which is comparable to the 2.39 times reported for private four-year nonprofit institutions during the same time frame. This means that, in 1985, a student could attend a public four-year institution for an average $2,918 a year, but in 2015–2016 that number climbs to an average of $9,410, which is still relatively low as some four-year public institutions have tuition and fees as high as $20,000 (Baum, 2015).

In 1985, the primary cost burden was placed on states through state-appropriated funds, but now that cost burden has shifted to students, which explains the higher fees, tuition, and additional costs to attend college (Ehrenberg, 2000; Gould, 2003; Kelchen, 2016). This helps explain why some schools have increased tuition by almost 200% over the last 15 years (The Chronicle of Higher Education, 2016). For example, The College of William and Mary, a four-year public institution in Virginia engaged in high research activity, has increased their tuition from a sticker price of $6,584 in 1999 (adjusted for inflation) to just under $20,000 in 2015 (The Chronicle of Higher Education, 2016). The difference in student enrollment is approximately 900 students from 1999 to 2015 (The College of William & Mary, 1999). Another example of a drastic increase in tuition includes Arizona State University, which saw a 216% increase in tuition from 1999 to 2015 ($3,226 to $10,184, respectively). It is important to note that in 1999, their enrollment was approximately 49,700 and in the fall of 2014 it was 71,049. Arizona State University experienced a significant reduction in state appropriation over that same time frame (Mitchell, Leachman, & Masterson, 2016).

Both of these examples are drastic and are more common among public institutions, whereas private institutions have seen their tuition increase around 50% over the last 15 years (The Chronicle of Higher Education, 2016), which speaks to why students attending private colleges have not seen their share of costs increase as much as students attending public institutions (8% shared cost to approximately 60%) (Desrochers & Hurlburt, 2014). Other examples of tuition increases from 1999 to 2015 include Christopher Newport University at 184%; the University of Tennessee at 181%; University of Georgia at 168%; University of Texas at Austin at 121%; and Ohio State University at 70%. This is not an exhaustive list, but demonstrates the point that tuition has risen considerably and varies from state-to-state and school-to-school. If we look at the last 10 years, and adjust for inflation, the overall increase in tuition and fees for public four-year institution is 40% (Baum, 2015).

These increases seem outrageous, but when we consider that institutions have experienced considerable growth in terms of capital projects for college amenities over the last 20 years it is not surprising. In 1995, the construction and capital projects cost was about $6.1 billion dollars and peaked in 2006 at $15 billion (Abramson, 2013). Construction costs did slowly decrease from 2007 ($14.5 billion) to 2009 ($10.7 billion), with it increasing slightly at $11 billion in 2010 and 2011 (Abramson, 2013). Approximately 70% of these figures were allocated to new buildings (Abramson, 2013), which was likely due to market demands for commercializing institutions of higher education and providing amenities that are desirable to students (Jacob et al., 2013).

Market Demand

Colleges and universities have succumbed to the capitalistic economy and are influenced by the economic market in terms of competition, supply and demand, profitability, and other aspects that comprise economies (Gardner, 2005). There are many reasons for tuition and fees increasing, some of which include decreased state appropriations. However, the major contributing factor includes the commercialization of higher education and administrative costs (Samuels, 2013). Higher education, over the last 30 years, has increasingly commercialized, subsequently resulting in a marketplace of competition (Bok, 2003; Gould, 2003). Higher education has deviated from the original purpose of educating students, but now serves more as a experiential country club (Jacob et al., 2013). As reported by Forbes magazine in 2014, this country club atmosphere becomes the definition of the college arms race (Newlon, 2014). The commercialization and market demand for lavish amenities has resulted in the college arms race and the idea that if colleges "build it," students will come. We have seen this principle in practice with student athletics.

Pope and Pope (2009) evaluated the impact of college sports on the quantity and quality of student admission's applications. They hypothesized that the better the collegiate sports, the school would see an increase in student applications with the quality of those applications also increasing. They were correct, and found that a school's admissions applications rose between 2% and 8% depending on the profile of the school. They also found the school's response to this success varied. Some schools would increase tuition rates with the increased number of students; other schools would deny more students to increase their selectivity rate; and some schools use the increase in applications to adjust enrollment and student quality (Pope & Pope, 2009). Regardless of the purpose, the overall theme presented is that schools can use student athletics to help increase their desirability among prospective students, which is the same principle as providing extravagant college amenities to increase desirability.

This becomes the crux of the college arms race. If schools increase the overall desirability of the school environment through lavish student centers, recreation facilities, and residence halls, then colleges can increase student applications, subsequently increasing their student profile. It is important to note that the increase in student applications is more likely to be from wealthy high-achieving students whereas the less academically oriented students who have fewer financial resources tend not to apply to these schools (Jacob et al., 2013). Therefore, these schools are unintentionally, or intentionally, excluding some students that can help diversify their student population; however, the schools with these amenities are increasing their application numbers and with increased denials increase the school's selectivity rate—both of which are factors used to consider US News & World Report Rankings.

It should be no surprise that colleges have responded the way they did to commercialization over the last 30 to 40 years. Not only have they desired to remain competitive in a pool of thousands of other schools, but colleges have to fight for resources (Bok, 2003). Therefore, what better way to find resources than to commercialize practices and increase marketability through college amenities that become a part of the "college experience." Institutions want to increase the number of services and amenities they provide to students to become competitive and meet student demands (Bok, 2003). However, where is the money going to come from to pay for these newly increased demands? Tuition and fees are one way, but it could also be speculated that the commercialization of higher education was really able to happen between the 1980s and 2010s with the increased access to federal funds from the development of the GI Bill, Stafford loans, PELL grants, and PLUS loans. There is no formal evidence to suggest as such, but the correlation is interesting nonetheless.

The increase in access to funds for students has resulted in a burden that the United States has not seen before with student loan debt equaling 6% of the national debt at $1.3 trillion. We have seen students increasingly share the cost of publically subsidized schools (Desrochers & Hurlburt, 2014). Although it begs the question—what are students receiving with the increase in student fees, tuition, and cost sharing because of the commercialization of colleges and universities?

College Amenities

Despite higher education becoming more commercialized, the development and building priorities along with resource allocation have been a direct result of the varied preference of students, according to Jacob et al. (2013). For example, highly selective private institutions have a greater incentive to invest in instructional activities since the academically average student is more interested in academic quality than they are in recreational amenities. This is in comparison to less selective schools that need to attract more students and feel compelled to invest in consumption amenities. Therefore, Jacob et al. (2013) have concluded that colleges do respond to the demand model as it relates to commercialization and market consumption.

The conclusions from Jacob et al. (2013) are relatively easy to find in present-day colleges. Most often, colleges focus on recreation centers, student housing, and student unions as the prize buildings on campus. High Point University, which was a fledging institution in the late 1990s and early 2000s, decided to invest in their college amenities and after $700 million of renovations since 2007 they are able to advertise a movie theatre, free arcade, ice cream truck, complementary housing, and a steak restaurant all provided to students "free." Since these renovations, High Point University has seen an increase in their application numbers and selectivity resulting in numerous top rankings from US News and World Report (Newlon, 2014).

The California State University, Fullerton (2016) has a recreation center that boasts 22,000 square feet of gymnasium space with three full indoor courts that can be converted into basketball courts, volleyball courts, or nine badminton courts. There is an indoor track measuring at 7,000 square feet that rises above 7,600 square feet of activity space for fitness classes not including the spin room. Students have access to two racquetball courts and a 35 feet high climbing wall as well as an outdoor pool (California State University at Fullerton, 2016). All of this was built for $41 million dollars (Newlon, 2014). A slightly upgraded version can be experienced at the University of Colorado. They spent $63 million (Newlon, 2014) on a 300,000 square feet recreation facility that provides over six basketball courts, five fitness studios, an ice rink, three tennis courts, four pools, four racquetball courts, an indoor turf gym, a climbing wall, and a wellness suite (University of Colorado, 2016). As wonderful as this facility is at the University of Colorado, it pales in comparison to Purdue University's recreation center (Purdue University, 2016). Purdue University built a new recreation center in 2012 for a little less than $100 million dollars (Newlon, 2014), which includes two spas, two pools, three saunas, two indoor tracks, 55 foot climbing wall, six gymnasiums, eight multipurpose rooms, 16 racquet ball and squash courts, and demonstration kitchens for healthy cooking (Purdue University, 2016).

If the facility at Purdue University was not enough, The Ohio State University built a $140 million (Newlon, 2014) recreation facility featuring a skyway that connects the facility to an academic building. In terms of amenities, there are five pools—a competitive swimming pool, a varsity swimming pool, a recreation lap pool, a class instructional pool, and a leisure pool—two spas, one as a dive pool spa and the other serves as a leisure whirlpool spa. To conclude the aquatic facilities, there are two dry saunas. In terms of recreation space, there is a special events gym designed for spectator seating for 500 people or the area configures to four 84-foot basketball courts. Students have access to four volleyball courts or an upper gym that divides into four basketball courts or four more volleyball courts. Two of the basketball courts can convert into six badminton courts. Two additional court gyms configure as two basketball, three volleyball, or six badminton courts. The weight and fitness area includes a weight area and multiple cardio areas across three different floors. Other amenities include racquetball and squash courts (10 and four, respectively), seven golf ball hitting stations, a simulator, a chipping and putting area, a walking and jogging track, aerobics and multipurpose rooms, a wellness center, gaming lounge, kids zone, kitchen space for demonstration cooking, and a members lounge (Ohio State University, 2016). The Recreation and Physical Activity Center is one of eight recreation facilities at The Ohio State University.

These recreation facilities all have one thing in common—to attract and retain students. However, at what cost? The building of grand recreation facilities is not the only method colleges employ to attract students. Residence living is probably as, if not more, popular in terms of extravagant buildings. One example of this comes from the University of Tennessee, Knoxville as they have built, and are building, two new residence halls. One residence hall, Fred D. Brown Jr. Residence Hall is a 250,000 square foot facility that houses 680 beds that opened in 2014. This building includes full-size beds, a lavish lobby with a glass staircase and a fountain, eateries, and many other features for $60 million (Saxon & Alapo, 2014). This may not sound too extravagant considering the current building costs of residence halls and the needs of students, but the University of Tennessee, Knoxville plans to open another facility in the Fall of 2017 at the cost of $85 million (University of Tennessee at Knoxville, 2016a). For $25 million more, one would expect significantly more beds because that is the purpose of a residence hall. The lodging difference, four beds (University of Tennessee at Knoxville, 2016b).

It is important to note, the cost and expansion of residence halls is not unique to the University of Tennessee, Knoxville. In fact, it has become the norm for large institutions to provide magnificent residential facilities, and schools often lose out when their housing pales in comparison to their peer institutions. Best College Value (2016), an organization committed to helping students find affordable options for college, reported the 30 most luxurious student-housing buildings. These buildings range from pools on rooftops to chandeliers to granite countertops in the students' rooms. These items are not "free," but are built into the cost of the room. So, what does this mean for college affordability and marketability? Often two competing principles, especially as the United States is beginning to see a decline in college admissions across the nation.

The End Result

Colleges that are not able to compete and increase or maintain their enrollment will not be able to continue to attract, retain, and graduate students—they will lose their relevance as was seen by Dowling College's lack of enrollment and funding (Pettit, 2016). The competition is real. In Knocking at the College Door, the Western Interstate Commission for Higher Education (WICHE) reports projections for high school graduation by region and state (Prescott & Bransberger, 2012). WICHE predicts that nationally there will be a 2% decline in high school graduates over the period between 2008 and 2020 (Prescott & Bransberger, 2012). The only region of the country that is growing is the South (4% increase by 2020), but that is offset by major declines in the Midwest and Northeast (–8% and –7%, respectively) and by a more moderate decline of 2% in the West. Several states (mostly in the Northeast) are experiencing double-digit declines of high school graduates over this period. Overall, there will be a net decline of more than 63,000 students nationally—resulting in colleges having less revenue and resources to serve students (Prescott & Bransberger, 2012). However, colleges and universities are not showing any decline in construction costs (Abramson, 2013).

Pair that with the cuts in state funding and there is a disaster looming in higher education as colleges and universities scramble to add new and exciting amenities to attract students in a declining student market (Prescott & Bransberger, 2012) while concomitantly increasing tuition and student fees to supplement state cuts (Baum, 2015). According to a report from the Center on Budget and Policy Priorities, during the period of 2008 through 2015, there were state budget cuts in 47 of the 50 states (Mitchell et al., 2016). Average state spending per student declined from a low of 2% (Montana) to a whopping 47% (Arizona), which explains the significant tuition increases reported earlier in this chapter at Arizona State University. Although state spending is not an issue for most private colleges, endowment return has finally begun to return to even after the devastating effects of the economic downturn in 2008.

Therefore, the crux of the arms race becomes less state-appropriated funds, fewer students, and increased market demand for outlandish amenities and buildings. The opulence that is displayed in these buildings is astounding—but it is all meant to gain an advantage over the competition, and attract new students and parents that want such amenities (Jacob et al., 2013). Such lavishness, as demonstrated earlier, has certainly received the attention of many that are concerned about the affordability of college and the high costs created by building to meet the luxury needs of students.

State legislatures, Boards of Trustees, and other governing agencies are closely evaluating how much the arms race is costing the state and their students. Although investing in the "arms race" for high-value amenities that attract students is only one of the factors for the high cost of college, it is one that state legislatures can control through reducing capital expenditures and diminishing a college's ability to use state funds to finance such projects, thereby passing the cost onto the student through tuition and fees (Samuels, 2013). As a result, higher education has come full circle as they need enrollment to continue to grow to demonstrate a need for state-appropriation funds, but cannot get that increased enrollment without being attractive to students resulting in a serious issue regarding affordability.

In 2012, the Commonwealth of Virginia undertook the challenge to study college affordability. The legislature created a Joint Legislative Audit and Review Commission (2014) that evaluated the cost of education in the Commonwealth of Virginia—a state that had the fifth highest net cost in the nation. They found that auxiliaries (student housing, student dining, intercollegiate athletics, security, etc.) accounted for 56% of the increase in student spending and, as such, was the primary factor for higher spending per student (Joint Legislative Audit and Review Commission, 2014). This is a compelling argument to reconsider the purpose of college and determine if participating in the "arms race" is important to the overall mission of higher education institutions. These questions raised by Virginia are not unique to the Commonwealth.

Other states have followed suit with their own studies, and affordability, finance, funding, and tuition policy are all major agenda items for the National Conference of State Legislators (2016). In 2016, the State Senate of Georgia commissioned an affordability study focusing on cost containment, tuition pricing and restraint, and maintaining or reducing ancillary fees for auxiliaries and other services (Millar, 2016). This is on the heels of some dramatic increases in tuition at Georgia's research institutions, large jumps in presidential salaries, and reports of opulent buildings built with state funds. Legislators are questioning the efficacy of state institutions participating in the arms race—opting more for a measured approach to construction of moderately attractive buildings and development of reasonable programs and services that can still assist students toward success (Millar, 2016).

Such moderation and restriction is spawning other creative ideas that reduce the state's exposure while at the same time allows institutions to respond to enrollment growth and the needs and wants of a millennial generation. For example, in Georgia, the Board of Regents, in response to legislation passed in 2014, has begun outsourcing all building and maintenance of residence halls and parking garages. The Public-Private-Partnerships legislation gives for-profit developers the same tax advantages as state agencies in Georgia. This allows them to build and maintain residence halls and parking garages on college campuses, and receive "rent" from the institution. In turn, institutions (and the state) do not have the debt obligation for the construction, and through student rent and fee collection, pay the concessionaire for the maintenance of the building while exercising control of the program operations. Even in this scenario, the buildings are adequately appointed, and serviceable to the needs of college residence hall programming and living, but they are far from lavish. In this way, the state is controlling the arms race (at least within its system) and produces value for the residents while maintaining a position of moderation, an act applauded by legislators and other constituents.

Conclusion

The college arms race is an interesting paradox challenging higher education. Students and parents alike want the lavish amenities that come with institutions participating in the arms race. However, repeatedly, they complain about the high cost of college. This leaves colleges and universities in a position to either build the extravagant facilities for students or risk of losing students to other institutions. Such extravagant amenities come at a cost, and many states are now reigning in those costs through restrictions, outsourcing, or privatizing components of higher education. The result comes full circle in terms of the purpose for postsecondary education and the need to reevaluate its actual purpose in the 21st century.

It is not unique for a profession to reevaluate its need for existence (Gardner, 2005). The college arms race is currently forcing higher education to do just that—reveal its true identity. Is the purpose of higher education to earn revenue and provide amenities that enable a unique college experience or is it to educate students and improve society? If colleges and universities are evaluated at their core, then higher education institutions are to convey to students the most important intellectual knowledge and skills that have been developed to the present moment; to develop in students deep disciplinary knowledge in at least one area; to foster critical thinking, analysis, and expression across a range of topics; to contemplate the relation between accumulated knowledge and skills, on one hand, and the issues facing contemporary society, on the other; to prepare students—in a broad rather than narrow sense—for civic life and productive work. (Gardner, 2005, p. 98)

Education in the United States has lost its purpose through capitalism, competition, and marketability.

References

Abramson, P. (2013). *College construction report*. Retrieved from College Planning & Management: https://webcpm.com/research/2013/02/college-construction-report.aspx

Baum, S. (2015). *Trends in college pricing*. Washington, DC: The College Board. Retrieved from https://trends.collegeboard.org/sites/default/files/trends-college-pricing-web-final-508-2.pdf

Best College Value. (2016). *The 30 most luxurious student housing buildings*. Retrieved from http://www.bestcollegevalues.org/best-college-dorms/

Bok, D. (2003). *Universities in the marketplace*. Princeton, NJ: Princeton University Press.

Brubacher, J. S., & Rudy, W. (1958). *Higher education in transition*. New York, NY: Harper & Brothers Publishers.

Brzezinski, M. (2007). *Red moon rising: Sputnik and the hidden rivalries that ignited the space race*. New York, NY: Times Books, Henry Holt and Company.

California State University at Fullerton. (2016). *Titan recreation features*. Retrieved from http://www.asi.fullerton.edu/src/features.asp

The Chronicle of Higher Education. (2016). *Tuition and fees, 1998-99 through 2015-16*. November 4, 2015. Retrieved from http://chronicle.com/interactives/tuition_fees

The College of William & Mary. (1999). *Enrollment factbook*. Retrieved from http://www.wm.edu/offices/ir/documents/factbook/Enrollment_2015_Final_New_add_Spring.pdf

Desrochers, D., & Hurlburt, S. (2014). Trends in college spending, 2001–2011: A Delta Data update. *Delta Cost Project*. Retrieved from http://www.deltacostproject.org/sites/default/files/products/15-4626%20Final01%20Delta%20Cost%20Project%20College%20Spending%2011131.406.P0.02.001%20....pdf

Ehrenberg, R. (2000). *Tuition rising: Why colleges cost so much*. Cambridge, MA: Harvard University Press.

Gardner, H. (2005). Beyond markets and individuals: A focus on educational goals. In R. Hersh & J. Merrow (Eds.), *Declining by degrees: Higher education at risk*. New York, NY: Palgrave Macmillan.

Gould, E. (2003). *The university in a corporate culture.* New Haven, CT: Yale University Press.

Jacob, B., McCall, B., & Stange, K. (2013). *College as a country club: Do colleges cater to students' preferences for consumption.* Paper presented at the NBER Working Paper Series, National Bureau of Economic Research. Retrieved from http://www.nber.org/papers/w18754

John F. Kennedy Presidential Library and Museum. (2016). *Address before a joint session of Congress,* 25 May 1961. Retrieved from http://www.jfklibrary.org/Asset-Viewer/xzw1gaeeTES6khED14P1Iw.aspx

Joint Legislative Audit and Review Commission. (2014). *Addressing the cost of public higher education in Virginia* (p. 461). Richmond, VA: Commonweath of Virginia.

Kelchen, R. (2016). An analysis of student fees: The role of states and institutions. *The Review of Higher Education, 39*(4), 597–619.

Millar, F. (2016). *Higher education affordability; create senate committee.* Retrieved from http://www.legis.ga.gov/Legislation/20152016/157650.pdf

Mitchell, M., Leachman, M., & Masterson, K. (2016). *Funding down, tuition up.* Retrieved from Center on Budget and Policy Priorities: http://www.cbpp.org/sites/default/files/atoms/files/5-19-16sfp.pdf

National Conference of State Legislators. (2016). *Higher education.* Retrieved from http://www.ncsl.org/research/education/higher-education.aspx

Newlon, C. (2014). The college amenities arms race. *Forbes Magazine.* Retrieved from http://www.forbes.com/sites/caranewlon/2014/07/31/the-college-amenities-arms-race/#da6c4941f3cc

Ohio State University. (2016). *Office of recreational sports.* Retrieved from https://recsports.osu.edu/facilities/recreation-and-physical-activity-center-rpac

Pettit, E. (2016). *Long-struggling dowling college is told it will lose accreditation.* Retrieved from http://chronicle.com/blogs/ticker/long-struggling-dowling-college-is-told-it-will-lose-accreditation/112495

Pope, D. G., & Pope, J. C. (2009). The impact of college sports success on the quantity and quality of student applications. *Southern Economic Journal, 75*(3), 750–780.

Prescott, B., & Bransberger, P. (2012). *Knocking at the college door: Projections of high school graduates* (8th ed.). Boulder, CO: Western Interstate Commission for Higher Education.

Purdue University. (2016). *Purdue University recreation & wellness.* Retrieved from http://www.purdue.edu/recwell/

Samuels, R. (2013). *Why public higher education should be free.* New Brunswick, NJ: Rutgers University Press.

Saxon, K., & Alapo, L. (2014). *First new residence hall in 45 years opens to students next week.* Retrieved from http://tntoday.utk.edu/2014/08/07/residence-hall-45-years-opens-students-week/

University of Colorado. (2016). *Student recreation center.* Retrieved from http://www.colorado.edu/recreation/facilities/student-recreation-center

University of Tennessee at Knoxville. (2016a). *Captial projects summary report.* Retrieved from http://facilitiesplanning.utk.edu/currentprojects_knoxville.pdf

University of Tennessee at Knoxville. (2016b). *Stokely Hall.* Retrieved from http://housing.utk.edu/halls/stokely-hall/

26. The Need for College Amenities and Their Benefit to the Student and Institution's Success

STEVEN TOLMAN AND CHRISTOPHER TRAUTMAN

With the ever-increasing cost of higher education, students, families, and tax-payers have begun to scrutinize the factors and expenses that are driving the skyrocketing cost of tuition. Adjusting for inflation, the average cost to attend a university (tuition, room/board, and fees) in 2014 was more than double than it was in 1984 (NCES, 2016). And unfortunately, this is a trend that is unlikely to change. It is projected that college tuition will continue to rise at a rate of 5% each year (Badkar, 2014). While the cost of a four-year degree is currently approximately $77,000, the same degree 18 years from now is pro-jected to cost a staggering $185,000. To put this into perspective, both the median home price in the Midwestern United States (NAR, 2016) and cost of a Ferrari sports car are approximately $175,000. To this end, students and their families are justifiably questioning the cost of higher education.

While the cause of rising tuition is outside the scope of this chapter and likely the book as a whole, it is worth mentioning that many believe the impetus for this increasing cost of higher education to be reduced state funding (Barnshaw & Dunietz, 2015; Mitchell & Leachman, 2015). While this change in appropriations funding higher education may result in lower taxes (or more likely tax dollars being appropriated elsewhere), institutions of higher education are often forced to pass these financial deficits onto students in the form of higher college tuition and fees. This is particularly notable, as these changes in the funding of higher education often go unnoticed publicly, except by those responsible for keeping the lights on at the university. For example, the state of Illinois recently withheld appropriations to institutions of higher education within the state (Brown, 2016; Douglas-Gabriel, 2016; Hassinger, 2016). After many months of surviving without these funds, several state institutions were forced to publicly announce their dire financial situation. This included institutions eliminating Spring Break and ending their semester early, layoffs and requiring employees to take pay cuts or furlough days, hiring freezes, scaling back course offerings, etc.

While many institutions are increasing the cost of tuition to offset lack of government funding and/or administrative costs that have become a necessity, these expenses are hidden behind the scenes and often not public. As these expenses drive up the cost of higher education, it is often the "frills" or amenities on a college campus that become the iconic symbol of rising tuition. The existence and addition of these amenities has become a punching bag for those calling for educational reform to address the rising cost of higher education. However, within reason, it can be contended that not only are the cost of these amenities overblown, but that they are actually both beneficial and necessary to the academic mission of the university.

Throughout this chapter we will explore the contested issue of amenities on college campuses and argue that amenities spending benefits students and the institution as a whole.

Reflecting on Our Past

In order to better understand the current landscape of amenities spending within higher education, it is important to briefly trace the evolution of the university model in the United States. Early universities assigned faculty and tutors to be responsible for the general comportment of their students, akin to the legal doctrine in loco parentis (Lake, 1999; Long 2012). This philosophy faded as faculty were exposed to the German model of higher education, becoming less interested in the outside management of their students and more interested in their own academic pursuits (Long, 2012). This distinction between academic learning and cocurricular development is where student affairs as a profession was born (Doyle, 2004). The ending of World War II also led to an expansion in the profession as returning soldiers and veterans began to take advantage of government-offered tuition assistance through the G.I. Bill, which saw new and large waves of diverse students entering university life, each population with different needs (Coomes & Gerda, 2016; Doyle, 2004).

The American Council on Education, established in 1918, took notice of this growing cocurricular profession and published what would become a seminal document in the field, The Student Personnel Point of View (Sandeen,

Albright, Barr, Golseth, Kuh, Lyons & Rhatigan, 1987). Published in 1937, The Student Personnel Point of View established the value of understanding and supporting the student as a whole, a tenant that remains at the heart of student affairs practice today (Patton, Renn, Guido, & Quaye, 2016). We assert that this was a turning point in our profession, as it reinforced the need to support students and create an exceptional experience for them in-and-out of the classroom. This movement has led to the creation of many of the resources, services, and amenities provided on college campuses today.

Reviewing the history of the profession reminds us that the amenities spending on student services in higher education is not a recent, problematic cultural and organizational shift; rather, this spending is a long-term investment in the development of the whole student, integral to the collegiate system.

Defining Amenities

We have the challenge of defining what amenities are on college campuses. Are college amenities anything that takes place outside of the classroom and extends beyond administrative offices with the sole purposes of enrolling/graduating students? In that working definition, would this exclude academic support services like tutoring, supplemental instruction, career services, and internship placement? We genuinely believe that college amenities are uniquely defined by each student. What would be considered an amenity by some, would be considered a necessity and integral component of their college education by others. With that being said, for the purposes of defining an amenity for this chapter, we will concede the common definition of amenities being the resources, services, and facilities that are committed by institutions that extend beyond academic support (i.e. tutoring, advising, career services, etc.) and the staples of student services (i.e. psychological services, health centers, etc.). These amenities could, in theory, be removed and students would still be able to successfully complete their academic studies.

Examining Common Amenities

Working with this definition of amenities, we will examine some of the more common, "hot button" amenities on college campuses that are often highly scrutinized and questioned. A simple Google search of college amenities will yield dozens of articles that balk at the luxury provided and cost to do so. However, many of these articles fail to expose the benefits of these amenities. We will briefly provide the benefit of such amenities by examining rock climbing walls, upscale restaurants, and modern residence halls. Through this exploration, we will illustrate the benefits and necessity of providing these amenities on college campuses. Doing so will provide the context and set the stage to further examine amenities through the lens of student development theory.

Rock Climbing Walls

Arguably, rock climbing walls are the pinnacle example of an amenity, as their large physical presence (60-foot-tall mountain) stands out and garners attention. While often criticized as an unnecessary amenity, these structures offer many benefits to the student and university. Rock climbing exposes students to a new recreational activity that they may otherwise never have explored. Whether students use the wall a single time or they become a regular fixture on the wall, it affords them a unique opportunity. Rock climbing walls can be used as venues for staff development, much in the way that high ropes courses are used. Many universities develop opportunities for students to further explore their interest in rock climbing by taking them on outdoor trips, which are an amazing experience for these students. Beyond the use of the university community, rock climbing walls also provide an additional revenue stream for the university, as they can be utilized by outside groups for events like birthday parties, rock climbing competitions, etc.

Upscale Restaurants

Many college campuses now include upscale restaurants like formal steak-houses. While these premium dining facilities may seem like an unnecessary luxury, they greatly contribute to the university and enhance students' experience. The restaurants provide students the opportunity to gain life experience by eating at them and learning formal dining etiquette. The wait staff at many of these restaurants are trained on formal etiquette and can assist the student/guest. This is an invaluable experience that will pay dividends later in the students personal and professional life. These upscale restaurants also provide an on-campus environment for formal meals. These can include meetings and interviews for faculty/staff, receptions and banquets for student organizations, and opportunities for students to have a nicer meal with friends and family.

The upscale restaurants also provide many opportunities for student employment and career development. There is the imminent opportunity for universities to utilize this facility and partner it with their academic programs in hospitality management and culinary arts. Students within those programs can utilize this space to gain real-life experience and be able to apply theory-to-practice from what they are learning in the classroom.

Residence Halls

As higher education enrollment increases, so too does the demand to live on campus in residence halls. This growth in the residential population is a win-win for the university, as it generates additional revenue and strengthens the sense of community and student engagement, especially in the evening and weekends. Furthermore, it has been shown that students who live on campus have higher GPAs than their counterparts who commute (de Araujo & Murray, 2010; Nicpon et al., 2007). Clearly, it is mutually beneficial for students to live on campus.

However, to attract students to live on-campus and reap these benefits, universities must provide facilities that meet students' needs and expectations. Driving this are the expectations of students and their families (Archibald & Feldman, 2010). In many college towns, students have a plethora of housing options. This includes recently constructed apartments and townhomes, to privately owned and operated residence halls near or directly adjacent to the university. To this end, institutions must provide on-campus housing that is competitive in terms of amenities in order to draw students in.

Generational increases in quality of life have grown students accustomed to a higher base standard of living than seen by previous generations. As that base standard rises, students will come to expect more out-of-college or university facilities (Archibald & Feldman, 2010). For traditionally aged students, campus appearance bears weight on the decision to enroll (Noel-Levitz Report, 2012) and there is a demand for new residence halls (Kirshtein & Kadamus, 2012). A 2005 survey found that over 42% of students consider the appearance of residence hall facilities "extremely important" or "very important" when considering which college to attend (Reynolds, 2007). These facilities are more than easy headlines for reporters; they are valuable recruitment tools and selling points in the increasingly competitive higher education market.

While the addition of college amenities is often described as an arms race between institutions, we argue that institutions are instead simply updating their facilities to catch up to the evolving expectations of society. This point is reinforced by Archibald and Feldman (2010) who assert that "…colleges and universities have increased the quality of their living options in an attempt to keep pace with what is happening to housing in general" (p. 9). Consider that many of the residence halls on college campuses were constructed before the invention of technology like computers, internet, HD TV, video game consoles, etc. So much so, many residence hall rooms are inadequately built to accommodate technology, such as only having two outlets per room (which was adequate when students only had an alarm clock and lamp).

Beyond drawing students to live on campus during the academic year, residence halls can be used year-round. For many campuses, summer conferences and housing of participants is a significant revenue stream. During the summer, our campuses often turn into conference space that can be utilized by outside organizations. Common examples are corporations hosting a day-long meeting with multiple breakout sessions (utilizing conference center and classroom spaces), cheerleading camps where students live on-campus for the week (and practice in the recreation center), to social events like weddings. Whether it is housing students who are taking summer classes or a group of accountants attending a conference hosted at the university, the residence halls are heavily utilized. By having modern facilities with the types of amenities that students and guests have come to expect, it enables universities to attract external use of our facilities, thus generating revenue for the university and paying for such amenities.

These modern residence halls provide amenities such as lounges with flat screen TVs, recreation rooms with pool and foosball tables, convenience stores, fitness centers, computer labs, and classroom space. As new residence halls are constructed, many of these spaces rival the private construction of luxury apartments off-campus. The difficult question that universities face is what is the fine line between a residence hall that is modern and meets the expectations of students/guests vs. what is unnecessary, lavish, and irresponsible?

Student Benefit: Examination Through the Lens of Student Development Theory

As student affairs professionals, it is our responsibility to inform our practice through the knowledge and application of student development theory. Student development theory concerns itself with the growth and learning of the college student outside of the classroom (Patton et al., 2016). As a field of study, it attempts to put student learning within a larger context, and its exploration of cocurricular development makes it an ideal framework to use when establishing the importance of amenities spending in higher education.

In particular, Bronfenbrenner's Developmental Ecology Model, Maslow's Hierarchy of Needs, and Chickering and Reisser's Seven Vectors of Development are useful in demonstrating this. It is important to distinguish though that Maslow's and Bronfenbrenner's theories did not originate in student development work; rather, their ideas have been adapted for use in higher education settings and their work helps provide a bedrock for student development theory.

Bronfenbrenner's Developmental Ecology Model

Bronfenbrenner's (1995) model consists of four components: process, person, context, and time (PPCT). Context, most relevant for our purposes, addresses the complex and layered interactions between person and environment, and consequently the impact of those interactions on the individual. Bronfenbrenner identified four systems for this environmental component of his model: the microsystem, which comprises the spheres of life which have the most immediate impact on people, such as close family relationships, work, occupation, etc.; the mesosystem, which comprises the interactions of the spheres within the microsystem; the exosystem, which comprises the broader spheres which hold indirect influence over the individual person; and finally the macrosystem, which comprises the larger sociological, historical, cultural, and political influences in a person's life (Bronfenbrenner, 1994; Bronfenbrenner & Morris, 2006; Renn & Reason, 2013).

The amenities model of higher education inherently builds an environment geared toward positive social interaction for comparatively little cost. The cost and total sum of resources dedicated to amenities facilities spending is relatively low. Data suggests that since 2005, less than 15% of new facilities management projects on college campuses were classified as "amenities," or nonacademic, residential, or miscellaneous buildings (Kirshtein & Kadamus, 2012). When that spending does occur, evidence suggests it can be beneficial to student development, especially if students themselves have a voice in the design process (McDowell & Higbee, 2014).

This spending develops settings in which students can feel safe, comfortable, and engaged, establishing campus spaces where positive microsystem interactions can occur. Development is of course an individual process, and Bronfenbrenner's model does more to demonstrate how external factors intertwine to affect students; however, it can still show that investments in the campus environment have the potential to support students (Renn & Reason, 2013). Campus climate is critical to student success, and a no-frills model of higher education simply does not allow for the level of contextualized student support that models with amenities offer.

Maslow's Hierarchy of Needs

Maslow's Hierarchy of Needs (1943) established a tiered system of needs for all people. In ascending order, the needs are: physiological, safety, love and belonging, esteem, and finally self-actualization (Maslow, 1943). The first four needs are classified as deficiency needs, meaning that an individual must satisfy them before moving on to the next developmental milestone. We contend that amenities provide value in guiding students from one of Maslow's needs to the next, with the most direct impact possible in both safety needs and love and belonging. Simply put, students cannot engage in learning and development, the mission of the college or university experience, until their most basic needs are met.

Figure 26.1 demonstrates the posited impact of amenities on development through Maslow's hierarchy. Amenity impact, indicated here by the orange shading, is darker in the two areas we believe amenities have the greatest positive impact, the so-called amenity zone. While other areas may be impacted by amenities as well, that is beyond the scope of this discussion; however, to acknowledge that possibility the other needs are shaded in a faded orange color.

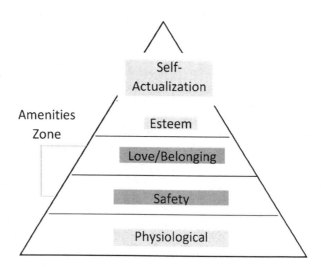

Figure 26.1. Maslow and Amenities.
Source: Author.

Safety needs address concerns for shelter, protection, and security (Maslow, 1943). In higher education, Housing/Residence Life departments meet these needs for residential students by providing students with housing for the school year. Most Residence Life departments also employ RAs (resident assistants or resident advisors) to provide first-line incident response on a nightly basis within the halls. Research indicates that well-trained RAs can also be useful in identifying and supporting students with mental health concerns (by encouraging them to seek Counseling support), particularly students at risk of suicide (Taub & Servaty-Seib, 2011; Taub et al., 2013). Residence halls offer many benefits when compared to off-campus housing, especially the built-in support system that is designed to meet basic safety needs, which arguably is the most important.

Love and belonging are at the third level in Maslow's hierarchy. If basic social interaction and integration are fundamental tenets of success, then expenditures that promote social interaction surely matter for students. Residence halls and campus recreation centers positively contribute to student success by creating social hubs for students. Campus recreation facilities for example achieve this through the promotion of student interactions, which leads to students feeling more enmeshed in the greater campus community (Huesman, Brown, Lee, Kellogg, & Radcliffe, 2009). Of course, this can only happen if students feel comfortable in these spaces and want to be a part of the building community, something that is much more easily achieved if the facilities themselves are appealing and well maintained. Residential students also benefit by being more involved with campus activities and are more likely than commuter students to be satisfied with their collegiate social experience (Astin, 1999). Upscale restaurant too, while they may seem frivolous, can encourage students to stay on campus and gather with peers, especially if institutions are in settings where they compete with many local businesses for students' attention and time.

In order for students to fully reap the developmental benefits of these amenities, they must desire to live on campus. Fostering this desire begins with building attractive facilities that are rich with amenities. This is why, as will be discussed later in more detail, it is critical for institutions to invest as much in their nonacademic buildings as they do in their academic ones.

Chickering and Reisser's Seven Vectors

In 1969, Chickering proposed what has come to be seen as a seminal theory of student development, later updated with Reisser. Their work suggests that students move through different vectors of development while in college, progressing through various vectors at different rates (Chickering & Reisser, 1993). A full review of the theory would be too extensive for this chapter, but here we will consider how Chickering and Reisser's Seven Vectors can broadly be used to understand the benefits of certain expenditures on student development and success.

Establishing Identity is a vector which builds on those coming before it (Chickering & Reisser, 1993). Though it addresses a multitude of privileged or marginalized identities, it also more fundamentally represents the needs of students to establish positive social relationships and negotiate their roles in their environment, in a similar way to Maslow's (1943) love and belonging needs. As discussed previously, nonacademic expenditures, particularly on facilities, provide opportunities for students to establish their identities outside of the classroom. It cannot be stressed enough that this identity formation can occur in the residence halls, at the gym, in a dining facility; institutions have the potential to build breeding grounds for positive socio-emotional growth, if only they are willing to seriously and responsibly invest. Stuart, Lido, Morgan, Solomon, and May (2011) found that alumni credit extracurricular activities as being positive influencers on self-identity development.

Built into Chickering and Reisser's (1993) theory is a consideration of environmental influences on student involvement, broken down into seven key influences. One of these is the significance of student-faculty relationships in student success. They posit that students benefit from seeing faculty in varied environments (i.e. outside of the classroom) and engaging with them in different ways (Evans, Forney, Guido, Patton, & Renn, 2010). Davenport and Pasque (2014) also note that faculty-student interactions provide a multitude of benefits to students, which include a higher cumulative GPA, increased enrollment in graduate school, and, most importantly, increased likelihood to continue college.

Amenities such as residence halls and campus recreational facilities can engender this bridge and solidify the benefits of collaboration between academic affairs and student affairs. Though the history between the two may seem contentious, the bridging of relationships has occurred over the past few decades and will only continue to serve students and the institution well (Doyle, 2004). This can be seen more specifically in faculty-in-residence programs, whereby faculty members live in residence halls with students and provide additional academic support and academic programming. Programs such as these indicate that nonacademic expenditures can have impacts, both direct and indirect, on student development when they are utilized in intentional ways.

Institutional Considerations

Using student development theory as a framework, we have demonstrated the benefit of amenities spending on the college student as an individual; however, it is also important to examine the ways in which spending produces practical gains for the campus beyond the goals of supporting student development. These college amenities are instrumental in the recruitment and retention of students.

It is important to note there are over 4,000 institutions of higher education in the United States, which provide a plethora of options for students' college choices. It is obvious that the amenities provided by a college impact students' decision of which institution to attend. It is believed that improving the campus environment and adding amenities will attract students and ultimately generate revenue (Jacob, McCall & Strange, 2013). Looking at these amenities through the lens of campus ecology (Strange & Banning, 2001, 2015), the presence or absence of amenities speaks volumes as to the priorities of the institution and the type of culture/community that is fostered at the institution.

Recruiting students though is only half of the equation for colleges and universities. Retention of students is also a high priority, and research indicates that spending on student-services expenditures such as Student Activities, Diversity and Cultural Events, and Athletics positively affects graduation and persistence rates, particularly at colleges or universities with student cohorts who have a lower average test score on standardized exams (Webber, 2012; Webber, & Ehrenberg, 2010). Though the impact of these expenditures does vary by institution type and student population, this is an affirming and positive indication that nonacademic expenditures have real value in keeping students on the path to success while in college.

Jacoby and Garland (2004) also identify a broad range of student services initiatives (including first-year orientation and other programming) which specifically work to retain commuter students, a population on college campuses which often (and inadvertently) does not receive as much attention or support. For all students though, data suggests that buildings such as campus recreation facilities marginally increase first-year student academic success (when such facilities are utilized), which itself is positively associated with retention (Huesman et al., 2009). Similarly, rock climbing walls appear to be frivolous on the surface, but their presence on college campuses draws students into the campus community and engages them, all for a comparatively low per-student cost.

The importance of the physical environment must not be underscored, as it reflects the values that the institution holds. So much so that it has been found that changes in both academic and quality-of-life reputations listed in college guidebooks are positively correlated with admissions numbers (Alter & Reback, 2012). At the heart of quality-of-life factors are the amenities on college campuses. Subsequently, this reinforces the benefit of amenities and supports Bronfenbrenner's model: environment (comprised of areas such as residence halls and other facilities) impacts student experience, which in turn impacts student perception of and satisfaction with the institution. Despite this, institutions must be cautious in how they market themselves and these (necessary and beneficial) amenities, especially during this tough economic time. Caution must be exerted, as "Advertising of this sort is a double-edged public relations sword" (Archibald & Feldman, 2010, p. 3). While this advertising illustrates the resources and amenities of the campus, it can also unintentionally send the message that tuition is unaffordable and/or that the institution is financially irresponsible.

Cost

An increasingly common headline in higher education is one that decries the so-called college "arms race," whereby institutions are modernizing not to better themselves and provide a more positive student experience, but to compete with sister schools in order to become more attractive to prospective students. This is often referred to as an "arms race" and implies the decision to incur these expenses is to simply one-up other institutions. While our chapter reinforces that the addition of these amenities benefits the institution as a whole and student development, it is important to examine the financial impact of these additions. The question is posed as to return on investment. Do these amenities drive up the cost of tuition and are they the gremlin responsible for the skyrocketing cost of higher education? Would eliminating these amenities ring in the cost of higher education? The ultimate answer is no (Archibald & Feldman, 2010; Kirshtein & Kadamus, 2012). The actual costs of these amenities to students is minimal.

For example, let's consider the "punching bag" amenity of a rock climbing wall. The cost of such a structure can easily be $100,000 (Kirshtein & Kadamus, 2012). While that is a significant amount of money, when dispersed over the entire student population, it becomes minimal. For example, at an institution of 10,000 students, this cost is covered by adding a one-time $10 fee to each student. At a larger institution of 50,000 students, this cost is one-time $2 fee per student (Table 26.1).

Table 26.1. One-time Fee per Student to Cover Cost of College Amenities.

	Institutional Size			
Amenity	5,000	10,000	20,000	50,000
$100K	$20	$10	$5	$2
$500K	$100	$50	$25	$10
$1M	$200	$100	$50	$20
$10M	$2,000	$1,000	$500	$200

While it is not true for all college amenities, many like rock climbing walls and campus recreation centers (with pools) are covered directly by student fees. We would assert that if you were to add up all of the fees for the cost of college amenities, it will make up a small percentage of the students' overall tuition. In the end, does not this small increase in overall price justify the existence of these amenities that we have demonstrated benefit both the institution and student directly?

Times Are Changing

We have to reimagine higher education and how it will evolve and grow in the future. To replicate the college environment of the past will inhibit our future. As we look at our current campuses and ask ourselves, "what were they thinking when they built this!", we owe it to our current and future students and community to develop a campus infrastructure of tomorrow – today.

With all of this being said, like others before us (Archibald & Feldman, 2010), we do not believe all amenities are worth their cost. Informed and strategic decisions, that are data driven, must be made when deciding which amenities to offer. The benefits of these amenities, to the student, university, and community, must outweigh the costs – now and in the future. In order to reframe the thinking behind institutional spending, we propose a model to be utilized during the financial decision-making process which attempts to contextualize the end product of spending on dimensions of cost to the institution (money and other resources) and student/institutional benefit (Figure 26.2).

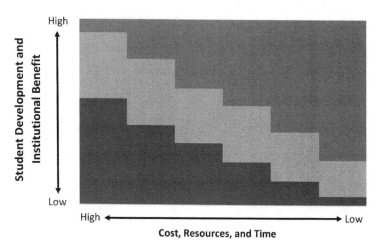

Figure 26.2. Responsible Spending Model.
Source: Author.

This is a recommended budgeting model administrators can use when deciding which amenities are worth funding. The x-axis represents the cost to the institution or department making the particular funding decision, moving from a comparatively high cost to a comparatively low one. Cost here represents both the money and time that would need to be allocated in order to execute the proposals. The y-axis indicates the overlapping benefits of amenities-spending for student development and institutions as described in Figure 26.2, ranging from a low benefit to a high benefit.

Sections of the graph are shaded in with one of three colors, each color indicating a particular level of consideration proposals should receive based on a data-driven, strategic decision-making process. Proposals falling in red sections offer a disproportionately low return for the projected costs, or comparatively low benefit at all, indicating that they should almost never be considered for funding. Proposals falling in yellow sections offer a stronger return on investment, meaning that administrators should consider these proposals with caution. Finally, proposals falling in the green offer the most benefit when compared to their cost, meaning that these should almost always (if not always) receive funding.

From the start of this chapter, our conceit has been that spending can provide deep and varied benefits to campus communities, but only if done responsibly. Thus, greater accountability is required when large financial decisions are being made. Senior administrators must involve key stakeholders (students, families, faculty, staff, and the local community) and ask themselves:

how could this purchase or allocation benefit students? How could it benefit the institution? Who is impacted by this decision? Do the benefits truly outweigh the costs? If we make it a practice of asking these questions and others like them, we can develop into an educational culture that views amenities not as luxuries, but as necessities which both round out and enhance the college experience.

Through this chapter, we have illustrated the importance of amenities on college campuses on the impact of student development and benefit to the university overall. In doing so, it is our hope to have combated the notion that these amenities are simply pawns being used in an arms race between colleges to attract the most/best students. Furthermore, Archibald and Feldman (2010) astutely attack this notion and assert that "A key part of an arm race story is the idea that a treaty that halted the arms race would leave all parties better off, including the students who are the ultimate consumer" (p. 12). We have illustrated the benefits of amenities to college students, who would clearly not be "better off" if this alleged arms race came to an end.

References

Alter, M., & Reback, R. (2012). True for your school. *How Changing Reputations.* Retrieved from http://www.columbia.edu/~rr2165/pdfs/trueforyourschool_dec2013.pdf

Archibald, R., & Feldman, D. (2010). *Are gold plated room and board charges important drivers of college cost* (Working Paper No. 99). Retrieved from Research Gate website: https://www.researchgate.net/profile/David_Feldman7/publication/254402902_Are_Gold_Plated_Room__Board_Charges_Important_Drivers_of_College_Cost/links/0deec53bee8b863a01000000.pdf

Astin, A. W. (1999). Student involvement: A developmental theory for higher education. *Journal of College Student Development, 40*(5), 518–529.

Badkar, M. (2014, May 30). *Here are some horrific projections for anybody who expects to pay for college some day.* Retrieved from http://www.businessinsider.com/cost-of-college-in-the-future-is-scary-2014-5

Barnshaw, J., & Dunietz, S. (2015). Busting the myths: The annual report on the economic status of the profession. *Academe, 101*(2), 4–82.

Bronfenbrenner, U. (1994). Ecological models of human development. In T. Husen & T. N. Postlethwaite (Eds.), *International encyclopedia of education* (2nd ed., Vol. 3, pp. 1643 – 1647). Oxford, UK: Pergamon Press.

Bronfenbrenner, U. (1995). Developmental ecology through space and time: A future perspective. In P. Moen, G. H. Elder, Jr., & K. Lu☐ scher (Eds.), *Examining lives in context: Perspectives on the ecology of human development* (pp. 619–647). Washington, DC: American Psychological Association.

Bronfenbrenner, U., & Morris, P. A. (2006). The bioecological model of human development. In W. Damon & R. M. Lerner (Eds.), *Handbook of child psychology, Vol. 1: Theoretical models of human development* (6th ed., pp. 793 – 828). New York, NY: Wiley.

Brown, S. (2016, June 2). Illinois still hasn't passed a budget. Here's what that means for its public universities. *The Chronicle of Higher Education*. Retrieved from www.chronicle.com

Chickering, A. W., & Reisser, L. (*1993*). *Education and identity*. San Francisco, CA: Jossey-Bass.

Coomes, M.D., & Gerda, J.J. (2016). A long and honorable history: Student affairs in the United States. In McClellan, G. S., & Stringer, J. (4th ed.). *The Handbook of Student Affairs Administration* (pp. 3-23). San Francisco, CA: John Wiley & Sons.

Davenport, A. M., & Pasque, P. A. (2014). Adding breadth and depth to college and university residential communities: A phenomenological study of faculty-in-residence. *The Journal of College and University Student Housing, 40*(2), 46–65.

de Araujo, P., & Murray, J. (2010). Estimating the effects of dormitory living on student performance. *Economics Bulletin, 30*, 866–878.

Douglas-Gabriel, D (2016, February 26). Chicago State University sends layoff notices to all employees amid Illinois budget battle. *The Washington Post*. Retrieved from https://www.washingtonpost.com/news/grade-point/wp/2016/02/26/chicago-state-university-sends-layoff-notices-to-all-employees-amid-illinois-budget-battle/?utm_term=.0ac1f50623d0

Doyle, J. A. (2004). Where have we come from and where are we going? A review of past student affairs philosophies and an analysis of the current student learning philosophy. *The College Student Affairs Journal, 24*(1), 66–83.

Evans, N. J, Forney, D. S., Guido, F. M., Patton, L. D., & Renn, K. A. (2010). *Student development in college: Theory, research, and practice* (2nd ed.). San Francisco, CA: Jossey-Bass.

Hassinger, A. (2016, June 3). Higher education in Illinois is dying. *The New York Times*. Retrieved from www.nytimes.com

Huesman, R., Jr., Brown, A. K., Lee, G., Kellogg, J. P., & Radcliffe, P. M. (2009). Gym bags and mortarboards: Is use of campus recreation facilities related to student success? *NASPA Journal, 46*(1), 50–71.

Jacob, B., McCall, B., & Stange, K. M. (2013). *College as country club: Do colleges cater to students' preferences for consumption?* (No. w18745). National Bureau of Economic Research.

Jacoby, B., & Garland, J. (2004). Strategies for enhancing commuter student success. *Journal of College Student Retention: Research, Theory & Practice, 6*(1), 61–79.

Kirshtein, R. J., & Kadamus J. A. (2012) Climbing walls and climbing tuitions. *The Delta Cost Project*. Retrieved from http://www.deltacostproject.org/sites/default/files/products/Delta-Cost-Climbing-Walls-Climbing-Tuitions.pdf

Lake, P. F. (1999). The rise of duty and the fall of in loco parentis and other protective tort doctrines in higher education law. *Missouri Law Review, 64*(1), 1–28.

Long, D. (2012). The foundations of student affairs: A guide to the profession. In L. J. Hinchliffe & M. A. Wong (Eds.), *Environments for student growth and development: Librarians and student affairs in collaboration* (pp. 1–39). Chicago, IL: Association of College & Research Libraries.

Maslow, A. H. (1943). A theory of human motivation. *Psychological Review, 50(4)*, 370–396.

McDowell, A. M., & Higbee, J. L. (2014). Responding to the concerns of student cultural groups: Redesigning spaces for cultural centers. *Contemporary Issues in Education Research, 7*(3), 227–236.

Mitchell, M., & Leachman, M. (2015). Years of cuts threaten to put college out of reach for more students. *Center on Budget and Policy Priorities*, 1–26.

National Association for Realtors (NAR). (2016). *Existing homes sales.* Retrieved from http://www.realtor.org/sites/default/files/reports/2016

National Center for Educational Statistics (NCES). (2016). *Digest of education statistics.* Retrieved from www. http://nces.ed.gov/programs/digest

Nicpon, M. F., Huser, L., Blanks, E. H., Sollenberger, S., Befort, C., & Kurpius, S. E. R. (2007). The relationship of loneliness and social support with college freshmen's academic performance and persistence. *Journal of College Student Retention: Research, Theory & Practice, 8*(3), 345–358.

Noel-Levitz. (2012). *The factors influencing college choice among nontraditional students.* Coralville, IA: Author. Retrieved from www.noellevitz.com/Factors2012

Patton, L. D., Renn, K. A., Guido, F. M., & Quaye, S. J. (2016). *Student development in college: Theory, research, and practice* (3rd ed.). San Francisco, CA: Jossey-Bass.

Renn, K. A., & Reason, R. D. (2013). *College students in the United States: Characteristics, experiences, and outcomes.* San Francisco, CA: Jossey-Bass.

Reynolds, G. L. (2007). The impact of facilities on recruitment and retention of students. *New Directions for Institutional Research, 135*, 63-80.

Sandeen, A., Albright, R. L., Barr, M. J., Golseth, A. E., Kuh, G. D., Lyons, W., & Rhatigan, J. (1987). *A perspective on student affairs: A statement issued on the fiftieth anniversary of The Student Personnel Point of View.* Washington, DC: National Association of Student Personnel Administrators.

Strange, C. C., & Banning, J. H. (2001). *Education by design: Creating campus learning environments that work. The Jossey-Bass Higher and Adult Education Series.* San Francisco, CA: Jossey-Bass.

Strange, C. C., & Banning, J. H. (2015). *Designing for learning: Creating campus environments for student success.* San Francisco, CA: Jossey-Bass.

Stuart, M., Lido, C., Morgan, J., Solomon, L., & May, S. (2011). The impact of engagement with extracurricular activities on the student experience and graduate outcomes for widening participation populations. *Active Learning in Higher Education, 12*(3), 203–215.

Taub, D. J., & Servaty-Seib, H. L. (2011). Training resident assistants to make effective referrals. *The Journal of College and University Student Housing, 37*(2), 10–24.

Taub, D. J., Servaty-Seib, H. L., Miles, N., Lee, J.-Y., Morris, C. A. W., Prieto-Welch, S. L., & Werden, D. (2013). The impact of gatekeeper training for suicide prevention on university resident assistants. *Journal of College Counseling, 16,* 64–78.

Webber, D. A. (2012). Expenditures and postsecondary graduation: An investigation using individual-level data from the state of Ohio. *Economics of Education Review, 31,* 615–618.

Webber, D. A., & Ehrenberg, R. G. (2010). Do expenditures other than instructional expenditures affect graduation and persistence rates in American higher education? *Economics of Education Review, 29,* 947–958.

Part Fourteen: Are Today's College Students Too Entitled?

In "Then and Now: The Relationship Between the College and the Student," Mark Bauman tracks how the traditional collegian relates to her institution. He traces the historical evolution of this changing association, particularly between student affairs professionals and university life from *in loco parentis*, to *alma mater*, to caveat emptor. The notion of "student as consumer" is vividly depicted, especially as neoliberals redefine it as a "caring service," a bridge between the historical mission of student affairs and student development and what some now call the "entitlement" of today's college students. Bauman points out that student demands for more amenities and a specific collegiate experience are not new historically. Instead, he contends that it is the brevity with which the university is responding to these demands that has purveyed a sense of entitlement.

In "Are College Students Too Entitled Today? The Role of Customer Service in Meeting Student Needs and Expectations," Denise L. Davidson and Amy A. Paciej-Woodruff argue that the question of "coddling" students is inappropriate and misguided in changing times (e.g., different student demographics and economic fluctuations) and more pronounced pressures on colleges and universities to operate in more effective ways. They reframe the notion of "customer service" as performance-driven, i.e., providing positive experiences for students, particularly those who have been traditionally underrepresented and underserved. This strategy includes the efficient resolution of complaints, listening to stakeholders, and inviting feedback. The authors are especially concerned about insuring suitable learning environments; they encourage university leaders to adjust their institutions to different groups of students on a continual basis.

27. Then and Now: The Relationship Between the College and the Student

MARK BAUMAN

Over the last several years the idea of student affairs as synonymous with, or at least informed by, a customer service philosophy has crept into the profession. As evidence, a quick search on higher education employment sites reveals the phrase "customer service" woven into some job descriptions and, at times, included in the actual position title. A "student affairs specialist," for example, was required to have a *high level of customer service skills*; similarly, *quality customer service* was expected of a "retention and student success" professional; and an "assistant dean for student development" had as its first bulleted requirement under knowledge, skills, and abilities a *knowledge of customer service techniques*. These examples, representing only three of many, suggest at least a preliminary movement away from the profession's core—that is, from its history of emphasizing the learning, development, and growth of the whole student, toward one that is focused on customer service, transactions, and commodities. If students are treated like customers the logical outcome is the creation of a consumer-oriented mindset—one complete with a sense of entitlement *as the customer.*

This movement toward customer service, and the subsequent entitled expectations that can befall students, is further evidenced by the case of Trina Thompson. Thompson earned her associates and then bachelors degree at Monroe College, studying information technology (Kessler, 2009). Thompson, assisted by personnel in the Monroe College Office of Career Advancement, could not secure professional, postgraduate employment (Kessler). Her frustrations led Thompson to file a lawsuit which claimed that a career advancement counselor in Monroe's Office of Career Advancement "…has not tried hard enough to help…" find her employment

(*Thompson v. Monroe College*, 2009). Thompson sued for the full cost of her degree—$70,000—plus an additional $2,000 for the stress created from the search for employment (Kessler). Despite extensive searching, no follow-on legal action could be found, though her initial filing in 2009 continues to receive widespread attention. Though the legal action appears to have not gained traction, Thompson's suit illuminates the shifting landscape of the student mindset—one that views itself as an entitled consumer, purchasing a product, rather than a learner focused on intellectual and personal growth. In Thompson's consumer mindset, Monroe's staffers are bound to "find" her employment. Certainly the Office of Career Advancement should help; they should seek to educate, to mentor, and to guide the student through a productive employment search. They should, in essence, engage in student development, as all those in student affairs should. But the notion that counselors must essentially find and secure employment while the student remains a passive observer runs afoul of the core ideas of both student affairs *and* higher education. Nowhere in the court filing does the student accept or acknowledge that a large portion of this responsibility falls on her own shoulders; similarly, the Thompson's filing does not acknowledge her middle-of-the-road 2.7 cumulative grade point average as a possible contributing factor to her lack of success. In essence, in Thompson's view, she has *purchased* the degree, much like any *customer* might purchase a product, and is thus *entitled* to postgraduation employment commensurate with her academic achievement.

Historical Foundations of Entitlement

Student Affairs Professionals

Taken together, these examples speak to the movement of both the student affairs profession *and* the students they serve toward a more consumer-oriented worldview. Perhaps the students moved first, thus prompting the profession to follow? Or maybe student affairs decision makers observed the trend in the larger society and endeavored to be proactive? Regardless of the precise etiology of this shift, what is clear is that this philosophy is contrary to the history of student affairs. Discussing the founding document of an early, emerging student personnel field, Evans and Reason (2001) noted that the American Council on Education (1937) codified the profession's early emphasis on the totality of the student via the publication of the Student Personnel Point of View (SPPV). The original authors of the SPPV, a group with roots in anthropology, asserted that this philosophy imposes upon educational institutions the obligation to consider the student as a whole—his [sic] intellectual capacity and achievement, his [sic] emotional make up, his [sic] physical condition, his social relationships, his [sic] vocational aptitudes and skills, his [sic] moral and religious values, his [sic] economic resources, his [sic] aesthetic appreciations. It puts emphasis, in brief, upon the development of the student as a person rather than upon his [sic] intellectual training alone. (American Council on Education, 1937)

Twelve years later, the American Council on Education (1949) published an update to their initial work. Given the rapid expansion of higher education, largely on the heels of the recently enacted GI Bill, the efforts of student personnel workers were even more critical. This update reaffirmed the roots of student personnel work, but offered a full-throated endorsement that the development of the student is an active participant in his or her own maturation. The authors stated with conviction that

the concept of education is broadened to include attention to the student's well-rounded development physically, socially, emotionally and spiritually,-as well as intellectually. The student is thought of as a responsible participant in his own development and not as a passive recipient of an imprinted economic, political, or religious doctrine, or vocational skill. (American Council on Education, 1949, p. 2)

Additional guiding documents shaping the philosophy and practice of student affairs were produced throughout the 20th century and largely echoed the profession's early emphasis on the holistic development of the student. And while this emphasis has ebbed and flowed since its inception, Evans and Reason assert that "student affairs professionals' responsibility to insure the total development of all students by creating supportive and responsive environments in collaboration with their faculty colleagues remains as vital now as it was in 1937" (p. 374). Nuss (2003) concurs, adding that one of the "enduring and distinctive concepts" (p. 65) of the student personnel movement is the "consistent and persistent emphasis on and commitment to the development of the whole person" (p. 65). Given this long and seemingly unified philosophical history, embracing the notion of customer service, and identifying students and their families as that customer, shifts our collective attention away from the learning and development process—indeed it shifts away from the core identity and mission of the student affairs profession, one that has served institutions of higher learning and their students well for multiple generations.

While the student affairs profession is a critical element of the larger higher education experience, it does not fully encapsulate all the activities of the campus. Is this shift to customer service and the associated sense of entitled confined, then, *only* related to the student affairs aspect of higher education? Is it only about getting an immediate, on-the-spot room change? Is it only about getting exactly the kind of cuisine a student demands from campus dining? Is it only about having a "rooftop infinity pool" (Olick, 2015, para. 1) as is the case at the University of Georgia at Athens? Or a lazy river, a feature of selected housing at the University of North Florida or Louisiana State University at Baton Rouge and others (Woodhouse, 2015)? While student affairs and their associated activities may seem an obvious spot for a consumer-oriented, entitled mindset to show itself, the academic affairs elements of higher education are by no means immune. As Angulo (2016) asserts, the goal of higher education is not "to produce cars, clothing" or "some other commodity" (para. 3). But while this may not be the stated goals, the shift to a customer service or market-based orientation (Angulo) suggests just that: That the degree is a product to be purchased, thus entitling the customer to simply exchange, discard, or modify the received commodity, a notion that aligns with other consumer transactions. A recent legal action amplifies Angulo's claim and also demonstrates that this consumerist, entitled mindset is not only present in the student affairs elements of higher education, but that it is equally present in the academic spheres.

In 2013, Megan Thode, a former graduate student in counseling psychology at Lehigh University (Shortell, 2013), filed a lawsuit seeking "$1.3 million in damages stemming from a grade of C+" (Segal, 2013, para. 1). The dollar amount was arrived at based on her projected earnings as a licensed professional counselor, her stated professional goal. And her C+ was granted largely due to her lack of classroom participation, for which points were awarded—or not, as was the case with Thode who earned a zero for this graded element. But it is the C+, the final mark in a required course, that summarily blocked Thode from her professional aspiration as a licensed counselor (Shortell, 2013). Both the Court of Common Pleas of Northampton County and the Superior Court of Pennsylvania rejected her claim (Hall, 2014), with the Superior Court writing that

> while another instructor might have given a more lenient grade than zero for these infractions, we are reluctant to make a judicial determination to overturn Thode's grade. Courts lack the expertise to micromanage the complex and highly subjective endeavor of academic grading. Attempting to do so would invite an increase in difficult and time-consuming lawsuits by students who are disgruntled over grades, courses, teachers or other academic requirements. (*Thode v. Ladany, Carr, & Lehigh University*, 2014)

Thode's complaint, and there are more like this (Kingkade, 2013), reveals a theme similar to the examples presented earlier in this chapter: That students are *owed* or *entitled* to something, simply by virtue of their enrollment and attendance at an institution of higher learning. Segal (2013) sums this sentiment perfectly: "Thode's argument is that she *needed* a higher grade. Well, yes, she did—but that did not mean that she was entitled to it" (para. 10).

The Professoriate and Academia

Much like the profession of student affairs has philosophical underpinnings that have guided professionals for generations, so too does the more general ideal of higher education, and this movement to a customer service philosophy is counter to those roots. Since their inception, institutions of higher learning have responded to the needs of the local, regional, and, eventually, their national community. Harvard, the first chartered college, was created in part to fulfill the need for a "...learned clergy..." (Elliot, 1936, p. 3). More broadly, the Puritans felt a strong desire to transplant and retain English culture in the New World; Harvard College was a prominent vehicle in accomplishing this mission (Elliot, 1936; Rudolph, 1962). Yale, along with the College of William and Mary, echoed Harvard's emphasis of a learned clergy. Geiger (1999) notes that "...the founding documents of all three schools speak to the aim of educating ministers..." (p. 40). Rudolph (1962) writes that successive early colleges held to similar ideals as they attempted to educate future clergy and public servants. In a philosophical sense, the "...college was expected to educate and morally uplift the coming generation" (Boyer, 1990, p. 4). Collectively, these early institutions identified needs in their community and sought collegiate education as a mechanism for their attainment. These patterns of addressing the community's needs continued as the New World evolved. And while strong elements of religion remained in some colleges, a shift in philosophy entered academia in 1746 with the establishment of the College of New Jersey (Princeton). Featuring a board of clergy and laypeople, the College of New Jersey practiced religious tolerance with preference given to certain denominations (Geiger, 1999). Subsequent colleges founded on these principles (Dartmouth, Queen's College) employed a spirit of religious openness while appreciating secular professions and public service as vocational goals upon culmination of one's education. Rudolph (1962) writes of the philosophy of institutions of this era: "...a college is useful: it helps men to learn the things they must know in order to manage the temporal affairs of the world; it trains a legion of teachers" (p. 13). Matters of religion and church, rather than paramount, were balanced with the needs of the regional lay community (Geiger, 1999).

In the early 19th century, the trend toward more practical and more secular aspects of education continued as the needs of the larger community evolved. The movement was sufficient to warrant ideological recoil from traditional colleges that adhered to the paradigm of classical liberal education. Perhaps the most notable reaction came in 1828 from the "academical faculty" of Yale. This doctrine, known as the Yale Report, espoused a commitment to knowledge, emphasized mental discipline and moral righteousness (Clifton & Wyer, 1980). Those unable to attend a college of this sort, or those not desiring this type of education, should be free to pursue educational interests at other, less rigorous institutions. "A defective education is better than none" (Yale Faculty, 1828, para. 15) states the Yale Report in an attempt to address growing utilitarian programs and institutions throughout the nation. This defective education was to be offered through professional and vocational schools and through partial courses, none of which would be housed at Yale. Many small, private, denominational institutions echoed Yale in distinguishing classical liberal arts colleges from the applied or professional courses of study. Though passionate in their beliefs, colleges with strict adherence to the traditional liberal curriculum "...declined dramatically in educational significance and impact with the rise of the comprehensive university..." in the middle to later 1800s (Clifton & Wyer, 1980).

The transient influence of the Yale report was overpowered by the needs of a post civil war and increasingly industrial society (Association of American Colleges, 1985). The citizenry, employers and local, state and national government were seeking a more practical, vocational education, allowing graduates to contribute fully to a growing nation (Boyer, 1990; Clifton & Wyer, 1980; Rudolph, 1962). Rudolph (1962) writes that "...the old ways and the old curriculum were too narrow, elementary or superficial" (p. 245). The traditional liberal curriculum could not adequately address the needs of this emerging nation, forcing a review of the baccalaureate curriculum. Curricular change, as Slaughter (2002) observes, is "...based on students, faculty and administration interpreting and acting in response to the various pressures and opportunities in their environment" (p. 265). Consequently, academic learning, once heralded as the pursuit of wisdom through mental rigor, transitioned to a more utilitarian focus in response to external forces (Gumport, 2002). Recognizing the need, vocationally oriented education was codified by the federal government through passage of the Morrill Act of 1862. This act gave states large parcels of land designed to be sold with the resultant revenue directed toward "...education in the liberal arts and training in the skills that ultimately would undergird the emerging agricultural and mechanical revolutions" (Boyer, 1990, p. 5). These land-grant colleges offered access to higher learning to largely untouched regional farming communities, many of whom were precisely the constituents seeking more practical postsecondary education (Boyer, 1990; Slaughter, 2002). Combining the mission of applied education with institutional service to the community, the land-grant colleges defined the notion of community-oriented higher learning. Through the application of research and knowledge, these institutions specifically endeavored to serve their community in addressing regional problems while concurrently providing widespread educational access (Boyer, 1990; Gumport, 2002).

In the early 20th century, the American university had taken shape. Borrowing largely from Germanic traditions of higher education, the American university presented a fairly standardized organization and curriculum. It is also in this period that student affairs arises as student personnel workers, buoyed by the previously mentioned *Student Personnel Point of View* (1937), carried out responsibilities that formerly rested with the faculty (Sandeen, 1985). Academically, however, Geiger (1999) observes, the American university "...admitted only bona fide high school graduates...provided them with two years of general education followed by two years of advanced or specialized courses" (p. 55). It was during this time that these institutions experienced explosive growth, more than four times that of the larger population (Rudolph, 1962). The service orientation of the universities, as initially established by the land-grant colleges, remained a popular mission in this era (Boyer, 1990; Rudolph, 1962). However, much as the industrial growth of the 1860s and beyond required a response from institutions of higher learning, the technological growth in the early 20th century also required curricular change. "Modern technology required a more highly educated population: the colleges and universities were called upon to provide the trained intelligence that would create, master, and find the terms on which man could live with that technology" (Rudolph, 1962, p. 463). Once again, universities were called upon to address the needs of a dynamic society.

The transformation of the state normal schools further exemplifies the historical responsiveness and philosophical fluidity of higher education. In the early 1800s, normal schools originated in an effort to address the lack of formal training for teachers (Gitlin, 1996). Normal schools in California, for example, began in 1862. By the end of 1920, most of the nation's 180 state normal schools followed California's lead, transitioning into state teachers colleges in an effort to address increased teacher demand (Gitlin, 1996; Ogren, 2003). Curricular and degree options were expanded, extracurricular activities were offered, summer sessions were added, and women and other historically underrepresented groups comprised a majority of the enrollment in these transitional colleges (Ogren, 2003). As state funding tightened across the country, teachers colleges expanded enrollment and began resembling "...small liberal arts colleges" (Ogren, 1995). In an effort to continue serving their regional communities, many modern teachers colleges have evolved into comprehensive undergraduate institutions, offering copious undergraduate and graduate choices, certificates, and other professionally oriented education. The remaining years in the 20th century saw significant developments in postsecondary education as well as the rekindling of old debates surrounding the purpose and function of higher education (Ehrlich, 1999). The passage of the GI Bill in 1944 opened the doors to college to millions of students that previously were unlikely to enroll (Blair, 1999). Twenty years later, the Civil Rights Bill, passed in 1964, called for, in part, equal opportunities in education (Bickel, 1998; Blair, 1999). The collective impact of these and other social forces allowed collegiate enrollment to climb steadily during the remainder of the 20th century as colleges and universities continually endeavored to address the dynamic needs of an unfolding society.

Social Foundations and Philosophy of Entitlement

Historical tracing aside, educational leaders and pioneers have long discussed the meaning, content, and purpose of the baccalaureate degree. In the earlier part of this century, John Dewey and Robert Maynard Hutchins, two educational giants, clashed over the nature and purpose of higher education. Dewey's emphasis rested firmly with the idea of civic education, real-world problem solving, and the fundamental improvement of democratic society (Ehrlich, 1997). Conversely, Hutchins' argument focused primarily on the pursuit of knowledge and truth (Ehrlich, 1997; Hutchins, 1936). Hutchins (1936) argued that a University's "...only excuse for existence...is to provide a haven where the search for truth may go unhampered by utility or pressure for results" (p. 43). In many ways, this debate continues today. Kirp (2003) describes the two philosophical orientations as a conflict between "...those who urge greater reliance on marketplace norms, with their promise of greater efficiency and productivity, against defenders of the community of scholars, with its promise of discovering and transmitting knowledge" (para. 1). Writing about this more recent movement toward the "marketization" of higher education in Britain, Hermanns (2015) asserts that "value for money has begun to consume higher education and student unions" and that this newly created "competitive environment is having a corrosive effect on learning: it already is forcing institutions to cut 'unprofitable' courses and academics to focus on revenue streams, while increasing debt and hardship take their toll on students' wellbeing" (para. 6).

Discussion

What insight, then, does this brief historical philosophy of higher education provide for the current discussion? Institutions of higher education are indeed responsive to their communities, to their regions, and to the larger national and global society. But this responsiveness does not equate to a dilution of the educational experience, one where the customer is always right. Higher education is *not* synonymous with Wal-Mart, where a consumer can browse the seemingly endless shelves for a pair of jeans or the latest gadget. Education— true learning, or, as the Yale Faculty called it, *the furniture of the mind*—is not something to simply be browsed for, purchased, and then turned in for employment assembling widgets.

Returning to Thode's and Thompson's complaints, there is subtle and more concerning idea reflected in these cases. There's the suggestion that purchasing an education, much like a customer would purchase any other product, *entitles* the buyer to something on the back-end—in the case of Thompson, that entitlement came in the form of postgraduate employment in her field, though with no apparent effort from the student. For Thode it was a better grade that was *needed*, but as Segal (2013) aptly clarifies, it was not a grade to which she was entitled.

But this is a two-way street, right? After all, students asking for, or perhaps demand, certain campus features is not a new phenomenon. What does seem new, however, is how some colleges are responding, and that response enables the customer service orientation that some students and their families have come to expect. Bruni (2016) captures this sentiment, stating that

> students at Oberlin and their counterparts elsewhere might not behave in such an emboldened fashion if they did not feel so largely in charge. Their readiness to press for rules and rituals to their liking suggests the extent to which they have come to act as customers—the ones who set the terms, the ones who are always right—and the degree to which they are treated that way. (para. 4)

Indeed there are entire student affairs divisions that have embraced all or a portion of the customer service philosophy, using it as a guiding theme for departmental mission statements and the hiring and training of professional and student staff, some of which is evidenced in the employment postings presented earlier in the chapter. To some degree, the pressure to serve the customer rather than develop the student is not surprising. My sense is that viewing students as customers to be served reflects the attempt to meet the current generation's (and their parent's/guardian's) expectations that education is some sort of tangible product; in an effort to be responsive to the demands of their constituents, colleges have therefore responded accordingly. As Kreuter (2013) writes high-end features and creature comforts clearly draw in students and families, which leads to paying customers, which leads to stable or growing enrollments. But such a changed relationship between the college and the student—a relationship that Bruni (2016) called "one of the most striking transformations in higher education over the last quarter-century" (para. 5)—can lead to a host of challenges. We can all imagine incidents on our respective campuses that have been laced with a similar sense of the customer-style entitlement: An immediate release from one's housing contract, a "free pass" from a judicial infraction, a changed or inflated grade, the "right" to not attend a class, parking adjacent to one's campus housing—and the list could easily continue. Unfortunately, the customer mentality suggests that these things are feasible simply because a fee has been paid. If coupled with a department, division, or institution that adheres to the customer service philosophy, I'm concerned about what we're actually teaching that student and how we might be *devaluing* that educational experience—an experience that's inherently *invaluable*. As we move forward, we should reflect on our founding philosophies of student development, the importance of intellectual and interpersonal growth, and a focus on the whole student, in all of their seemingly infinite nuance. These guiding ideas served us well then, and can continue to serve us well now, as we look ahead to the next generation.

References

American Council on Education. (1937). *The student personnel point of view* (Series I, Vol. I, Number 1). Washington, DC: Author.

American Council on Education. (1949). *The student personnel point of view* (Series VI—Student Personnel Work—Number 13). Washington, DC: Author.

Angulo, A. J. (2016, July 6). Don't turn students into consumers—The US proves it's a recipe for disaster. *The Guardian*. Retrieved from https://www.theguardian.com/higher-education-network/2016/jul/06/dont-turn-students-into-consumers-the-us-proves-its-a-recipe-for-disaster?CMP=share_btn_tw

Association of American Colleges. (1985). *Integrity in the college curriculum: A report to the academic community*. Washington, DC: Author.

Bickel, R. D. (1998). A brief history of the commitment to inclusion as a facet of equal educational opportunity. *New Directions for Community Colleges, 83*, 3–13.

Blair, J. (1999). GI bill paved the way for a nation of higher learners. *Education Week, 18*, 32–33.

Boyer, E. L. (1990). *Scholarship reconsidered.* New York, NY: Jossey-Bass.

Bruni, F. (2016, June 22). In college turmoil, signs of a changed relationship with students. *The New York Times.* Retrieved from http://www.nytimes.com/2016/06/23/educ ation/in- college-turmoil-signs-of-a-changed-relationship-with-students.html

Clifton, C. F., & Wyer, J. C. (1980). *Liberal education in transition.* AAHE-ERIC/ Higher Education Research Report Number 3 (pp. 3–18). Washington, DC: American Association for Higher Education.

Ehrlich, T. (1997). Civic Learning: "Democracy and education" revisited. *Educational Record, 78*(3–4), 56–65.

Ehrlich, T. (1999). Dewey versus Hutchins: The next round. In R. Orrill (Ed.), *Education and democracy* (pp. 225–262). New York, NY: The College Board.

Elliot, S. E. (1936). *Three centuries of Harvard.* Cambridge, MA: Harvard University Press.

Evans, N. J., & Reason, R. D. (2001). Guiding principles: A review and analysis of student affairs philosophical statements. *Journal of College Student Development, 42*(4), 359–377.

Geiger, R. L. (Eds.). (1999). *The American college in the nineteenth century.* Nashville, TN: Vanderbilt University Press.

Gitlin, A. (1996). Gender and professionalization: An institutional analysis of teacher education and unionism at the turn of the twentieth century. *Teachers College Record, 97*(4), 588–624.

Gumport, P. J. (2002). *Academic pathfinders: Knowledge creation and feminist scholarship.* Westport, CT: Greenwood Press.

Hall, P. (2014, November 7). Superior court affirms rejection of Lehigh student's grading lawsuit. *The Morning Call.* Retrieved from http://www.mcall.com/news/breaking/ mc-megan-thode-ruling-20141107-story.html

Hermanns, D. (2015, October 30). We must resist the market forces destroying our universities. *The Guardian.* Retrieved from https://www.theguardian.com/commenti sfree/2015/oct/30/market-forces-education-system-conservative-privatised-stud ents-march

Hutchins, R. M. (1936). *The higher learning in America.* New Haven & London: Yale University Press.

Kessler, J. (2009). Alumna sues college because she hasn't found a job. *CNN.* Retrieved from http://www.cnn.com/2009/US/08/03/new.york.jobless.graduate/

Kingkade, T. (2013, February 13). Megan Thode, Lehigh University grad, files $1.3 million lawsuit over C+ grade. *The Huffington Post.* Retrieved from http://www.huffi ngtonpost.com/2013/02/13/megan-thode-lehigh-university-lawsuit_n_2671739. html

Kirp, D. L. (2003). *Message in a bottle.* Retrieved from http://www.highereducation.org/ crosstalk/ct0403/voices0403-message.shtml

Kreuter, N. (2013). Customer mentality. *Inside Higher Ed*. Retrieved from https://www. insidehighered.com/views/2014/02/27/essay-critiques-how-student-customer-idea-erodes-key-values-higher-education#.V4-dD-vw2ik.twitter

Nuss, E. M. (2003). The development of student affairs. In S. R. Komives, D. B. Woodard Jr., & Associates (Eds.), *Student services: A handbook for the profession* (4th ed., pp. 65–88). San Francisco, CA: Jossey-Bass.

Ogren, C. A. (1995). Where coeds were coeducated: Normal schools in Wisconsin 1870–1920. *History of Education Quarterly, 35*, 1–26.

Ogren, C. A. (2003). Rethinking the "nontraditional" student from a historical perspective: State normal schools in the late nineteenth and early twentieth centuries. *The Journal of Higher Education, 74*, 640–664.

Olick, D. (2015, September 3). Tricked out student housing equals big developer profits. *CNBC*. Retrieved from http://www.cnbc.com/2015/09/03/tricked-out-student-housing-equals-big-developer-profits.html

Rudolph, F. (1962). *The American college and university*. Athens, GA: The University of Georgia Press.

Sandeen, A. (1985). The legacy of values education in college student personnel work. In J. C. Dalton (Ed.), *Promoting values development in college students* (pp. 9–23). Washington, D.C.: National Association of Student Personnel Administrators.

Segal, C. F. (2013, February 19). The curious case of Megan Thode. *Inside Higher Ed*. Retrieved from https://www.insidehighered.com/views/2013/02/19/lessons-learned-case- lawsuit-over-c-essay

Shortell, T. (2013, November 25). Lehigh university student's bid rejected for new trial in $1.3 million C-plus lawsuit. *Lehigh Valley Live*. Retrieved from http://www.lehigh valleylive.com/bethlehem/index.ssf/2013/11/judge_rejects_new_trial_for_le.html

Slaughter, S. (2002). The political economy of curriculum-making in American universities. In S. Brint (Ed.), *The future of the city of intellect* (pp. 260–289). Stanford, CA: Stanford University Press.

Thode v. Ladany, Carr, & Lehigh University. (2014). In the Superior Court of Pennsylvania.

Thompson v. Monroe College Office of Career Advancement. (2009). Supreme Court of the State of New York County of the Bronx.

Woodhouse, K. (2015, June 15). Lazy rivers and student debt. *Inside Higher Ed*. Retrieved from https://www.insidehighered.com/news/2015/06/15/are-lazy-rivers-and-climbing-walls-driving-cost-college

Yale Faculty. (1828). *The Yale report*. Retrieved from http://www.higher-ed.org/resources/Yale_Report.htm

28. Are College Students Too Entitled Today? The Role of Customer Service in Meeting Student Needs and Expectations

DENISE L. DAVIDSON AND AMY A. PACIEJ-WOODRUFF

In the summer of 2015, American politicians drew attention to the perceived excessive comforts made available on some college campuses (Woodhouse, 2015). Climbing walls and lazy rivers were contrasted against the increasing costs of higher education, with claims that these "amenities" were extravagances that students—and by extension, parents and society—could ill-afford. Within higher education circles, attention focused on the perception that college students are increasingly coddled, entitled, and demanding of a customer service approach that many find contrary to the essential purposes of higher education.

In this chapter, we explore the role and utility of customer service in contemporary higher education as a logical means to address the needs of an increasingly diverse student population and changing society. In particular, we examine the economic notions of public and private goods and their relationship to a customer service orientation. To put this in context, we briefly trace historical events and include an examination of the varied characteristics of today's college students. Noting that customer service can be a means to provide a high-quality education, we conclude that it is a natural response to a changing society, altered student population, and evolving role of American higher education.

The Present Climate

In separate speeches in 2015, Elizabeth Warren, the U.S. Senator from Massachusetts, and Chris Christie, Governor of New Jersey, drew attention in public speeches to the high cost of college and the expensive amenities provided to students by some institutions of higher learning. A number of colleges and universities have invested heavily in construction of what might be considered "amenities," that is, extras or supplements to the core educational mission. These included a barbershop in the University of Oregon's football performance center (Biemiller, 2013), a wave rider at Pensacola Christian College (Rubin, 2014), a sunken garden at the University of Albany (Biemiller, 2013), and music activated by "washing your hands in the restrooms" (Biemiller, 2013, para. 9) at the Colby College Museum of Art. Simultaneously, popular press publications have addressed the growing importance of a bachelor's degree for financial security and have discussed the long-term benefits of a college education (Adams, 2013; Leonhardt, 2015; Weiner, 2014). Further, various researchers have demonstrated the societal contributions of a learned citizenry (Baum & Payea, 2005; Bloom, Hartley, & Rosovsky, 2007; Trostel, n.d.). Tension is evident between meeting the perceived demands of prospective and enrolled students and the need for an educated populous.

Public Good Versus Private Good

American society is unclear about the role of higher education, evidenced, in part, by the lack of a national system and coherent agreement about its purposes (Brubacher & Rudy, 2008). Sometimes viewed as a debate, the question is posed as: is higher education a public good or a private good? Some argue that it is the degree or the credential—a "good" that can be used to obtain a job or advance in a career. Some say it is the experience of college and the structured opportunity to gain knowledge and skills in order to have a "better" life—financially, socially, intellectually, and emotionally. Still others point to the value accrued by society when its people are educated, that is, that we all benefit when we know more and are well-prepared for work, which then contributes to a continually advancing society. From an economic perspective, a public good benefits many people, as well as the individual receiving the good, even though not everyone has paid for it (Shaw, 2010). Shaw (2010) used learning to read and write as an example of a public good, abilities that advance the welfare of the individual while also making "people better citizens, acquaintances, and colleagues—contributing to the lives of others, even though they do not pay for those benefits" (p. 241). Conversely, a private good advantages only the individual and has no added value for society at large, as in the purchase of a car.

Yet viewing advanced education as a dichotomy, purely a public or private good, is not an effective frame for contemporary institutions of higher education. The boundaries between public and private goods are blurry because the student is not the only beneficiary. Beyond the student contributing to society via her increased education, the institution transfers benefits to the local, regional, and national communities via faculty research, performances and cultural events, economic development, institutional spending and employment, and more (Baum & McPherson, 2011). In a meta-analysis of a decade of studies concerning the effects of college, Pascarella and Terenzini (2005) found that college attendance has a broad range of enduring impacts on the individual in regard to occupation and earnings; cognitive, moral, and psychosocial characteristics; values and attitudes; and indices of the quality of life. Thus, both society *and* the student benefit.

Historical Foundations

The evolution of higher education as a "good" is confusing. The original Colonial colleges were affiliated with, if not established by, religious congregations with the aim of educating the young men of those communities (Thelin, 2011). Colleges were created largely so that educated students would contribute to these nascent communities through leadership and service (Thelin, 2011; Thelin & Gasman, 2010). The development of publically funded institutions, with the enactment of the Morrill Land Grant Act of 1862, emphasized the value of public education for the good of an expanding nation through "the liberal and practical education of the industrial classes in the several pursuits and professions in life" (7 U.S.C. § 304). Using the lens of the Land Grant Act, higher education was intended to benefit the citizenry directly through advanced education and indirectly via an educated populace (Wilhite & Silver, 2005).

An alternate perspective reveals additional motives. Modeled after Cambridge and Oxford universities in England, Harvard "welcomed 'fellow commoners' as well as serious degree students, 'gentlemen' who paid double tuition for the privilege of residing in the college and dining with the Fellows" (Brubacher & Rudy, 2008, p. 3). The purpose of higher education in the early days was to *not only* transmit knowledge but to continue class and culture for an American aristocracy, to sustain and promulgate the "intellectual and political elite of English America" (Brubacher & Rudy, 2008, p. 22).

The notion of college as an individual benefit has its origins in our earliest institutions.

In the early centuries, resources were scarce. As microcosms of society, industry and wealth started to grow in America and so too did the amenities in colleges. For instance, after the 1880s, Yale students no longer had to provide and chop their own firewood (Dodd, 1921). America also adopted the student center, or student union, trend that began in Oxford, England, as early as 1823, where an entire building was erected and dedicated for student activities outside of the classroom (University of Pennsylvania University Archives and Records Center, 2013). The first such center in the United States was built at the University of Pennsylvania in 1896 and contained a pool, bowling alley, gym, theater, music and billiards rooms, as well as socializing spaces and was run by students (University of Pennsylvania University Archives and Records Center, 2013). At the same time, an overall laissez-faire attitude toward students emerged as institutions adopted the German research university approach. According to Brubacher and Rudy (2008), a singular focus on academic development within newly emerging universities that focused on research and graduate students resulted in disregard of student activities outside of the classroom, treating students more as adults responsible for their own motivation and care. Providing housing for students was not a priority of the college. Fraternities grew in this era as they afforded needed shelter that the institutions did not. Other private housing ventures, such as Yale's "Hutch" and Harvard's "Gold Coast," were built by business entrepreneurs who also provided for the student housing need. Competition for students became an issue as more institutions were founded across the country. Some institutions reacted by constructing neo-Gothic buildings in the late 1800s and early 1900s that were purposefully designed to woo wealthy students to enroll and outshine their competition (Brubacher & Rudy, 2008), a direct response to meeting the needs and wants of students.

Collegiate athletic opportunities grew much in the same way as the fraternity system while the administration and faculty focus remained on academics alone. As athletics' popularity grew in the 1800s, wealthy alumni donated funds to support the thought that a "winning football team was considered 'good business' by many college administrators" (Brubacher & Rudy, 2008, p. 132). Students and alumni wanted organized athletics and pursued it, while colleges began to see it as a way to increase enrollment, prestige, and popularity. An example of how thoroughly athletic programs were embraced in higher education was the fact that in 1905 U.S. President Theodore Roosevelt brainstormed with Harvard, Yale, and Princeton to decide how to save football after the release of statistics detailing serious injuries and 18 deaths in collegiate sports (Brubacher & Rudy, 2008), which triggered nationwide reform. A strong message is sent when a U.S. president gets involved.

Contemporary College Students

Today's college student population has changed from even a few decades ago. No longer is the majority comprised of 18- to 22-year-olds who live in campus housing and enroll full-time. Accordingly, their needs and expectations of higher education have changed. Responses to the CIRP Freshman survey (Berrett & Hoover, 2015) demonstrate a dramatic shift in opinions about the purpose of a college education from "developing a meaningful philosophy of life" (65% "very important" or "essential" in 1974 to 45% in 2014) to "being well off financially" (44% in 1974; 82% in 2014).

The college-going population and higher education are not immune to external events such as the Great Recession, increased accessibility for persons with invisible disabilities, legal mandates concerning campus safety, attention to student loan default rates, and intense pressure to demonstrate the value of postsecondary education. Chambers and Gopaul (2008) suggest a tension between internal constituents' views of the purpose of higher education and external constituents (e.g., parents, students, taxpayers) who want bang for their buck. These external stakeholders want to know that this expensive venture is worth an investment of time, effort, and resources.

When we consider their experiences, it is not surprising that contemporary college students and their families want—and expect—campuses that are considered safe, accessible, financially sound, efficient, and comfortable. For instance, increases in high school and campus shootings have drawn attention to institutional responsibility for prevention and response. Greater national attention—via the Americans with Disabilities Act of 1990, 2008 amendments, and the Individuals with Disabilities Education Act—has been drawn to providing students with reasonable accommodations. Students and parents are accustomed to asking for assistance in meeting essential educational needs and this carries over to other areas. New interpretations of the Fair Housing Act of 1968 have solidified the right to assistance of animals in campus housing (Grieve, 2014). Few housing professionals envisioned that campuses would be required to permit dogs, cats, guinea pigs, and any variety of creature into the residence halls; now, students—with appropriate need and documentation—can do just that. Are these students entitled and coddled or are we meeting previously unrecognized student needs?

Other statutory changes have impacted how students and families perceive the role of the institution in relation to providing various opportunities,

services, and experiences for students, including adjustments to, and reaffir-
mations of, the Family Educational Rights and Privacy Act's provisions for
engaging parents in student conduct matters and the continued evolution of
the Clery Act's mandate for information sharing. Though higher education
practitioners may complain that current students, as Millennials, are more
protected than prior generations (Howe & Strauss, 2000), this is their experience of the world and the reality of their world view.

Looking forward, further changes are expected in college-going populations. Hussar and Bailey (2013) project, for instance, a 23% increase in
enrollment of students aged 35 and over between 2012 and 2022. In comparison, they estimate a 9% increase in students between 18 and 24 years of
age for this same time period. Similar increases are expected in relation to age,
race, and enrollment status. Labeled Generation Z (Williams, 2015), the next
cohort has been described as loyal, compassionate, thoughtful, open-minded,
responsible, and determined (Seemiller & Grace, 2016). Considered digital
natives, Generation Z is racially diverse (Williams, 2015). These factors are
expected to influence college students' notions of community, means of interaction, conceptions of learning, and presumptions of the college experience
and degree attainment (Seemiller & Grace, 2016).

What Is Customer Service?

Today's definition of customer service is a far cry from the notion articulated
by retailers Marshall Field and Jon Wannamaker as "the customer is always
right" (McBain, 1944). Defined as "the assistance and advice provided by a
company to those people who buy or use its products or services" (Oxford
Dictionaries, 2016, para. 1), customer service is generally perceived as aligned
with business and the exchange of goods. "Customer experience is the core
of customer service, not efficiency" (Greenberg, 2009, para. 16) and is bol-
stered by staff attention to solving a customer's problems (Greenberg, 2009;
Verduyn, 2013). Yet, there is no overall foundational theory in the business
world that addresses customer service within a particular industry. Absent
such an explanation, it is conventional to adopt commonly accepted interpretations of customer service. As long as customer service equals "the student is
always right," there is likely to be anger and resentment among some others
(beyond students) in academe.

A more thorough definition of customer service may parallel best practices in higher education. The most common components of customer service
seem to include a charge to provide an overall positive experience (Greenberg, 2009; Verduyn, 2013), to resolve complaints quickly and efficiently at

all levels (Greenberg, 2009; Schieltz, 2016), to ensure stakeholders feel heard (Greenberg, 2009; Schieltz, 2016), and to seek feedback to improve services and programs (Greenberg, 2009; Schieltz, 2016).

Overall Positive Experience

As a means to provide students with an overall positive experience, it is common for colleges to seek excellence in their functions, for instance, by providing correct information, demonstrating faculty and staff competence, offering a welcoming and respective campus climate, enacting best practices within specific departments, and framing work within the institutional mission. Additionally, cultivating institution-wide respect and care for others by treating everyone with dignity, enacting and educating the community concerning social justice, engaging in community service, and providing fair and just student conduct policies and processes all support an orientation toward ensuring students feel their college experience is affirmative and encouraging of their learning. As part of her presentation to families during new student orientation, Amy, as senior student affairs officer, discusses the importance of how families can assist their students in fixing their own problems without detracting from learning opportunities. Then, she closes by reminding them that she and her staff are available for them for the next four years. This reinforces the role of the student in her experience within the context of an institution and people who care about that experience.

Resolve Complaints Quickly and Efficiently at All Levels

Unfortunately, complaints from students, family members, and even internal constituents about getting the run-around are not uncommon. Some campuses may have several positions titled "dean," including within academic affairs and student affairs. Not surprisingly, many student concerns expressed to the dean of students are actually intended for an academic dean. Although not technically within the dean of students' purview, a service orientation suggests that the dean aids the student in understanding organizational structure and assists the student in figuring out who it is she should contact. Even though the issue may not be related to one's functional area, college personnel still help the complainant, perhaps making a few calls to get things straightened out and calling the complainant to ensure accurate information and a direct connection to the person who can rectify the matter. No matter our position within the institution, one avoids saying, "that's not my job"; instead, we respond promptly to resolve problems.

Ensure Stakeholders Feel Heard

From some perspectives, this may be the most important element of customer service. Though we often think of service as a means to resolve complaints, this element is a way to *prevent* problems from arising. First, devoting personal attention and institutional processes to listening means we have potentially useful data that enables us to appropriately design and implement services toward student needs. This does not mean students get everything they want, but that our efforts are attuned to our specific student populations, their needs, and their interests. Listening is involved when working with students seeking internship opportunities within student affairs offices. Some practitioners routinely share a list of potential projects with the student as she shares her goals and future aspirations. In partnership, the practitioner and student sift through the lists, discuss congruence, and examine possible opportunities. Internship goals are defined according to what the student would like as a learning outcome that also fit within a broader practitioner goal. There is a mutuality in this approach that is proactive and service oriented. It is much easier to develop appropriate learning opportunities by listening to students and empowering them to manage routine and unexpected issues.

Seek Feedback

Most can agree that the student is always right about their perception of her experience including occasions when she has felt welcomed on campus, challenged, connected, and engaged. When practitioners reject this information, we are, in essence, invalidating that student's perspective and experience. Rejecting the student is likely to result in undesirable outcomes, including upset and disgruntled students. At the least, good practice in assessment in student affairs and higher education calls for gathering feedback from students about their experience. In addition to validating students' experiences, this aids our efforts toward continual improvement and achievement of learning outcomes. We gather this information via institutional surveys, focus groups, and other intentional, systemic approaches. However, seeking feedback can also be as simple as routinely asking students—and other stakeholders—about their experiences and perspectives. This approach to customer service includes understanding students' preferred means of communication (Greenberg, 2009). While some practitioners are more effective than others, many make the attempt to adjust to the medium students prefer and thereby successfully gather information essential to the feedback loop.

These four elements of customer service, when applied to higher education, offer useful ways of thinking about how this approach can enhance the student experience while remaining congruent with the underlying tenets of student development and learning. The customer—or in this case, student—retains their sense of agency and remains responsible for her choices and decisions. Meanwhile, the practitioner and institution gain important insights into their daily work and how to more effectively meld students' desires with intended learning and development outcomes.

A Contemporary View of Customer Service

There is no agreement within higher education circles on the desired outcomes of postsecondary education or who should benefit from it. This lack of clarity aligns with confused notions of customer service. Though some interpret customer service as always doing what the customer wants, we suggest that service is not divorced from the history of higher education. Though often perceived as a dichotomy—customer service *or* education—today's students, society, and educational stakeholders benefit from adopting a blended approach: customer service *and* education. We view service as consistently providing appropriate environments that facilitate student learning and degree attainment.

Rivard (2014) describes a recent Gallup study that found college graduates were more engaged at work and had greater overall sense of well-being if they experienced someone at their school who cared about them, was concerned about their future careers, and had inspired them to learn. It is possible to conclude that a customer service approach promotes students' feeling that they and their opinions matter, that their experiences are important to faculty and staff and the institution. This expression of interest and attentiveness mirrors the essence of customer service.

Many institutions effectively consider service in their approach to institutional functioning. Particularly within Catholic institutions, hospitality is a core element of institutional philosophy. This includes being in community with other people, breaking bread, making the stranger or enemy a friend, and making people welcome in order to feel safe, comfortable, and valued so that meaningful dialogue and learning can take place (Hagstrom, 2013). These beliefs, enacted through tangible behaviors, sound suspiciously like customer service; and only with difficulty can one object to these essential convictions.

The notion of mattering, of making a difference, suggests a customer service orientation will promote student learning, retention, and degree attainment:

> [I]nstitutions that focus on mattering and greater student involvement will be more successful in creating campuses where students are motivated to learn, where their retention is high, and ultimately, where their institutional loyalty for the short-and long-term future is ensured. (Schlossberg, Lynch, & Chickering, 1989, p. 14)

Students, however, are not passive recipients of institutional services. The foundational documents articulating the philosophy of the student affairs profession express the fundamental agency of students as responsible for, and active contributors to, their own development and learning. This includes self-advocacy and the ability to provide feedback to others, completing the communication loop and larger benefit of soliciting and then using student input.

Our conception of customer service relies upon an existing foundation of higher education as a genuine service. Whether the student or society is the beneficiary is a question we cannot resolve here. Rather, we maintain that service does not mean providing everything an individual may want. Customer service, in our opinion, involves helping the student understand the reasoning behind decisions and institutional actions, how the student can effect desired change, the student's role in her own development, and generally developing a broader perspective. We do not suggest that a student must always be satisfied—the student is *not* always right—but, instead, that service includes educating the student about what is not and is possible and its congruence with institutional philosophy.

Many institutions hold to core values and are also able to adjust to changing times. Not too long ago, residence halls were equipped with hall phones, one per floor—or perhaps only located in the main lounge with a monitor to ensure opposite sex visitors did not venture from the lobby. Staff may have implemented bed checks and compulsory chapel attendance. Students were segregated by race and sex and institutions functioned *in loco parentis*. These circumstances are closely tied to a past macroculture and are a sign of prior generations. Yet, much has changed since the founding of Harvard College in 1636. Our role, as facilitators of student learning and development, is to meet students where they are instead of complaining that students are not what they once were. It is important to situate customer service within current societal context. The force of the economy, questions about the value of a college education, and changing thinking about societal equity, access, justice, and fairness all influence the nature of higher education and student environments. As students change—as our national changes—we must be prepared to adjust to new needs and expectations. We argued here that a new notion of customer service is appropriate for contemporary college students who are embedded within a culture that expects—nay demands—excellence in their experiences and supportive services. An important question is not whether today's students are coddled or entitled, but is higher education able to adjust—and provide appropriate support—to continually different student populations.

References

Adams, S. (2013, January 10). It still pays to get a college degree. *Forbes*. Retrieved from http://www.forbes.com/sites/susanadams/2013/01/10/it-still-pays-to-get-a-col lege-degree/#1cb477517892

Baum, S., & McPherson, M. (2011, January 18). Is education a public good or a private good? *Chronicle of Higher Education*. Retrieved from http://chronicle.com/blogs/ innovations/is-education-a-public-good-or-a-private-good/28329

Baum, S., & Payea, K. (2005). *The benefits of higher education for individuals and society*. New York, NY: The College Board. Retrieved from http://www.collegeboard.com/ prod_downloads/press/cost04/EducationPays2004.pdf

Berrett, D., & Hoover, E. (2015, February 5). College freshmen seek financial security amid emotional insecurity. *Chronicle of Higher Education*. Retrieved from http:// chronicle.com/article/College-Freshmen-Seek/151645/

Biemiller, L. (2013, August 29). New buildings greet students (mostly without construc tion fences). *Chronicle of Higher Education*. Retrieved from http://chronicle.com

Bloom, D. E., Hartley, M., & Rosovsky, H. (2007). Beyond private gain: The public ben efits of higher education. In J. J. F. Forest & P. G. Altbach (Eds.), *The international handbook of higher education* (Vol. 18, pp. 293–308). Dordrecht, the Netherlands: Springer.

Brubacher, J. S., & Rudy, W. (2008). *Higher Education in transition: A history of Amer ican colleges and universities* (4th ed.). New Brunswick, NJ: Transaction Publishers.

Chambers, T., & Gopaul, B. (2008). Decoding the public good of higher education. *Jour nal of Higher Education Outreach and Engagement, 12*(4), 59–91. Retrieved from http://openjournals.libs.uga.edu/index.php/jheoe/article/view/94/82

Dodd, W. E. (1921). *Woodrow Wilson and his work* (4th and revised edition). Garden City, NY: Doubleday, Page.

Greenberg, P. (2009, October 9). *Whole lot of Shakin' going on: The new customer service model*. Retrieved from http://www.mycustomer.com/service/management/whole- lot-of-shakin-going-on-the-new-customer-service-model

Grieve, K. A. (2014). *Reasonable accommodations? The debate over service and emotional support animals on college campuses.* Retrieved from https://www.naspa.org/rpi/posts/reasonable-accommodations-the-debate-over-service-and-emotional-support-ani

Hagstrom, A. A. (2013). The role of charisma and hospitality in the academy. *Integritas, 1*(1), 1–14. doi:10.6017/integritas.v1i1p1

Howe, N., & Strauss, W. (2000). *Millennials rising: The next great generation.* New York, NY: Vintage Books.

Hussar, W. J., & Bailey, T. M. (2013). *Projections of Education Statistics to 2022* (NCES 2014-051). U.S. Department of Education, National Center for Education Statistics. Washington, DC: U.S. Government Printing Office.

Land Grant Aid of Colleges, 7 U.S. Code § 301.

Leonhardt, D. (2015, April 24). College for the masses. *New York Times.* Retrieved from http://www.nytimes.com/2015/04/26/upshot/college-for-the-masses.html

McBain, H. M. (1944, November). Are customers always right? *The Rotarian Magazine, 65*(5), 32–33. Retrieved from https://books.google.com/books?id=qUIEAAAAMBAJ&pg=PA5&lpg=PA5&dq=Are+customers+always+right?+The+Rotarian+Magazine.&source=bl&ots=D12M5yAE7z&sig=r-eUNfPHJmC--HCuieloVw6gBQ8&hl=en&sa=X&ved=0ahUKEwi03bK1lf3NAhXSMx4KHcF9AjAQ6AEIHjAA#v=onepage&q=Are%20customers%20always%20right%3F%20The%20Rotarian%20Magazine.&f=false

National Survey of Student Engagement. (2013). *A fresh look at student engagement—Annual results 2013.* Bloomington, IN: Indiana University Center for Postsecondary Research.

Oxford Dictionaries. (2016). *Customer service.* Retrieved from http://www.oxforddictionaries.com/us/definition/american_english/customer-service

Pascarella, E. T., & Terenzini, P. T. (2005). *How college affects students: A third decade of research* (Vol. 2). San Francisco, CA: Jossey-Bass.

Rivard, R. (2014, May 6). Gauging graduates' well-being. *Inside Higher Ed.* Retrieved from https://www.insidehighered.com/news/2014/05/06/gallup-surveys-graduates-gauge-whether-and-why-college-good-well-being

Rubin, C. (2014, September 21). Making a splash on campus. *New York Times.* Retrieved from www.nyt.com

Schieltz, M. (2016) *How to develop a customer service model.* Retrieved from http://www.ehow.com/how_5856047_develop-customer-service-model.html

Schlossberg, N. K., Lynch, A. Q., & Chickering, A. W. (1989). *Improving higher education environments for adults.* San Francisco, CA: Jossey-Bass.

Seemiller, C., & Grace, M. (2016). *Generation Z goes to college.* San Francisco, CA: Jossey-Bass.

Shaw, J. S. (2010). Education—A bad public good? *The Independent Review, 15*(2), 241–256.

Thelin, J. R. (2011). *A history of American higher education* (2nd ed.). Baltimore, MD: Johns Hopkins University.

Thelin, J. R., & Gasman, M. (2010). Historical overview of American higher education. In J. H. Schuh, S. R. Jones, & S. R. Harper (Eds.), *Student services: A handbook for the profession* (5th ed., pp. 3–23). San Francisco, CA: Jossey-Bass.

Trostel, P. (n.d.). *It's not just the money: The benefits of college education to individuals and to society.* Indianapolis, IN: Lumina Foundation. Retrieved from https://www.luminafoundation.org/files/resources/its-not-just-the-money.pdf

University of Pennsylvania University Archives and Records Center. (2013). Undergraduate student governance at Penn, 1895-2006. *The Houston Club.* Retrieved from http://www.archives.upenn.edu/histy/features/studtorg/stugovt/housclub.html

Verduyn, D. (2013, November 7). *Discovering the Kano model.* Retrieved from www.kanomodel.com

Weiner, J. (2014, August 22). Do the benefits of a college education outweigh the cost? *Washington Post.* Retrieved from https://www.washingtonpost.com/blogs/she-the-people/wp/2014/08/22/do-the-benefits-of-a-college-education-outweigh-the-cost/

Wilhite, S. C., & Silver, P. T. (2005). A false dichotomy for higher education: Educating citizens vs. educating technicians. *National Civic Review, 94*(2), 46–54. Retrieved from EBSCO Host database.

Williams, A. (2015, September 18). Move over Millennials, here comes Generation Z. *New York Times.* Retrieved from http://www.nytimes.com/2015/09/20/fashion/move-over-millennials-here-comes-generation-z.html

Woodhouse, K. (2015, June 15). Lazy rivers and student debt. *Inside Higher Ed.* Retrieved from www.insidehighered.com

Part Fifteen: Are Fraternities and Sororities Still Relevant in Higher Education?

In "Are Fraternities and Sororities Still Relevant?" Ashley Tull and Kathy Cavins-Tull analyze Greek life, including its associated umbrella organizations, to distill the larger context of its national network and influence on American higher education. They argue for its continuing relevance despite widespread media criticism. The authors claim that fraternities and sororities offer opportunities for a sense of belonging, student success, and social support systems for mental health. For culturally based Greek organizations, in particular, they can afford feelings of mutual identity and community service benefits. In general, they crystallize values and augment leadership development. Tull and Cavins-Tull urge such organizations to reaffirm their commitment to the academic mission—one that requires consistent support from university leadership and concerned alumni.

In "Fraternities and Sororities in the Contemporary Era Revisited: A Pendulum of Tolerance," Pietro A. Sasso provides a brief history of the academy's relationship with Greek life and argues that the latter is no longer relevant to university ideals. He claims that residential functions and developmental gains can be replicated by other campus programs and initiatives. The chapter cites case examples at several universities where Greek organizations have been eliminated or curtailed in their activities. Sasso contends that, if fraternities and sororities are to continue, the parent institutions will need to exert greater jurisdiction and accountability through certified advisors and additional supervisors. Greek groups will need to be measured on outcomes focused primarily on student learning.

29. Are Fraternities and Sororities Still Relevant?

ASHLEY TULL AND KATHY CAVINS-TULL

Introduction

This chapter will address the historical and contemporary relevancy of fraternities and sororities (Greek organizations) on college and university campuses. While the degrees to which some or all of the important outcomes of Greek membership are relevant for members, this chapter accepts this notion for members of any type of Greek organization. These include traditionally White organizations such as fraternities in the North American Interfraternity Conference (NIC) and sororities in the National Panhellenic Conference (NPC); traditionally African American fraternities and sororities in the National Pan-Hellenic Conference (NPHC); fraternities and sororities in the National Multicultural Greek Council (NMGC); traditionally Latino/a fraternities and sororities in the National Association of Latino Fraternal Organizations (NALFO), traditionally Asian and Pacific Islander fraternities and sororities in the National Asian Pacific Islander American Panhellenic Association (NAPA) and LGBT fraternities and sororities.

Contents of this chapter will include the historical and contemporary relevancy of fraternities and sororities; current relevancy for undergraduates to include values; principles and ideals; leadership; community service and the development of altruism; cultural identity and awareness; diversity; student success; and support systems for academic, social, mental health, and accountability. Relevancy for alumni members of Greek organizations will be addressed and will include personal and professional networking/mentorship, public and philanthropic service, and affinity for alma mater and donor relations.

Historical and Contemporary Relevancy of Greek Organizations

Today more than 350 national fraternities and sororities exist that are social in nature. This number is exclusive of the many honor societies on college and university campuses that also use the Greek alphabet to name their organizations. The Greek subculture that has grown, and is still growing, since the early 19th century has done much to promote both educational and cocurricular experiences for generations of men and women. It has been and remains a staple of college life for many. We contend that it was relevant in many important ways then and remains so today. America's first Greek organizations were born out of early literary societies with the express purpose of developing more social outlets for members. Early literary societies did much to develop students scholastically, but were lacking in the social opportunities that students sought at the time.

As colleges and universities became home to women, students of color, and non-Christian students, new organizations were formed by "disenfranchised segments of the students—beginning with a handful of industrious college women in the Midwest" (DeSantis, 2007). Feeling that there was little support for their presence on college campuses, women began to form organizations that provided a place of support, enhanced their learning, and expressed their leadership.

By the turn of the 20th century, Greek organizations whose membership focus was on ethnic and multicultural student populations have continued to thrive. In addition to groups established primarily in the early 19th century that make up the NPHC and are historically African-American groups, groups for Latino/a's, Asian, multicultural, and LGBT students were founded and continue to grow in membership and influence. Latino/a groups were first founded in the 1970s and became noticed in the 1990s as a vehicle for promoting student success and cultural heritage among their members (Munoz & Guardia, 2009). Multicultural Greek organizations got their start along the same time as groups for Latino/as in the 1980s and 1990s. Their groups were founded because, "there were students coming from multicultural and multiethnic backgrounds, households, schools, and neighborhoods who often were able to identify with bicultural or multicultural identities" (National Multicultural Greek Council, 2016, para. 2). Like Latino/a groups, multicultural groups, "founding members were also students who exemplified cultural pride and wanted to share it with their peers, while simultaneously seeking to learn of other cultures" (NMGC, 2016, para. 4). Asian and Pacific Islander fraternities and sororities are relatively new and are members of NAPA founded in 2006 to "advocate, collaborate, and educate…members and constituent[s] for the greater good" (NAPA, 2016, para. 1). LGBT fraternities and sororities are the latest to emerge as a primary means for students who identify as LGBT to develop community among like student peers without concerns for acceptance or discrimination by other groups (Funke, 2015).

Fraternities and sororities, since their founding, have promoted scholarship, mentorship, community service, and best efforts for their communities (Ross, 2000). Rhinehimer (2014) outlined contemporary benefits of belonging to a fraternity or sorority that are as relevant today as they have been historically. These included,

> you expand your cultural circle...you gain a network of loyal friends...opportunity and experience are everywhere...you are recognized as a leader...you get to help others through community service...the future networking possibilities are invaluable...you learn how to work well as a team. (para. 5–11)

While the historical and contemporary relevancy outlined above might appear primarily for undergraduates, Greek organizations continue to be relevant for their membership after graduation. These groups serve as large personal and professional networks benefiting members for a lifetime, as will be discussed later. Historical examples of this include published newsletters, directories, and detailed catalogs (Syrett, 2009). Many of these include personal and professional contact information, "as well as military, political, civil and collegiate titles of individuals when they were particularly distinguished" (Syrett, p. 95).

Current Relevancy for Undergraduates

Values, Principles, and Ideals

Membership in Greek organizations provides undergraduate students opportunities to identify with values, principles, and ideals that are greater than themselves. In most cases these are aligned with universally accepted values such as self-transcendence, self-enhancement, conservation, and openness to change (Schwartz, 2012; Tull & Shaw, 2016). Results of research on Greek membership have found many positive outcomes to be associated with the espoused and enacted values experienced by undergraduates. Some of these include personal relationships, civic engagement, participation in extracurricular activities, philanthropic endeavors, and academic achievement (Asel, Seifert, & Pascarella, 2009; Hayek, Carini, O'Day, & Kuh, 2002; Whipple & Sullivan, 1998). Espoused values are best represented by the outward and open values systems that are adopted and communicated by Greek organizations to stakeholders and the broader public. Examples of espoused values include: loyalty, duty, respect, service & stewardship, honor, integrity, and personal courage (Lambda Chi Alpha); personal growth, friendship, service, and loyalty (Sigma Kappa); brotherhood, service, and scholarship (Phi Beta Sigma); scholarship, service, sisterhood, finer womanhood (Zeta Phi Beta); sisterhood, leadership, service, diversity, strength, unity, and scholarship (Gamma Eta); and unity, honesty, integrity, and leadership (Kappa Delta Chi). Each of these espouse values enacted by respective members through many of the activities described below.

Leadership

Leadership is an important outcome of membership in a Greek organization on two major fronts. First, members are able to learn important leadership skills through educational training programs offered on the local, regional, national, and international level. Second, they are able to practice their leadership skills through multiple opportunities to hold appointed and/or elected positions within their organizations. These too can be practiced through student positions on each of the levels mentioned earlier.

Members of Greek organizations have also been found to develop their leadership skills through higher levels of engagement in leadership opportunities across campus, when compared to their non-Greek peers (Bureau, Ryan, Ahern, Shoup, & Torres, 2011; Harms, Woods, Roberts, Bureau, & Green 2006; Kelley, 2008). Asel, Seifert, and Pascarella found, "fraternity/ sorority members as a group appeared to spend substantially more hours per week participating in co-curricular or extracurricular activities...than other students" (p. 5). In addition to their levels of engagement, Greek members have also scored significantly higher on leadership skills assessment measures and achieved higher general educational gains than their non-Greek peers (Asel et al., 2009; Astin, 1993; Hevel, Martin, & Pascarella, 2014).

Membership of African-American undergraduates in Greek organizations has also proven to be a valuable place for leadership development. This is true at a variety of institutional types, particularly historically black colleges and universities (HBCUs) and predominately white institutions (PWIs), where Greek organizations can serve, for some, as a place to more easily connect and develop and practice their leadership (Harper, 2008; Harper & Harris 2006; Hevel et al., 2014; Kimbrough, 1995; Kimbrough & Hutcheson, 1998; Patton, Bridges, & Flowers, 2011). African-American men, who are members of Greek organizations, have been found to hold more campus-wide leadership positions and to be involved in greater levels as a result of their membership (Patton et al., 2011). African-American male and female undergraduate students have also been found to be more engaged, than their non-Greek African-American peers, in "effective educational practices" (Patton et al., p. 119) at PWIs.

Community Service and the Development of Altruism

Like the important outcome of leadership explicated earlier, service and the development of altruism are also key as a by-product of the Greek experience (Bureau et al., 2011; Harms et al., 2006; Kelley, 2008). Participation in service activities fosters engagement on many levels that include: locally, statewide, regionally, nationally, and internationally. Undergraduate members are able to gain a greater appreciation for the communities and world around them and in many cases participate in service related to their chosen field of study or career interests (Harper, 2008; Harper & Harris, 2006; Kimbrough, 1995; Patton et al., 2011).

Community service activities are often overseen on the local level by an appointed or elected member of the chapter who organizes activities for members. Both leadership and service skills are practiced contemporaneously though these activities. Previous research has found Greek membership to lead to significantly greater levels of participation in service or volunteer activities as compared to non-Greek peers. "Some researchers suggest fraternity/ sorority affiliation is associated positively with increased levels of volunteerism and civic responsibility" (Asel et al., 2009, p. 1). Additionally, many national organizations have chosen national philanthropic organizations to partner with for greater impact. A secondary development outcome for members of Greek organizations results when, through their participation, undergraduates develop a greater sense of altruism and sense of duty to engage in community or public service beyond their college years. The experiences that Greek members have while an undergraduate can not only *pay dividends* for them, but also their alma mater and society. Bruggink and Siddiqui (1995) stated, "…altruism to his/her college may be driven by a social sense of obligation to provide collective goods and services to society, sharpened by feelings of allegiance and empathy to his/her school" (p. 53).

Improved Student Success

There has been a substantial amount of research on the transition of first year students to campus and the impact of that transition on persistence (Schlossberg, 1989; Tinto, 1998; Tinto, Goodsell, & Russo, 1993). The quality and effort students devote to educationally purposeful activities, their involvement with faculty members, and relationships with peers have been identified as some of the most critical factors in the outcomes of the first college year and persistence to graduation (Astin, 1993; Pascarella & Terrenzini, 2005). For many college students, transition to college coincides with their recruitment and early membership activities of joining a fraternity or sorority. While Greek organizations are often criticized for their perceived role as antithetical to the academic mission of their college and university hosts, there is competing evidence of outcomes that challenge the claim.

Every nationally recognized fraternal organization was founded on the value of scholarship and each continues today to espouse academic values as central to the organization's core. Every organization has structured educational programs designed to support the educational goals of its members and most have structured recognition and remediation programs for individual members and chapters. Several researchers have tried to capture the effect of affiliation on the scholarship goals of students, although much of the research is centered in single university studies or the scope of the research is so small that it is difficult to generalize.

In a study of more than 42,000 students at 192 institutions of higher education, Hayek et al. (2002) examined the levels of engagement in educationally purposeful activities of affiliated students against those who were not affiliated with Greek organizations. They looked specifically at how much time students spent studying, participating in cocurricular activities, interacting with faculty and peers using the data collected from the National Study of Student Engagement (NSSE) that assesses collegiate quality. The researchers concluded that "students who belong to Greek-letter organizations do not fare worse and in many cases fare better than other students in terms of their levels of engagement in educationally effective practices" (p. 657). Affiliated men and women, first year and senior students were found to engage as much or more than their unaffiliated peers in the "amount of effort they put forth inside and outside the classroom (including experiences and exposure to diversity), to self-reported gains in various educational and personal growth areas and to perceptions of the campus environment" (p. 657).

Another national study attempted to answer the question of academic outcome of affiliation using educational records instead of self-reports. DeBard and Sacks (2010) sought to determine the impact of involvement in a fraternity or sorority on the transition of the first year student to campus. The researchers used academic records to determine the outcomes of the first year and concluded, after controlling for precollege factors, that students who affiliated in their first year "earned significantly higher grade point averages than non-affiliated students" (p. 16). The same study found new members "retained to their sophomore year at significantly higher rates than their non-affiliated peers" (p. 16).

Ahren, Bureau, Ryan, and Torres (2014) studied over 179,000 college seniors through the NSSE data collected in 2006, 2007, and 2008 to determine if there was a difference in engagement for first-generation students who were also members of fraternities and sororities. They found that compared to their first-generation college student peers who were unaffiliated with Greek-letter organizations and their peers who were not first-generation college students, those who were first-generation college students and members of Greek-letter organizations scored higher than their peers in self-reported areas of "gains in general education, higher order learning, integrative learning and reflective thinking" (p. 9). Students who report higher engagement in educationally purposeful activities generally have greater satisfaction, higher grades, and persist to graduation at greater rates (Kuh, Kinzie, Buckley, Bridges, & Hayek, 2006).

In a smaller study, Nelson, Halperin, Wasserman, Smith, and Graham (2006) studied affiliation and student retention and grade point averages over the course of 10 semesters and found substantially higher retention rates for members of sororities and fraternities than students who were not affiliated. The researchers found in two of the cohorts a negative effect on grade point average during the semester of new membership, but then improved performance that aligned with the performance of their nonaffiliated peers. The researchers provide the caveat that when the subcultures are aligned with the values and mission of the host university, they can "positively influence peer behavior, promote loyalty to an alma mater, and increase students involvement and persistence to graduation" (p. 70).

Presence of Support Systems

When many of the social Greek organizations were formed, colleges and universities were enrolling mostly white, male students. Women and students of color were often underrepresented on campus and sororities and black fraternal organizations were created to provide a place for intellectual inquiry, support, social acceptance, and opportunities for leadership for their members. Issues of mattering (Schlossberg, 1989) and belonging are concerns that remain unchanged on college campuses today. Student success and persistence continue to be linked to interaction with supportive adults on campus, strong peer-to-peer relationships, diversity, cocurricular activity, and student satisfaction with their college or university (Kuh et al., 2006).

Relationships with faculty, advisors, and peers have consistently been factors that correlate with the success and satisfaction with the college experience (Asel et al., 2009; Kuh et al., 2006; Patton et al., 2011). In their study of first year and senior year students, Asel et al. found that for seniors, "affiliation was related positively to both quality and impact of personal relationships with peers and frequency of contact with student affairs professionals" (p. 5).

Patton et al. (2011) studied the effects of affiliation on the engagement of African-American students on different college campuses. They found that students who were members of Black Greek Letter Organizations (BGLOs) indicated better overall engagement in their education than their nonaffiliated peers. Even greater was the engagement of members of BGLOs at HBCUs than their peers at PWIs. The researchers explain that many students who attend PWIs feel the effects of racism and discrimination on their abilities to engage in educationally purposeful activities. They cite the need for BGLOs as a place where students develop their leadership, find support, and assist students with their relationships with faculty members and classmates. Similarly, Kimbrough and Hutcheson (1998) found that students who were members of BGLOs were more involved in their campus and reported greater confidence in their ability to lead at both HBCUs and PWIs than their unaffiliated peers.

Lounsbury and DeNeui (1996), in their study of collegiate psychological sense of community, determined that participation in a fraternity or sorority contributes to a greater sense of community based on their emphasis on belongingness, cohesion, and shared identity. Similarly, Pike (2003) found that students involved in Greek life reported higher gains in social involvement and integration of college experiences, resulting in greater increases in their general abilities associated with cognitive development.

Greek-letter organizations were established by students to fulfill a need for community, affinity, and connection since 1776. Pike concluded that fraternal organizations are strong engines for socialization of students and suggested that their connection to student success is often tied to how integrated the organizations are with the institutional culture.

Future Relevancy for Alumni

Personal and Professional Network/Mentoring

Personal and professional networking and mentoring for members of a Greek organization can have significant outcomes for both undergraduate members and alumni members. In many cases undergraduates develop relationships among their peers that aid in personal and professional networking and mentoring. These relationships are enhanced even more when members are afforded opportunities to network and be mentored by alumni members on the local and national levels through their organizations. "Undergraduates generally enjoy meeting their older brothers and sisters who are professionally successful and domestically happy" (DeSantis, 2007, p. 226). This can also help "promote and encourage academic achievement and community service" (Patton et al., 2011, p. 113).

For members of BGLOs, those belonging to the NPHC, networks on both local and national levels have been found to be important for alumni to serve as role models and for continued emphasis on the importance of community engagement. Schuh, Triponey, Heim, and Nishimura (1992) and Patton et al. (2011) found that membership in a BGLO provided bonding networks both locally and nationally, allowed members to act as role models, and stressed the importance of community engagement both for undergraduates and alumni members. Each party benefits as the undergraduate participates in an important developmental relationship and the alum gives back to their local chapter and/or the national organization.

To develop and strengthen those relationships between members at all levels of a Greek organization, many have developed alumni chapters or associations, hosted reunions and philanthropic events, and received regular correspondence through a variety of means. Each of these has helped members to continue to invest in important relationships that will be meaningful throughout the member's lifetime (Syrett, 2009). These have been built upon continued interaction with members that is maintained through, "good feelings engendered by a college experience fondly remembered" (Syrett, p. 101).

Public and Philanthropic Service

Groups, such as the NIC and NPC, as well as their member fraternities and sororities have touted their members who hold public office as well as contributions to national and local nonprofit organizations. This brings great pride for these groups and their membership and helps to promote membership as a launchpad for success in business, public service, and many other fields. A recent review of the NIC website showed that 19 (44%) U.S. Presidents were members of fraternities; 39 (39%) of the U.S. Senate membership are members of fraternities or sororities; and 106 (24.6%) of the U.S. Congress are members of fraternities or sororities (NIC, 2016a).

Groups, such as those mentioned earlier, along with NPHC, NALFO, and NMGC also regularly track monetary contributions and number of service hours annually to national and local nonprofits. Recent data for NPC showed annual monetary donations of $34,880,415 and 2,958,395 hours for the 2014–2015 academic year (NPC, 2016); NIC showed annual monetary donations of $20,300,000 raised and 380,487 hours for the same time period (NIC, 2016b); and NMGC showed annual monetary donations of $819,516 raised and 35,523 hours for the same time period (NMGC, 2014). In addition to large monetary contributions and many hours of service, national Greek organizations have long-standing partnerships with leading organizations aimed at social impact. The NPHC regularly partners with the United Negro College Fund (UNCF) and the St. Jude's Children's Hospital and is highly engaged in voter empowerment initiatives (NPHC, 2016). NALFO has regularly coordinated a national day of service for member organizations that has resulted in many groups and persons being served on a national and local level by these efforts (NALFO, 2016).

Affinity for Alma Mater and Donor Relations

Membership in a Greek organization has been shown to deepen one's affinity for their alma mater (Bureau et al., 2011; Kelley, 2008). This is likely due to students' inward and outward demonstration of the positive outcomes outlined above. The "Greek experience [has] increased one's gratitude to the college, and this does not disappear even if the actual fraternity [or sorority chapter] does" (Bruggink & Siddiqui, 1995, p. 57).

Alumni members of Greek organizations have also been shown to have an improved inclination toward contributing to philanthropic causes at greater levels than their non-Greek peers (Asel et al., 2009). These can include both those connected to the undergraduate institution and beyond. "Direct benefits [could] include the advantages of the college's continued or improved reputation, and any special privileges or attention that giving confers on alumni donors..." (Bruggink & Siddiqui, p. 54). Related to the outcome of community service and the development of altruism outlined earlier, research on those who actively volunteer in college has shown that they contribute 120% more than their nonvolunteer peers as alumni (Wunnava & Lauze, 2001). This improves the importance of service while in college, more importantly for Greek students who have been found to have higher affinity and greater inclination to give already.

Conclusion

Since the establishment of Phi Beta Kappa in 1776 and the onset of social fraternities as early as 1825, students have considered Greek-letter organizations to be an important source for socialization, service, and support during their college experience and well beyond. Fraternities and sororities have served colleges and universities as outlets for leadership, community engagement, and social connection during some of most defining years for young people. And it is through fraternities and sororities that many graduates remain connected to and supportive of their universities.

In many cases, colleges and universities are quick to highlight the risks and liabilities associated with fraternities and sororities and a review of the literature provides plenty of fodder for these claims. Whether one supports or opposes the establishment of fraternal organizations on college campuses, research indicates the strong influence of peer-to-peer relationships as a central source for student success, satisfaction, and persistence. Aligning fraternities and sororities to the mission and values of the university and providing them with consistent support and leadership development provides the scaffolding for the success colleges and universities expect to see in their students and alumni.

References

Ahren, C., Bureau, D., Ryan, H. G., & Torres, V. (2014). First to go to college and first to "go Greek": Engagement in academically oriented activities by senior year first generation students who are fraternity/sorority members. *Oracle: The Research Journal of the Association of Fraternity/Sorority Advisors, 9*(1), 1–19.

Asel, A. M., Seifert, T. A., & Pascarella, E. T. (2009). The effects of fraternity/sorority membership on college experiences and outcomes: A portrait of complexity. *Oracle: The Research Journal of the Association of Fraternity/Sorority Advisors, 4*(2), 1–15.

Astin, A. W. (1993). *What matters in college? Four critical years revisited.* San Francisco, CA: Jossey-Bass.

Bruggink, T. H., & Siddiqui, K. (1995). An econometric model of alumni giving: A case study for a liberal arts college. *The American Economist, 39*(2), 53–60.

Bureau, D., Ryan, H. G., Ahern, C., Shoup, R., & Torres, V. (2011). Student learning in fraternities and sororities: Using NSSE data to describe members' participation in educationally meaningful activities in college. *Oracle: The Research Journal of the Association of Fraternity/Sorority Advisors, 6*(1), 1–22.

DeBard, R., & Sacks, C. (2010). Fraternity/sorority membership: Good news about first-year impact. *Oracle: The Research Journal of the Association of Fraternity/Sorority Advisors, 5*(1), 12–23.

DeSantis, A. (2007). *Inside Greek U: Fraternities, sororities, and the pursuit of pleasure, power, and prestige*. Lexington, KY: University of Kentucky Press.

Funke, D. (2015, March 18). LGBT fraternities and sororities look to make Greek life more inclusive. *USA Today College*. Retrieved July 27, 2016 from http://college.usatoday.com/2015/03/18/lgbt-fraternities-and-sororities-look-to-make-greek-life-more-inclusive/

Harms, P. D., Woods, D., Roberts, B., Bureau, D., & Green, M. (2006). Perceptions of leadership in undergraduate fraternal organizations. *Oracle: The Research Journal of the Association of Fraternity Advisors, 2*(2), 81–94.

Harper, S. R. (2008). The effects of sorority and fraternity membership on class participation and African American student engagement in predominately White classroom environments. *College Student Affairs Journal, 27*(1), 94–115.

Harper, S. R., & Harris, F. (2006). The role of Black fraternities in the African American male undergraduate experience. In M. J. Cuyjet (Ed.), *African American men in college* (pp. 129–153). San Francisco, CA: Jossey-Bass.

Hayek, J. C., Carini, R. M., O'Day, P. T., & Kuh, G. D. (2002). Triumph of tragedy: Comparing student engagement levels of members of Greek-letter organizations and other students. *Journal of College Student Development, 43*(5), 643–663.

Hevel, M. S., Martin, G. L., & Pascarella, E. T. (2014). Do fraternities and sororities still enhance socially responsible leadership? Evidence from the fourth college year. *Journal of Student Affairs Research and Practice, 51*(3), 233–245.

Kelley, D. R. (2008). Leadership development through the fraternity experience and the relationship to career success after graduation. *Oracle: The Research Journal of the Association of Fraternity Advisors, 3*(1), 1–12.

Kimbrough, W. M. (1995). Self-assessment, participation, and value of leadership skills, activities, and experiences for Black students relative to their membership in historically Black fraternities and sororities. *Journal of Negro Education, 64*(1), 63–74.

Kimbrough, W. M., & Hutcheson, P. A. (1998). The impact of membership in Black Greek-letter organizations on Black students' involvement in collegiate activities and their development of leadership skills. *Journal of Negro Education, 67*(2), 96–105.

Kuh, G. D., Kinzie, J., Buckley, J. A., Bridges, B. K., & Hayek, J. C. (2006). *What matters in student success: A review of the Literature*. Commissioned Report for the National Symposium on Postsecondary Student Success: Spearheading a Dialog on Student Success, National Postsecondary Educational Cooperative. Retrieved August 8, 2016 from http://nces.ed.gov/npec/pdf/kuh_team_report.pdf

Lounsbury, J. W., & DeNeui, D. (1996). Collegiate psychological sense of community in relation to size of college/university and extroversion. *Journal of Community Psychology, 24*(4), 381–394.

Munoz, S. M., & Guardia, J. R. (2009). Nuestra historia y future (Our history and future): Latino/a fraternities and sororities. In C. L. Torbenson & G. S. Parks (Eds.), *Brothers and sisters: Diversity in college fraternities and sororities*. Cranbury, NJ: Farleigh Dickinson University Press.

National Asian Pacific Islander American Panhellenic Association. (2016). *Welcome to NAPA*. Retrieved August 13, 2016 from http://www.napahq.org

National Association of Latin Fraternal Organizations. (2016). *National Day of Service*. Retrieved August 8, 2016 from http://nalfo.org/national-day-of-service/

National Multicultural Greek Council. (2014). *Membership demographic report*. Retrieved August 9, 2016 from http://nationalmgc.org/wp-content/uploads/2008/12/NMGC-2014-Membership-Demographic-Report.pdf

National Multicultural Greek Council. (2016). *About*. Retrieved July 27, 2016 from http://nationalmgc.org/about/

National Panhellenic Conference. (2016). *Meet NPC*. Retrieved August 9, 2016 from https://www.npcwomen.org/about.aspx

National Pan-Hellenic Council. (2016). *Social action taskforce*. Retrieved August 8, 2016 from http://www.nphchq.org/quantum/social-action-taskforce/

Nelson, S. M., Halperin, S., Wasserman, T. H., Smith, C., & Graham, P. (2006). Effects of fraternity/sorority membership and recruitment semester on GPA and retention. *Oracle: The Research Journal of the Association of Fraternity Advisors, 2*(1), 61–70.

North American Interfraternal Conference. (2016a, July 27). *Political leaders*. Retrieved from http://www.nicindy.org/political-leaders.html

North American Interfraternal Conference. (2016b, August 9). *Fraternity statistics*. Retrieved from http://www.nicindy.org/fraternity-statistics.html

Pascarella, E. T., & Terrenzini, P. T. (2005). *How college affects students: A third decade of research*. San Francisco, CA: Jossey-Bass.

Patton, L. D., Bridges, B. K., & Flowers, L. A. (2011). Effects of Greek affiliation on African American students' engagement: Differences by college racial composition. *College Student Affairs Journal, 29*(2), 113–123.

Pike, G. R. (2003). Membership in a fraternity or sorority, student engagement, and educational outcomes at AAU public research universities. *Journal of College Student Development, 44*(3), 369–382.

Rhinehimer, J. (2014, November 21). 10 ways Greek life prepares you for real life. *USA Today College*. Retrieved July 27, 2016 from http://college.usatoday.com/2014/11/21/10-ways-greek-life-prepares-you-for-real-life/

Ross, L. C. (2000). *The divine nine: The history of African American fraternities and sororities*. New York, NY: Kensington Publishing.

Schlossberg, N. K. (1989). Marginality and mattering: Key issues in building community. *New Directions for Student Services, 48*, 5–15.

Schuh, J. H., Triponey, V. L., Heim, L. L., & Nishimura, K. (1992). Student involvement in historically Black Greek letter organizations. *NASPA Journal, 29*(4), 274–282.

Schwartz, S. H. (2012). An overview of the Schwartz Theory of Basic Values. *Online Readings in Psychology and Culture, 2*(1). doi:10.9707/2307-0919.1116

Syrett, N. L. (2009). *The company he keeps: A history of White college fraternities*. Chapel Hill, NC: University of North Carolina Press.

Tinto, V. (1998). Colleges as communities: Taking research on student persistence seriously. *Review of Higher Education, 21*(2), 167–177.

Tinto, V., Goodsell, A., & Russo, P. (1993). Building community among new college students. *Liberal Education, 79*, 16–21.

Tull, A., & Shaw, A. (2016). *Universally espoused fraternal values on college and university campuses: Commonplace or coincidence?* Unpublished manuscript.

Whipple, E. G., & Sullivan, E. G. (1998). Greeks as communities of learners. *New Directions for Student Services, 81*, 87–94.

Wunnava, P. V., & Lauze, M. A. (2001). Alumni giving at a small liberal arts college: Evidence from consistent and occasional donors. *Economics of Education Review, 20*(6), 533–543.

30. Fraternities and Sororities in the Contemporary Era Revisited: A Pendulum of Tolerance

PIETRO A. SASSO

Introduction

An attempt to revivify the fraternity/sorority experience was begun in 2003 and is commonly termed the "values-based movement." It was spearheaded by the Franklin Square Group—an assembly of 20 college and university presidents and inter-/national fraternal organization leaders representing several organizations, campus representatives, and academic consortia—which met in Washington, D.C. to consider the state of fraternities and sororities (Franklin Square Group, 2003).

In 2003, the Franklin Square Group issued *A Call for Values Congruence* to express concerns over the focus of the "liquid culture" of the fraternity/sorority system and to establish recommendations regarding the sustainability of fraternity and sorority chapters across the nation. This convening and leadership group supported the notion that fraternities and sororities were a bastion for alcohol misuse that caused a dichotomy between their stated missions and their actual behaviors. The report also supported the notion that fraternities and sororities impact student culture in ways that no other student organization can through experiential learning opportunities outside the classroom. This juxtaposition led the authors to call for "the development of programs and policies addressing alcohol abuse based upon research findings and established best practices and oversee their implementation" (p. 6).

A Call for Values Congruence advocated the use of a periodic "certification process" to involve multiple external stakeholders, ranging from local alumni to faculty. This certification process is reflected within the Collegiate Greek

Community Standard (CGCS). The CGCS is a framework for creating minimum policy and programming standards processes that fraternity and sorority chapters must meet to be recognized annually. It is a certification process for which each fraternity and sorority chapter must show how it has respectively met the listed standards. An external committee of alumni, faculty, and staff volunteers reviews this evidence. The Franklin Square Group (2003) devised a certification process model for fraternity/sorority standards programs within *A Call for Values Congruence*. It was the goal of the program to provide an active approach for programming and community standards for a campus system to address and ultimately reduce binge drinking and other related negative effects of fraternity/sorority involvement. This plan was lauded by campus administrators—particularly those who work directly as advisors to fraternities and sororities—as a way to conceptualize reframing the fraternity/sorority experience by emphasizing the historical founding values of brotherhood/sisterhood, service, and leadership connected with the academic experience. This was a well-intentioned attempt to facilitate campus-based change; however, it is the view of the author that this movement failed.

Recent narratives related to hazing deaths and injuries at Rutgers University, West Virginia, and the University of Virginia provide face validity for these criticisms. Once again, fraternities and sororities are under increased scrutiny. Yet, fraternities and sororities at American colleges and universities remain pervasive, enduring social institutions. They have yet to falter despite widespread criticism related to their involvement in sexual assault, hazing, binge drinking, racism, and elitism (Sasso, 2016). Such events have led to increased introspection regarding the purpose of collegiate fraternal organizations. Faculty, students, college administrators, and the public have called for increased supervision and accountability over chapters. Many campuses have rebirthed the notion of restricting their membership, reducing their campus influence, or eliminating the fraternity/sorority community. This circumstance demonstrates an apparent "pendulum of support." In some temporal frames, they are vigorously supported; and in others, the compass swings right, negating their existence (Sasso, 2015).

The more neoliberal strategy of P's (policy, procedure, process, and protocol) may not be the answer. If the mere existence of a "Greek life" in undergraduate collegiate culture is going to be sustainable, then college administrators need to put forth more consistent support for fraternities and sororities if they are to remain relevant. Otherwise, they may have to be eliminated altogether. This chapter will discuss the pendulum of tolerance and support for fraternities and sororities and then propose a new model to reframe the undergraduate fraternity/sorority experience.

Perspectives on the Fraternity/Sorority Experience

We know from the most recent research that fraternity/sorority organizations, particularly fraternities, demonstrate developmental and learning gains that are equal to those of their nonaffiliated peers. Students affiliated with collegiate fraternity/sorority organizations self-report increased leadership gains, community citizenship through service, and connectedness to their alma mater. They also report higher levels of self-esteem and interdependence.

Research also shows that "Going Greek" does not inhibit overall academic performance. However, during the initial period of affiliation, often commonly referred to as "pledging," members can experience a marked decline in academic achievement. It appears that "Going Greek" provides an individual benefit to its student members, but continues to be a burden on the academic community and institution. Furthermore, studies reveal that off-campus fraternity houses are bastions for underage drinking—which can be related to petty crime, binge drinking, mild drug experimentation, and sexual assault. For example, a fraternity house from Thursday evening to Saturday evening (the traditional college "party" nights) remains one of the most dangerous environments in which students can socialize (Sasso & Schwitzer, 2016).

Joining a fraternity or sorority is a predictor of increased binge drinking, sexist attitudes, and cocooning of conformity. While much more organized and supported, sororities also are linked to increased groupthink or conformity. Sororities often draw criticism from feminist leaders who suggest members encourage male hegemony and traditional patriarchal systems (Sasso, 2016).

In my estimation, fraternities and sororities are not artifacts from the past intended to be shelved and studied. In an era when most students develop friendships via social media and become "digital natives," fraternities and sororities have value in providing students with more authentic social development opportunities. Students are able to generate a depth and breadth of friendships based on personal interactions.

Thus, fraternities and sororities present an opportunity for students to develop meaningful lifelong friendships and leadership opportunities. However, colleges and universities need to do more to provide stewardship of the student experience within these organizations. More advising and administrative staff should be hired to facilitate learning experiences. Institutional structures and personnel need to produce proper accountability throughout campus.

Myriad issues associated with sorority and fraternity membership remain. Some, such as binge drinking and hazing, persist regardless of their value to society and their individual members. In some instances, fraternities and sororities have become cocurricular social outlets for institutional liabilities, viewed as no more than *speakeasies* or *drinking clubs* that engage in homoerotic hazing rituals (Sasso, 2016). This has caused increased scrutiny of fraternities and sororities in an effort to reduce institutional liability. Challenges to their existence have caused many colleges to question their relevancy.

The *raison d'être* of fraternities and sororities is thus being questioned more frequently. Recent events across the country have further put their relevancy into question. Many college administrators feel that they are not consistent with their individual institutional mission or that they are not related to desired learning outcomes. This has led to the dissolving of fraternity/sorority systems at Alfred University, Colby College, Williams College, and Bowdoin College, among others, within the last 40 years (Kaplin & Lee, 2014).

The Slow Erosion of the Fraternity/Sorority Experience

Prior to 1880, fraternities and sororities largely avoided antifraternity rules and operated sub rosa chapters. Almost half of men, by 1840, joined these social groups for the purpose of the "extracurriculum," that is a more active social life. Fraternities, and the modern conception of the "Greek system," traces its roots to both Union College and Dartmouth College. In the antebellum college, their mere existence created much antifraternity sentiment (Dartmouth, 1936).

In 1846, the Dartmouth Board of Trustees banned any elections to secret societies after 1849. Thus, Dartmouth President Nathan Lord, in 1847, banned freshman and sophomores from joining fraternities. President Lord advocated a general antifraternity sentiment in his report of 1847, noting that the two lower classes (freshman and sophomores) seemed predominantly opposed. A Dartmouth freshman, in 1846, described the societies as "the cause of division, envy, and malice. About one-half the men in college belong to them, these are the most talented" (Dartmouth, 1936). However, Dartmouth did not enforce its 1840s ban on fraternities. Furthermore, by the mid-1850s, the societies' public standing had improved. It took much agitation at Union for fraternities to become so highly supported.

The president of Union College, Dr. Eliphalet Nott, led a significant attempt to undermine student membership in fraternities. He went so far as to ban roasted potatoes and candied apples because they were selected by rebellious students in previous uprisings and food fights in the dining commons. He authored an edict to expel all men who were members of social fraternities. Nott felt that fraternities interfered with his grand ideals of transforming the classicist curriculum to one of scientific inquiry and mathematics. This initial lack of tolerance for the existence of fraternities eventually receded as the relationship between fraternities and sororities evolved (Trowbridge, 1926).

Unfortunately, the proliferation of fraternities and sororities and their antecedents have not been revitalized by the values-based movement spawned by the *Call for Values Congruence*. Currently, the pendulum is shifting to removing fraternities and sororities on many campuses. Particularly, this is permissible on private college and university campuses where case law establishes a legal precedent to do so (Kaplin & Lee, 2014).

Many institutions previously found that the development of community standards was a singular best-fit policy for addressing behaviors (Harvey, 1990). The relevancy question of fraternities and sororities, therefore, was answered and further made distinct through a relationship statement. Relationship statements defined the scope of the association between the host institution and the fraternity or sorority chapter. Such statements typically included a description of the limited purpose of recognition; acknowledgment that the fraternity/sorority letter organization was independently chartered; confirmation that the college assumed no responsibility for supervision, control, safety, security, or other services with respect to the fraternity/sorority organization; and a requirement that the fraternity or sorority provide evidence that it carried sufficient insurance to cover its risks (Gulland & Powell, 1989).

A relationship statement can be restrictive and overbroad in its scope. This has led to several instances on college campuses questioning the actual relationship between the fraternity/sorority community and the institution (Harvey, 1990). Although the existence of such a recognition statement might defeat a claim that the institution has assumed a duty to supervise fraternity and sorority chapters, it might also limit the institution's authority to regulate the organization's activities (Kaplin & Lee, 2014). However, the poor design and implementation of relationship statements led to several institutions facing liability issues because they failed, leading others to consider eliminating their existence or forcing coeducational mandates in lieu of recent Title IX federal legislation expansion.

Colby College

Colby College in Waterville, Massachusetts, is a private liberal arts college often clustered into a number of institutions often fondly referred to as the "New England Hilltop Colleges." They are often referred to by this nick-name because of closely situated campuses that overbook a bucolic scene with residence halls nestled amidst ivy-covered walls and substantial green space with manicured lawns. These colleges typically include Union College, Williams College, Middlebury University, Amherst University, and Colby. These colleges and universities are among the elite liberal arts college in both the Northeast and the United States and were some of the early colo-nial colleges that were replicated by others as models for the Midwestern and Southern liberal arts colleges. They were traditionally reflective of the "collegiate culture." That is, they define themselves as educating a primarily traditional residential, full-time student who is characterized as receiving an education strongly grounded and in the liberal educations. The students are enveloped in *artes liberals,* with an emphasis in the humanities—particu-larly English, history, philosophy as well as an emphasis on critical thinking coupled with a large swath of courses in the social sciences, e.g., political science, sociology, and psychology. The underpinning of the culture in the liberal arts college is very connected to the ethos of life of the mind. Frater-nities and sororities were part of the extracurriculum that is often perceived as antithetical to the educational mission and collegiate culture. This was the case at several of the New England Hilltop Colleges, including Williams, Colby, and Middlebury.

At Colby, the administration recognized that Williams may have been ahead of the curve. A College task force was appointed and cited a similar peer institution at Hamilton College, which had enacted an ill-fated series of reforms for its fraternity/sorority community. Hamilton opted to maintain the status quo, but with one restriction. They banned their members from dining or living together. Colby College, which sits six hours north across the tundra of Maine, nicely followed Williams' lead. Colby also eliminated recog-nition and privileges for its fraternity/sorority community in 1984.

In 1983, Colby President Cotter appointed a task force entitled the "Trustee Commission," which was comprised of alumni, faculty, and even students. The Commission held hearings on campus and interviewed alumni, and engaged in an environmental scan of fraternities and sororities. Then in early 1984, the Commission unsurprisingly voted unanimously to eliminate the fraternity system. The students were enraged by the news and burned furniture outside of their chapter houses in protest.

As with Middlebury, there was no coeducational mandate and as with Williams, some fraternities became sub rosa chapters. However, whatever influence that was extorted by fraternities on campus life later phased itself out. Five fraternities filed suit in an effort to block the new policy, but the legal maneuvering was in vain. The result was that the number of women in campus leadership positions swiftly rose.

Williams College

The prestigious Williams College, perched on 450 acres in scenic northwestern Massachusetts, led the charge a generation prior. The fraternity system was phased out when the institution was still all-male. The concern about the impact of the fraternity system in collegiate culture began a little before World War II. During that era fraternities dominated the campus. Their houses were populated by the affluent graduates of private New England boarding schools, including Exeter, Andover, and Deerfield. After the end of the war the arrival of student-veterans flooding campus with the GI Bill helped to unravel this traditional social structure. The student-veterans hailed from more modest backgrounds, often citing the fraternity system as "Mickey Mouse," referring to it as a waste of time. There was also a disdain for the entire caste system. Additionally, the system was highly discriminatory as there was a pattern of blackballing and secret agreements between some fraternities and their national bodies to exclude African-Americans and Jews. When the first fraternity, Sigma Phi, opted to admit black students, its new member class fell by almost half.

In Fall, 1961, a committee was formed to examine the influence of fraternities on the social life of students at Williams. Fraternities, it concluded, had compromised "the primary educational purposes of the College." In 1962, its Board of Trustees set in motion the transition away from the system. Initial anger by alumni and students was ferocious for about two years. However, shortly thereafter the decision was made to admit women and become coeducational. The outcome was that Williams' academic standing and perceived prestige increased. There was also a greater ability to raise money as alienated alumni who had been the victims of the fraternity system came back to the College.

Bowdoin College

Fifteen years later, Bowdoin College would join the ranks of those colleges eliminating its fraternity and sorority community. In March of 1997, the Board of Trustees approved the recommendations of the Trustee Commission on Residential Life. Fraternities at Bowdoin were phased out and a new system of inclusive "College Houses" was implemented. Interest in fraternities and sororities had waned. After more than a century and a half of fraternities at Bowdoin, their abolition was a historic shift for the College. The houses were restored into independent-living communities linked by common dining facilities that were remodeled as part of recommendations made by the Trustee Commission on Residential Life. Outcomes included a greater sense of community, but the elimination of fraternity/sorority life did not lead to a reduction in alcohol consumption by its undergraduates.

Middlebury College

Just as Colby was wrapping up its transition period by 1990 (as the last students with any organizational affiliation were graduating), the fraternity/sorority relevance question at Middlebury College was arising. A series of embarrassing public incidents, particularly involving fraternities, called into question the relevance and role of its own fraternity/sorority community. One such incident involving a mannequin being thrown out of a house onto the front lawn of the fraternity house in direct view of the university president, certainly appeared to conjure up images of the revel of *Animal House.*

The mannequin become a metaphor of unbridled influence the six fraternities had exerted over campus life. This truly marked the beginning of the end, as the drinking age was raised to 21 in 1986 in Vermont. The fraternities had simply become speakeasies and unruly bastions for underage drinking. Shortly thereafter, the Middlebury president Olin Robison declared it "a point beyond which our tolerance cannot and must not be stretched." The mannequin fraternity, Delta Upsilon, was suspended for a full year. A generation of college students passed and, by 1990, the Board of Trustees had reached its limit. In late 1989, a task force study stated, "The narrowly defined, fraternity-dominated social life on campus is incompatible with our vision of the future." Through a vote in early 1990, it was insisted that the fraternities include women and become coeducational. The fraternities realized that they would then have to forfeit their national affiliations or dissolve. Within one academic year, the fraternity community had been officially abolished. Several of them transitioned into coeducational "social houses."

A new type of residential system was also set in place in 1991, combining elements of the colonial residential college system with the contemporary conception of living-learning communities. First-year Middlebury students were put in cohorts and tracked into one of five coeducational living learning communities. The response was not completely cordial on the part of all the fraternities; one, in particular, resisted the new social order on campus. Delta Kappa Epsilon attempted to keep its house and later trashed it in the vein of 1980s rock stars when they were forced to vacate the premises. They reportedly ripped off bannisters, broke windows, and put many holes in the walls. The College later repaired the house and made it one of the coeducational houses. The chapter waged a legal battle that ended up being fruitless. The group also attempted to meet in secret at an off-campus warehouse through 1994. Similarly, Swathmore College students voted in favor of coeducational fraternity and sororities, but the College made no formal policy changes or mandates.

Amherst College

In 1984, Amherst College eliminated its fraternity/sorority system with a vote from its Board of Trustees. Amherst had allowed them to operate as sub rosa chapters until a 2014 task force addressing sexual assault cited their potential risk to students. The Sexual Misconduct Oversight Committee, composed of faculty, students, staff, administrators, and trustees, cited its "underground" fraternity/sorority community. They had considered recognizing the fraternities to bring them under institutional control to reduce liability. However, the Board instead reaffirmed its 1984 decision and decided as well to ensure its administration follow through on its enforcement. This decision is particularly related to a public relations issue resulting from a mishandled sexual assault case.

In October 2012, Angie Epifano, an undergraduate at Amherst, authored an op-ed article in the student newspaper which accused the College of mishandling her sexual assault case. She stated that the College admitted her to a psychiatric ward in response to her comments about being depressed as it was concerned that she might have suicidal ideations. Later, Epifano filed a federal complaint against the College in December 2013, with the U.S. Department of Education, as whether Amherst violated the Title IX gender equity law. In that complaint, Epifano cited a sexually hostile climate created and fostered by the underground fraternities. Amherst responded by bolstering its student services for Title IX compliance, revising related policies, increasing awareness programming, and augmenting counseling services. Its reaffirmation of the decision against the support of fraternities/sororities was part of this change.

Alfred University

Alfred University is located in western New York just south of Rochester in the same town as the State University of New York at Alfred. Ironically, the private liberal arts college eliminated its fraternity/sorority community in 1984, but SUNY Alfred has a vibrant one across the street in this very small college town. Alfred University phased out its fraternity/sorority community after citing that it was "unsuccessful" following the death of an undergraduate student in 2002. Benjamin Klein was a 21-year-old junior majoring in economics. He was involved in the University orchestra and was pledging Zeta Beta Tau. In February 2002, his body was found in a creek behind the town post office. The University suspended his fraternity once it looked into reports that fraternity brothers had beaten him. Members were merely charged with assault in the wrongful death.

Additional Cases

Additional narratives have been constructed that involve antifraternity sentiment, including Harvard University, Trinity College, and Cornell University. Cornell initially attempted reform of its fraternity/sorority community rather than outright eliminate it. After a string of very public and continued hazing incidents followed by the death of a 19-year-old freshman, Cornell President David J. Skorton, in 2011, attempted to eliminate the pledge system through mandate. The enforcement was truly never codified and instead the current president, Elizabeth Garrett, continues the practice whereby additional fraternities have been cited for hazing. The University has been unsuccessful in eliminating hazing or the traditional pledge model with a number of incidents occurring during the 2016–2016 academic year. Dartmouth began the same approach in 2014 with modest results.

At Harvard University, arguably one of the most prestigious postsecondary institutions in the United States, an "all-comers" policy was instituted which included a ban on unrecognized organizations. An all-comers policy is a neoliberal nondiscrimination standard that student organizations cannot discriminate on the basis of religion, class, sexual orientation, gender, race, or culture. This supersedes rights to intimate association and assembly. An example would be the administration enforcing the right of an atheist student to become the president or vice-president of the Newman organization, a collegiate Catholic organization. Consistent with implementing this policy and beginning with Harvard's Class of 2021, undergraduate members of any unrecognized single-gender social organization will be banned from holding athletic team captaincies and leadership positions in all recognized student groups. They will also be ineligible for endorsement from the institution for top fellowships such as the Rhodes and Marshall scholarships. For the organizations to be recognized, sponsored, and use University facilities, they must be coeducational and follow a modified all-comers policy. The policy was implemented by a Title IX compliance task force to protect students from sexual assault. The new policy extends to fraternities, sororities, and "final clubs." A final club is a highly selective, esoteric upperclassmen organization and serves as the last possible organization a Harvard student may join. These organizations were historically all-male, which later fostered the organization of all-female final clubs and sororities.

At Harvard, these final clubs are antecedents of social organizations for collegiate undergraduate seniors. In 1984, Harvard attempted to pressure the clubs to adopt gender-neutral policies. This led to many organizations disaffiliating from the University and led to the formation of many sororities and all-female final clubs in the 1990s. Similarly, at Trinity College a previous 2012 edict for its fraternities and sororities to become coeducational was actually rescinded in 2015. It was felt that it would not truly achieve the sentiment of gender equity that was originally intended.

The aforementioned cases exhibit a continued historical timeline demonstrating the failed narrative of regulating fraternities and sororities that often leads to their elimination or a lack of support. Clearly, more policy does not support their existence or reduce institutional liability. This produces a conundrum regarding the best approach to coping with the fraternity/sorority "problem." The answer may lie in returning to a modified form of *in loco parentis*, by simply improving the supervision of fraternities and sororities through effective advising.

Improving Chapter Advising

The support for college fraternal organizations traditionally is facilitated in the form of leadership training as well as advising. Advising is facilitated by alumni/alumnae advisors who are approved by the national organization or from an administrator who is traditionally located in a centralized "Greek Affairs" office with other related staff or within the student activities office. Within a chapter, alumni/alumnae advisors may be an individual advisor or consist of an advisory board. It is more commonplace for a sorority than a fraternity to have an alumnae advisory board; fraternities typically have a singular advisor. NPHC and NAFLO chapters may have the local support of a graduate chapter consisting entirely of alumni/alumnae (Gregory, 2003).

Formal training regarding how to advise fraternities and sororities does not exist. Therefore, it is the opinion of the author that many chapter members and student leaders are not the beneficiary of the advisors, but are the victim of their efforts. Simply put, there are a significant number of bad advisors. On the campus side, the majority of fraternities and sororities at large universities are advised by graduate assistants who are overseen by a small, but often dedicated, staff of administrators.

At smaller institutions there may be one individual responsible for advising. The age range of these individuals is traditionally under 30; many are only a few years removed from graduate school and traditionally serve in the role less than four years (Gregory, 2003). In other circumstances the advisor may be a graduate assistant, often the same age or close to the age of traditional undergraduate students. Within the traditional national organizations or the chapter, support structures vary for advising. Sororities traditionally have an advisory board, and each has a delineation of responsibility that represents a specific functional area of the chapter such as leadership or recruitment. There appears to be greater age range and more experience within sororities. These advisory boards are also supported by traveling staff members from the inter/national headquarters who undergo extensive training. Within fraternities, support for chapters varies. Traditional fraternities have traveling staff members like sororities and traditionally have an alumni advisor. The alumni advisor appointment structure varies by organizations, but is predominantly a loosely coupled structure. Fraternity alumni advisory boards, like those found within sororities, are all too rare. In some instances, it is not uncommon, in situations where the chapter has private housing, that the local incorporated housing corporation oversees the residence assumes responsibilities for advising. NPHC and NAFLO groups are supported by a decentralized structure with volunteer-driven staff members who irregularly visit chapters. Their greatest support comes from their alumni/alumnae advisor or the local graduate chapter. Advising fraternities and sororities is most often based on little or no professional preparation.

The Council for the Advancement of Standards in Higher Education (CAS) has outlined specific criteria for advising college fraternal organizations (Council for the Advancement of Standards in Higher Education, 2015). However, it does not outline the required educational requirements or competencies. The Association of Fraternity/Sorority Advisors (AFA) has outlined several competencies (Association of Fraternity/Sorority Advisors, 2011). While these overarching standards from CAS and complementary AFA competencies for the profession of advising fraternities and sororities exist, they do not facilitate any programming to formally educate and certify advisors. It is the view of the author that students receive a disservice when it is assumed an advisor is capable just because he/she has a master's degree related to higher education administration or has graduated from college. This notion assumes that advisors will learn simply based on their experiences (Kolb, 1984). Furthermore, based on the CAS standards for higher education administration graduate programs, advising is not among the required competencies that graduates must have.

Therefore, graduate preparation does not prepare students to advise fraternities and sororities. Additionally, alumni/alumnae advisors receive little professional development or training. There is sometimes a guide or manual provided, and there may be an orientation with an inter-/national staff member about expectations, but this does not support consistent quality advising. Ignorant chapter-based advisors are dangerous since they can reinforce negative traditions such as hazing and encourage further homogeneity of membership (Kimbrough, 2003; Nuwer, 1999). This phenomenon can become a significant liability and must be addressed. Advising fraternities and sororities, in its current form, is extremely provincial and is literally "folksy." The majority of advisors draw from their undergraduate experience to inform their advising of chapters. Little evidence supports the notion that any student development or learning theory is intentionally applied in the advising of fraternity chapters (Sasso, 2008).

Instead of advising, community standards have been developed in an attempt to legitimize interactions with students. This has led to greater bureaucracy and removed the focus on developmental outcomes of students. Programs with clear measureable outcomes should be focused and facilitated to support student learning and not used to establish more administrative protocol, procedure, and policy. They should not be utilized to replace interactions with students. What would better legitimize interactions with students is not needless bureaucratic community standards programs, but further education concerning how to advise fraternities and sororities. There are bad advisors, not because they are inherently poor at facilitating their responsibilities, but because they have received no formal training. No forum for formal training currently exists that could support a structure to assist in creating fraternal advisor training or a certification process to mark successful completion. Therefore, a certification process should be established to train and educate fraternity and sorority advisors, on campus and within the chapter, to establish a consistent advising approach across all campuses.

Too few advisors are knowledgeable of best practices in advising and of the vast diversity and complexity found within fraternities and sororities. Therefore, an advisor certification process should include content such as student development theory, learning theories, effective advising approaches, contemporary issues in higher education, history of fraternal organizations, and issues specific to fraternities and sororities such as alcohol, hazing, and academic achievement. An advisor certification process would not serve as a panacea for the ills of advising fraternities and sororities, but it would help advisors navigate the complexity and ambiguity of their roles. Such a program would help to establish consistency and, if mandated for all advisors, would additionally further the fraternal movement and help to centralize the ideal that fraternal organizations are about the development of its members as students and eventually as lifelong members.

Supervision in Residential Experiences

Princeton University President Woodrow Wilson (1902–1910) and Harvard University President Abbott Lawrence Lowell (1909–1933) were two vociferous opponents of the influence of German research universities. Lowell believed that the residential experience was an integral part of undergraduate education and curriculum alone could not direct the development of students' character. Similarly, Wilson understood that a close personal relationship between student and faculty that had existed in the old-time college had been undone by the indifference of German-trained research scholars to the personal development of students. These two men, as well as many other American educators, enabled the restoration the English model. Oxford and Cambridge were again viewed as a prime example for student housing. These institutions were set up to provide opportunities for interaction among students to aid the social and intellectual development of students. As a result, the Oxford and Cambridge man seemed to display social and intellectual skills beyond those of the typical American undergraduate. Concurrent with the Oxford/Cambridge model of a residential campus and curriculum, fraternities and sororities were relied on to provide a component of these experiences as independent living groups.

Fraternities and sororities are now the largest collegiate nonprofit private housing network, valued at three billion dollars. They house over a quarter million individuals. However, the historical evolution to their formation as a private housing provider is far removed from their origins. American fraternities were created as social organizations, and they retain that characteristic to the present day. However, by the middle of the 19th century, a change occurred on the campus that caused fraternities to acquire a secondary characteristic: the fraternity house. Due to many factors and circumstances, most of them economical, a number of schools were unable to maintain housing for their students. Consequently, campuses were ringed with boarding houses where students secured their own lodging and meals. In 1846, at the University of Michigan, Chi Psi built a 20- by 14-foot log cabin in which to hold its meetings. This marks the first instance of the fraternity as a social living group and the end to it as a social outlet (Baily, 1949).

Built by the University in the woods near Ann Arbor, it was the prototype of the modern fraternity house—a place where a meeting could be held peacefully and secretly (Baily, 1949). Delta Kappa Epsilon's 1853 occupation of a cabin at Kenyon College in Gambier, Ohio, is the second freestanding fraternity hall in the country. The first known instance of fraternity ownership of real estate came when Kappa Alpha Society purchased a lot and house at Williams College in 1864. As sizes of chapters were increased, fraternities began to rent halls and houses, a few even buying them outright (Baily, 1949). Other fraternities then copied this archetype for communal housing.

The change from being a group that *met* together to being a group that *lived* together was a marker in the evolution of the men's fraternity movement. It altered the entire concept of fraternity experience. This had its own advantages and disadvantages. It strengthened the unity, discipline, activities, and friendships of its members. It also provided opportunities for these newly residential groups to become more engaged and invested within campus life. On some campuses the fraternities began fostering extracurricular activities, such as athletics, newspapers, homecoming, and school dances. Many colleges concerned themselves solely with the educational process and took no responsibility for other facets of student life. Dartmouth and Union were examples of the Oxford model that proliferated a large residential fraternity/sorority housing system.

It has been aforementioned that the transition from meeting in dormitory rooms to houses caused a need for space, which eventually caused the formation of the Fraternity Quad at Union and the formation of the Greek Row at Dartmouth as they moved from halls to houses. However, this evolution and iconic shift of the fraternity from a social outlet to a social living group naturally mirrored a larger national trend that really did originate at Dartmouth and Union. Students' reaction to the need—for meeting rooms and for living quarters—was to lease, and finally to build, their own homes. The author of the 1895 *American University Magazine* article on Dartmouth fraternities wrote:

> The idea of chapter houses as it came from other colleges was discussed by many of the chapters, and the prevalent belief was that a chapter house would tend to isolate its occupants from the rest of the college, or worse still, might create factions in college affairs. The Dartmouth man has alwlays looked with abhorrence

upon anything savoring of an aristocracy. Gradually there has come a change in the attitude of the students toward this question, not that they have weakened in principle, but it appears that the chapter house does not destroy the unity of the College. (Dartmouth, 1936, p. 30)

The move mirrored a rather national change in the meaning of fraternity/sorority life as fraternities had previously been shifting to an outlook that valued socializing more than secrecy and the fellowship of meetings more than literary aspects. The new emphasis was on the "good times" one could have in college and the associations one could make. During this period the collegiate ideal was returning after a period of "Germanification" inspired by the research university. Fraternities experienced a great growth in popularity. Dartmouth faculty member Ashton Willard observed this change in 1897, noting that, "the students who belong to these organizations have close social relationship with each other, and find it agreeable to be quartered under the same roof" (Dartmouth, 1936). Willard insightfully commented on the architectural component of this shift.

Also, campus housing during the early era of campus life left a growing number of students becoming used to living in boarding houses rather than in dormitories as more students had a greater personal wealth than in earlier periods and could afford to board in fraternity houses. The effect of the fraternity entering the housing business has been many and varied. Owning and maintaining property required the cooperation of the alumni, many of whom in the past had simply graduated and disappeared. They became involved with the management of the chapters, which indirectly benefited the colleges by keeping alumni interested and engaged in the affairs of their alma mater. Likewise, private ownership of these houses relieved many colleges and universities of the financial burden of building dormitories. Fraternities have a practical benefit of housing people when an expanding college or university cannot cope, and many institutions at this time relied on fraternities in that way.

In fact, the willingness of sororities and fraternities to assume responsibility for housing has gradually led to many arrangements on the part of the institutions, such as "leased land" agreements, whereby the school owns the land and the fraternity constructs the building. These complicated arrangements caused many tensions between fraternities and their host institution. This even happened at Dartmouth.

Its trustees saw a danger in the new houses and the potential it promised for what was happening elsewhere. They saw the existence of separate dining facilities and *de facto* private dormitories as segregating their members into cliques (Dartmouth, 1936). In 1902, they decided, in the "interest of democracy," that no more than fourteen members could live in a fraternity and that no house could have a dining facility (Dartmouth). These rules made their way into the deeds for Webster Avenue properties that the school sold to many of the fraternities (Dartmouth). This later caused much tension between students and the administration, which led to several food fights involving frozen potatoes and tomatoes (Huffcut, 1899). While Dartmouth did not truly accept fraternity houses as Union embraced them so early on, some schools approved of such separation. However, they did provide the foundation for what the modern conception a Fraternity Quad or a Greek Row. This helped position the men's collegiate fraternity as an independent social living group. This legacy is the true impact of the fraternity/sorority systems at Dartmouth and Union.

Shortly after 1925, Stanford University allowed fraternities to build or purchase houses around the campus in order to facilitate the original idea of campus planner Frederick Law Olmsted's for a cottage system modeled after Dartmouth (Hering, 1925). Though it came to fruition in one form with fraternities, Olmsted's ideal was a domestically scaled residence where small number of students could live and dine together in familial camaraderie (Hering). By 1915, approximately 600 chapters owned houses of such descriptions, mostly private dwellings adapted to their use (Brown, 1915). It is estimated that 60 to 70 percent of fraternities lived in their own houses—either leased or owned (Brown). The rest had lodges, suites, or rented meeting rooms. A great boom in fraternity construction had swept the country in the first quarter century of the 20th century (Baily, 1949). Millions of dollars had been invested by the fraternities in their buildings and their furnishings—only to be phased out on many campuses.

Opponents of fraternity/sorority life often argue that another type of student organization will arise in place of fraternities and sororities. The proliferation of fraternity housing gave way to the larger sorority community with the advent of coeducation in the 1950s and 1960s. However, its necessity for housing has outlived its purpose as many colleges support their existence only for tradition. They are merely an artifact of a past existence as many colleges have attempted to eliminate or reduce their influence. Whether a new residential model is to replace the fraternity and sorority remains an enigma.

For over about a century, visitors to Union College stood at its gates and were greeted by three regal mansions. The houses were occupied by fraternities; their presence was a symbol of the centrality of fraternity/sorority organizations. However, they have been reframed into a residential model inspired by the Greek goodness of Wisdom, Minerva.

Minerva housing at Union College has replaced the three former fraternity/sorority mansions with an additional four other houses and relocated the fraternities to other residences. In Minerva housing, incoming first-year students are placed into a first-year preceptorial class, which is connected to their Minerva House assignment. Students are also connected to a faculty member as these houses serve as living-learning communities as well. Each house is also governed independently and is given a programming budget. Students are encouraged to develop a governance structure that is unique in character and spirit. Each House Council is led by a House Council chair and a residential upperclassman mentor.

While Minerva housing has failed to produce the alternative that the college administration sought, it has allowed for students to create a different sense of community outside of the one created by members of fraternities and sororities. Additional support now exists for the proliferation of theme houses, Minervas, and other alternative fraternity/sorority institutions. This approach will ideally starve fraternities and sororities of potential new members, pushing the remaining ones off-campus. This has begun to happen in a subtle fashion.

Toward a Mutable Administrative Approach

The relationship statements set forth in broad terms the mutual responsibility of the institution and its recognized fraternity and sorority chapters. This approach led to even more serious liability concerns for institutions that poorly implemented them. What has typically worked is the development of fraternity/sorority standards programs that are effective in aligning the institution's mission with that of the fraternity/sorority system. This closes the gap that *A Call for Values Congruence* (2003) claims had existed. Kohlberg (1984) echoed this notion when he stated that "right action tends to be defined in terms of general individual rights and standards that have been critically examined and agreed upon by the whole society" (p. 39). Moreover, the current nature of standards programs and advising support for fraternities and sororities remains somewhat provincial. Measuring learning outcomes, the application of a developmental approach, and embedding a theoretical framework should be the next evolution of the traditional standards programs for a fraternity/sorority community. If this cannot be accomplished, then colleges and universities should simply consider phasing out their existence.

It is additionally necessary to have learning outcomes rooted in student development theory. These theories exist to support the notion that the undergraduate experience facilitates cognitive, identity, and behavioral change through growth. They provide a framework by which to author learning outcomes and serve as a philosophical basis for a theory of change for an overall evaluation plan. For example, one could easily utilize Magolda's (2004) Self-Authorship Theory. Learning outcomes could be framed around the developmental areas of epistemological, interpersonal, and intrapersonal development. These outcomes would address the questions of: (1) how do I know; (2) who am I; and (3) how do I want to construct relationships with others (Magolda, 2004). A learning outcome might be written as, "Students will self-author their own narrative through participation in the summer fraternity/sorority retreat as measured by results of XXX survey."

Fraternity/sorority professionals serve as champions and advocates for both the fraternal movement and the undergraduate experience involving fraternities and sororities. Therefore, it is necessary to conceptualize that it is a part of the professional responsibility to advance this learning that has been documented through research and to further its impact (Keeling, 2004; Sandeen & Barr, 2006). The method by which this advocacy of the advancement of learning can be accomplished is through intentionally creating conditions that support and facilitate learning (Schuh & Upcraft, 2001). This means that as educators it is necessary to facilitate programs that engage these students across the duration of their experience, are grounded in student development theory, and include learning outcomes connected to assessments (Perlow, 2007; Strayhorn & Colvin, 2006; Whipple & Sullivan, 1998). Therefore, it is necessary to develop student learning outcomes and assessment measures, analyze results, and then share results to encourage continuous improvement and enhance future learning (Green, Jones, & Aloi, 2008). These assessments should be a piece of the larger evaluation of the fraternity/sorority advising program.

It is important that fraternity/sorority professionals consider the greater impact the fraternal movement has on the campus community through engagement. Many times this is misinterpreted as involvement. Remember that engagement is much broader than involvement, and it is easy to confuse the two concepts. Engagement builds on involvement theory (Astin, 1993). Involvement is simply a binary measure of whether or not a student is involved in a club, organization, or university activity (Astin, 1993). Engagement is a larger, broader concept that: (1) measures the amount of time and effort students expend for their academic pursuits and activities that facilitate student success; and (2) how the institution or in this case, fraternity/sorority life office, organizes learning opportunities to facilitate student involvement in these activities that will create student success (Wolf-Wendel, Ward, & Kinzie, 2009).

Therefore, measures of determining how many members are in other clubs are only nominally addressing the educational impact that the fraternity/sorority experience has across the institution and on its members. They measure only involvement. Fraternity/sorority professionals should consider measuring engagement by determining participation rates in clubs, learning communities, signature programs within the division of student affairs, undergraduate research, and other important factors. This quantitative approach determines if the students' fraternal membership helps contribute to their involvement in these activities, and how the fraternity/sorority life office contributed to this engagement of fraternity/sorority students in broader activities across the institution. Remember that retention, persistence, and graduation are not the same. Retention is the capacity of the institution to facilitate support services and programs that ensure students remain enrolled. Persistence is the capacity of the student to interface and move through her undergraduate degree and experience. Graduation is when a student completes the duration of her undergraduate experience and degree. Therefore, fraternity/sorority advisors should simply consider partnering with the institutional research office on their campus to track the persistence of students to determine if their fraternal membership experience potentially has an impact on retention and graduation. Additionally, it would be advisable to consider the potential confounding variable of membership retention. It is easy to track the retention of membership by verifying its authenticity and examining its consistency to determine the retention of membership across the duration of the student experience. Reconsider the current definition of academic standards. Currently, the best practice is to simply calculate the mean grade point average (GPA) for the chapter and the differences between new members and active members. However, one can determine the greater impact of membership on academics by examining the individual change over time for each student as well as the impact on the cumulative GPA. Given the variability over time of GPA by semester, it also necessary to measure individual and chapter GPA over an academic year rather than one semester.

Fraternity/sorority advisors and campuses should work to frame their programs on student learning outcomes. Without this grounding, administrators may be merely encouraging programming and utilizing standards programs as a locus of control. However, the question remains: what are students gaining from these programs? Incorporating tenets of fundamental student development theories would help frame desired learning outcomes embedded in a standards program. Documenting learning outcomes from participation would help address relevancy questions raised by the Franklin Square Group (2003).

Conclusion

It is acknowledged that the recommended structure is a radical departure from the current social status composition ceded to alcohol. The "ceded to alcohol" phrase seems strange—what is its meaning for traditional fraternities and sororities. Potentially adapting the structure from the residential fraternities and sororities may result in stronger student development outcomes if the housing component is reduced in emphasis. Identity and lesser conformity among members may occur. Administratively, they would be easier to manage given the smaller chapter sizes, resulting in the capacity to refocus some human capital to developing programmatic support structures to aid in the development of individual fraternity and sorority members. Students will potentially be the beneficiaries of a more intimate experience and greater opportunity for leadership involvement, and perhaps a more welcoming environment in which students can explore and better define them within the academic space of the university. This change may once again shift the pendulum toward support.

References

Association of Fraternity/Sorority Advisors. (2011). *Core competencies for excellence in the profession* (3rd ed.). Indianapolis, IN: Author.

Astin, A. (1993). *What matters in college: Four critical years revisited.* San Francisco, CA: Jossey-Bass.

Baily, H. J. (Ed.). (1949). *Baird's manual of American college fraternities.* Menasha, WI: The Collegiate Press.

Brown, J. T. (Ed.). (1915). *Baird's manual of American college fraternities.* New York, NY: Author.

Council for the Advancement of Standards in Higher Education. (2015). *CAS professional standards for higher education* (9th ed.). Washington, DC: Author.

Dartmouth College. (1936). *Survey of the social life in Dartmouth college: Fraternities.* Hanover, NH: Dartmouth College Publications.

Franklin Square Group. (2003). *A call for values congruence.* Carmel, IN: Association of Fraternity Advisors.

Green, A. S., Jones, E., & Aloi, S. (2008). An exploration of high-quality student affairs learning outcomes and assessment practices. *NASPA Journal, 45,* 133–157.

Gregory, D. E. (2003). *The administration of fraternal organizations on North American campuses: A pattern for the new millennium.* St. Johns, FL: College Administration Publications.

Gulland, D., & Powell, M. (1989). *Colleges, fraternities, and sororities. A white paper on tort liability issues.* Washington, DC: American Council on Education.

Harvey, J. (1990). Fraternities and the constitution: University-imposed relationship statements may violate student associational rights. *Journal of College & University Law, 17*, 11–42.

Hering, O. (1925). *Designing and building the chapter house.* Minneapolis, MN: Minnesota University Press.

Huffcut, E. W. (1899). *The shield of theta delta chi.* New York, NY: Author.

Kaplin, W. A., & Lee, B. A. (2014). *The law of higher education: A comprehensive guide to legal implications of administrative decision making* (5th ed.). San Francisco, CA: Jossey-Bass.

Keeling, R. P. (Ed.). (2004). *Learning reconsidered: A campus-wide focus on the student experience.* Washington, DC: NASPA: Student Affairs Administrators in Higher Education and ACPA—College Student Educators International.

Kimbrough, W. M. (2003). *Black Greek 101: The culture, customs, and challenges of Black fraternities and sororities.* Madison, NJ: Fairleigh Dickinson University Press.

Kolb, D. A. (1984). *Experiential learning: Experience as the source of learning and development.* Englewood Cliffs, NJ: Prentice Hall.

Kohlberg, L. (1984). *The psychology of moral development: The nature and validity of moral stages.* San Francisco: Harper & Row.

Magolda, M. B. (2004). *Making their own way.* Sterling, VA: Stylus.

Nuwer, H. (1999). *Wrongs of passage: Fraternities, sororities, hazing, and binge drinking.* Bloomington, IN: Indiana University Press.

Sandeen, A., & Barr, M.J. (2006). *Critical issues for student affairs: Challenges and opportunities.* San Francisco, CA: Jossey-Bass.

Perlow, E. (2007, Summer). Refresh, reframe, refocus: Using assessment as an improvement framework. *Perspectives, 6*(2), 13–16.

Sasso, P. A. (2008). From administrator to educator: Facilitating student learning in Greek affairs practice (Unpublished master's thesis). University of Rochester, Rochester, NY.

Sasso, P. A. (2015). White boy wasted: Compensatory masculinities in fraternity men. *Oracle: The Research Journal of the Association of Fraternity/Sorority Advisors, 10*(1), 14–30.

Sasso, P. A. (2016). Towards a more coherent typology of Greek standards programs: A content analysis. *Best of Issue Celebrating 10 Years of Oracle: The Research Journal of the Association of Fraternity/Sorority Advisors, 1*(1), 56–76. (Reprinted from *Oracle: The Research Journal of the Association of Fraternity/Sorority Advisors, 6*(3), 54–75).

Sasso, P. A., & Schwitzer, A. M. (2016). Social desirability and expectations of alcohol in fraternity members. *Oracle: The Research Journal of the Association of Fraternity/Sorority Advisors, 10*(2), 17–35.

Schuh, J. H., & Upcraft, M. L. (2001). *Assessment practice in student affairs: An applications manual.* San Francisco, CA: Jossey-Bass.

Strayhorn, T. L., & Colvin, A. J. (2006). Assessing student learning and development in fraternity and sorority affairs. *Oracle: The Research Journal of the Association of Fraternity Advisors, 2*(2), 95–107.

Trowbridge, A. B. (1926). *Kappa alpha record: 1825-1925.* New York, NY: Publisher's Printing Co.

Whipple, E. G., & Sullivan, E. G. (1998). Greeks as communities of learners. In E. G. Whipple (Ed.), *New challenges for Greek letter organizations: Transforming fraternities and sororities into learning communities* (pp. 87–94). New Directions for Student Services, No. 81. San Francisco, CA: Jossey-Bass.

Wolf-Wendel, L., Ward, K., & Kinzie, J. (2009). A tangled web of terms: The overlap and unique contribution of involvement, engagement, and integration to understanding college student success. *Journal of College Student Development, 50,* 407–428.

Part Sixteen: Can College Athletics and Academics Coexist?

In "Are Collegiate Athletics Necessary in Contemporary Higher Education," Curtis M. Clock and Thalia M. Mulvihill argue that athletics and academics can ideally coexist despite some claims to the contrary. They view athletics as important to the mission of the university by providing a broad historical account of intercollegiate athletics and input from both student-athletes and nonathlete students. Presenting a rich review of the literature, Clock and Mulvihill also discuss such issues as role conflicts, skill-building sets in athletics as preparation for postcollege careers, stereotypes about "jocks" and gender in sports, and the opportunities that athletics allow underrepresented groups in society.

In "Academics and Athletics: Struggles and Strategies in the Pursuit of (A) Grades and (A) Games," Sally Dear-Healey shares her personal experiences as a whistleblower in the basketball scandal at Binghamton University in upstate New York. She profiles a hierarchical structure that perpetuates itself through recruitment pipelines used to entice teens who have "big dreams of playing ball." They are often academically unprepared, and then tracked through a college education that is subpar. Dear-Healey cites several studies and National Collegiate Athletic Association (NCAA) commission reports that suggest the need to redirect the focus of college athletics toward the primary academic mission of the university. She concludes that it is the collective responsibility of the professoriate to be guardians of the curriculum against transgressions that demean students' learning needs.

31. Are Collegiate Athletics Necessary in Contemporary Higher Education?

Curtis M. Clock and Thalia M. Mulvihill

The growing often vitriolic debate over whether or not collegiate athletics is necessary within contemporary higher education has reached a crescendo. Athletics Departments are increasingly requiring higher percentages of the overall university budget and institutions of higher education are under intense scrutiny to produce winning teams, model student-athletes, and Title IX compliant programs. And groundbreaking court cases such as *O'Bannon v. National Collegiate Athletics Association, 2009* and *EA Sports and the Commonwealth of Pennsylvania v. NCAA, 2013* served as catalysts for a wholesale reexamination of the relationship between higher education and athletics. At the same time, athletics is a key part of the overall strategic planning for most institutions, and is used to help generate broad public interest and involvement with higher education. Athletics represents a primary reason many donors decide to contribute time and money.

This chapter examines why collegiate athletics remains an integral part of the college experience, even within this context, and puts forth an argument for continued inclusion of collegiate athletics as part of the overall mission of higher education. Specifically, the authors argue that collegiate athletics contributes to, more than it hinders, the overall mission of higher education within a democratic society. Two types of student perspectives will be used to analyze and bring forward a more nuanced understanding of the tenets of the argument, and student points-of-view (athletes and nonathletes) also figure prominently within the examination of this issue.

Athletics Today

Over the years, scholars have continued to question whether or not intercollegiate athletics is contradictory to the mission of higher education (Elinson, 2013; McCormick & McCormick, 2006; Sack & Staurowsky, 1998; Sperber, 1990, 2000; Zimbalist, 1999). Despite the mixed reception of intercollegiate athletics today and throughout its history, it remains an essential component of the U.S. campus (Jayakumar & Comeaux, 2016). Athletics can provide opportunities normally outside the reach of disadvantaged youth, instill important values, and provide entertainment and publicity to supporters of the institution (Sylwester & Witosky, 2004). Students who choose to participate in intercollegiate athletics can expect to enjoy several social and academic benefits (Brown, Brown, Jackson, Sellers, & Manuel, 2003; Ryan, 1989; Wolf-Wendell, Toma, & Worphew, 2001). For example, participation can have positive impacts on students' level of self-esteem, persistence, and college satisfaction (Brown et al., 2003; Pascarella, Edison, Hagedorn, Nora, & Terenzini, 1996; Taylor, 1995; Wolf-Wendell et al., 2001). While the authors of this chapter support the continued inclusion of athletics within higher education, we recognize a few critical issues in need of reexamination, which we intend to explain through the use of two student perspectives.

The National Collegiate Athletics Association (NCAA) has been scrutinized for its involvement and decision making within the realm of collegiate athletics. A recent landmark decision, in the antitrust class action case of *O'Bannon v. NCAA and EA Sports*, illustrates some of the contemporary issues. In this case, Ed O'Bannon, former All-American student-athlete at UCLA, found that an avatar of himself in a video game resembled his likeness so exactly (including his jersey number) that he decided to mount a legal challenge. Having waived his right to compensation as a requirement to participate in the NCAA, he was never compensated for the use of his image in the game—usage for which he never provided permission. Shortly after, O'Bannon sought out a suit against the NCAA and EA Sports for their use of his likeness without his permission. The suit claimed that upon graduation student-athletes ought to be financially compensated for when the NCAA uses their images. This litigation climbed to the 9th District Court of Appeals, initially claiming a small victory in that student-athletes could be paid $5,000 in deferred money; but after the NCAA appealed, this ruling was thrown out because it was not as restrictive as the NCAA's current regulations.

Student-athletes can now be compensated with a cost of attendance stipend of up to $5,000 because it is education based. However, that may change. On March 15, 2016, O'Bannon's attorneys asked the U.S. Supreme

Court (USSC) to hear this case. The request comes at an interesting time as the USSC has one seat vacant due to the February 13, 2016 death of USSC Justice Antonin Scalia, and the decision of whether or not this case will be taken up by the USSC cannot be predicted.

The NCAA's contention that student-athletes remain amateurs, and therefore not financially compensated, is the crux for appealing the court's decision (Sheetz, 2016). The competing argument recognizes that college sports is an 11 billion dollar sports industry that uses student-athletes as the generators of that money, yet student-athletes are never financially compensated (Edelman, 2013). In some respect, this decision could permanently reshape the bonds between collegiate athletics and colleges if the USSC decides to hear the case and further decides that the NCAA is violating section one of the Sherman Antitrust Act. The USSC could change the landscape of collegiate athletics as conferences might dissolve and reform as new entities; television rights and contracts would need to be redrawn. As major organizational bodies prepare for potential outcomes, student-athletes look on, wondering how this will affect their future. The arguments inherent within this piece of litigation help shed light on one aspect of the climate within collegiate athletics today. They help contextualize the broader discussion about the ongoing inclusion of athletics within the mission of higher education. We continue our examination of this issue, "Are Collegiate Athletics Necessary in Contemporary Higher Education?" by first providing a brief historical overview, then by unpacking the arguments surrounding the issue, and then offering some closing thoughts.

Historical Overview

Athletics, as we know them today, has seemingly been with us for as long as we can remember; but in reality, it is a relatively young tradition. The first form of organized physical activity was instituted around 1830 when institutions such as Yale, Harvard, Amherst, Williams, Brown, Virginia, the College of Charleston (South Carolina), and Dartmouth opened gymnasiums (Lewis, 1970). However, these gymnasiums were not created with the intent to create competitive sports; they were built to help facilitate the health of their students and lessen some of the focus placed upon them by their academics. During this period in higher education, students sought out to rebel against those with authority over them, namely their faculty, in any way possible. By creating gymnasiums, it was thought that physical activity would eliminate excess energy they might have. In many ways it was designed as a behavior-management strategy.

With the introduction of the gymnasiums came further discourse and arguments for and against involving women in any kind of physical activity surfaced. Formal higher education for women was growing in acceptance only when it was for the purpose of training teachers. By the early 19th century, a strong case was made for the inclusion of physical activity in the curriculum to maintain a sound body and mind. For example, Emma Hart-Willard [1787–1870], founder of the Troy Seminary Academy; Catherine Beecher [1800–1878], founder of Hartford Female Seminary; and Mary Lyon [1797–1849], founder of Mount Holyoke Seminary, each established institutions of higher education to prepare women to be teachers that placed physical education as a required part of the curriculum (Mulvihill, 2002). These curriculum developments were occurring alongside vigorous debates about the effects of physical activity on a woman's body. These debates were renewed by Dr. Edward Clarke, who instilled a sense of fear in the general public that increased physical activity would lessen a woman's ability to reproduce (Clarke, 1874). By the mid-19th century, the number of women in physical education programs preparing students to be high school teachers and university professors began to grow, enhancing the field of women's health and physiology.

By the 1840s, other sports began to develop for the purpose of entertainment with the introduction of football, baseball, cricket, and others; but each sport had infrequent schedules and no formal associations had yet been established (Lewis, 1970). It was not until the 1852 Yale and Harvard boating competition that competitive sports would become part of the college experience. These events generated broad public interest and soon became part of the overall strategic planning for institutions of higher education.

19th- and 20th-Century Expansion

During the 1890s and early 1900s, women's physical education had turned its focus from building muscular strength to games and other structured activities to focus on the whole body (Mulvihill, 2002). This was viewed by some as a departure from the traditional program's rigor and academic seriousness and drew harsh criticism from some. However, this change was gathering national attention as professional organizations of physical education were gaining strength and creating an agenda on how curricula ought to be structured. "A sport for every girl" and "every girl in a sport" represented the stance of the Committee on Women's Athletics and the National Section of Women's Athletics. By the 1920s and 1930s, arguments were made that sports should be available for all girls and women, not just a select few who would compete among themselves. Despite these positive changes, women physical educators understood the power of organization and sought to strengthen their standing during the 1930s and 1940s (Mulvihill, 2011). By 1972, athletics grew closer to being equitable for both sexes with the passage of Title IX, which prohibited exclusion of participation in educational programs or activities that received federal financial aid funding on the basis of sex (Hoffman, 2011).

As modern athletics began to burgeon following the first intercollegiate football contest in American history in 1869 between Rutgers and Princeton, inconsistencies regarding rules of each sport, and its growing commercialization, incited concern for more institutional control (Crowley, 2006). After several failed attempts at establishing a regulatory body, President Theodore Roosevelt called for the formation of a joint committee. In 1906, the Intercollegiate Athletic Association of the United States was born and in 1910 was renamed the NCAA. The NCAA went forward without any enforcement or regulatory role until 1951, when Walter Byers was named the first Executive Director of the NCAA and led the negotiation of the NCAA's first contract deal for televised football estimated to be over one million dollars (Smith, 2000).

Collegiate women saw the 1971 creation of The Association of Intercollegiate Athletics for Women (AIAW), which started with 280 institutional members and held the first national tournaments for women's collegiate athletics in 1972. After the passage of Title IX, the NCAA received advice from legal counsel to rescind its rule prohibiting female student-athletes from participating in NCAA events. Yet, it was not until 1981 when the NCAA created a full governance plan for female collegiate athletics, including allocating positions for women on the NCAA Council. The NCAA was a robust competitor for the AIAW because of its wealth and political influence and its storied history (Bell, 2008).

Competition between the two organizations culminated in the eventual collapse of the AIAW when the NCAA decided to introduce women's championships for intercollegiate by offering interested institutions a proposition. The NCAA proposition included: "(a) pay all expenses for teams competing in a national championship, (b) charge no additional membership fees for schools to add women's programs, (c) create financial aid, recruitment, and eligibility rules that were the same for women as for men, and finally, (d) guarantee women more television coverage" (p. 5). On June 30, 1982, the AIAW was forced to cease operations because it could not compete with the NCAA proposition in place, which caused the AIAW the loss of membership, income, championship sponsorship, and media rights (Festle, 1996). As a last effort, the AIAW sued the NCAA for allegedly violating the Sherman

Anti-Trust Act. This suit was unsuccessful because the courts ruled the market open for competition with respect to women's athletics, thereby no antitrust laws had been violated (Schubert, Schubert, & Schubert-Madsen, 1991).

The collegiate athletics industry and the NCAA have grown tremendously in the past 116 years, with nearly 350 member schools in Division I athletics and operating as an 11 billion dollar industry. Collegiate athletics has provided a myriad of opportunities for students, both student-athletes as well as student-fans, including providing scholarship monies and creating environments for camaraderie and institutional pride.

Two Types of Student Perspectives

As mentioned previously, we selected two types of student perspectives to assist with a more nuanced examination of the issue, "Are Collegiate Athletics Necessary in Contemporary Higher Education?" as student perspectives are often absent from the literature surrounding college athletics. First, we will analyze this issue from the perspective of a student-athlete by examining their weekly struggles as a student-athlete and the barriers that they must overcome to enjoy the vast amount of rewards that the public often believes they are already enjoying. Following this analysis, the perspective of a nonathlete, full-time equivalent (FTE) student will also be analyzed. These perspectives will provide readers with a more nuanced understanding for why a strong argument can be made in favor of the necessary inclusion of collegiate athletics in contemporary higher education.

Student-Athletes

Today critics of intercollegiate athletics cite its ballooning budget as the reason for diverting tangible resources away from the "real" mission of higher education, specifically degree-attainment. However, a subpopulation exists that is not often examined, namely student-athletes who fuel the machine that is collegiate athletics. For the purposes of this examination, we will focus on Division I student-athletes.

Scholarships, Jobs, and Pay

High school students engaged in athletics seeking a college education are typically interested in an athletic scholarship. For many students identified as being in a lower socioeconomic status (SES), including high percentages of students of color, securing some form of scholarship is perceived as the only way to finance college. According to the NCAA, 53% of student-athletes in Division I schools receive some level of aid, which could range from 1 dollar all the way to full tuition coverage (NCAA, 2014). This is not to say that obtaining a scholarship in any form is easy. Because Division I institutions manage larger budgets and have larger overall programs, they also attract the most talented student-athletes vying for a limited amount of scholarships. Additionally, once a student-athlete obtains a scholarship, it is far from secure as injury or athletic performance may, in some cases, cause student-athletes to lose their scholarship.

Assuming that a student-athlete is able to stay healthy through her entire college career and maintain her athletic performance, she also has numerous other barriers to overcome. Wolverton (2008) suggests that student-athletes spend at least 40 hours per week on sports-related activities consisting of practice and traveling, which does not include additional conditioning hours for physical injuries. Being a FTE student has traditionally been likened to a full-time job as students will attend class roughly for 15 hours per week, and they would need to study at least 1–3 hours per week for each credit hour they take. If we consider the perspective of the student-athlete, she is essentially working two full-time jobs. A sample student-athlete schedule has been included in Table 31.1 to provide further insight into her extremely active schedule.

Role Conflict and Cognitive Dissonance

Adler and Adler (1991) found that male athletes from revenue-producing programs, with all of the institutional attention placed on them, enter college with feelings of optimism and pragmatism about their academics, but many quickly devalue classroom activities as soon as their second semester because of the demands of their sports programs. To eliminate internal role conflict (which is also a psychological phenomenon called cognitive dissonance) many athletes will change their behavior to match commitments (Aaronson, 1968; Bem, 1967). Student-athletes who will likely experience cognitive dissonance are those that are purely committed to their academics (Snyder, 1985). Conversely, the pure athlete will have minimal interest in academics, which will lead to little or no cognitive dissonance. Ideally, a student-athlete would balance the two roles, which would reflect a high level of commitment to both athletics and academics. Achieving this balance is difficult but possible; if student-athletes make the right choices, they will likely succeed in both roles (Jayakumar & Comeaux, 2016). While there is a real issue with underpreparedness that puts student-athletes at a disadvantage, what is often forgotten is how difficult it can be to strike a balance between the role of being a student and the role of being an athlete (Comeaux & Harrison, 2011). Because of the immense difficulty of managing this balancing act, support services primarily focus on academic scheduling, academic tutoring, and time management (Comeaux, 2010b; Shriberg & Brodzinski, 1984). Understanding this information and how educational environments can contribute to resolving cognitive dissonance is a crucial piece to improving academic success and graduation rates of student-athletes (Jayakumar & Comeaux, 2016).

Table 31.1. Representative Example of a Student-Athlete's Daily Schedule.

Time	Monday	Tuesday	Wednesday	Thursday	Friday
6:00 a.m.	Conditioning	Conditioning	Conditioning	Conditioning	Conditioning
7:00 a.m.	Conditioning	Conditioning	Conditioning	Conditioning	Conditioning
8:00 a.m.	Math	Biology	Math	Biology	Math
9:00 a.m.	English	Biology	English	Biology	English
10:00 a.m.	Psychology	History	Psychology	History	Psychology
11:00 a.m.					
12:00 a.m.					
1:00 p.m.	Treatment	Treatment	Treatment	Treatment	Treatment
2:00 p.m.	Practice	Practice	Practice	Practice	Practice
3:00 p.m.	Practice	Practice	Practice	Practice	Practice
4:00 p.m.	Practice	Practice	Practice	Practice	Practice
5:00 p.m.	Practice	Practice	Practice	Practice	Practice
6:00 p.m.	Practice	Practice	Practice	Practice	Practice
7:00 p.m.	Study Tables	Study Tables	Study Tables	Study Tables	Study Tables
8:00 p.m.					
9:00 p.m.					
10:00 p.m.–6:00 a.m.	Sleep	Sleep	Sleep	Sleep	Sleep

The pay-for-play arguments have been ongoing. Opponents cite that student-athletes knew about the commitments when they decided to play sports at the collegiate level; however, a fundamental error exists in this retort. For a FTE student, she can supplement her education by seeking academic scholarships, which in many cases are just as competitive as athletic scholarships; but in contrast to student-athletes, FTE students can obtain a job. For the student-athlete who plays a sport to provide financial support for her education, there is no time available to obtain a job to supplement anything. This means no money for gas to go on the weekends to see family, no money for an extra snack or drink after practice if it is outside of the provided meal time, and finally, no extra money for her own hobbies (e.g., going to the movies or dinner). Controlling for the true cost of attendance has assisted with this to some extent, but issues still exist with respect to the stipend amount that students receive as a direct result of the O'Bannon decision.

The "Dumb Jock" Stereotype

Student-athletes must also navigate through several vicious stereotypes in college, and the "dumb jock" stereotype is the most prevalent. Evidence exists demonstrating that faculty hold more prejudicial attitudes toward male and female student-athletes than their nonathlete peers (Baucom & Lantz, 2001; Comeaux, 2011; Engstrom, Sedlacek, & McEwen, 1995). For example, Engstrom et al. (1995) note that faculty expressed a degree of astonishment when male student-athletes, from revenue-producing sports, received an "A" in their class. They were also more likely to display negative attitudes toward student-athletes receiving specialized academic tutorial services (Comeaux, 2012). Even though faculty–student interaction remains central to student success in college, student-athletes face a complex dynamic in developing relationships with faculty (Kuh, 2001).

Scott, Paskus, Miranda, Petr, and McArdle (2008) suggest that "as new data are becoming available it is incumbent upon research in this field to challenge traditional assumptions that often go untested within college athletics" (p. 224). These assumptions that are made by faculty, staff, students, and observers from outside the institution can quickly transition to stereotypes if data are not analyzed and reported out regarding how student-athletes perform academically. For example, it was once believed that student-athletes could benefit from longer seasons of play and more structured practice time; but data did not support this (Milton, Freeman, &Williamson, 2012). Additionally, findings by Sellers (1992) demonstrate that academic success (a student-athlete's GPA) is not correlated to motivation, which was measured by hours spent studying and the desire to obtain a degree. By unpacking the more widely held stereotypes regarding student-athletes, readers can develop a better understanding of the perspectives of student-athletes and the contextual barriers they must navigate.

Racially Charged Stereotypes about Student-Athletes

Black male student-athletes at Division I schools often must endure the most demeaning and deep-rooted racial stereotypes (Comeaux, 2010a; Edwards, 1984; Harrison, 1998; Johnson, Hallinan, & Westerfield, 1999; Sailes, 1993; Simons, Bosworth, Fujita, & Jensen, 2007; Singer, 2005). Comeaux (2010a) examines faculty perceptions of White and Black student-athletes at a Division I institution and finds that some White faculty utilized "racial coding," which was an effort crafted to not arouse suspicions of racism. Similar to racial coding, many Black student-athletes also experience micro-aggressions. Racial microaggressions are defined by Solorzano, Ceja, and Yosso (2000) as "subtle insults (verbal, nonverbal, and/or visual) directed toward people of color, often automatically or unconsciously" (p. 60). While offenders may be completely unaware of their subtle racial epithets, they can be destructive to the victim's self-esteem and feeling of comfort. Unfortunately, microaggressions and stereotypes extend beyond faculty as Sailes (1993) notes that White and male students believe African-American student-athletes to be unprepared for academic work in college, and not as intelligent, nor receive grades as high as White student-athletes. As one can plainly see, the stereotypes, microaggressions, and outright racism that Division I student-athletes face have been long-standing and detrimental. The nature of these racial stereotypes can cause harmful damage to a student's psyche and cause him or her to lose focus as she balances the roles of being a student and an athlete.

Gender-Based Stereotypes

Since their inception, sports have widely been considered a space created by men for men (Fink, 2008; Hartmann-Tews, & Pfister 2003; Hoeber, 2007; Shaw & Hoeber, 2003). Despite the gendered legacy of sport, women's athletics have made tremendous strides since Title IX and today women constitute approximately 40 percent of all sports participants (Women's Sports Foundation, 2016). Yet, women still experience inequities from the sports media who often describe them by their role as a mother or wife rather than by their athletic ability (Kane & Buysse, 2005; Kane & Lenskyj, 1998). Additionally, many female athletes immediately have their sexual orientation called into question because of the prevailing stereotype, which often results in them being labeled as a lesbian (Griffin, 1998). More recently, the NCAA has been actively engaged in ensuring a safe climate for students who identify as transgender. In 2011, the NCAA's office of inclusion released guidelines on how to best provide access that is fair, legal, and respectful of students who identify as transgender (Griffin & Carroll, 2011). Among these guidelines exist restrictions on which student-athletes undergoing treatment or not, trans males (female to male) and trans females (male to female), may be permitted to participate on men's, women's, or either athletic team. While there is a considerable amount of progress yet to be made, the NCAA has demonstrated a step forward in understanding the complex narrative of gender and collegiate athletics

Why Do Student-Athletes Play?

For some students hoping to go to college, the determining factor is their success in sports. Not only would they need to be successful, but they would also need to secure an athletic scholarship, which can be rare even for the highest caliber of athletes. Full- ride scholarships exist only in a few sports: football, men's and women's basketball, gymnastics, volleyball, golf, track and field, and tennis. Approximately 2% of high school athletes receive an athletic scholarship from an NCAA school, which averages $11,000 (O'Shaughnessy, 2012). Despite the scarcity of these scholarships for students from lower SES, these scholarships can be the determining factor between going to college or not. With the difficulties that student-athletes face in the college arena, one might logically wonder why they would willingly subject themselves to potentially damaging stereotypes and an extremely hectic schedule that has the potential to endanger their academics.

There are a few crucial reasons as to why, year after year, student-athletes continue to suit up. Many students from a lower SES perceive that an athletic scholarship is their only opportunity to earn a degree. Without it, they would most likely enter the workforce immediately after high school or perhaps attend a community college that has an athletic program. Additionally, many students choose to initially pursue athletics at the college level for social reasons, so they have the opportunity to make new friends or stay in touch with old friends that enjoy similar activities. By default, socialization evolves into the camaraderie aspect of sports, which is the other crucial reason student-athletes choose to continue sports in college. Student-athletes enjoy several intangible benefits from working together with their team, including developing a set of skills that are highly coveted by employers when these student-athletes transition from college to the workforce.

Student-Athlete Characteristics in the Workforce

Participation in collegiate athletics became associated with leadership development when a sociologist observed the ability of sports to develop moral authority and exemplary characteristics as a means of proving themselves by displaying courage, teamwork, and team spirit (Armstrong, 1984), eventually giving rise to the aphorism, "sports build character" (Sage, 1998). In a recent study, Chaflin, Weight, Osborne, and Johnson (2015) recognize a gap in the literature regarding outcomes of participating in athletics related to the job search. This study focused on two companies (www.careerathletes.com and Game Theory Group) whose mission was to connect former student-athletes to companies who hire former student-athletes to determine what characteristics employers are searching for in new student-athlete graduates. The population used in this study was not meant to reflect the entire corporate population hiring new graduates, but rather to reflect companies that have already expressed an interest in targeting new student-athlete graduates. The results of their study suggest that there are direct dispositional characteristics associated with participating in athletics that employers seek to maximize by targeting new student-athlete graduates such as "competitiveness, goal-orientation, ability to handle pressure, strong work ethic, confidence, coachability, ability to work with others, self-motivation, mental toughness, and time management skills to these athletes" (p. 15). This study supports existing research that participating in intercollegiate athletics can develop these skills (Duderstadt, 2009; Henderson, Olbrecht, & Polachek, 2006; Long & Caudill, 1991; Ryan, 1989; Soshnick, 2013; Williams, 2013). While these employers would desire a team captain or an All-American more than an individual with just membership on an athletic team, participation in athletics was valued higher by employers than any other campus leadership position other than vocational experience (Chaflin et al., 2015). The implications this has for continuing the dialogue of how intercollegiate athletics meshes with the mission of higher education are great. This subset of the literature reinforces the tangible, positive impact of participating in intercollegiate athletics as it demonstrates the potential for long-term benefits for student-athletes post-degree employment.

Nonathlete, Full-Time Equivalent Students

After exploring the perspective of a student-athlete, it is helpful to consider the perspective of a nonathlete, FTE student, specifically as it relates to her perceptions of the necessity of intercollegiate athletics. FTE students can be classified as any student, athlete or not, who is enrolled in at least 12 credit hours of coursework at an accredited institution. As we previously mentioned, aspects of intercollegiate athletics such as camaraderie and attachments to community in sports extend beyond simply the athletes to include the fans as well. From the perspective of student-athletes, postdegree opportunities are positive considerations.

Let's now consider the perspectives of nonstudent-athletes who are FTE students. The desired outcome is directly in line with strategic plans for most institutions of higher education and linking participating in athletics to employment success. Many students develop a sense of the "college experience" by participating as fans of their teams. For example, this might include pregame activities such as tailgating and cooking-out to face-painting, wearing decorative clothing, making signs, to watching the game and cheering on their team with other members of the student-body. Each institution of higher education has a vastly different climate as it relates to its athletics program, but without doubt, there are students on each campus who love and support their institution regardless of the sport. There are also those who may have very strong opinions against the institution spending millions of dollars on athletics for which they may not see or understand the tangible benefits. Given this information, it is easy to understand how dismayed nonathlete FTE students can be when they discover that a portion of their student fees are going exclusively to athletics, especially if they have no aspirations of attending a sporting event. While it may be difficult for most students to understand the economy of college athletics, many still could not imagine their collegiate experience without sports.

Athletics Program Spending

There is seemingly no longer a need to question whether or not athletic programs are netting any revenue because, for the most part, they are not. In 2013, the NCAA found that only 20 FBS athletic programs reported positive net generated revenues, which is down from 2012, when there were 23 programs in the black (Burnsed, 2014). This means that 8.5 percent of Division I athletic programs are actually making money. Further, only seven, or three percent of Division I institutions did not receive any money in the form of subsidies (USA Today, 2014). There is no shortage of metrics that all seem to gesture in the direction of financial doom for athletic programs; however, it would be incorrect to postulate that because of these metrics that intercollegiate athletics is in bad shape (Kirk, 2014). If we examine these factors put forward, the first three boost revenue, while the fourth factor controls for costs. As one can quickly tell, the casual observer may or may not be aware of the complex underpinnings that help athletic departments remain float. While it may be more simplistic to compare expenditures and revenue by athletic departments, it does not provide the observer with all the details.

To a FTE student (nonathlete), athletic spending may seem reckless and exorbitant, especially for FTE students who have no interest in sports, or those who do not wish to attend sporting events. However, students must remember that each student, athlete or not, pays a student fee each semester that helps the institution provide programming and services that benefit the general population of the institution. For example, while one particular student might not enjoy sports, perhaps she enjoys frequenting the university theater for a play or attending a concert sponsored by the institution. Indeed, student fees support these activities. Institutions of higher education set percentages of this student fee to be allocated to each activity, so that it can be adequately supported by the funds provided by enrolled students that might attend it. The notion of buyback exists because very few students will exercise their privilege to attend or utilize all of the programs and activities sponsored by their student fees; so by default, their fees help support the ventures of other students that establishes an environment where programs and activities thrive because they enjoy a mutually beneficial, symbiotic relationship created by all of the students. It may well be students' first lesson in how community-funded, or publicly funded, services are appropriated and allocated for the good of the whole.

Closing Thoughts

The question posed to the authors of this chapter was, "Has collegiate athletics become too contradictory to the academic mission of higher education?" We answer with a resounding no, and support it with current, relevant literature that examines the question by first exploring the storied history of collegiate athletics and then analyzing two student perspectives to gain a more nuanced position on the question. Collegiate athletics generates broad public interest through competitive activities that develop pride among many of the institution's faculty, staff, and students.

Yet there are considerable concerns that surround the entire enterprise of intercollegiate athletics such as the continuing series of legal battles that the NCAA faces over the notion of amateurism and paying student-athletes and finding a balance for athletic program expenditures, as well as the continuing struggles related to identity issues. While it is tempting to examine collegiate athletics through the lens of whether or not it is revenue producing, it simply cannot be reduced to money outcomes alone. Collegiate athletics provides opportunities to higher education that would ordinarily be out of the grasp of students from a lower SES, creates and allows camaraderie to flourish both for athletes and nonathletes, and further develops the future leaders of our nation through skill sets derived through participating in sports. Overall, the benefits of including athletics in contemporary higher education outweigh the complications and still serve as an arena, not only for athletic contests, but also simultaneously for teaching students (student-athletes and nonstudent-athletes alike) many essential lessons.

References

Aaronson, E. (1968). Dissonance theory: Progress and problems. In R. P. Abelson, E. Aronson, W. J. McGuire, T. M. Newcomb, M. J. Rosenberg, & P. H. Tannenbaum (Eds.), *Theories of cognitive consistency: A sourcebook* (pp. 5–27). Chicago, IL: Rand McNally.

Adler, P., & Adler, P.A. (1991). Backboards and blackboards: College athletics and role engulfment. New York, NY: Columbia University Press.

Armstrong, C. F. (1984). The lessons of sports: Class socialization in British and American boarding schools. *Sociology of Sport Journal, 1*, 314–331.

Baucom, C., & Lantz, C. D. (2001). Faculty attitudes toward male division II student athletes. *Journal of Sports Behavior, 24*, 265–276.

Bell, R. C. (2008) A history of women in sport prior to Title IX. *U.S. Sports Academy-The Sport Journal.* Retrieved from http://thesportjournal.org/article/a-history-of-women-in-sport-prior-to-title-ix/

Bem, D. J. (1967). Self-perception: An alternative interpretation of cognitive dissonance phenomena. *Psychological Review, 74*, 183–200.

Brown, K. T., Brown, T. N., Jackson, J. S., Sellers, R. M., & Manuel, W. J. (2003). Teammates on and off the field? Contact with Black teammates and the racial attitudes of White student-athletes. *Journal of Applied Social Psychology, 333*, 1379–1403.

Burnsed, B. (2014). *Growth in Division I athletics expenses outpaces revenue increases: And no Division II or Division III institutions generate more revenue than they spend, according to a recent study.* Retrieved from http://www.ncaa.org/about/resources/media-center/news/growth-division-i-athletics-expenses-outpaces-revenue-increases

Chaflin, P., Weight, E., Osborne, B., & Johnson, S. (2015). The value of intercollegiate athletics participation from the perspective of employers who target athletes. *Journal of Issues in Intercollegiate Athletics, 8*, 1–27.

Clarke, E. H. (1874). *Sex in education: or a fair chance for girls.* Boston, MA: James R. Osgood and Company.

Comeaux, E. (2010a). Racial differences in faculty perceptions of collegiate student-athletes' academic and post-undergraduate achievements. *Sociology of Sport Journal, 27*(4), 390–412.

Comeaux, E. (2010b). Mentoring as an intervention strategy: Toward a (re)negotiation of first year student-athlete role identities. *Journal for the Study of Sports and Athletes in Education, 4*(3), 257–275.

Comeaux, E. (2011). Examination of faculty attitudes toward division I college student-athletes. *College Student Affairs Journal, 30*(1), 75-87.

Comeaux, E. (2012). Unmasking athlete microaggressions: Division I student-athletes' engagement with members of the campus community. *Journal of Intercollegiate Sport, 5*, 189–198.

Comeaux, E., & Harrison, C. K. (2011). A conceptual model of academic success for student-athletes. *Educational Researcher, 4*, 235–245.

Crowley, J. N. (2006). *The NCAA's first century in the arena.* Retrieved from https://www.ncaapublications.com/p-4039-in-the-arena-the-ncaas-first-century.aspx

Duderstadt, J. J. (2009). *Intercollegiate athletics and the American university: A university president's perspective.* Ann Arbor, MI: University of Michigan Press.

Edelman, M. (2013). A short treatise on amateurism and antitrust law: Why the NCAA's no-pay rules violate section 1 of the Sherman Act. *Case Western Reserve Law Review, Fall*, 1–35.

Edwards, H. (1984). The Black "dumb jock": An American sports tragedy. *The College Board Review, 131*, 8–13.

Elinson, Z. (2013, June 21). Lawsuit could alter college athletics. *The Wall Street Journal,* p. A6.

Engstrom, C., Sedlacek, W., & McEwen, M. (1995). Faculty attitudes toward male revenue and nonrevenue student-athletes. *Journal of College Student Development, 36*(6), 217–227.

Festle, M. J. (1996). *Playing nice: Politics and apologies in women's sports.* New York, NY: Columbia University Press.

Fink, J. S. (2008) Gender and sex diversity in sport organizations: Concluding remarks. *Sex Roles, 58*, 1–2.

Griffin, P. G. (1998). *Strong women, deep closets: Lesbians and homophobia in sport.* Champaign, IL: Human Kinetics.

Griffin, P., & Carroll, H. (2011). *NCAA inclusion of transgender student-athletes.* Retrieved from https://www.ncaa.org/sites/default/files/Transgender_Handbook_2011_Final.pdf

Harrison, C. K. (1998). Themes that thread through society: Racism and athletic manifestation in the African American community. *Race, Ethnicity and Education, 1*(1), 63–74. doi:10.1080/1361332980010105

Hartmann-Tews, I., & Pfister, G. (2003). *Social issues in women and sport: International and comparative perspectives.* London: Routledge.

Henderson, D. J., Olbrecht, A., & Polachek, S. W. (2006). Do former college athletes earn more at work? A nonparametric assessment. *Journal of Human Resources, 41*(3), 558–577.

Hoeber, L. (2007). Exploring the gaps between meanings and practices of gender equity in a sport organization. *Gender, Work and Organization, 14*(3), 259–280.

Hoffman, J. L. (2011). Each generation of women had to start anew: A historical analysis of Title IX policy and women leaders in the extracurriculum. In P. Pasque & S. Errington (Eds.), *Empowering women in higher education and student affairs: Theory, research, narratives, and practice from feminist perspectives.* Sterling, VA: Stylus Publishing.

Jayakumar, U. M., & Comeaux, E. (2016). The cultural cover-up of college athletics: How organizational culture perpetuates an unrealistic and idealized balancing act. *The Journal of Higher Education, 87*(4), 488–515.

Johnson, D., Hallinan, C., & Westerfield, C. (1999). Picturing success: Photographs and stereotyping in men's collegiate basketball. *Journal of Sport Behavior, 22*, 45–53.

Kane, M. J., & Buysse, J. (2005). Intercollegiate media guides as contested terrain: a longitudinal analysis. *Sociology of Sport Journal, 22*(2), 214–238.

Kane, M., & Lenskyj, H. (1998). Women in the sport media: Issues of gender and sexualities. In L. Wenner (Ed.), *MediaSport: Cultural sensibilities and sport in the media age* (pp. 186–201). London: Routledge.

Kirk, J. (2014, June 6). *College athletic departments aren't necessarily as broke as you think.* Retrieved from http://www.sbnation.com/college-football/2014/6/6/5783394/college-sports-profits-money-schools-revenues-subsidies

Kuh, G. D. (2001). Assessing what really matters to student learning: Inside the national survey of student engagement. *Change, 33*(3), 10–17, 66. doi:10.1080/00091380109601795

Lewis, G. (1970). The beginning of organized collegiate sport. *American Quarterly, 22*(1). Retrieved from http://www.jstor.org/stable/2711645

Long, J. E., & Caudill, S. B. (1991). The impact of participation in intercollegiate athletics on income and graduation. *The Review of Economics and Statistics, 73*, 525–531.

McCormick, R. A., & McCormick, A. C. (2006). The myth of the student-athlete: The college athlete as employee. *Washington Law Review, 81*, 71–157.

Milton, P. R., Freeman, D., & Williamson, L. M. (2012). Do athletic scholarships impact academic success of intercollegiate student-athletes: An exploratory investigation. *Journal of Issues in Intercollegiate Athletics, 5*, 329–338.

Mulvihill, T. M. (2002). Physical education. In A. M. Aleman & K. A. Renn (Eds.), *Women in higher education: An encyclopedia* (pp. 184–188). Santa Barbara, CA: ABC-CLIO.

Mulvihill, T. M. (2011). The powerful collaboration between deans of women and directors of physical education: Syracuse University's contributions to the history of student affairs, 1930s–1950s. In: P. Pasque & S. E. Nicholson (Eds.), *Empowering women in higher education and student affairs: Theory, research, narratives and practice from feminist perspectives* (pp. 47–60). Sterling, VA: Stylus Publishing.

NCAA. (2014). *NCAA recruiting facts*. Retrieved from https://www.ncaa.org/sites/default/files/Recruiting%20Fact%20Sheet%20WEB.pdf

O'Shaughnessy, L. (2012). *8 things you should know about sports scholarships*. Retrieved from http://www.cbsnews.com/news/8-things-you-should-know-about-sports-scholarships/

Pascarella, E.T., Edison, M., Hagedorn, L.S., Nora, A., & Terenzini, P.T. (1996). Influences of students' internal locus attribution for academic success in the first year of college. *Research in Higher Education, 37*, 731–753.

Ryan, F. J. (1989). Participation in intercollegiate athletics: Affirmative outcomes. *Journal of College Student Development, 30*, 122–128.

Sack, A. L., & Staurowsky, E. J. (1998). *College athletes for hire: The evolution and legacy of the NCAA's amateur myth*. Westport, CT: Praeger.

Sage G. H. (1998) *Power and ideology in American sport: A critical perspective* (2nd ed). Champaign, IL: Human Kinetics.

Sailes, G. (1993). An investigation of campus stereotypes: The myth of Black athletic superiority and the dumb jock stereotype. *Sociology of Sport Journal, 10*, 88–97.

Schubert, A. F., Schubert, G. W., & Schubert-Madsen, D. L. (1991). Changes influenced by litigation in women's intercollegiate athletics. *Seton Hall Journal of Sport Law, 1*, 237–268.

Scott, B., Paskus, T., Miranda, M., Petr, T., & McArdle, M. (2008). In-season vs. out-of-season academic performance of college student-athletes. *Journal of Intercollegiate Sports, 1*, 202–226.

Sellers, R. M. (1992). Racial differences in the predictors for academic achievement of student-athletes in Division I revenue producing sports. *Sociology of Sport Journal, 9*, 48–60.

Shaw, S., & Hoeber, L. (2003). "A strong man is direct and a direct woman is a bitch": Gender discourses and their influence on employment roles in sports organizations. *Journal of Sport Management, 17*, 347–375.

Sheetz, A. C. (2016). Student-athletes vs. NCAA: Preserving amateurism in college sports amidst the fight for player compensation. *Brooklyn Law Review, Winter*, 1–35.

Shriberg, A., & Brodzinski, F. R. (1984). Rethinking services for college athlete. New directions for student-athletes in division I revenue producing sports. *Sociology of Sport Journal, 9*, 48–59.

Simons, H. D., Bosworth, C, Fujita, S., & Jensen, M. (2007). The athlete stigma in higher education. *College Student Journal, 41*(2), 251–273.

Singer, J. N. (2005). Understanding racism through the eyes of African American male student-athletes. *Race, Ethnicity and Education, 5*(4), 365–386. doi:10.1080/13613320500323963

Smith, R. (2000). A brief history of the national collegiate athletic association's role in regulating intercollegiate athletics. *Marquette Sports Law Review, 11*(1), 9–22.

Snyder, E. E. (1985). A theoretical analysis of academic and athletic roles. *Sociology of Sport Journal, 2*, 210–217.

Solorzano, D., Ceja, M., & Yosso, T. (2000). Knocking on freedom's door: Race, equity, and affirmative action in U.S. higher education. *The Journal of Negro Education, 69*(1), 60–73.

Soshnick, S. (2013). *Wall Street hires losers turned winners after college athletics.* Retrieved from http://www.bloomberg.com/news/2013-10-16/wall-street-hires-losers-turned-winners-after-college-athletics.html

Sperber, M. (1990). *College Sports, Inc.,* New York, NY: Henry Holt and Co.

Sperber, M. (2000). *Beer and circus: How big-time college sports is crippling undergraduate education,* New York, NY: Henry Holt and Co.

Sylwester, M., & Witosky, T. (2004). Athletic spending grows as academic funds dry up. *USA Today.* Retrieved from http://usatoday30.usatoday.com/sports/college/2004-02-18-athletic-spending-cover_x.htm

Taylor, D. L. (1995). A comparison of college athletic participants and nonparticipants on self-esteem, *Journal of College Student Development, 36,* 444–451.

USA TODAY Sports. (2014, October 6). *NCAA Finances.* Retrieved from http://sports.usatoday.com/ncaa/finances

Williams, D. (2013). *Why you should fill your company with 'athletes'.* Retrieved from http://www.forbes.com/sites/davidkwilliams/2013/10/02/why-you-should-fill-your-company-with-athletes/

Wolf-Wendell, L. E., Toma, D., & Worphew, C. C. (2001). There's no "I" in team: Lessons from athletics on community building. *Review of Higher Education, 24,* 369–396.

Wolverton, B. (2008). *Athletes' hours renew debate over college sports.* Retrieved from https://chronicle.com/article/Athletes-Hours-Renew-Debate/22003

Women's Sports Foundation. (2016). *Frequently asked questions.* Retrieved from https://www.womenssportsfoundation.org/home/about-us/faq

Zimbalist, A. (1999). *Unpaid professionals: Commercialism and conflict in big-time college sports.* Princeton, NJ: Princeton University Press.

32. Academics and Athletics: Struggles and Strategies in the Pursuit of (A) Grades and (A) Games

SALLY DEAR-HEALEY

Human beings first—athletes second.
    —Raj Bhavsar, Gymnast and Member of the 2008 Olympic Team

Most people attend colleges and universities to get an education. Some have other goals or purposes in mind, one of which is to "play ball." While the benefits of getting an education are undisputed, there are also advantages associated with participating in college sports, such as "providing critical lessons in discipline, teamwork, dedication to purpose, and other virtues" (Hyman & Van Jura, 2009). The National Collegiate Athletic Association (NCAA) states that "Participating in college sports provides opportunities to learn, compete and succeed (and) student-athletes as a group graduate at higher rates than their peers."[1] Unfortunately, the path to "success" for "student athletes" is neither simple nor clear cut.

In fact, some emphatically argue that the two roles—academics and athletics—are both counterproductive and counterintuitive. Accordingly, in an article published by the John William Pope Center for Higher Education Policy (2000), Jon Ericson argues that we should use the phrase "students who are also athletes" and stop using the term "student-athletes" since the latter "perpetuates the myth of the student who participates in sports as someone special, distinctive, set aside from other students." For example, there have been a number of cases where, while millions of dollars were lavished on Division I athletics, there were also flagrant violations of NCAA rules, college athletes were "used and abused," academic fraud was rampant, and faculty who served as whistleblowers were summarily dismissed.

While it is evident that conversations about academics and athletics embody both positive and negative components, the overarching goal should be to offer quality athletic programs while remaining committed to the academic mission of the institution and preserving academic freedom and integrity. It is also important to recognize the various influences, including economics, and potential problems, such as human rights abuses.

Varsity sports, especially at Division I schools, drive enrollments, fueling the current business model of the university. Unfortunately, the funding generated from ticket sales, royalties, endorsements, and licensing deals, as well as the goodwill generated among legislators, alumni, and donors, tends to blur the lines between the academic role of the institution and its athletic programs. A 2015 article in the *Washington Post* highlights an even more troubling issue. Hobson and Rich report, "While big-time college sports departments are making more money than ever before…poorer departments such as Rutgers have taken millions in mandatory fees from students and siphoned money away from academic budgets to try to keep up."

However, there are still some administrators and organizations that have kept their eye on the educational ball. For example, as Drew Faust so aptly stated in her 2007 inaugural address as President of Harvard, "A university is not about results in the next quarter; it is not even about who a student has become by graduation. It is about learning that molds a lifetime: learning that transmits the heritage of millennia; learning that shapes the future." In fact few could argue against the premise that lessons about human rights should be an indispensable part of the higher education curriculum. Further, according to a 2015 report by the United National Educational, Scientific and Cultural Organization, "The right to education has been internationally recognized as an overarching right: it is a human right in itself and is indispensable for the exercise of other human rights." Accordingly, the American Association of University Professors' (AAUP) 1915 Declaration specifically recognized that "academic freedom has traditionally had two applications—the freedom of the teacher to teach (Lehrfreiheit) and that of the student to learn (Lernfreiheit)" (AAUP Redbook, 1967).

Those of us who teach, realize that lessons often reach far beyond the classroom. We also recognize that it is challenging for students to balance their academic work with other personal goals and interests, especially when students also have required practices, games, and travel. Moreover, it is challenging for teachers when students are not academically prepared for college- and university-level work and are "clustered" into particular curriculums and classes. Many times they are "strongly encouraged" to be "athlete-friendly," often to the point where they are unable to hold all students equally account-able to the same standards of work and evaluation.

This chapter engages in a discussion about the pros and cons of the recruitment, retention of athletically promising students who are also "questionably qualified" for academia, and "remedial academic support." This chapter will also examine the varied and often competing roles of the various "players"; including admissions, administrations, students, teachers, coaches, and athletic departments. The overall goal of the chapter is to increase awareness and to reveal methods for maintaining academic integrity and ethical standards for teachers *and* students, specifically for those who find themselves standing at the thresholds of both the classroom and the locker room. We begin with a discussion of institutional accountability and the impact of the Buckley Amendment.

Institutional Accountability and the Buckley Amendment

The word transparent is defined as "free of pretense or deceit; readily under-stood; characterized by visibility or accessibility of information."[2] The concept of transparency is a critical criterion when it comes to business practices and relationships and directly applies to the relationship between the university as an institution, students, and teachers. Consequently, one of the major debates in academia today is whether or not colleges and universities are educational institutions or business enterprises whose major role is the hierarchical and orderly management of people, property, productivity, and finance for profit (Greenberg, 2004). In other words, are administrators, teachers and coaches treating students as students or as potential revenue sources? This question is especially relevant to the discussion of students who are also athletes since their recruitment often has more to do with their ability to "play ball" and subsequently earn money and fame for the institution than attend classes, *earn* grades, and leave with an education that will benefit them, and their families and communities, in the future.

The Buckley Amendment, enacted by Congress in 1974, was created to curb the abuse of student education records and to ensure that admitted students were not only academically qualified, but that provisions were in place to appropriately and effectively support their academic efforts and success. However, Salzwedel and Ericson, in their 2010 *Dartmouth Law Journal* article entitled "The University——The Closed Society," provide numerous examples of how the Buckley Amendment has been routinely abused and argue that the idea that students who are also athletes are going to get anything resembling a college education is a charade, or what Jon Ericson called the "big lie." As examples, in their 2003 *Wisconsin Law Review* article "Cleaning up Buckley: How the Family Educational Rights and Privacy Act Shields Academic Corruption in College Athletics," Salzwedel and Ericson (2003) share several illustrative and illuminating cases which clearly illustrate abuses and fraudulent practices within the system:

- Neel Sheth completed nearly a year's worth of classes in electrical engineering and physics in just one semester, all while earning a 3.62 GPA.
- Eric Berger completed 24 credit hours at two institutions in a period of 74 days.
- Ricky Clemons, who with no high school diploma or GED, completed 24 credit hours in three different states, half of which were correspondence courses.

Salzwedel and Ericson went on to argue for the appeal of the Buckley Amendment and for Congress to enact a statute that was "consistent with the original intent of its authors—a law that protects students' academic performance and provides for institutional accountability" (2010).

Herein lie some of the questions inherent to this discussion. Is it ethical to admit a student who is not qualified academically, even (or especially) if he (or she) is believed to be an exceptional athlete? How, and by whom, is eligibility determined and maintained; and finally, are the standards for passing classes and making progress toward graduation the same for all students? Here Binghamton University (BU) serves as an excellent example of what can happen when the focus on winning on the court trumps the focus on academic integrity in the classroom.

"At What Price Glory?"—The "Perfect Storm" at Binghamton University

While corruption in big-time college sports is not new, BU's athletic scandal, described by some as the "perfect storm" of events, is unusual in that Binghamton is not a "big-time" sports school. As former Vermont coach Tom Brennan stated, "At what price glory? They (Binghamton) just might be a little car on the big highway, but they were emblematic of what goes on at a whole lot of places."[3] Perhaps this is one of the reasons that BU's case was so interesting, and so sadly tragic. As was true with so many other schools like them, the fall from grace at BU began with the adoption of a "do whatever it takes to win" philosophy that threw academic integrity, ethical teachers, and students out the window.

I first became aware of what was going on in the fall of 2008, when I was teaching *Prenatal, Infant, and Toddler Development* in the department of Human Development in the College of Community and Public Affairs (CCPA). Among the forty plus students in my class were three students who were also key players on the men's basketball team. That semester was different right from the start in some not-so-subtle ways. For example, starting at the beginning and continuing throughout the semester, I received numerous emails and phone calls from the Associate Athletic Director for Student Services Ed Scott, who not only directly questioned my assignments and grading policy, but went so far as to suggest that I was being discriminatory and unfair in my grading practices. Coach Broadus entered my classroom while I was teaching, silently stood there for a while, and then just turned and walked out.[4] I also received pressure from the administration to give students who were also athletes "breaks" that weren't available to other students. For example, although the university attendance policy stated that missing more than 25% of the classes would result in failure of the class, I was asked to overlook 9 out of 15 class absences for one of the basketball players. Not only that, the students who were also basketball players frequently came 15–20 minutes late to the 3-hour class and left half-way through, missed scheduled meetings and presentations, signed in for each other on the attendance sheet, and were either missing or turned in substandard assignments. Equally disturbing was a visit I received from a member of the administration who informed me that "it would be in my best interests" not to fail basketball players. What I soon came to realize was the Department of Human Development was being used as a holding pen to "cluster"[5] basketball players who, when they were in danger of failing other courses, were being given independent study courses or "paper classes"[6] with "athlete-friendly" professors.

Confident that I fairly assessed student work and held true to the class contract/syllabus and clearly stated universities guidelines, I turned in grades. I was also supported by my department chair Al Dekin, who had made it clear that he was "most interested in protecting faculty rights and responsibilities for academic programs, especially in the face of administrative pressures and possible interference."[7] At that point we both considered the entire matter done and over with and I started preparing for my spring classes. Yet, when I received that first phone call in early February (2009) from *New York Times* reporter Pete Thamel, whose investigative efforts had followed Coach Broadus from Georgetown University,[8] I quickly realized that I had opened up a hornet's nest and that quite a few people, including me, were likely to get stung.

In February of 2009, immediately after the publication of the first *New York Times* article, I received my first nonrenewal letter in over ten years of teaching in the same department. I was also approached by a CCPA colleague in front of the elevator. In a hushed voice she said "I heard what happened to you. They did the same thing to me!" Not at all surprised by her admission, I asked her what she had done and she unabashedly responded, "Why I changed the grade of course!" This was the first of what was to become a flurry of clandestine admissions from people at all levels of the university who, with good reason, were too frightened to come forward to the administration with what they knew or had experienced. Even so, I was wholly unprepared for the breadth and depth of corruption or the "scandal" that would ensue, which included a million-dollar investigation of the university in 2010. The story it told was not a positive one. In a March 2012 article, Thamel reflected:

> Shortly after that flickering moment of glory in 2009 (when BU went to the NCAA), the university's basketball program imploded. Binghamton, a part of the State University of New York system, has been cleaning up—and paying out millions—ever since. The president, provost, two top athletic officials and the men's basketball head coach have been replaced amid a scandal that proved costly to both university's reputation and its bottom line.[9]

That reputation included Binghamton's history of admitting students with high academic qualifications. Unfortunately, these standards did not apply equally to students who were recruited for their athletic capabilities. In the February 2009 *New York Times* article "At Binghamton, Division I Move Brings Recognition and Regret," Dennis Lasser, who was removed as a Faculty Athletic Representative after Coach Broadus arrived, was quoted as saying "It appears to me that minimum qualifications as specified by the NCAA are the only academic criteria currently needed for the men's basketball team to be admitted to Binghamton University."[10] The question was how were these students able to make it to graduation?

In that same article (then) BU President Lois DeFleur claimed "All of our basketball players are eligible and are making progress toward graduation." To the vast majority of people who read this statement this went a long way toward alleviating any concerns that BU students who were also athletes were somehow not academically prepared or capable of university study. However, those of us who had these students in our classes were vividly aware that most of them were not.[11] DeFleur also stated that "Since we've been Division I, all of the players that have stayed in the program have graduated," although it was not clear which "program" she was talking about, for example, the major program, the sports program, or the special program of paper classes and inflated grades which allowed students who were also athletes to remain eligible to play ball. The top-down influence was undeniable. Not only did Justice Kaye's (2010) report state that "The President had a blind spot regarding athletics," it also reported that CCPA Dean Pat Ingraham said that she had "added another 'local' layer toward ensuring the academic success (of the student)—she (had) a faculty member in Human Development who (would) serve as an additional mentor and advisor."

As Bruce Svare, Professor of Psychology at SUNY Albany, former Drake Group member, and Founder/Director of the National Institute for Sports Reform stated in a March 21, 2010 *Albany Times Union* commentary, "The real story here, and in every other college sports scandal, is about the enabling faculty who create phony curriculum and independent (often no-show) study courses, give grades when little or no work is done and change grades when pressured. As 'friends' of the intercollegiate sports program on campus, they keep athletes eligible but prevent them from receiving a real education like every other student."[12]

Men's basketball Coach Broadus also went on record to say that his players had been "exceptional in the classroom," and that "giving young men a second chance was part of his job."[13] Justice Kaye's report also highlighted "repeated reference to the *admirable* (author's emphasis) University commitment to give second (or more) chances to disadvantaged youths, some with troubled backgrounds."[14] While there are certainly circumstances where individuals should be given second chances, giving second chances to deserving students and justifying academic corruption are two entirely different conversations. It soon became crystal clear that there was a huge dichotomy between actual student qualifications—what the administration and the athletic department saw as "academically capable" and "making progress"—and what teachers knew constituted "exceptional" academic capabilities.

It is also obvious from what happened at Binghamton and other schools who experienced similar problems that some of these incoming students lacked initial opportunities for success and, once admitted, they were denied the provision of appropriate and ethical remedial and institutional support. It is also clear that what these and other students experienced was—at least in part—the result of structural and environment factors as well as socially learned behavior.

Factors Affecting the Educational Attainment of College Students Who Are Also Athletes

Carbonaro (2005), whose work focuses on education and social stratification, looked at how "the systemic organizational and institutional characteristics of schools shape academic outcomes." Similarly, Sørensen and Hallinan (1977) suggest that differences in student achievement are the result of three factors: learning opportunities, effort, and ability. Students who are athletically gifted, but who are not academically prepared or qualified for university study, often due to a lack of early educational opportunities, are deliberately recruited to colleges to play sports even though they are not expected to function academically. In other words they are labeled and then "handled,"[15] thus never really giving them a chance—nor the desire or need—to exert the effort needed to prove themselves capable, both on *and* off the court. While we realize that all students are individuals and they all learn in different ways, not even giving these students a chance is, quite literally, an entirely different—and qualitatively unfair—"ball game." This targeted tracking is described as circular tracking, "a social structure that differentially provides opportunities and imposes constraints upon what students have the potential to learn" (Carbonaro, 2005).

This tracking toward inequality mechanism starts early on. For example, while minority male participation in sport-based afterschool programs has been reported to offer positive results (Fuller, Percy, Bruening, & Cotrufo, 2013), Jay MacLeod's book "Ain't No Makin' It: Aspirations and Attainment in a Low-Income Neighborhood" (2008) epitomizes the social reproduction theorist's view that families, neighborhoods, and schools serve to reinforce social inequality. MacLeod argues that while some may believe that "Any child can grow up to be president," the reality is that others are highly pessimistic about their prospects for social mobility and openly dispute the education system's ability to "deliver the goods." Similarly, in terms of the opportunities provided by athletics and sports to break out of these cultural milieus, afterschool recreation and sport programs do not necessarily extend across sociodemographic boundaries such as gender, race, and social class (Woodland, Martin, Hill, & Worrell, 2009). Still, the lure of becoming a professional athlete is considerable for these youth who might not otherwise have a chance to make it out of their neighborhood, let alone become famous.

Inequities are further articulated in the article "Four Years a Student-Athlete: The Racial Injustice of Big-Time College Sports." Michigan State Professor Robert McCormick states, "It was incredible. I realized all of the people being paid or getting pleasure out of the game were white, and the vast majority of the people playing and risking their health were black" (Hruby, 2016).[16] McCormick and his wife Amy, also a professor at Michigan State, coauthored another article, "Major College Sports: A Modern Apartheid," which argued that the labor produced by revenue-producing campus football and men's basketball holds racial minorities "in legal servitude for the profit and entertainment of the racial majority" (Hruby, 2016). In the end it remains painfully clear that, no matter how some things change, others remain the same.

Despite the history and challenges associated with academically challenged students who are also athletes, change is possible. Claims that "it has always been this way" and "it is what it is" can be countered with evidence that other practices and methods can—and should—be employed to turn the situation around for the betterment of everyone concerned. Here we turn to organized efforts to make academic integrity a basis for athletics reform.

Making Academic Integrity a Basis for Athletics Reform

Academic integrity for all students, including students who are also athletes, is not only the goal; it must be the practice, within and outside the classroom. This is accomplished through organized and consistent efforts at the intuitional level—which includes administration, faculty, and staff—to alleviate academic fraud. Equally important, faculty who serve as the "guardians of the curriculum"—as well as the students themselves as representatives of their own learning—must have a voice and be protected against retribution for truth-seeking and whistleblowing.

As Bruce Svare argues in his article "The 'Big Lie' and Intercollegiate Sports in America: Time to Tame the Monster that is Enabled by Academic Corruption":

> If we are serious about providing an effective and long-lasting remedy for academic corruption in college sports, then we would choose disclosure, transparency and truth-telling. Academic fraud begins and ends with faculty who are sympathetic to athletes and sports program on their campuses. (n.d.)[17]

But schools often don't, or won't, set and monitor standards. This is why organizations such as the AAUP, the NCAA, the Carnegie Foundation, The Knight Commission (KC), The Drake Group (TDG), the Coalition on Intercollegiate Athletics (COIA), and the National Institute for Sports Reform must step forward in order to create and enforce the rules and hold all the various players equally accountable. Education is also a key component of their work. Even as far back as 1929, the Carnegie Foundation released a 311 page report on the negative influence of big-time college sports on our educational system. Similarly, the Knight Commission on Intercollegiate Athletics (KC) has engaged the problem of corruption in college athletics and encouraged action. More specifically, their "blueprint" called for "restoring educational values and priorities," a process they claimed begins with strengthening accountability for athletics programs in the following three ways:

1. Require greater transparency and the reporting of better measures to compare athletics spending to academic spending;
2. Reward practices that make academic values a priority; and
3. Treat college athletes as students first and foremost—not as professionals.[18]

The overarching goal of the KC is to ensure that intercollegiate athletics programs operate within the *educational* mission of their colleges and universities. One of the challenges to the educational mission is the concept of remedial support. While all students should have the benefit of remedial support, that support is often differentially applied. For example, an article on the website *Paper Class Inc.* claims that "During the recruiting process, promises are made with regards to the academic resources available to student athletes, such as class advising, scheduling and tutoring. Therefore, once a school admits an underprepared student, they have a duty to provide them with these services and resources."[19] Unfortunately, and as we've already seen, these remediation efforts often include paper classes and grade inflation, but they also can involve "excessive" help with writing papers and completing class assignments.

TDG is another example of an organization initiating positive and proactive change. TDG, formally the National Association of Faculty for Collegiate Athletic Reform, is a national organization consisting of faculty, staff, and other committed individuals whose mission is to "defend academic integrity in higher education against the corrosive aspects of commercial college sport, encourage personal and intellectual growth for all students, as well as excellence and professional integrity from faculty charged with teaching."[20] TDG was founded in 1999 when Jon Ericson organized members of faculty senates, journalists, and athletic directors, along with members of the NCAA and the KC, with the goal of ending academic corruption in college sports. In addition to producing policy position papers and proactive education and media campaigns focused on intercollegiate athletics governance association reforms, TDG is active politically. Following the lead of presidentialfootball.com, where college presidents were asked "What is the future of football at your university?" TDG has partnered with journalist and Kent State associate professor Karl Idsvoog to sponsor *The Academic Integrity Project*, the focus of which is to determine the level of academic corruption among students who are also athletes and what, if anything, is being done about it. The project initiated a "Dear Provost so and so" letter, which was sent to every university in the ACC, Big 12, Big 10, PAC 12, and SEC. Last but not least, inspired by Robert Maynard Hutchins, former President of the University of Chicago

(1929–1951), TDG presents the Robert Maynard Hutchins Award to honor faculty and staff who take a courageous stand to defend academic integrity in collegiate sports at their institutions, often at great professional and personal risk.[21]

Conclusion

During the past several years, similar to the KC and TDG, the COIA has produced a number of white papers and other documents that lay out recommendations for reform that can be used by schools to examine their own policies and practices with regard to intercollegiate athletics, many of which have been brought to the NCAA as possible action items. Another of COIA's missions is to provide a national faculty voice on intercollegiate sports issues.[22]

These organization's individual and collective efforts to challenge the status quo, along with initiatives and actions taken at the college and university level to increase transparency and oversight and encourage "sufficient objectivity and self-inquiry," have the potential to reform college athletics as we know it, eliminate fraudulent and coercive tactics, and improve educational opportunities for all students. And, while there are thousands of voices that have chosen to be silent about what they have witnessed or experienced, it is also our collective responsibility to "report what we see" so that meaningful change can take place and everyone—students, faculty, administration, and staff—can experience fairness, trust, and respect. Moreover, it is our collective responsibility to maintain faculty as "guardians of the curriculum," so that within academia there remains both the right to teach and the right to become educated.

Notes

1. http://www.ncaa.org/student-athletes/future
2. Merriam-Webster.com
3. http://www.nytimes.com/2012/03/01/sports/ncaabasketball/after-a-costly-scandal-binghamton-begins-rebuilding.html
4. The double-standard was obvious as you can only imagine what would have happened to me had I stepped out on the court and just stood there during a game.
5. Considered by some as "taking the path of least resistance," clustering involves placing students who are also athletes in certain majors/fields because the time demands of their sports discourage, if not rule out, disciplines that require lots of work and/or are not receptive or conducive to their practice, game, and travel schedules. At Binghamton, the "go to" department for athletes was Human Development. Not only was Human Development considered to be an "easy" major for these students, some of

the teachers in that department had been determined by the athletic department and the administration to be especially "athlete friendly."

6. "Paper classes are essentially no-work independent studies involving a single paper that allowed functionally illiterate players to prop up their GPAs, thus satisfying the NCAA's eligibility requirements." (http://www.slate.com/blogs/money box/2014/03/27/the_unc_fake_class_scandal_athlete_got_an_a_for_a_one_para graph_paper.html).

7. Private email from Al Dekin to Sally Dear-Healey.

8. Coach Broadus had reportedly recruited players from a notorious Philadelphia diploma mill, Lutheran Christian Academy, while he was an assistant at Georgetown and at "George Washington University" before coming to Binghamton University. (http://www.nytimes.com/2009/02/22/sports/ncaabasketball/22binghamton. html?pagewanted=1&_r=2).

9. http://www.nytimes.com/2012/03/01/sports/ncaabasketball/after-a-costly-scan dal-binghamton-begins-rebuilding.html

10. http://www.nytimes.com/2009/02/22/sports/ncaabasketball/22binghamton. html?pagewanted=all&_r=0

11. Issues related to academic preparedness, "clustering" into specific programs and classes, grade inflation, and problems related to "academic support" tend to be more common for students who play basketball and football, primarily because these are the sports which generate the largest fan base and revenue.

12. Albany Times Union, 21 March 2010, p. B1, Perspectives.

13. http://www.nytimes.com/2009/02/22/sports/ncaabasketball/22binghamton. html?pagewanted=2&_r=2

14. While others never (publically) made the connection, I can't help but question Justice Kaye's lack of bias in conducting this audit given that she has a strong history publically and legally advocating for "misguided" and disadvantaged African-American youth.

15. The Free Dictionary defines a handler as "One that handles or directs something or someone." The Black Cager; A Black Perspective on Collegiate Athletics blog featured a post in 2014 titled "'Frustrated' Black Parents and the Rise of 'Handlers.'" The author, Delgreco K. Wilson, who has spent the last 20 years advising and mentoring "student-athletes" in the Greater Philadelphia Region, admonishes that, "Never, ever should a parent relinquish control over their child's athletic and educational development." He goes on to say that "It is highly unlikely that others will care about their child's education as much as they do. As a parent you must, at all times, remember that academics are more important that athletics." The problem is, as Wilson readily admits; "Only a relatively small segment of working class and poor Black parents have a keen and thorough understanding of the college preparation and application process." This is compounded by the fact that, "Revenue producing college basketball and college football are dominated by Black athletes" and the vast majority of those same Black athletes come from homes where the parents, often single mothers, are unemployed and underemployed, receive public assistance, and are struggling to make ends meet. Here Wilson sets the stage for what comes next. "Eventually, someone will notice the poor, talented, determined and hungry boy that just wants to play ball. They will approach his mother and offer to 'handle' her son's basketball development (and) if she allows hi the work with her son he will earn an

athletic scholarship to pay for college" (https://delgrecowilson.com/2014/02/24/ frustrated-black-parents-and-the-rise-of-handlers). Needless to say these families are highly motivated, but that in itself does not guarantee that their son is, nor does it guarantee that he will succeed academically.

16. https://sports.vice.com/en_us/article/four-years-a-student-athlete-the-racial-injus tice-of-big-time-college-sports
17. https://www.inter-disciplinary.net/probing-the-boundaries/wp-content/ uploads/2012/10/bbsvare_dpaper.pdf
18. http://www.knightcommission.org/academic-integrity/academic-integrity-com mission-report
19. http://paperclassinc.com/athletics-v-academics/
20. https://thedrakegroup.org
21. In 2010, the author of this chapter was honored by TDG with the Robert Maynard Hutchins award for "courageous defense of academic integrity in college sports."
22. http://blogs.comm.psu.edu/thecoia/

References

AAUP Redbook. (1967). *Joint statement on rights and freedoms of students.* Washington, D.C.: American Association of University Professors.

Carbonaro, W. (2005). Tracking, students' effort, and academic achievement. *Sociology of Education, 78*(1), 27–49.

Fuller, R., Percy, V., Bruening, J., & Cotrufo, R. (2013). Positive youth development: Minority male participation in a sport-based afterschool program in an urban environment. *Research Quarterly for Exercise & Sport, 84*(4), 469–483.

Greenberg, M. (2004). The university is not a business (and other fantasies). *EDUCAUSE Review, 39*(2), 10–16.

Hobson, W., & Rich, S. (2015, November 12). Playing in the Red. *The Washington Post.*

Hruby, P. (2016, April 4). Four years a student-athlete: The racial injustice of big-time college sports. Retrieved from https://sports.vice.com/en_us/article/ezexjp/four-years-a-student-athlete-the-racial-injustice-of-big-time-college-sports

Hyman, J., & Van Jura, M. (2009). *Elite collegiate athletics and the academy: Criticisms, benefits, and the role of student affairs.* The Vermont Connection, *30*, 42-52.

Kaye, J. S. (2010). *Report to the Board of Trustees of the State University of New York.* Retrieved from http://www.suny.edu/Files/sunynewsFiles/Pdf/KayeReport.PDF

MacLeod, J. (2008). *Ain't no makin' it: Aspirations and attainment in a low-income neighborhood.* Boulder, CO: Westview Press.

McCormick, R. A., & Amy, C. (2010). Major college sports: A modern apartheid. *Texas Review of Entertainment & Sports Law, 12*(1), 12–51.

Salzwedel, M., & Ericson, J. (2003). Cleaning up Buckley: How the family educational rights and privacy act shield's academic corruption in college athletics. *Wisconsin Law Review, 6*, 1053–1113.

Salzwedel, M., & Ericson, J. (2010). The University: The closed society. *Dartmouth Law Journal, 8*(2), 88–108.

Sørensen, A., & Hallinan, M. (1977). A reconceptualization of school effects. *Sociology of Education, 50,* 273–289.

Svare, B. (n.d.). *The 'Big Lie' and intercollegiate sports in America: Time to Tame the Monster that is enabled by Academic Corruption.* Retrieved from https://www.inter-dis ciplinary.net/probing-the-boundaries/wp-content/uploads/2012/10/bbsvare_ dpaper.pdf

The John William Pope Center for Higher Education Policy. (2000). *Cut athletic scholarships, reduce number of athletic contests, professors say.* Raleigh, NC: Staff.

United Nations Educational, Scientific and Cultural Organization (UNESCO). (2015). *Document prepared for the 12th session of the Committee of Experts on the Application of the Recommendations concerning Teachers (CEART).* The Right to Education and the Teaching Profession; Overview of the Measures Supporting the Rights, Status and working Conditions of the Teaching Profession reported on by Member States, Paris, France.

Woodland, M, Martin, J., Hill, R., & Worrell, F. (2009). The most blessed room in the city: The influence of a youth development program on three young black males. *The Journal of Negro Education, 78*(3), 233–244.

Contributors

Mark Bauman is an assistant professor and program coordinator for the Counseling and College Student Affairs program at Bloomsburg University of Pennsylvania. Prior to assuming those positions, Mark spent 14 years in various student affairs roles at BU, including residence life and judicial affairs. Since 2009, Mark has focused his research and service efforts on student-veterans and was one of the first to write and speak about that population. Mark is currently in the United States Coast Guard Reserve.

Paul Gordon Brown is Director of Curriculum, Training, and Research for Roompact, a technology software company, where he conducts research on social media's impact on college student development and identity. He has over 15 years of professional experience in higher education and student affairs in a variety of functional areas, including as an instructor in the Boston College and Merrimack College higher education programs. Dr. Brown has given over 50 refereed presentations at international and regional conferences.

Lindsey M. Burke is the Will Skillman Fellow in Education Policy at The Heritage Foundation. She researches and writes on federal and state education issues. Her work has appeared in various newspapers and magazines, and she has been featured on education reform nationally and internationally, including on radio and television. Ms. Burke also serves on the Speaker's Bureau for the Friedman Foundation for Educational Choice and has conducted in-depth evaluations of education savings account use for the Foundation. A Ph.D. student in education policy and research methodology at George Mason University, she holds a bachelor's degree in politics from Hollins University and a master of teaching degree in foreign language education from the University of Virginia.

Monica Galloway Burke is an associate professor in the Department of Counseling and Student Affairs at Western Kentucky University. She has 18 years of experience as a faculty member and practitioner in student affairs and higher education. Dr. Burke has published in several peer-reviewed journals, contributed chapters to various books, and coauthored, with Jill Duba Sauerheber and Aaron W. Hughey, *Helping Skills for Working with College Students: Applying Counseling Theory to Student Affairs Practice* (Routledge, 2016).

Colin Cannonier is an assistant professor of economics at Belmont University. He is a former first-class cricketer and central banker who began his career as a country economist in the Eastern Caribbean. His research interests include health economics, economic demography, applied economics, public policy, and labor economics. He has a Ph.D. in economics from Louisiana State University.

Kathy Cavins-Tull is Vice Chancellor for Student Affairs at Texas Christian University, where she is also an adjunct professor of higher education. She was previously Vice President for Student Affairs at Illinois Wesleyan University and Associate Vice President for Student Services as Dean of Students at Western Illinois University. Dr. Cavins-Tull has been on the Advisory Board of the National Association of Student Personnel Administrators (NASPA) Center for Women, the James E. Scott Academy Advisory Board, and a faculty member of the Small College Institute. She currently serves as National Co-Chair of NASPA's Fraternity and Sorority Knowledge Community.

Curtis M. Clock is an academic advisor and doctoral student in Adult, Higher, and Community Education at Ball State University, where he holds an M.A. in Adult and Community education, with a higher education focus. His research interests include investigation of the dynamics of Division I collegiate athletics, increasing persistence of first-year students on academic probation, and innovative teaching methodologies, specifically collaborative learning.

Denise L. Davidson is an assistant professor In the Educational Leadership and College Student Affairs program at Bloomsburg University of Pennsylvania. She has 20 years of experience in residence life, student conduct, academic advising, student financial aid, student activities, fraternity/sorority life, and alumni affairs. Recipient of two awards for outstanding teaching and one for research, Dr. Davidson's academic interests include new professionals' job satisfaction and turnover, student affairs work at for-profit institutions, students with disabilities in campus housing, and the scholarship of teaching and learning.

Sally Dear-Healey has been a visiting professor in the Department of Sociology, Anthropology, and Criminology and coordinator of the Women's

Studies Program at SUNY-Cortland. She has served as an adjunct faculty member at SUNY-Oneonta, Syracuse University, and Binghamton University. Dr. Dear-Healey was Vice President of the New York State Chapter of the American Association of University Professors (AAUP) and chair of its Committee on the Status of Women in the Academic Profession. Her academic interests include interpersonal and family relationships; violence; social deviance; women's family and community health; and social activism. In 2010, she received the Robert Maynard Hutchens Award from The Drake Group (TDG) for her support of academic integrity in intercollegiate athletics. She is now a member of its Board of Directors.

Joseph L. DeVitis is a retired professor of educational foundations and higher education. He is a past president of the American Educational Studies Association (AESA), the Council of Learned Societies in Education, and the Society of Professors of Education. Dr. DeVitis is the recipient of the Distinguished Alumni Award from the University of Illinois at Urbana-Champaign. Two of his books have earned *Choice* Awards from the American Library Association; and four others have won Critics Choice Awards from AESA as outstanding books of the year, including his most recent book, *Popular Educational Classics* (Peter Lang, 2016). He lives with his wife Linda in Palm Springs, California.

J. Bennett Durham is Coordinator of Exploratory Studies, a program for first-year students who do not declare a major, at DeSales University. Additionally, he is Coordinator of Choral Activities and Liturgical Music and an instructor of music. He holds a M.M. in choral conducting from Westminster Choir College of Rider University.

Frank Fernandez is a fellow with the Institute of Higher Education at the University of Florida. He researches policy issues in higher education, including doctoral education, the preparation of future faculty, and faculty work. On the latter topic, he focuses on academic freedom and the roles that faculty and universities play in knowledge production.

Michael Sean Funk is a clinical assistant professor in the Steinhardt School of Culture, Education, and Human Development at New York University. He has worked in academic affairs, student affairs, academic advising, and residence life, including serving as a faculty fellow in residence at NYU. His honors include the NASPA (Student Affairs Administrators in Higher Education) inaugural Emerging Faculty Leader Academy Award (2016); a Distinguished Teaching Award from the University of Massachusetts, Amherst, where he received his doctorate; induction into his High School Hall of Fame for his work on social justice; and service as the NYU faculty ambassador at its Free State Global Leadership Conference in Africa. Dr. Frank is the coauthor of "racism and White Privilege" in *Teaching for Diversity and Social Justice*, 3rd ed., by Maurianne Adams and Lee Ann Bell (Routledge, 2016).

Dennis E. Gregory is an associate professor of higher education at Old Dominion University. He has served in numerous student affairs leadership roles, including as a senior student affairs officer. He has authored or co-authored over 50 publications, including a book on Greek life. His current academic interests include enrollment management, higher education law, and comparative education. Dr. Gregory is a charter member and past president of the Association for Student Conduct Administration (ASCA) and the International Association of Student Affairs and Services (IASAS).

Richard Guarasci is president of Wagner College in New York City. He has chaired the Board of Directors of both Campus Compact and the Coalition of Urban and Metropolitan Universities as well as other organizations devoted to community service-learning. A leading proponent of civic education in liberal education, President Guarasci is the coauthor, with Grant H. Cornwell, *of Democratic Education in an Age of Difference: Redefining Citizenship in Higher Education* (1997).

Valerie A. Guerrero is a doctoral student in the Department of Educational Leadership and Policy at the University of Utah. Her research interests include critical pedagogy, faculty teaching preparation, campus climate, and social justice education. She was the Associate Director of the Center for Intercultural Development and Student Success at Allegheny College, where she designed and led hundreds of workshops and training sessions aimed at fostering the inclusion of diverse identity groups.

Bruce W. Hauptli is a professor emeritus of philosophy at Florida International University. He taught there from 1976 to 2015 and has written on epistemology, early modern philosophy, American philosophy, and philosophy of education. He is the author of *The Reasonableness of Reason: Explaining Rationality Naturalistically* (Open Court, 1995). He lives with his wife, Laurie, in Bath, Maine.

Aaron W. Hughey is a professor in the Department of Counseling and Student Affairs at Western Kentucky University, where he oversees the graduate program in Student Affairs in Higher Education. Previously, he spent 10 years in administrative positions, including 5 years as the Associate Director of University Housing at WKU. He has authored over 60 refereed publications on a wide range of issues, including student learning and development, standardized testing, diversity, and leadership. Dr. Hughey regularly presents at national and international conferences and consults extensively with companies and schools. He also provides training programs on a variety of topics centered on change management.

Neal H. Hutchens is a professor of education at the University of Mississippi. Previously, he held positions at Pennsylvania State University and the University of Kentucky. Dr. Hutchens's research centers on law and policy issues in higher education. He earned his Ph.D. from the University of Maryland and his J.D. from the University of Alabama.

Philo A. Hutcheson is a professor and chair in the Department of Educational Leadership, Policy and Technology at the University of Alabama. He is a past president of the History of Education Society and author of *A Professional Professoriate: Unionization, Bureaucratization, and the AAUP* (2000) and numerous book chapters and articles. He is completing a manuscript on the 1947 President's Commission on Higher Education and has a book contract with Routledge to write a history of United States higher education.

Ezekiel Kimball is an assistant professor of higher education at the University of Massachusetts, Amherst. He studies the roles that individual agency, institutional practices, and social structures play in the construction of postsecondary experiences. Dr. Kimball's research examines the way student affairs professionals use scholarly knowledge in practice and how disability status shapes students services in higher education.

Kimberly A. Kline is a professor and Chair of the Higher Education Administration Department at Buffalo State College, State University of New York. Her research focuses on professional development, social justice and agency in higher education, well-being, and student learning outcomes assessment. In 2013–2014, she was a Fulbright Scholar at the National University of Kyiv-Mohyla in Ukraine and received another Fulbright in 2014–2015 to study the student-initiated protests that led to its revolution. Dr. Kline has over 20 years of experience in higher education and student affairs. Her book *Reflections in Action: A Guidebook for Faculty and Student Affairs Professionals* (Stylus, 2013) was named a 2015 Diamond Honoree by the ACPA Educational Leadership Foundation.

David S. Knowlton is a professor of instructional technology at Southern Illinois University Edwardsville, where he teaches courses in instructional technology and educational psychology. His research interests include higher education pedagogy, creativity, innovation, and instructional technology design in corporate and nonprofit settings. Dr. Knowlton is coeditor of *From Entitlement to Engagement: Affirming Millennial Students' Egos in the Higher Education Classroom,* with Kevin Jack Hagopian (Jossey-Bass, 2013) and *Problem-Based Learning in the Information Age: New Directions for Teaching and Learning,* with David Sharp (Jossey-Bass, 2003).

Nathan R. Kuncel is the Marvin D. Dunnette Distinguished Professor of Industrial and Organizational Psychology and a McKnight Presidential

Fellow at the University of Minnesota. His research focuses of how individual characteristics influence work, academic, and life success as well as efforts to model and measure success. Recently, he has examined the meaning and measurement of critical thinking and the effects of judgment and decision making on the utility of college admissions and hiring. Dr. Kuncel edited the Industrial and Organizational section of the three-volume APA *Handbook of Testing and Assessment in Psychology* (2013). He received the Anne Anastasi Award from the American Psychological Association—Division 5, the Cattell Research Award from the Society of Multivariate Experimental Psychology, and the Jeanneret Award from the Society for Industrial and Organizational Psychology.

Scott L. Lingrell has been Vice President for Student Affairs and Enrollment Management at the University of West Georgia since 2005 after having served as the Associate Vice President since 2005. He had held numerous positions in enrollment management, admissions, and academic advising at Wayne State University, Bowling Green State University, the University of Toledo, and Rhodes State University. He has presented at numerous national conferences on issues related to organizational leadership and strategic decision making and enrollment planning. Dr. Lingrell is the 2009 inaugural recipient of the American Association of College Registrars and Admissions Officers' (AACRAO) Strategic Enrollment Management Award and the author of "Getting It Right: Data and Good Decisions" in Bob Bontrager and Doris Ingersoll (Eds.), *Strategic Enrollment Management: Transforming Higher Education* (AACRAO, 2012).

R. Scott Mattingly is Assistant Dean of Academic Life and an adjunct instructor in the Division of Liberal Arts and Social Sciences at DeSales University. He possesses 14 years of experience in higher education, including positions in a variety of functional areas. He earned his Ed.D. in educational administration at Temple University.

Patricia A. McGuire has been President of Trinity University Washington since 1989. Previously, she was Assistant Dean for Development and External Affairs and an adjunct professor of law at Georgetown University Law Center. She serves on numerous boards, including the Consortium of Universities, the Cafritz Foundation, the College Success Foundation—District of Columbia, Catholic Charities of DC, United Educators, and the Ameritas Holding Company. Her prior board service includes the American Council on Education, the National Association of Independent Colleges and Universities, the Middle States Commission on Higher Education, the Meyer Foundation, and the Community Foundation of the National Capitol Region, among others. President McGuire has received numerous awards and honors: the Hesburgh Award for Leadership Excellence from the Teachers Insurance and Annuity Association of America (TIAA) in 2016; the Carnegie Award for Academic Leadership from the Carnegie Foundation in 2015; and the Henry Paley Award from the National Association of Independent Colleges and Universities in 2012. She holds honorary degrees from Georgetown, Howard, Liverpool, Hope the College of New Rochelle, and others. She has received recognition in the *Washington Post, Washingtonian* magazine, *Washington Business Journal,* and other media outlets. In 2007, she was named "Leader of the Years" by the Greater Washington Board of Trade.

Michael T. Miller is Dean and a professor of higher education in the College of Education and Health Professions at the University of Arkansas, Fayetteville. He formerly served as associate dean and department chair. Dr. Miller has also worked in administration at San Jose State University and as a faculty member at the University of Alabama, where he was the Director of the National Data Base on Faculty Involvement in Governance. His most recent books are *Staff Governance and Institutional Policy Formation,* edited with John W. Murry, Jr. (Information Age, 2011); *College Student-Athletes: Challenges, Opportunities, and Policy Implications,* edited with Daniel B. Kissinger (Information Age, 2009); and *Training Higher Education Policy Makers and Leaders: A Graduate Program Perspective,* edited with Diane Wright (Information Age, 2007).

Thalia M. Mulvihill is a professor of social foundations of education and higher education and an affiliate faculty member in the Women's and Gender Studies Program and Honors College at Ball State University. She is the Chair of the University Athletics Committee, and a member of the American Educational Research Association (AERA) Special Interest Group (SIG)—Research Focus on Education and Sports. Dr. Mulvihill's recent books include *Critical Approaches to Life Writing Methods in Qualitative Research* (Routledge, 2017) and *Critical Approaches to Questions in Qualitative Research* (2016), both with Raji Swaminathan, and *The Show Choir Handbook,* with Alan L. Alder (Rowman & Littlefield, 2016).

Johann N. Neem is a professor of history at Western Washington University. He is the author of *Creating a Nation of Joiners: Democracy and Civil Society in Early Massachusetts* (Harvard Historical Studies, 2008) and the forthcoming *Democracy's Schools.* Dr. Neem writes regularly about higher education for *Inside Higher Ed* and other venues.

Sergio Ossorio is a community director at the University of North Carolina, Asheville. He is a recent graduate of the Higher Education and Student Affairs Administration Graduate Program at Buffalo State. He served as the Graduate Intern within the Office of the President. He is originally from the

Bronx, New York. He also earned a B.A. in English writing from DePauw University.

Amy A. Paciej-Woodruff is Assistant Vice President for Student Life at Marywood University. Her service in student affairs has encompassed housing and residence life, orientation, student activities, student conduct, athletics, counseling, student health, and leadership development. Dr. Paciej-Woodruff has 22 years of experience in six institutions, including serving as dean of students for seven years at Marywood, where she earned her M.S. and Ph.D. in human development in higher education administration.

Nicolle Parsons-Pollard is Vice Provost for Academic and Faculty Affairs and a professor in the Criminal Justice Program at Monmouth University. Her current research includes juvenile delinquency, truancy, disproportionate minority conduct (DMC), and program evaluation.

Sean Robinson is an associate professor of higher education administration at Morgan State University in Baltimore. He has over 20 years' experience in both academic and student affairs work. His teaching areas include higher education administration, policy, and legal issues; organizational behavior and theory; student development theory; and qualitative research methodology. His primary research interests are related to identity development and sexual orientation/gender expression in youth and young adults, particularly as portrayed in popular culture and mass media and an exploration of the lived experiences of LGBTQ faculty and administrators in colleges and universities. Dr. Robinson has published over a dozen articles and book chapters and regularly presents on gender and sexual diversity themes.

Juan Manuel Ruiz-Hau is a doctoral candidate in Educational Policy and Leadership at the University of Massachusetts, Amherst. He supervises and advises Student Bridge, a student-run organization that supports the access and success of underrepresented students at the University of Massachusetts, Amherst. His research centers on organizational behavior in postsecondary institutions, with an emphasis on systemic inequity and oppression and social justice for populations historically marginalized from participation in higher education.

Cristobal Salinas, Jr. is an assistant professor in the Department of Educational Leadership and Research Methodology at Florida Atlantic University. He previously served as the College of Design's multicultural liaison officer at Iowa State University, where he earned his M.Ed. and Ph.D. in higher education. He also has a B.A. in Spanish and ESL from the University of Nebraska at Kearney. He is the coauthor of *Iowa's Community Colleges: A Collective History of Fifty Years of Accomplishment* (Iowa State University College of Human Sciences, 2015). *Cristobal is the cofounder and managing editor of the*

Journal Committed to Social Change on Race and Ethnicity. Dr. Salinas's academic interests promote access and quality in higher education and explore the social, political, and economic contexts of educational opportunities for historically marginalized groups, with an emphasis on Latino/a communities.

Pietro A. Sasso is an assistant professor and Director of the College Student Personnel Administration Program at Southern Illinois University Edwardsville. He has over 10 years of professional and teaching experience in postsecondary education. He is co-editor, with Joseph L. DeVitis, of *Today's College Students* (Peter Lang, 2014) and *Higher Education and Society* (Peter Lang, 2015). He is co-author of the text, *The Dynamic Student Development Meta-Theory: A New Model for Student Success* (Peter Lang, 2017) with the Center for Learning Outcomes at Indiana State University. Dr. Sasso is a reviewer for several peer-reviewed journals, facilitated over 20 regional or national conference presentations, and authored over 25 scholarly publications which include identity construction in traditional undergraduates (college student development), alcohol misuse in higher education (student health outcomes), the impact of the college fraternity experience, and masculinity in higher education.

Dilys Schoorman is a professor and Chair of the Department of Curriculum, Culture and Educational Inquiry at Florida Atlantic University, where she teaches multicultural/global education, curriculum theory, and critical theory. Her professional and scholarly interests in faculty governance emerge from a commitment to integrate her professional philosophy grounded in critical pedagogy and leadership for social justice to her academic service in faculty governance. She strives to support and preserve the academy as a site for democratic praxis.

David Shiner has been a member of the faculty at Shimer College (now The Shimer Great Books School at North Central College) in Illinois since 1976. He has taught all 16 of the required courses in the Shimer curriculum as well as numerous electives. He has also served as Shimer's academic dean (13 years) and as chief operating officer (5 years) in addition to a brief stint as acting president. Dr. Shiner is a member of the American Philosophical Association.

Matthew R. Shupp is an assistant professor in the Department of Counseling and College Student Personnel at Shippensburg University of Pennsylvania. He worked as a student affairs administrator for 12 years prior to that appointment. Dr. Shupp is both a National Certified Counselor (NCC) through the National Board for Certified Counselors (NBCC) and a Distance Certified Counselor (DCC). He is Past-President of the Pennsylvania College Personnel Association (PCPA). His Ed.D. is from Widener University.

Everett A. Smith is an assistant professor of higher education at the University of Cincinnati. He previously served as Director of Assessment at the University of Arkansas, Fayetteville and as an admissions counselor at Christian Brothers University. His research focuses on public funding for higher education and collaborative decision making, including faculty governance. Dr. Smith holds a Ph.D. in public policy from the University of Arkansas.

Ashley Thorne is Executive Director of the National Association of Scholars (NAS). She is the lead author of four studies of college "common reading" programs, *Beach Books: What Do Colleges and Universities Want Students to Read Outside Class?* (NAS, 2010–2014). She is also the author of "Ducking the Coffins: How I Became an Edu-Con," in Jonah Goldberg (Ed.), *Proud to Be Right: Voices of the Next Conservative Generation* (Broadside Books, 2010) and "Hate Crimes on College and University Campuses," in Donald Altschiller (Ed.), *Hate Crimes: A Reference Handbook*, 3rd ed. (Contemporary World Issues, 2015). Ms. Thorne has a master's degree in linguistics from the City University of New York Graduate Center and an undergraduate degree in politics, philosophy, and economics from The King's College (NY).

Steven Tolman is an assistant professor of Higher Education at Georgia Southern University and was coordinator of the Higher Education Program at Montclair State University. Prior to his faculty role, he was a student affairs administrator for twelve years in residence life, student conduct, and student involvement. His research focuses on the organization and leadership practices in student affairs and the residential life of students. He earned his Ed.D. in education at Rutgers University.

Christopher Trautman is currently a Community Director at the University of North Carolina Chapel Hill. He earned his graduate degree in higher education leadership at Montclair State University, where he served as an assistant community director in the Office of Residence Life. He received a bachelor's degree in world literature from Fairleigh Dickinson University.

Ashley Tull is a clinical associate professor and Program Director of the Ed.D. Program at Southern Methodist University. He has also served as the Director of Assessment and Strategic Initiatives at SMU. His research inters center of management concepts and supervision in student affairs and higher education. Dr. Tull is the editor of *The Handbook for Student Affairs in Community Colleges*, with Linda Kuk, Paulette Dalpes, and Florence B. Brewer (Stylus, 2014); *New Realities in the Management of Student Affairs: Emerging Specialist Roles and Structures for Changing Times*, with Linda Kuk (Stylus, 2012); and *Becoming Socialized in Student Affairs: A Guide for*

New Professionals and Their Supervisors, with Joan B. Hirt and Sue Saunders (Stylus, 2009). He also serves on the editorial boards of the *Journal of College and Character, Journal of Applied Research in the Community College. Journal of College Student Development, Community College Review, Journal of Community College Research and Practice, College Student Affairs Journal*, and *the Journal of Student Affairs Research and Practice.*

Fermin Valle is a doctoral student in Higher Education at the University of Massachusetts, Amherst. He is an academic advisor with the Commonwealth Honors College. Informed by critical theory and social justice, his research and public engagement analyze how imperialism, capitalism, racism, sexism, heterosexism, and multiple systems of oppression are simultaneously reproduced and challenged across higher education. A committed activist in his free time, Valle believes that true learning for liberation can occur both inside and outside the classroom.

Matthew Varga is an associate professor of counselor education and college student affairs in the Department of Clinical and Professional Studies at the University of West Georgia. His central research explores substance (especially prescription) abuse among graduate students and resiliency. For eight years Dr. Varga worked in university housing. His recent articles appear in the *Journal of Evidenced-Based Social Work*. He holds a Ph.D. in higher education administration and a M.S. in college student personnel from the University of Tennessee, Knoxville, and a B.A. in philosophy from Christopher Newport University.

Isis N. Walton is an associate professor of criminal justice at Virginia State University. She earned her doctorate at Wayne State University. Her current research interests include juvenile justice issues such as delinquency, truancy, and minority disenfranchisement.

Martin C. Yu is a doctoral student in the Industrial/Organizational Psychology program at the University of Minnesota. He received his B.Sc. in Psychology from the University of British Columbia. His research interests are focused on decision making in organizational settings, particularly in personnel selection and retention scenarios. His other research interests include complex problem solving, expert performance, assessments, and psychometrics.

Studies in Criticality

General Editor
Shirley R. Steinberg

Counterpoints publishes the most compelling and imaginative books being written in education today. Grounded on the theoretical advances in criticalism, feminism, and postmodernism in the last two decades of the twentieth century, Counterpoints engages the meaning of these innovations in various forms of educational expression. Committed to the proposition that theoretical literature should be accessible to a variety of audiences, the series insists that its authors avoid esoteric and jargonistic languages that transform educational scholarship into an elite discourse for the initiated. Scholarly work matters only to the degree it affects consciousness and practice at multiple sites. Counterpoints' editorial policy is based on these principles and the ability of scholars to break new ground, to open new conversations, to go where educators have never gone before.

For additional information about this series or for the submission of manuscripts, please contact:

Shirley R. Steinberg
c/o Peter Lang Publishing, Inc.
29 Broadway, 18th floor
New York, New York 10006

To order other books in this series, please contact our Customer Service Department:

(800) 770-LANG (within the U.S.)
(212) 647-7706 (outside the U.S.)
(212) 647-7707 FAX

Or browse online by series:
www.peterlang.com